Computer Science, Technology and Applications

nova
science publishers
www.novapublishers.com

Computer Science, Technology and Applications

Information and Knowledge Systems
Manaswini Pradhan, PhD (Editor)
Satchidananda Dehurl (Editor)
2023. ISBN: 979-8-89113-303-7 (Softcover)
2023. ISBN: 979-8-89113-390-7 (eBook)

Emerging Applications of Blockchain Technology
Vinod Kumar Shukla, PhD (Editor)
Sonali Vyas, PhD (Editor)
Shaurya Gupta, PhD (Editor)
Suchi Dubey, PhD (Editor)
2023. ISBN: 979-8-89113-101-9 (Hardcover)
2023. ISBN: 979-8-89113-185-9 (eBook)

Digital Transformation – Modernization and Optimization of Wireless Networks
Ram Krishan, PhD (Editor)
Manpreet Kaur, PhD (Editor)
Jagtar Singh, PhD (Editor)
Shilpa Mehta, PhD (Editor)
Vikas Goyal (Editor)
2023. ISBN: 979-8-89113-042-5 (Softcover)
2023. ISBN: 979-8-89113-116-3 (eBook)

Digital Twins: The Industry 4.0 Use Cases: The Technologies, Tools, Platforms and Application
Kavita Saini, PhD (Editor)
Pethuru Raj Chelliah, PhD (Editor)
2023. ISBN: 979-8-89113-057-9 (eBook)

More information about this series can be found at https://novapublishers.com/product-category/series/computer-science-technology-and-applications/

A. Anitha Kamaraj
and Debi Prasanna Acharjya
Editors

Explainable Artificial Intelligence in Healthcare Systems

nova science publishers
www.novapublishers.com

DOI: https://doi.org/10.52305/GOMR8163

NOTICE TO THE READER

Library of Congress Cataloging-in-Publication Data

Names: Kamaraj, A. Anitha, editor. | Acharjya, D. P., 1969- editor.
Title: Explainable artificial intelligence in healthcare systems / (editors) A. Anitha Kamaraj, School of Information Technology and Engineering, Vellore Institute of Technology, Vellore, Tamil Nadu, India, Debi Prasanna Acharjya, School of Computer Science and Engineering, Vellore Institute of Technology, Vellore, Tamil Nadu, India.
Description: New York : Nova Science Publishers, [2024] | Series: Computer science, technology and applications | Includes bibliographical references and index. |
Identifiers: LCCN 2024010654 (print) | LCCN 2024010655 (ebook) | ISBN 9798891135987 (hardcover) | ISBN 9798891136670 (adobe pdf)
Subjects: LCSH: Artificial intelligence--Medical applications.
Classification: LCC R859.7.A78 E9695 2024 (print) | LCC R859.7.A78 (ebook) | DDC 610.285--dc23/eng/20240313
LC record available at https://lccn.loc.gov/2024010654
LC ebook record available at https://lccn.loc.gov/2024010655

Published by Nova Science Publishers, Inc. † New York

Contents

Preface

Explainable Artificial Intelligence (XAI) is a next-generation research field that aims to make AI and deep models more human-interpretable without compromising performance. Healthcare and its services are built around trust and high ethical standards to provide quality of life through automated tasks to produce more accurate diagnoses and treatment plans; it helps healthcare be more predictive and proactive by analyzing big data to develop improved patient preventive care recommendations. The methods should be more promising in adaptability and immunity against the observatory variables with cost-effective solutions. The book aims to encourage and invite the researcher with novel ideas and multi-disciplinary transformers to introduce the practical approach for analyzing various healthcare data to exhibit the unique challenges in the healthcare domain. This edited book covers 360-degree views of the development and automation of the healthcare domain using XAI to analyze smart healthcare systems. The wide variety of topics presented in this book offers the readers multiple perspectives on various disciplines.

Artificial Intelligence (AI), machine learning, and deep learning models have paved a solid predictive path in numerous real-life applications, including medical imaging and healthcare tasks. In healthcare, decisions and investigation process is taken with great care, but risks are associated with diagnosing a disease. The diagnosis of the patient's illness is analyzed based on various symptoms, observations, test reports, and experience. However, there is a chance of uncertainty while analyzing the data. Additionally, a second opinion is sought in many cases. Using AI, it is possible to automate the model to mimic the process of a domain expert so that a physician can think of alternative decisions while making decisions. Specifically, XAI provides a clear picture of prediction concerning deep learning models and the use of predicted results in healthcare applications. This book aims to provide the basic and intermediate notions of XAI and its application to healthcare applications.

The book includes four sections comprising primitive concepts under XAI, XAI in smart telemedicine and telehealth, public health applications using XAI, and medical imaging classification using XAI. The first five chapters comprise section 1, followed by four chapters in section 2. Six chapters further follow it in section 3. The final section, 4, includes five chapters.

Healthcare professionals can use XAI to understand better how an AI system generates a particular diagnosis concerning a disease. It aids in enhanced diagnosis and treatment, improved patient outcomes, safety and risk assessment, ethical AI use, regulatory compliance, patient trust and acceptance, research and knowledge, and patient trust and acceptance. XAI is essential to bridge the gap between sophisticated AI algorithms and human comprehension. It enables medical practitioners to fully utilize AI's capabilities while making wise judgments that benefit patients and the healthcare sector. Chapter 1 provides the development of XAI, especially for safety and risk assessment. Its advantages go beyond technological ones, including user acceptance, ethical considerations, and the proper usage of AI technologies.

AI is increasingly used in medical and distant healthcare applications, yet most AI systems are frequently too complex for human comprehension. In hopes of providing insight into their accuracy, tolerance, and transparency, the authors define the fundamentals of XAI. The objective of Chapter 2 is to provide a concise introduction to XAI algorithms employed in various healthcare services and present the role of federated learning with XAI in smart healthcare.

Healthcare 5.0 strongly emphasizes real-time patient monitoring, ambient control, welfare, and privacy compliance with aided technologies, including AI, the Internet of Things (IoT), big data, and facilitated networking channels. By utilizing the models' outputs for decision-making and prediction, XAI, a contemporary disruptive AI movement, seeks to improve the comprehension of traditional AI models. Chapter 3 presents the use of SWOT analysis while employing XAI in healthcare. A thorough analysis of XAI's advantages, disadvantages, opportunities, and threats concerning healthcare is discussed in this chapter.

Despite advancements, many AI models are perceived as black boxes, lacking transparency for end users provided that XAI is vital for the deployment phase. These human-centered design approaches ensure the explanations generated are helpful, understandable, and aligned with users' mental models. More complex models tend to offer better performance but are more complicated to interpret, resulting in the challenging trade-off between performance and explanation of XAI research. Chapter 4 presents a survey that includes XAI's principles, applications, and advancements. Besides, it also offers future research directions and potential opportunities regarding XAI.

The healthcare field has seen revolutionary developments due to AI, which has applications from diagnosis to treatment planning to create new medications. XAI aims to increase the transparency and interpretability of AI systems. To identify potential biases in the data, Chapter 5 elaborates on some of the XAI methods used in the healthcare industry and discusses their applicability along with the limitations and future prospectus of XAI in healthcare organizations.

Section 2 of the book mainly focuses on XAI in telemedicine and telehealth. Telemedicine is the delivery and support of healthcare services over long distances using electronic information and communication technology. At the same time, telehealth allows your healthcare practitioner to treat you without a face-to-face appointment. All these practices are being observed because of computer and information technology advancements. This section comprises four chapters. Due to the world's expanding population, a significant need exists to provide acceptable healthcare services. With the arrival of modern technologies, the need gap may widen. The sensor is one such technology that could be used in a health monitoring system built on the Internet of Things. The implementation of such a system is discussed in Chapter 6.

Recently, the novel acute respiratory infection coronavirus has spread quickly around the globe. It takes longer to classify photos using traditional diagnostic methods. Effective and quick identification is a crucial first step in reducing the spread of COVID-19 and related death rates. Early diagnosis and management of COVID-19 can be accomplished with the help of chest X-rays (CXRs). To this end, Chapter 7 presents a transfer learning-enhanced CNN framework for COVID-19 classification using CXR.

The AI-powered vest-coat stethoscope has several advantages over conventional auscultation methods. It offers accurate and consistent assessments, lessens reliance on a patient's interpretation of sounds, and enables remote patient monitoring. The system also has the potential to help less experienced healthcare workers by boosting diagnostic accuracy and offering real-time coaching. The identification of aberrant lung sounds is essential in the diagnosis of respiratory disorders. Several techniques have recently demonstrated outstanding performance in identifying abnormal lung sounds. Chapter 8 uses deep learning algorithms and a vest coat stethoscope for disease diagnosis with unusual lung sounds.

Heart disease is increasing rapidly because of many reasons. Both cardiologists and surgeons find it difficult to anticipate when heart failure might occur. This diagnosis is a difficult task that demands precision and effectiveness. Chapter 9 investigates machine learning techniques such as naïve Bayes, support vector machine, logistic regression, and random forest over heart disease. The use of XAI techniques will aid in early cardiac disease diagnosis.

Public health is the science and art of avoiding illness, extending life, fostering physical and mental well-being, controlling infectious diseases, and setting up health services. Section 3 presents how XAI helps public health applications. To begin with maternal care, chapter 10 illustrates an overview of AI and machine learning (ML) techniques in maternal care, focusing on pregnancy risk assessment. It examines how AI and ML identify high-risk pregnancies and forecast problems, highlighting the significance of precise risk assessment. Predicting preterm labor, gestational diabetes mellitus, and preeclampsia, determining gestational age, determining fatal risk using cardiotocographic data, and identifying fatal growth limitation are just a few of the specific applications for assessing pregnancy risk covered in this chapter.

According to WHO data, almost 18 million individuals worldwide are affected by heart disorders yearly. Detection of heart disease can prevent millions of deaths. Today, ML and AI are commonly employed in the healthcare industry to find a disease's cure. Since different methodologies have varying degrees of accuracy, predicting conditions when data and features change becomes more challenging. With this intention, Chapter 11 implements the categorization models in an XAI framework. Its dependability can be achieved using ML while analyzing heart diseases based on electronic health data.

A universal goal shared by all people is achieving and sustaining excellent health. But, for various reasons, the ordinary person faces serious health hazards. The rate of public health hazards can be reduced with the early detection of diseases. With this objective, chapter 12 uses five ML algorithms to predict conditions based on user-inputted symptoms because it recognizes the importance of early disease detection. It, in turn, significantly reduces the health risks of the ordinary person.

Public health organizations can better understand potential hazards and population vulnerabilities by predicting disease outbreaks, which can help them build policies to stop future attacks. Analyzing various elements, such as environmental conditions, population density, and individual behaviors, makes this challenging. To this end, chapter 13 discusses the methodologies of association rule mining and graph node classification that have been applied to anticipate disease outbreaks. Graph node categorization adds international airline networks, which act as a stand-in for human movement and connectivity and present a fresh framework for capturing the temporal and spatial spread of diseases across various locations with better accuracy rate.

Healthcare has transformed with the development of AI technology to medical image processing. Besides, interpreting predictions from classifiers on picture data is quite challenging. As a result, XAI has attracted much interest in the healthcare industry, notably in the analysis of medical images. Chapter 14 examines the use of XAI in healthcare, concentrating on its use in the study of biopsy medical images.

From moderate symptoms to significant sickness and death, COVID-19 symptoms might vary. The COVID-19 patient displayed signs including fever, insomnia, and a dry cough. The COVID-19 virus mutates and is still present in some parts of the world. To this end, chapter 15 presents a review describing how and where to use a database of X-ray and CT-Scan pictures, MRI scans from people who frequently had respiratory infections, established COVID-19 infection, and common instances to diagnose coronavirus infection. The support vector machine, logistic regression, and random forest techniques are considered for classification purposes. Each algorithm's experimental results are contrasted with one another and with the categorization models' traditional implementation methods. Further Comparison of the XAI-based classification models with other state-of-the-art models is done.

The process of categorizing and labeling sets of pixels or vectors inside an image following predetermined rules is known as image classification. Developing the classification legislation using one or more spectral or textural properties is possible. The prime objective of section 4 is to provide the use of XAI in medical image classification. Healthcare applications of AI now include patient data and diagnostics, clinical decision-making, service delivery and management, and predictive medicine. Despite functioning on par with humans, AI models still need to be viewed as a mystery and only have a limited number of applications. However, there is a challenge with the black box operation of AI model judgments, which has led to a lack of responsibility and faith in produced decisions. Chapter 16 discusses the XAI as a technique that can boost confidence in the predictions generated by the model by detailing how the projections are made to promote the use of AI systems in healthcare.

As technology has advanced quickly, healthcare organizations have been the subject of numerous data breach assaults in recent years. In many industries, notably this one, healthcare content must be protected from theft, interference, and fabrication since it is valuable. Steganography adds a layer of security for medical imaging. Chapter 17 presents a DeoxyRibo Nucleic Acid (DNA) algorithm for protecting medical images. The LSB substitution method, algorithmic selection, and DNA encoding are the three phases of this phase. This steganographic image's quality is evaluated using various measures, including MSE, PSNR, SSIM, and BER. Besides, it also compared with several existing methods.

Recently, the COVID-19 has spread quickly around the globe. It takes longer to classify images using traditional diagnostic methods. The primary goal of Chapter 18 is to use conceptual transfer learning-enhanced CNN framework models while analyzing COVID-19 chest X-ray images. A confusion matrix and several performance metrics were used to evaluate various model's performance, including accuracy, recall, precision, f1-score, and loss.

Chapter 19 explores how XAI and visualization techniques enhance readability and transparency in healthcare informatics. The demand for understandable and transparent AI-driven insights has reached a critical juncture due to the growing complexity of healthcare data and the increasing popularity of AI technology. A powerful answer is provided by XAI-driven visualization, which presents AI-generated outcomes in an understandable visual format for policymakers, patients, and healthcare practitioners. Line, area, bar, histogram, scatter plot, heat map, geographic information system (GIS) mapping, interactive dashboards, and decision trees are just a few of the data visualization techniques examined in detail.

Nearly every part of medicine has the potential to be transformed in the near and distant future by ML and AI in general. However, a lack of transparency in AI applications has proven more troublesome in numerous domains, including outside health. It is very apparent in situations where users must interpret the output of AI systems. Chapter 20 conducted a thorough literature evaluation of the work done in applying XAI in healthcare decision support systems.

The XAI is a field of study that has attracted several researchers in numerous organizations worldwide. Conversely, considerable data analysis and cloud computing techniques are developing concurrently. It will enter a new dimension thanks to the union of XAI with these modern methods and technologies. We kept the book reader-friendly so they could follow this progress unified. The main goal is to precisely present the majority of the essential findings in the field, as described above so that it can guide other researchers. Researchers interested in XAI in healthcare informatics will find this edited book helpful in staying current on new developments and applications.

Dr. A. Anitha
School of Computer Science Engineering and Information Systems
Vellore Institute of Technology
Vellore, Tamilnadu, India

Dr. D. P. Acharjya
School of Computer Science and Engineering
Vellore Institute of Technology
Vellore, Tamilnadu, India

Section 1. Primitive Concepts under Explainable AI

Chapter 1

XAI in Healthcare: Black Box to Interpretable Models

Shikha Verma[1]
Sandhya Avasthi[2,1]
Priya Mishra[1]
Meghna Gupta[1]
and Gunjan Agarwal[1]
[1]MCA Department, ABES Engineering College, Ghaziabad, India
[2]Department of CSE, ABES Engineering College, Ghaziabad, India

Abstract

Explainable Artificial Intelligence (XAI) is a critical aspect of AI development, particularly in sensitive and high-stakes applications. Its benefits extend beyond technical aspects to encompass ethical considerations, user acceptance, and the responsible deployment of AI technologies. It refers to the techniques and methods used to make AI models and their decisions more transparent and interpretable to humans. Traditional machine learning algorithms, such as deep learning neural networks, are often considered "black boxes" because they lack transparency, making it challenging to understand how they arrive at specific conclusions or predictions. XAI aims to address this limitation by providing human-readable explanations for AI model outputs. There are many benefits of XAI including Transparency, Trust, and Confidence, Identifying Biases, Debugging and Improvements, Regulatory Compliance, Human-AI Collaboration, Education and Understanding, Insights, and Research.

XAI can help healthcare professionals understand how an AI system arrives at a specific diagnosis or treatment recommendation it helps in Enhanced Diagnosis and Treatment, Improved Patient Outcomes, Safety and Risk Assessment, Ethical AI Use, Regulatory Compliance, Patient Trust and Acceptance, Enhanced Diagnosis and Treatment, Improved Patient Outcomes, Safety and Risk Assessment, Ethical AI Use, Regulatory Compliance, Patient Trust and Acceptance, Research and Knowledge Discovery, Continuous Learning and Improvement. XAI is crucial in bridging the gap between complex AI algorithms and human understanding. It empowers healthcare professionals to harness the potential of AI while making informed and responsible decisions for the benefit of patients and the healthcare industry.

In: Explainable Artificial Intelligence in Healthcare Systems
Editors: A. Anitha Kamaraj and Debi Prasanna Acharjya
ISBN: 979-8-89113-598-7

Keywords: XAI, NLP, machine learning, explainable Model, LIME, SHAP

1.1 Introduction

Applications of AI make it possible for autonomous systems to sense their environment, educate themselves, and come to their conclusions. The systems are specifically designed to handle extensive collections of data and employ advanced technologies such as machine learning and natural language processing (NLP) to yield outcomes. Nevertheless, a significant quandary arises from the fact that existing systems fail to provide us with the underlying rationale behind their decision-making processes. The provided output is presented without accompanying elucidation regarding the underlying causative factors responsible for its generation. It is imperative to acknowledge that within this context, there exists a discernible prediction, albeit lacking in accompanying justification.

The current situation can be characterized as a "black box" scenario, wherein the contents and mechanisms of the box are unknown to observers. Hence, it is plausible that this enigmatic "black box" possesses the potential to confine the utilization and scope of artificial intelligence (AI). If artificial intelligence (AI) machines are incapable of engaging in transparent discourse with humans, their potential for achieving true intelligence will remain unattainable. Explainable artificial intelligence (AI) serves the purpose of enhancing the transparency of the "black box" phenomenon, thereby facilitating the ability of practitioners to engage in comprehensive analysis and comprehension of AI systems. The recent development represents a significant advancement toward enhancing the ethical framework of artificial intelligence.

Explainable AI (XAI) is an artificial intelligence program that explains the thought process behind reaching a particular result. Introducing a novel learning process that not only provides accurate predictions but also offers comprehensive explanations for the rationale behind each prediction (Merrick and Taly, 2020). In the construction of an Explainable AI model, an additional layer is incorporated into the machine learning (ML) design to enhance its explanatory capabilities as shown in Figure 1. 1.

The inclusion of an additional layer is of utmost importance due to its pivotal role in the enhancement of decision-making objectivity through the facilitation of explainability (Gunning et al. 2019). This technique facilitates the process of discerning and mitigating any inherent biases that may be present within the datasets.

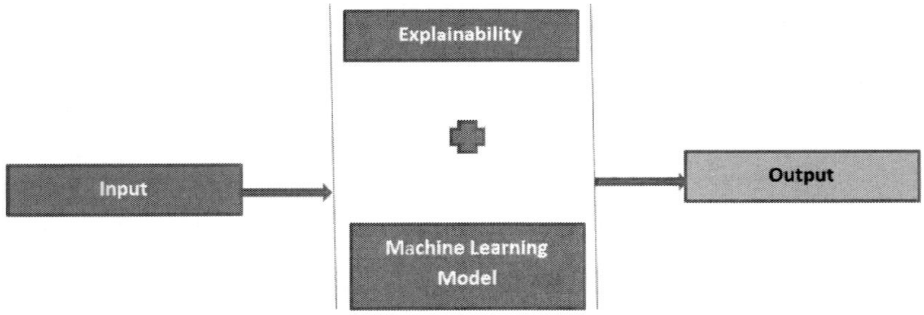

Figure 1.1 Explainable AI Model.

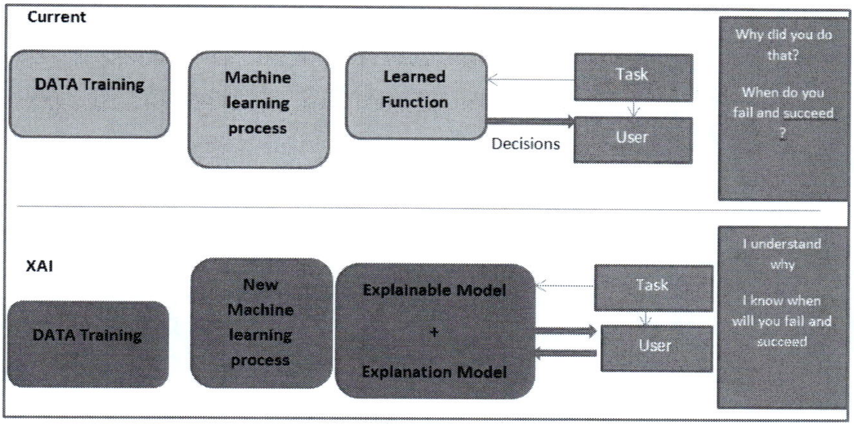

Figure 1.2. Comparison of XAI with the Traditional Model.

The concept of explainability directs our focus toward various factors that have the potential to influence the outcome of a prediction. Explainable AI (XAI), alternatively referred to as Interpretable AI, is a burgeoning domain that directs its attention toward a diverse array of methodologies aimed at mitigating the inherent opacity of Machine Learning models, thereby engendering elucidations that resonate with human-level comprehension. Explainable artificial intelligence (XAI) refers to a comprehensive array of systematic procedures and methodologies that facilitate the comprehension and establishment of trust among human users about the outcomes and outputs generated by machine learning algorithms. The primary objective of the Explainable AI (XAI) program is to develop a comprehensive set of machine learning methodologies that fulfill two key objectives. Firstly, these methodologies should generate models that are more transparent and interpretable, without compromising their ability to achieve high levels of learning performance, specifically in terms of prediction accuracy. Secondly, they should empower human users to comprehend, place appropriate trust in, and proficiently oversee the forthcoming cohort of artificially intelligent collaborators (Gunning et al. 2019).

Future iterations of machine-learning systems will possess the remarkable capability to elucidate the underlying reasoning behind their decisions, delineate their inherent advantages and limitations, and effectively communicate their projected behavior in forthcoming scenarios are shown in Figure 1.2. The proposed approach to attaining the objective involves the cultivation of novel or adapted machine-learning methodologies, which will yield models endowed with enhanced interpretability (Confalonieri et al. 2021). The integration of these models will be complemented by cutting-edge human-computer interface methodologies, which can convert them into comprehensible and valuable explanation dialogues for the end user.

1.2 Significance of XAI

The significance of Explainable Artificial Intelligence (XAI) cannot be overstated, as it addresses a critical limitation of traditional black-box machine learning models. By providing interpretability and transparency, XAI offers a multitude of benefits that have far-reaching implications for various domains. Firstly, XAI enhances trust and accountability in AI systems. By elucidating Explainable Artificial Intelligence (XAI) presents a range of benefits that encompass transparency, accountability, trust, and compliance within decision-making procedures. Additionally, XAI aids in the identification and mitigation of biases that may otherwise result in inequitable decision-making. Through the provision of lucid and all-encompassing elucidations about the intricate process of decision-making, Explainable Artificial Intelligence (XAI) possesses the potential to facilitate the formulation of well-informed and resolute judgments by decision-makers (Confalonieri et al. 2021). Given the prevailing regulatory landscape, wherein industries and organizations are compelled to adhere to transparent and interpretable decision-making protocols, the integration of Explainable Artificial Intelligence (XAI) emerges as a viable solution to fulfill these mandates. Hence, explainable artificial intelligence (XAI) assumes a pivotal position in facilitating the attainment of organizational objectives and ensuring a competitive edge in a rapidly changing and dynamic landscape as shown in Figure 1.3.

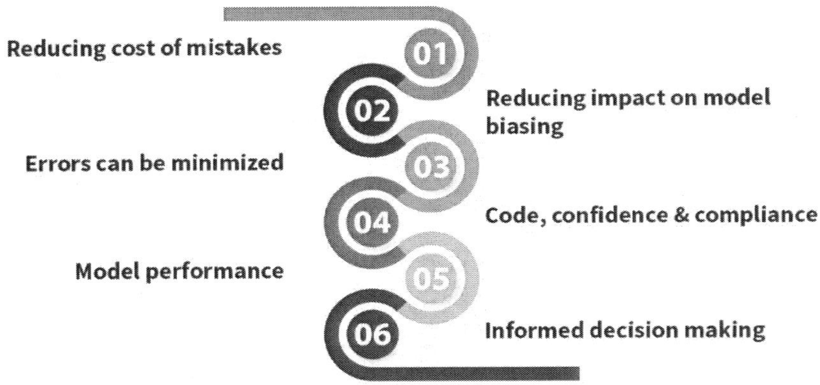

Figure 1.3. XAI Benefits.

The acceleration and extensive deployment of artificial intelligence systems are directly proportional to the level of confidence instilled in them. By strategically positioning your business, you will enhance its capacity to cultivate innovation and gain a competitive edge in the realm of developing and embracing the cutting-edge capabilities of the next generation.

- *Reducing the cost of mistakes:* Erroneous prognostications exert a substantial influence on decision-centric sectors such as healthcare, finance, jurisprudence, and the like. The act of monitoring the outcomes serves to mitigate the potential ramifications of erroneous discoveries and facilitates the identification of the fundamental factors, thereby enhancing the foundational framework (Vilone and Longo, 2021). Consequently, the advent of advanced artificial intelligence (AI) technologies has engendered a notable enhancement in the credibility and authenticity of AI writers, rendering them increasingly reliable and practical for utilization.
- *Reducing Impact of Model Biasing:* The empirical findings have indicated a substantial presence of bias within AI models. Instances of bias have been observed in various domains, such as the presence of gender bias in the Apple Cards system, the

manifestation of racial bias in autonomous vehicles, and the identification of gender and racial bias in Amazon Recognition. An explainable system possesses the potential to mitigate the deleterious consequences stemming from biased predictions by elucidating the underlying decision-making criteria.

- *Errors can be minimized:* It is a well-established fact that AI models inherently possess a certain degree of fallibility in their predictive capabilities. However, the integration of a human agent who possesses the qualities of responsibility and accountability can significantly enhance the system's overall efficiency.
- *Code Confidence and Compliance:* Each instance of inference, accompanied by its corresponding explanation, has the propensity to augment the level of confidence within the system (Vilone and Longo, 2021). Certain user-critical systems, including autonomous vehicles, medical diagnosis tools, and the finance sector, necessitate a heightened level of code confidence from users to achieve optimal utilization. Considering the escalating demands imposed by regulatory bodies, enterprises find themselves compelled to swiftly embrace and operationalize Explainable Artificial Intelligence (XAI) to ensure compliance with governing authorities.
- *Performance evaluation:* To optimize performance, it is imperative to possess a comprehensive comprehension of the potential vulnerabilities that may impede progress. Enhancing the comprehension of model behavior and the underlying causes of occasional failures facilitates the process of refining said models. The concept of explainability holds significant potential in artificial intelligence research (Vilone and Longo, 2021). By enabling the detection of flaws within models and biases inherent in the data, explainability serves as a potent tool for fostering trust among all users. The utilization of this approach facilitates the validation of prognostications, the enhancement of computational models, and the acquisition of novel perspectives about the issue under consideration. The identification of biases within the model or dataset is facilitated by a comprehensive comprehension of the model's underlying mechanisms and the rationale behind its predictive outcomes.
- *Informed Decision Making:* Machine learning applications have emerged as a pivotal tool in the realm of business, primarily serving the purpose of facilitating automated decision-making processes. However, it is frequently desirable to employ models primarily to extract analytical insights. As an illustration, one could employ a model to forecast sales within an expansive retail conglomerate by leveraging a comprehensive dataset encompassing variables such as geographical coordinates, operational hours, meteorological conditions, temporal context, product assortment, and physical outlet dimensions, among others. The proposed model exhibits the capability to prognosticate sales across multiple retail establishments, encompassing a comprehensive temporal scope spanning every day of the calendar year, while accommodating diverse meteorological circumstances. By constructing a comprehensible model, one can discern the primary catalysts behind sales and leverage this knowledge to enhance revenue generation.

1.3 Motivation for Applying XAI in Health Care

The prevailing sentiment is one of profound optimism regarding the potential of artificial intelligence (AI) to yield significant enhancements across the entire spectrum of healthcare, encompassing diagnostics as well as treatment modalities. The prevailing consensus posits that artificial intelligence (AI) tools are poised to serve as facilitators and augmenters of human labor, rather than supplanting the roles of physicians and other healthcare personnel outright. Artificial intelligence (AI) has reached a level of maturity where it can effectively assist healthcare professionals across a wide range of responsibilities. These encompass not only administrative tasks and workflow management but also extend to critical areas like clinical documentation, patient outreach, and even specialized domains such as image analysis, medical device automation, and patient monitoring. The integration of AI into healthcare systems holds immense potential for enhancing the efficiency and effectiveness of healthcare personnel, ultimately leading to improved patient care outcomes. The integration of artificial intelligence (AI) has become increasingly prevalent in various domains of healthcare, including health services management, clinical decision-making, predictive medicine, patient data analysis, and diagnostics. Notwithstanding its remarkable accomplishments, artificial intelligence continues to be perceived as an enigmatic entity, commonly referred to as a black box.

Explainable AI (XAI) in the domain of healthcare encompasses a suite of technologies that empower medical professionals with the capacity to comprehend the underlying rationales behind the decision-making processes of AI systems. This elucidation of the "why" behind the system's choices serves as a crucial component in fostering trust, transparency, and interpretability within the healthcare AI landscape (Dosilovic et al. 2018).

Put simply, this elucidates the fundamental reasoning of the artificial intelligence system. Numerous state-of-the-art black-box models often employ suboptimal or perplexing variables to attain their impressive performance levels. An illustrative example involves the utilization of a deep learning network that has been meticulously trained on a cohort of individuals afflicted with asthma, with the invaluable guidance and expertise of medical professionals. Regrettably, this network erroneously deduced a much lower mortality rate associated with pneumonia cases. The utilization of extraneous data, such as the positional attributes of the scanner, was observed in another instance of a deep learning architecture employed for pneumonia detection in X-ray images. In a subsequent iteration, a novel framework was devised to discern patients with varying degrees of risk by leveraging X-ray data, wherein hardware-related features were harnessed to forecast the likelihood of adverse outcomes (Zhang, Weng and Lund, 2022). These illustrative instances demonstrate the insufficiency of relying solely on the dependability of the models. The current landscape of artificial intelligence research necessitates the development of supplementary frameworks that cultivate a sense of assurance, notably in the form of explainable AI. With the progressive proliferation of explainable artificial intelligence (AI) within the realm of healthcare, it is reasonable to anticipate a heightened level of convergence between this burgeoning technology and wearable devices. Wearable devices have emerged as a valuable reservoir of patient data, as they diligently track and record individuals' health metrics throughout their daily activities. Explainable AI can harness.

1.4 Advantages in Healthcare

- *Improved Accuracy:* Through the elucidation of the underlying mechanisms employed by an AI system to derive a specific inference, explainable artificial intelligence (XAI) methodologies foster a culture of transparency within the realm of healthcare procedures. The augmentation of openness and comprehension, consequently, engenders elevated levels of trust. Furthermore, the elucidations provided by explainable Artificial Intelligence (XAI) methodologies can facilitate the monitoring of the influence exerted by various components on the predictive capabilities of an AI system.
- *Model Improvement: In AI research, a crucial aspect is the continuous enhancement of models.* These models, which are imbued with the ability to learn from vast amounts of data, possess the remarkable capability to generate accurate forecasts. At times, it is observed that the prevailing norms and regulations may prove to be fallible, leading to the generation of imprecise prognostications. The utilization of explainable Artificial Intelligence (XAI) methodologies facilitates the assessment of acquired rules, thereby enabling the identification of errors and subsequent enhancement of models.
- *Enhanced precision:* Through elucidating the underlying processes employed by an AI system, explainable artificial intelligence (XAI) in the realm of healthcare has the potential to augment the precision of medical diagnoses and therapeutic protocols. This facilitates the comprehension of physicians and other medical practitioners regarding the rationale behind the recommendation of a particular diagnostic strategy, thereby fostering enhanced precision and efficacy in subsequent therapeutic interventions.
- *Knowledge transfer:* Explainable Artificial Intelligence (XAI) serves as a conduit for the seamless transfer of knowledge from AI systems to medical personnel, thereby empowering them to leverage this knowledge to optimize patient outcomes. As an illustration, an AI system can unearth a heretofore unacknowledged correlation between a given symptom and a specific ailment. Through the elucidation of its underlying reasoning, the AI system engenders a paradigm shift within practitioners, illuminating novel interconnections that can be harnessed for subsequent diagnostic endeavors (Tiddi and S. Schlobach, 2022).
- *Early Detection:* The utilization of Explainable Artificial Intelligence (XAI) holds great potential in the realm of early detection, as it possesses the capability to meticulously scrutinize vast quantities of patient data. By doing so, XAI can uncover intricate patterns that may elude the discernment of medical professionals, thereby facilitating timely diagnoses of various illnesses. Explainable Artificial Intelligence (XAI) possesses the remarkable capability to elucidate the underlying factors contributing to an individual's susceptibility to specific diseases. This advanced system achieves this feat by employing a rigorous process of analysis and inference, enabling it to discern the intricate patterns and correlations within vast amounts of data (Antoniadi et al. 2021). Consequently, XAI can provide comprehensive explanations regarding its conclusions, shedding light on the precise reasoning behind its determinations. Moreover, XAI goes beyond mere diagnosis, as it is equipped to propose proactive measures aimed at averting the onset of these diseases. By leveraging its extensive knowledge base, XAI offers valuable insights into preventive

strategies, empowering individuals to take informed actions in safeguarding their health.

1.5 XAI Methods

The efficacy of explainable artificial intelligence (XAI) techniques is contingent upon several key factors. These include the specific model employed, the domain within which the problem resides, the desired degree of interpretability, and the intended recipients of the explanations. Various explainable artificial intelligence (XAI) methodologies exhibit distinct trade-offs concerning their accuracy, fidelity, and comprehensibility.

Explainable Artificial Intelligence (XAI) is an encompassing term denoting a collection of methodologies and approaches that are designed with the noble objective of furnishing lucid and comprehensible explanations for the discerning human mind regarding the intricate decision-making processes executed by artificial intelligence (AI) and machine learning (ML) models. These elucidations serve to facilitate comprehension for users and stakeholders, shedding light on the underlying rationale behind model predictions, thereby fostering trust and promoting transparency in the realm of artificial intelligence systems. Numerous explainable Artificial Intelligence (XAI) methodologies have been devised to attain this objective.

1.6 Commonly Used XAI Methods

There are several different approaches that XAI takes, some of them are as follows:

- *Local Interpretable Model-agnostic Explanations (LIME):*
  LIME is a well-known method used to produce local explanations for black-box machine learning models. Using perturbed data points, it creates a simple model that is easily interpretable (for example, a linear model) to get an approximation of the decision boundary that surrounds a particular instance (Kotriwala et al. 2021, Machlev et al. 2022).
  The LIME approach consists of some critical steps, which are as follows:
  - *Data Manipulation*: The first step that LIME takes in the process of generating local explanations is to pick the instance that requires an explanation. After that, the data for this instance is altered to generate a collection of cases that are comparable to one another but have some subtle differences.
  - *Model Prediction:* The black-box model is applied to each instance that has been disrupted, and the associated predictions are derived from this process. The black-box model is regarded as a "black box" in the sense that we do not need to know its internal architecture or parameters. This allows us to approach the model as if it were a "black box."
  - *Local Data Weighting*: In LIME, weights are assigned to the perturbed instances based on how closely they resemble the initial instance. Higher weights are assigned to instances that occupy a location in the feature space that is geographically closer to the initial instance. This indicates these instances are of

greater significance when approximating the local behavior of the black-box model.

- *Interpretability Model:* After that, a more straightforward interpretable model is educated with the help of the perturbed examples and the black-box model predictions corresponding to those instances. The interpretable model used may be anything as straightforward as a decision tree or linear model. The interpretable model's goal is to provide a close approximation of the behavior predicted by the black-box model near the instance of interest.
- *Local Explanation:* Once the interpretable model has been trained, it can be used to create explanations for the prediction of the initial instance. This may be done once the model has been trained. The coefficients or decision rules of the interpretable model bring attention to the features and various contributions each feature had to the forecast that the black-box model had made for that instance.

- *SHapley Additive exPlanations (SHAP)*
  The SHAP (SHapley Additive exPlanations) framework is rooted in the principles of cooperative game theory, a branch of mathematics that deals with the analysis of strategic interactions among multiple agents. By leveraging this theoretical foundation, SHAP can provide valuable insights into the inner workings of machine learning models. One of the key outputs of the SHAP framework is the assignment of a SHAP value to each feature. These values serve as indicators of the relative importance or contribution of a particular feature to a given prediction. By quantifying the impact of each feature, SHAP enables researchers and practitioners to gain a deeper understanding of the factors driving model predictions (Saranya and Subhashini, 2023). The proposed framework offers a comprehensive and cohesive structure for elucidating the outcomes generated by machine learning models across various domains.
- Partial Dependence Plots (PDP) and Individual Conditional Expectation (ICE) Plots:
  - The use of Partial Dependence Plots (PDP) and Individual Conditional Expectation (ICE) plots has become increasingly prevalent in artificial intelligence research. These visualizations serve the purpose of providing a comprehensive understanding of the average impact that one or a select few features have on the predictions generated by a given model. By employing these plots, researchers can gain valuable insights into the intricate relationships between features Partial Dependence Plots (PDPs) provide a comprehensive overview of the average impact of a single feature on the model's predictions. On the other hand, Individual Conditional Expectation (ICE) plots offer a more granular perspective by illustrating the individual effect of a feature on each specific instance.
  - *Global Surrogate Models*
    Global surrogate models refer to interpretable models trained to approximate predictions made by a black-box model. Surrogate models possess the advantageous characteristic of enhanced interpretability, thereby facilitating the acquisition of valuable insights into the behavioral patterns exhibited by black-box models.
  - *Decision Trees and Rule-Based Models*
    Decision trees and rule-based models possess an inherent characteristic of interpretability. Decision-making processes are effectively represented by

artificial intelligence researchers as a sequence of uncomplicated rules or nodes within a tree structure, thereby facilitating comprehension and interpretation.

- *Attention Mechanisms*
  Attention mechanisms are widely used in deep learning architectures, with emphasis on their application in natural language processing. The salient aspects of the input that the model prioritized during its cognitive deliberation are duly emphasized.
- Methods for assessing feature importance, such as permutation feature importance and feature importance derived from tree-based models (e.g., Gini importance), facilitate the ranking of features according to their respective contributions to the predictive capabilities of a given model (Van der Waa et al. 2021).
- *Feature Importance Methods*
  Methods for assessing feature importance, such as permutation feature importance and feature importance derived from tree-based models (e.g., Gini importance), facilitate the ranking of features according to their respective contributions to the predictive capabilities of a given model.
- *Rule-based Explanations*
  Rule-based explanations offer explicit and interpretable rules that articulate the reasoning behind the predictions made by the model. The rules are derived from the internal representation of the model.
- *Contrastive Explanations*
  Contrastive explanations, in the realm of artificial intelligence research, involve the process of comparing a model's prediction for a given instance with the prediction it would have generated had certain features possessed alternative values. This technique allows for a deeper understanding of the model's decision-making process and sheds light on the impact of different feature values on the final prediction. This facilitates the comprehension of users regarding the impact of varying feature values on the output of the model (Mendel and Bonissone, 2021).
- *Anchors*
  Anchors, in the context of machine learning, can be conceptualized as concise and interpretable if-then statements that serve as adequate conditions for the predictions made by the model. The authors offer succinct elucidations about the precise outputs of the model.

1.7 Interprétable Machine Learning Model

Interpretable Machine Learning (ML) models, colloquially referred to as Explainable AI (XAI) models, have been meticulously crafted to offer comprehensible and transparent elucidations for their prognostications. These models play a pivotal role in situations where the transparency and interpretability of the model are of utmost importance, as observed in domains like medical diagnosis, finance, and legal systems. Presented below are a few illustrations of interpretable machine learning (ML) models that have been employed in the realm of explainable artificial intelligence (XAI).

1. *Decision trees, a prevalent model in artificial intelligence, are highly regarded for their interpretability.* These models can dissect complex datasets by systematically partitioning the data into a series of hierarchical decisions. This hierarchical decision-making process is elegantly represented as a tree structure, which further enhances the comprehensibility of the model. In the context of the tree structure, it is important to note that every individual node is inherently associated with a specific feature. Furthermore, it is crucial to acknowledge that each branch emanating from said node signifies a decision that is contingent upon the feature.
2. *Random Forests*, a prominent ensemble technique, are composed of numerous decision trees. This approach's use yields enhanced predictive capabilities while preserving a degree of interpretability. By scrutinizing the constituent trees, one can discern the significance of features and the rationale behind decision-making processes.
3. *Generalised Linear Models* (GLMs) represent a distinguished category of linear models that effectively broaden the scope of simple linear regression (Verma et al. 2022) by incorporating diverse target variables, such as binary or count data. The interpretability of linear models is frequently observed owing to their inherent linearity.
4. *Linear regression*, a fundamental statistical modeling technique, is characterized by its simplicity and interpretability. This model effectively establishes a linear association between the input features and the target variable.
5. *Logistic regression*, akin to its linear regression counterpart, is a statistical modeling technique employed for binary classification tasks. Its interpretability is derived from its inherent linearity, which allows for a clear understanding of the relationship between the input variables and the predicted outcome (Kumar et al. 2023).
6. *Rule-based models*, encompassing rule-based decision systems and expert systems, leverage human-readable rules to generate predictions and exhibit a commendable level of interpretability (Gade et al. 2019, Linardatos, Papastefanopoulos and Kotsiantis, 2018).
7. *Additive models*, a class of predictive models, leverage the combination of various elementary functions, such as linear, spline, or tree-based functions, to generate accurate predictions. By integrating these simple functions, additive models can capture complex relationships and patterns within the data, ultimately enhancing their predictive capabilities. Interpretability can be significantly enhanced, particularly in the context of linear components.
8. *Partial Least Squares (PLS)* is a regression technique that has gained considerable attention in the field of artificial intelligence research. It offers a valuable solution for addressing the challenges posed by multicollinear data, a common issue encountered in various domains. PLS has demonstrated its efficacy in producing results that are not only statistically sound but also readily interpretable, making it a preferred choice among researchers and practitioners alike.
9. *Naive Bayes, a probabilistic model rooted in Bayes' theorem, has emerged as a prominent tool in text classification.* Its popularity stems from its ability to effectively handle many classification tasks of textual data. The inherent simplicity of the subject matter facilitates its interpretability.

10. *The LASSO*, also known as the Least Absolute Shrinkage and Selection Operator, is a linear regression technique that combines the benefits of variable selection and regularization. By incorporating both aspects, the LASSO method offers a comprehensive approach to modeling and analysis. L1 regularization, also known as Lasso regularization, possesses the remarkable property of inducing sparsity in the coefficient space. This property endows the model with enhanced interpretability, as it allows certain coefficients to be precisely zero.
11. *The Elastic Net model* is a sophisticated linear regression technique that effectively integrates both L1 and L2 regularization methods. By striking a delicate balance between variable selection and regularization, the Elastic Net model offers enhanced interpretability compared to conventional linear regression models.
12. *Symbolic AI, also known as symbolic reasoning systems, is a paradigm in artificial intelligence that encompasses the representation of knowledge through symbols and rules.* Human-readable explanations of the decision-making process are permitted by these entities (Linardatos et al. 2018, Emmert-Streib et al. 2020).

The interpretability of these models exhibits a spectrum of degrees, and the selection of a model is contingent upon the utilization scenario and the desired level of transparency. Achieving a harmonious equilibrium between interpretability and performance is of utmost importance when employing interpretable models within the realm of Explainable AI applications. It is imperative to meticulously deliberate upon the inherent trade-offs that arise in such scenarios.

1.8 Comparative Study of Four Models

Naive Bayes, a probabilistic classification algorithm rooted in Bayes' theorem, is renowned for its simplicity and effectiveness. The term "naive" is employed in this context to denote the underlying assumption that the features within the dataset exhibit conditional independence concerning the class label. Despite the initial assumption of naivety, it is noteworthy that Naive Bayes exhibits remarkable performance in numerous practical classification endeavors, particularly in the domains of text classification and spam filtering. The Least Absolute Shrinkage and Selection Operator (LASSO) is a regression technique that introduces a penalty term to the conventional ordinary least squares (OLS) regression. The incorporation of an L1 penalty into the regression coefficients serves a dual purpose, facilitating both feature selection and regularization. The L1 penalty, also known as the Lasso regularization, exerts a powerful influence on the coefficients of a model by driving some of them to precisely zero. This remarkable property endows the L1 penalty with the ability to perform feature selection, thereby simplifying the model.

The Elastic Net algorithm represents a significant advancement in linear regression, building on the foundations of the LASSO technique. By integrating both L1 (LASSO) and L2 (Ridge regression) penalties, Elastic Net achieves a harmonious balance between feature selection and regularization, resulting in enhanced predictive performance and improved model interpretability. The integration of L1 and L2 penalties in a regularization framework offers a harmonious equilibrium between the virtues of feature selection, as exemplified by the LASSO method, and the enhanced treatment of correlated features, akin to the principles underlying Ridge regression. The utilization of Elastic Net proves to be advantageous in scenarios where the dataset exhibits a substantial quantity of features, and a subset of these features demonstrates a notable degree of correlation.

Symbolic AI, colloquially referred to as classical AI or rule-based AI, is an esteemed discipline within the realm of artificial intelligence that operates on the foundation of explicit rules and symbols. This paradigmatic approach entails the representation of knowledge and the subsequent decision-making process through the utilization of meticulously crafted rules and symbols. This particular methodology entails the representation of knowledge through the utilization of logical rules, thereby facilitating the process of reasoning through the application of deduction and inference rules. This stands in stark contrast to the machine learning methodologies that acquire knowledge of patterns and interdependencies through the analysis of data. Symbolic AI, once a dominant paradigm in the early stages of AI development, has witnessed a notable shift in recent times. This shift has been propelled by the emergence of machine learning, deep learning, and neural networks, which possess the remarkable capacity to acquire knowledge autonomously from vast amounts of data, thereby obviating the necessity for explicit rule-based systems.

Naive Bayes, a renowned probabilistic classification algorithm, has garnered significant attention in artificial intelligence research. It leverages the power of probability theory to classify data points with remarkable accuracy. However, LASSO and Elastic Net, two prominent regularization techniques, have emerged as indispensable tools in linear regression. These techniques effectively combat overfitting by imposing constraints on the model's coefficients.

1.9 Applications of XAI

Machine learning and artificial intelligence (AI) possess immense potential, both in the present and the future, to revolutionize nearly every facet of the medical field. Nevertheless, the issue of opacity in AI applications has become progressively troublesome in various domains, extending beyond the realm of medicine. The phenomenon is conspicuous in situations where users must decipher and comprehend the generated outcomes of artificial intelligence systems (Antoniadi, 2021). The concept of Explainable AI (XAI) encompasses the provision of a coherent and comprehensible rationale, enabling users to gain insight into the underlying factors that have contributed to a system's generation of a specific output. The resulting output possesses the potential for interpretation within a predetermined context. In recent years, there has been a growing body of evidence showcasing the remarkable efficacy of Artificial Intelligence (AI) systems across various domains (Zhang et al. 2022). These systems have consistently demonstrated their ability to produce exceptionally precise outcomes (Antoniadi, 2021). Machine Learning (ML) models that exhibit commendable performance, characterized by minimal occurrences of false positives and false negatives, such as Deep Learning networks, Support Vector Machines, or ensemble methods (e.g., Random Forest), are, nevertheless, regarded as black box models. In addition to their principal output, which typically involves anomaly detection, event prediction, or failure anticipation, these systems tend to provide minimal elucidation regarding the underlying methodologies employed to attain such outcomes. Furthermore, it is worth noting that certain machine learning models exhibit a rather disconcerting phenomenon. These models, while demonstrating commendable performance during the training and test phases, are unfortunately plagued by an enigmatic bias present within the available data. Consequently, when deployed in real-world scenarios, these models falter and struggle to generalize effectively. Two notable challenges arise from this situation. Firstly, the reliability of the machine learning model's output is called into question. Secondly, additional inquiries are necessary to confirm, pinpoint, and comprehend the underlying issue that prompted the machine learning model's response. The field of Explainable Artificial Intelligence (XAI) has emerged as a prominent research domain, aiming to tackle the challenges. Consequently, it has garnered significant attention across various disciplines and industries. Given the escalating need to enhance the transparency of intricate systems for comprehensibility and safeguarding the rights of end-users, explainable artificial intelligence (XAI) possesses the capability to facilitate heightened acceptance and dependability of AI systems (Kotriwala et al. 2021).

The domain of Clinical Decision Support Systems (CDSSs) presents a compelling case for the integration of Explainable Artificial Intelligence (XAI) techniques. These computational systems assist medical professionals in their clinical decision-making processes. However, the lack of explainability in these systems can potentially result in challenges related to either excessive or insufficient reliance on their outputs. The provision of comprehensive explanations regarding the derivation of recommendations will enable practitioners to engage in more sophisticated decision-making processes, thereby potentially leading to outcomes that are not only more nuanced but also capable of preserving human lives in critical scenarios. The imperative for explainable artificial intelligence (XAI) within clinical decision support systems (CDSS), as well as the broader medical domain, is underscored by the imperative for ethical and equitable decision-making. It is crucial to recognize that AI models, when trained on historical data, have the potential to perpetuate and reinforce historical actions and biases that warrant scrutiny and examination. In the realm of artificial intelligence research, it is observed that tabular data processing explainable Artificial Intelligence (XAI)-enabled systems have gained significant prominence. These systems, which facilitate the interpretation and understanding of the underlying mechanisms driving their decision-making processes, have become widely prevalent in literature. Conversely, it is worth noting that XAI-enabled Clinical Decision Support Systems (CDSS) specifically designed for text analysis purposes are comparatively less prevalent in the existing body of scholarly work. Numerous studies have elucidated the advantageous implications of Explainable Artificial Intelligence (XAI) [6]. These investigations have highlighted notable merits, including the augmentation of decision confidence among clinicians. Furthermore, XAI has demonstrated its capacity to generate hypotheses on causality, thereby fostering an environment of heightened trustworthiness and acceptability for the system. Consequently, these findings have underscored the potential for XAI's seamless integration into clinical workflows. Clinical Decision Support Systems (CDSS) are a class of computer systems meticulously designed to augment healthcare service delivery. These systems have recently witnessed the integration of Machine Learning (ML) techniques, which are being effectively harnessed to further enhance their development and functionality.

The process industry pertains to the intricate and multifaceted domain of converting discrete and distinct raw materials into their ultimate and consummate manifestations as finished products. The proliferation of Artificial Intelligence (AI) systems within various industries has resulted in a notable enhancement of production efficiency, a commendable reduction in energy consumption, and a significant improvement in operational safety. Notwithstanding the considerable level of automation, the involvement of human agents and their cognitive faculties continues to hold significance and indispensability in facilitating the requisite operational processes (Kotriwala et al. 2021). The utilization of Explainable Artificial Intelligence (XAI) within the process industry presents a notable set of challenges, primarily stemming from the multifaceted demands that emerge from a diverse range of AI end-users and AI application scenarios. The process industry, also known as the manufacturing sector, encompasses a range of industries that are involved in the transformation of raw materials into finished products. This transformation is achieved through the application of specific recipes or formulas, which dictate the precise steps and parameters required to convert the input materials into the desired output. The process industry distinguishes itself from other sectors by its focus on the systematic and controlled manipulation of materials, rather than the assembly of pre-existing parts. Illustrative instances encompass sectors such as oil and gas, chemical, pulp and paper, metal, cement, or food and beverage industries. The operational aspects of these processes pertain to the routine activities carried out within the production facility (Antoniadi et al. 2021). These activities encompass the vigilant oversight and regulation of the process itself, the diligent monitoring and upkeep of the equipment, the strategic planning and scheduling of production activities, and the ongoing pursuit of enhancing the production process (Machlev et al. 2022). This pursuit may involve implementing alterations to the recipe or refining the control processes, all to achieve continuous improvement. The operational procedures within these various industries exhibit a remarkable degree of automation, yet it remains imperative to acknowledge the indispensable contributions made by human operators, engineers, and maintenance personnel. A control room operator plays a pivotal role in ensuring the optimization of operational processes, guaranteeing both productivity and effectiveness. Their primary objective is to uphold the highest standards of product quality, while simultaneously adhering to the operational and business requirements that govern their domain (Confalonieri et al. 2021).

1.10 Limitations of XAI and Future Developments and Trends

While the concept of Explainable Artificial Intelligence (XAI) holds great promise in enhancing transparency and interpretability in AI systems, it is imperative to acknowledge and address the inherent limitations associated with this approach. Firstly, it is imperative to acknowledge the absence of a universally accepted norm of the desired outcomes of explainability (Machlev et al. 2022). The requirements for comprehending AI models vary between developers and users, encompassing technical comprehension, as well as norms and decision-making procedures, contingent upon the domain. In addition to the manifold advantages of Explainable Artificial Intelligence (XAI), it is imperative to acknowledge the existence of certain limitations. These limitations encompass concerns of data privacy and security, the intricate nature of AI models, the potential for human bias, and the challenge of ensuring user comprehension. It is imperative to acknowledge the extant constraints of explainable artificial intelligence (XAI) in the present context. Several notable constraints of Explainable Artificial Intelligence (XAI) can be identified.

The domain of explainable artificial intelligence (XAI) encompasses various approaches and methodologies that often exhibit computational complexity, necessitating substantial computational resources and processing capabilities for the generation and interpretation of the valuable insights and information they offer. The computational complexity associated with XAI poses a significant obstacle when it comes to real-time and large-scale applications, thereby constraining the utilization and implementation of XAI within these domains (Streib et al. 2020, Gunning et al. 2019, Avasthi et al. 2022).

The prevailing challenge in the field of explainable artificial intelligence (XAI) lies in the limited scope and domain-specificity exhibited by various approaches and methods. It is crucial to acknowledge that these techniques may not possess universal applicability or relevance across the entire spectrum of machine learning models and applications (Machlev et al. 2022). The inherent limitations in the scope and domain-specificity of Explainable Artificial Intelligence (XAI) pose a formidable challenge, impeding the widespread adoption and application of this cutting-edge technology across various domains and use cases.

One of the primary challenges in the domain of Explainable Artificial Intelligence (XAI) pertains to the absence of standardization and interoperability (Saranya and Subhashini, 2023). Presently, various XAI approaches and methodologies employ disparate metrics, algorithms, and frameworks. This heterogeneity poses a significant hurdle in effectively comparing and evaluating these approaches, thereby impeding the widespread adoption and deployment of XAI across diverse domains and applications.

The inherent constraints associated with explainable artificial intelligence (XAI) pose formidable obstacles that impede the widespread adoption and implementation of this cutting-edge technology across various domains and applications. The deployment of Explainable Artificial Intelligence (XAI) presents a multitude of advantages, as well as certain obstacles and constraints. However, it is imperative to recognize that the significance of Explainable Artificial Intelligence (XAI) cannot be disregarded, as it signifies a pivotal advancement toward attaining enhanced and accountable implementations of AI models in forthcoming endeavors.

As the Future developments and trends the trajectory of Explainable AI (XAI) appears to be highly auspicious, propelled by an escalating need for transparency and confidence in the realm of AI systems. With the increasing ubiquity of Artificial Intelligence across diverse domains, it is imperative to acknowledge the pivotal significance of Explainable Artificial Intelligence (XAI) in guaranteeing the responsible and ethical deployment of AI systems. Future advancements in the field of artificial intelligence are expected to primarily revolve around the refinement and development of deep learning models that possess increased interpretability (Saranya and Subhashini, 2023). This pursuit aims to enable a deeper understanding of the inner workings of these models, thereby facilitating their comprehension and trustworthiness. Additionally, there will be a strong emphasis on enhancing the interaction between humans and computers in the context of explainable artificial intelligence. The implementation of standardized evaluation metrics will play a pivotal role in facilitating the process of benchmarking and effectively comparing explainable artificial intelligence (XAI) techniques. Furthermore, the seamless incorporation of explainable Artificial Intelligence (XAI) within the broader framework of AI pipelines, coupled with the progressive advancement of tailor-made interpretability tools, will undoubtedly expedite the pragmatic deployment of XAI in diverse real-world scenarios. As the field of Explainable Artificial Intelligence (XAI) progresses, it is poised to play a pivotal role in facilitating the democratization of AI. By enabling users to comprehend and make well-informed choices grounded in the predictions generated by Artificial Intelligence systems, XAI holds the potential to cultivate a more transparent and reliable AI ecosystem [1].

Increased adoption of XAI methods for the burgeoning prevalence of Explainable AI (XAI) techniques can be attributed to the growing need for enhanced transparency, trustworthiness, and accountability within the realm of artificial intelligence systems. The necessity for explanations in AI decision-making is propelled by a confluence of factors, namely regulatory requirements, user trust, and fairness concerns. Explainable Artificial Intelligence (XAI) plays a pivotal role in facilitating and enhancing critical applications by ensuring transparency and interpretability. By adhering to legal obligations, XAI fosters a regulatory-compliant environment, thereby mitigating potential risks and liabilities (Machlev et al. 2022). Moreover, XAI contributes to optimizing business outcomes by providing actionable insights and facilitating informed decision-making processes. The utilization of human-in-the-loop artificial intelligence (AI) systems is facilitated, thereby enhancing the overall performance and capabilities of the AI models. This approach capitalizes on advances in research and education, thereby fostering continuous improvement in AI. Furthermore, the integration of enhanced explainable AI (XAI) tools further amplifies the benefits derived from this paradigm, enabling a more transparent and interpretable AI ecosystem. The practical applications of this technology in real-world scenarios serve as compelling evidence of its inherent value, while the prevailing public sentiment places a significant emphasis on the ethical implications that accompany its deployment. In the broader context, the burgeoning recognition of responsible AI underscores the significance of interpretability in constructing dependable and advantageous Artificial Intelligence (AI) systems, thereby propelling the ascendance of Explainable AI (XAI) across various sectors and use cases. There are several compelling rationales for endowing explainable artificial intelligence (XAI) systems with the capacity for justification.

Fostering user confidence in the system's capabilities is the primary motivation for pursuing Explainable AI (XAI) lies in the user's desire to establish a sense of trust and confidence in the AI system. This factor is consistently cited as the most prominent rationale behind the pursuit of XAI.

Safeguarding against bias for ensuring its mitigation is a paramount concern in artificial intelligence research. Bias, whether explicit or implicit, can significantly impact the fairness and equity of AI systems. Consequently, it is imperative for researchers. The imperative of transparency arises from the need to scrutinize the utilization of data by an AI system, particularly with its potential to engender inequitable consequences.

Meeting regulatory standards or policy requirements and ensuring compliance with regulatory standards and policy requirements is a critical aspect of any AI research endeavor. Adhering to these guidelines is essential to promote ethical and responsible AI development. By meeting regulatory standards, researchers can demonstrate their commitment to transparency, fairness, and accountability in their work. Improving system design for considering transparency and explainability holds significant weight when implementing legal frameworks on artificial intelligence systems. The empirical evidence substantiates the assertion that a given product or service has successfully satisfied the requisite regulatory benchmarks.

Estimating risk, robustness, and vulnerability to increase the capacity of the AI system to provide explanations can greatly facilitate the comprehension of its decision-making processes by developers, thereby enabling them to discern the underlying rationale behind its behaviour and subsequently devise appropriate enhancements. The task at hand involves the estimation of risk, robustness, and vulnerability. This multifaceted endeavor necessitates a comprehensive understanding of the potential hazards, the ability to withstand and recover from adverse events, and the susceptibility to harm or damage. By employing rigorous methodologies and advanced analytical techniques, we aim to quantify

Understanding and verifying the outputs from a system for gaining a comprehensive understanding of the underlying mechanisms governing a system's operation can prove instrumental in effectively assessing and quantifying associated risk factors (Gade et al. 2019). The imperative nature of conducting thorough evaluations arises when a system is introduced into an unfamiliar environment, thereby engendering uncertainty regarding its efficacy. This attribute's incorporation holds significant merit within the realm of safety-critical domains, such as airports, automated teller Figmachines (ATMs), and aircraft operations.

The task at hand involves comprehending and validating the outcomes generated by a given system. The incorporation of interpretability techniques within the evaluation process of an AI system can prove to be highly advantageous in the context of verifying its outputs (Machlev et al. 2022). This elucidates the intricate interplay between modeling decisions and the selection of data, both of which exert discernible influence on the resultant outcomes of the system.

There is a growing recognition that the ethical implications of black box artificial intelligence systems render the notion of the ends justifying the means untenable. Historically, the mere acquisition of insights sufficed as evidence for the feasibility of an AI platform. However, in the realm of critical use cases, it has become imperative for AI platforms to demonstrate their capacity to elucidate the underlying rationale behind their decision-making processes. New methods and approaches are highly probable that forthcoming epochs will witness the emergence of novel methodologies and approaches, which shall bestow upon us the ability to procure machine learning models that are endowed with enhanced transparency and interpretability. The methodologies and approaches under consideration may be predicated upon diverse principles and perspectives, thereby affording a more holistic and nuanced comprehension of the inner workings of machine learning models.

Increased demand and adoption are plausible to anticipate a surge in demand and widespread adoption of explainable AI in the forthcoming era. This projection is rooted in the growing realization among various entities and individuals regarding the inherent merits and favorable outcomes associated with the utilization of transparent and interpretable machine learning models (Vilone and Longo, 2021). The surge in demand and subsequent adoption of artificial intelligence (AI) has the potential to catalyse the advancement and implementation of novel explainable AI techniques and methodologies. Consequently, this could pave the way for the proliferation of AI applications that possess a greater degree of transparency and comprehensibility, thereby amplifying their reach and influence across various domains (Avasthi et al. 2023, Rachha and Seyam, 2023, Hasib et al. 2022).

Regulatory and ethical considerations for the forthcoming era will undoubtedly witness an intensified emphasis on the regulatory and ethical dimensions of explainable artificial intelligence (AI), as a growing number of entities and individuals acknowledge the profound implications and ramifications that this cutting-edge technology may entail. The exploration of this avenue holds the potential to engender the emergence of novel benchmarks, protocols, and conceptual frameworks in the domain of explainable artificial intelligence (Mendel and Bonissone, 2021). Moreover, it stands poised to furnish a structural scaffold that facilitates the conscientious and principled deployment of this technology, thereby ensuring its responsible and ethical utilization (Avasthi et al. 2022).

Considering these forthcoming advancements and emerging patterns in the realm of explainable artificial intelligence, they will probably yield substantial ramifications and find diverse utility across various domains and contexts. The advancements can engender novel prospects and complexities within the realm of explainable artificial intelligence (AI), thereby exerting a profound influence on the trajectory of this cutting-edge technology.

1.11 Conclusion

Explainable AI (XAI), although still in its nascent phase, holds significant promise in fostering consumer confidence and trust in the deployment of increasingly sophisticated AI applications. In the interim, enterprises shall be compelled to address the lacunae and engage in conjecture regarding the algorithms employed by the artificial intelligence system to arrive at a decision. The explainable artificial intelligence (AI) is teeming with many forthcoming advancements and emerging trends. These developments possess the potential to yield profound consequences and find practical utility across diverse domains and applications. There are several significant accomplishments and developing trends in the field of explainable artificial intelligence (AI) that deserve attention. The chapter provides a comprehensive overview of Explainable AI and its diverse range of applications within the healthcare industry. XAI in healthcare offers a multitude of advantages, including the timely identification of diseases, enhanced model performance, increased accuracy and precision, as well as efficient knowledge transmission. Furthermore, this paper examines different interpretable models that are commonly employed in the implementation of Explainable Artificial Intelligence (XAI). Additionally, the limitations and challenges of XAI are also addressed in this study.

References

Antoniadi, A. M., Du, Y., Guendouz, Y., Wei, L., Mazo, C., Becker, B. A., and Mooney, C. (2021). Current challenges and future opportunities for XAI in machine learning-based clinical decision support systems: a systematic review. *Applied Sciences*, 11(11), 5088.

Avasthi, S., Chauhan, R., and Acharjya, D. P. (2021). Processing large text corpus using N-gram language modeling and smoothing. In *Proceedings of the Second International Conference on Information Management and Machine Intelligence : ICIMMI* 2020 21-32. Springer Singapore.

Avasthi, S., Chauhan, R., and Acharjya, D. P. (2023). Extracting information and inferences from a large text corpus. *International Journal of Information Technology*, 15(1), 435-445.

Avasthi, S., Prakash, A., Sanwal, T., Tyagi, M., and Yadav, S. (2023, January). Tourist reviews summarization and sentiment analysis based on aspects. In *2023 13th International Conference on Cloud Computing, Data Science and Engineering (Confluence)*, 452-456. IEEE.

Confalonieri, R., Coba, L., Wagner, B., and Besold, T. R. (2021). A historical perspective of explainable Artificial Intelligence. Wiley Interdisciplinary Reviews: *Data Mining and Knowledge Discovery*, 11(1), e1391.

Došilović, F. K., Brčić, M., and Hlupić, N. (2018, May). Explainable artificial intelligence : A survey. In *2018 41st International convention on information and communication technology, electronics and microelectronics (MIPRO)* 0210-0215. IEEE.

Emmert-Streib, F., Yli-Harja, O., and Dehmer, M. (2020). Explainable artificial intelligence and machine learning: A reality rooted perspective. Wiley Interdisciplinary Reviews: *Data Mining and Knowledge Discovery*, 10(6), e1368.

Gade, K., Geyik, S. C., Kenthapadi, K., Mithal, V., and Taly, A. (2019, July). Explainable AI in industry. In *Proceedings of the 25th ACM SIGKDD international conference on knowledge discovery and data mining* 3203-3204.

Gunning, D., Stefik, M., Choi, J., Miller, T., Stumpf, S., and Yang, G. Z. (2019). XAI—Explainable artificial intelligence. *Science robotics*, 4(37), eaay7120.

Gunning, D., Stefik, M., Choi, J., Miller, T., Stumpf, S., and Yang, G. Z. (2019). XAI—Explainable artificial intelligence. *Science robotics*, 4(37), eaay7120.

Hasib, K. M., Rahman, F., Hasnat, R., and Alam, M. G. R. (2022, January). A machine learning and explainable ai approach for predicting secondary school student performance. In *2022 IEEE 12th Annual Computing and Communication Workshop and Conference (CCWC)* 0399-0405). IEEE.

Kotriwala, A., Klöpper, B., Dix, M., Gopalakrishnan, G., Ziobro, D., and Potschka, A. (2021). XAI for Operations in the Process Industry-Applications, Theses, and Research Directions. In AAAI Spring Symposium : *Combining Machine Learning with Knowledge Engineering* 1-12).

Kumar, K., Pradeepa, M., Mahdal, M., Verma, S., RajaRao, M. V. L. N., and Ramesh, J. V. N. (2023). A Deep Learning Approach for Kidney Disease Recognition and Prediction through Image Processing. *Applied Sciences*, 13(6), 3621.

Linardatos, P., Papastefanopoulos, V., and Kotsiantis, S. (2020). Explainable ai: A review of machine learning interpretability methods. *Entropy*, 23(1), 18.

Machlev, R., Heistrene, L., Perl, M., Levy, K. Y., Belikov, J., Mannor, S., and Levron, Y. (2022). Explainable Artificial Intelligence (XAI) techniques for energy and power systems: Review, challenges and opportunities. *Energy and AI*, 9, 100169.

Mendel, J. M., and Bonissone, P. P. (2021). Critical thinking about explainable AI (XAI) for rule-based fuzzy systems. *IEEE Transactions on Fuzzy Systems*, 29(12), 3579-3593.

Merrick, L., and Taly, A. (2020). The explanation game: Explaining machine learning models using shapley values. In *Machine Learning and Knowledge Extraction: 4th IFIP TC 5, TC 12, WG 8.4, WG 8.9, WG 12.9 International Cross-Domain Conference,* CD-MAKE 2020, Dublin, Ireland, August 25–28, 2020, Proceedings 4 17-38). Springer International Publishing.

Rachha, A., and Seyam, M. (2023). *Explainable AI In Education : Current Trends, Challenges, And Opportunities. SoutheastCon* 2023, 232-239.

Saranya, A., and Subhashini, R. (2023). A systematic review of Explainable Artificial Intelligence models and applications : Recent developments and future trends. *Decision analytics journal,* 100230.

Tiddi, I., and Schlobach, S. (2022). Knowledge graphs as tools for explainable machine learning: A survey. *Artificial Intelligence*, 302, 103627.

van der Waa, J., Nieuwburg, E., Cremers, A., and Neerincx, M. (2021). Evaluating XAI: A comparison of rule-based and example-based explanations. *Artificial Intelligence*, 291, 103404.

Verma, S., Mishra, M. P., Verma, M. P., and Gupta, M. M. (2022). Student's Behavior and Regularity Effects Result. *Journal of Pharmaceutical Negative Results*, 6995-7003.

Vilone, G., and Longo, L. (2021). Notions of explainability and evaluation approaches for explainable artificial intelligence. *Information Fusion*, 76, 89-106.

Zhang, Y., Weng, Y., and Lund, J. (2022). Applications of explainable artificial intelligence in diagnosis and surgery. *Diagnostics,* 12(2), 237.

Chapter 2

Healthcare XAI: A Systematic Study

N. V. Neeraja*
and J. Kamalakannan
School of Information Technology and Engineering,
Vellore Institute of Technology, Vellore

Abstract

Now-a-days Artificial intelligence is increasingly widely used in medical and distant healthcare applications, yet the most efficient AI systems are frequently too complex for human comprehension. The authors define explainable AI approaches to provide insight into their accuracy, tolerance, and transparency. According to IBM, Explainable Artificial Intelligence (XAI), often referred to as Interpretable AI or Explainable Machine Learning is a group of methods that enhances people's capacity to comprehend and trust the results of machine learning programs. The ability of an AI model to articulate its goal, intended outcome, and ingrained biases is referred to as "explainable AI." A few of the businesses that have used XAI include banking financial services insurance (BFSI), healthcare, automobiles, the legal system, insurance, manufacturing, the military, and more. As the healthcare system has always maintained, centralized agents presented their raw data. Without sending raw data, FL maintains communication based on the desired system model. The primary objective of this chapter is to provide a concise introduction to XAI algorithms that are employed in various healthcare services and to present the role of Federated learning with XAI in smart healthcare. By describing how the forecast is made, XAI is a technique that can build confidence in the model's prediction, promoting the usage of AI systems in healthcare. This book chapter aims to present a comprehensive and perceptive overview of XAI and XAI in healthcare and the role of federated learning with XAI in the health sector.

Keywords: Artificial intelligence, explainable artificial intelligence, explainable machine learning, federated learning

* Corresponding Author's Email: neeraja.nv2022@vitstudent.ac.in.

In: Explainable Artificial Intelligence in Healthcare Systems
Editors: A. Anitha Kamaraj and Debi Prasanna Acharjya
ISBN: 979-8-89113-598-7

2.1 Introduction

Recently, artificial intelligence and machine learning, in general, have demonstrated remarkable performances in many tasks, from image processing to natural language processing, especially with the advent of deep learning (DL) (Tioa and Cuntai, 2020). Now-a-days although the use of artificial intelligence in medicine and remote healthcare applications is growing, the most effective AI systems are frequently too sophisticated for human comprehension. The authors define eXplainable AI techniques to shed insight into their precision, tolerance, and transparency. New XAI techniques use domain-specific terms and concepts for application domains and modelling. XAI is used in machine learning, robotics, multi-agent systems, computer vision, knowledge representation, reasoning, etc (Kaadoud et al. 2021). According to IBM, "Explainable Artificial Intelligence (XAI), often referred to as Interpretable AI or Explainable Machine Learning is a group of methods that enhances people's capacity to comprehend and trust the results of machine learning programs. The ability of an AI model to articulate its goal, intended outcome, and ingrained biases is referred to as explainable AI." The authors need AI that can explain machine learning methods, which are hard to grasp. The authors need AI that can justify its actions because traditional ML techniques are hard to comprehend and examine. The models are transparent "black boxes," making assertions based on data without providing any justification. It lacks interpretability and transparency. It is challenging to trust and validate traditional ML algorithms. The models are opaque and impenetrable, making them difficult to understand and forecast. These models may not be deployed or adopted due to a lack of trust and understanding. Biased and unjust machine learning models were another issue. Since they learn from biased, incomplete, or unrepresentative data, these models can encode these biases in their predictions. It can impair these models' fairness and impartiality and lead to prejudiced judgments. XAI was created because machine learning algorithms are unfair, biased, untrustworthy, unverifiable, and lack interoperability and transparency. XAI's main goal is to overcome the aforesaid issues (Arrieta et al. 2019).

In Arrieta et al. (2019), and Kavya et al. (2021), the authors observed the XAI's conceptual framework uses machine learning model methodologies and techniques to provide transparency and interoperability. Explainable AI combines these three critical components to make machine learning models clear and simple. The design improves the fairness, credibility, and transparency of ML techniques. XAI's architecture integrates three main components: (a) ML Model: Explainable AI relies on a machine learning model. It includes data analysis algorithms and procedures. Supervised, unsupervised, and reinforcement learning can be used for this phase. Medical imaging, natural language processing, and computer vision employ it. (b) Explanation algorithm: Explainable AI's explanation algorithm reveals the model's most significant factors. This section uses AI methods including feature importance, attribution, and visualization. It can explain the machine learning model. (iii) Interface: Explainable AI's interface displays the explanation algorithm's findings. Web apps, mobile apps, and visualizations can build this part. It simplifies access to the explainable AI system's insights and information. In Arrieta et al. (2019), and Miller, Tim, (2019), the authors observed and concluded some fundamental principles of XAI are transparency, interpretability, and accountability. XAI should offer the most important factors that influence model predictions for purposes of transparency. Openness can help people accept XAI and provide useful insights and benefits for various industries and purposes. Interpretability is the ability of XAI to ensure that the ideas and information it generates are simple to understand as well as to use. Interpretation can overcome the limitations of typical machine learning models, which are difficult to understand and use. It offers insights and benefits in several fields and applications. Accountability requires that XAI take responsibility for the ethical and legal concerns raised by machine learning and offer a solution to these issues. This responsibility ensures that XAI is utilized responsibly and provides relevant insights and advantages in various domains and applications. These principles can ensure XAI is utilized ethically and provide important insights and advantages in various fields and applications.

The book chapter's contributions are as follows:

a. Framework from machine learning to XAI.
b. Knowledge representation of XAI.
c. Interpretability and Explainability.
d. XAI approaches and analysis in sustainable smart healthcare informatics.
e. Role of AI.
f. XAI approaches.
g. On federated learning and the role of federated learning with XAI in the health sector.
h. Threats of XAI in healthcare.
i. Opportunities of XAI.
j. Results and conclusion.

2.2 Framework from Machine Learning to XAI

The goal of Explainable AI (XAI) is to provide a rationale for the predictions made by complex "black box" AI models. Due to their unreliability as forecasting tools, AI models have been under heavy scrutiny in recent years. Both individuals who work on AI and those who use it have concerns about the possibility of generating biased and unfair models. This has led to the development of many laws intended to streamline the inner workings of AI applications at the regulatory level. Therefore, Explainability is crucial, and it can be achieved using several XAI techniques. There were 9 XAI frameworks recommended here. They are Local Interpretable Model-Agnostic Explanations (LIME), Shapley Additive explanation (SHAP), Testing with Concept Activation Vector (TCAV), model Agnostic Language for Exploration and eXplanation (DALEX), Explainer dashboard, InterpretML, ALIBI, Diverse Counterfactual Explanations (DiCE), Explain Like I'm Five (ELI5) (Sheu and Pardeshi, 2022).

In this study, the researchers proposed and discussed a taxonomy of recent contributions related to the Explainability of various machine learning models, including those intended for explaining deep learning methods, for which a second taxonomy was constructed and examined in depth. The classification criteria of the Explainable machine learning model were based on the transparent models and the post-hoc Explainability. This framework was developed using the author's earlier research (Arrieta et al. 2019). In this article, the researcher discusses the latest uses of Explainable deep learning for medical imaging modalities and the broad taxonomy of Explainability approaches. The researcher represents a flowchart that represents the taxonomy based on their literature study. Figure 2.1 presents a flowchart representing the taxonomy of XAI technique classifications.

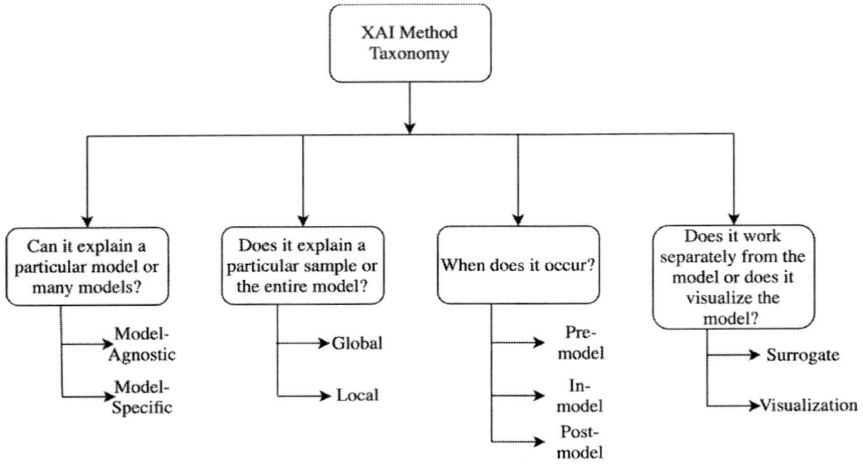

Figure 2.1. Taxonomy of XAI methods.

Model-Specific vs Model-Agnostic

Model-specific techniques are white boxes that use reverse engineering to explain how the individual DL or ML algorithm is making the relevant decision. Examples of model-specific techniques are GNN, CNN, etc. Model-agnostic techniques are black boxes, and they find explanations by disrupting and changing input data and measuring the sensitivity of these mutations on the original data performance. These reveal the input's relative localization, which increases sensitivity

Global Methods vs Local Methods

Locally interpretable methods can be used for just one of the model's results, this can be done by coming up with ways to explain why a certain prediction or result happened the way it did. For instance, it is interested in certain parts and how they work. Global approaches utilize knowledge of the model, its training, and related data to concentrate on the model's internal processes. They are designed to show how the model functions generally, such as by identifying which attributes among a variety improve the model's overall performance. Global methods include PDP, and ICE, while local methods include LIME, and SHAPley

Before-Modelling vs During-Modelling vs After-Modelling

Before-modelling Explainability uses many ways to improve dataset knowledge for model construction. The dataset used to train an AI model drives its behavior, motivating this method. During-modelling Explainability summarises a dataset's primary features. This summary usually includes the dataset's dimensionality, mean, standard deviation, range, missing samples, and so on. After-modelling extracts explanations for pre-developed models. Post-modeling Explainability using perturbation mechanism, backward propagation, proxy models, and activation optimization.

Surrogate Techniques vs Visualization Techniques

Surrogate techniques employ a collection of models to evaluate black-box models by comparing their decisions against substitute models. This aids in comprehending the functioning of black-box models. An exemplary illustration can be found in the form of a decision tree. Visualization techniques, rather than novel models, elucidate components of models such as activation maps by illustrating their underlying mechanisms.

From the perspective of a deep learning researcher creating a system for clinical end-users, Singh, Sengupts, and Lakshminarayanan highlight the different techniques, problems for clinical deployment, and areas requiring future investigation. A new XAI classification criterion was established through the research of Arrieta et al. (2019). The authors observed that XAI classification methods vary greatly based on their characteristics; hence, there is no single "best" taxonomy of XAI methods.

2.3 Knowledge Representation of XAI

Knowledge processing must be automated. Knowledge representation uses reasoning to obtain knowledge. Humans learn more than machines can understand. Knowledge representation is needed. AI agents reason using knowledge representation techniques. Deep thinking lets them solve complex, time-consuming challenges.

This article's objective is to develop a broad theoretical framework for talking about the essential features of explanation and the methods by which problems may be fixed and occurrences can be rationalized. The phenomenological approach to reconstructing complex systems (which includes sophisticated AI-based systems) provides the epistemological foundation for this method. The logical point of view is like that of debate and induction (as a mode of learning). From the perspective of the knowledge representation and reasoning paradigm, and more specifically computational logic, the validity and restrictions of the methods are discussed. Concerning the latter, the suggestion is interwoven with several related explanation concepts from the philosophy of science (Borrego-Díaz, Joaquín, and Juan Galán Páez, 2022).

The focus of this research is on knowledge and neural networks, two areas where XAI has been shown to have strong implicit connections. Both (i) the knowledge domain, which focuses on knowledge discovery and representation, and (ii) the domain of representation learning is included in this narrative evaluation of research publications. Similarities and connections between these fields and XAI were highlighted by the researchers. They concluded that XAI methods could benefit from looking to the past and contemporary works in the knowledge and representation learning domains if they were to make black boxes more understandable (Kaadoud et al. 2021).

Based on semantic technologies and AI, the researcher presents a new architecture for XAI. The architecture is adapted to the field of demand forecasting and is then tested in a real-world scenario. Knowledge fusion about concepts characterizing features important to a given forecast, linked media events, and metadata regarding external datasets of interest leads to the offered explanations. Because it provides information at a higher degree of abstraction than individual traits, the knowledge graph improves the quality of explanations. In this way, proprietary information about the demand forecasting algorithms is protected while still being adequately explained. The knowledge graph provides insights into actionable elements and facilitates the connection of domain knowledge, projected values, and forecast interpretations (Rožanec, Jože M., Blaž Fortuna, and Dunja Mladenić, 2022).

The benefits of knowledge representation and reasoning (KRR) for improving XAI in data science were explored by Joaqun Borrego-Daz and Juan Galan Paez. Knowledge extraction in a deep neural network, and consequently XAI, relies heavily on latent space, latent representation, and hierarchical representation, which have been the focus of research by Kaadoud et al. (2021). Relationships among KDP, KR, RL, and XAI were also studied and brought to light. A semantic explainable framework using explanation graphs has been presented by Roanec, Joe M., Bla Fortuna, and Dunja Mladeni. As a result, the authors can enhance our understanding of black-box output and reason about its origins. Knowledge representation, as shown by the research, is crucial for healthcare systems to exhibit intelligent behavior to accurately diagnose patients.

2.4 Interpretability and Explainability

Interpretability

Interpretability is defined as the ability to explain or to provide meaning in understandable terms to a human (Arrieta et al. 2019).

Explainability

Explainability is associated with the notion of explanation as an interface between humans and a decision-maker that is, at the same time, both an accurate proxy of the decision-maker and comprehensible to humans (Arrieta et al. 2019).

Importance of Interpretability and Explainability

According to Tim Miller the terms "interpretability" and "explainability" are Explainable Artificial Intelligence (XAI): Concepts, taxonomies, opportunities, and challenges toward responsible AI equivalent. Some models may not require explanations (interpretability) because they are used in low-risk environments, the method has been extensively studied and evaluated, the model has no substantial impact, and the problem has been thoroughly investigated (Miller, Tim, 2019).

In this paper, the researcher provides a survey of the most recent XAI techniques used in healthcare and related medical imaging applications. They summarize and categorize the XAI types, and highlight the algorithms used to increase the interoperability in medical imaging applications. The researcher categorized and summarised the XAI method as Explanation forms, Interpretation types, model specificity, and Explanation scopes. Feature map, Textual, and Example-based are the methods that comes under Explanation forms, Intrinsic, and post-hoc are the methods that comes under interpretation types, Model-specific, and model-agnostic methods comes under model-specificity, local and global explanation methods are comes under explanation scopes.

Interpretability vs Explainability

Researchers frequently use the phrases interpretability and explainability synonymously, however despite their near resemblance; several works highlight the distinctions between the two ideas. It is impossible to define interpretability or explainability mathematically in precise terms. Researchers frequently use the phrases interpretability and explainability synonymously, however despite their near resemblance; several works highlight the distinctions between the two ideas. However, many attempts have been made (Lipton-Zachary, 2018; Gilpin et al. 2018; Adadi, Amina, and Mohammed Berrada, 2018; Miler-Tim, 2019) to clarify not only these two terms but also related notions like comprehensibility. Neither an explicit mathematical definition nor a metric have been developed for interpretability or Explainability. All these formulations, however, lack formality and rigor in mathematics (Adadi, Amina, and Mohammed Berrada, 2018). As stated by Miller's definition of interpretability is the extent to which a human can understand the decision's cause, which is intuitive and devoid of mathematical formality and rigor (Adadi, Amina, and Mohammed Berrada, 2018; Linardatos, Pantelis, Vasilis Papastefanopoulos, Sotiris Kotsiantis, 2020).

According to the interpretability is primarily related to the logic underlying a model's outputs (Adadi, Amina, and Mohammed Berrada, 2018). Interpretability in machine learning systems makes it simpler to identify cause-and-effect relationships between inputs and outputs. For instance, in image recognition tasks, the system may determine an object's component in the output by considering notable patterns in the input. Explainability is related to the internal logic and mechanics of a machine learning system, and as a model learns or makes judgments, humans gain a better knowledge of its workings. Interpretability does not always imply that users can understand a system's underlying logic or activities Gilpin et al. (2018) provided support for the idea that explainability is equally important to interpretability and that the absence of either is insufficient. According to the literature review, interoperability and explainability are crucial in many applications, particularly in healthcare systems. The authors envision, for the future of interoperability and explanation in healthcare, that by conducting additional research on how programs and machines can explain themselves, they will gain a better comprehension of intelligence and be able to create more intelligent machines.

2.5 XAI Approaches and Analysis in Sustainable Smart Healthcare Informatics

The WHO's 2020-2024 digital health strategy aims to "improve health for everyone, everywhere, by accelerating the adoption of appropriate digital health". "The field of knowledge and practice associated with any aspect of adopting digital technologies to improve health, from inception to operation" is a more inclusive definition of digital health (World Health Organization, 2021). The strategy helps countries optimize digital healthcare technology in a sustainable, equitable, accessible, and scalable way to help patients manage their health better, improve communication with healthcare providers, and monitor health policy impact for further improvement (Dhingra, Dhulika, Aashima Dabas, 2020).

The Ayushman Bharath Digital Mission (ABDM) was initiated by the National Health Authority (NHA) on September 27, 2021, by the World Health Organization's Global Strategy for Digital Health, 2020-2024. The main objective of ABDM was to utilize health data analytics and medical research to improve the administration of the healthcare industry. To facilitate the enhancement of the efficacy and efficiency of government at all levels. After pandemics, sustainable, intelligent healthcare is crucial because it focuses primarily on scaling up health promotion, disease prevention, diagnosis, and management etc. Several digital initiatives have already been adopted by the Indian government, including the mother and child monitoring system, hospital information system, drug and vaccine distribution system, and ASHA-soft among others. Some of the ethical issues faced by users include:

Healthcare digitization and mobile and IoT data collection devices present many ethical issues. The precise role of consumer tech giants like Amazon, Apple, Google, Facebook, and Samsung in digital health is a frequent theme (Sharon, Tamar, 2016). These companies acquire, store, and analyze health data, raising privacy, data protection, and informed consent concerns (Sharon, Tamar, 2016; Schmietow, Bettina, and Georg Marckmann, 2019). Social media and wearable technologies are generating more private user-generated health data than ever before.

Literature (Kostkova, Patty, Helen Brewer, Simon de Lusignan, Edward Fottrell, Ben Goldacre, and Graham Hart, 2016) often considers data ownership ethics in addition to privacy, protection, and consent. Consumer-oriented apps and technology blur medical and non-medical gadgets and pose ethical questions about how to govern them (Schmietow, Bettina, and Georg Marckmann; Cortez, Nathan, 2018). Technological advancement and healthcare globalization worsen this issue (Cortez, Nathan, 2018; Cummins, Nicholas, and Björn W. Schuller, 2020).

2.6 Role of AI

Digital health system data can help AI improve diagnosis, therapy selection, and clinical outcome prediction. Digital health technologies raise safety, explainability, and justice problems. No standard exists for verifying and validating AI-based systems, and the risk they represent to human life is poorly studied. AI models have trouble generalizing promising outcomes from "limited" training sets on real-world data. Few research on deep learning solutions for medical imaging were high-quality enough for clinical use (Liu et al. 2019). Clinicians and patients now have the right to know how an AI decision was made. Trust and transparency in AI systems assist clinicians, patients, and the system's accuracy and generalizability. Thus, the next clinical AI technology must be transparent, intelligible, explicable, and fair.

AI has performed well in health-based detection tasks, but improving explainability is difficult. Due to "black box" methods, many of these results are difficult to interpret. Thus, data input yields a predictive output without explanation. Deep learning algorithms in digital health worsen this issue. To address the preceding issue, XAI was built (Cummins, Nicholas, and Bjorn W. Schuller, 2020).

2.7 XAI Approaches

This paper examines the field of medical Explainable Artificial Intelligence (XAI), encompassing several aspects such as model modifications, evaluation techniques, case studies, open box architecture, medical open datasets, and potential areas for future progress. Recent methods in Explainable Artificial Intelligence (XAI) encompass many approaches such as local and global pre-processing techniques, algorithms based on knowledge bases, and interpretable machine learning methods. These methods may differ from AI methods. A great deal of algorithms falls under these categories. Under Global and Local Methods for Pre-processing are the algorithms Gradient Weighted Class Activation Mapping (Grad-CAM), Layer-Wise Relevance Propagation (LRP), Statistical Functions for the feature Analysis and Processing, Shapely Additive explanations (SHAP), Attention Maps, and Local Interpretable Model-agnostic Explanations (LIME). Convolutional/Deep/Recurrent Neural Networks (CNN/DNN/RNN), Long Short-Term Memory (LSTM), Recent Machine Learning-based Approaches, Rule-based Systems, and the database of knowledge, and this process encompasses a range of algorithms, together with other XAI methods for plots, objectives, and explanations. Interpretable Machine Learning is further subdivided into two subcategories: (a) Intrinsic Interpretability and (b) Post-hoc Interpretability. Intrinsic Interpretability encompasses algorithms such as Interpretable CNN, Mimic Learning (Ensemble Tree), and Attention Mechanism. Post-hoc Interpretability algorithms consist of Model Agnostic Explanations, generalized linear Models, and LASSO (Sheu et al. 2022).

This study developed reliable deep learning (DL) prediction models for skin cancer classification, addressed a typical severe class imbalance problem (the skin-affected patient's class is significantly smaller than the healthy class), and interpreted model output to better understand the decision-making mechanism. Propose an Android-based smart healthcare system. The suggested DL approach was compared to six well-known classifiers for generalization capability and classification accuracy. An optimized CNN and the HAM10000 dataset identified seven skin cancer types. The model was trained using two optimization functions (Adam and RMSprop) and three activation functions (Relu, Swish, and Tanh). An XAI-based skin lesion classification system used Grad-CAM and Grad-CAM++ to explain model decisions. With 82% classification accuracy and 0.4% loss accuracy, this technology helps doctors diagnose early-stage skin cancer (Mridha, et al. 2023).

The study examines smart city XAI technology advances. It illustrates the society, Industrial, and technological that drive smart cities. It details enabling XAI technologies for smart cities. This article also examines smart cities, XAI technology use cases, problems, applications, possible alternatives, and current and future research advancements. XAI research and standardization for smart cities are detailed. Summarising state-of-the-art research and discussing technical challenges illuminates future research opportunities. This first-of-its-kind, thorough, and detailed study on XAI for smart cities will help future researchers construct XAI-driven frameworks, systems, and applications.

Despite its merits, training the recommended framework involves more labeling components than existing models, such as instance-level bounding boxes and mask labeling, limiting its scalability to large-scale generation difficulties. In this study, the researcher examined the literature review and found several promising research avenues to address such issues. End-to-end instruction permits unsupervised semantic construct analysis. The construct finds the concrete data structures by regularising intermediate output structures. Medical ethics and world safety require diagnostic and therapeutic explainability. Competence, unpredictability, data nonlinearity, and context dependency inhibit the XAI model. Clinical assistance and decision-making applications with dependency inferences complicate model interpretation and explanation. Clinical regimens with lots of human-machine interaction may benefit from XAI models. Dynamic clinical functions complicate model integration and measurement. Explaining problems encourages people to fix them. These models can make regulated decisions automatically (Srinivasu et al. 2022).

Many researchers have already implemented XAI strategies in smart healthcare. Our literature review shows that the XAI system is an important part of healthcare. Our review of the relevant literature showed that model-specific and model-agnostic techniques, as well as global and local techniques (like LIME and SHAP), play an important role.

2.8 On Federated Learning and the Role of Federated Learning with XAI in Health Sector

Federated learning (FL) is a decentralized strategy in which local devices train models using their data while a central server oversees the overall learning process (Lim et al. 2020). This is especially helpful in the healthcare and educational sectors since it is possible to alter vast amounts of data, such as hospital data, to cause system disruption. This technique protects patient privacy by exchanging and modifying model parameters without disclosing raw data. Thus, FL uses privacy-preserving methods and machine learning models to solve many healthcare system issues (Long, Guodong et al. 2021; Pokhrel, Shiva Raj, and Jinto Choi, 2020).

Federated artificial intelligence can solve the problem of explaining deep learning predictions, which are frequently inexplicable due to the black-box nature of the method. This is of utmost importance in the field of healthcare because the author must persuade both medical professionals and patients that the predictions are accurate. Deep learning with FL has created a substantial impact on healthcare, especially in diagnosis and surgery, outperforming physicians despite its black-box nature, which limits its explainability and medical application.

Amoroso et al. (2021) proposed an XAI framework for mammary cancer treatment. Through segmentation and decreased dimensionality, the framework successfully identified critical clinical aspects of a patent and designed oncological medications. Dindorf et al. (2021) proposed an explicable sickness in a vertebra deportment-based classifier. EI-Sappagh et al. (2021) proposed a random forest model for AD diagnosis and progression.

To help both patients and doctors understand the AI model, the knowledge-based technique may generate natural language forms. To aid clinicians in making prognosis predictions for their hepatitis patients, Peng et al. (2021) developed an Explainable Artificial Intelligence framework. Models of interpretable AI (Support Vector Machine, Extreme Gradient Boosting, and Random Forest) are compared in this research. Complex post-hoc approaches such as LR, DT, and K. Nearest Neighbour were generated using SHAP, LIME, and PDPs. Sarp et al. (2021) employed the XAI technique LIME to describe their CNN-based chronic wound categorization model. In Rucco et al. (2020) developed a topological-texture XAI program to diagnose glioblastoma (Rahman, Anichur, et al. 2022). Our study of the literature showed that model-specific and model-agnostic techniques, as well as global and local techniques (SHAP, LIME, PDP, LR, DT, KNN, etc), play important roles in smart healthcare. Along with these models, federated learning also plays an important role in smart healthcare.

2.9 Threats of XAI in Healthcare

According to She et al. (2022), some challenges of XAI are: Explainability ratings for the new models; Measurement system for the XAI evaluation. The authors support Sheu et al. (2022) in their efforts to address the threats of XAI in healthcare.

Explainability ratings for the new models: No rating-based exists for modern XAI-compliant works. Thus, a system can be tested for pre-processing techniques and model explanation after evaluation, which point-based evaluations increase, Explainability is XAI system-dependent prediction and classification and ease of comprehension. Language compatibility and parameter options increase transparency. Data statistics and interpretability at every DNN layer could improve transparency with more details. The user is unaware of the quick decision change because decision transparency is rarely addressed. Thus, every decision should be communicated to the user to avoid false alarms and hospital staff chaos.

Measurement method for the XAI examination: the outcomes of the XAI examination are not quantifiable. Bots and robot-based explanations use diverse classification models like Class Activation Mapping, Gradient weight class activation mapping, network dissection, etc. CXR models may showcase different features. The user's identity consideration might contain a lot of priorities. Amy is used to define preferences using inherent and ad hoc XAI analysis methods. An autonomously adaptive system that chooses the optimum classification and prediction methods is still unknown. The ensemble algorithm is a possibility; however, its brute force method compromises performance. Local datasets bias classification and are ineffective on global data. Adversarial attacks pose a serious threat to model training bias. Thus, detecting bias is difficult.

Explainable Artificial Intelligence research has recently made strides that have led to the development of hyper-tuned classification models that may overfit certain datasets or display feature alterations. Thus, transfer learning models will also perform poorly. The XAI system must be flexible to accommodate additional features, including vital signs, CXR images, ICU parameters, clinical testing, and more. System adaptability and model expansion through user input. To perform at its best, a model that receives input from various data sources must be able to categorize based on only one source of vital signs, or on several sources of ICU parameters, on different sources of clinical tests.

With vital signs or CXR image data, saliency map analysis has difficulty identifying features. During model training, medical examiner-based data labeling is required to enhance model quality and classification output. High hopes for XAI have resulted in a smart system that can persuade doctors of its classification for wise treatment choices. Explainable artificial intelligence development is accelerated by involving human export. Without losing performance, XAI must allow multi-specialty hospitals with separate departments. Users must also be able to customize layer size and weights for efficient diagnostic or severity analyses. This degree of adaptability is essential for making sure that XAI can meet the unique needs and specifications of various medical specialties. Furthermore, the ability to customize layer weights and sizes enables more precise and trustworthy diagnostic and severity analysis. Human specialists' input and knowledge can help XAI consistently develop and strengthen its performance, which will ultimately result in more sensible treatment choices in multi-specialty institutions.

2.10 Opportunities of XAI

Alibi explains and detects how ML models reached their results and identifies unusual data that reduces model accuracy. This lets doctors and people make decisions using their judgment and machines. Providing evidence for ML model conclusions will boost AI adoption due to bias concerns. Explainable AI is also important for healthcare machine learning ethics concerns. Proponents say it improves diagnostics, decision-making, and operational efficiency. To move AI solutions beyond hype and optimism in medicine, models must be trusted to give clinicians the information they need to treat their patients. Due to the FDA's late 2018 advice on ML models, healthcare data scientists will need to uncover or create explainability frameworks that explicitly illustrate how models analyze data. Many medicinal items can benefit from AI, but they will be regulated. Clinical instructions, prescriptions, tests, and discharge papers are examples. Before regulatory enforcement, machine learning pipelines containing these medicinal items should integrate explainability methodologies.

2.11 Results and Analysis

The authors use metrics and evaluations from several published articles, including top FL AI algorithms, to describe binary classification assessment measures. Authors utilize these to demonstrate how different metrics provide varying evaluations of an artificial intelligence model's quality; authors do not evaluate the study themselves. For binary classification tasks, a mixture model can model the data distribution as given in eqn. (1)

$$P(x,\alpha) = \alpha Pp(x) + (1-\alpha)PN(x) \tag{1}$$

$P_{P/N}$ stands for the positive/negative class distributions, and α is the positive class parameter, where x represents data samples, derived as $\alpha = \frac{N_P}{(N_P+N_N)}$,

with $N_{P/N}$ the overall amount of class data samples that are positive or negative. The confusion matrix's 4 entries determine binary classifier metrics, as detailed in eqn. (2).

$$\mathrm{M}=(TP\ FN\ FP\ TN\ ) \tag{2}$$

The term "True Positive" (TP) denotes the quantity of positive samples that have been accurately classified. Similarly, "True Negative" (TN) represents the number of negative samples that have been correctly classified. On the other hand, "False Positive" (FP) signifies the count of samples that have been incorrectly classified as positive, while "False Negative" (FN) indicates the count of samples that have been incorrectly classified as negative.

The effectiveness of popular AI algorithms and models deployed in FL is evaluated using the following metrics:

Accuracy (ACC): Accuracy can be defined as the proportion of samples in an evaluation dataset that have been accurately identified. This is a popular statistic used in machine learning for medical purposes. Accuracy falls on a scale from 0 to 1, with 1 indicating perfect success at predicting the outcomes of all samples and zero indicating no success at all as given in eqn. (3)

$$ACC = \frac{TP+TN}{TP+Fp+TN+FN} \tag{3}$$

Area Under the ROC Curve (AUC): It is a measure of overall classification accuracy. The AUC measures how well samples are classified as positive. It evaluates the orderliness of predictions rather than their absolute values. It evaluates how well the model predicts outcomes across different levels of classification.

Specificity (SPEC): Specificity measures how well negative samples are classified. Accuracy is assessed as the percentage of false-negative samples that were correctly classified. Limiting the range of specificity to [0,1] means that only perfect negative class predictions and inaccurate negative class sample predictions using eqn. (4)

$$SPEC = \frac{TN}{TN+Fp} SPEC = \frac{TN}{TN+Fp} \tag{4}$$

Sensitivity/Recall (REC): The recall, which is also called the sensitivity or True Positive Rate (TPR), is the number of positive samples that were properly labeled as positive and all positive samples. It is calculated as the ratio of properly labeled positive samples to all positive samples. The recall is limited to the range [0,1], where 1 is a perfect guess of the class and 0 is an inaccurate prediction of the class as provided in eqn. (5).

$$REC = \frac{TP}{TP+FN} \tag{5}$$

Precision (PREC): By dividing the total number of samples that were correctly recognized, one can calculate a method's precision. It shows how many of the recovered samples are relevant. The precision metric is constrained within the range of 0 to 1. A value of one (1) indicates that all samples in the class have been accurately predicted, while a value of zero (0) signifies that there are not any right predictions in the class as depicted in eqn. (6)

$$PREC = \frac{TC}{TC+FC} \tag{6}$$

In the context of binary classification, the variable C represents the "class" and can assume two distinct values, namely positive (P) or negative (N).

The results of several research studies that have been mentioned in this book chapter are presented in Table 2.1 in terms of accuracy and ACC.

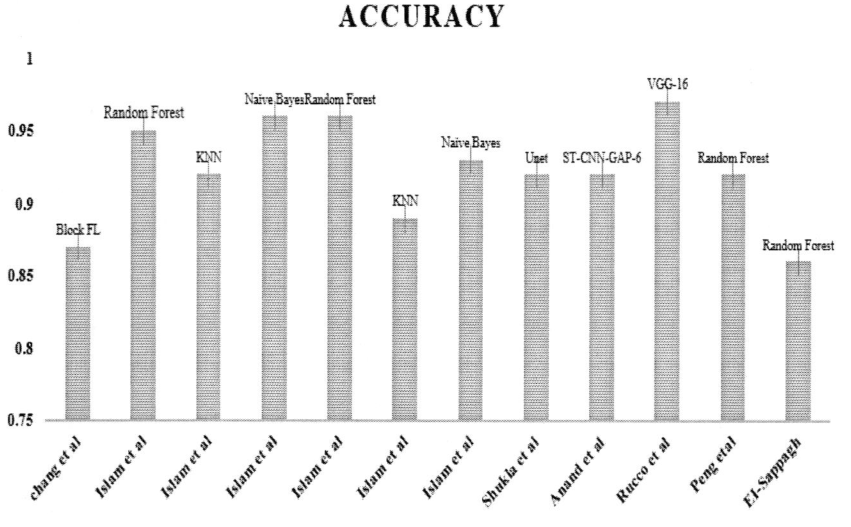

Figure 2. 2. Analysis of various research studies in terms of Accuracy (%).

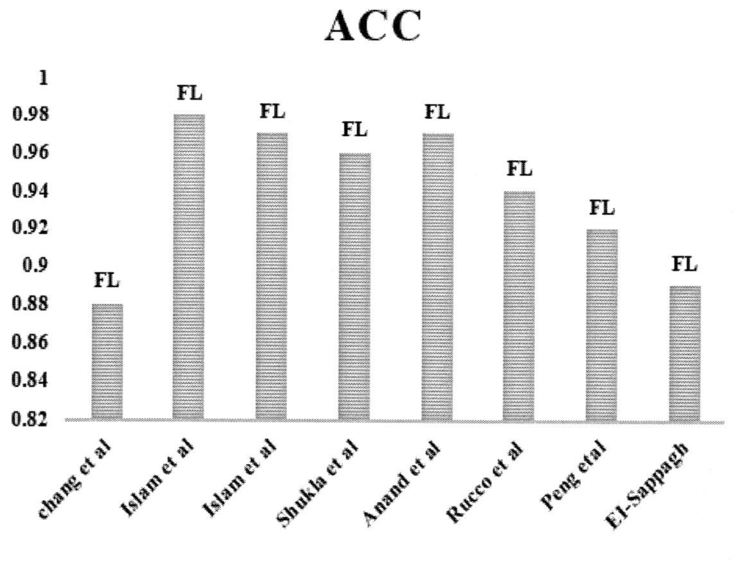

Figure 2. 3. Analysis of multiple investigation results in terms of ACC (%).

Figures 2.2 and Figure 2.3 illustrate the accuracy and AUC findings of the different studies discussed in this article. The graph's Y-axis shows performance scores as percentages, while the X axis identifies the studies that obtained them. Each bar displays the method on top, and the data used in the work is indicated inside the bar.

Table 2.1. Evaluation of accuracy and ACC

Papers	Database	Techniques		Accuracy
Chang et al. (2021)	Pima Indians diabetes dataset	Block FL	FL	0.87
Islam et al. (2021)	Abalone database	RF	FL	0.95
Islam et al. (2021)	Abalone database	KNN	FL	0.92
Islam et al. (2021)	Abalone database	Naïve Bayes	FL	0.96
Islam et al. (2021)	Wine Database	RF	FL	0.96
Islam et al. (2021)	Wine dataset	KNN	FL	0.89
Islam et al. (2021)	Wine dataset	Naïve Bayes	FL	0.93
Shukla et al. (2022)	CT scans from 398 people	U-Net	FL	0.92
Anand et al. (2022)	ECG of erythema victims	ST-CNN-GAP-6	FL	0.92
Rucco et al. (2020)	the carcinoma imaging achieves (TCIA)	VGG-16	FL	0.96
Peng et al. (2021)	Hepatitis classification database	RF	FL	0.92
EI-Sappagh et al. (2021)	Alzheimer's disease real database	RF	FL	0.86

When the dataset was utilized using federated learning algorithms, Chang et al. (2021), Islam et al. (2021), Shukla et al. (2022), Anand et al. (2022), and Rucco et al. (2020) achieved the highest performance, whereas peng et al. (2021), EI-Sappagh et al. (2021) produced the lowest result. The results demonstrate that, when applied to different datasets, federated learning yields superior performance than that of existing machine learning techniques.

2.12. Conclusion

This study makes a thorough investigation of the vast amounts of knowledge about three new topics: federated learning, explainable artificial intelligence, and astute medical care. Additionally, the author discussed an overview of XAI, the various frameworks of XAI, threats, opportunities, and the importance and role of FL along with XAI in the healthcare sector. Additionally, the researcher examined a comparative analysis of FL in the health sector. The researchers believe that it is possible to improve accuracy by utilizing both the already available XAI approaches and the FL techniques.

References

Adadi, Amina, and Mohammed Berrada (2018)."Peeking inside the black-box : a survey on explainable artificial intelligence (XAI)." *IEEE Access*. 52138-52160.

Amoroso, Nicola, Domenico Pomarico, Annarita Fanizzi, Vittorio Didonna, Francesco Giotta, Daniele La Forgia, Agnese Latorre et al. (2021). "A roadmap towards breast cancer therapies supported by explainable artificial intelligence." *Applied Sciences* 11, no. 11. 4881.

Anand, Atul, Tushar Kadian, Manu Kumar Shetty, and Anubha Gupta. "Explainable AI decision model for ECG data of cardiac disorders." *Biomedical Signal Processing and Control* 75 (2022): 103584.

Arrieta, Alejandro, Natalia Díaz-Rodríguez, Nikola Kasabov, Adrien Bennetot, Siham Tabik, Alberto Barbado, Salvador Garcíal et al. (2019). "Explainable Artificial Intelligence (XAI) : Concepts, Taxonomies, Opportunities and Challenges Toward Responsible AI." *Information Fusion* 58. 82–115.

Borrego-Díaz, Joaquín, and Juan Galán Páez. (2022). "Knowledge representation for explainable artificial intelligence : modeling foundations from complex systems." *Complex & Intelligent Systems* 8, no. 2. 1579-1601.

Chang, Yuxia, Chen Fang, and Wenzhuo Sun (2021). "A blockchain-based federated learning method for smart healthcare." *Computational Intelligence and Neuroscience.* 12.

Cortez, Nathan. (2018). "The evolving law and ethics of digital health." *Digital Health: Scaling Healthcare to the World*, 249-269.

Cummins, Nicholas, and Björn, Schuller (2020) "Five crucial challenges in digital health." *Frontiers in Digital Health*, 536203.

Dhingra, Dhulika, and Aashima Dabas. (2020). "Global strategy on digital health." *Indian Pediatrics*, 356-358.

Dindorf, Carlo, Jurgen Konradi, Claudia Wolf, Bertram Taetz, Gabriele Bleser, Janine Huthwelker, Friderike Werthmann et al. (2021). "Classification and automated interpretation of spinal posture data using a pathology-independent classifier and explainable artificial intelligence (XAI)." *Sensors* 21, no. 18. 6323.

EI-Sappagh, Shaker, Jose M. Alonso, S. M. Islam, Ahmad M. Sultan, and Kyung Sup Kwak. (2021). "A Multilayer multimodal detection and prediction model based on explainable artificial intelligence for Alzheimer's disease." *Scientific Reports* 11, no. 1. 1-26.

Gilpin, Leilani H., David Bau, Ben Z. Yuan, Ayesha Bajwa, Michael Specter, and Lalana Kagal. (2018). "Explaining explanations: An overview of interpretability of machine learning." In *2018 IEEE 5th International Conference on data science and advanced analytics (DSAA)*, pp. 80-89.

Islam, Saiful, Umme Sara, Abu Kawsar, Anichur Rahman, Dipanjali Kundu, Diganta Das Dipta, A. R. Karim, and Mahedi Hasan. (2021). "Sgbba: An efficient method for prediction system in machine learning using imbalance dataset." *Int. J. Adv. Comput. Sci. Appl,* 430-441.

Kaadoud, Ikram Chraibi, Lina Fahed, and Philippe Lenca. (2021). "Explainable AI: a narrative review at the crossroad of Knowledge Discovery, Knowledge Representation and Representation Learning." In *MRC 2021: Twelfth International Workshop Modelling and Reasoning in Context*, vol. 2995, pp. 28-40.

Kavya, Ramisetty, Jabez Christopher, Subhrakanta Panda, and Bakthasingh Lazarus (2021). "Machine learning and XAI approaches for allergy diagnosis." *Biomedical Signal Processing and Control* 69, 102681.

Kostkova, Patty, Helen Brewer, Simon de Lusignan, Edward Fottrell, Ben Goldacre, and Graham Hart. Phil Koczan. (2016). "Who Owns the Data? Open Data for Healthcare," *Frontiers in Public Health* 4, no. 7: 1-6.

Lim, Wei Yang Bryan, Nguyen Cong Luong, Dinh Thai Hoang, Yutao Jiao, Ying-Chang Liang, Qiang Yang, Dusit Niyato, and Chunyan Miao. (2020). "Federated learning in mobile edge networks : A comprehensive survey." *IEEE Communications Surveys & Tutorials* 22, no. 3. 2013-2063.

Lipton, Zachary. (2018)."The mythos of model interpretability: In machine learning, the concept of interpretability is both important and slippery." *Queue* 16, no. 3. 31-57.

Liu, Xiaoxuan, Livia Faes, Aditya U. Kale, Siegfried K. Wagner, Dun Jack fu, Alice Bruynseels, Thushika Mahendiran. (2019). "A comparison of deep learning performance against health-care professionals in detecting diseasesfrom medical imaging: a systematic review and meta-analysis." *The lancet digital health* 1, no. 6, e271-e297.

Long, Guodong, Tao Shen, Yue Tan, Leah Gerrad, Allison Clarke, and Jing Jiang (2021). "Federated learning for privacy-preserving open innovation future on digital health." In Humanity Driven AI : Productivity, Well-being, *Sustainability and Partnership*, pp. 113-133. Cham: Springer International Publishing.

Miller, Tim. (2019). "Explanation in artificial intelligence : Insights from the social sciences." *Artificial Intelligence* 267, 1-38.

Mridha, Krishna, Md Mezbah Uddin, Jungpil Shin, Susan Khadka, and Mridha. (2023). "An Interpretable Skin Cancer Classification using Optimized Convolutional Neural Network for a smart Healthcare System." *IEEE Acces.*

Peng, Junfeng, Kaigiang Zou, Mi Zhou, Yi Teng, Xiongyong Zhu, Feifei Zhang, and Jun Xu. (2021). "An explainable artificial intelligence framework for the deterioration risk prediction of hepatitis patients." *Journal of Medical Systems* 45 : 1-9.

Pokhrel, Shiva Raj, and Jinto Choi. 2020. "A decentralized federated learning approach for connected autonomous vehicles." In *2020 IEEE Wireless Communications and Networking Conference Workshops* (WCNCW), pp. 1-6.

Rožanec, Jože M., Blaž Fortuna, and Dunja Mladenić. (2022) "Knowledge graph-based rich and confidentiality preserving Explainable Artificial Intelligence (XAI)." *Information Fusion* 81. 91-102.

Rucco, Matteo, Giovanna Viticchi, and Lorenzo Falsetti. (2022)."Towards personalized diagnosis of glioblastoma in fluid-attenuated inversion recovery (FLAIR) by topological interpretable machine learning." *Mathematics* 8, no. 5. 770.

Sarp, Salih, Murat Kuzlu Emmanuel Wilson, Umit Cali, and Ozgur Guler. (2021)."The ehlightening role of explainable artificial intelligence in chronic wound classification." *Electronics* 10, no. 12. 1406.

Schmietow, Bettina, and Georg Marckmann. (2019)."Mobile health ethics and the expanding role of autonomy." *Medicine, Health Care and Philosophy* 22.623-630.

Sharon, Tamar. (2016)."The Googlization of health research: from disruptive innovation to disruptive ethics," *Personalized Medicine* 13, no. 6.563-574.

Shukla, Piyush Kumar, Mohammed Zakariah, Wesam Atef Hatamleh, Hussam Tarazi, and Basant Tiwari. (2022). "AI-DRIVEN novel approach for liver cancer screening and prediction using cascaded fully convolutional neural network." *Journal of Healthcare Engineering.*

Srinivasu, Parvathaneni Naga, Sandhya, Ruthvij, Jhaveri, and Roshani Raut. (2022). "From blackbox to explainable AI in healthcare: existing tools and case studies," *Mobile Information Systems*, 1-20.

Tioa, Erico and Cuntai Gaun. (2020). "A survey on explainable artificial intelligence (XAI): Toward medical XAI." *IEEE Transactions on Neural Networks and Learning Systems* 32, no. 11,4793-4813.

Chapter 3

XAI in Healthcare: A SWOT Analysis

Anitha K.*
Department of Management Studies,
Meenakshi Academy of Higher Education and Research, Chennai

Abstract

With the help of aided technologies including artificial intelligence (AI), the Internet of Things (IoT), big data, and facilitated networking channels, healthcare 5.0 emphasizes real-time patient monitoring, ambient control and wellbeing, and privacy compliance. Explainable AI (XAI), a recent disruptive movement in AI, aims to make classic AI models more comprehensible by leveraging the models' decision-making and prediction outputs. The explainability factor gives black-box models new potential and gives healthcare stakeholders the confidence to interpret machine learning (ML) and deep learning (DL) models. The requirement for XAI in healthcare historical data can operate as a reinforcer of past behaviors and prejudices that need to be exposed. The present chapter reports the advantages of using XAI in healthcare by conducting a SWOT analysis. For instance, it may increase clinicians' decisional confidence or generate causality hypotheses, both of which increase the system's acceptability and trustworthiness and open the door to its integration into clinical workflow. As with the adoption of any new technology, some substantial obstacles and constraints must be surmounted for XAI to accomplish its goals. The pillars of XAI and the process are outlined in the chapter. A detailed perspective of strengths, weaknesses, Opportunities, and Threats in XAI of healthcare is discussed.

Keywords AI, XAI, explainability, artificial intelligence, healthcare, SWOT

3.1 Introduction

Technology has played a transformative role in the healthcare industry, revolutionizing the way medical services are delivered, improving patient outcomes, and enhancing overall efficiency. The integration of technology in healthcare has given rise to a wide range of innovations and advancements that continue to shape the future of medicine. From electronic health records

* Corresponding Author's Email: anitharamesh211@gmail.com.

In: Explainable Artificial Intelligence in Healthcare Systems
Editors: A. Anitha Kamaraj and Debi Prasanna Acharjya
ISBN: 979-8-89113-598-7

(EHRs) to telemedicine, robotics to artificial intelligence, and wearable devices to genomic medicine, technology has permeated every aspect of healthcare delivery. These technologies can streamline workflows, improve diagnostics, enhance communication and collaboration among healthcare professionals, and empower patients to take control of their health.

Artificial intelligence can currently be executed well and swiftly and is used widely in many fields. This is the outcome of machine learning algorithms being continuously developed and improved to handle numerous challenges, including those in the healthcare industry, making the application of AI to medical imaging one of the most significant scientific pursuits (Nazar M, et al. 2021). AI (Artificial Intelligence) has emerged as a powerful tool in the healthcare industry, offering the potential to revolutionize various aspects of patient care, diagnostics, research, and administrative tasks. Deep learning-based AI is opaque, though, which leaves practitioners unsure of the symptoms of a diagnosis. The crucial query is then how to offer strong support for the answers. But there is a "black box" transparency gap between human cognition and AI models today. (Von Eschenbach, 2021). The explainable AI (XAI) paradigm was created in 2015 by the US Defense Advanced Research Projects Agency (DARPA). Later, in 2021, a project on trust in artificial intelligence (AI) demonstrated that the XAI may be applied to interdisciplinary application challenges in the fields of psychology, statistics, and computer science and may offer justifications that foster user trust (Gunning, D. and Aha, D, 2019). XAI refers to the ability of an artificial intelligence system or algorithm to provide understandable explanations or justifications for its decisions or predictions. Traditional AI models often operate as "black boxes," meaning they produce results without explicitly revealing the underlying reasoning or factors that influenced those outcomes. In contrast, XAI aims to address this limitation by making the decision-making process of AI systems transparent and interpretable.

3.2 Healthcare 5.0

Healthcare 5.0 is a concept that represents the future of healthcare, emphasizing a patient-centric approach and the integration of advanced technologies. Some of the key characteristics and principles associated with healthcare 5.0 are:

- *Personalized and Precision Medicine:* Healthcare 5.0 objects to bring personalized and precise medical care by considering individual characteristics, genetic information, lifestyle factors, and preferences. It emphasizes tailoring treatment plans and precautionary measures to each patient's unique needs, thereby improving patient outcomes.
- *Patient Empowerment and Engagement:* Healthcare 5.0 emphasizes active patient participation in decision-making and care management. Patients are fortified to take accountability for their health, access their health data, and participate in shared decision-making with healthcare providers. It endorses patient education and encourages patients to make informed choices about their healthcare.
- *Integration of Technology:* Healthcare 5.0 influences advanced technologies such as artificial intelligence (AI), machine learning, Internet of Things (IoT), and big data analytics to transmute healthcare delivery. These technologies facilitate remote

monitoring, predictive analytics, real-time data analysis, and personalized interventions, enabling more efficient and effective healthcare.

- *Interdisciplinary Collaboration:* Healthcare 5.0 encourages association among healthcare professionals from diverse disciplines, including doctors, nurses, pharmacists, therapists, social workers, and technologists. It identifies the reputation of interdisciplinary teams in bringing holistic care, addressing the diverse needs of patients, and promoting inclusive well-being.
- *Value-based Care:* Healthcare 5.0 highlights value-based care rather than volume-based care. It focuses on outcomes that matter to patients, such as quality of life, functional status, and overall well-being, rather than just the number of procedures performed, or services delivered. Value-based care encourages cost-effective interventions and the efficient use of healthcare resources.
- *Continuous Learning and Innovation:* Healthcare 5.0 embraces a culture of continuous learning and improvement. It encourages healthcare professionals to stay updated with the latest research, adopt evidence-based practices, and embrace innovation in healthcare technologies and processes. Continuous learning and innovation drive progress in patient care and healthcare delivery.

Healthcare 5.0 envisions a future healthcare system that is patient-centered, technologically advanced, collaborative, and focused on delivering personalized, precise, and value-based care to improve patient outcomes and experiences. This chapter primarily focuses on the integration of technology such as XAI in healthcare.

3.3 XAI

Explainable AI techniques allow humans, such as healthcare professionals, and end-users, to realize and trust the output of AI systems. XAI methods provide insights into how the AI model arrived at a particular decision, which features or variables were considered important, and the logic or rules followed by the algorithm. This explanation can be textual descriptions, visualizations, graphs, or other interpretable formats.

3.3.1. Definitions

To develop a useful definition, thorough analysis of the currently used explanation techniques in machine learning. They offer the definitions listed below:

- "An explanation is an 'interface' between humans and a decision-maker that is both an accurate proxy of the decision-maker and understandable to humans," according to the definition.
- Interpretability is referred to as comprehensibility.'
- ""Interpretability" gives meaning in understandable terms, according to this quote.

Before providing details of the taxonomy and examples, the researchers first provide a nomenclature of explanations, classifying them as model elucidations (explaining the logic of a classifier), outcome explanations (explaining the reasons for a given decision), or model inspection (explaining how the model behaves internally). They make a distinction between regional and global explanations within this taxonomy. While global explanations encompass the entire model and all conceivable predictions, local explanations are exclusive to a single prediction or action. If you can explain one prediction, you can explain all forecasts made by globally explainable models, which are a subset of locally explainable models. The difficulty of solving the global explanation problem is increased by the fact that many local solutions are not universal.

The definition of agents engaged in this set of definitions as being humans and the decision-maker, as well as the assertion that an explanation is a proxy for being accessible, interpretable, and understood, are both crucial elements. Numerous explainable AI techniques share this definition. It heavily relies on a variety of terms, especially those that are synonymous, such as "interpretability," "comprehensibility," and "understandable," to create a linked definition. It stops short of properly defining those concepts, though. The decision-makers and individuals in the setting are quite broadly defined, while the specifics of the practical actions are very detailed. An explanatory method and a certain model are supposed to be held generally.

In the literature, they point out two different methods of explanation: the idea of proxy explanation; and the concept of interpretability in the context of an application. They describe the first by saying that it must be interpreted in some way if it is beneficial in a practical application or a condensed version of it. They suggest that "interpretability is defined as the ability to explain or to present in terms that are understandable to a human" in place of these two approaches, which they reject as being inadequate. They do not formalize the meaning of "explain" or "understandable" in the context of the work at hand, they consider the judgment in terms of "whether [the explanation] results in better identification of errors, new facts, or less discrimination." If a person can complete the task more effectively than the model, like in the case of a student performing better on an exam, the model is interpretable.

3.4 XAI Process

Because it is believed that XAI will be useful for system enhancements in the future. As a result, the following are the primary stages needed for the XAI process. The process is illustrated in Figure 3.1.

a. *Pre-processing*: This phase describes data purification, recovery/imputation, and top feature analysis. The management of inaccurate, duplicate, corrupted, or incomplete datasets is referred to as data cleaning, as opposed to the use of substitute values to fill in the gaps left by missing data, which is referred to as data imputation. The top dominating features of SHapley Additive exPlanations (SHAP), a game theoretic strategy for better prediction outcomes, are found. (Muller et al., 2021).
b. *Methodology:* The model was built specifically for the improvement and development of deep learning or machine learning. Neural networks are used to simulate human brains by offering several algorithms for identifying relationships within the dataset

(Erico, T.; Guan, C.; Ye, Q.; Xia, J, 2022). There are many machine learning algorithms, such as naive Bayes, linear regression, decision trees, support vector machines (SVM), etc. Interpretable deep learning covers related concepts, but it looks at data processing at each layer, helping the designer to control data flow and underlying mathematical operations. The activation functions, max pooling, completely linked classification, and feature learning via convolution are additional possibilities for setting up the layers.

c. *Explanation:* This stage thoroughly describes each selection so that the user may comprehend its meaning and the actions taken by the algorithm. Every decision made inside the model, including pre-processing, prediction method, classification, evaluation, and conclusion, is thoroughly justified in the explanation. The explanations that make up the bulk of XAI's content make the deployed system easier for the end user, professionals in the field, or clients to accept.
d. *Re-evaluation:* A feedback mechanism was developed to understand constraints as the difference between algorithmic and user decisions. At the algorithm's completion, the user can interact with the system by providing the right information regarding each option and set of parameters, which can then be successfully evaluated by reconfiguring in a later version. As a result, it not only promotes user-friendliness but also includes the user in the system, which can improve future iterations of the augmentation of training data and weights.

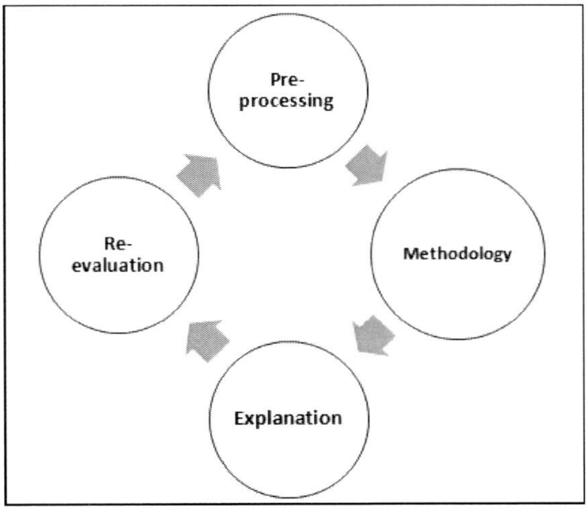

Figure 3.1. Process of XAI..

3.5 Pillars of XAI

The fundamental guidelines that every XAI system must adhere to make sure that the explanations are understandable, inclusive, and ultimately beneficial to people have been divided into five pillars illustrated in Figure 3.2. To have a comprehensive and all-encompassing strategy towards explainability and to provide reliability in such systems, every

XAI-based solution should follow these 5 pillars when developing and building its ML models (Anai, 2022).

- *Explanation*
  The techniques offered by Explainable AI must include explainability since they help open the black box of ML models and reveal the hidden meaning underlying an algorithm's decision. It can discover biased models and establish a culture of fairness and trust by using the explanations produced by an AI. To help the stakeholders understand how the model is working, XAI must offer evidence for each of the outputs.
- *Accuracy*
  An explanation's accuracy is determined by how well it enables various groups and individuals to comprehend the explanations produced by the system. Christmas can produce a variety of accurate explanations that convey the message to all parties involved as simply as possible.
  Research is continuously ongoing, and new approaches to obtaining correctness for an explanation are still being developed. However, an XAI system must produce explanations in several formats because even if a thorough explanation may be thought to be extremely correct, it might not make sense to all audiences.
- *Relevance*
  An XAI system's explanations are only useful if they enable the stakeholder to comprehend the choice made by the system. The XAI systems should be able to explain an output's logic to everyone who will be impacted by it.
  But depending on the explanations themselves, the individual's past experiences, and their thought processes, the applicability of such explanations can change. Consequently, XAI-based systems ought to handle this as well.

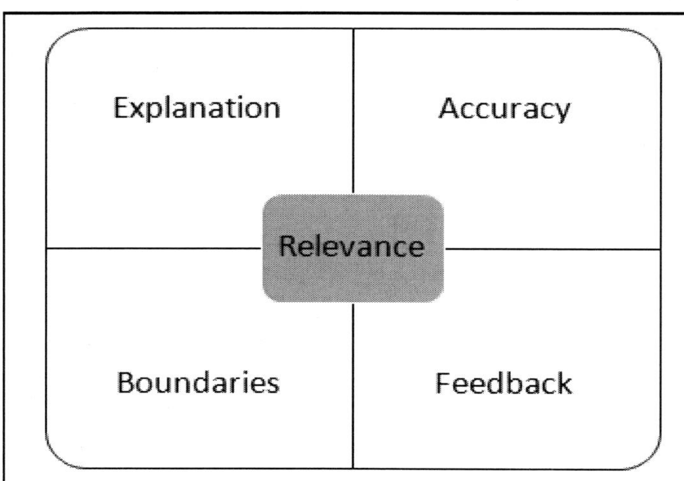

Figure 3.2 Five Pillars of Explainable AI.

- *Boundaries*
  Additionally, XAI systems must always be aware of their limitations and refrain from attempting to provide justifications when none exist. These limitations aid in building a trustworthy system and stop it from providing inaccurate and occasionally dangerous explanations.
  To ensure that users receive explanations only when they are necessary and not just for the sake of it or even if there is nothing to explain, the right XAI technique must be utilized to produce explanations for a specific use case.
- *Feedback*
  Any system needs feedback because it keeps the system in check and aids in systematic progress. The greatest XAI systems should be able to provide comments on what can be improved along with the justifications, albeit it is not essential. Such feedback can hasten the creation of fair and reliable ML models by assisting model developers in quickly identifying systemic issues.

3.6 XAI – SWOT Analysis

This section of the chapter deals with SWOT – Strengths, Weaknesses, Opportunities, and Threats of XAI in healthcare. An outline is tabulated in Table 3.1 followed by a detailed explanation.

3.6.1 Strength

- *Transparency and Interpretability*
  A recent survey on medical XAI emphasizes entirely interpretability (Erico T, Guan C, 2020). The prerequisite for improved interpretability is due to the high level of accountability and transparency found in the medical industry. The expansion of interpretability should be principally focused on refining medical practices, and using data based on exact understanding for technical applications is encouraged even though interpretability is treated similarly across all hospitals. Both perceptual and mathematical structures fall under the many interpretability groups mentioned below. Some of the key points highlighting the importance and benefits of transparency and interpretability which are major strength of XAI are:

  - *Improved Trust*: By increasing the transparency of AI systems' decision-making, XAI techniques aid in the restoration of confidence and acceptability. Users are more inclined to trust and rely on AI systems when they understand how these systems come to their conclusions or suggestions.
  - *Explainability:* AI models and algorithms may now be explained using XAI approaches in a way that is understandable to regular people. This makes it easier for users, stakeholders, and decision-makers to understand how AI-driven decisions are made, which is crucial in crucial sectors like healthcare, finance, and justice.

- *Insights into Model Behaviour*: Users can spot biases, mistakes, or unexpected actions by using XAI approaches, which offer insights into the behavior and operation of AI models. This helps to ensure justice and accountability by making it easier to identify and mitigate any risks and biases associated with AI systems.
- *Legal and Ethical Compliance*: The transparency and interpretability of AI systems are mandated by many laws and ethical frameworks. By supplying justifications for AI judgments and guaranteeing that they are not based on unfair or discriminatory standards, XAI strategies assist organizations in adhering to these rules.
- *User Empowerment*: End-users are empowered by transparent and interpretable AI systems because they can comprehend the justification for decisions made by the AI. The results of the system can be contested or questioned by users, which can improve system performance or reveal biases or inaccuracies.
- *Domain Expert Collaboration*: Collaboration between domain experts and AI practitioners is facilitated by XAI approaches. Domain experts can contribute their knowledge and skills to validate and improve AI models by offering comprehensible explanations, leading to more accurate and dependable systems.
- *Education and Knowledge Transfer*: By allowing users to gain an understanding of the inner workings and decision-making processes of AI models, XAI fosters education and knowledge transfer. This information can be shared across various stakeholders, promoting a deeper comprehension of AI and its ramifications.

  Accountability, fairness, and user acceptance of AI systems depend heavily on openness and interpretability in XAI. These advantages enable a more efficient and responsible application of AI across a variety of sectors by bridging the gap between AI technology and human decision-making.

- *Improved Trust and Adoption*

  One of the significant strengths of XAI is its ability to improve trust and adoption of AI systems. Transparency and interpretability in XAI contribute to improved trust as follows:

  - *Understanding AI Decisions*: XAI approaches offer justifications for AI decisions, making it simpler for people to comprehend why a specific choice or suggestion was made. Users are more inclined to believe and accept decisions made by AI systems when they understand how those decisions were made.
  - *Reduced "Black Box" Perception:* Traditional AI models, like deep neural networks, are frequently referred to as "black boxes" due to the complexity and obscurity of their inner workings. This problem is addressed by XAI approaches, which increase the transparency and comprehension of AI models by offering insights into the decision-making process.
  - *Identifying Bias and Discrimination*: XAI makes it possible to find bias and prejudice in AI systems and to mitigate them. XAI approaches assist in identifying any potentially biased patterns or unfair criteria in the data or model by offering understandable explanations. Organizations can correct prejudices and advance justice because of this transparency.

- *Error Detection and Correction*: The discovery of mistakes or inconsistencies in AI systems is made possible by XAI approaches. Users are more likely to identify abnormalities or errors when they can comprehend and interpret the decision-making process. As a result, AI models become more accurate and reliable as they are improved and refined.
- *Accountability and Responsible AI:* Holding artificial intelligence systems accountable requires transparency and interpretability. The decision-making process can be traced using XAI methodologies, and the people accountable for mistakes or abuse can be identified together with the variables that affect the decision's outcome. This accountability encourages the appropriate design and use of AI technologies.
- *User Feedback and Collaboration:* XAI approaches promote user input and cooperation. Users can offer insightful criticism and suggestions for change when they can understand the decision-making process. By working together, users and AI practitioners may better develop trust and develop AI systems that meet user needs and expectations.
- *Regulatory Compliance:* To follow rules and ethical standards, many sectors and governments demand transparency and interpretability in AI systems. To ensure accountability and transparency in their AI applications, organizations can achieve these compliance criteria with the use of XAI approaches.

Table 3.1 SWOT Analysis of XAI

Strength	**Weakness**	**Opportunities**	**Threats**
Transparency & Interpretability	Complexity of Explanations	Minimized Error	Data Privacy & Security
Improved Trust and Adoption	Limited Generalization	Model Performance	Human Bias
Enhanced Clinical Decision Support	Potential for Overconfidence	Informed Decision Making	User Understanding
Error Detection and Mitigation	Data Bias and Interpretation	--	--
Regulatory Compliance	Complex Implementation and Integration	--	--
Patient Empowerment and Education	--	--	--

- *Enhanced Clinical Decision Support*

  One of the areas where XAI can have a significant impact is in enhancing clinical decision support systems. XAI can contribute to improved clinical decision-making as follows:

- *Interpretability of AI Models:* Healthcare practitioners can comprehend and analyze the forecasts and recommendations offered by AI models thanks to XAI approaches. In clinical settings, where choices directly affect patient care, interpretability is essential. Clinicians can more effectively trust and make use of AI-driven recommendation systems by outlining the logic behind them.
- *Transparency in Risk Assessment:* Clinical decision support systems that use XAI can conduct transparent risk assessments. Clinicians can make defensible

decisions by comprehending the variables and circumstances that affect risk predictions. Patient safety is enhanced through the identification of high-risk patients, potential adverse events, or missed diagnoses.

- *Identification of Relevant Features*: The most pertinent aspects or contributing factors to a forecast can be found with the aid of XAI algorithms. This can help doctors understand which patient traits or clinical variables have the greatest bearing on the suggested course of action in clinical decision support. It aids clinicians in concentrating on the most important information and weighing it against their own experience.
- *Detection of Bias and Discrimination*: XAI approaches make it easier to find biases in clinical decision support systems and to reduce their impact. These techniques enable interpretability, which enables the determination of whether the AI models unfairly favor or discriminate against patient groups. This promotes equity and fairness in healthcare decisions.
- *Accountability and Justification*: Clinical professionals can explain their choices to patients or coworkers using XAI. When AI systems produce clear and comprehensible outputs, practitioners can explain the thinking behind their suggestions and win over patients' and colleagues' trust. It helps patients comprehend the rationale behind their treatment regimens and encourages joint decision-making.
- *Continuous Learning and Improvement*: XAI techniques shed light on the effectiveness and bounds of AI models. Clinicians can pinpoint situations when the model might have erred or neglected to take crucial clinical considerations into account. The AI system may learn and develop continuously thanks to this feedback loop, which over time improves accuracy and dependability.
- *Education and Collaboration*: XAI endorses an alliance between AI experts and healthcare professionals. XAI approaches help these two groups communicate and share knowledge by offering understandable explanations. Clinical decision support systems will be more reliable and efficient as a result of clinicians' domain experience and improved understanding of the AI models.
- By bringing accountability, transparency, and interpretability to clinical decision support systems, XAI has the potential to transform them. XAI can assist doctors in making knowledgeable decisions, improving patient outcomes, and building trust in AI-driven healthcare systems by improving the comprehension of AI models and their outputs.

- *Error Detection and Mitigation*

  Error detection and mitigation are crucial aspects of XAI to ensure the reliability and accuracy of AI systems. Error detection and mitigation role in XAI is listed below:

  - *Identification of Systematic Errors*: AI models may contain systematic flaws or biases, which can be found using XAI approaches. These methods help researchers and practitioners comprehend the model's decision-making process and recognize patterns of errors or biases that may develop owing to data restrictions, algorithmic biases, or other factors by offering interpretability.

- *Detection of Outliers and Anomalies*: Outliers and abnormalities that may have an impact on the performance of AI systems can be found using XAI approaches. XAI approaches can identify situations where the input data significantly deviates from the norm, possibly revealing errors or misleading information, by analyzing the contributions of various variables or features in the model's decision-making process.
- *Error Quantification and Confidence Estimation*: The degree of uncertainty and confidence surrounding AI predictions or choices can be quantified using XAI methodologies. Users can assess the accuracy of the outputs of the AI system using XAI approaches by providing confidence intervals or uncertainty estimations. Unusually high uncertainty or low confidence levels could be a sign of mistakes or performance constraints in the model.
- *Feedback Loop for Error Correction*: XAI allows a feedback loop for model improvement and error correction. XAI techniques can be used to explore the root causes of mistakes or anomalies and direct changes to the AI system. The model's accuracy and performance are improved over time by using an iterative process of error analysis and correction.
- *Data Quality Assessment*: XAI approaches can be used to evaluate the accuracy and reliability of the input data. XAI approaches can spot situations where the data may be missing, inconsistent, or corrupted by studying the connections between the input variables and the model's output. This makes it possible to execute data cleaning and pre-processing operations to reduce potential errors and enhance the performance of the AI system.
- *Model Robustness Testing*: XAI techniques can be used to assess an AI model's resistance to different scenarios or disturbances. XAI approaches can assess a model's performance under various scenarios and pinpoint any potential flaws or failure modes by doing sensitivity studies or stress tests. This makes it possible to recognize and correct mistakes that can occur during actual deployment.
- *Explainability for Error Understanding*: XAI offers interpretability, enabling people to comprehend how mistakes or inaccurate predictions happen. Using XAI approaches, users can identify the sources of errors and learn more about the model's limitations by looking at the variables or components that go into a particular decision or output. Improvements to systems and tactics for error mitigation are made easier by this insight.

  XAI intends to enhance the robustness, dependability, and trustworthiness of AI systems by incorporating error detection and mitigation procedures. It enables proactive error detection and correction, resulting in more precise and reliable decision-making across a range of domains.

- *Regulatory Compliance*

  Regulatory compliance is a significant consideration in the development and deployment of XAI systems through:

  - *Transparency and Accountability*: Transparency and accountability are requirements in many regulatory regimes for AI systems. AI judgments are made more transparent and intelligible with XAI approaches, which offer explanations.

This makes it possible for businesses to adhere to laws that demand an explanation of AI outputs, assuring accountability for the choices the system makes.

- *Fairness and Non-discrimination*: In regulatory rules, the significance of fairness and non-discrimination in AI systems is frequently emphasized. XAI techniques can be used to spot prejudices and biased trends in decision-making. By supplying interpretability, XAI enables businesses to evaluate the fairness of their AI models and take the appropriate action to reduce any potential biases.
- *Ethical Guidelines*: Ethics standards for AI applications are frequently established by regulatory agencies and professional organizations. By offering transparency, interpretability, and explainability, XAI can help with adherence to these rules. This makes it easier to ensure that AI systems follow moral standards like respect for privacy, autonomy, and justice.
- *Data Protection and Privacy*: Laws governing the handling of personal data, such as the General Data Protection Regulation (GDPR), impose requirements. By offering tools to comprehend how personal data is used in AI models and ensuring that data protection and privacy principles are respected, XAI approaches can help with compliance with these rules.
- *Algorithmic Auditing and Validation*: A few regulatory frameworks might demand that AI systems be audited and validated. By offering comprehensible explanations and insights into the decision-making process, XAI approaches can assist these demands. As a result, businesses may evaluate the accuracy and legitimacy of their AI models and fulfill their legal duties for auditing and validation.
- *Consent and User Rights*: XAI can help ensure that laws about user rights and consent are followed. Users can better understand how their data is used and the effects of AI-driven results by offering explanations for AI judgments. This makes it possible for businesses to have users' informed consent and respect their right to view, correct, and delete their data by any applicable laws.
- *Documentation and Reporting*: Requirements for reporting and documentation are frequently part of regulatory compliance. Through the provision of traceability and documentation of the decision-making process, XAI approaches can assist these duties. Organizations can document the factors, variables, and rationale behind AI choices thanks to the interpretability and transparency of XAI methodologies, which helps with regulatory reporting and compliance.

It is significant to keep in mind that certain regulatory requirements may change based on the jurisdiction and the specific application domain. To ensure compliance during the development, deployment, and continuous operation of their AI systems, organizations creating XAI systems should carefully evaluate the pertinent laws and policies.

- *Patient Empowerment and Education*

Patient empowerment and education are essential aspects of XAI that can positively impact healthcare and are listed below:

- *Transparency in Medical Decisions*: Patients can better grasp the thinking behind AI-driven medical decisions by using XAI approaches, which offer explanations for those judgments. XAI gives patients the ability to take an active role in their healthcare and make knowledgeable judgments about their treatment alternatives by making the decision-making process clear and understandable.

- *Shared Decision-Making*: XAI enables patients and healthcare professionals to make decisions together. Patients can actively participate in talks with their healthcare providers, express their preferences, and jointly choose the best treatment options when they have access to clear explanations of AI recommendations. Patients are given more authority to participate in their healthcare decisions thanks to this shared decision-making process.
- *Improved Health Literacy*: By more clearly articulating difficult medical terms and concepts, XAI approaches help improve health literacy. Patients can learn more about their diseases, possible therapies, and anticipated results. Patients are more equipped to make educated decisions about their care thanks to this knowledge, which also encourages them to look for more information.
- *Educational Resources*: XAI can aid in the creation of patient education materials. To help patients understand the reasoning behind AI-driven suggestions, educational materials can be made using the explanations offered by XAI approaches, such as patient-friendly summaries or visualizations. By educating patients about their medical issues and available therapies, these resources promote patient empowerment and self-management.
- *Risk Communication*: The risks and uncertainties related to medical decisions can be communicated with the help of XAI approaches. XAI can explain the elements impacting the risk assessments produced by AI systems by offering transparency and interpretability. Patients can make decisions that are in line with their preferences and values by being informed about the potential advantages, dangers, and trade-offs of various treatment alternatives.
- *Trust and Confidence in AI Systems*: Patients can grow to trust and have confidence in the AI systems employed in their care when they have access to explanations for AI-driven suggestions. Concerns and cynicism can be reduced by understanding the underlying decision-making process and the variables the AI system considers. When patients understand the rationale behind the suggestions, they are more likely to follow the treatment programs.
- *Empowered Advocacy*: XAI gives patients the ability to speak up for their demands and rights within the healthcare system. Patients can contest decisions that seem to go against their preferences or values by understanding the elements that affect AI-driven decisions. This advocacy supports patient-centered treatment and encourages collaboration between patients, medical professionals, and AI systems.

By giving open and understandable justifications for AI-driven medical decisions, XAI supports patient empowerment and education. It enables patients to take an active role in their healthcare, create wise judgments, and improve their well-being. Patients are given the tools they need to take charge of their health and actively participate in the healthcare process thanks to XAI's enhancement of health literacy and facilitation of shared decision-making.

3.6.2 Weakness

- *Complexity of Explanations*
  One of the weaknesses of XAI is the complexity of explanations it provides. XAI techniques aim to provide transparent and understandable explanations for the decisions made by AI models. However, in complex and highly sophisticated AI systems, the explanations generated by XAI methods can be difficult to understand for non-experts. A list of a few reasons why the complexity of explanations can be a weakness is explained below:

  - *Interpretability Gap*: XAI approaches frequently produce explanations for the AI model's internal workings or feature relevance at a lower level of representation. Although theoretically correct, these explanations may be difficult for users without technical knowledge to understand. The usefulness of explanations for non-experts who need to comprehend the decision-making process is constrained by this interpretability gap.
  - *Lack of Context*: AI models frequently use complicated mathematical techniques and enormous amounts of data to operate. It might be challenging to simply and intuitively explain the choices that these models make. Due to the complexity of the underlying AI system, it can be challenging to give explanations that fully account for contextual information, which might result in explanations that are either inaccurate or incomplete.
  - *Scalability*: It may be difficult for XAI techniques to scale deeper learning models that are more complicated than simple AI models. It gets harder to come up with explanations that fully describe the behavior of AI models as they become more complex and have millions or even billions of parameters. The complexity of the model may cause a large rise in the complexity of the explanations, making it more difficult to study and comprehend the underlying decision-making process.
  - *The trade-off between Accuracy and Simplicity*: Finding the ideal mix between precision and simplicity is a problem when creating explanations. Complex AI models may include complex decision boundaries and dependencies that are challenging to comprehend straightforwardly. While more accurate explanations could be too complex for consumers to comprehend, simplifying them risks losing crucial information and lowering their accuracy.
  - Continuous XAI research and improvement are necessary to address these flaws. Some of the areas where researchers are actively working to reduce the complexity of explanations in XAI include finding a balance between precision and simplicity, enhancing the contextualization of explanations, and creating user-friendly interfaces that can effectively communicate complex AI decisions.

- *Limited Generalization*
  One more weakness of XAI is its limited generalization competence. XAI techniques often emphasize amplifying the decisions made by a specific AI model for a given set of inputs. However, these clarifications may not always simplify well to diverse scenarios or variations of the problem, which limits their broader applicability. A few reasons why limited generalization a weakness in XAI can be as follows:

- *Contextual Dependence*: XAI approaches frequently depend on the context to deliver their explanations. They rely on the data and distribution that were utilized to train the AI model. The explanations may not adequately describe the decision-making process or may fall short of offering insightful information when the model encounters inputs that considerably deviate from the training data.
- *Lack of Robustness*: XAI methods might not be resilient to modifications made to the AI model itself. The explanations produced by the XAI methods may no longer be valid or need to be reevaluated if the model design or parameters are changed. The applicability of XAI techniques in dynamic situations where AI models change over time may be constrained by this lack of robustness.
- *Limited Coverage*: Instead, then offering a comprehensive knowledge of the behavior of the AI model, XAI techniques frequently concentrate on explaining specific predictions or actions. Even though explanations for specific cases can be helpful, they might not represent the broad trends and guiding ideas influencing the model's judgement. As a result, the explanations might not apply well to other inputs or scenarios.
- *Domain Specificity*: XAI approaches are frequently created and tested within certain applications or domains. When applied to a new domain with distinct characteristics or constraints, the explanations developed for one area might not translate well. When using XAI approaches in new domains or attempting to comprehend AI models that function across several domains, this lack of generalizability can be a constraint.
- The problem of restricted generalization in XAI is a topic of active research. Instead of concentrating simply on instance-level explanations, developing methodologies that capture the underlying principles and high-level behaviors of AI models can aid in improving generalization. Additionally, investigating transfer learning methods and techniques that apply XAI approaches across many domains may expand the range of applications for the explanations produced by XAI procedures.

- *Potential for Overconfidence*
  Another flaw with XAI is its propensity towards arrogance. While XAI techniques try to explain AI model decisions, there is a chance that doing so could give users a false sense of security or confidence in the model's precision and dependability. In some circumstances, this arrogance might have detrimental effects. A few explanations as to why XAI may be susceptible to overconfidence are listed below:

  - *Incomplete or Misleading Explanations*: Due to the intricacy of the AI model or the technique's limits, XAI approaches may produce explanations that are inaccurate or incomplete. Users may overestimate the efficacy of the model because they believe these explanations to be complete and accurate depictions of the decision-making process. However, not all pertinent issues may be covered by the explanations given.
  - *Lack of Uncertainty Quantification*: AI models inherently deal with uncertainty, especially in complex real-world scenarios. XAI Methods frequently have trouble expressing and quantifying this ambiguity. Users may have a higher level of

confidence than is necessary when given explanations that fail to express the degree of uncertainty or probable inaccuracies in the model's conclusions. A misplaced faith in the AI system can result from relying too heavily on these explanations without comprehending their limitations.

- Human Bias and Interpretation: Because XAI techniques are created by people, they may unintentionally include their biases or presumptions in the explanations. The explanations may also be interpreted incorrectly or biased by humans. When people accept the answers without questioning their underlying presumptions or potential biases, this might result in overconfidence.
- *Sensitivity to Adversarial Attacks*: Adversarial assaults entail changing the input data in a way that leads the AI model to make the wrong judgements while keeping the justifications the same. Users may be duped into believing the model is reliable even while it is susceptible to adversarial attacks if they simply rely on the explanations to make this determination. In industries where safety is crucial, like healthcare or driverless vehicles, this arrogance can have disastrous effects.
- XAI's potential for overconfidence must be addressed in a balanced manner. The restrictions and uncertainties related to the justifications produced by XAI approaches must be made clear. Users can make more informed judgements and avoid having blind faith in the model's answers by quantifying and communicating uncertainty and potential inaccuracies. Moreover, encouraging XAI's transparency, auditability, and independent assessment can mitigate the risks of overconfidence and ensure a more realistic understanding of the model's performance.

- Data Bias and Interpretation
  XAI's susceptibility to skewed data and problems with interpretation is another flaw. The data used to train AI models and the interpretations made by humans to produce explanations are both important components of XAI methodologies. However, biases in the data and subjective interpretations might contribute to errors and strengthen preexisting biases, perhaps making the explanations given insufficient. Data bias and interpretation may be flaws in XAI for the following reasons:

  - *Bias in Training Data*: The historical data that AI models use to train can reflect societal preconceptions and biases that may have been present during the data collection process. The explanations produced by XAI algorithms may reinforce any biases present in the training data. Because the explanations' biases cannot be obvious or simple to spot, users who rely on them might unintentionally encourage unfair or discriminatory practices.
  - *Interpretation Challenges*: To properly comprehend and make use of the explanations produced by XAI techniques, human interpretation is frequently necessary. However, because interpretation is a subjective process, biases or incorrect interpretations may be introduced. The same model's choice may be explained differently by many interpreters, resulting in inconsistencies and even misunderstandings. It can be challenging to maintain the impartiality and accuracy of the interpretation because of this subjective aspect.

- *Lack of Contextual Understanding*: The context and subtleties of the data may be difficult for XAI algorithms to fully capture. The explanations offered by XAI approaches could concentrate on certain traits or correlations without taking the decision-making process' larger context into account. Due to insufficient contextual knowledge, significant interactions or factors may be missed or presented incorrectly, resulting in incomplete or misleading explanations.
- *Limited Diversity in Training Data*: The training data used to build AI models lacks diversity, which might lead to explanations that are biased or have a narrow scope. The explanations might not be relevant or applicable to people or groups outside of that group if the training data predominantly represents that group in terms of demographics, culture, or socioeconomic status. This may result in discriminatory or biased explanations that do not consider the needs and perspectives of diverse populations.
- Fairness, openness, and inclusivity in XAI must be ensured by addressing data bias and interpretation issues. Through rigorous data collection procedures, data pre-processing methods, and routine audits of the training data for biases, efforts should be taken to mitigate biases in training data. Subjective biases can be found and addressed by promoting a diversity of viewpoints and integrating interdisciplinary teams in the interpretation process. Furthermore, encouraging transparency in the interpretation process and permitting user comment and inspection might aid in locating and resolving potential biases in the explanations given by XAI approaches.

- Complex Implementation and Integration

  The difficulty of XAI's implementation and integration with current AI systems is another flaw in the technology. Although XAI techniques provide useful insights into AI model choices, efficiently implementing them can be difficult and resource-intensive, creating impediments to their wider adoption. XAI may have a drawback due to sophisticated implementation and integration for the following reasons:

  - *Technical Complexity*: Deep technical knowledge and an understanding of the underlying AI models and algorithms are frequently needed to implement XAI techniques. These methods might entail enhancing or changing current models, adding new modules, or creating unique architectures. Because of this complexity, adopting and integrating XAI into systems may prove challenging for businesses or developers with limited AI expertise.
  - *Performance Trade-offs*: The incorporation of XAI approaches may result in increased computing overhead, which may influence the AI system's performance. Some XAI techniques call for completing several rounds or additional calculations to generate explanations, which can lengthen the inference time and demand more resources. It can be difficult to strike a compromise between the intended amount of explanation and the influence on the system's performance.
  - *Integration Challenges*: The designs, frameworks, and infrastructure of existing AI systems are frequently complicated and may not be easily adaptable to XAI methodologies. It could be time-consuming and expensive to retrofit, construct, or

make significant changes to the infrastructure to integrate XAI into these systems. The difficulty of seamless integration is made more difficult by the absence of standardized tools and interfaces for integrating XAI techniques.

- *Need for Domain Expertise*: Domain-specific knowledge and experience are frequently needed for effective XAI technology deployment and integration. Different areas have criteria for interpretability, considerations, and data characteristics. It can be difficult to adapt XAI techniques to domains and to guarantee that the explanations that are produced are meaningful and helpful to domain specialists.

For XAI techniques to be more widely adopted, the implementation and integration challenges must be addressed. Lowering the technical hurdles can be accomplished by streamlining the implementation procedure through the creation of user-friendly tools, libraries, and standardized interfaces. Organizations may negotiate the difficulties by offering clear standards, best practices, and documentation for incorporating XAI into current AI systems. Furthermore, encouraging cooperation among domain experts, AI researchers, and practitioners can guarantee that the integration and implementation procedures adhere to the distinct needs and specifications of various domains.

3.6.3 Opportunities

- *Minimized Error*

The ability to reduce AI system faults is one of the major opportunities presented by XAI. XAI approaches can aid in the identification and correction of errors, hence reducing the likelihood of unfavorable outcomes, by offering explicit and understandable justifications for the decisions made by AI models. A few XAI changes that help to reduce errors are:

- *Error Detection and Diagnosis*: XAI approaches make it possible to spot biases or flaws in the judgements made by AI models. Users can learn more about how the model arrived at a specific choice and spot any inconsistencies or inaccuracies by studying the explanations given. This enables users to identify and assess potential problems or errors in AI systems.
- *Error Correction and Model Improvement*: AI model flaws can be fixed, and models enhanced with the use of XAI explanations. Targeted changes or updates to the model are possible by understanding the elements and traits that lead to poor choices. Models can be improved with the help of XAI, which will improve performance, lower mistakes, and increase reliability.
- *Human-AI Collaboration*: Collaboration between humans and AI systems is facilitated by XAI techniques by increasing the transparency of the decision-making process. Users can use justifications to supplement their knowledge and discretion, effectively validating or contesting the conclusions reached by AI models. By combining the advantages of AI technology and human intellect, this collaborative strategy reduces errors.

- *Bias Mitigation*: By addressing biases in AI systems, XAI can lessen unfair or discriminating outcomes. The identification and mitigation of biases are made possible by XAI approaches by revealing the underlying elements and characteristics that affect decisions. This chance enables the creation of more egalitarian and fair AI systems that reduce bias-related errors.
- *Safety and Trust*: XAI approaches help make AI systems more trustworthy and safer. Users are better able to comprehend the behavior and logic of the system when they have access to justifications for the decisions made by AI models. This knowledge fosters confidence and trust, lowering the possibility of mistakes brought on by a blind dependence on the AI system and assuring a safer and more responsible use of AI technology.

  By leveraging these opportunities, XAI can play a critical role in minimizing errors and improving the overall performance and reliability of AI systems across various domains and applications.

- *Model Performance*

  Opportunities for enhancing model performance are provided by XAI. XAI approaches can help uncover problem areas, improve model performance, and raise the overall efficacy of AI systems by giving insights into the decision-making process of AI models. Here are some XAI chances that help improve model performance:

  - *Feature Importance and Understanding*: The significance and contribution of various aspects or inputs in the decision-making process of AI models can be revealed via XAI approaches. This knowledge enables feature engineering and selection, making it possible to identify the most pertinent and instructive traits. Model performance can be enhanced by concentrating on the most important elements, which will result in more precise forecasts and higher overall performance.
  - *Error Analysis and Debugging*: XAI offers justifications for specific predictions or judgements, enabling users to spot and investigate mistakes or incorrect classifications made by AI models. Adjustments can be made to address the underlying causes of mistakes by knowing the precise instances or circumstances where the model fails. By lowering inaccurate predictions and raising correct ones, this repeated process of error analysis and debugging enhances the model's performance.
  - *Model Optimization and Fine-tuning*: The optimization and fine-tuning of AI models can be aided by XAI explanations. Users can find areas where the model is making poor decisions or where improvements can be made by studying the explanations given. To improve the performance of the model, this information can be used to guide parameter adjustment, architecture changes, and other optimization strategies.
  - *Domain-Specific Insights*: XAI approaches offer comprehensible justifications that enable subject-matter professionals to understand how AI models are making judgments in their areas. Based on requirements and knowledge relevant to the domain, these insights can be used to modify the behavior of the model. Model

performance can be adjusted to application areas by incorporating domain expertise into the model design and decision-making process, producing predictions that are more precise and pertinent to the context.

- *Robustness and Generalization*: The robustness and generalization capacities of AI models can be improved through XAI. XAI approaches can aid in locating situations when the model may be too sensitive to inputs or prone to overfitting by explaining them. This realization makes it possible to create more reliable models that are less prone to performance degradation and that generalize effectively to new data.
- By making use of these possibilities, XAI can increase model performance, resulting in predictions that are more accurate and dependable, higher generalization abilities, and more overall efficacy of AI systems across a range of domains and applications.

- *Informed Decision Making*
  The ability to facilitate informed decision-making is one of Explainable Artificial Intelligence's (XAI) main opportunities. The application of XAI approaches enables users to make more informed and responsible decisions by providing clear and understandable explanations for AI model judgements. The following XAI opportunities help people make well-informed decisions:

- *Trust and Confidence*: By making the decision-making process of AI systems clear and understandable, XAI explanations aid in increasing user confidence. Users' trust in the system's dependability is increased when they can observe how the model reached a given conclusion. Users can make judgments based on the AI system's outputs thanks to this confidence, especially in important fields where accountability and openness are crucial.
- *Risk Assessment and Mitigation*: XAI approaches can shed light on the elements and characteristics that affect the choices made by AI models. Based on the information given, users can assess any risks connected to certain inputs or scenarios. When the stakes are high or the repercussions are severe, this understanding enables the assessment and reduction of risks, enabling more informed decision-making.
- *Explanation Comparison and Validation*: Users can assess and validate the judgements produced by AI models using XAI explanations in comparison to their domain expertise or outside data sources. Users can check the explanations against their knowledge or speak with subject matter experts to guarantee the accuracy and dependability of the model's conclusions. With the aid of this possibility, users can make judgments that incorporate both human and AI-generated insight.
- *Insights into Complex Models*: A better understanding of complicated AI models is possible thanks to the use of XAI approaches, which can shed light on their inner workings. Users can learn more about the connections, trends, and decision-making processes the model has discovered. This comprehension aids users in navigating the complexity of AI models and aids them in making judgements based on a greater grasp of the model's information processing capabilities and making predictions.

- *Ethical Considerations*: The identification and evaluation of ethical factors in AI decision-making are made easier by XAI approaches. By highlighting potential biases, injustice, or discrimination in the model's judgements, XAI explanations help users make decisions that are in keeping with moral principles and ethical standards. This change encourages the deployment and application of AI technologies ethically and responsibly.
- By taking advantage of these chances, XAI enables users to make better-informed choices, assuring accountability, transparency, and ethical concerns in AI systems. Users may assess risks, validate decisions, and develop trust thanks to the insights offered by XAI explanations, which ultimately promote more responsible and effective decision-making.

3.6.4 Threats

- *Data Privacy and Security*
  - *Model Inversion Attacks*: The goal of explainable AI techniques is to increase openness by disclosing how AI models think and make decisions inside. However, adversaries may also use model inversion attacks to take advantage of this transparency. In these assaults, the attackers reconstitute sensitive training data using the justifications offered by the XAI system, thus jeopardizing patient privacy.
  - *Unintended Disclosure of Sensitive Information*: XAI approaches frequently produce explanations by emphasizing crucial characteristics or aspects that are employed in judgement. These justifications may result in privacy violations and discrimination if they unintentionally reveal private patient data, like racial or ethnic origin, gender, or medical conditions.
  - *Link ability and Re-identification*: While XAI techniques attempt to offer individually interpretable insights, there is a chance that the explanations will be tied to certain people. By integrating them with other data sources, adversaries may use these justifications to re-identify patients, invading their privacy.
  - *Inadequate Data Anonymization*: To produce precise interpretations, XAI algorithms rely on huge datasets. It may be feasible to recreate patient identities or sensitive information from the explanations if the data used for training and explanation generation is not appropriately anonymized, jeopardizing privacy.
  - *Insider Threats and Unauthorized Access*: When implementing XAI systems, healthcare organizations must make sure that only authorized people have access to patient data and the XAI models. Patient information can be purposely misused or disclosed by workers or contractors with bad intentions, creating privacy breaches.
  - *Adversarial Attacks on Explanations*: XAI techniques are susceptible to adversarial assaults, in which nefarious individuals trick the XAI system by manipulating the input or the explanation-generating process. Due to this, decisions may be made that are biased or deceptive, jeopardizing patient privacy.
  - *Data Governance and Data Sharing*: For XAI models to offer trustworthy explanations, they need access to a variety of representative datasets. However,

there are privacy and security hazards when sharing patient data between healthcare organizations or with outside partners. Patient information may be accessed or used inadvertently due to poor data governance procedures and data-sharing agreements.

– It is possible to use the advantages of XAI in healthcare while preserving patient data privacy and security by addressing these concerns through a mix of technical safeguards, legal frameworks, and ethical practices.

- *Human Bias*

  Human bias is a serious risk that Explainable AI (XAI) in healthcare poses. In the design, development, and implementation of AI systems, particularly XAI models, human bias refers to the presence of subjective preconceptions or unjust assumptions that may be unintentionally integrated. Here are some examples of how human bias could appear in XAI used in healthcare and its potential effects:

  – *Bias in Training Data*: XAI models rely on extensive datasets for training, and if the data are biased or unrepresentative, they may accentuate already-existing societal biases. Biased training data can result in biased justifications and suggestions, which could influence healthcare choices and results.
  – *Biased Feature Selection*: Selecting the features or variables to include in the explanation can induce bias when creating an XAI model. Explanations for decisions may be unjust or discriminatory if some deciding variables are left out or given an excessive amount of weight.
  – *Interpretation Bias*: It can be difficult to objectively interpret and comprehend the justifications offered by XAI models. The same explanation may be interpreted differently by several people, including healthcare workers and patients, which could result in skewed perceptions and conclusions.
  – *Feedback Loop Bias*: User feedback and interactions are used to train XAI models, which might lead to a feedback loop. If there are biases in the initial XAI system, those biases may be reinforced and maintained over time via the feedback loop, resulting in a skewed and distorted understanding of healthcare data and decision-making.
  – *Bias in Implementation and Use:* Biases might appear during the implementation and use of an XAI model, even if the model was created without bias. Unfair results in healthcare delivery might be caused by biases introduced by the selection of patient populations, biased data-gathering techniques, or the context in which the XAI model is employed.
  – *Amplification of Historical Bias*: XAI models can be trained using historical healthcare data that reflects biases that exist in the healthcare system, such as differences in treatment between demographic groups. If these biases are not sufficiently addressed, XAI models may reinforce them, resulting in biased decision-making and unequal access to care.

- *User Understanding*

  User understanding is a significant risk that Explainable AI (XAI) in healthcare poses. The ability of patients, healthcare providers, and other stakeholders to comprehend and interpret the justifications offered by XAI systems is referred to as user understanding. Here are some reasons why user understanding could be dangerous and what that means:

- *Complexity of Explanations*: Complex algorithms used in XAI models, such as deep learning, might produce explanations that are difficult to understand. Healthcare professionals and patients may find it difficult to fully comprehend the underlying logic and elements impacting the AI's decision-making process due to the technical complexity of these explanations.
- *Limited Technical Expertise*: It is possible that patients and healthcare professionals might not have the necessary technical knowledge to interpret and assess the explanations offered by XAI systems. Without adequate comprehension, people could be unable to use explanations to guide healthcare decisions or might interpret the material incorrectly.
- *Misplaced Trust or Over-Reliance*: Users could put too much faith in the explanations given if they are unaware of the constraints and potential biases of XAI systems. Without a thorough grasp of the XAI systems' capabilities and constraints, there is a risk of making poor decisions and compromising patient care.
- *Lack of Contextual Knowledge*: XAI-generated explanations might not include all the pertinent details or insights about the patient in question, their medical history, or the larger clinical environment. Without this background information, patients and healthcare providers may find it difficult to appropriately grasp the explanations and make decisions.
- *Interpretation Bias*: User comprehension can be arbitrary, and depending on their cognitive biases or ingrained ideas, different people may interpret the same explanation in various ways. This interpretative bias may result in an erroneous judgement and maybe different healthcare results.

  The benefits of XAI systems can be used more successfully by patients and healthcare professionals by addressing the user's understanding difficulties, which will improve healthcare.

3.7. Conclusion

AI technology has been extensively used in healthcare and medicine. However, as AI technologies become more complicated, it gets more and harder to explain and articulate the applications that go along with them. This issue led to the conception of XAI as a solution. Not only can XAI increase the transparency of an AI program, but it can also help it get better. Current XAI tools and methods, however, are not designed for a particular AI application and instead require background knowledge from a variety of different domains. As a result, the AI application's explainability could not be adequate. To provide readers with a thorough grasp of XAI, this chapter covered its methodology and pillars. A SWOT analysis is done to highlight the effects of XAI in healthcare.

The strength of XAI brings enhanced transparency, improved trust, compliance, accountability, and valuable insights for decision-making. It has the potential to address fairness and bias concerns in AI systems. Weaknesses in XAI may present challenges regarding complexity, user understanding, and the limitations of explanations, which could hinder its effective utilization and interpretation. XAI Opportunities include opening doors for collaboration between AI experts, healthcare professionals, and stakeholders to collectively address challenges and develop more user-friendly and contextually relevant explanations. It also enables the development of new applications and innovations in healthcare. The Threats for XAI face threats such as human bias, data privacy, security risks, and the potential for misinterpretation or misplaced trust. These need to be carefully managed to ensure the responsible and ethical deployment of XAI in healthcare.

By capitalizing on its strengths, addressing weaknesses, seizing opportunities, and mitigating threats, XAI can pave the way for more transparent, trustworthy, and effective AI systems in healthcare, promoting better patient care and outcomes.

References

Erico, T., and Guan, C. (2021). A survey on explainable artificial intelligence (xai) : Toward medical xai. *IEEE Trans. Neural Netw. Learn. Syst.* (32), 4793–4813.

Eschenbach, W. J. (2021). Transparency and the black box problem, Why we do not trust AI. *Philos. Technol.* (34), 1607–1622.

Guang, Ye (2022). Xia Unbox the black box for the medically explainable ai via multi-modal and multi-centre data fusion : A mini-review, two showcases and beyond. *Inf. Fusion* (77), 29–52.

Gunning, D. and Aha, D. (2019). DARPA's explainable artificial intelligence (XAI) program. *AI Mag.* (40), 44–58.

Lipton Z. C. (2018). The mythos of model interpretability. *Commun ACM*; 61(10) :36–43.

Muller, H., Mayrhofer, M., Van Veen, E., and Holzinger, A. (2021). The Ten Commandments of Ethical Medical AI. *Computer* (54), 119–123.

Nazar, Alam, M. M., Yafi, E., and Mazliham, M. (2021). A systematic review of human-computer interaction and explainable artificial intelligence in healthcare with artificial intelligence techniques. *IEEE Access* 9, 153316–153348.

Chapter 4

A Comprehensive Review on the Developments in Explainable Artificial Intelligence

Durga Shree N.[1]
Steve Mathew D. A.[1]
Bodi Harshavardhan Reddy[1]
Tamil Priya D.[1,*]
and Thinagaran Perumal[2]
[1]Vellore Institute of Technology, Vellore, Tamil Nadu, India
[2]Universiti Putra Malaysia, Malaysia

Abstract

Artificial intelligence has been widely used in various applications over the past decade to handle large amounts of data and identify patterns and conclusions that may not be discernible to the human brain. However, to gain user trust and provide explanations for AI decision-making strategies, it is necessary to understand the consequential decisions through backpropagation. Moreover, the trustworthiness and reliability of AI systems are crucial for their integration into real-world scenarios. Despite advancements, many AI models are perceived as black boxes, lacking transparency for end users provided that XAI is vital for the deployment phase. Explainable AI (XAI) aims to address this issue by designing inherently interpretable AI models, where the model's architecture is transparent, and the decision-making process is more easily understandable. XAI research also emphasizes the importance of involving end-users in the design and evaluation of explanation methods by establishing the use of tools, techniques, and taxonomies. These human-centered design approaches ensure that the explanations generated are useful, comprehensible, and aligned with users' mental models. More complex models tend to offer better performance but are harder to interpret, resulting in the challenging trade-off between performance and explanation of XAI research. This survey examines the principles, applications, and advancements of XAI, while also discussing future research directions and potential opportunities in this field of AI.

* Corresponding Author's Email: tamilpriya.d@vit.ac.in.

In: Explainable Artificial Intelligence in Healthcare Systems
Editors: A. Anitha Kamaraj and Debi Prasanna Acharjya
ISBN: 979-8-89113-598-7

Keywords: Explainable AI, data-driven explainability, trustworthiness, model behavior, XAI systems

4.1 Introduction

Artificial Intelligence is a "black box" providing solutions to problems that cannot be hardcoded due to their composition of numerous variables and varying associated environments. Explainable AI explains the resulting reasons for a particular prediction or classification. Several methods and algorithms used the account for explaining the model generated on training, explaining a prediction, and interpreting the counterfactual and example-based explanations (Liao et al. 2020). Liao, Q. Vera et al. developed an XAI question bank that also describes requirements of questioning on data, output, performance, how, why, why not, how to be that, how to still be this, what if, and other relevant reasoning and explanation-oriented questions. The idea of AI is in demand due to incompetence in accumulating programs that run depending on huge amounts of data and their patterns. Explainable AI is vital to analyze the decisions of models with artificial intelligence to enhance user understanding, user experience, and user-interpretation. Explanations are crucial for users to comprehend, believe in, and manage these new artificially intelligent partners for many key applications such as defense, medical, finance, and law.

Explainable AI aims for contextual explanatory models capable of addressing uncertain real-world entities. Considering the practicality of ML, the involvement of experts from various fields is required to contribute to the integrated approach of Integrative Machine Learning by combining Human-Computer Interaction and Knowledge Discovery/Data Mining (Andreas et al. 2014). Understanding is the intellectual comprehension of the context in which facts emerge, in addition to identifying, perceiving, and reproducing—or simply "re-presenting"—things (Andreas, 2018). To bridge the difference between perceiving and reasoning, understanding is essential. AI needs to improve further to satisfy the role.

The development of XAI-based applications requires the inclusion of two phases, the understanding and explaining phases of the ML pipeline. The understanding phase aims to interpret the structure and functioning of a model to debug it and remove any bias resulting from training data on the trained model. The e-explaining phase involves examining the performance of the model in the real world (Rudresh Dwivedi, 2023). Understandability can either be in terms of data or model. Data understandability is explained based on samples or features.ple explanations are in terms of case-based reasoning and feature explanations require them to be meaningful. The model understandability provides local and global explanations based on the stakeholder. The contribution of input features to model output is shown by feature-based model explainability techniques such as feature importance, partial dependence plots, individual conditional expectation, ALE plot, global surrogate, local interpretable model-agnostic explanations, and shapely values. Example-based XAI techniques include anchors, counterfactual explanations, contrastive explanations method, kernel and tree SHAP, and integrated gradients.

One of the main advantages that can be harnessed through explainable AI or any methodology that is based on interpreting the decisions made by intelligent systems is reliability. There is an ingredient of skepticism for the end-user when organizations are asked to decide based on the insights gained by artificial intelligence systems because it often seems hard to make decisions based on a process that is not tangible to them (Hani Hagras, 2018). The reason for this field's conception can be broadly attributed to five main qualities addressed by the organizations that make decisions based on data: transparency, causality, bias, fairness and safety. They can be elaborated as: (1) Decisions that affect organizations must be presented to them in terms, formats, and languages that they can comprehend. (2) Can organizations that learn a model from data use it to explain the underpinning events and accurate inferences? (3) How can businesses make sure that the artificially intelligent system does not pick up a biased perspective of reality due to flaws in the training data or objective function? (4) Can the organizations validate the fairness of decisions made using an AI system? (5) Without a description of how it makes decisions, can businesses have faith in their AI system's dependability?

Artificial intelligence (AI) is a breakthrough technology, but there are obstacles that tamper the widespread use of AI in certain applications. Examples include neural networks' high complexity preventing their use in environments and devices with limited resources, the lack of resilience to adversarial attacks, which poses a serious threat in applications like autonomous driving, and the lack of transparency and explainability, which decreases confidence in, and the validity of choices taken by an Artificial intelligence system (Wojciech Samek, 2019).

In machine learning, a model's constituents, such as the weight of an attribute in a linear model, and the path in a decision tree can be directly examined to comprehend the model's projections when using ML algorithms like decision trees, Bayesian classifiers, additive models, and spare linear models. These models enable traceability and openness in their outcome while using a very small quantity of internal components (such as pathways, rules, or characteristics). These methods offer the clarity to comprehend decisions made by the AI system, provided the model is satisfactory for the predicting objective (Arun Rai, 2020). Deep learning algorithms, on the other hand, are a subset of machine learning algorithms that compromise predictability for visibility and understandability. These techniques are already being used to build software for speech recognition, image recognition, natural language processing, and consumer behavior prediction. CNNs, for instance, are used in facial recognition software to convert pixel-level input from images into linked properties that relate to the face. Instead of expecting the programmer to choose the pertinent characteristic, the model learns the characteristics that are crucial on its own. The model is intrinsically incomprehensible to humans because it uses pixel-level inputs and intricate linkages across network layers that produce extremely non-linear relationships among inputs and outputs.

Rapid innovations in interpretability methods, which replace deep learning black-box models with simplistic decipherable models that can be examined to help us understand the black-box models, have significantly reduced the trade-off between forecasting and reasoning attributed to neural network models (Michael Hind, 2019). As they convert black-box models into white-box models, these methods are known as Explainable Artificial Intelligence methods and are attracting a lot of interest because they provide a method for achieving the goals of model performance and comprehensibility with AI applications. Future algorithms and artificial intelligence must go beyond technical accuracy and superficial fairness to really satisfy consumer needs and be explained in order to assure the user of the credibility of the output (Donghee Shin, 2021).

4.2 Explainable Artificial Intelligence Literature Review

The research of self-explanatory AI is not a recent topic. Since the 1980s, when Pierce's abductive reasoning was first applied to expert systems, reasoning architectures have been developed to allow complex artificial intelligence systems to perform an explanation role. Applications for these reasoning systems include complicated multi-component design, real-world reasoning, and medical diagnosis. Hence, explainability is a natural outcome of how AI systems are designed and has existed from at least the early stages of AI (Lindsay Wells, 2021). Early expert systems lacked learning capabilities and could only manage uncertainty in basic ways, but they were composed of manually created knowledge bases that permitted reasoning across tightly focused and well-defined areas. Yet, the issue of collecting and exploiting uncertain information has been made simpler to cope with by the advent of formal reasoning frameworks that incorporate principled probabilistic reasoning (Lindsay Sanneman, 2020).

Recent and relatively swift progress in AI and machine learning has been attributed to neural network architectures. Recent events have given birth to this feat. To benefit from the practical application of statistical and algebraic learning techniques in spaces of any huge size, a new generation of neural learning algorithms may now scale. The usefulness of these systems is nevertheless limited by their inability to be debugged and their inability to "explain" their conclusions in a way that is both human-comprehensible and reconstructable, despite their vast accomplishments, the most of which can be recast as classification issues.

Even if we have a firm knowledge of the mathematical foundations supporting the machine learning architectures of today, it is not always easy to gain access to the models themselves. To explain how and why a certain outcome was achieved, formal modeling and reasoning skills are required (Adadi et al. 2018). We also know that contextual adaptation, which is the term for systems that gradually assist in the generation of explanatory models intending to address real-world problems, will be a significant barrier to the advancement of future AI. It would be better in this case to use artificial intelligence to supplement human intelligence rather than to replace it.

From a practical perspective, when we wish to ensure that machine learning models are explainable, the toughest of all the model types to explain is the deep learning family of models. As compared to more traditional machine learning algorithms like decision trees and support vector machines, deep learning techniques have significantly outperformed them in a range of prediction tasks. Yet, when it comes to detailing their inference procedures and end results, deep neural networks (DNNs) fall short of other neural network types (Feiyu Xu, 2019).

Explainable Artificial Intelligence aims to develop analytical tools that reveal hidden workings in a model, yet it does not yet provide a normative framework to judge the explanatory potency of these methods. Building such a framework is the aim of Carlos Zednik's work (Carlos Zednik, 2021), with an emphasis on respecting the many stakeholders' demands for explanation. This framework is based on an investigation of "opacity" from the perspective of scientific philosophy and is based on descriptions of explanation from the perspective of cognitive science. The framework distinguishes the explanation-seeking questions that are expected to be posed by different stakeholders and outlines the broad approaches that should be taken to provide answers to these questions so that these stakeholders may fulfill their responsibilities within the machine learning ecosystem. By using the normative framework to recently developed techniques like input heat mapping, feature-detector visualization, and diagnostic classification, it is possible to determine whether and to what extent techniques from Explainable Artificial Intelligence can be used to make opaque computing systems transparent and, as a result, whether they can be used to solve the Black Box Problem.

4.3 Explainable AI Systems

Authors provides a framework for the design and evaluation of explainable AI systems (Sina Mohseni et al. 2021). The authors explore various perspectives on explainability, including human factors, machine learning, psychology, and ethics. They propose a multidisciplinary approach to designing and evaluating explainable AI systems, including considering the needs and expectations of users, the interpretability of machine learning models, the role of human biases, and ethical considerations. A framework for evaluating the effectiveness of explainable AI systems based on their interpretability, fidelity, usability, and trustworthiness is proposed.

Core, Mark G et al. (2006) discuss the importance of building explainable artificial intelligence (XAI) systems, which are designed to provide clear and understandable explanations of their decisions and actions (Mark G. Core et al. 2006). It is argued that XAI systems are essential for building trust and promoting the responsible deployment of AI in society. Several key challenges in building XAI systems, including the need for interpretable machine learning models, effective visualization techniques, and tools for detecting and mitigating bias and discrimination are identified. Various approaches to designing XAI systems, such as rule-based systems, case-based reasoning, and model-based explanations are evaluated. XAI systems with multidisciplinary research collaborations involving experts in AI, cognitive science, ethics, and other fields will advance its development.

Buçinca, Zana, et al. (2020) discuss the potential limitations of using proxy tasks and subjective measures to evaluate the effectiveness of explainable artificial intelligence (XAI) systems (Zana Bucinca et al. 2020). It is argued that such methods may be misleading and fail to provide an accurate assessment of XAI's ability to promote transparency, accountability, and trustworthiness in AI systems. Proxy tasks, which involve using simplified or artificial scenarios to evaluate XAI, may not accurately reflect the complexity and variability of real-world situations. Subjective measures, such as self-reported trust or understanding, may be biased or influenced by factors such as cognitive load, prior beliefs, and social desirability. It is proposed that a more robust evaluation framework for XAI should include objective measures of performance, such as accuracy and speed of decision-making, as well as user-centered measures, such as usability and satisfaction. The importance is emphasized considering the broader social and ethical implications of XAI and involving diverse stakeholders in the evaluation process.

4.4 Applications of XAI

4.4.1 XAI in Various Domains

In domains demanding reliability and safety, such as healthcare and automated transportation, as well as crucial industrial applications with large economic ramifications, model explainability is a necessity for establishing trust and promoting the adoption of AI systems.

Khosravi, Hassan, et al. discuss the need to ensure students and teachers understand (transparency and interpretability) how AI is making decisions and recommendations in the learning process. XAI helps stakeholders to trust the potential of AI in revolutionizing the learning process by providing personalized and adaptive learning experiences. Various approaches such as model-based explanations, example-based explanations, and rule-based explanations support achieving explainability. XAI can improve student engagement, increase learning outcomes, and support teacher decision-making (Hassan Khosravi et al. 2022).

Imran Ahmed, et al. state that the industrial sector can use explanations for the working of AI in autonomous decision-making and process optimization systems to facilitate the improvement of trust and acceptance of AI systems enabling human-AI collaboration. XAI combined with ML and DL models, IoT devices, cloud computing, and cyber-physical systems can revolutionize the outcomes of an industrial product (Imran Ahmed et al. 2022, Van der Velden et al. 2022, Krishna Gade et al. 2020, Leopoldo Bertossi et al. 2020, Alberto Fernandez et al. 2019).

Tantithamthavorn, et al, (2021) discuss the need for AI systems to be explainable to build trust and ensure the safety and security of software. Rule-based systems, decision trees, and neural networks are considered to develop explainable models for software engineering. The challenges of building explainable AI models for software engineering are the trade-off between interpretability and accuracy, the need to balance transparency and privacy, and the difficulty of explaining complex models. XAI is applied in software testing, debugging, and maintenance (Tantithamthavorn, 2021).

XAI is used in fraud detection, credit risk assessment, and anti-money laundering. Challenges of building explainable AI models for fintech risk management include dealing with imbalanced data, handling missing data, ensuring model stability over time, addressing regulatory requirements, credit scoring, loan underwriting, and collections. XAI to improve the accuracy and transparency of loan approval decisions, reduce the risk of bias and discrimination, and increase trust in the lending process (Niklas Bussmann et al. 2020, Branka Hadji Misheva et al. 2021, Swati Sachan et al. 2020).

XAI supports the need for interpretability and transparency. The challenge would be the need for robust data preprocessing, feature selection, and model validation. Human-computer interaction (HCI) in XAI systems should possess a user interface designed to facilitate understanding and trust in the AI model. XAI for healthcare applications, including medical imaging, diagnosis, treatment planning, and clinical decision support. Integration of big data, AI, and other advanced technologies into healthcare with XAI will support personalized, preventive, and participatory healthcare. XAI can integrate AI with human expertise and decision-making. XAI should possess a user-centered design to consider the needs and preferences of patients, healthcare providers, and other stakeholders (Prashant Gohel et al. 2021; Hui Wen Loh et al. 2022; Deepti Saraswat et al. 2022).

XAI supports improving the efficiency and effectiveness of the drug development process. It helps understand how the AI model arrives at its predictions and recommendations to improve the accuracy and reliability of drug discovery efforts. XAI applications in drug discovery include the identification of novel drug targets, the prediction of drug efficacy and toxicity, and the optimization of drug design (José Jiménez-Luna et al. 2020).

A patient-centric approach to XAI in medical diagnosis emphasizes the importance of involving patients in the process of developing and implementing XAI systems. "Contestable AI diagnostic" (CAD) is an XAI system that is transparent, interpretable, adaptable, and responsive to patient needs and preferences. XAI applications in medical diagnosis include the use of decision trees and rule-based systems to predict disease risk and recommend treatment options. Patient involvement in development through feedback and preferences can improve the acceptability and accuracy of XAI systems. "Multi-modal causability" (MMC) is an XAI system to identify and reason about multiple causes of an event or outcome, considering different modalities such as genetics, environment, and lifestyle. XAI has applications in medical decision-making, including the prediction of disease risk and treatment outcomes. MMC of XAI for medical decision-making can identify and address the underlying causes of disease and the potential for personalized and precision medicine (Thomas Ploug et al. 2020; Andreas Holzinger, 2021; Guang Yang et al. 2022; Henry Han et al. 2021; Khodabandehloo et al. 2021; Simon Meyer Lauritsen et al. 2020).

XAI can assist pathologists in analyzing images and making diagnoses from predictions made by AI systems. It can also help identify errors or biases in AI systems, which is important for ensuring the accuracy and fairness of diagnoses.XAI in anatomic pathology provides improved accuracy, efficiency, and consistency in diagnoses (Tosun et al. 2020). Small-unit tactical behavior is an important aspect of military operations. AI can assist in decision-making processes, but the AI system must be transparent and understandable for military personnel (Michael et al. 2004). XAI models are constructed using data from military experts, and the system is validated through simulation experiments. These models are also used to improve energy and power systems to optimize the consumption of these resources (Hans et al. 2022; Machlev et al. 2022).

4.4.2 XAI in Industrial Applications

XAI supports in anomalies behavior prediction where the model with interpretability can identify anomalies in the present and forecast their likelihood in the future (Rocco Langone et al. 2020), manufacturing system operations where real-time predictive analytics and the multivariate time series approach are presented visually to draw attention to potential mistakes, alerts, and hostile intrusion attempts (Dy D. Le et al. 2019). XAI is integrated with deep meta-learning paradigms for cyber-physical systems (Evren Daglarli, 2021) and explainable process prediction in smart industries (Jana-Rebecca Rehse et al. 2019) with justifications for customer buying practices (Alex Gramegna et al. 2020) in business.

In manufacturing processes, nonlinear modelling and SHAP values from explainable AI are combined in a data-driven decision model to enhance manufacturing process quality (Julian Senoner et al. 2021). Fiber layup defect detection is done using a DL-based classification technique in autonomous composite manufacture (Meister et al. 2021). In the production of steel plates, XAI-based fault analysis and penetration harvesting is applied (Athar Kharal, 2020). Industrial machinery uses the development and justifications of an industrial data-based residual life estimate based on machine learning (Oscar Serradilla et al. 2020). In predictive process and maintenance, a local post-hoc explanation method for monitoring problems (Nijat Mehdiyev et al. 2021) and explanation models for prediction of errors and tool failures in industry are implemented (Bahrudin Hrnjica et al. 2020). XAI supports black-box model interpretation in rotating machinery using fault diagnostic and anomaly detection techniques (Lucas C. Brito et al. 2022). Smart cities are being developed with XAI for flood monitoring (Dhavalkumar Thakker et al. 2020), weather prediction and climate information (Abhirup Dikshit et al. 2021).

4.5 Advancements in XAI

4.5.1 Logic-Based Strategy

Alexey Ignatiev (Alexey Ignatiev, 2020) outlines how to apply the logic-based strategy to provide appropriate explanations for machine learning predictions. In addition, the study contends that heuristic explanations are unreliable, a claim that is reinforced by experimental data from prior research that throws doubt on the validity of the heuristic explanations that were utilized. The research hypothesizes that there is an innate possibility of inaccuracy in the techniques for calculating model-independent heuristic explanations. Also, mathematical reasoning and combinatorial methods are used to explain decisions taken by AI systems (D. Richard Kuhn et al. 2020).

4.5.2 Taxonomies

In today's XAI world, many approaches are generally used. The main contribution in (Pantelis Linardatos et al. 2020) is a taxonomy of the various interpretability strategies for machine learning. This taxonomy enables the comparison of different approaches from many viewpoints. The key categories for interpretability approaches in this taxonomy are ways for enhancing fairness and limiting the occurrence of discrimination, followed by methods for analyzing the sensitivity of model predictions. The list also includes techniques for developing white-box models, developing sophisticated black-box models, encouraging fairness, and analyzing the sensitivity of model predictions.

The great majority of interpretability methods for explaining the operation of deep learning models pertain to the classification of images and produce saliency maps, which display the effect of distinct visual regions. This goal is often accomplished by using gradient information traveling through the various layers of the network. Saliency maps are made using deconvolutional neural networks, which is not only an extra technique used to create them but also the method that has the greatest overall effect when measured using the same metric. For displaying feature interactions and feature significance, the LIME and SHAP approaches are by far the most thorough and well-established in the literature, but Friedman's PDPs, while being considerably older and less complex, are still a common option. The LIME and SHAP techniques are the most popular approaches for visualizing feature interactions and feature significance when discussing any black-box model. The LIME and SHAP techniques are not only independent of any specific model, but it has been shown that they can be used to any kind of data.

Different approaches for interpreting ML models are explored in terms of Taxonomy of XAI techniques (Rudresh Dwivedi, 2023). White box and black box model techniques based on suitability with the AI model at hand, model-specific techniques and model-agnostic techniques based on the components used for interpretability (structure, intermediate representations, features and outputs), global interpretation and local interpretation based on the scope of interpretation are the different dimensions to understand the interpretability of models.

The primary goal of (Alejandro et al. 2020) is to provide newcomers to the area of XAI with a comprehensive taxonomy that can be utilized as a resource to stimulate future research developments. Its secondary objective is to encourage specialists and professionals working in domains unrelated to AI to acknowledge the benefits of using AI in their areas of expertise, without having any preconceived preconceptions about how easily it can be interpreted. The authors of (Sina Mohseni et al. 2018) provide a taxonomy of Explainable AI design goals and evaluation methods. The classification demonstrates how distinct Explainable AI user groups' design goals, and their assessment methods relate to one another. The data are used to build a framework with precise design principles and assessment methods to assist transdisciplinary explainable AI teams in completing their iterative design and evaluation cycles.

4.5.3 Real-Time Explanations

The process of creating real-time explanations using automatic reasoning generation is a method in which a computer model is trained to interpret the internal status and action data representations of an autonomous agent in regular language. By obtaining training on human explanation data, agents may learn to provide reasons for their behavior that are like those produced by humans. The authors of the article (Upol et al. 2019) explain how to compile a corpus of explanations, train a neural reasoning generator to create various forms of justifications, and explain how people react to these justifications in the context of an agent that plays Frogger. The research is comprised of two different user studies. In the first piece of study, the plausibility of each kind of created reason is investigated, and users' perspectives are mapped out according to criteria such as assurance, human likeness, adequate justification, and understandability. In the second research, the preferences of users are investigated further in connection to user trust in the autonomous agent, unsuccessful communication, and unexpected behavior. It has been determined, overall, that the discrepancies between the intended qualities of the created rationales and the differences as viewed by users agree with one another.

4.5.4 Using Graph Neural Networks in XAI

A study covers how counterfactual routes may be used for intuitive explainability and causability, how embeddings can be learned in a distributed manner safely & quickly, and how multi-modal representations allow cooperative learning of a single result in (Andreas Holzinger et al. 2021). To enable information fusion for multi-modal causability, this paper recommends adopting graph neural networks as the technique of choice. A key premise is that employing conceptual knowledge as a model of reality will make it easier to train machine learning models that are more resilient, less biased, and can learn from fewer amounts of data.

4.5.5 Wikipedia Knowledge Graph

A system's decision is explainable by XAI systems in the presence of domain knowledge. Knowledge Graphs are best suited for this purpose of information representation. Heading toward the advancement of XAI, Kamruzzaman Sarker et al. propose Wikipedia Knowledge Graphs where articles in Wikipedia are transformed to graph structures. These provide a concept hierarchy of an article in Wikipedia, contributing to structured domain knowledge (Kamruzzaman Sarker, 2020).

4.5.6 Frameworks

The authors, Wencan Zhang et al. recommend the use of the XAI Perceptual Processing Framework and the RexNet model for relevant explainable AI with contrarian saliency, contrarian synthetic explanations, and contrarian signals explanations (Wencan et al. 2022). In order to predict and clarify emotions from speech, the study looked at the usage of vocal emotion detection and developed a modular multi-task deep neural network. In think-aloud and controlled experiments, counterfactual explanations were found to be beneficial, and their effectiveness was improved with the addition of semantic cues, whereas saliency explanations were not (Ruth, 2019).

4.5.7 Changes Suggested in XAI

It is necessary to reframe the pursuit of interpretable models and judgments in artificial intelligence (Andrés, 2020) in terms of the larger mission of providing a practical and realistic explanation of understanding in AI. It makes perfect sense that the purpose of discussing a model or choice is to assist its stakeholders in better understanding that model or decision. It is impossible to satisfy the activity condition on explanation in many machine learning models, but if we focus on understanding, we can relax this condition and instead pay attention to the pragmatic conditions that determine how well a model fits with the techniques and tools that are used to understand it. The conclusion is that interpretative or approximation models are not only the best way to achieve the objection understanding of a machine learning model, but that they are also a necessary condition to achieve post hoc interpretability. This is based on a review of the various types of understanding discussed in philosophical and psychological literature.

4.6 Advantages and Disadvantages of XAI Systems

Given the scope of XAI systems in proving the trustworthiness of AI systems, they also excel by reducing the cognitive demand of the user to understand the working of the models on their own, emulating a think-aloud method on agent behavior, helping people make good decisions reliably, computer-based Decision Support Systems (DSS) have been used across numerous disciplines, mitigating cognitive biases in decision-making which introduce self-awareness and self-monitoring of decision-making, evaluating the human's mental model of the system when the human is actively attending to the system's predictions and explanations, but do not necessarily evaluate how well the human is able to perform real decision-making tasks with the system.

Though this advancement in artificial intelligence shows better human-computer interaction, it also faces challenges and possesses unanswered questions to accomplish the purpose completely. These challenges (David Gunning et al. 2019) include the perspective and scope of explanations to bring the user into the loop of learning by providing interactive feedback, the need for interpretability that requires slight compromises with accuracy and fidelity (accounting for the ideal balance between interpretability, accuracy and tractability opens door to more explorations), simplification of explanations to provide abstractions with high-level patterns (automating the discovery of these abstractions has been a challenge), the extent of successfully completing ability of the AI system is to be acknowledged to the user in order to reflect further on the decisions from the systems.

The challenges for the research community as stated by Krishna Gade are defining the model explainability, defining explainability tasks to comprehend model behavior and creating solutions for these tasks and defining evaluation criteria for model performance in explainability tasks (Krishna Gade, 2019).

4.7 Conclusion and Future Scope

From a human-centered research standpoint, studies on competences and knowledge may enable XAI to do tasks more than just describing specific XAI systems and guiding users toward the proper level of confidence (Andrea, 2020). XAIs could play important social roles in the future. In addition to learning and explaining to people, these roles might also involve working with other agents to connect knowledge, creating cross-disciplinary insights and common ground, collaborating in teaching f and other agents, and using previously discovered knowledge to speed up knowledge discovery and application. The future of XAI is just getting started from such a social perspective of knowledge-understanding and generation.

Research opportunities in XAI include developing more interpretable machine learning models, designing effective visualization techniques, and exploring the ethical implications of explainability (Christian Meske et al. 2022). There is growing judicial demand for explainable artificial intelligence (XAI) in legal contexts, particularly in the areas of criminal justice and discrimination law. XAI systems are essential for ensuring transparency, accountability, and fairness in legal decision-making, as well as for promoting public trust in the justice system. The various challenges in implementing XAI in legal contexts, such as the need for clear standards and guidelines for XAI systems and the difficulty of balancing transparency and privacy concerns are to be dealt with (Ashley Deeks, 2019). End-users, developers, regulators, and society can be seen as the key stakeholders of XAI. Langer, Markus, et al. (Markus Langer et al. 2021) propose a conceptual model for XAI research that incorporates four dimensions: (1) the technical dimension, which focuses on developing interpretable and transparent machine learning models; (2) the human dimension, which considers the needs and preferences of end-users and the role of human biases in decision-making; (3) the ethical dimension, which addresses the ethical implications of XAI, such as fairness, accountability, and privacy; and (4) the societal dimension, which considers the broader social and political implications of XAI.

References

Adadi, A. and Berrada, M. (2018). "Peeking Inside the Black-Box : A Survey on Explainable Artificial Intelligence (XAI)," *IEEE Access,* 6, 52138-52160.

Ahmed, Imran, Gwanggil Jeon, and Francesco Piccialli. (2022). "From artificial intelligence to explainable artificial intelligence in industry 4.0: a survey on what, how, and where," *IEEE Transactions on Industrial Informatics* 18(8), 5031-5042.

Alejandro Barredo Arrieta, Natalia Díaz-Rodríguez, Javier Del Ser, Adrien Bennetot, et al. (2020). Explainable Artificial Intelligence (XAI) : Concepts, taxonomies, opportunities, and challenges toward responsible AI, *Information Fusion*, 58, 82-115,1566-2535.

Alexey Ignatiev, Towards Trustable Explainable AI, *Proceedings of the Twenty-Ninth International Joint Conference on Artificial Intelligence* (IJCAI-20).

Andreas Holzinger, Bernd Malle, Anna Saranti, Bastian Pfeifer, (2021). "Towards multi-modal causability with Graph Neural Networks enabling information fusion for explainable AI," *Information Fusion*, 71,28-37,1566-2535.

Bertossi, Leopoldo, and Floris Geerts, (2020). "Data quality and explainable AI." *Journal of Data and Information Quality (JDIQ)*, 12.2, 1-9.

Brennen, Andrea. (2020). "What Do People Really Want When They Say They Want" Explainable AI ?" We Asked 60 Stakeholders." *Extended Abstracts of the 2020 CHI Conference on Human Factors in Computing Systems.*

Brito, L. C., G. A. Susto, J. N. Brito, and M. A. Duarte. (2022). "An explainable artificial intelligence approach for unsupervised fault detection and diagnosis in rotating machinery," *Mech. Syst. Signal Process*, 163, 108105.

Buçinca, Zana, Phoebe Lin, Krzysztof Z. Gajos, and Elena L. Glassman. (2020)."Proxy tasks and subjective measures can be misleading in evaluating explainable ai systems". In *Proceedings of the 25th international conference on intelligent user Interface*, 454-464.

Bussmann, Niklas, Paolo Giudici, Dimitri Marinelli, and Jochen Papenbrock. (2020). "Explainable AI in fintech risk management." *Frontiers in Artificial Intelligence,* 3,26.

Byrne, M. J. Ruth. (2021). "Counterfactuals in Explainable Artificial Intelligence (XAI): Evidence from Human Reasoning." *Proceedings of the Twenty-Eighth International Joint Conference on Artificial Intelligence (IJCAI).*

Core, Mark G., Chad Lane, Michael Van Lent, Dave Gomboc, Steve Solomon, and Milton Rosenberg. (2006). "Building explainable artificial intelligence systems." In *AAAI,* 1766-1773.

Daglarli, E. (2021). "Explainable artificial intelligence (XaI) approaches and deep meta-learning models for cyber-physical systems," In *Proc. Artif. Intell. Paradigms Smart Cyber-Phys. Syst.* 42–67.

Dayama, P., Jain, V. and Jinwala. D. C. (2021). Explainable AI in Healthcare : A Comprehensive Survey. *Journal of Healthcare Engineering*, 1-20.

De Bruijn, Hans, Martijn Warnier, and Marijn Janssen. (2022), "The perils and pitfalls of explainable AI : Strategies for explaining algorithmic decision-making." *Government Information Quarterly*, 39.2, 101666.

Deeks, Ashley. (2019). "The judicial demand for explainable artificial intelligence," *Columbia Law Review* 119, 1829-1850.

Dhavalkumar Thakker, B. K. Mishra, A. Abdullatif, S. Mazumdar, and S. Simpson, (2020), "Explainable artificial intelligence for developing smart cities solutions," *Smart Cities*, 3, 4, 1353–1382.

Dikshit, Abhirup, and Biswajeet Pradhan. (2021)."Interpretable and explainable AI (XAI) model for spatial drought prediction." *Science of the Total Environment* 801, 149797.

Donghee Shin, (2021). The effects of explainability and causability on perception, trust, and acceptance : Implications for explainable AI, *International Journal of Human-Computer Studies*, 146, 10255.

Dwivedi, Rudresh, Devam Dave, Het Naik, Smiti Singhal, Rana Omer, Pankesh Patel, Bin Qian et al. (2023). "Explainable AI (XAI) : Core ideas, techniques, and solutions." *ACM Computing Surveys* 55, 9, 1-33.

Ehsan, Upol, Pradyumna Tambwekar, Larry Chan, Brent Harrison, and Mark O. Riedl. (2019). "Automated rationale generation: a technique for explainable AI and its effects on human perceptions." In *Proceedings of the 24th International Conference on Intelligent User Interfaces*, 263-274.

Fernandez, Alberto, Francisco Herrera, Oscar Cordon, Maria Jose del Jesus, and Francesco Marcelloni. (2019). "Evolutionary fuzzy systems for explainable artificial intelligence : Why, when, what for, and where to ?" *IEEE Computational intelligence magazine* 14,1, 69-81.

Gade, Krishna, Sahin Cem Geyik, Krishnaram Kenthapadi, Varun Mithal, and Ankur Taly. (2019). "Explainable AI in industry." In *Proceedings of the 25th ACM SIGKDD international conference on knowledge discovery & data mining*, 3203-3204.

Gade, Krishna, Sahin Geyik, Krishnaram Kenthapadi, Varun Mithal, and Ankur Taly. (2020). "Explainable AI in industry: Practical challenges and lessons learned." In *Companion Proceedings of the Web Conference 2020*, 303-304.

Gramegna, A. and Giudici, P. (2020). "Why to buy insurance? an explainable artificial intelligence approach," *Risks,* 8(4), 137.

Hagras, H. (2018). "Toward Human-Understandable, Explainable AI," in *Computer*, 51, 9, 28-36.

Han, Henry, and Xiangrong Liu. (2021). "The challenges of explainable AI in biomedical data science." *BMC Bioinformatics*, 22, 12 : 1-3.

Hind, Michael. (2019), "Explaining explainable AI." XRDS : Crossroads, *The ACM Magazine for Students* 25.3, 16-19.

Holzinger, Andreas, and Igor Jurisica. (2014). "Knowledge discovery and data mining in biomedical informatics: The future is in integrative, interactive machine learning solutions." *Interactive knowledge discovery and data mining in biomedical informatics.* Springer, Berlin, Heidelberg, 1-18.

Holzinger, Andreas. (2018). "From machine learning to explainable AI." 2018 *world symposium on Digital Intelligence for Systems and Machines* (DISA), IEEE.

Holzinger, Andreas. (2021). "Explainable AI and multi-modal causability in medicine", *i-com* 19, 171-179.

Hrnjica B. and S. Softic, (2020). "Explainable AI in manufacturing: A predictive maintenance case study," In *Proc. IFIP Int. Conf. Adv. Prod. Manage. Syst.*, 66–73.

Jiménez-Luna, José, Francesca Grisoni, and Gisbert Schneider. (2020). "Drug discovery with explainable artificial intelligence." *Nature Machine Intelligence*, 2,10, 573-584.

Kharal, A. (2020). "Explainable artificial intelligence based fault diagnosis and insight harvesting for steel plates manufacturing," *arXiv*:2008.04448.

Khodabandehloo, Elham, Daniele Riboni, and Abbas Alimohammadi. (2021). "HealthXAI: Collaborative and explainable AI for supporting early diagnosis of cognitive decline." *Future Generation Computer Systems*, 116, 168-189.

Khosravi, Hassan, Simon Buckingham Shum, Guanliang Chen, Cristina Conati, Yi-Shan Tsai, Judy Kay, et al. (2022) : "Explainable artificial intelligence in education." *Computers and Education : Artificial Intelligence*, 3, 100074.

Kuhn, D. Kuhn, D. Richard, Raghu N. Kacker, Yu Lei, and Dimitris E. Simos. (2020). "Combinatorial methods for explainable AI." In *2020 IEEE International Conference on Software Testing, Verification and Validation Workshops (ICSTW),* 167-170. IEEE.

Langer, Markus, Daniel Oster, Timo Speith, Holger Hermanns, Lena Kästner, Eva Schmidt, Andreas Sesing, and Kevin Baum. (2021). "What do we want from Explainable Artificial Intelligence (XAI)? –A stakeholder perspective on XAI and a conceptual model guiding interdisciplinary XAI research." *Artificial Intelligence* 296, 103473.

Langone, R. Cuzzocrea, A and Skantzos, N. (2020). "Interpretable anomaly prediction: Predicting anomalous behavior in Industry 4.0 settings via regularized logistic regression tools," *Data Knowl. Eng.*, 130, 101850.

Lauritsen, Simon Meyer, Mads Kristensen, Mathias Vassard Olsen, Morten S. L., (2020). "Explainable artificial intelligence model to predict acute critical illness from electronic health records." *Nature Communications,* 11, 1, 3852.

Liao, Q. Vera, Daniel Gruen, and Sarah Miller. (2020). "Questioning the AI : informing design practices for explainable AI user experiences." *Proceedings of the 2020 CHI Conference on Human Factors in Computing Systems.*

Linardatos, P., Papastefanopoulos, V. and Kotsiantis. S. (2021). "Explainable AI : A Review of Machine Learning Interpretability Methods," *Entropy*, 23(1), 18.

Loh, Hui Wen, Chui Ping Ooi, Silvia Seoni, Prabal Datta Barua, Filippo Molinari, and U. Rajendra Acharya. (2022). "Application of explainable artificial intelligence for healthcare: A systematic review of the last decade (2011–2022)." *Computer Methods and Programs in Biomedicine*, 107161.

Machlev, R., L. Heistrene, M. Perl, K. Y. Levy, J. Belikov, S. Mannor, and Y. Levron. (2022), "Explainable Artificial Intelligence (XAI) techniques for energy and power systems: Review, challenges and opportunities." *Energy and AI,* 9, 100169.

Mehdiyev, N. and Fettke, P. (2021). "Explainable artificial intelligence for process mining: A general overview and application of a novel local explanation approach for predictive process monitoring," *Interpretable Artif. Intell.: Perspective Granular Comput.*, Springer, Cham, 937,1.

Meister, S. Wermes, M. Stüve, J. and Groves, (2021) R. M. "Investigations on explainable artificial intelligence methods for the deep learning classification of fibre layup defect in the automated composite manufacturing," *Composites Part B: Eng.,* 109160.

Meske, Christian, Enrico Bunde, Johannes Schneider, and Martin Gersch. (2022). "Explainable artificial intelligence : objectives, stakeholders, and future research opportunities." *Information Systems Management* 39,1, 53-63.

Misheva, Branka Hadji, Joerg Osterrieder, Ali Hirsa, Onkar Kulkarni, and Stephen Fung Lin. (2021). *"Explainable AI in credit risk management."* arXiv preprint arXiv :2103.00949.

Mohseni, Sina, Niloofar Zarei, and Eric D. Ragan. (2021). "A multidisciplinary survey and framework for design and evaluation of explainable AI systems." *ACM Transactions on Interactive Intelligent Systems (TiiS)*, 11.3-4, 1-45.

Páez, Andrés. (2019). "The pragmatic turn in explainable artificial intelligence (XAI)." *Minds and Machines,* 29, 3, 441-459.

Ploug, Thomas, and Søren Holm. (2020). "The four dimensions of contestable AI diagnostics patient-centric approach to explainable AI." *Artificial Intelligence in Medicine*, 107, 101901.

Rai, Arun. (2020), "Explainable AI : From black box to glass box," *Journal of the Academy of Marketing Science,* 48.1, 137-141.

Rehse, J. R., Mehdiyev, N. and Fettke, P. (2019). "Towards explainable process predictions for Industry 4.0 in the dfki-smart-lego-factory," *KI-Künstliche Intelligenz,* 33, 2, 181–187.

Sachan, Swati, Jian-Bo Yang, Dong-Ling Xu, David Eraso Benavides, and Yang Li. (2020). "An explainable AI decision-support-system to automate loan underwriting." *Expert Systems with Applications* 144, 113100.

Samek, Wojciech, and Klaus-Robert Müller. "Towards explainable artificial intelligence. (2019). *"Explainable AI : interpreting, explaining and visualizing deep learning."* Springer, Cham, 5-22.

Sanneman, Lindsay, and Julie A. Shah. (2020). "A situation awareness-based framework for design and evaluation of explainable AI," Explainable, Transparent Autonomous Agents and Multi-Agent Systems: Second International Workshop, *EXTRAAMAS 2020*, Auckland, New Zealand, Springer.

Saraswat, Deepti, Pronaya Bhattacharya, Ashwin Verma, Vivek Kumar Prasad, Sudeep Tanwar, Gulshan Sharma, Pitshou N. Bokoro, and Ravi Sharma. (2022). "Explainable AI for healthcare 5.0: opportunities and challenges." *IEEE Access.*

Sarker, Md Kamruzzaman, Joshua Schwartz, Pascal Hitzler, Lu Zhou, Srikanth Nadella, Brandon Minnery, Ion Juvina, Michael L. Raymer, and William R. Aue. (2020). "Wikipedia knowledge graph for explainable AI." In *Knowledge Graphs and Semantic Web : Second Iberoamerican Conference and First Indo-American Conference,* KGSWC 2020, Mérida, Mexico, 72-87. Springer International Publishing.

Senoner, J. Netland, T., and. Feuerriegel, S. (2021). "Using explainable artificial intelligence to improve process quality: Evidence from semiconductor manufacturing," *Manage. Sci.,* 224,1.

Serradilla, O. Zugasti, E. Cernuda, C. Aranburu, A. de Okariz, J. R. and Zurutuza, U. (2020). "Interpreting remaining useful life estimations combining explainable artificial intelligence and domain knowledge in industrial machinery," In *Proc. IEEE Int. Conf. Fuzzy Syst*., 1–8.

Tantithamthavorn, Chakkrit Kla, and Jirayus Jiarpakdee. (2021). "Explainable ai for software engineering." 2021 36th IEEE/ACM International Conference on Automated Software Engineering (ASE), *IEEE.*

Tosun B., Akif, Filippo Pullara, Michael J. Becich, D. Lansing Taylor, Jeffrey L. Fine, and S. Chakra Chennubhotla, (2020). "Explainable AI (xAI) for anatomic pathology", *Advances in Anatomic Pathology* 27, 4, 241-250.

Van der Velden, Bas HM, Hugo J. Kuijf, Kenneth GA Gilhuijs, and Max A. Viergever. (2022), "Explainable artificial intelligence (XAI) in deep learning-based medical image analysis," *Medical Image Analysis*, 79, 102470.

Van Lent, Michael, William Fisher, and Michael Mancuso. (2004)."An explainable artificial intelligence system for small-unit tactical behavior," *Proceedings of the national conference on artificial intelligence.* Menlo Park, London.

Vilone, Giulia, and Luca Longo. (2021). "Classification of explainable artificial intelligence methods through their output formats." *Machine Learning and Knowledge Extraction*, 3.3, 615-661.

Wells, Lindsay, and Tomasz Bednarz. (2021). "Explainable AI and reinforcement learning—a systematic review of current approaches and trends." *Frontiers in artificial intelligence*, 4, 550030.

Xu, Feiyu, Hans Uszkoreit, Yangzhou Du, Wei Fan, Dongyan Zhao, and Jun Zhu. (2019). "Explainable AI : A brief survey on history, research areas, approaches and challenges." In *Natural Language Processing and Chinese Computing: 8th CCF International Conference, NLPCC 2019,* Dunhuang, China, 9–14, 2019, 563-574. Springer International Publishing.

Yang, Guang, Qinghao Ye, and Jun Xia. (2022). "Unbox the black-box for the medical explainable AI via multi-modal and multi-centre data fusion : A mini-review, two showcases and beyond." *Information Fusion* 77,29-52.

Zednik, Carlos. (2021), "Solving the black box problem: A normative framework for explainable artificial intelligence," *Philosophy & technology,* 34, 2, 265-288.

Zhang, Wencan, and Brian Y. Lim. (2022), "Towards relatable explainable AI with the perceptual process." *Proceedings of the 2022 CHI Conference on Human Factors in Computing Systems*.

Chapter 5

Unveiling the Algorithms: How Explainable AI Reshapes Healthcare

A. Thriveni[1,*]
J. Balajee[2]
and R. Vasanthselvakumar[3]
[1,3]Department of Computer Science and Engineering - Software Engineering, Viswam Engineering College, Madanapalli, Andhra Pradesh, India
[2]Department of Computer Science and Engineering, Mother Theresa Institute of Engineering and Technology, Palamaner, Andhra Pradesh, India

Abstract

Artificial intelligence (AI) has brought revolutionary changes in the domain of healthcare, with its applications ranging from diagnostics to treatment planning and medication development. One of the difficulties with AI is that it might be difficult to grasp how AI systems make judgments. This makes it challenging for healthcare practitioners to trust AI systems and for patients to comprehend why they are receiving a certain diagnosis or therapy. Explainable AI (XAI) is a branch of artificial intelligence research that aims to make AI algorithms more visible and interpretable. XAI approaches may be used to explain why an AI decision was made, highlight potential biases in the data, and pinpoint areas where the AI system can be improved. This chapter explores the relevance of XAI in healthcare and examines some of the XAI approaches utilized in this sector. In addition to these, the article explores the constraints and prospects of XAI in the domain of healthcare.

Keywords: Explainable AI, healthcare, transparency, interpretability, bias, diagnosis, treatment planning, drug discovery

5.1 Introduction

Artificial Intelligence (AI) is quickly reshaping healthcare, with applications in areas such as diagnostics, treatment planning, and drug development. AI systems can analyze enormous

* Corresponding Authors Email: thrivenialamanur@gmail.com.

In: Explainable Artificial Intelligence in Healthcare Systems
Editors: A. Anitha Kamaraj and Debi Prasanna Acharjya
ISBN: 979-8-89113-598-7

volumes of data and detect patterns that humans might find difficult to see. This can lead to improved patient outcomes and more informed decisions. One of the difficulties with AI is that it might be difficult to grasp how AI systems make judgments. This makes it challenging for healthcare practitioners to trust AI systems and for patients to comprehend why they are receiving a certain diagnosis or therapy. Baldoni, et al. (2019) suggested that Explainable AI (XAI) is a branch of artificial intelligence research that aims to make AI algorithms more visible and interpretable. XAI approaches may be used to explain why an AI decision was made, highlight potential biases in the data, and pinpoint areas where the AI system can be improved. This book chapter covers the relevance of XAI in healthcare and examines some of the XAI approaches utilized in this subject. In addition, the chapter explores the problems and prospects of XAI in healthcare.

5.2 Role of AI in Healthcare

- Beam and Kohane (2018) suggested some concrete instances of how artificial intelligence is being applied in healthcare today:
- AI-powered diagnostic technologies can assist clinicians in more swiftly and correctly identifying ailments.
- Artificial intelligence-powered treatment planning systems can assist clinicians in developing tailored treatment regimens for patients.
- AI-powered drug discovery technologies can assist researchers in identifying novel drug targets and developing new disease therapies.
- Artificial intelligence-powered patient monitoring technologies can assist doctors in tracking patient health and identifying possible concerns early on.

AI has the potential to change healthcare, and it is currently being utilized in many ways to improve patient care are shown in Table 5.1.

Table 5.1. Importance and its Pros and Cons of XAI

Importance	Pros	Cons
Build trust	AI systems may be trusted by healthcare practitioners and patients provided they understand how they function and why they make the judgments they do.	This can be challenging, especially for complicated AI systems.
Identify bias	When AI systems are trained on data that is not representative of the population, they might become prejudiced. XAI can assist in identifying and mitigating any biases	This can be challenging, especially for big AI systems.
Improve decision-making	Healthcare professionals can make better judgments if they understand the elements that influence AI system decisions. This might take time and require specific understanding.	This might take time and requires specific understanding.
Enhance debugging	Developers may more readily rectify problems in AI systems if they understand how the systems function and why they make the judgments they do.	This can be challenging, especially for complicated AI systems.
Foster patient engagement	Patients can be more engaged in their treatment if they understand how AI systems make care decisions.	This can be challenging, especially for complicated AI systems.

5.3 The Importance of XAI in Healthcare

Here are some additional benefits of XAI in healthcare:

- *Error reduction*: Cabitza, et al. (2017) says XAI can assist in lowering the risk of mistakes in AI systems by making it simpler to discover and correct faults.
- *Improved transparency*: XAI can help to improve AI system transparency, making it easier for people to comprehend how the systems function and why they make the judgments they do.
- *Enhanced accountability*: XAI can assist in improving accountability for AI systems by making it easier to identify who is responsible for the systems' choices.
- *Improved compliance:* XAI can aid with regulatory compliance by making it easier to demonstrate that AI systems are fair and equal.

Here are some other XAI in healthcare considerations:

- *Explainability:* The amount of explainability required varies according to the application. Caruana et al. (2009) says that for some applications, such as diagnostics, a full explanation of how the AI system arrived at its choice may be required. A more generic explanation may suffice for other applications, such as drug discovery.
- *The intended audience*: The amount of explainability necessary will also be influenced by the audience for the explanations. It may be important for healthcare personnel to offer thorough explanations that are specialized to the medical area. For patients, more broad explanations that are simple to grasp may suffice.
- *The cost of explainability*: The cost of explaining AI systems varies depending on the approach chosen. Some procedures cost more than others.

Table 5.2. Pros of Interpretable AI and Explainable AI

Interpretable AI	Explainable AI
Easy to understand and explain	Can be used with complex models
Can build trust with users	Can identify and address bias in models
Can be used for debugging and troubleshooting	Can be used to improve model performance

The author Caruana (2015) says Overall, XAI has the potential to give several advantages to healthcare practitioners, patients, and the whole healthcare system. XAI can assist in enhancing the quality of care, cutting expenses, and raising patient happiness by making AI systems more visible and interpretable are shown in Table 5.2.

5.4 Interpretable vs. Explainable AI

- *Interpretable AI:* Examples of interpretable AI models include decision trees, linear regression models, and naive Bayes classifiers. Castelvecchi, D. (2016). Suggested that even non-technical consumers will find these models simple to grasp and convey.

- *Explainable AI:* Explainable AI models include neural networks, support vector machines, and random forests. Although these models are more complicated than interpretable models, they may be explained using approaches like feature importance, counterfactual explanations, and local interpretability methods.

Here are some instances of AI that are interpretable and explainable AI are shown in Table 5.3:

Table 5.3. Cons of Interpretable AI and Explainable AI

Interpretable AI	**Explainable AI**
Models that are not interpretable may not be as accurate.	It might be more computationally expensive.
It may not be appropriate for all usage situations.	It is possible that it will not be able to describe all elements of model behavior.

5.5 The Impact of Black Box AI in Healthcare

A sort of artificial intelligence (AI) that is difficult or impossible to understand or explain is known as black box AI. Challen et al. (2018) says this is because black-box AI models are generally trained on vast quantities of data using complicated algorithms, and their decision-making process is frequently opaque.

The usage of black box AI in healthcare is becoming more popular. These models are used for a range of activities, including:

- *Disease diagnosis*: Black box AI algorithms can evaluate medical pictures and data to diagnose illnesses. For example, a black box AI model that can diagnose diabetic retinopathy with the same accuracy as a human ophthalmologist was recently built.
- *Therapy recommendations*: Black box AI models may be used to make therapy recommendations for illnesses. Char et al. (2018) explained that for example, a black box AI model that can offer tailored cancer treatment methods was recently built.
- *Personalizing medicine: By considering unique patient aspects such as genetics, lifestyle, and environment, black box AI models may be used to tailor medication.* For example, a black box AI model that can predict which patients are most likely to benefit from a certain cancer therapy was recently built.

In healthcare, the application of black-box AI can improve patient care in a variety of ways. However, there are certain reservations about using black-box AI in healthcare. Chen et al. (2018) says One problem is that these models may be prejudiced, resulting in unfair or incorrect conclusions. Another worry is that these models may be difficult to trust because it is unclear how they make judgments.

5.6 Case Studies of XAI in Healthcare

Following are some examples of Explainable AI (XAI) in healthcare:

- *IBM Watson Health*: IBM Watson Health is a cloud-based platform that employs artificial intelligence to assist healthcare providers in making better decisions. One of IBM Watson Health's advantages is its capacity to explain its judgments. Chen et al. (2019) tells this enables healthcare practitioners to understand why IBM Watson Health made a certain decision, which can help them trust the platform and make better judgments on their own.
- *Google Health:* Google Health is a personal health platform that enables users to track and analyze their health data. Chen et al. (2018) says that Google Health also has a "My Explanations" tool that allows you to explain the judgments made by Google Health's AI-powered algorithms. This tool can help consumers comprehend their health data and make better health decisions.
- *Palantir Health*: Palantir Health is a healthcare analytics firm that employs artificial intelligence to assist healthcare practitioners in improving patient care. (Dandl et al. 2019) says Palantir Health's platform includes a tool called "Patient Explanations" that may explain Palantir Health's AI-powered algorithms' choices. This feature can assist healthcare practitioners in better understanding their patients' health data and making more informed decisions regarding their care.

These are just a few instances of how XAI is now being utilized in healthcare. As XAI technology advances, it is expected that XAI will be employed more broadly in healthcare.

5.7 XAI Techniques

Several XAI strategies may be used to explain AI system choices. Among the most prevalent XAI approaches are shown in Table 5.4.

5.7.1 User-Centered Design for Explainable AI

The process of building and assessing explainable AI systems that consider the users' requirements and comprehension is known as user-centered design. The author (Greenberg et al. 2018) suggested that understanding the user's objectives, tasks, and knowledge, as well as the context in which they will use the system, is part of this process. The purpose of user-centered design for explainability is to build systems that are simple to comprehend, trust, and employ.

5.8 Advantages and Limitations of Explainable AI

Here are some specific user-centered design principles for explainability:

- *Recognize the user:* The first stage is to comprehend the user's objectives, duties, and knowledge. Interviews, surveys, and observations can all be used to accomplish this.
- *Contextual design:* The system should be built for the context in which it will be utilized. (Greenberg et al. 2018) covers things like the user's surroundings, culture, and language.
- *Use a variety of explaining techniques*: There is no one optimal explanation for AI judgments. To suit the demands of diverse users, the system should employ a range of explanation strategies.
- *Gather user feedback*: The system should be tested with users to ensure that it is simple to comprehend, trust, and utilize.

User-centered design for Explainable AI is a critical step in developing successful and accessible explainable AI systems. Gunasekar et al. (2017) tells the various advantages and limitations of XAI are shown in Table 5.5.

5.9 Challenges and Opportunities of XAI in Healthcare

In healthcare, XAI presents a variety of obstacles and potential. Among the difficulties are:

- *AI system complexity:* AI systems may be exceedingly complicated, making it challenging to explain their conclusions.
- Holzinger et al. (2019) discussed a lack of standardized XAI techniques: No one XAI approach is ideal for all applications.
- *The requirement for human knowledge:* XAI approaches frequently necessitate the use of human skills to comprehend the explanations.

There are, nevertheless, several prospects linked with XAI in healthcare. Among these possibilities are:

- *The potential to enhance patient care*: By making AI systems more visible and interpretable, XAI has the potential to improve patient care.
- *The potential to decrease healthcare expenses*: By enhancing the accuracy and efficiency of AI systems, XAI has the potential to lower healthcare expenditures.
- *The potential to increase the quality of life*: The author Kim, B, and Wattenberg, M. (2019). XAI has the potential to improve a patient's quality of life by delivering more information about their health and treatment alternatives.

Table 5.4. Key Techniques for Explainable Healthcare AI

Techniques	Description
Local explanation technique	These strategies describe an AI system's judgment for a specific instance. A local explanation approach, for example, may explain why an AI system categorized a patient as having cancer.
Global explanation techniques	These approaches illustrate the general decision-making process of an AI system. A global explanation approach, for example, may describe how an AI system evaluates several criteria when reaching a diagnosis.
Interactive explanation techniques	These strategies enable people to engage with an AI system to learn more about the decision-making process. An interactive explanation approach, for example, may enable a person to observe how the AI system's judgment would alter if other data were utilized.
Feature importance	This approach determines the elements that are most significant to an AI system's judgment. For example, feature significance might be used to determine which symptoms are most indicative of a specific illness.
SHAP values	This method provides a score for each feature in an AI system, indicating how much that feature contributes to the system's conclusion. SHAP values, for example, might be used to discover the characteristics that are most significant in a patient's diagnosis.
LIME	This approach gives a local explanation for a specific instance by showing how the AI system's predictions vary when the feature values are altered. LIME, for example, might be used to explain why an AI system identified a patient as having cancer by demonstrating how the system's predictions alter when the values of the patient's symptoms are adjusted.
Partial dependence plots	These plots demonstrate how an AI system's predictions alter as the value of a certain characteristic varies. A partial dependency plot, for example, might be used to demonstrate how an AI system's estimates for a patient's risk of heart disease alter as the patient's age grows.
Counterfactual explanations	These explanations demonstrate how the AI system may have categorized a certain occurrence differently. A counterfactual explanation, for example, might demonstrate how a cancer patient could have been classed as not having cancer if their symptoms were different.

Table 5.5. Advantages and Limitations

Advantages	Limitations
Increased transparency	Explainable AI can assist in improving the transparency of AI systems, allowing users to better understand how the systems function and why they make the decisions they make. This can aid in the development of trust and confidence in AI systems.
Improved decision-making	Explainable AI can aid in decision-making by giving users insights into the elements that influence AI system judgments. This can assist users in making more informed judgments, particularly in complicated or unclear situations.
Reduced bias	Explainable AI might help reduce bias in AI systems by identifying and addressing potential causes of bias in data or algorithms. This can contribute to the fairness and equity of AI systems.
Enhanced debugging	Explainable AI can aid debugging by offering insights into the faults caused by AI systems. This can assist developers in repairing mistakes and improving system efficiency.
Fostering trust	Explainable AI can assist in developing trust between people and AI systems by making the systems easier to comprehend and trust. This is especially critical in situations where AI systems make judgments that affect people's lives, such as healthcare and finance.
Complexity	Explainable artificial intelligence approaches can be sophisticated and difficult to deploy. This can be difficult, particularly for small or resource-constrained enterprises.
Data requirements	Large volumes of data are frequently required for explainable AI strategies. This can be difficult, especially for businesses without access to massive databases.
Interpretability	Explainable AI approaches can be challenging to understand, particularly for non-technical consumers. This might make it difficult for consumers to understand and apply the explanations to make decisions.
Bias	AI approaches that can be explained can be biased, especially if they are not carefully built. This might result in incorrect or misleading explanations.

5.10 Real-World Use Cases of Explainable AI in Healthcare

Some real-world examples of explainable AI in healthcare:

- *Diagnosis:* Use explainable AI to explain how AI-powered diagnostic systems draw conclusions. This can assist clinicians in developing faith in and adoption of these systems, as well as in better understanding the outcomes of the analysis. The author Lipton, (2016). tells an AI system, for example, can be used to evaluate medical pictures to identify cancer. The system may then explain its decision-making process to the doctor, allowing him to comprehend why the system reached the conclusion it did.
- *Treatment:* Use explainable AI to explain how AI-powered treatment planning systems make judgments. This can help doctors tailor treatment strategies to specific patients and better understand the risks and advantages of various therapies. Lundberg and Lee (2017). It says that an AI system, for example, may be used to offer therapy alternatives for cancer patients. The system may then explain its decision-making process to the clinician, allowing him to comprehend why the system recommended the treatment alternatives it did.
- *Research:* Use explainable AI to explain how AI-powered research systems make judgments. This can assist researchers in identifying patterns in data and better understanding the outcomes of their analysis. (Montavon, et al. 2018) suggested an example that, an AI system may analyze medical information to discover illness risk factors. The system may then explain its decision-making process to the researchers, allowing them to comprehend why the system recognized the risk variables that it did.
- *Policymaking*: Explainable AI may be used to illustrate how decision-making systems powered by AI are made. This can assist policymakers in making educated decisions on the use of AI in healthcare, as well as mitigating the dangers of prejudice and discrimination. (Panch et al. 2018) tells An AI system, for example, may be used to evaluate healthcare data to find locations where resources are most required. The system may then explain its decision-making process to policymakers, allowing them to understand why the system picked the locations with the greatest need for funding.

These are only a few instances of how explainable AI is now being applied in healthcare. Rajkomar et al. (2019) says that as explainable AI technology advances, it is expected that explainable AI will be employed more broadly in healthcare.

5.11 Future Trends

The future of Explainable AI (XAI) in healthcare is set to bring about substantial changes in medical procedures, research, and patient care. (Rajkomar et al. 2018) tells several significant themes and orientations are predicted to impact XAI in healthcare's future:

- *Improved Patient-Centric Care*: By offering explicit explanations for treatment suggestions, XAI will allow patients to actively participate in their healthcare journey.

Ribeiro et al. (2016) tells Patients will comprehend the reasoning behind AI-driven decisions, resulting in more compliance and better patient outcomes.

- *Individualized Medicine*: XAI will be critical in the advancement of individualized medicine. Rudin, (2019) says that XAI will enable healthcare providers to adjust interventions to unique patient features by explaining the rationale of AI-generated treatment plans, resulting in more accurate and successful therapies.
- *Clinical Decision Support*: XAI will be integrated into clinical decision support systems, giving doctors transparent insights into AI-driven suggestions. This collaborative approach will improve the quality of medical choices and patient care.
- *Alignment of Ethical and Regulatory issues*: The future of XAI will place a major focus on ethical issues and regulatory compliance. Strickland (2019) says that XAI systems must follow ethical criteria to ensure justice, transparency, and accountability in AI-driven choices while also complying with data protection and medical legislation.
- *Interdisciplinary Collaboration*: Interdisciplinary collaboration among AI researchers, healthcare practitioners, ethicists, and politicians will be critical in determining the future of XAI in healthcare. This partnership will guarantee that XAI systems are consistent with medical knowledge, ethical norms, and societal values.
- *AI-Augmented Medical Research*: XAI will transform medical research by revealing the inner workings of AI models that analyze massive volumes of medical data. This will hasten the identification of novel therapies, medication candidates, and disease patterns.
- *Detection and Mitigation of Biases*: XAI will continue to advance in its approach to tackling biases and discrimination in healthcare AI models. Topol, (2019). Tells that Bias identification and mitigation techniques will be improved, increasing justice and inclusion in healthcare decision-making.

5.12 Conclusion

"Unveiling the Algorithms: How Explainable AI Reshapes Healthcare" is a revolutionary trip into the intersection of technology and healthcare, demonstrating how Explainable AI (XAI) is altering the medical environment. This investigation has demonstrated that XAI is a paradigm change that provides healthcare professionals and patients with transparent insights into AI-driven choices. The book has thrown light on how important XAI is in medical imaging, diagnostics, therapy customization, and clinical decision support. It is underlined that XAI is more than just a tool to improve diagnostic accuracy and treatment efficacy; it is also a catalyst for fostering trust, cooperation, and ethical AI deployment in healthcare. It is concluded that XAI deployment is dependent on multidisciplinary collaboration among AI researchers, healthcare specialists, ethicists, and politicians. The future of healthcare is positioned for patient-centric care, individualized therapies, and responsible AI adoption by ensuring regulatory compliance, resolving ethical concerns, and showcasing the value of transparent AI explanations. 'Unveiling the Algorithms' serves as an illuminating guide, highlighting the potential of XAI to redesign healthcare into a domain where human expertise and AI-driven insights coexist, fostering a future that is not only technologically advanced but also ethically compassionate, equitable, and driven by healthcare's core values: precision, empathy, and excellence.

References

Baldoni, S., Baroglio, C., and Martelli, A. (2019). "Explainable AI for healthcare: Introducing the EUXAI framework," *Artificial Intelligence in Medicine*, 95, 38-42.

Beam, A. L., and Kohane, I. S. (2018). "Big data and machine learning in health care," *Jama*, 319(13), 1317-1318.

Cabitza, F., Rasoini, R., and Gensini, G. F. (2017). "Unintended consequences of machine learning in medicine," *Jama*, 318(6), 517-518.

Caruana, R., Kangarloo, H., and Dionisio, J. D. (2009). "Case-based explanation of non-case-based learning methods," In *AMIA Annual Symposium Proceedings* (Vol. 2009, p. 2009).

Caruana, R., Lou, Y., Gehrke, J., Gomes, C., and Harry, D. (2015). "Intelligible models for healthcare: Predicting pneumonia risk and hospital 30-day readmission," In *Proceedings of the 21th ACM SIGKDD International Conference on Knowledge Discovery and Data Mining* (pp. 1721-1730).

Castelvecchi, D. (2016). "Can we open the black box of AI?," *Nature News*, 538(7623), 20.

Challen, R., Denny, J., Pitt, M., Gompels, L., Edwards, T., and Tsaneva-Atanasova, K. (2018). "Artificial intelligence, bias and clinical safety," *BMJ Quality and Safety*, 27(8), 627-630.

Char, D. S., Shah, N. H., and Magnus, D. (2018). "Implementing machine learning in health care—addressing ethical challenges," *New England Journal of Medicine*, 378(11), 981-983.

Chen, I. Y, Caruana, R., and Lou, Y. (2018). "Can AI predict severe community-acquired pneumonia?," *MLHC,* 203-218.

Chen, I. Y., Caruana, R., and Lou, Y. (2019). "Compas in ProPublica data set: A closer look at a case in automated fairness," *Big Data,* 7(4), 2045-2061.

Chen, J. H., Asch, S. M, and Moshfegh, J. (2019)."Machine learning approaches to predict 6-month mortality among patients with cancer," *JAMA Network Open*, 2(10), e1915997.

Dandl, S., Mourtada, R., Breitinger, C., and Müller, C. A. (2019). "Explainability in artificial intelligence: A survey," In *Europa Conference on Explainable Artificial Intelligence* (pp. 1-25).

Greenberg, M. D, Rosenfeld, J, and Lee, D. D. (2018). "How important is a black-box explanation?", *In International Conference on Learning Representations.*

Gunasekar, S., Lee, J., Soudry, D., Srebro, N., and Yin, H. (2017). "Implicit regularization in matrix factorization," In *Advances in Neural Information Processing Systems* (pp. 4123-4133).

Holzinger, A., Langs, G., Denk, H., Zatloukal, K., and Müller, H. (2019). "Causability and explainability of artificial intelligence in medicine," *Wiley Interdisciplinary Reviews: Data Mining and Knowledge Discovery,* 9(4), e1312.

Kim, B., and Wattenberg, M. (2019). "Interpretability beyond feature attribution: Quantitative testing with concept activation vectors (TCAV)," In *Proceedings of the 33rd AAAI Conference on Artificial Intelligence* (pp. 2673-2682).

Lipton, Z. C. (2016). "The mythos of model interpretability," In *Proceedings of the 2016 ICML Workshop on Human Interpretability in Machine Learning* (pp. 1-8).

Lundberg, S. M., Lee, S. I. (2017). "A unified approach to interpreting model predictions," *In Advances in Neural Information Processing Systems* (pp. 4765-4774).

Montavon, G., Samek, W., Müller, K. R. (2018). "Methods for interpreting and understanding deep neural networks," *Digital Signal Processing*, 73, 1-15.

Panch, T., Mattie, H., Celi, L. A. (2018). "The "inconvenient truth" about AI in healthcare," *Digital Medicine,* 1(1), 1-3.

Rajkomar, A., Dean, J., Kohane, I. (2019). " Machine learning in medicine," *New England Journal of Medicine*, 380(14), 1347-1358.

Rajkomar, A., Oren, E., Chen, K., Dai, A. M., Hajaj, N., Hardt, M., Corrado, G. (2018). "Scalable and accurate deep learning with electronic health records," *Digital Medicine*, 1(1), 18.

Ribeiro, M. T., Singh, S., Guestrin, C. (2016). " Why should I trust you? Explaining the predictions of any classifier," In *Proceedings of the 22nd ACM SIGKDD International Conference on Knowledge Discovery and Data Mining* (pp. 1135-1144).

Rudin, C. (2019). "Stop explaining black box machine learning models for high stakes decisions and use interpretable models instead," *Nature Machine Intelligence*, 1(5), 206-215.

Strickland, E. (2019). "How AI-powered chatbots could revolutionize mental health care," *Nature*, 572(7768), S8-S10.

Topol, E. J. (2019). "High-performance medicine: the convergence of human and artificial intelligence," *Nature Medicine*, 25(1), 44-56.

Section 2. Explainable AI in Smart Telemedicine and Telehealth

Chapter 6

Sensor Scheduling in an IoT Health Monitoring System with Interference Awareness

M. Sirish Kumar[1,*]
G. Nagendra Babu[1]
Jasmine Sabeena[2]
Ponnala Vaishnavi[1]
and Sanamreddy Sandhya[3]
[1]School of Computing, Mohan Babu University, Tirupati, India
[2]Dept. of CSE, SVCE, Tirupati, India
[3]Computer Science and Engineering, Mohan Babu University, Tiruapati, India

Abstract

Providing adequate healthcare services is in great demand due to the world's growing population. The need gap could widen with the introduction of contemporary technology. One such technology that may be applied to a healthcare monitoring system based on the Internet of Things is the sensor. The following chapter describes how such a system is put into practice. In a continuous wellness surveillance system, a regional analysis unit is linked to a variety of sensors over a common link with a predetermined capacity. There are many various network prerequisites for such sensors. To guarantee that every sensor has access to the required speed and latency on the common channel, the channel should only be reachable through distinct pathways. In the present research, an approach to planning for the Internet of Things-based system is proposed. This strategy prevents sensor interference and the resulting falsification of important nutritional information. The use of this technique within our concept medical treatment surveillance software is discussed in this chapter. In order to validate the planning procedure, we employed two detectors as a demonstration within the IoT-enabled assessment of satisfaction paradigm. Electrocardiogram shows a significant occurrence incidence but an insufficient amount of knowledge. Low example rate and high material quantity heat within the system level.

Keywords: IoT, scheduling, prerequisites

---

* Corresponding Author's Email: drmsk2102@gmail.com.

In: Explainable Artificial Intelligence in Healthcare Systems
Editors: A. Anitha Kamaraj and Debi Prasanna Acharjya
ISBN: 979-8-89113-598-7

6.1 Introduction

The infrastructure for healthcare is generally relatively weak in impoverished nations. In comparison to the expanding population, there are remarkably few hospitals. The few hospitals are ill-equipped, there aren't enough physicians working there, and most importantly, the essential diagnostic tools needed to identify life-threatening illnesses aren't available. Building new hospitals, giving them advanced medical infrastructure, and selecting doctors to be employed by such institutions is now an expensive and planned process. Nevertheless, believe that we might connect with a large audience and provide them with top-notch medical advice if we could develop a mobile, affordable wellness-detecting gadget that could measure the distinctive characteristics of the human body and communicate with the cloud. Once one of the authorities from a network of specialists spread out around the world examines those health factors on the Cloud, the pharmaceutical service is offered. We may gain the favour of a substantial populace.

However, if the health monitoring equipment interacts with a tablet or cellphone that already has the potential to interface with the internet via the cloud, the entire network would be significantly more expensive. This is because most individuals now have access to these modern information and communication gadgets, which have also decreased in price significantly. Moreover, the system may be made M2M machines-to-machines and IoT (Internet of Things) compliant. This article goes over the implementation of this sort of healthcare surveillance system. Each sensor has different needs for data quantity or size and bitrate in a health monitoring system.

To get a credible and trustworthy result, it must measure the health parameter. One difficult task is concurrently gathering intelligence from several sensors. Making data from sensors discrete correctly is necessary to transmit it to the data generator via a shared channel with fixed bandwidth (Rodríguez et al, 2010). Every detector must correctly gather input while adhering to the parameter's suitable bitrates, and the data must be supplied to the microcontroller without distortion or redundancy for the system for medical surveillance to be accurate.

This article proposes a programming technique that prevents any interference between several detectors and the ensuing data leakage. The two factors that matter when determining the sensor data schedule are the pulse width necessary when evaluating an attribute and the amount of data quantity per specimen required when detecting an attribute. While factors, especially if they involve image data along with sound, require much lower specimen rates but have much larger data lengths per sample, echocardiography, Lexicon, Signals Were Recorded, RR, and other linear measurements mean increased signal processing techniques that have shorter records lengths per specimen.

This chapter proposes a rescheduling method that prevents any interference between different sensors and the ensuing data loss. Two elements are critical when choosing sensor data scheduling: two items are required to measure a parameter: The sampling rate, (i) sample size, and (ii) the quantity of specimen or data length. When compared to parameters involving images (such as palpable images and other microscopic pictures) and sound (such as heart and lung sounds), graph-based parameters (such as electrocardiograms, electroencephalograms, electromyograms, and respiration rates) require higher sampling rates but have shorter data lengths per sample.

As a result, we want to provide every value the same importance while delivering health data across a common channel and allocate a specific window of duration. If the sensor characteristic information cannot be compressed inside the scheduled intervals, the data must be divided into several bits that do.

The remainder of the chapter is organized as shown below. Section 6.2 discusses the Internet of Things and its possible applications in the healthcare sector. The architecture of a healthcare system based on the Internet of Things is then proposed within Section 6.3 The problem of continuously gathering information via several wellness detectors is discussed in Section 6.4 along with a management approach.

Section 6.5 discusses how effective the scheduling technique is with a simple example. Lastly, we give a path for further research in Section 6.6 as conclusion of the chapter.

6.2 Internet of Things

The phrase "Internet of Things" describes a network of real-world and online gadgets that operate in smart settings and link as well as interact with one another in consumer, interpersonal, and physical environments.

The Internet of the Future, when everything is connected, could be seen as this. In the network, each object is assigned a special identification. This enables anytime, everywhere remote device access across the network. Smart, ubiquitous, and constantly connected environments are created when IoT-enabled products interact with humans, communicate with one another, and access information through the Internet.

The Internet of Things (IoT) also enables machine-to-machine (M2M) connectivity, allowing devices to be controlled both by other machines and by the Internet.

When machines take over, this might alter how technology is utilised since it would remove the barriers that prevent people from connecting with digital systems. The vast amounts of important data which computers can track monitors throughout the globe supply would take years for a person to acquire.

IoT brings the ideas of distributed computing and the Internet of Things to life by enabling everyday objects like automobiles, highways, heart rate monitors, meds-shaped cameras in our digestive tracts, signs that adjust to motorists, freezers, and even cattle equipped with sensors to communicate with humans and assist them in every step.

The next section emphasises the use of IoT in the healthcare sector.

6.3 IoT in Healthcare

A patient connected to IoT-enabled medical equipment for remote monitoring is sometimes referred to as a "virtual patient" in the digital era. The virtual patient's physiological circumstances mirror those of the real patient exactly. A doctor can only check on a patient a few times per day, yet medical crises can arise at any time. Continuous monitoring of health data becomes necessary.

Because of a patient's capacity to be accessed by other devices and the Internet thanks to the Internet of Things, their health may be continuously monitored. This makes it possible for serious illnesses to be identified early on, allowing for the implementation of effective measures.

IoT may also be used to gather medical records. Machines can produce statistical data relating to health conditions. It is feasible to collect data more quickly, in large quantities, and without errors than human approaches could possibly manage. Remote health data can be used for illness surveillance, risk mapping, and statistics generation (Beck, 2000).

This section discusses an approach for connecting to the internet of wellness tracking. Multiple sensors attached to a person make up a system for keeping track of health. These sensors connect with information-gathering and analysis equipment. One possibility for the information collector and analysis device is a smartphone or specialist device.

The information unit must gather data from each sensor using a predetermined sample rate to build the Human Body Awareness Association (Chen, 2010; Patel, 2011). As an aggregating unit in our architecture, we employed an Arduino microcontroller, and protothreads were used for scheduling. Our health monitoring system's processing centre is a portable computer. The Arduino aggregator communicates with the data processing unit using wired USB serial connections or short-range wireless communication technologies including Router, Internet, Lorawan, as well as Zigbee.

The information gathered from the collector unit is processed by the data processing unit, sometimes known as a portable computer.

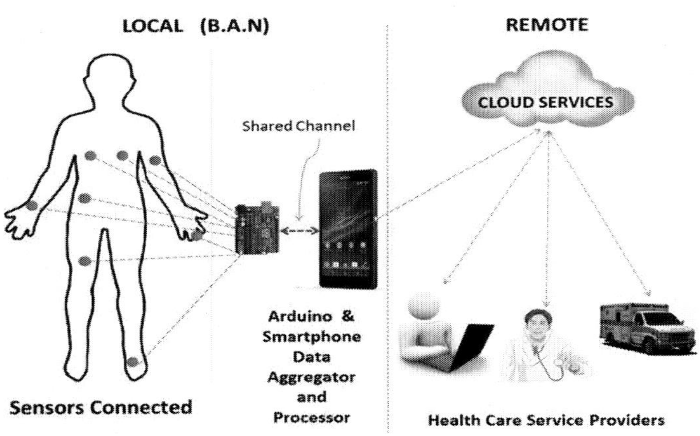

Figure 6.1. Layout of the health monitoring system.

The information might also be used to create interesting features for users, such as interactive graphs and charts. (including variables such as an ECG monitoring data graph). By using this tool, patients may obtain crucial medical advice from their doctors and set alarms or reminders for appointments and medications that must be taken on time.

The layout of the health monitoring system is depicted in Figure 6.1. There are two components to the system: local and remote. Data can be saved and sent to distant suppliers, such as urgent care doctors, including carers, thanks to the remote component. Input via detectors linked to a patient is gathered by the neighbouring component. Furthermore, software analyses the raw data gathered to deliver knowledge that experts and medical professionals can understand. The processed data is then displayed and sent to the remote servers after that.

6.4 Create a Framework for Monitoring Health

Open-Source Hardware

A data microcontroller Open-source hardware is employed. It can quickly enable the Internet of Things. An Arduino board includes a sixteen MHz version of the AT CPU, thirty-two thousands of portable storage, and two kilobytes of Memory. For connecting various sensors and actuators, it features fourteen electronic pins and Six analogue interfaces. This kind of project and other Bluetooth Sensory web systems benefit greatly from its high processing capacity and ability to link to a variety of sensors and communication devices. It speaks of an Arduino-powered wireless sensor network,

The open-source hardware is linked to a portable information handling and interaction device through a fixed bandwidth serial connection. Given that the Arduino and the handheld data handling device share a channel, each sensor's communication across this shared channel should be handled separately.

Sensor

SPO_2 Sensor: This device is also known as a pulse oximeter. This sensor offers unobtrusive tools that capture numerous essential physical characteristics of the human body known as health sensors. All the system's sensors are discussed in this section. To allow communication with data aggregator hardware, these have been updated. Upon request from the Open-source hardware-based information collector device, the sensor records a specific property value as well as communicates it back to the data aggregator. Some sensors employed in the system are shown in Figure 6.2 below.

- A technique for determining the amount of oxygen in our blood's haemoglobin. Additionally, the pulse rate is measured.
- An ECG sensor measures the power supply and contractions in the coronary artery.
- An airway detector, also known as a respiration detector, tracks the patterns of rate of breathing variations that may indicate serious functional disturbance. The subject is a vital medical tool for quickly identifying a lack of oxygen and insomnia.
- Temp Sensor: This sensor measures a person's temperature.
- Blood pressure cuff: This instrument measures artery blood pressure. The pulse value and diastolic value, which indicate the level of fluid in blood vessels during cardiac contraction and heart dilation, respectively, are the two values provided by this measurement.
- The human body's status, including being in a position, seated, lying flat, and other positions, is determined by its internal motion detector. There are several illnesses where it's crucial to pay attention to the body's movements. In one case, it could be helpful in determining a neurological patient. This sensor can also detect dizziness or tumbling, making it crucial for elderly people.
- GSR detector measures the electric conductivity and stiffness of the outermost layer of skin, as it varies with the amount of moisture in the skin. Since the sympathetic

nervous system influences sweat glands, intense emotional states alter the skin's resistance to electricity and conductance. This sensor assists in identifying both emotional and physical arousal.

- Glucometer: A glucose detector that estimates the blood's estimated glucose concentration.
- A sensor called an electromyogram (EMG) measures the nerve impulses of muscles in the body both at relaxation and when they are contracting. This is used to identify kinesiological anomalies, quantify low back pain, identify neuromuscular illnesses, and examine the biological mechanisms that influence human motion. Additionally, it can aid in the detection of medical anomalies, activation levels, recruitment patterns, and motor control issues. The sensors mentioned above are used by this healthcare system. But a lot more detectors might be included within this remote surveillance network if advised to do so by qualified medical personnel.

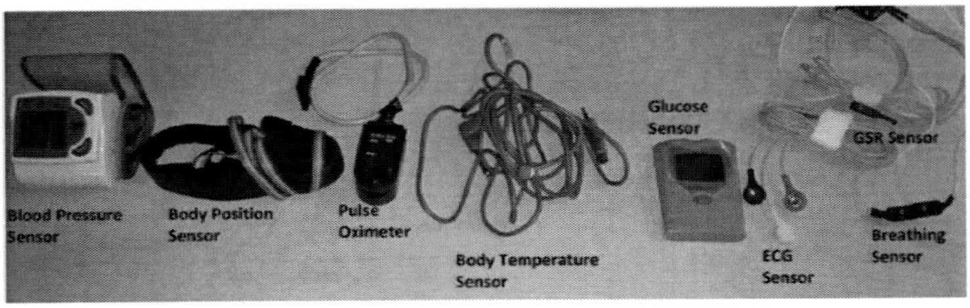

Figure 6.2. Detectors for wellness tracking.

Connection for Application

There is also an Android app that has been developed. It can be used by any smartphone or tablet running Android that has a Wireless connection. The sensors are connected to the Arduino, and the code communicates with them over a Wireless network. Additionally, this program displays an electrocardiogram visualization, heart rate charts, body temp, blood pressure, O2 saturation, and arterial pressure. The Android application's user interface is depicted in Figure 6.3.

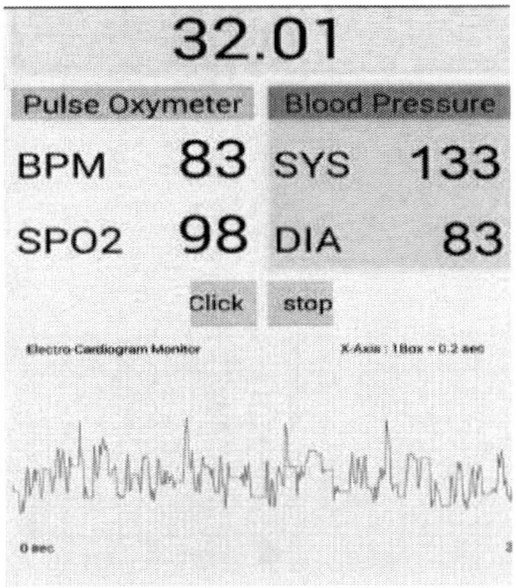

Figure 6.3. Android app UI.

6.5 Acquiring Information from Sensors

The data gathered by the detectors in the wellness tracking equipment is transmitted via an individual conventional interface between the CPU and the data accumulator module. Different measuring measurements, widths, and sample frequencies are required depending on the sensor. To produce a trustworthy and dependability-oriented result, these two factors must be considered. Input must consistently flow across the common link to every data analysis module to keep up with the specimen rate.

The sampling rate is faster for measures like the electrocardiogram (ECG), electroencephalogram (EEG), electromyogram (EMG), respiratory rate (RR), and other graph-based metrics, but the data length per sample is less. Although there is still a huge amount of data in each sample, sampling rates for parameters like visuals (such as micro pictures) and sound (containing variables like cardiac, and respiratory sounds) are significantly lower.

Every sensing device should perform accurate readings while keeping to the prescribed frequency of samples for the parameter. Additionally, there should be no loss of data or overlap when sending it to the data processor. To prevent data loss while using an established communication channel, sensor data from several sensors must be interleaved. It should be put into practice in a way that ensures every specimen from all sensors is collected, and that results are given within the allotted period.

In this case, our main goal is to offer a suitable method of linking data across the shared channel.

6.6 Suggested Method

Health metrics that depend on time have a very limited tolerance for delays. The latency and sample rate should be kept constant to preserve the integrity and significance of the data. As a result, a data interleaving technique is used to distribute the obtainable memory across the sensors, allowing each to preserve its testing frequency, delay and input size.

Where Bc be the overall communication channel high frequency (in bit values per sec). One or more slots may be created out of the bandwidth.

The goal is to split the bandwidth between several such positions. Data Size = Slotd for 1 millisecond. The needed rate of sampling as well as the information duration for a sensor are represented by Slot, fi, Si, and Ldi, respectively. Si, Ti = Sensor cycle times or lengths.

LdiMax is short for maximum data length. In a 115200bps bandwidth, the single sensor's maximum data length is provided by:

$$\text{SlotdXTi} = \text{LdiMax} \quad (1)$$

Slot d = Bc/(10008), in Bytes, calculates the data size for each millisecond slot. (2)

From useful execution experience, it is expected that the absolute data transmission (Bc) of the correspondence channel is 115200 pieces/sec. In this way, applying Condition 2, the information size per opening becomes:

Slotd = 14 Bytes.

We know,

Time period = 1/f (3)

where we can measure time period or cycle length and f = recurrence.

We can observe two instances right now to see how our technique works.

1. *Scenario 1:* A single detector, designated S1, is connected through a passive line. Accept that the required information length (Ld1) for the detected boundary is 25 Bytes and the anticipated examination rate (f1) is 125 Hz. The time duration for S1 is T1 = 8 milliseconds based on Condition 3. It indicates that we receive 8 slots, each of 14 bytes.
   To keep up with the necessary information stream, openings anticipated for the information length of the sensor S1 should be saved every 8 ms. With the set testing rate from Condition 1, we can compute the maximum allowable information length (Ld1Max) for this sensor.
   Ld1Max = 14x8, or 112 bytes.
   The S1 sensor data may be appropriately obligated within the cable transmission frequency because of Ld1 Ld1Max. Sensor S1 needs a pair of holes of length Slotd, over instance, 14 Bytes, since Ld1 = 25 Bytes. Subsequently, there are 6 empty areas between each pair of samples. There are 84 free bytes (6 x 14).

2. *Scenario 2: The primary means of communication is expanded to include a second sensor (S2), which has several criteria.* For S2, the data dimension (Ld2) is equal to 300 Bytes, and the scrutinizing frequency (f2) is equal to 10 Hz. The time period, T2, equals 100 milliseconds due to Condition 3 being done.

This will allow us to keep delivering data from sensor S2 each one hundred ms at the current rate. Considering scenario 1, we get the following maximal informative amount:

For every millisecond, Ld2Max is 14 times 100, or 1400 bytes.

Currently, a few recognized knowledge evaluations from sensor S1 are supposed to be delivered within this 100 ms time period for sensor S2 when transferring information from the two sensors across the same channel since S1 has a greater scrutinizing velocity. The number of tests from S1 that will be included in S2 during one sample period is as follows: (4) The following criterion defines the available data transfer for sensor

S2:Ld2Actual = Ld2Max (f1/f2)X(2XSlotd) (5)

From Condition 5, it is possible to calculate the available broadcast ability: Ld2Actual = 1400 ((2X14)X12) = 1064 Bytes.

When looking at scenario 1, we saw that the most extreme 84 Bytes may be allotted between two samples from sensor S1 for delivering data from the additional sensor S2. Then data from S1 ought to be provided. Then, further data from S1 must be sent. After that, 84 more bytes are available, and S2 data may be delivered. As a result, data from the two sensors may be combined, as shown in Table 6.1.

Table 6.1. Arranging for medical treatment

Data size per milli sec for bandwidth 115200 bit/s	Sensor 1: sample rate 125 Hz and data size 25B	Sensor 2: sample rate 10Hz and data size 300B
1 ----- 14 bytes	25 Bytes	
2 ----- 14 bytes	25 Bytes	
3 ----- 14 bytes		84 Bytes
4 ----- 14 bytes		84 Bytes
5 ----- 14 bytes		84 Bytes
6 ----- 14 bytes		84 Bytes
7 ----- 14 bytes		84 Bytes
8 ----- 14 bytes		84 Bytes
9 ----- 14 bytes	25 Bytes	
10 ----- 14 bytes	25 Bytes	
11 ----- 14 bytes		84 Bytes
12 ----- 14 bytes		84 Bytes
13 ----- 14 bytes		84 Bytes
14 ----- 14 bytes		84 Bytes
15 ----- 14 bytes		84 Bytes
16 ----- 14 bytes		84 Bytes
17 ----- 14 bytes	25 Bytes	
18 ----- 14 bytes	25 Bytes	
19 ----- 14 bytes		84 Bytes
20 ----- 14 bytes		84 Bytes
21 ----- 14 bytes		84 Bytes
22 ----- 14 bytes		84 Bytes
23 ----- 14 bytes		84 Bytes
24 ----- 14 bytes		84 Bytes
25 ----- 14 bytes	25 Bytes	
26 ----- 14 bytes	25 Bytes	
27 ----- 14 bytes		48 Bytes
28 ----- 14 bytes		48 Bytes
29 ----- 14 bytes		48 Bytes
30 ----- 14 bytes		48 Bytes
31 ----- 14 bytes		
32 ----- 14 bytes		

For S2, a large information length of 300 Bytes is required. To maintain the required example pace of S1, the information produced by S2 should be divided into 3 parts, each of which should be 84 Bytes in size. The remaining 48 Bytes can then be required in the subsequent free opening. Therefore, we design the sensors such that lengthy information cannot be divided into smaller portions and necessitate the opening of saved information from another sensor.

6.7 Results

To validate the planning procedure, we employed two detectors as a demonstration within the IoT-enabled assessment of satisfaction paradigm.

- Electrocardiogram shows a significant occurrence incidence but insufficient amount of knowledge
- Low example rate and high material quantity heat within the system level

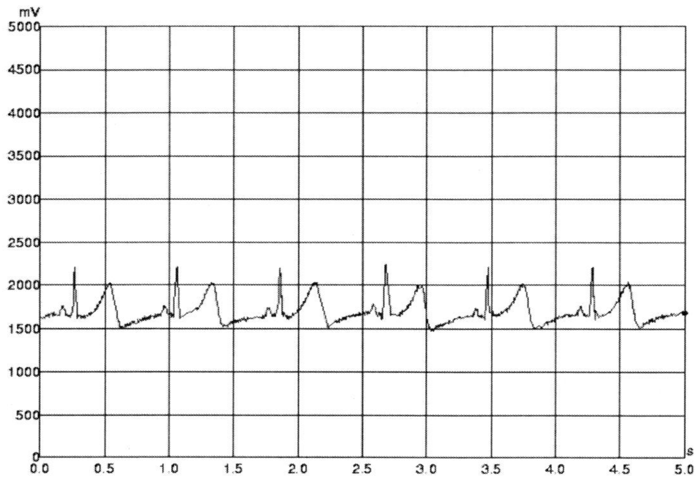

Figure 6.4. Information will overlap with the ECG information.

Since the electrocardiogram (ECG) detector demands a speed of, for instance, 125 Hz, we actually want to deliver the ECG data every 8 ms. Given that the two sensors use the same channel, it is now required that the data from the inside temperature content sensor be shared amongst both samples. However, if the body's internal heat level signal is not separated between the ECG sensor instances, this information will overlap with the ECG information and the translation of the information at the processing unit will be distorted, as shown in Figure 6.4. The ECG tests are not delayed at that point, and the ECG is faithfully decoded at the data performing unit of service, considering that we figure out the free openings throughout each instance from the ECG sensor and subsequently break down the information from the internal heat level sensor as indicated by the size of the free spaces between the ECG tests. Figure 6.4 shows what data was obtained after using our suggested technique.

It's crucial to look at Figure 6.4 of the paradigm. Due to the limited transmission speed, it is important to strategically position each sensor, as was covered in this study, to sustain a rapid checking frequency and data integrity. We have shown that by incorporating what is available according to the required testing rate and excluding larger information with the largest permitted information size, it is possible to maintain the inspection rate for a number of sensors while ensuring a high-quality exchange of data and effective use of data transfer capacity.

6.8 Conclusion

For the sensors to operate successfully, an illness tracking system must satisfy each detector's inspection frequency and duration specifications. As the velocity of transmission is constrained, we ought to organise every detector sensibly, as discussed in this study, so that the testing rate is maintained, and the caliber of data is high. By dividing bigger knowledge by having the biggest permitted features analysis and interleaving the information according to the needed monitoring severity, we have shown this.

References

Beck, L. R., Lobitz, B. M., and Wood, B. L. (2000). Remote sensing and human health: new sensors and new opportunities. *Emerging infectious diseases*, *6*(3), 217.

Bisoi, S., Bhunia, S. S., Roy, S., and Mukherjee, N. (2013). iSENSE: intelligent sensor monitoring services with integrated WSN Testbed. *Procedia Technology*, *10*, 564-571.

Chen, M., Gonzalez, S., Vasilakos, A., Cao, H., and Leung, V. C. (2011). Body area networks : A survey. *Mobile networks and applications*, *16*, 171-193.

Paschou, M., Sakkopoulos, E., Sourla, E., and Tsakalidis, A. (2013). Health Internet of Things: Metrics and methods for efficient data transfer. *Simulation Modelling Practice and Theory*, *34*, 186-199.

Patel, M., and Wang, J. (2010). Applications, challenges, and prospective in emerging body area networking technologies. *IEEE Wireless communications*, *17*(1), 80-88.

Rodríguez, C. C. G., Riveill, M., and Antipolis, S. (2010). e-Health monitoring applications: What about Data Quality?. In *Proc. of the Health Ambiant Information Systems Workshop*.

Chapter 7

A Time Series-Based Artificial Neural Networks for Predicting COVID-19 Positive Cases in Indonesia

Balakrishnama Manohar[1]
Raja Das[2,*]
and Biju Vasudevan[3]
[1,2]Department of Mathematics, School of Advanced Sciences,
Vellore Institute of Technology (VIT), Vellore, Tamil Nadu, India
[3]Department of General Studies, Jubail University College, Jubail Industrial City,
Saudi Arabia

Abstract

Artificial neural networks (ANN) have been extensively utilized in recent years to forecast the COVID-19 outbreak. However, most research using ANN to estimate COVID-19 cases is only trained on limited COVID-19 datasets using one method. The main objective of this research is to design an ANN model that trains using three different algorithms to predict COVID-19 cases in the time frame of January 1, 2022, to March 30, 2023 (451 Days) in Indonesia. This paper covers a research gap on how to use numerous ANN training algorithms with large COVID-19 datasets to estimate future COVID-19 cases. For training the ANN model, the LM, BFGS, and SGC algorithms are used in this work. The results show that the ANN-LM model achieved the best fit in regression analysis compared to the other two models. The ANN-LM method provides the higher values of EC (0.9990, 0.9999, 0.9998), R^2 values (0.999, 1.000, 1.000) and the lowest *RMSE* (346.5, 1859.5, 1855.5), *MAPE* (16.17, 19.776, 21.53), CRM (0.0016, 0.0257, 0.0263) during training, validation, and testing, respectively. Based on the results, the ANN-LM model is much better at making predictions compared to ANN-BFGS and ANN-SCG models. Finally, the authors conclude that the ANN-LM model developed in this work offers increased prediction accuracy with a higher EC, R^2 and lower *RMSE, MAPE, and CRM* when compared to the other two models. Therefore, the ANN-LM method has been identified as one of the most suitable models for predicting COVID-19 cases.

Keywords: Artificial neural network, BFGS, COVID-19, LM, prediction models, SCG

* Corresponding Author's Email: rajadasrkl@gmail.com.

In: Explainable Artificial Intelligence in Healthcare Systems
Editors: A. Anitha Kamaraj and Debi Prasanna Acharjya
ISBN: 979-8-89113-598-7

7.1 Introduction

The COVID-19 epidemic has been recognized as a threat to world health. Many different virus species in the coronavirus family may infect both humans and animals and cause sickness. Several coronaviruses may infect the respiratory system in people, causing everything from common colds to more serious conditions like Middle East Respiratory Syndrome (MERS) and other severe acute respiratory syndromes (SARS). COVID-19 is an infectious infection that has just been identified and has spread globally (Chan et al. 2015). The disease's emergence was unknown until it was discovered in Wuhan, a Chinese city, in December 2019. Fever, tiredness, and a dry cough are COVID-19's three most prevalent symptoms. Some individuals get the virus without displaying any signs or getting sick. Most patients (80%) are likely to recover from the infection without requiring any special care. One in six individuals with COVID-19 infection gets severe symptoms (Fu et al. 2016). Fever, coughing, sore throat, headaches, weariness, muscle soreness, and shortness of breath are among the usual clinical symptoms of COVID-19. Tiny droplets that become airborne if the person who is infected coughs or sneezes may transfer the sickness from one person to another. The items and surfaces near the sick individual are covered by these droplets. COVID-19 may spread to people who contact certain things or surfaces and then touch their eyes, nose, or mouth. These airborne droplets can cause those who breathe them to develop COVID-19. As a result, it is crucial to maintain around one meter (3 feet) from sick people. Globally, between January 20, 2022, to April 01, 2023, approximately 764.38 million people were infected, resulting in more than 6.93 million deaths cases; and from Indonesia, 6.77 million people (about twice the population of Oklahoma) were infected positively, resulting in 0.161 million deaths cases.

Recent research on the computational, mathematical, and statistical features of many viruses has already been published in several articles on COVID-19. The dynamics of COVID-19 are studied mathematically using a variety of models. The Susceptible Infectious Recovered (SIR) model is one of the models used the most to study the dynamics of different illnesses. This model uses a set of time-dependent differential equations to predict the spread of the epidemic. The SIR framework and its several modified versions have been widely used by researchers to explore the diseases AIDS and Ebola (Khaleque et al. 2016; Zakary et al. 2016). Such models were recently employed to model the spread of the coronavirus outbreak. Numerous statistical techniques have been employed to forecast the COVID-19 pandemic's spread, such as regression techniques (Namasudra et al. 2023), the Susceptible-Infectious-Quarantined-Recovered (SIQR) technique (Crokidakis, 2020), the autoregressive integrated moving average (ARIMA) and suttee ARIMA technique (Zhang, 2003) and the Composite Monte-Carlo (CMC) simulation technique (McClarren 2018). All these models have their unique benefits, but none of them are flexible, which means that the forecasting error is not utilized in an iterative process to better the model.

Many investigators are working on the COVID-19 forecasting task since it is critical. The model that gives higher performance and quicker training is preferred among the available models. In this study, a model called "artificial neural networks" was used to predict the no. of confirmed positive cases in Indonesia for the next few days based on the data from 01 January 2022 to 19 March 2023.

Many research papers using ANN models to predict COVID-19 cases have already been published. However, each has its own set of advantages and drawbacks. However, no research has been done to ascertain the most efficient ANN training technique and structure using COVID-19 examples. The goal of this work was to build and demonstrate ANN-based approaches to forecast COVID-19 cases for upcoming outbreaks. To choose the optimal method for building a forecasting model, we developed and evaluated three ANN training algorithms.

7.2 Literature Review

In recent years, researchers have employed different machine learning and deep learning methods to make predictions about COVID-19 data. Table. 7.1 provides a summary of some of the related literature.

Table 7.1. An overview of the relevant previous work

Authors	Title	Period	Models	Inputs	Outputs	Outcomes
(Niazkar and Niazkar 2020)	Application of artificial neural networks to predict the COVID-19 outbreak	2020	ANN Model	Daily Counts of Confirmed Instances	The ANN-based model that considers the preceding 14 days (about 2 weeks) performs better than the other models.	To anticipate daily confirmed cases, the prior fourteen days are recommended.
(Ahmad and Asad, 2020)	Predictions of coronavirus COVID-19 distinct cases in Pakistan through an artificial neural network	2020	ANN-ADAM	Daily, confirmed, recovered, and dead instances	Prediction of Next 7 days	The suggested method has produced forecasts for the next seven days.
(Borghi et al. 2021)	A COVID-19 time series forecasting model based on MLP ANN	2021	ANN - MLP Model	Daily Counts of Confirmed Instances	future 20 days (about 3 weeks)	Model archives More than accuracy 90%
(Hamadneh et al. 2021)	Artificial Neural Networks for Prediction of COVID-19 in Saudi Arabia	2021	PPA-ANN Model	Daily confirmed, recovered cases collected from Saudi Arabia.	Forecast of new verified instances and recovered instances	The number of sick people will rise over the next several days to at least 9789. 2000 to 4000 recoveries will occur each day.
(Shetty and Pai 2021)	Forecasting of COVID-19 Cases in Karnataka State using Artificial Neural Network (ANN)	2021	ANN-CS	Cumulative confirmed cases	The suggested approach can accurately analyze the epidemic's pattern.	On the training data, the MAPE had a value of 6.62%, whereas, on the test data, it had a value of 7.03%.
(Manohar and Das 2022a)	Artificial Neural Networks for the Prediction of Monkeypox Outbreak	2022	ANN LSTM, and GRU	Daily Counts of Confirmed Instances	Prediction of confirmed cases	ANN-LM gives better results compared to the LSTM and GRU.

Table 7.1. (Continued)

Authors	Title	Period	Models	Inputs	Outputs	Outcomes
(Shaibani et al. 2022)	Investigation of the robustness of hybrid artificial neural network with artificial bee colony and firefly algorithm in predicting COVID-19 new cases: a case study of Iran	2022	ANN-ABC, ANN-FA	Daily Confirmed Cases	The suggested approach can precisely analyze the epidemic's trend.	Based on the R-squared values of the best model are ANN-ABC and ANN-FA, 96% and 98%, respectively.
(Manohar and Das 2022b)	Artificial neural networks for prediction of COVID-19 in India by using backpropagation	2023	ANN-BP	Daily Confirmed Cases	The ANN-based model that considers the preceding 14 days (about 2 weeks) performs better than the other models.	To anticipate daily confirmed cases, the prior fourteen days are recommended.

The novelties of the proposed model in this paper are the following:

- Using current as well as historical data, this study develops ANN prediction models that provide the best results for predicting confirmed positive COVID-19 cases in Indonesia.
- To choose the optimal method to develop a prediction model, we built an ANN model with three learning algorithms.
- The widely used algorithms are considered: Levenberg (LM) Marquardt, Broyden-Fletcher (BFGS) Goldfarb-Shanno Quasi-Newton, Scaled (SCG) Conjugate Gradient.
- The tansig and purelin activation functions used for ANN models in this Study.
- Three different metrics (RMSE, MAPE, CRM, EC, and R^2) were utilized to analyse each model's prediction performance.
- The resulting model offers quicker training and enhanced prediction performance.

7.3 Proposed Methodology

The main aim of this study is to design a time-series-based ANN model for the prediction of COVID-19 cases using different algorithms like LM, BFGS, and SCG. In this research, the model with the most accurate outcome is picked as the best model. The proposed methodology is shown in Figure 7.1.

7.3.1 Data Collection

The Indonesian COVID-19-positive case data was collected from the worldindata.org website link. The COVID-19-positive cases in Indonesia from January 1, 2022, to March 30, 2023, were used to train, validate, and test the proposed techniques in this study. The whole set of data is split into three parts: training (70%), testing (15%), and validation (15%) from January 1, 2022, to March 19, 2023, and the remaining data we keep separately for future forecasting from March 20 to March 30, 2023. A complete dataset time interval for training, validating, and testing is shown in Table 7.2.

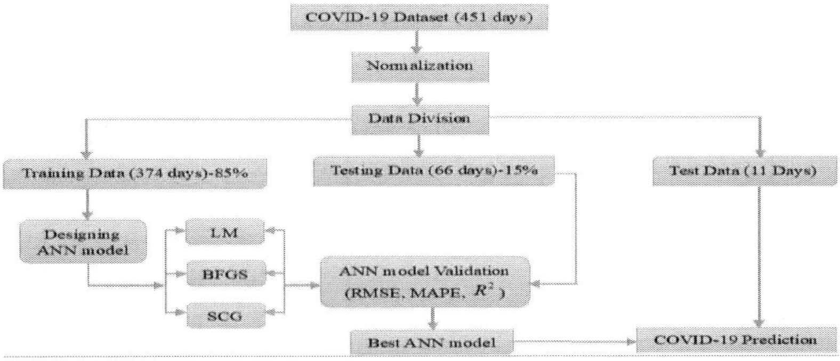

Figure 7.1. Flowchart of the proposed methodology.

Table 7.2. COVID-19 dataset for Training, Validation, Testing

	Dataset	Training dataset	Validation dataset	Testing dataset	Test data
Time Interval	01/01/2022 - 19/03/2023	01/01/2022 - 05/11/2022	06/11/2022 - 11/01/2023	12/01/2023 - 19/03/2023	20/03/2023 - 30/03/2023

7.3.2 Data Normalization

Normalization is a scaling method in which numbers are moved and rescaled so that they fall between -1 and 1. It is also called "Min-Max scaling," and Eq. 1 is used to figure it out:

$$y = \frac{(y_{max} - y_{min}) * (x - x_{min})}{(x_{max} - x_{min})} + y_{min} \quad (1)$$

where, y_{max} and x_{max} is the maximum, y_{min} and x_{min} is the minimum value of the feature (Manohar and Das 2022a).

7.4 Artificial Neural Networks (ANNs)

Artificial Intelligence (AI) is a promising field for handling a variety of challenges, including those involving prediction (forecasting). (Tata Hardinata et al. 2017) AI is an immensely significant field that comprises a variety of well-established fields, such as ANN. (Shanbehzadeh et al. 2022; Li, et al. 2021) A method called a neural network, which draws inspiration from the neurons in the human brain, is designed to find patterns in complex data. The neural network is produced by the method in which individuals think. When artificial neurons are used to form neural networks, they are called artificial neural networks. A huge number of neurons are layered in three layers to form an artificial neural network (ANN): A layer that receives input, an outcome layer, and one or more hidden layers. The first layer is the input layer, which has one node for each of the issue's input parameters. The second layer is the hidden layer, which is utilized for parameter interactions. This is the output layer, which is used to generate anticipated values. Neurons receive an input signal and then process it before emitting an output signal. Weights are associated with every neuron. Below is an explanation of the connection between the output and the input x : (Qiu and Song, 2016) Several neurons, which are single processing components, are grouped in layers. Every neuron in a layer is linked to every neuron in the layer underneath it, and each link has a different weight. As shown in Figure 7.2, the method involves sending numbers from a single neuron to another via numerous connections to enter the input information into the input layers. Once it reaches the output layer, it will be able to achieve any desired number.

Here, represents the input data. w denotes the weight of every neuron that is linked to another neuron. Bias, represented b , approximates the point at which the value of a new neuron becomes relevant. σ represents the activation value between -1 and 1 for each neuron. Furthermore, an activation function has to be defined by σ . The most important weights may be determined with the help of activation. By either adding or removing a bias from the activation and weights product, it might calculate the value of a new neuron. The Eq. 2 and Eq. 3 represents a new neuron value:

$$y_j(x)=\sum_{i=1}^{n} w1_{ji}x_i + b1_j \quad (2)$$

$$z_j(x)=\frac{1}{1+e-\left(w1_{ji}x_i + b1_j\right)} \quad (3)$$

In a structure with more than one layer, the process keeps going in the same order: Information is gathered by the input neurons and sent to the first hidden layer of neurons. From there, the behavior of every node is figured out. Then, the following layer receives the outputs from the primary hidden layer, where each neuron's behavior is determined. Until the output layer has been reached and the required output is generated, this process is continued.

There are a variety of criteria that can be applied to evaluate a model's performance. Researchers utilize an average cost function, whose value will be optimized later, to assess the model's performance.

The network is then trained once the ANN's structure has been designed. Training the networks consists mostly of locating and gaining the optimal solutions for the network's various biases and weights. In this study, three distinct training algorithms are used to get the optimal value for the network.

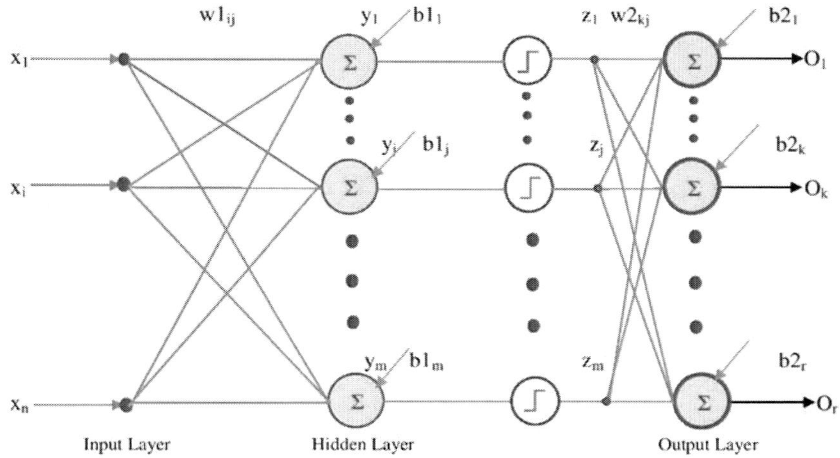

Figure 7. 2. Schematic diagram of the artificial neural network with backpropagation (BPNN).

7.5 ANNs Training Algorithms

As indicated in the introduction, investigators are progressively using artificial neural networks to forecast real-world events. These ANN algorithms optimize the weights of feed-forward neural networks using local or global nonlinear optimization techniques (Wanto, 2018). Local searches are restricted to local results, but global searches circumvent this restriction. The performance of training varies depending on the objective function of the optimization process, the error surface underlying a specific issue, and the network architecture. Variants of gradient-based backpropagation algorithms are the most prevalent optimization approaches. The gradient information of the error surface is accessible to these techniques (Qiu and Song, 2016). The widely used methods are LM, BFGS, and SGC. The goal of training an ANN is to minimize the global error (E), which is defined as follows in Eq. 4:

$$E = \frac{1}{S}\sum_{s=1}^{S} E_s \tag{4}$$

where S represents the total number of training patterns and ES is the error for pattern S. The following Eq. 5 is used to compute ES:

$$E_S = \frac{1}{n}\sum_{i=1}^{n}(O_i - t_i) \tag{5}$$

Here, the total number of output nodes is represented by n, the network output at the kth output node is represented by o_k, and the desired output at the kth output node is represented by t_k. By modifying the weights and biases of the training process, the global error is decreased. These are descriptions of the most popular training algorithms for neural networks.

7.5.1 Evaluation Metric Performance

Three different metrics (RMSE, MAPE, CRM, EC and R^2) were utilized to analyse each model's prediction performance. When the forecasting model produces lower RMSE, MAPE, and CRM values and higher EC, R^2 values, it is more effective. In the mathematical Eq. 6 to Eq. 10, n stands for the sample size, o , $\overline{o}$ represents the actual value, and average of actual values, respectively, and t represents the target value (Muhammad et al. 2022; Veza et al. 2022).

The square root of the mean square error is the term "Root Mean Square Error" is expressed as RMSE:

$$RMSE = \sqrt{\frac{1}{n}\sum_{i=1}^{n}\left(o_i - t_i\right)^2} \tag{6}$$

The Mean Absolute Percentage Error is expressed as MAPE:

$$MAPE = \frac{1}{n}\sum_{i=1}^{n}\left|\left(\frac{o_i - t_i}{t_i}\right)\right| \times 100\% \tag{7}$$

The Coefficient of Residual Mass is expressed as CRM:

$$CRM = \frac{\sum_{i=1}^{n} t_i - \sum_{i=1}^{n} o_i}{\sum_{i=1}^{n} o_i} \tag{8}$$

The Efficiency Coefficient is expressed as EC:

$$EC = 1 - \frac{\sum_{i=1}^{n}\left(o_i - t_i\right)^2}{\sum_{i=1}^{n}\left(o_i - \overline{o}\right)^2} \tag{9}$$

The coefficient of determination is expressed as R^2:

$$R^2 = 1 - \left(\frac{\sum_{i=1}^{n}\left(o_i - t_i\right)^2}{\sum_{i=1}^{n} t_i^2}\right) \tag{10}$$

7.6 Experimental Results

In this section, we present the results of the experiments, and the outputs will be analyzed quantitatively and qualitatively.

In this study, MATLAB 2012 was implemented for ANN modelling. As stated previously, the LM, BFGS, and SCG algorithms are chosen for ANN training. Determining the optimal number of hidden nodes is crucial to designing an ANN. Typically, the trial-and-error method is used to accomplish this. This study employs rating systems and trial-and-error techniques. In this way, several structures have been scored by considering various numbers of hidden neurons (from 1 to 15). The results are shown based on the correlation coefficient at the training, testing and validation steps for trainlm, trainbg and trainscg as Figure 7.3a, Figure 7.3b, Figure 7.3c respectively. According to the ANN-LN model, 9 neurons give the best correlation coefficient values in the training, validation, and test stages. Similarly, 13 neurons for BFGS and 15 neurons for SCG gave the best correlation coefficient values in the training, testing and validation steps. As shown in Table 7.3, the structures of ANN models are the ANN-LM (9-9-1), ANN-BFGS (9-13-1), and ANN-SCG (9-15-1). The Error tolerance was fixed at 0.001 and a maximum of 1000 epochs. Training the ANN-LM model takes only 19 epochs to reach error tolerance as shown in Table 3. The ANN-LM model converges fast, and the only time it takes to converge is 0.01 sec. For the ANN-BFGS, ANN-SCG models take 422, 17 epochs and 0.05, and 0.02 sec, respectively as shown in Table 7.3.

Table 7.3 Parameter values of ANN models

Parameters	Values		
Training algorithm	LM	BFGS	SGC
No. of nodes in the input layer	9	9	9
No. of nodes in hidden layer	9	13	15
No. of nodes in output layer	1	1	1
Error tolerance	0.001	0.001	0.001
Maximum epochs	1000	1000	1000
Learning rate	0.1	0.1	0.1
Number of epochs	19	422	17
Momentum	0.1	-	-
Training speed (Sec)	00.01	00.05	00.02

The effectiveness of the network is validated using regression plots, which also show how the proposed system's results relate to the desired outcomes. The network output in connection with desired outcomes for training, validation, and testing datasets has been displayed using regression graphs. In each graph, the best outcome is shown by the dashed line. The outputs-to-targets linear regression line with the best fit is shown by the solid line. A perfect linear connection (R=1) exists between the outputs and the objectives. When R values are close to 0, there is no linear connection between output and objectives.

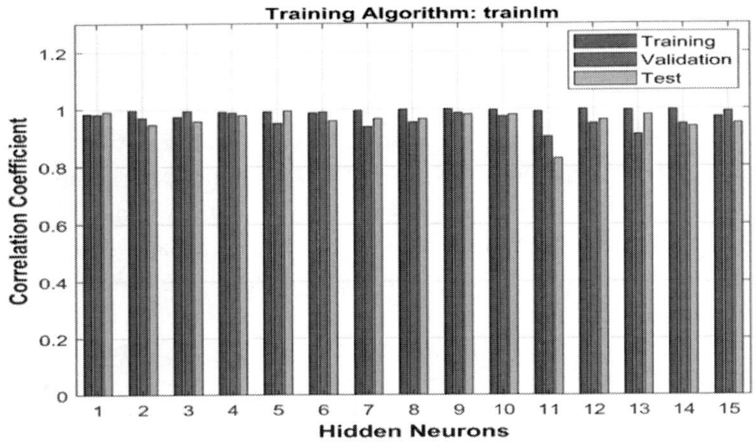

Figure 7.3a. Selection of the number of neurons in the hidden layer for trainlm.

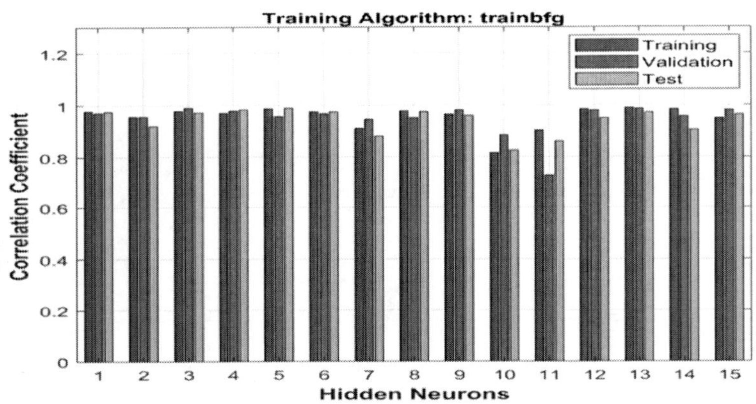

Figure 7.3b. Selection of the number of neurons in the hidden layer for trainbg.

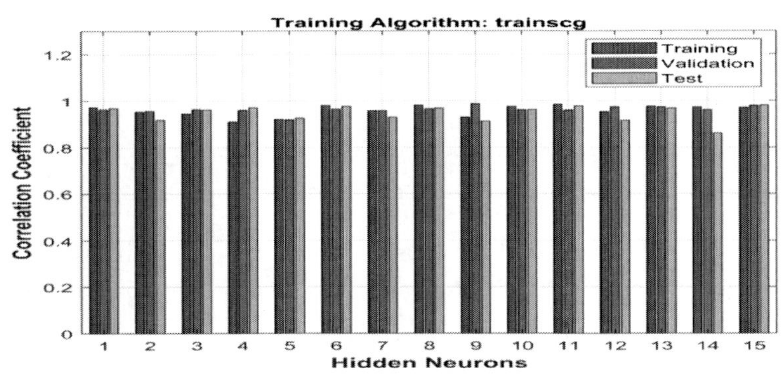

Figure 7.3c. Selection of the number of neurons in the hidden layer for training.

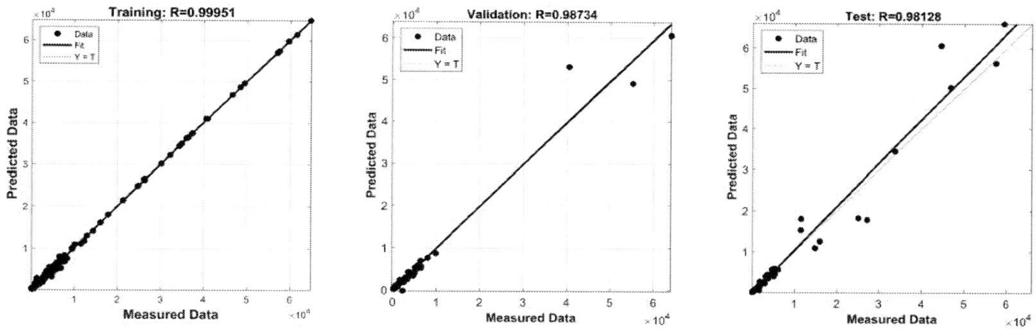

Figure 7.4. Regression analysis of ANN-LM model (Training, Validation, Testing).

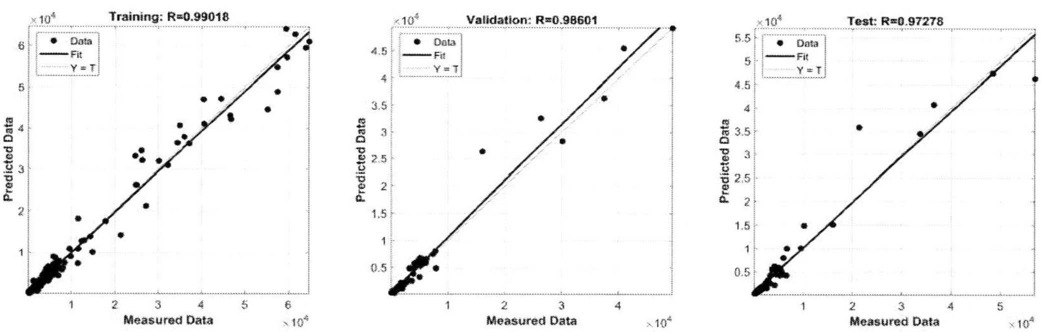

Figure 7.5. Regression analysis of ANN-BGFS model (Training, Validation, Testing).

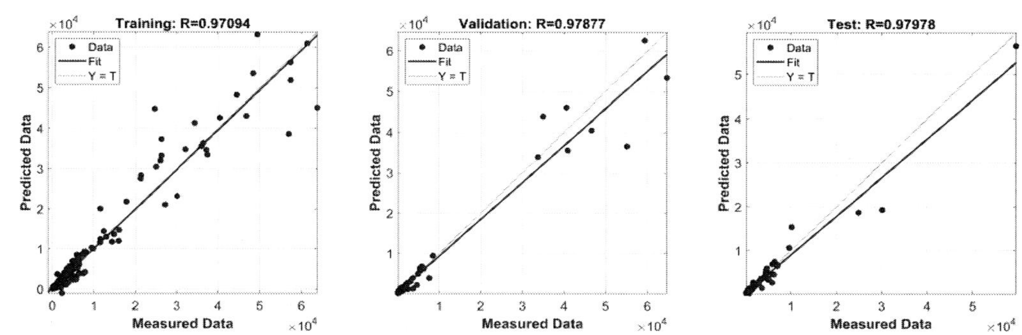

Figure 7.6. Regression analysis of ANN-SCG model (Training, Validation, Testing).

It was noticed that the fit is very good for three ANN models for the anticipated COVID-19 cases, as the R values are all 0.98 or higher in each model. In Figure 7.4, the LM algorithm shows R-values for training (0.99951), validation (0.98734), and testing (0.98128). On the contrary, in Figure 7.5 the BFGS algorithm shows R-values for training (0.99018), validation (0.98601), and testing (0.97278), in Figure 7.6 the SCG algorithm shows R-values for training (0.97094), validation (0.97877), testing (0.97978). Overall, the LM algorithm got better R-values (99%) compared to the BFGS (98%) and SCG (97%) algorithms for COVID-19 case prediction.

In this work, three ANN models are developed for the forecast of COVID-19 cases in Indonesia during the period of January 1, 2022, to March 19, 2023. The whole set of data is split into three parts: training (70%), testing (15%), and validation (15%). We used data from 01 January 2022 to 05 November 2022 for training the ANN models, 06 November 2022 to 11 January 2023 for validation, and 12 January 2023 to 19 March 2023 for testing.

7.6.1 Results of ANN-LM

Figure 7.7 displays the actual and predicted confirmed cases of COVID-19 using the ANN-LM model. The structure of ANN-LM decided on 9-9-1 (9 inputs, 9 hidden nodes, 1 output) for the forecast of COVID-19 cases in Indonesia. 308 (70%) days of COVID-19 cases are used to train the ANN-LM model, and 66 (15%) days of COVID-19 cases are used to validate and test the ANN-LM model. The results of the predicted and actual (training, validation, and testing)

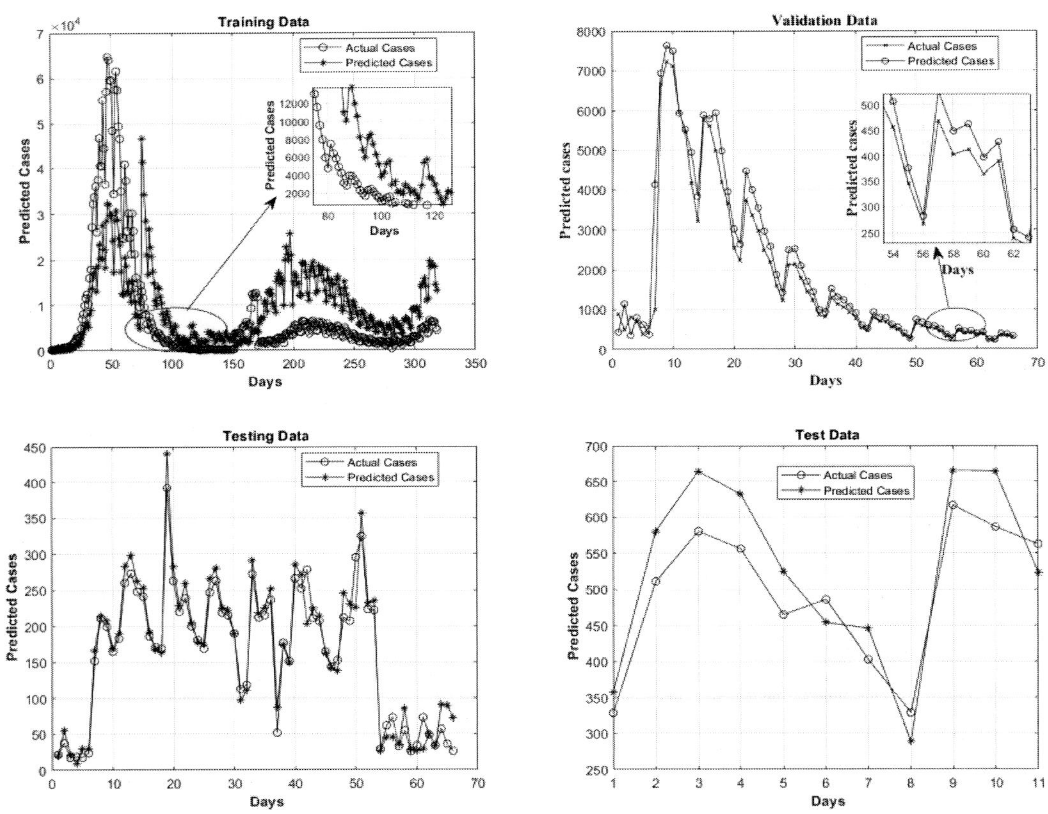

Figure 7.7. Comparison of actual and predicted COVID-19 positive cases of the ANN-LM model (Training, Validation, Testing, and next 11 days (about 1 and a half weeks) of testing).

COVID-19-positive cases are shown in Figure 7.7. Using RMSE, MAPE, CRM, EC and R^2, the performance measurement of ANN-LM models (Train, Validate, and test) is shown in Table

4. As per Table 4, The ANN-LM model archives the best lower values of RMSE (346.5, 1859.5, and 1855.5), MAPE (16.17, 19.776, and 21.53), CRM (0.0016, 0.0257, 0.0263) and best higher EC (0.9990, 0.9999, 0.9998), (0.9999, 0.9998, 0.9999) values during training, validation, and testing, respectively. Apart from the total dataset, we keep separately the next 11 days (about 1 and a half weeks) of COVID-19 case data for testing the ANN-LM model. The predicted 11-day COVID-19 cases are shown in Figure 7.7. According to Figure 7.7, the predicted COVID-19 cases are close to actual cases and the prediction was performed well using the ANN-LM model.

7.6.2 Results of ANN-BFGS

Figure 7.8 illustrates the actual and predicted confirmed cases of COVID-19 using the ANN-BFGS model. The structure of ANN-BFGS was decided on 9-13-1 (9 inputs, 13 hidden nodes, 1 output) for the forecast of COVID-19 cases in Indonesia. The results of the predicted and actual (train, validate, and test) COVID-19-positive cases are shown in Figure 7.8.

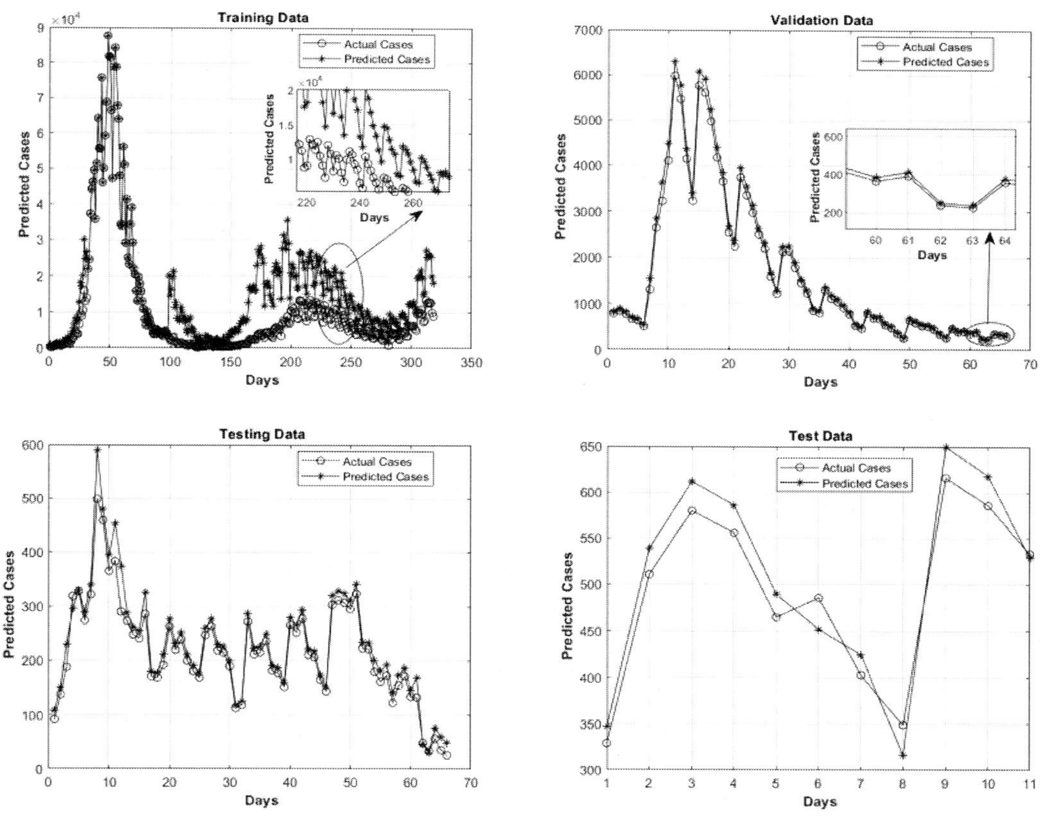

Figure 7.8. Comparison of prediction and actual COVID-19 positive cases of the ANN-BFGS model (Training, Validation, Testing, and next 11 days (about 1 and a half weeks) of testing).

Using RMSE, MAPE, CRM, EC and R^2, the performance measurement of ANN-BFGS models (Training, Validation, and testing) is shown in Table 7.4. As per Table 7.4, The ANN-BFGS model archives the best lower values of RMSE (1661.3. 1741.7, and 2501.5), MAPE (33.26, 40.795, and 36.36), CRM (0.0029, 0.0513, 0.0489) and best higher EC (0.9804, 0.9683, 0.9450), R^2 (0.984, 0.9749, and 0.956) values during training, validation, and testing, respectively.

Apart from the total dataset, we keep separately the next 11 days (about 1 and a half weeks) of COVID-19 case data for testing the ANN-BFGS model. The anticipated next 11 days (about 1 and a half weeks) of COVID-19 cases are shown in Figure 7.8. The predicted COVID-19 cases, as shown in Figure 7.8, closely correspond to actual cases, although the ANN-BFGS model did not perform well for the prediction.

7.6.3 Results of ANN-SCG

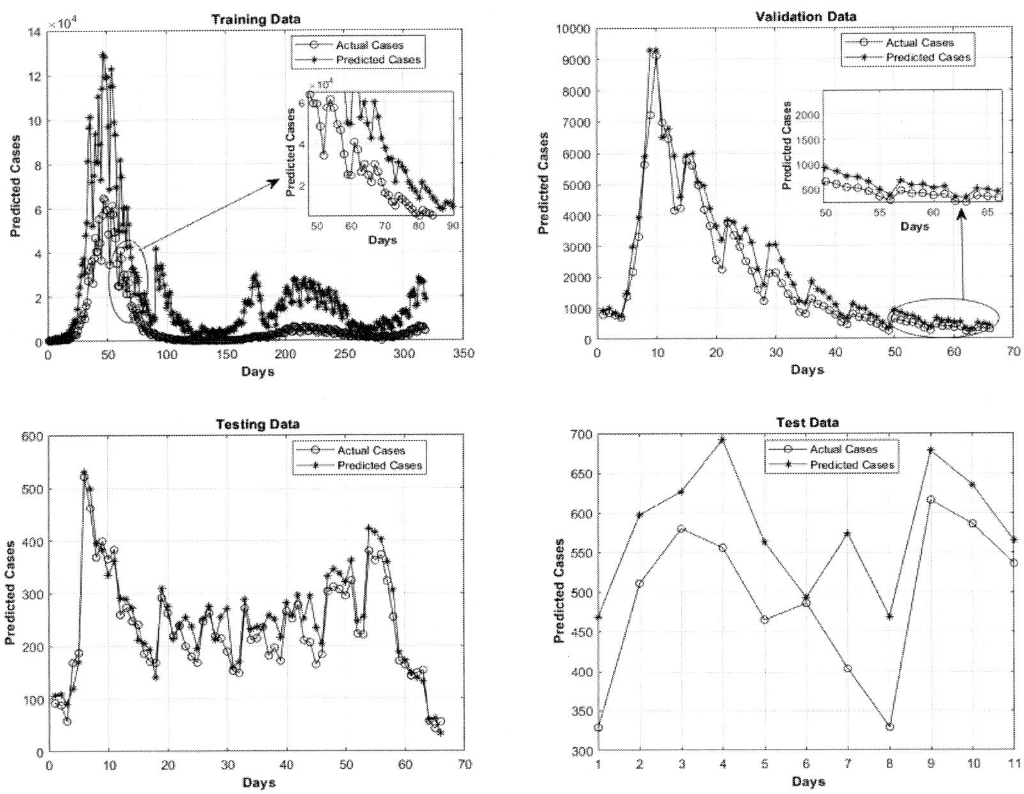

Figure 7.9. Comparison of actual and prediction COVID-19 positive cases of the ANN-SCG model (Training, Validation, Testing, and next 11 days (about 1 and a half weeks) of testing).

Figure 7.9 depicts the actual and predicted confirmed cases of COVID-19 using the ANN-SCG model. The structure of ANN-SCG decided on 9-15-1 (9 inputs, 15 hidden nodes, 1 output) for the forecast of COVID-19 cases in Indonesia. The results of the predicted and actual (train, validate, and test) COVID-19 positive cases are shown in Figure 7.9. Using RMSE, MAPE,

CRM, EC, and R^2, the performance measurement of ANN-SCG models (Training, Validation, and testing) is shown in Table 4. As per the Table 4, The ANN-SCG model archives the best lower values of RMSE (2658.2, 3253.1, 2867.1), MAPE (29.74, 35.791, 33.67), CRM (0.0225, 0.0550, 0.0722) and best higher EC (0.9408, 0.9550, 0.9523), R^2 (0.953, 0.9634, 0.961) values during training, validation, and testing, respectively.

Apart from the total dataset, we keep separately the next 11 days (about 1 and a half weeks) of COVID-19 case data for testing the ANN-SCG model. The anticipated next 11 days (about 1 and a half weeks) of COVID-19 cases are shown in Figure 7.9. Moreover, Figure 7.9 shows that the predicted COVID-19 cases correspond to the actual cases, although the prediction did not perform well using the ANN-SCG model.

Table 7.4. Performance measurement of ANN models (Training, Validation, Testing)

Performance	Models			
		ANN-LM	ANN-BFGS	ANN-SCG
RMSE	Training	346.53	1661.3	2658.2
	Validation	1859.5	1741.7	3253.1
	Testing	1855.5	2501.5	2867.1
MAPE	Training	16.173	33.265	29.748
	Validation	19.776	40.795	35.791
	Testing	21.534	36.368	33.677
CRM	Training	0.0016	0.0029	0.0225
	Validation	0.0257	0.0513	0.0550
	Testing	0.0263	0.0489	0.0722
R^2	Training	0.9999	0.9847	0.9535
	Validation	0.9998	0.9749	0.9634
	Testing	0.9999	0.9567	0.9612
EC	Training	0.9990	0.9804	0.9408
	Validation	0.9999	0.9683	0.9550
	Testing	0.9998	0.9450	0.9523

7.7 Conclusion

In this research, three ANN models were developed, and their predictive abilities for Indonesia's COVID-19 cases were examined. All three models are able to accurately depict the transmission trend in Indonesia. The findings of the evaluation measures RMSE, MAPE, CRM, and EC and show that the ANN-LM model has the best overall performance. We also want to point out that, when compared to other research that used ANN models to predict SARS-CoV-2 cases, our model demonstrates an improvement with a lower error. We next predicted the COVID-19 victims of 11 days (about 1 and a half weeks) outside the training and test datasets for Indonesia in the investigation using the top-performing ANN-LM model. Creating such models may be essential for preparing for pandemics and for combating COVID-19 more successfully. The proposed models and teaching methods can be used in other countries in addition to the one that was studied. They can also be used to measure how well the policies are working to stop the spread of the virus. In the future, we hope to add more information about the types of SARS-CoV-2 versions, whether people have been vaccinated, the health care facilities, etc., as features to improve the model's performance and capacity. So, ANN models would help make choices about controlling variables and making policies and decisions that are more accurate.

References

Ahmad, I., and Asad, S. M. (2020). "Predictions of coronavirus COVID-19 distinct cases in Pakistan through an artificial neural network." *Epidemiology and Infection*, *148*, e222.

Borghi, P. H., Zakordonets, O., and Teixeira, J. P. (2021). "A COVID-19 time series forecasting model based on MLP ANN." *Procedia Computer Science*, *181*, 940-947.

Chan, J. F., Lau, S. K., To, K. K., Cheng, V. C., Woo, P. C., and Yuen, K. Y. (2015). "Middle East respiratory syndrome coronavirus: another zoonotic betacoronavirus causing SARS-like disease." *Clinical microbiology reviews*, *28*(2), 465-522.

Crokidakis, N. (2020). "Modeling the early evolution of the COVID-19 in Brazil: Results from a Susceptible–Infectious–Quarantined–Recovered (SIQR) model." *International Journal of Modern Physics C*, *31*(10), 2050135.

Fu, L., Wang, B., Yuan, T., Chen, X., Ao, Y., Fitzpatrick, T., et al. (2020). "Clinical characteristics of coronavirus disease 2019 (COVID-19) in China: a systematic review and meta-analysis." *Journal of Infection*, *80*(6), 656-665.

Hamadneh, N. N., Khan, W. A., Ashraf, W., Atawneh, S. H., Khan, I., and Hamadneh, B. N. (2021). "Artificial neural networks for prediction of covid-19 in Saudi Arabia." *Comput. Mater. Contin*, *66*, 2787-2796.

Khaleque, A., and Sen, P. (2017). "An empirical analysis of the Ebola outbreak in West Africa." *Scientific reports*, *7*(1), 42594.

Li, D., Sun, X., Gao, F., and Liu, S. (2021). "An improved real-valued negative selection algorithm based on the constant detector for anomaly detection." *Journal of Intelligent and Fuzzy Systems*, *40*(5), 8793-8806.

Manohar, B., and Das, R. (2022). "Artificial neural networks for the prediction of monkeypox outbreak." *Tropical Medicine and Infectious Disease*, *7*(12), 424.

Manohar, B., and Das, R. (2023). "Artificial neural networks for prediction of COVID-19 in India by using backpropagation." *Expert Systems*, *40*(5), e13105.

McClarren, R. G. (2018). "Introduction to Monte Carlo methods." *Comput. Nucl. Eng. Radiol. Sci. Using Python*, 381-406.

Muhammad, L. J., Haruna, A. A., Sharif, U. S., and Mohammed, M. B. (2022). "Cnn-lstm deep learning based forecasting model for covid-19 infection cases in Nigeria, South Africa and Botswana." *Health and Technology*, *12*(6), 1259-1276.

Namasudra, S., Dhamodharavadhani, S., and Rathipriya, R. (2021). "Nonlinear neural network based forecasting model for predicting COVID-19 cases." *Neural processing letters*, 1-21.

Niazkar, H. R., and Niazkar, M. (2020). "Application of artificial neural networks to predict the COVID-19 outbreak." *Global Health Research and Policy*, *5*(1), 1-11.

Qiu, M., and Song, Y. (2016). "Predicting the direction of stock market index movement using an optimized artificial neural network model." *PloS one*, *11*(5), e0155133.

Shaibani, M. J., Emamgholipour, S., and Moazeni, S. S. (2021). "Investigation of robustness of hybrid artificial neural network with artificial bee colony and firefly algorithm in predicting COVID-19 new cases : case study of Iran." *Stochastic Environmental Research and Risk Assessment*, 1-16.

Shanbehzadeh, M., Nopour, R., and Kazemi-Arpanahi, H. (2022). "Design of an artificial neural network to predict mortality among COVID-19 patients." *Informatics in medicine unlocked*, *31*, 100983.

Shetty, R. P., and Pai, P. S. (2021). "Forecasting of COVID 19 cases in Karnataka state using artificial neural network (ANN)." *Journal of The Institution of Engineers (India): Series B*, *102*(6), 1201-1211.

Veza, I., Panchal, H., Paristiawan, P. A., Idris, M., Fattah, I. R., Putra, N. R., and Silambarasan, R. (2022). "Improved prediction accuracy of biomass heating value using proximate analysis with various ANN training algorithms." *Results in Engineering*, *16*, 100688.

Wanto, A., Zarlis, M., and Hartama, D. (2017, December). "Analysis of artificial neural network backpropagation using conjugate gradient fletcher reeves in the predicting process." In *Journal of Physics: Conference Series* (Vol. 930, No. 1, p. 012018). IOP Publishing.

Zakary, O., Larrache, A., Rachik, M., and Elmouki, I. (2016). "Effect of awareness programs and travel-blocking operations in the control of HIV/AIDS outbreaks: a multi-domains SIR model." *Advances in Difference Equations*, *2016*(1), 1-17.

Zhang, G. P. (2003). "Time series forecasting using a hybrid ARIMA and neural network model." *Neurocomputing*, *50*, 159-175.

Chapter 8

Abnormal Sound Detection in Lungs Using Vest-Coat Stethoscope Using Deep Learning Algorithm

B. Vishnu Vardhan[1,*]
M. Kalaiselvi Geetha[1]
G. Syam Prasad[2]
and C. S. Khiran Kumar[3]
[1]Department of Computer Science and Engineering, Annamalai University, India
[2]Department of Information Technology, Narasaraopeta Engineering College, Narasaraopeta
[3]University of Maryland Baltimore County, MD, USA

Abstract

In recent years, advancements in artificial intelligence (AI) have revolutionized the field of medical diagnostics. This abstract presents several models for detecting abnormal sounds from the lungs using an AI-powered vest-coat (AI-VC) stethoscope. The proposed system combines a stethoscope's traditional acoustic capabilities with AI algorithms' computational power, enabling accurate and efficient diagnosis of respiratory conditions. The AI-powered vest-coat stethoscope consists of a wearable vest-coat embedded with multiple miniature microphones strategically positioned to capture lung sounds. The proposed system consists of a vest coat stethoscope with multiple sensors to capture lung sounds. These sensors are designed to record high-quality audio data, then pre-processed to remove noise and artifacts. The pre-processed audio data is then fed into a deep learning model, specifically a CNN, to automatically classify lung sounds into normal or abnormal categories. A large dataset of labeled lung sounds is collected from patients with various respiratory conditions to train the CNN. Finally, this study presents an automated system for detecting abnormal lung sounds using a vest coat stethoscope and deep learning algorithms. The design shows promising results in accurately classifying odd lung sounds, which can assist healthcare professionals in promptly diagnosing and treating respiratory conditions. Further research and validation on larger datasets and clinical trials are warranted to enhance the system's performance and ensure clinical viability.

* Corresponding Author's Email: bvishnuvardhan84@gmail.com.

In: Explainable Artificial Intelligence in Healthcare Systems
Editors: A. Anitha Kamaraj and Debi Prasanna Acharjya
ISBN: 979-8-89113-598-7

Keywords: artificial intelligence (AI), machine learning, deep learning, convolutional neural networks (CNNs) and recurrent neural networks (RNNs).

8.1 Introduction

Lung disease diagnosis and detection are critical for early intervention, effective treatment, and improved patient outcomes. Wheezing, crackles, and rhonchi, which are abnormal sounds produced by the lungs, provide valuable clinical information that can aid in identifying and classifying various lung conditions (Chen et al. 2019). The human respiratory system comprises the lungs, airways, and other structures in charge of the exchange of oxygen and carbon dioxide. When the lungs are affected by diseases or abnormalities, airflow can be disrupted, resulting in abnormal breathing sounds.

Auscultation, a method of listening to lung sounds with a stethoscope, has traditionally been used by healthcare professionals to identify abnormal respiratory sounds. This approach, however, is subjective and heavily dependent on the clinician's experience and expertise. Furthermore, certain lung conditions can have similar sounding abnormalities, making accurate diagnosis difficult. Technological advancements have developed electronic auscultation devices and digital signal processing techniques to improve lung sound detection and analysis (Gairola et al. 2021). These devices can capture and amplify respiratory sounds, allowing for more precise analysis and automated detection of abnormal patterns.

Machine learning and pattern recognition algorithms are commonly used to detect and classify abnormal lung sounds. These algorithms can be learned to accurately determine the difference between normal and abnormal respiratory sounds by training on a dataset of known lung conditions. This allows healthcare providers to detect lung diseases such as asthma, chronic obstructive pulmonary disease (COPD), pneumonia, and pulmonary fibrosis more quickly (Demir et al. 2020).

The current state of research and technologies used in diagnosing and detecting lung diseases based on abnormal sounds will be discussed in this chapter. We will review the various types of abnormal lung sounds, their clinical significance, and the difficulties in accurately detecting them. In addition, we will investigate the emerging trends and prospects for leveraging artificial intelligence and machine learning in this field to improve the accuracy, speed, and accessibility of lung disease diagnosis and monitoring.

8.2 Types of Detection of Abnormal Sounds from Lungs

The diagnosis of lung diseases and abnormalities often requires the detection of abnormal sounds in the lungs, known as adventitious lung sounds. These sounds can provide important diagnostic information and aid in the identification of various respiratory conditions. Healthcare professionals employ several diagnostic methods to detect and analyze these abnormal lung sounds by Fraiwan et al. (2021). This article will explore some of the commonly used diagnostic methods for detecting abnormal sounds in the lungs.

Auscultation
Auscultation is the most basic and commonly used method for diagnosing abnormal lung sounds. It involves using a stethoscope to listen to the sounds produced during breathing. By placing the stethoscope on different areas of the chest, healthcare professionals can detect various abnormal lung sounds, such as crackles, wheezes, and rhonchi. Auscultation provides valuable initial information about the presence and location of abnormal lung sounds.

Pulmonary Function Tests (PFTs)
Pulmonary function tests are a series of non-invasive tests that assess lung function and aid in the diagnosis of respiratory disorders. These tests measure various parameters, such as lung volumes, airflow rates, and gas exchange efficiency. Abnormal lung sounds can be associated with specific lung function abnormalities, and PFTs can help identify the underlying cause of these sounds.

Imaging Techniques
Imaging techniques, such as chest X-rays, computed tomography (CT) scans, and lung ultrasound, play a crucial role in diagnosing lung diseases and abnormalities. These techniques can provide detailed images of the lungs, allowing healthcare professionals to identify structural abnormalities, fluid accumulation, or tumors that may contribute to abnormal lung sounds.

Bronchoscope
A bronchoscope is an invasive diagnostic procedure that involves inserting a thin, flexible tube with a light and camera (bronchoscope) into the airways to visualize the lungs. It allows direct visualization of the airways and collection of samples for further analysis. Bronchoscopy is particularly useful in diagnosing conditions that may cause abnormal lung sounds, such as tumors, foreign body aspiration, or infections.

Blood Tests
Blood tests may not directly detect abnormal lung sounds, but they can provide valuable information about the underlying causes of these sounds. For example, blood tests can measure levels of inflammatory markers, antibodies, or specific enzymes that indicate infection, autoimmune diseases, or other systemic conditions that can manifest as abnormal lung sounds.

Summary
The diagnosis of abnormal lung sounds requires a comprehensive approach that combines different diagnostic methods. Auscultation serves as a primary screening tool, while pulmonary function tests, imaging techniques, bronchoscopy, and blood tests provide additional insights into the underlying causes of abnormal lung sounds. The integration of these diagnostic methods enables healthcare professionals to accurately diagnose respiratory conditions and develop appropriate treatment plans.

8.3 Literature Survey

This section discussed several ML and DL models and their performances. They also discussed the advantages and disadvantages of the models discussed.

8.3.1 Machine Learning (ML) Algorithms for Detecting Abnormal Sounds in Lungs

Machine learning algorithms have become increasingly popular in the medical field for their ability to analyze complex data and assist in diagnosis. One area where these algorithms have shown great promise is in the detection of abnormal sounds in lungs using CT scan images. Abnormal sounds, such as crackles or wheezes, can indicate various respiratory conditions, including pneumonia, asthma, or lung fibrosis. Early detection of these abnormal sounds can aid in timely treatment and improve patient outcomes. CT scans provide detailed cross-sectional images of the lungs, allowing for a thorough examination of lung tissue. However, manually analyzing these images to identify abnormal sounds can be time-consuming and prone to human error. Machine learning algorithms offer a potential solution by automating the detection process and providing accurate and efficient analysis.

This chapter's objective is to explore different machine learning algorithms for detecting abnormal sounds in lungs using CT scan images. By training these algorithms on a large dataset of CT scans, we aim to develop a robust and reliable system that can accurately identify abnormal lung sounds and assist radiologists in their diagnostic process. This chapter discussed various machine learning algorithms commonly used in medical image analysis, including CNNs, SVMs, and random forests (RFs). We will evaluate the performance of these algorithms in terms of accuracy, sensitivity, specificity, and computational efficiency. Additionally, we will explore techniques for feature extraction and selection to enhance the algorithms' performance.

These studies have the potential to significantly improve the efficiency and accuracy of abnormal lung sound detection using CT scan images. This technology can aid radiologists and physicians in the early detection and diagnosis of respiratory conditions, leading to improved patient care and outcomes Fraiwan et al. (2021). Moreover, the developed algorithms can be integrated into existing medical systems, providing a valuable tool for routine clinical practice.

8.3.2 SVM for Abnormal Sound Detection in Lungs Using Vest Coat Stethoscope

SVMs are a type of ML algorithm that can be used for classification tasks. In the context of abnormal sound detection in the lungs, an SVM can be trained to distinguish between normal lung sounds and abnormal lung sounds. To use an SVM for this task, you would first need a dataset of lung sound recordings. These recordings can be obtained using a vest coat stethoscope, which is a wearable device designed to capture and record lung sounds. The dataset should consist of labeled examples, where each example is associated with a class label indicating whether the sound is normal or abnormal. Once you have your dataset, you would typically preprocess the lung sound recordings to extract relevant features. These features could include frequency-based measures, time-domain characteristics, or statistical properties of the sound signals Jacome et al. (2019). The choice of features would depend on the specific characteristics of abnormal lung sounds you are interested in detecting.

It's worth noting that SVMs are just one of many possible machine-learning algorithms that can be used for this task. Other algorithms, such as deep learning models (e.g., convolutional neural networks), may also be applicable and might provide better performance depending on the complexity of the problem and the size of the available dataset.

8.3.3 Random Forest (RF) for Abnormal Sound Detection in Lungs Using Vest-Coat Stethoscope

Recently, ML algorithms have shown significant factors in healthcare systems. One area where machine learning can be useful is in the detection of abnormal sounds in the lungs, which can provide valuable insights into respiratory conditions. In this context, a random forest algorithm can be employed for accurate and efficient abnormal sound detection using a vest-coat stethoscope kanavati et al. (2020).

An RF is the algorithm that merges the number of DT to predict accurate patterns. It is mainly compatible with classification tasks that involve assigning labels to input data based on their features. In the case of abnormal sound detection, the input data would consist of audio recordings captured by the vest-coat stethoscope, while the labels would represent the presence or absence of abnormal lung sounds.

To utilize the random forest algorithm, a training dataset is required, consisting of a large number of lung sound recordings labeled as normal or abnormal. These recordings should cover a wide range of respiratory conditions and be representative of the population under consideration. Additionally, relevant features can be extracted from the audio signals, such as frequency content, duration, intensity, and temporal patterns.

After preparing the training dataset, the random forest algorithm can be trained by constructing a forest of decision trees. Each decision tree is built with a subset of the training data and a randomly selected subset of features. During the training process, the decision trees learn to classify lung sound recordings based on the provided labels and extracted features. Once the random forest model is trained, it can be used to predict the presence of abnormal lung sounds in new, unseen recordings. The model takes as input the extracted features from the audio signal and passes them through each decision tree in the forest. To evaluate the performance of the random forest model, a separate test dataset can be used, consisting of lung sound recordings that were not used during the training phase. Various evaluation metrics can be employed, such as accuracy, precision, recall, and F1-score, to assess the model's ability to correctly classify normal and abnormal lung sounds. Overall, employing a random forest algorithm for abnormal sound detection in lungs using a vest-coat stethoscope holds great potential in improving respiratory condition assessment. By leveraging machine learning techniques, healthcare professionals can benefit from accurate and efficient identification of abnormal lung sounds, aiding in early diagnosis and intervention for various respiratory disorders.

8.3.4 Decision Tree for Abnormal Sound Detection in Lungs Using Vest-Coat Stethoscope

The accurate detection of abnormal lung sounds plays a vital role in diagnosing various respiratory disorders. Traditional stethoscopes have been widely used by healthcare professionals for auscultation, but their limitations in capturing subtle sounds have led to the development of advanced technologies. One such innovation is the Vest-Coat stethoscope, which incorporates multiple sensors and wearable technology to enhance the detection of abnormal lung sounds.

This article introduces a decision tree (DT) approach for abnormal sound detection in the lungs using the Vest-Coat stethoscope. Decision trees are powerful machine learning models that can effectively classify and predict outcomes based on a series of hierarchical decisions. By utilizing a decision tree algorithm, we can create a systematic and automated method for analyzing lung sounds and identifying potential abnormalities.

The Decision Tree Approach

The decision tree algorithm consists of a hierarchical structure comprising nodes and branches. Each node represents a decision based on specific features or attributes, and each branch corresponds to a possible outcome of that decision. The tree's root node reflects the decision-making process's beginning point, and the leaf nodes indicate the final classifications.

Using the Vest-Coat stethoscope abnormal sounds can be detected, the decision tree can be constructed based on relevant acoustic features, such as pitch, duration, intensity, and frequency. These features are extracted from the lung sound recordings obtained through the Vest-Coat stethoscope's sensors. The decision tree algorithm learns from a labeled dataset, where abnormal and normal lung sounds are appropriately categorized Chen et al. (2015).

During the training phase, the decision tree algorithm analyzes the dataset and determines the most informative features and decision points to differentiate abnormal from normal lung sounds. The algorithm recursively splits the data based on these features, creating decision nodes that progressively refine the classification process. This iterative process continues until the algorithm reaches leaf nodes, which provide the final classification outcomes Bardou et al. (2018).

Benefits of the Decision Tree Approach

The decision tree approach offers several advantages for abnormal sound detection in the lungs using the Vest-Coat stethoscope. Firstly, it provides a transparent and interpretable model, allowing healthcare professionals to understand the reasoning behind the classification decisions. This transparency helps build trust in the algorithm and its outcomes.

Secondly, decision trees are computationally efficient and can handle large datasets with numerous features. The algorithm's ability to select the most informative features simplifies the decision-making process and reduces computational complexity. Furthermore, decision trees can handle both categorical and numerical features, making them adaptable to a wide range of acoustic features extracted from lung sounds. The algorithm is also robust to noise and outliers, ensuring reliable performance even in less ideal recording conditions. The decision tree approach for abnormal sound detection in lungs using the Vest-Coat stethoscope presents a promising method for improving respiratory disorder diagnosis. By leveraging the Vest-Coat stethoscope's advanced sensor technology and the power of decision tree algorithms, healthcare professionals can benefit from automated and accurate abnormal sound classification. This approach has the potential to enhance the efficiency and effectiveness of diagnosing respiratory disorders, leading to improved patient outcomes and better overall healthcare.

8.3.5 K-Means Algorithm for Abnormal Sound Detection in Lungs Using Vest-Coat Stethoscope

Medical diagnostics has made significant advances in recent years, owing to the incorporation of artificial intelligence (AI) techniques. The detection of abnormal sounds in the lungs, which can aid in the early diagnosis of respiratory disorders, is one such area of interest. This section introduces the utilization of the K-Means algorithm in combination with a Vest-Coat stethoscope for efficient abnormal sound detection in lung auscultation.

Background

Auscultation is a common method used by healthcare professionals to assess the respiratory system. By analyzing the sounds produced during breathing, valuable insights about the underlying health condition of the lungs can be obtained. However, accurate identification and interpretation of abnormal lung sounds can be challenging, as they often overlap with normal sounds. This is where the integration of AI algorithms becomes crucial in enhancing diagnostic capabilities Petmezas et al. (2022).

K-Means Algorithm

K-Means is a well-known unsupervised machine learning algorithm that divides a dataset into K distinct clusters. It works by iteratively assigning data points with the closest mean value to the collection and updating the cluster centers based on the newly identified issues. This iterative process continues until convergence, resulting in a set of clusters with minimized intra-cluster distances.

Application in Abnormal Sound Detection

To apply the K-Means algorithm for abnormal sound detection in lung auscultation, a Vest-Coat stethoscope is employed. The Vest-Coat stethoscope incorporates multiple sensors distributed across the vest worn by the patient. These sensors capture lung sounds from various positions, allowing for a comprehensive analysis of the entire lung area. The captured sound data is then preprocessed to extract relevant features that represent different sound characteristics.

Next, the K-Means algorithm is utilized to cluster the extracted features into distinct groups. By training the algorithm with a labeled dataset comprising both normal and abnormal lung sounds, it learns to identify patterns and differences between the two classes. Once the algorithm has converged, it can be used to classify new, unlabeled sound data into the appropriate clusters, enabling the detection of abnormal lung sounds.

Benefits and Challenges

The integration of the K-Means algorithm with a Vest-Coat stethoscope offers several benefits. Firstly, it allows for real-time analysis of lung sounds, enabling prompt diagnosis and intervention. Secondly, the algorithm can be learned from a large dataset, improving its accuracy over time. Furthermore, the Vest-Coat stethoscope provides a non-invasive and comfortable experience for patients during auscultation.

However, there are challenges to overcome. The K-Means algorithm relies on accurate feature extraction, which may require expertise and careful consideration. Additionally, the algorithm's performance can be influenced by the quality and variability of the acquired sound data. Ongoing research and development are needed to address these challenges and optimize the algorithm for reliable abnormal sound detection. The combination of the K-Means algorithm with a Vest-Coat stethoscope holds significant potential for enhancing the detection of abnormal lung sounds. By leveraging the algorithm's clustering capabilities and the extensive coverage of the Vest-Coat stethoscope, healthcare professionals can benefit from improved diagnostic accuracy and expedited decision-making. Further advancements in this area could revolutionize respiratory diagnostics, leading to more effective treatments and improved patient outcomes Padilla-Ortiz et al. (2018).

8.3.6 Linear Regression for Abnormal Sound Detection in Lungs Using Vest-Coat Stethoscope

The diagnosis of lung diseases and abnormalities plays a crucial role in the healthcare industry. Traditional methods, such as auscultation using a stethoscope, are widely employed by medical professionals for this purpose. However, accurately identifying abnormal lung sounds can be challenging, especially for less experienced practitioners. To address this issue, the concept of a vest-coat stethoscope equipped with advanced technologies has emerged, enabling more accurate and efficient detection of abnormal lung sounds.

Linear Regression for Abnormal Sound Detection

It establishes a linear relationship between two variables. In the context of abnormal sound detection in the lungs using a vest-coat stethoscope, linear regression can be employed to analyze the relationship between the recorded lung sounds and the presence of abnormalities. By identifying patterns and correlations within the data, linear regression can aid in the development of algorithms to automate the detection process.

Data Collection and Preprocessing

To train a linear regression model, a dataset comprising lung sound recordings and corresponding labels indicating the presence or absence of abnormalities is required. These recordings can be obtained using the vest-coat stethoscope, which captures lung sounds in a non-invasive manner. The data should be carefully collected from a diverse set of patients, considering factors such as age, gender, and lung conditions, to ensure the model's generalizability.

Before applying linear regression, data preprocessing steps may be necessary. This can involve cleaning the data to remove any artifacts or noise, normalizing the sound recordings to a consistent format, and extracting relevant features. Feature extraction techniques, such as Mel-frequency cepstral coefficients (MFCCs) or wavelet transforms, can be used to represent lung sounds in a format suitable for analysis.

Model Training and Evaluation

The training and testing set work when the data is ready. The training set is used to train the linear regression model by fitting a line that best represents the relationship between the features extracted from the lung sounds and the corresponding abnormality labels. The model's performance is then evaluated using the testing set to assess its accuracy, precision, recall, and other relevant metrics.

Potential Challenges and Future Directions

While linear regression can provide a straightforward approach to abnormal sound detection in the lungs, there are several challenges to consider. Variations in lung sounds among individuals, the presence of overlapping sounds, and the influence of environmental factors can all impact the accuracy of the model Rocha et al. (2020). Moreover, future research could focus on incorporating additional data sources, such as patient demographics, medical histories, or imaging results, to enhance the accuracy of the abnormal sound detection system. By integrating multiple modalities, a more comprehensive and reliable diagnostic tool can be developed to aid healthcare professionals in detecting lung abnormalities. Linear regression provides a promising approach to detecting abnormal lung sounds using a vest-coat stethoscope. By analyzing the relationship between lung sound features and abnormality labels, this technique can aid in the development of automated detection algorithms. However, further research is needed to overcome challenges related to variability in lung sounds and explore advanced machine-learning methods. Ultimately, an accurate and reliable abnormal sound detection system can significantly improve the diagnosis and treatment of lung diseases.

8.4 Deep Learning Algorithms for Abnormal Sound Detection in Lungs Using Vest-Coat Stethoscope: An Introduction

The detection of abnormal lung sounds plays a crucial role in diagnosing various respiratory conditions. Traditional stethoscopes have long been used by medical professionals for auscultation, but they are limited in their ability to accurately identify subtle abnormalities. However, recent advancements in deep learning algorithms, combined with the development of innovative medical devices such as the vest-coat stethoscope, have opened up new possibilities for improving the accuracy of abnormal sound detection in the lungs by Chamberlain et al. (2012).

The vest-coat stethoscope is a wearable device equipped with multiple sensors distributed across the chest area. These sensors capture acoustic signals from the lungs during the respiratory cycle. By combining these sensor readings with deep learning algorithms, it becomes possible to automatically analyze the acquired data and identify abnormal lung sounds indicative of various respiratory disorders.

Deep learning algorithms, specifically CNNs and RNNs, have shown remarkable success in various audio-processing tasks. These algorithms excel at learning complex patterns and features from large datasets, making them well-suited for abnormal sound detection in lung auscultation. By training these algorithms on annotated datasets containing normal and abnormal lung sounds, they can learn to differentiate between different types of respiratory conditions.

The key advantage of deep learning algorithms lies in their ability to automatically extract high-level features from raw audio signals. Traditional signal processing techniques often require manual feature engineering, which can be time-consuming and may not capture all relevant information. Deep learning algorithms, on the other hand, can automatically learn and represent features that are most discriminative for abnormal sound detection, leading to improved accuracy and efficiency. In addition to CNNs and RNNs, other deep learning architectures, such as hybrid models combining CNNs and RNNs (e.g., CNN-RNN), or attention-based models, can also be explored for abnormal sound detection. These models can capture both spatial and temporal dependencies in the acoustic signals, enabling a more comprehensive analysis of lung sounds.

To train these deep learning algorithms, large and diverse datasets of lung sounds need to be collected. These datasets should encompass a wide range of respiratory conditions, including common abnormalities like crackles, wheezes, and bronchial breath sounds. The data collection process can involve collaborations with healthcare institutions and the inclusion of patients with known respiratory disorders. Once the deep learning algorithms are trained, they can be integrated into real-time monitoring systems or mobile applications that provide instant feedback to healthcare professionals. By enabling timely and accurate identification of abnormal lung sounds, these algorithms can assist in early detection and diagnosis of respiratory conditions, leading to improved patient outcomes and enhanced healthcare delivery.

Finally, the combination of deep learning algorithms and the vest-coat stethoscope holds great promise for enhancing abnormal sound detection in the lungs. By leveraging the power of machine learning, these algorithms can automatically analyze large volumes of lung sound data and accurately identify abnormalities. With further research and development, this technology has the potential to revolutionize respiratory diagnostics and improve patient care.

8.5 Proposed AI-Powered Vest-Coat (AI-VC)

In this section, the proposed approach is combined with CNN and autoencoders as shown in Figure 8.1. Identifying unusual lung sounds, such as coughing, squeaks, or other signs of respiratory problems, can be critical for early detection and treatment of respiratory disorders. Detecting these sounds with CNNs and autoencoders in conjunction with a device like a "vest coat" is intriguing.

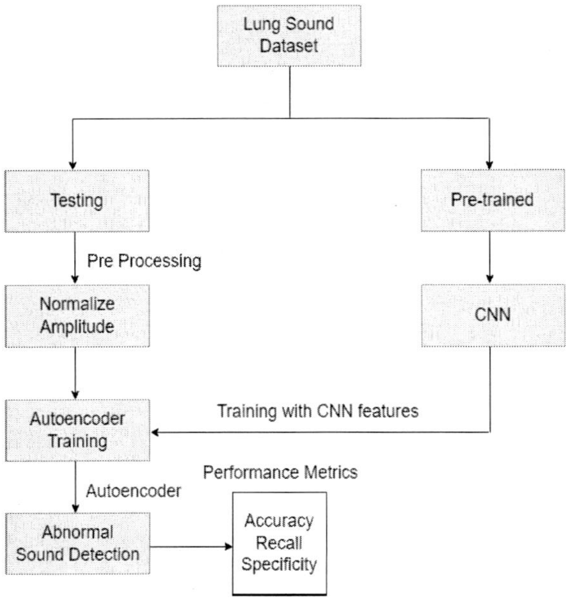

Figure 8.1. CNN with Autoencoder Architecture for Abnormal Lung Sound Detection.

Dataset Description

The dataset contains 112 samples, with 35 healthy and 77 unhealthy. The age of humans who participated in this experiment is 21 to 90, with 43 females and 69 males. The training also used the same samples. The dataset is collected from Kaggle.

8.6 CNN for Abnormal Sound Detection in Lungs Using Vest-Coat Stethoscope

The early detection of abnormal lung sounds can play a vital role in diagnosing respiratory conditions and improving patient outcomes. Traditional stethoscopes have been the primary tool used by healthcare professionals for auscultation, but they have limitations in terms of accuracy and portability. In recent years, advancements in technology have led to the development of novel stethoscope variants, such as the vest-coat stethoscope, which integrates wearable sensors and wireless communication capabilities. This paper presents an introduction to the use of a Convolutional Neural Network (CNN) for abnormal sound detection in lungs using a vest-coat stethoscope. The CNN-based approach aims to enhance the accuracy and efficiency of lung sound analysis, leading to earlier and more accurate diagnosis of respiratory conditions.

Introduction

The ability to accurately interpret lung sounds is crucial in the diagnosis of various respiratory conditions, including pneumonia, chronic obstructive pulmonary disease (COPD), asthma, and others. Traditional stethoscopes have served as the primary tool for auscultation, relying on the expertise and subjective judgment of healthcare professionals. However, due to the limitations of human perception and the variation in auscultation skills among practitioners, the accuracy and consistency of lung sound interpretation can vary.

Vest-Coat Stethoscope

The vest-coat stethoscope is a novel wearable device that integrates sensors into a wearable vest or coat. These sensors capture lung sounds and transmit them wirelessly to a connected device, such as a smartphone or computer, for analysis. This integration of technology enables continuous monitoring, remote diagnosis, and the potential for real-time feedback to healthcare professionals. The vest-coat stethoscope offers improved portability, ease of use, and the ability to record and store lung sound data for future reference.

Convolutional Neural Network (CNN) for Abnormal Sound Detection

To enhance the accuracy and efficiency of lung sound analysis, a CNN-based approach is proposed. CNNs have shown remarkable success in various audio and image classification tasks, making them suitable for abnormal sound detection in lung auscultation. The CNN model can be trained using a large dataset of labeled lung sound recordings, encompassing both normal and abnormal respiratory conditions. Figure 8.2 shows the CNN layers connected with each other to continue the process of abnormal data detection. The network learns to extract meaningful features from the audio data, allowing it to differentiate between healthy and abnormal lung sounds.

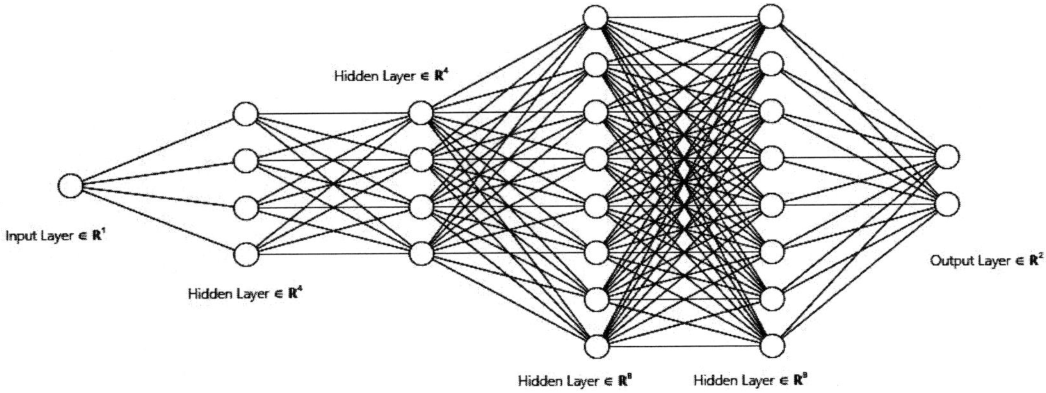

Figure 8.2. CNN Layers connected to each other to process the data.

Benefits and Potential Applications

By utilizing a CNN-based approach with the vest-coat stethoscope, several benefits can be achieved. First, the accuracy of abnormal sound detection can be significantly improved compared to traditional auscultation methods. Second, the vest-coat stethoscope allows for continuous monitoring of lung sounds, providing valuable longitudinal data for tracking the progression of respiratory conditions. Additionally, wireless connectivity enables remote diagnosis and consultation, facilitating access to healthcare services in remote or underserved areas. The combination of a vest-coat stethoscope and a CNN-based approach for abnormal sound detection in the lungs holds great promise for enhancing respiratory diagnostics. This technology has the potential to improve the accuracy and efficiency of lung sound analysis, leading to earlier detection of respiratory conditions and better patient outcomes. Further research and development in this field are necessary to refine the CNN models, optimize the vest-coat stethoscope design, and validate its performance through clinical studies.

8.7 Auto Encoder for Abnormal Sound Detection in Lungs Using Vest-Coat Stethoscope

The identification and early detection of abnormal sounds in the lungs can significantly aid in the diagnosis and treatment of respiratory conditions. Traditional auscultation techniques with a stethoscope are limited in their ability to accurately detect and analyze these sounds. A novel approach using an auto-encoder framework coupled with a vest-coat stethoscope to improve the detection of abnormal lung sounds. This introduction provides an overview of the research objective, the significance of the study, and a brief outline of the methodology. Respiratory diseases pose a significant global health challenge, with conditions such as pneumonia, bronchitis, and chronic obstructive pulmonary disease (COPD) affecting millions of individuals worldwide. The auscultation of lung sounds plays a crucial role in diagnosing and monitoring these respiratory conditions. However, the subjective nature of traditional stethoscope-based auscultation methods often leads to inconsistencies and inaccuracies in sound interpretation.

Limitations of Traditional Auscultation

Traditional stethoscope-based auscultation suffers from several limitations. Firstly, the sound signals captured by the stethoscope are affected by external noises, making it challenging to distinguish abnormal lung sounds from background interference. Secondly, the perception and interpretation of these sounds vary among healthcare professionals, leading to diagnostic discrepancies. Finally, the lack of standardized training in lung sound analysis further compounds the challenges faced by healthcare practitioners.

Proposed Solution

To address these limitations, we propose the integration of an autoencoder, a type of artificial neural network, with a vest-coat stethoscope. The autoencoder's ability to learn and represent latent features within sound signals can aid in the identification and classification of abnormal lung sounds. The vest-coat stethoscope, equipped with multiple sensors and microphones, provides enhanced signal acquisition capabilities, reducing the impact of external noise and interference.

Methodology

The proposed methodology involves the following steps:

a. Data Acquisition: Collecting a diverse dataset of lung sound recordings, including both normal and abnormal sounds, using the vest-coat stethoscope.
b. Preprocessing: Applying appropriate signal processing techniques to remove noise, normalize amplitude, and segment the lung sound recordings.
c. Autoencoder Training: Developing autoencoder architecture and training it on the preprocessed lung sound dataset to learn the underlying features and patterns.
d. Abnormal Sound Detection: Employing the trained autoencoder to classify lung sound recordings as normal or abnormal based on the learned representations.
e. Evaluation: Assessing the performance of the proposed system through quantitative metrics, such as accuracy, sensitivity, and specificity, and comparing it with traditional auscultation methods.

Significance of the Study

Integrating an autoencoder with a vest-coat stethoscope can revolutionize lung sound analysis. By leveraging advanced machine learning techniques, this approach can enhance the accuracy and objectivity of abnormal sound detection in the lungs. The proposed system could assist healthcare professionals in making more informed diagnoses, facilitating early intervention and improving patient outcomes.

8.8 Performance Metrics

The performance metrics are used to analyze the strength of the proposed approach by using a confusion matrix. The confusion matrix contains the following attributes True positive (TP), True Negative (TN), False Positive (FP) and False Negative (FN). Table 8.1 shows the comparison of algorithms based on detecting abnormal sounds. Figure 8.3 shows the comparative performance of different algorithms.

The following parameters show the strength of the proposed approach as given in eqn(1), eqn(2) and eqn(3).

$$accuracy = \frac{TP+TN}{TP+TN+FP+FN} \quad (1)$$

$$Recall = \frac{TP}{TP+FN} \quad (2)$$

$$Specificity = \frac{TN}{TN+FP} \quad (3)$$

Table 8.1. A list of Algorithms shows the comparison based on detecting the abnormal sounds

Algorithms	Accuracy	Recall	Specificity
CNN	81.89	82.12	83.23
Autoencoders	86.87	86.98	85.34
Proposed (CNN_Autoencoders)	91.78	92.34	93.65

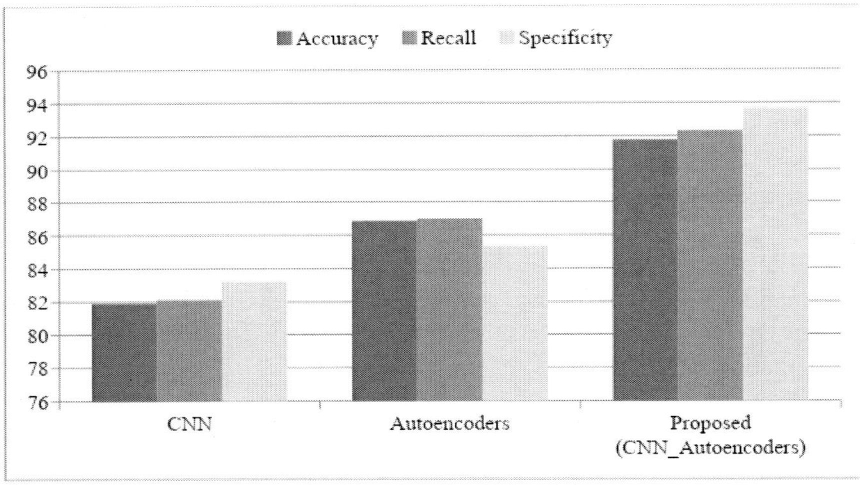

Figure 8.3. Comparative performance of list of algorithms.

8.9 Conclusion

In conclusion, the use of a Vest-Coat Stethoscope equipped with a deep learning algorithm has proven to be an effective method for the detection of abnormal sounds in the lungs. This innovative approach combines the convenience and mobility of a wearable vest-coat with the advanced capabilities of deep learning algorithms, resulting in a powerful tool for healthcare professionals.

By leveraging deep learning techniques, the stethoscope can analyze lung sounds and identify patterns associated with respiratory conditions, such as pneumonia, bronchitis, or lung tumors. The algorithm can distinguish between normal lung sounds and abnormal ones, providing valuable insights for accurate diagnosis and treatment planning. The Vest-Coat Stethoscope offers several advantages over traditional stethoscopes. Firstly, it provides continuous monitoring, allowing healthcare providers to capture and analyze lung sounds over extended periods, which can be particularly useful for patients with chronic respiratory conditions. Additionally, the wearable nature of the vest coat allows for increased patient comfort and mobility during the monitoring process.

The deep learning algorithm integrated into the stethoscope has demonstrated high accuracy in identifying abnormal lung sounds. By training on large datasets of labeled lung sound recordings, the algorithm has learned to recognize specific acoustic patterns associated with different respiratory disorders. This enhances diagnostic capabilities and can potentially lead to earlier detection and intervention, improving patient outcomes.

Moreover, the Vest-Coat Stethoscope can be connected to a digital platform or medical records system, enabling the seamless integration of lung sound data into a patient's healthcare records. This facilitates data sharing, remote monitoring, and collaboration among healthcare professionals, ultimately enhancing the quality and efficiency of patient care.

While the Vest-Coat Stethoscope with a deep learning algorithm holds great promise for improving respiratory diagnostics, further research and validation are necessary. Large-scale clinical trials and comparative studies should be conducted to assess its performance in real-world settings and compare it with existing diagnostic methods.

Overall, the combination of a Vest-Coat Stethoscope and deep learning algorithm presents a promising approach for the early detection and monitoring of respiratory disorders. By leveraging the power of artificial intelligence, this technology has the potential to revolutionize lung sound analysis, enabling more accurate diagnoses and better management of lung-related conditions, ultimately improving patient outcomes and quality of life.

References

Bardou, D., Zhang, K., and Ahmad, S. M. (2018). "Lung sounds classification using convolutional neural networks." *Artificial intelligence in medicine*, *88*, 58-69.

Chamberlain, D., Kodgule, R., Ganelin, D., Miglani, V., and Fletcher, R. R. (2016). "Application of semi-supervised deep learning to lung sound analysis." In *2016 38th Annual international conference of the IEEE engineering in medicine and biology society (EMBC)* (pp. 804-807). IEEE.

Chen, C. H., Huang, W. T., Tan, T. H., Chang, C. C., and Chang, Y. J. (2015). "Using k-nearest neighbor classification to diagnose abnormal lung sounds." *Sensors*, *15*(6), 13132-13158.

Chen, H., Yuan, X., Pei, Z., Li, M., and Li, J. (2019). "Triple-classification of respiratory sounds using optimized s-transform and deep residual networks." *IEEE Access*, *7*, 32845-32852.

Demir, F., Ismael, A. M., and Sengur, A. (2020)." Classification of lung sounds with CNN model using parallel pooling structure." *IEEE Access*, *8*, 105376-105383.

Fraiwan, L., Hassanin, O., Fraiwan, M., Khassawneh, B., Ibnian, A. M., and Alkhodari, M. (2021). "Automatic identification of respiratory diseases from stethoscopic lung sound signals using ensemble classifiers." *Biocybernetics and Biomedical Engineering*, *41*(1), 1-14.

Fraiwan, M., Fraiwan, L., Khassawneh, B., and Ibnian, A. (2021). "A dataset of lung sounds recorded from the chest wall using an electronic stethoscope." *Data in Brief*, *35*, 106913. doi: 10.1016/j.dib.2021.106913.

Gairola, S., Tom, F., Kwatra, N., and Jain, M. (2021). "Respirenet: A deep neural network for accurately detecting abnormal lung sounds in limited data setting." In *2021 43rd Annual International Conference of the IEEE Engineering in Medicine and Biology Society (EMBC)* (pp. 527-530). IEEE.

Jacome, C., Ravn, J., Holsbø, E., Aviles-Solis, J. C., Melbye, H., and Ailo Bongo, L. (2019). "Convolutional neural network for breathing phase detection in lung sounds." *Sensors*, *19*(8), 1798.

Kanavati, F., Toyokawa, G., Momosaki, S., Rambeau, M., Kozuma, Y., Shoji, F., et al. (2020). "Weakly-supervised learning for lung carcinoma classification using deep learning." *Scientific reports*, *10*(1), 9297.

Petmezas, G., Cheimariotis, G. A., Stefanopoulos, L., Rocha, B., Paiva, R. P., Katsaggelos, A. K., and Maglaveras, N. (2022). "Automated lung sound classification using a hybrid CNN-LSTM network and focal loss function." *Sensors*, *22*(3), 1232.

Padilla-Ortiz, A. L., and Ibarra, D. (2018). "Lung and heart sounds analysis: state-of-the-art and future trends". *Critical Reviews™ in Biomedical Engineering*, *46*(1).

Rocha, B. M., Pessoa, D., Marques, A., Carvalho, P., and Paiva, R. P. (2020). "Automatic classification of adventitious respiratory sounds: A (un) solved problem?" *Sensors*, *21*(1), 57.

Section 3. Public Health Application using Explainable AI

Chapter 9

Heart Diseases Prediction Based on Multiple Machine Learning Models

Sreekumar[1,*]
Suman Halder[1]
Alex Khang[2]
and Sambhu Dutta[3]
[1]Rourkela Institute of Management Studies, Rourkela, Odisha, India
[2]AI and Data Scientist, Universities of Science and Technology, Vietnam and United States
[3]Internal Medicine and Intensive Care Medicine, St. Ann's JM Hospital, Visakhapatnam, India

Abstract

Heart disease cases are rising at an alarming rate every day, it's critical and worrisome to anticipate these due to various factors of illness. The most lethal illness and one of the main reasons for mortality in the world is heart disease. Each year, its impacts are felt by over 20 million individuals (about the population of New York) globally. It is challenging for both cardiologists and surgeons to predict when heart failure may occur. This diagnosis is a challenging task that requires accuracy and efficiency. The medical field is heavily reliant on machine learning. Medical data classification and prediction models enable deeper understanding. One of the main objectives of the paper for using the heart disease dataset is to improve heart failure [HF] projection. Using information extracted from a medical database and analyzed using machine learning techniques, the likelihood of heart failure [HF] is predicted. This study and a comparative analysis have demonstrated that cardiac disease may be predicted with great accuracy. The research paper mainly focuses on which patient is more likely to have a heart disease based on various medical attributes. In this research paper, a built-in dataset is being used. Implementation of the different techniques with the same dataset is done to predict heart disease. These implemented algorithms are Naïve Bayes (NB), support vector machine (SVM), Logistic Regression (LR) and Random Forest (RF). This paper investigates which technique gives more accuracy in predicting future heart disease/attack/failure or cardiovascular disease/arrest/failure based on health parameters. These study findings show that early detection and proper management of heart

* Corresponding Author's Email: kumarsree42003@gmail.com.

In: Explainable Artificial Intelligence in Healthcare Systems
Editors: A. Anitha Kamaraj and Debi Prasanna Acharjya
ISBN: 979-8-89113-598-7

disease can significantly reduce the risk of heart failure. The application of machine learning and data mining techniques will help in early diagnosis of heart disease. On implementing different machine learning algorithms, it was found that the best result was obtained from Random Forest, which resulted in the highest accuracy of 98.05%, with 100.00% sensitivity, 96.36% specificity, and 98.18% balanced accuracy. Future studies could focus on further applicability to various contexts in medical education.

Keywords: Cardiovascular Disease (CVD), heart diseases (HD), Heart Failure (HF), Data Mining Techniques, Naïve Bayes (NB), Support Vector Machine (SVM), Logistic Regression (LR) and Random Forest (RF)

9.1 Introduction

Heart disease also known as cardiovascular disease (CVD), is a major global health concern with an increasing number of people being diagnosed every year. According to the World Health Organization, heart disease is the leading cause of death worldwide, accounting for 17.9 million deaths annually (Ali et al. 2021). The prevalence of heart disease is expected to rise in the coming years due to factors such as an aging population, sedentary lifestyles, unhealthy diets, and increasing levels of stress (Bharti et al. 2021). Research has identified core connections between cardiovascular disease, cholesterol, blood sugar level, and having too much body fat (Gao et al. 2021). Heart patients frequently must go through multiple types of testing, causing undue financial, emotional, and mental strain on them. This can be particularly burdensome for those who are already dealing with health issues and can lead to delays in treatment and misdiagnosis, which can have serious consequences (Gao et al. 2021; Segar et al. 2019). Therefore, healthcare providers need to prioritise efficient and accurate diagnostic processes that minimize the burden on patients (Segar et al. 2019). Heart disease can be a silent killer-many people die of it without symptoms. Anyone, including children, can develop heart disease. Early diagnosis is crucial because decisions about lifestyle changes and medical treatment help reduce the complications that come with heart disease (Ahmad et al. 2017; Turkmenoglu et al. 2021).

Heart disease can be categorized into three different conditions: "coronary heart disease, cardiomyopathy, and cardiovascular disease." The term "heart disease" refers to a wide range of conditions that impact the blood vessels, and the flow of fluid through the body's circulatory system (Chicco et al. 2020). Cardiovascular disease is a major cause of death, disability, and a variety of illnesses (Wong et al. 2021; Zahid et al. 2019). A critical and difficult task in medicine is disease diagnosis (Kathare et al. 2021; Chen et al. 2021; Srivenkatesh et al. 2020). Early medical diagnosis is viewed as a necessary yet challenging task that must be completed correctly and rapidly (Mehta et al. 2021). To correctly diagnose a patient's condition, one needs a wide range of information, expertise, and analytical abilities (Marbaniang et al. 2020; Jindal et al. 2021). The accuracy and dependability of medical diagnoses have increased with technological innovation.

Machine learning simplifies decision-making and forecasting from the immense volume of data gathered by the healthcare sector (Ayers et al. 2021; Haq and Xu, 2021; Mortazavi et al. 2016). As a result, healthcare professionals can make more accurate diagnoses, develop more effective treatment plans, and ultimately improve patient outcomes. Machine learning also has the potential to reduce healthcare costs by identifying inefficiencies and streamlining processes (Benjamin et al. 2019; Jayakrishnan et al. 2021; Wang et al. 2018). With continued advancements in technology, machine learning is poised to revolutionize the healthcare industry in the coming years. Using patient data for analysis exploring different machine learning techniques and making better use of healthcare data. Machine learning algorithms help determine if they have heart disease, the goal of this project is to predict future cases. Machine learning techniques can be extremely helpful in this situation (Marbaniang et al. 2020; Jindal et al. 2021). Despite heart disease manifesting in various ways, a common set of fundamental risk factors determines whether a person will be at risk for developing the condition. It can be said that this technique can be very well adapted to the problem by gathering the data from different sources, organizing them under appropriate headings, and then analyzing them to extract the desired data (Solanki and Sharma, 2019).

9.1.1 Classification

The retrieval of knowledge or relevant information from an enormous data collection can be called data mining. Data from numerous sources, including a database, online resources, social networking sites, and other digital platforms, are analyzed and summarized throughout this process. Finding patterns, trends, and correlations in data that may be utilized to enhance forecasting, decision-making, and other business operations is the aim of data mining. Overall, data mining is a crucial process that helps businesses and organizations make informed decisions based on the patterns and trends found in large amounts of data from various sources. It has become an essential tool in today's digital age, allowing companies to gain valuable insights and improve their operations.

Data mining is used in healthcare to find disease risk factors, forecast patient outcomes, and enhance patient treatment. In summary, clustering, predictive modelling, and association rule mining are important techniques used in data mining. Many industries, such as marketing, banking, healthcare, and manufacturing, rely heavily on data mining to make informed decisions. In healthcare, data mining is used to identify disease risk factors, predict patient outcomes, and improve patient treatment.

Classification methods are widely used in various fields to make predictions and decisions based on the data. These methods can also be used for anomaly detection and outlier analysis. In healthcare, classification is used to predict the risk of developing diseases and to develop personalized treatment plans.

Classification is a popular technique used in data mining to categorize data into predefined classes or categories. The goal of classification is to develop a model that accurately predicts the class of new data based on the characteristics of the existing data. In classification, the data set is divided into two parts: the training set and the testing set. The training set is used to build the classification model, while the testing set evaluates its performance.

Several algorithms are used in classification, such as decision trees, naive Bayes, k-nearest neighbors, and support vector machines. Decision trees are a popular classification algorithm that uses a tree-like structure to classify data based on a series of decisions. Naive Bayes is a probabilistic algorithm that calculates the probability of each class based on the characteristics of the data. K-nearest neighbors is a non-parametric algorithm that classifies data based on the similarity to the nearest neighbors. Support vector machines are a more complex algorithm that separates data into different classes using a hyperplane.

Details of the algorithms and classification techniques used are discussed in section 9.5.3.

The objectives of the study are:

1. Predicting Heart Disease using a categorized data set of medical records.
2. Comparing the various classifications' accuracy using the methods stated above.
3. Based on the results of the comparison, it suggests a more accurate prediction system.

9.2 Background Study

Many researchers have been conducting the diagnosis of Cardiovascular or heart disease using Machine Learning algorithms has motivated this work. This paper contains a brief literature survey. An efficient cardiovascular disease prediction has been made by using various algorithms. Some of them include Logistic Regression, Support Vector Machine, KNN, Random Forest Classifier etc. (Grubb et al. 2020; Ishaq et al. 2021; Nashif et al. 2018). Machine learning models and analysis can be found in heart failure (Baccouche et al. 2020). To create a model for the prediction of cardiac disease, researchers have used a variety of data mining techniques, including association rules, classification, and clustering (Vijayashree and Iyengar, 2016; Marimuthu et al. 2018; Golande and Pavan, 2019). A more accurate death prediction model might be used to identify patients in intensive care unit teams who are likely to benefit from tighter monitoring, extended treatment, or hospice assistance (Ayers et al. 2021). Several risk models can be used to predict heart failure-related death (Haq and Xu, 2021; Mortazavi et al. 2016). Numerous problems in data science have been resolved using machine learning. Machine learning can anticipate outcomes with the use of existing data. The authors studied ensemble classification as a potent machine learning approach to enhance several classifiers.

Most applications rely on common clinical risk factors like chest pain, high blood sugar and hypertension (Haq and Xu, 2021). It might be more difficult to set a baseline for normalcy when lab findings are assessed more realistically. For calculating risk, using trustworthy survival models is essential (Ayers et al. 2021; Haq and Xu, 2021; Mortazavi et al. 2016). Using computational techniques, traditional proportional risk models can increase their ability to find significant predictors by automatically establishing links between components and large data response values. When the heart is unable to adequately pump blood throughout the body, heart failure results. The leading contributors to cardiovascular disease mortality are heart attacks and strokes. It resembles many people's ultimate fate.

9.3 Generalised Prediction and Analysis

Medically, a myocardial infarction, commonly known as a heart attack or heart failure, occurs when the blood supply to a portion of the heart muscle is inadequate. The longer a period that goes by without seeking treatments to improve blood flow, the more collateral harm the heart muscle sustains. The primary factor for heart attacks is coronary artery disease (CAD). A coronary artery contraction, which is a violent sudden contraction, is less frequent the cause and can cut down blood supply to the heart muscle.

Clinically there are various factors for the basic diagnosis of heart disease; the factors include age, blood pressure, blood sugar level, chest pain, family history, etc. of the patient. Most heart attacks are characterised by pain in the middle of the chest that lasts for longer than a few minutes or that disappears and reappears. It may feel like painful pressure, squeezed, or uncomfortable pressure. For both men and women chest pain (Angina) is the most typical heart attack symptom. However, women may also have other symptoms including shortness of breath, nausea, and vomiting, as well as back or jaw pain, which are often less indicative of heart problems. On the basis of these factors, a generalised graph is represented in Figure 9.1.

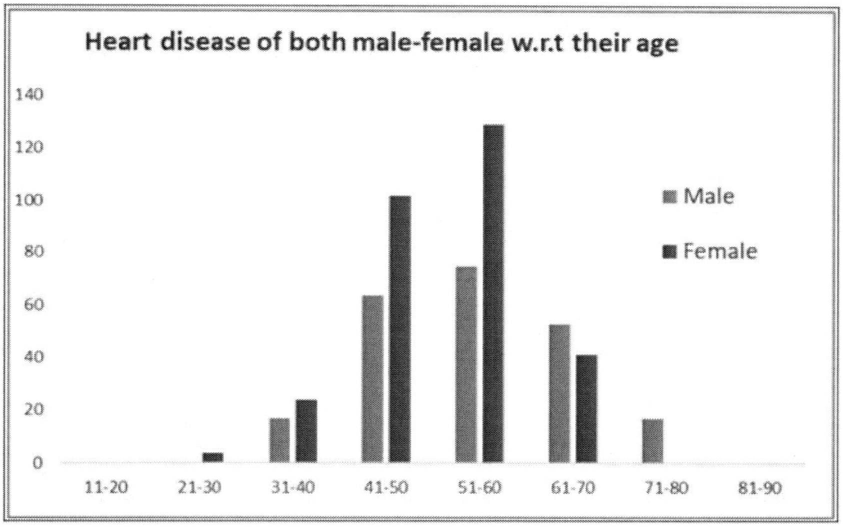

Figure 9.1. Generalized graph for Heart dataset.

9.4 Methodology

Machine learning in heart disease treatment is growing in popularity. Finding the most practicable method for heart disease datasets, despite the abundance of machine learning techniques, remains a difficulty. The main objective of the suggested research project is to suggest a highly accurate machine learning heart disease detection method. According to the inputs provided by clinical data, accurate prediction using machine learning algorithms such as SVM, Logistic Regression, Random Forest, Naïve Bayes etc. are to be used for heart disease detection. The optimum machine learning algorithm for handling instances associated with heart illness is therefore found based on the effectiveness of the chosen classification technique.

The research methodology, a heart entails several steps to accomplish the stated research objectives: gathering a Heart dataset with pertinent patient attributes, pre-processing the values of numerical facts, using various machine learning classification techniques, and performing the necessary predictive analysis using these data. These steps are briefly described in Figure 9.2.

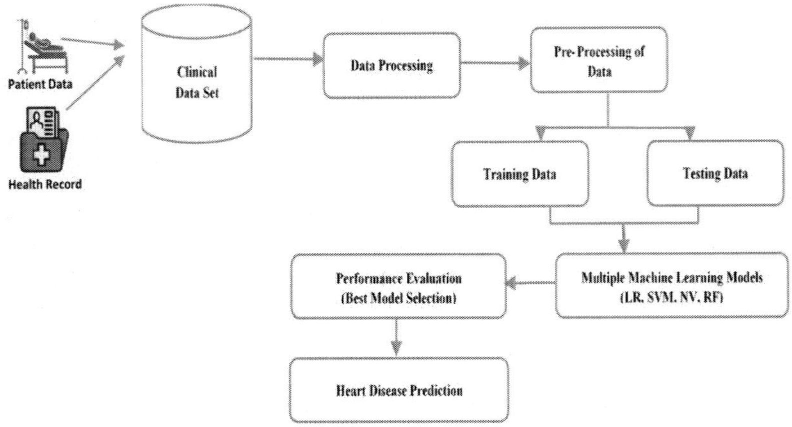

Figure 9.2. Architecture Diagram.

9.4.1. Metrics to Evaluate Performance

To determine which classification method performed the best in terms of accuracy, four (04) classification algorithms were applied to the dataset. Support Vector Machine (SVM), Random Forest (RF), Logistic Regression (LR), and Naive Bayes (NV) were the methods used. Based on the performance evaluation metrics, these algorithms were compared.

To determine the sensitivity, specificity, and accuracy of the outcome for each method, a confusion matrix was created. All the parameters were calculated using the formulas shown below.

$$Sensitivity = \frac{TruePositive}{TruePositive + FalseNegative}$$

$$Specificity = \frac{TrueNegative}{TrueNegative + FalsePositive}$$

or

$$Specificity = \frac{TruePositive + TrueNegative}{TruePositive + FalsePositive + TrueNegative + FalseNegative}$$

$$TruePositiveRate = \frac{TruePositive}{TruePositive + FalseNegative}$$

$$FalsePositiveRate = \frac{FalsePositive}{FalsePositive + TrueNegative}$$

Here, Sensitivity is the number of positive predictions that the classifier properly recognized as well as the proportion of real positives that are appropriately defined as data by the classifier. Whereas Specificity is the correctly distinguishing negative outcomes recognized by the classifier. The percentage of occurrences that a classifier correctly classifies is known as accuracy. For more efficiency of the models, further ROC (Receiver Operating Characteristics) are determined for each model.

9.5. Experimental Setup

This section deals with the data description, data preprocessing, analysis using statistical and supervised learning algorithms

9.5.1. Data Description

Keeping in mind their history of cardiac issues and in accordance with other medical concerns, a structured dataset of individuals was chosen. The many disorders that harm the heart collectively are referred to as heart disease. The data source consists of the medical history of 1025 different patients of different age groups. This dataset gives us the much-needed information i.e., the medical attributes such as age, blood pressure, blood sugar level,

Table 9.1 Detail Data Description

Sl. No.	Attribute	Attribute Range	Type	Attribute Description
1	AGE	Age range 29 - 77	Numeric	Age: Age of patient in years
2	SEX	Sex: 0-Male and 1-Female	Boolean	Gender: Male/Female
3	CP	0-typical angina; 1-atypical angina 2-non-anginal pain; 3-asymptomatic	Boolean	Chest Pain type (4 values)
4	TRESTBPS	Blood Pressure	Numeric	Resting Blood Pressure (140 mm (about 5.51 in)/Hg)
5	CHOL	Cholesterol	Numeric	Serum Cholesterol in mg/dl (289 mg (about the weight of ten grains of rice)/dl)
6	FBS	Diabetes	Boolean	Fasting blood sugar > 120 mg (about the weight of a business card)/dl (1 = Present and 0 = Not Present)
7	RESTECG	ECG: 0-normal, 1-having ST-T, 2-hypertrophy	Numeric	Resting electrocardiographic results (values 0,1,2)
8	THALACH	Heart rate (Range 71-202)	Numeric	Maximum Heart Rate Achieved
9	EXANG	Angina Phenomenon: 0 and 1	Boolean	Exercise Induced Angina (1 = Present and 0 = Not Present)
10	OLDPEAK	Myocardial Ischemia/Oxygen Deprivation (0-6.2)	Numeric	ST depression induced by exercise relative to rest
11	SLOPE	ST segment/heart rate slope (0-2)	Numeric	The slope of the peak exercise ST segment (0-upsloping, 1-flat, 2-downsloping)
12	CA	Fluoroscopy Reading (0-3)	Numeric	Number of major vessels coloured by fluoroscopy
13	THAL	Thalassemia (0-2)	Numeric	0 = normal; 1 = fixed defect; 2 = reversible defect
14	TARGET	Diagnosis class	Boolean	Diagnosis of heart disease (1 = Present/Disease and 0 = Not Present/No Disease)

chest pain, etc. of the patient that helps us in detecting whether the patient is diagnosed with any heart disease or not. This dataset contains 14 medical attributes of 1025 patients that help us detect if the patient is at risk of getting heart disease or not. This Heart Disease dataset is taken from the Kaggle data set. According to this dataset, Accuracy, sensitivity, and specificity were the metrics used to gauge performance on 1025 samples, and the pattern led to the detection of patients prone to heart disease. The following areas of data are included in this dataset and are listed here in Table 9.1.

9.5.2. Data Preprocessing

The data from the real world includes numerous incomplete and inaccurate values at the beginning phase of data processing. To avoid these issues and produce precise forecasts, these data have been pre-processed. The available raw data is inadequate and unreliable. One can eliminate the values that are missing or use the mean value in their stead. Because of employing a filtering policy, the data received must be slightly modified to carry out a good analysis. The final data is obtained after multiple filtering.

9.5.3. Supervised Machine Learning Algorithms Classification Techniques

Some well-known classification methods are used to forecast heart disease once the data has been prepared for modelling. An introduction to these methods is given before going on to the findings and analysis. These classification methods include decision trees, logistic regression, and support vector machines, which have been widely used in the medical field for disease prediction. The findings and analysis of these methods can provide insights into the risk factors and potential interventions for heart disease prevention.

9.5.3.1. Logistic Regression

Logistic regression is a method of statistical analysis that uses one or more types of explanatory variables to produce a binomial outcome. This method intends to identify the category into which an element instance belongs. Applications like rate of success and item sales forecasting can benefit from the usage of regression. LR also helps in predicting long-term risk factors from clinical data analysis. The probability that a new observation will be classified into a particular class is determined by LR, with the result ranging between 0 and 1 as it is a probability.

9.5.3.2. Support Vector Machine

Support vector machines (SVM) can be applied to classification and regression problems. Indeed, one of the most significant machine learning techniques is being used mostly in pattern recognition problems, such as categorising network traffic and recognising images. SVM is basically implemented in categorising the problems. The SVM algorithm's objective is to establish the optimal path or decision boundary that can divide n-dimensional space into classes, allowing us to quickly classify fresh data points in the future. SVM selects the extreme vectors and points to assist in the creation of the hyperplane.

9.5.3.3. Naïve Bayes

Naive Bayes is a clear and simple classification algorithm that helps in making use of past data to anticipate how new data will be categorized. Determines the likelihood that an event will take place in another event's presence. Conditions for the incident at issue are known. Examining news articles about technology, politics, or sports and categorizing emails as spam are two real-world applications of Naive Bayes classification. In conclusion, Naive Bayes is a well-liked algorithm for classifying data, particularly around natural language processing. Based on previous data and known circumstances, it predicts the classification of new data using statistical models. Overall, Naive Bayes is a flexible and popular algorithm that has shown success in a variety of classification tasks, including those involving facial recognition and natural language processing. It is useful for the prediction of outcomes-based models on probability theory and historical data.

9.5.3.4. Random Forest

Random Forest is one of the popular machine learning algorithms, as a part of the supervised learning methodology. It can be applied to machine learning problems involving both classification and regression. It is based on the idea of ensemble learning, which is a method of combining various classifiers to address complex issues and enhance model performance. Random decision forests are ML actors that can be used to troubleshoot classification and regression challenges, according to RF. The output is obtained by enhancing every DT's output to settle a single outcome. They function by building a different number of DT classifiers or regressions. Combining these DTs is known as ensemble learning, which aims to improve the model's accuracy and robustness by reducing overfitting and bias. Ensemble methods such as bagging, boosting, and random forests are commonly used in machine learning.

9.5.4. Analysis Using Logistic Regression (LR)

The analysis of Heart Data was done using the LR model of machine learning and the result of the prediction is presented in Table 9.2.

Table 9.2. Model Prediction value of LR Model

Sl. No	Dimensions	LR Value
01	Accuracy	0.8339
02	95% CI	(0.7874, 0.8737)
03	No Information Rate	0.5375
04	P-Value [Acc > NIR]	< 2e-16
05	Kappa	0.6637
06	Mcnemar's Test P-Value	0.09289
07	Sensitivity	0.7746
08	Specificity	0.8848
09	Pos Pred Value	0.8527
10	Neg Pred Value	0.8202
11	Prevalence	0.4625
12	Detection Rate	0.3583
13	Detection Prevalence	0.4202
14	Balanced Accuracy	0.8297
15	'Positive' Class	X0

The model's accuracy now stands at 83.39%, while its sensitivity and specificity are, respectively, 77.46% and 88.48%. It shows that the model is proactive and that the expected outcomes have occurred. The classification issue is satisfied, as indicated by the positive class, which equals 0. The kappa value of 0.6637 suggests a decent match. For each of the two groups, the forecasts at 95% CI (Confidence Interval) are 78.74% and 87.37%, respectively. While the model's balanced accuracy is 0.8297.

In Table 9.3 and Figure 9.3, the confusion matrix for the LR model is displayed. The confusion matrix predicts that 110 and 146 cases will be properly categorized, whereas 19 and 32 instances will be incorrectly classified. The model's accuracy, which is 83.39%, shows that it is functioning well. The model, however, has a high rate of false negatives compared to false positives, which means that it is more likely to categorize occurrences mistakenly as negative when, they are positive. In some situations where false negatives are extremely expensive, this might be an issue. Further investigation should be done to see whether the examples that were incorrectly categorized have any traits or patterns in common that may be used to enhance the model. Even though the LR model appears to be functioning well overall based on its accuracy score, there are still some things that may be done to make it better.

Table 9.3. Confusion Matrix of LR Model

Prediction class	Reference instance	
	0	1
0	110	19
1	32	146

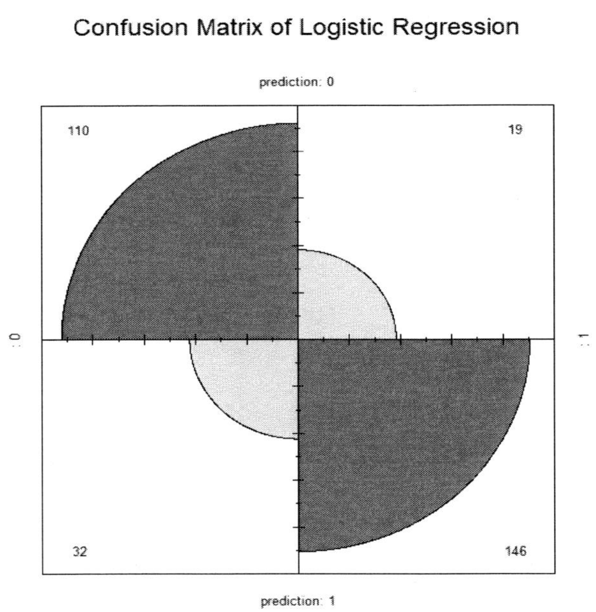

Figure 9.3. Confusion Matrix of LR Model.

While Figure 9.4 shows the analysis's ROC curve. Sensitivity is plotted on the vertical axis while 1-specificity is plotted on the horizontal axis. It ought to show that the area in the top left corner has the best cut-off score discrimination. This line is clearly above the ROC curve.

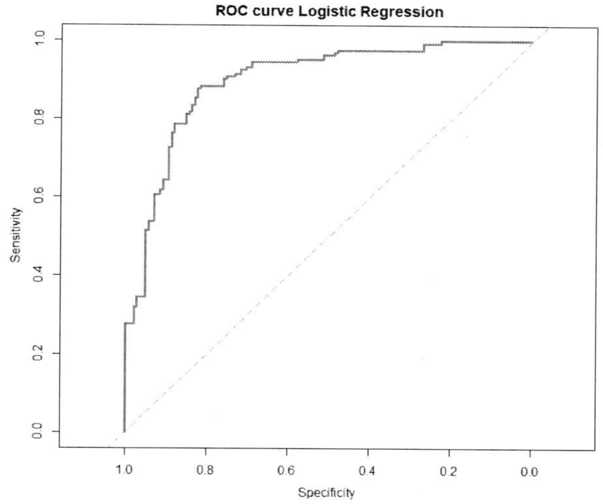

Figure 9.4. ROC Curve of LR Model.

9.5.5. Analysis Using Support Vector Machine (SVM)

The analysis of Heart Data was done using the SVM model of machine learning and the result of the prediction is presented in Table 9.4.

Table 9.4. Model Prediction value of SVM Model

Sl. No	Dimensions	SVM Value
01	Accuracy	0.8632
02	95% CI	(0.8196, 0.8996)
03	No Information Rate	0.5244
04	P-Value [Acc > NIR]	< 2e-16
05	Kappa	0.7240
06	Mcnemar's Test P-Value	0.00337
07	Sensitivity	0.7877
08	Specificity	0.9317
09	Pos Pred Value	0.9127
10	Neg Pred Value	0.8287
11	Prevalence	0.4756
12	Detection Rate	0.3746
13	Detection Prevalence	0.4104
14	Balanced Accuracy	0.8597
15	'Positive' Class	X0

Table 9.5. Confusion Matrix of the SVM Model

Prediction class	Reference instance	
	0	1
0	115	11
1	31	150

The model's accuracy now stands at 86.32%, while its sensitivity and specificity are, respectively, 78.77% and 93.17%. It shows that the model is proactive and that the expected outcomes have occurred. The classification issue is satisfied, as indicated by the positive class, which equals 0. The kappa value of 0.7240 suggests a decent match. For each of the two groups, the forecasts at 95% CI (Confidence Interval) are 81.96% and 89.96%, respectively. While the model's balanced accuracy is 0.8597.

In Table 9.5 and Figure 9.5, the confusion matrix for the SVM model is displayed. The confusion matrix predicts that 115 and 150 cases will be properly categorized, whereas 11 and 31 instances will be incorrectly classified. The model's accuracy, which is 86.32%, shows that it is functioning well.

The model, however, has a high rate of false negatives compared to false positives, which means that it is more likely to categorize occurrences mistakenly as negative when, they are positive. In some situations where false negatives are extremely expensive, this might be an issue. Further investigation should be done to see whether the examples that were incorrectly categorized have any traits or patterns in common that may be used to enhance the model. Even though the SVM model appears to be functioning well overall based on its accuracy score, there are still some things that may be done to make it better.

While Figure 9.6 shows the analysis's ROC curve. Sensitivity is plotted on the vertical axis while 1-specificity is plotted on the horizontal axis. It ought to show that the area in the top left corner has the best cut-off score discrimination. This line is clearly above the ROC curve.

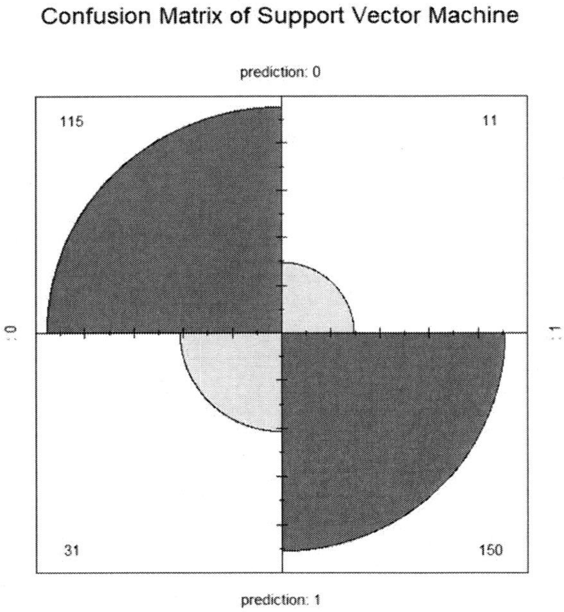

Figure 9.5. Confusion Matrix of SVM Model.

9.5.6. Analysis Using Naïve Bayes (NV)

The analysis of Heart Data was done using the NV model of machine learning and the result of the prediction is presented in Table 9.6.

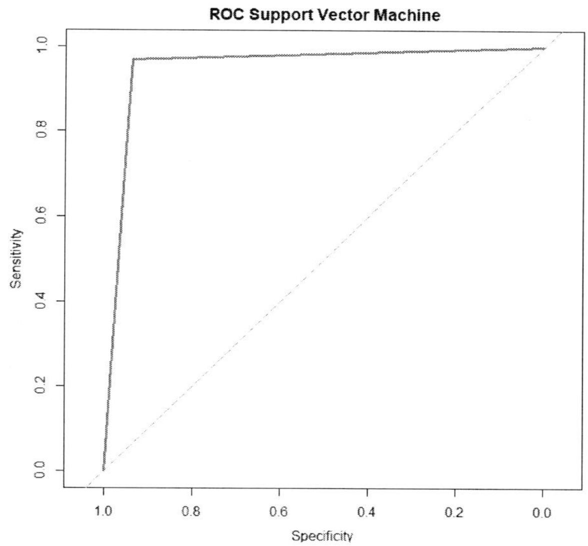

Figure 9.6. ROC Curve of SVM Model.

The model's accuracy now stands at 82.41%, while its sensitivity and specificity are, respectively, 80.14% and 84.47%. It shows that the model is proactive and that the expected outcomes have occurred. The classification issue is satisfied, as indicated by the positive class, which equals 0. The kappa value of 0.6469 suggests a decent match. For each of the two groups, the forecasts at 95% CI (Confidence Interval) are 77.68% and 86.50%, respectively. While the model's balanced accuracy is 0.8230.

Table 9.6. Model Prediction value of NV Model

Sl. No	Dimensions	NV Value
01	Accuracy	0.8241
02	95% CI	(0.7768, 0.8650)
03	No Information Rate	0.5244
04	P-Value [Acc > NIR]	<2e-16
05	Kappa	0.6469
06	Mcnemar's Test P-Value	0.06831
07	Sensitivity	0.8014
08	Specificity	0.8447
09	Pos Pred Value	0.8239
10	Neg Pred Value	0.8242
11	Prevalence	0.4756
12	Detection Rate	0.3811
13	Detection Prevalence	0.4625
14	Balanced Accuracy	0.8230
15	'Positive' Class	X0

In Table 9.7 and Figure 9.7, the confusion matrix for the NV model is displayed. The confusion matrix predicts that 117 and 136 cases will be properly categorized, whereas 25 and 39 instances will be incorrectly classified. The model's accuracy, which is 82.41%, shows that it is functioning well. The model, however, has a high rate of false negatives compared to false positives, which means that it is more likely to categorize occurrences mistakenly as negative when, they are positive. In some situations where false negatives are extremely expensive, this might be an issue. Further investigation should be done to see whether the examples that were incorrectly categorized have any traits or patterns in common that may be used to enhance the model. Despite the NV model functioning well based on its accuracy score, there are still some things that may be done to improve it.

Table 9.7. Confusion Matrix of NV Model

Prediction class	Reference instance	
	0	1
0	117	25
1	29	136

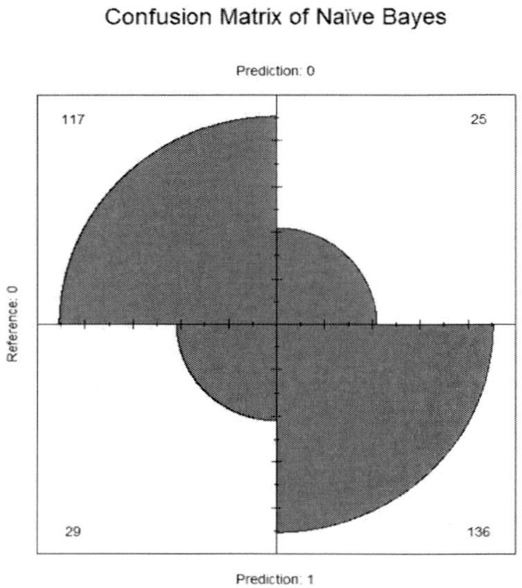

Figure 9.7. Confusion Matrix of NV Model.

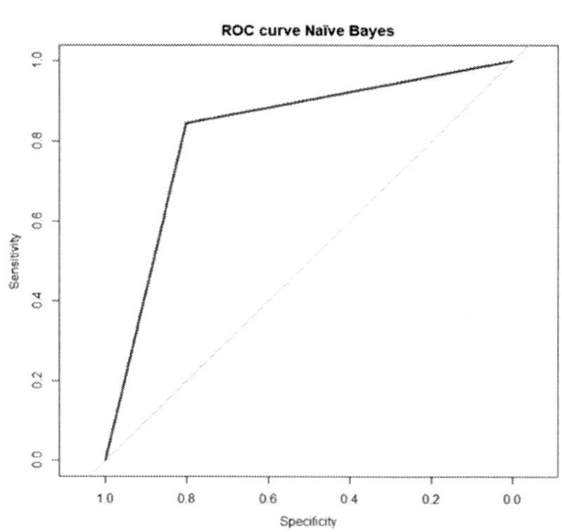

Figure 9.8. ROC Curve of NV Model.

While Figure 9.8 shows the analysis's ROC curve. Sensitivity is plotted on the vertical axis while 1-specificity is plotted on the horizontal axis. It ought to show that the area in the top left corner has the best cut-off score discrimination. This line is clearly above the ROC curve.

9.5.7. Analysis Using Random Forest (RF)

The analysis of Heart Data was done using the RF model of machine learning and the result of the prediction is presented in Table 9.8.

The model's accuracy now stands at 98.05%, while its sensitivity and specificity are, respectively, 100% and 96.36%. It shows that the model is proactive and that the expected outcomes have occurred. The classification issue is satisfied, as indicated by the positive class, which equals 0. The kappa value of 0.9608 suggests a decent match. For each of the two groups, the forecasts at 95% CI (Confidence Interval) are 95.79% and 99.28%, respectively. While the model's balanced accuracy is 98.18%.

In Table 9.9 and Figure 9.9, the confusion matrix for the RF model is displayed. The confusion matrix predicts that 142 and 159 cases will be properly categorized, whereas 0 and 6 instances will be incorrectly classified.

Table 9.8. Model Prediction value of RF Model

Sl. No	Dimensions	RF Value
01	Accuracy	0.9805
02	95% CI	(0.9579, 0.9928)
03	No Information Rate	0.5375
04	P-Value [Acc > NIR]	< 2e-16
05	Kappa	0.9608
06	Mcnemar's Test P-Value	0.04123
07	Sensitivity	1.0000
08	Specificity	0.9636
09	Pos Pred Value	0.9595
10	Neg Pred Value	1.0000
11	Prevalence	0.4625
12	Detection Rate	0.4625
13	Detection Prevalence	0.4821
14	Balanced Accuracy	0.9818
15	'Positive' Class	X0

Table 9.9. Confusion Matrix of RF Model

Prediction class	Reference instance	
	0	1
0	142	6
1	0	159

The model's accuracy, which is 98.05%, shows that it is functioning very well. The model, however, has a high rate of false negatives compared to false positives, which means that it is more likely to categorize occurrences mistakenly as negative when, they are positive. In some situations where false negatives are extremely expensive, this might be an issue. Further investigation should be done to see whether the examples that were incorrectly categorized have any traits or patterns in common that may be used to enhance the model. Even though the RF model appears to be functioning very well overall based on its accuracy score, there are still some things that may be done to make it better.

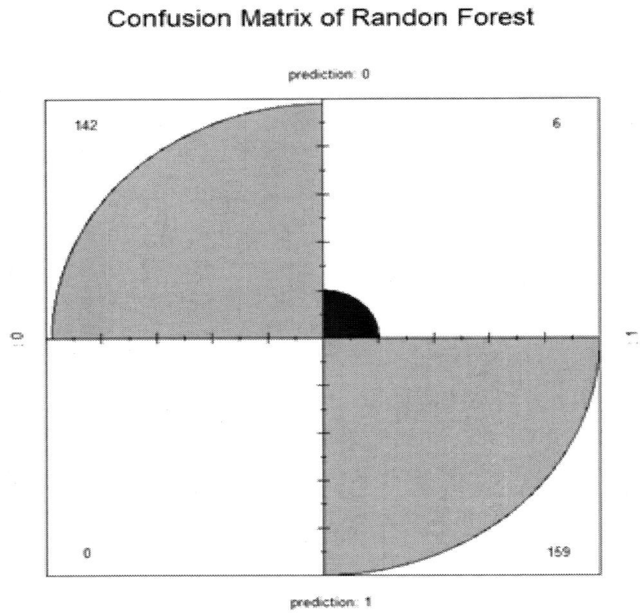

Figure 9.9. Confusion Matrix of RF Model.

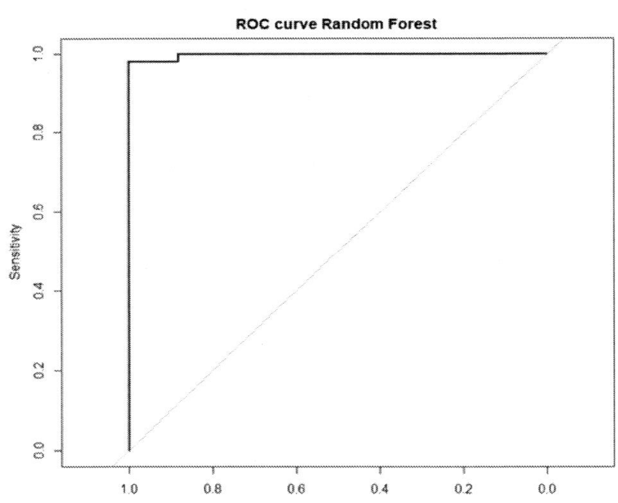

Figure 9.10. ROC Curve of RF Model.

While Figure 9.10 shows the analysis's ROC curve. Sensitivity is plotted on the vertical axis while 1-specificity is plotted on the horizontal axis. It ought to show that the area in the top left corner has the best cut-off score discrimination. This line is clearly above the ROC curve.

9.6. Prediction Comparative and Result Analysis among Different Models

After the execution of multiple algorithms, the subsequent action is to compare the various machine learning algorithms used to perform these and select the algorithm that provides the highest level of accuracy. Table 9.10 shows an overall comparison between all the models used for the prediction of heart disease. Figure 9.11 depicts the accuracy and balanced accuracy prediction of real-time machine learning using LR, SVM, NV and RF models on the heart data set. At this point, it appears the accuracy of various models is represented. The greatest degrees of accuracy are earned by RF.

RF (98.05%), SVM (86.32%), LR (83.39%), and NV (82.41%) are subsequent accurate linear regression models for heart disease prediction. Based on the comparison the best accuracy that can be used to predict heart attacks is achieved by Random Forest (98.05%). Whereas SVM, LR and NV are good as they have nearly the same accuracy. The most efficient linear regression models for heart disease prediction are RF (98.05%), SVM (86.32%), LR (83.39%), and NV (82.41%). Random Forest (98.05%) has the best accuracy and can be used to predict heart attacks. By considering real-time information about patients, the machine learning approach suggested by this work may be utilised to enhance the prediction of heart failure (HF) as well as various disorders. Multiple performance measurements are employed, for instance, to compare the results of these studies. A summary of algorithms using True Positive, False Positive, False Negative and True Negative is shown in Table 9.11.

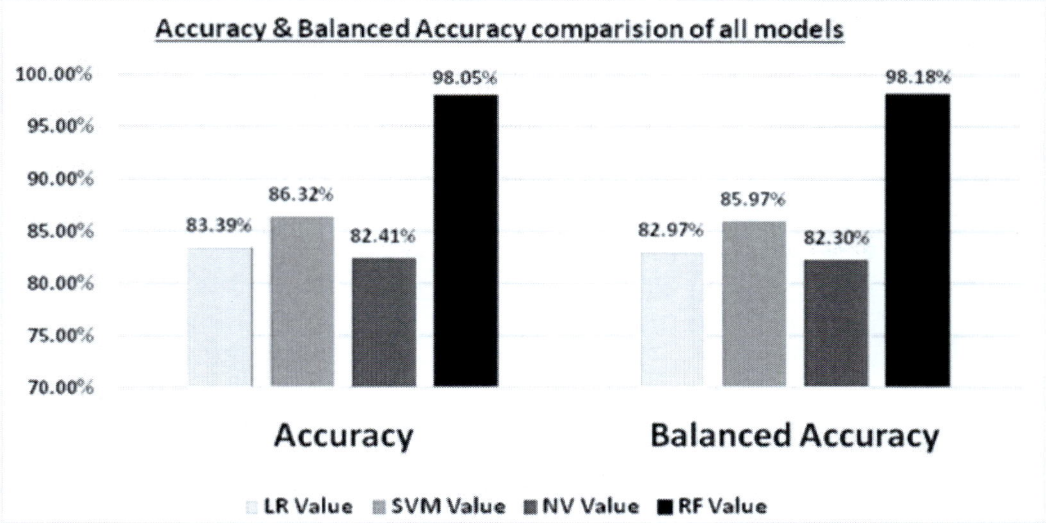

Figure 9.11. Summary of Accuracy and Balanced Accuracy of Different Algorithms.

As everybody is aware, heart disease is a delicate and serious condition affecting millions of lives every year. It is better to relieve people from their disease when the diagnosis is accurate and made sooner rather than later. As a result, algorithms are projected to detect cardiac patients with high accuracy. A consequence of the above algorithms shows that Random Forest would be prudent for the most accurate heart disease prediction. Additionally, medical professionals might focus on how to employ the suggested machine learning model to enhance clinical data analysis for heart disease.

Table 9.10. Overall result comparison between LR, SVM, NV and RF

Sl. No	Dimensions	LR Value	SVM Value	NV Value	RF Value
1	Accuracy	83.39%	86.32%	82.41%	98.05%
2	95% CI	78.74%, 87.37%	81.96%, 89.96%	77.68%, 86.50%	95.79%, 99.28%
3	No Information Rate	53.75%	52.44%	52.44%	53.75%
4	P-Value [Acc > NIR]	< 2e-16	< 2e-16	<2e-16	< 2e-16
5	Kappa	66.37%	72.40%	64.69%	96.08%
6	Mcnemar's Test P-Value	09.29%	00.34%	06.83%	04.12%
7	Sensitivity	77.46%	78.77%	80.14%	100.00%
8	Specificity	88.48%	93.17%	84.47%	96.36%
9	Pos Pred Value	85.27%	91.27%	82.39%	95.95%
10	Neg Pred Value	82.02%	82.87%	82.42%	100.00%
11	Prevalence	46.25%	47.56%	47.56%	46.25%
12	Detection Rate	35.83%	37.46%	38.11%	46.25%
13	Detection Prevalence	42.02%	41.04%	46.25%	48.21%
14	Balanced Accuracy	82.97%	85.97%	82.30%	98.18%
15	'Positive' Class	X0	X0	X0	X0

Table 9.11. Overall performance measures between LR, SVM, NV and RF

Sl. No	Algorithms	True Positive	False Positive	False Negative	True Negative
1	LR	110	19	32	146
2	SVM	115	11	31	150
3	NV	117	25	29	136
4	RF	142	6	0	159

9.7 Conclusion and Future Scope

In the modern era, heart failure (HF) is a common condition that can be fatal. Every year around a million people throughout the world contracts the disease. It can be difficult to foresee when a patient may experience heart failure in cardiology and surgery. Early detection and proper management of the disease can significantly reduce the risk of heart failure in patients with cardiology and surgery-related illnesses. By using data on cardiovascular disease and machine learning techniques to predict the occurrence of heart failure in a medical database, the accuracy of HF projections will be increased. This approach can help doctors identify high-risk patients and provide them with timely interventions to prevent heart failure. It also can improve patient outcomes and reduce healthcare costs associated with managing heart failure.

As heart disease advances slowly, early diagnosis and successful treatment are the keys to reducing the impacts that this disease can cause. The application of data mining techniques in healthcare, namely in the early diagnosis of heart disease, was this work's major emphasis. Heart disease is a serious condition that can result in death. The following algorithms, Logistic Regression, Support Vector Machine, Naïve Bayes, and Random Forest were used to create data mining techniques. Performance is evaluated using several algorithms and the following metrics: Accuracy, Balanced Accuracy, True Negative, False Positive, False Negative, and True Positive rate. The best result was obtained from RF, which resulted in the highest accuracy of 98.05%, with 100.00% of sensitivity, 96.36% of specificity, and 98.18% of balanced accuracy.

It is recommended that one should use more algorithms in future studies to see whether they can generate superior outcomes. Additionally, using a dataset with more cases would be crucial for creating a larger, more balanced dataset that would increase the validity of this research. Apart from that, multiple metrics may be applied to assess additional criteria, leading to more reliable results.

The vast potential for applications of healthcare data mining is demonstrated through a literature study. The paper focuses on classifying HD patients into the expected HD and Non-HD categories using SPSS 27.0 and R-project, a free software environment for statistical computation. The research project compares Logistic Regression, Support Vector Machine, Naïve Bayes and Random Forest. The clinical dataset on heart disease (HD) is collected from Kaggle for this research.

References

Ahmad, T., Munir, A., Bhatti, S. H., Aftab, M., and Raza, M. A. (2017). "Survival analysis of heart failure patients : A case study." *PloS one*, *12*(7), e0181001.

Ali, M. M., Paul, B. K., Ahmed, K., Bui, F. M., Quinn, J. M., and Moni, M. A. (2021). "Heart disease prediction using supervised machine learning algorithms: Performance analysis and comparison." *Computers in Biology and Medicine*, *136*, 104672.

Ayers, B., Sandholm, T., Gosev, I., Prasad, S., and Kilic, A. (2021). "Using machine learning to improve survival prediction after heart transplantation." *Journal of Cardiac Surgery*, *36*(11), 4113-4120.

Baccouche, A., Garcia-Zapirain, B., Castillo Olea, C., and Elmaghraby, A. (2020). "Ensemble deep learning models for heart disease classification : A case study from Mexico." *Information*, *11*(4), 207.

Benjamin, E. J., Muntner, P., Alonso, A., Bittencourt, M. S., Callaway, C. W., Carson, A. P., et al. (2019). "Heart disease and stroke statistics—2019 updates : a report from the American Heart Association." *Circulation*, *139*(10), e56-e528.

Bharti, R., Khamparia, A., Shabaz, M., Dhiman, G., Pande, S., and Singh, P. (2021). "Prediction of heart disease using a combination of machine learning and deep learning." *Computational Intelligence and Neuroscience*, *2021*.

Chen, X. J., LaPorte, E. T., Olsen, C., Collins, L. M., Patel, P., Karra, R., and Mainsah, B. O. (2021). "Heart sound analysis in individuals supported with left ventricular assist devices." *IEEE Transactions on Biomedical Engineering*, *68*(10), 3009-3018.

Chicco, D., and Jurman, G. (2020). "Machine learning can predict survival of patients with heart failure from serum creatinine and ejection fraction alone." *BMC Medical Informatics and Decision Making*, *20*(1), 1-16.

Gao, X. Y., Amin Ali, A., Shaban Hassan, H., and Anwar, E. M. (2021). "Improving the accuracy for analyzing heart diseases prediction based on the ensemble method." *Complexity*, *2021*, 1-10.

Golande, A., and Pavan Kumar, T. (2019). "Heart disease prediction using effective machine learning techniques." *International Journal of Recent Technology and Engineering*, *8*(1), 944-950.

Grubb, A. F., Pumill, C. A., Greene, S. J., Wu, A., Chiswell, K., and Mentz, R. J. (2020). "Tobacco smoking in patients with heart failure and coronary artery disease: A 20-year experience at Duke University Medical Center." *American Hear Journal*, *230*, 25-34.

Haq, I. U., Haq, I., and Xu, B. (2021). "Artificial intelligence in personalized cardiovascular medicine and cardiovascular imaging." *Cardiovascular Diagnosis and Therapy*, *11*(3), 911.

Ishaq, A., Sadiq, S., Umer, M., Ullah, S., Mirjalili, S., Rupapara, V., and Nappi, M. (2021). "Improving the prediction of heart failure patients' survival using SMOTE and effective data mining techniques." *IEEE Access*, *9*, 39707-39716.

Jayakrishnan, A., Visakh, R., and Ratheesh, T. K. (2021). "Computational approach for heart disease prediction using machine learning." In *2021 International Conference on Communication, Control and Information Sciences (ICCISc)* (Vol. 1, pp. 1-5). IEEE.

Jindal, H., Agrawal, S., Khera, R., Jain, R., and Nagrath, P. (2021). "Heart disease prediction using machine learning algorithms." In *IOP conference series: Materials Science and Engineering* (Vol. 1022, No. 1, p. 012072). IOP Publishing.

Kathare, S., and Gaikwad, S. (2021). "Practicability of heart attack prediction using machine learning." *International Journal of Research Publication and Reviews*, *2*(7), 1473-1477.

Marbaniang, I. A., Choudhury, N. A., and Moulik, S. (2020). "Cardiovascular disease (CVD) prediction using machine learning algorithms." In *2020 IEEE 17th India Council International Conference (INDICON)* (pp. 1-6). IEEE.

Marimuthu, M., Abinaya, M., Hariesh, K. S., Madhankumar, K., and Pavithra, V. (2018). "A review on heart disease prediction using machine learning and data analytics approach." *International Journal of Computer Applications*, *181*(18), 20-25.

Mehta, D., Naik, A., Kaul, R., Mehta, P., and Bide, P. J. (2021). "Death by heart failure prediction using ML algorithms." In *2021 4th Biennial International Conference on Nascent Technologies in Engineering (ICNTE)* (pp. 1-5). IEEE.

Mortazavi, B. J., Downing, N. S., Bucholz, E. M., Dharmarajan, K., Manhapra, A., Li, S. X., et al. (2016). "Analysis of machine learning techniques for heart failure readmissions." *Circulation : Cardiovascular Quality and Outcomes*, *9*(6), 629-640.

Nashif, S., Raihan, M. R., Islam, M. R., and Imam, M. H. (2018). "Heart disease detection by using machine learning algorithms and a real-time cardiovascular health monitoring system." *World Journal of Engineering and Technology*, *6*(4), 854-873.

Segar, M. W., Vaduganathan, M., Patel, K. V., McGuire, D. K., Butler, J., Fonarow, G. C., et al. (2019). "Machine learning to predict the risk of incident heart failure hospitalization among patients with diabetes: the WATCH-DM risk score." *Diabetes Care*, *42*(12), 2298-2306.

Solanki, Y., and Sharma, S. (2019). "A survey on risk assessments of heart attack using data mining approaches." *International Journal of Information Engineering and Electronic Business*, *11*(4), 43-51.

Srivenkatesh, M. (2020). "Prediction of cardiovascular disease using machine learning algorithms." *Int. J. Eng. Adv. Technol*, *9*(3), 2404-2414.

Türkmenoğlu, B. K., and Yildiz, O. (2021). "Predicting the survival of heart failure patients in unbalanced data sets." In *2021 29th Signal Processing and Communications Applications Conference (SIU)* (pp. 1-4). IEEE.

Vijayashree, J., and SrimanNarayanaIyengar, N. C. (2016). "Heart disease prediction system using data mining and hybrid intelligent techniques : A review." *International Journal of Bio-Science and Bio-Technology*, *8*(4), 139-148.

Wang, S. B., Mitchell, P., Liew, G., Wong, T. Y., Phan, K., Thiagalingam, A., et al. (2018). "A spectrum of retinal vasculature measures and coronary artery disease." *Atherosclerosis*, *268*, 215-224.

Wong, T. Y., Klein, R., Klein, B. E., Tielsch, J. M., Hubbard, L., and Nieto, F. J. (2001). "Retinal microvascular abnormalities and their relationship with hypertension, cardiovascular disease, and mortality." *Survey of ophthalmology*, *46*(1), 59-80.

Chapter 10

Artificial Intelligence and Explainable Artificial Intelligence Applications for Predicting and Preventing Complications in Maternal Health

Karthik Balajee Laksham[1,*]
Nanthini Saravanan[2]
and Surendiran Balasubramanian[3]
[1]Department of Community Medicine, JIPMER Karaikal, Karaikal, India
[2]Department of Obstetrics and Gynecology, JIPMER Karaikal, Karaikal, India
[3]Department of Computer Science and Engineering,
National Institute of Technology (NIT) Puducherry, India

Abstract

This chapter presents an overview of Artificial Intelligence (AI) and Machine learning (ML) applications in maternal care, focusing on pregnancy risk assessment. It explores how AI and ML predict complications and identify high-risk pregnancies, emphasizing the importance of accurate risk assessment. The chapter outlines specific applications in pregnancy risk assessment, including predicting preterm labor, gestational diabetes mellitus, and preeclampsia, estimating gestational age, assessing foetal risk using cardiotocographic data, and detecting foetal growth restriction. It also covers real-time labor monitoring, breastfeeding support, predicting postpartum depression, ensuring medication safety, and developing clinical decision systems. Furthermore, the chapter introduces Explainable Artificial Intelligence (XAI) and highlights the significance of transparent and interpretable AI models. It discusses ethical and legal considerations in maternal care AI and the field's challenges and future directions. In conclusion, AI and ML hold substantial potential for improving pregnancy outcomes and providing personalized care. They enhance risk assessment, facilitate early detection of complications, and support decision-making. Addressing ethical concerns, ensuring explainability, and overcoming challenges are critical for fully harnessing the benefits of AI in maternal care.

* Corresponding Author's Email: dr.balajeelaksham@gmail.com.

In: Explainable Artificial Intelligence in Healthcare Systems
Editors: A. Anitha Kamaraj and Debi Prasanna Acharjya
ISBN: 979-8-89113-598-7

Keywords: artificial intelligence, machine learning, explainable AI, pregnancy risk assessment, pregnancy complications, preterm labor

10.1 Introduction

Maternal mortality is a significant global health challenge. The World Health Organization estimated that 287,000 women (about half the population of Wyoming) died due to pregnancy in 2020 (World Health Organization 2023). The leading causes of maternal deaths are postpartum hemorrhage, high blood pressure during pregnancy (such as preeclampsia and eclampsia), and infections. Furthermore, preterm birth is a significant contributor to infant morbidity and mortality. An estimated 13.4 million babies are born prematurely, and 900,000 die due to complications associated with preterm birth in a year. (World Health Organisation 2023) Most preterm births happen spontaneously, some due to pregnancy complications. Fetal distress is a common complication of pregnancy that can lead to emergency cesarean delivery.

Predicting and diagnosing maternal and foetal complications is challenging, especially when the clinical findings and investigations are inconclusive. Therefore, addressing these issues requires innovative approaches. In this chapter, we will explore the potential applications of artificial intelligence and machine learning in predicting and preventing complications in pregnancy.

10.1.1. Overview of Pregnancy and Maternal Care

When a woman experiences a missed menstrual period, the Urine Pregnancy Test (UPT) determines the pregnancy status. This test is available at all health facilities, including primary health centers and sub centers. Ultrasonography can diagnose pregnancy as early as five weeks of gestational age. The pregnancy period, divided into three trimesters, spans 40 weeks from the Last Menstrual Period (LMP). The first trimester spans from conception to 12 weeks, followed by the second trimester from 13 to 27 weeks, and finally, the third trimester from 28 to 40 weeks. After confirming pregnancy, women are enrolled and encouraged to undergo regular AnteNatal Care (ANC) check-ups to monitor maternal health and foetal growth and development. The World Health Organization recommends a minimum of four Antenatal visits.

During the first trimester, the ANC visits assess maternal vital signs, weight, and blood pressure. Laboratory tests, including blood hemoglobin, Blood grouping and typing, and urine for protein, are done to detect complications like anemia, Rh incompatibility, and preeclampsia. Healthcare providers routinely screen mothers for infectious diseases, HIV, and syphilis. An ultrasound (USG) examination confirms pregnancy and assesses the foetus's position within the uterus. Diabetes during pregnancy is Gestational Diabetes Mellitus (GDM), which leads to foetal complications and mortality. A glucose tolerance test is done in the second trimester to screen for GDM. An anomaly scan is done in the second trimester to evaluate the growth of the foetus and detect any congenital abnormalities.

Women with any risk factors detected during ANC visits are considered High-risk pregnancies and referred to higher centers for further investigations and follow-up. Higher centers conduct a Doppler ultrasound to evaluate the blood flow in the umbilical cord and placenta. In selected cases, healthcare providers conduct non-invasive tests such as analyzing foetal DNA in maternal blood and invasive tests like amniocentesis and chorionic villus sampling to assess the risk of congenital anomalies in women. During labor, the electronic foetal monitoring device is placed on the mother's abdomen to monitor foetal heart rate and uterine contractions, assess foetal wellbeing, and detect signs of distress.

Obstetricians face challenges in predicting and preventing pregnancy complications like Preterm birth (delivery before 37 completed weeks), Gestational Diabetes Mellitus (GDM), and pre-eclampsia and assessing foetal well-being. These challenges arise from the complex interactions of diverse biological and genetic factors. After delivery, any woman may develop complications like Postpartum hemorrhage or infection, and the probability is uncertain. The obstetricians rely on their clinical skills and interpretation of the investigations with a subjective component to detect complications. Often, they face a dilemma between the risks and benefits of a clinical decision. Moreover, optimizing limited resources like time, staff, and medicine is challenging. Artificial Intelligence is a promising technology which can play a significant role in assisting obstetricians.

10.1.2. Artificial Intelligence and Machine Learning in Maternal Care

Machine learning algorithms can analyze data from medical records and physiological parameters, enabling early detection of high-risk pregnancies. This valuable capability aids obstetricians in predicting and preventing complications and identifying high-risk patients who may require enhanced monitoring or interventions. Figure 10. 1 illustrates the development and application of ML algorithms in maternal health.

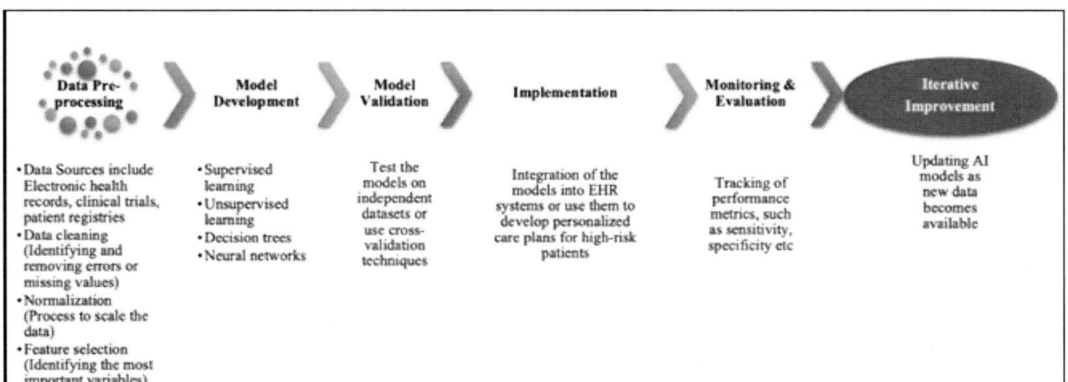

Figure 10.1. Flowchart on applying ML algorithm in maternal health.

Machine learning can assess individualized risk profiles for pregnant women and provide personalized recommendations. ML algorithms can analyze ultrasound and other medical images, enabling the detection of foetal abnormalities, placental disorders, and maternal complications. This advanced analysis assists obstetricians in making accurate diagnoses and developing effective treatment plans. Machine learning can assist in monitoring and managing postpartum complications such as postpartum hemorrhage, infections, or depression. Table 1 describes the different AI applications used in maternal health.

Table 10.1. AI application in maternal health and their application

AI application	Description	Application in Maternal Health
Machine learning algorithms	They are trained on large datasets and can identify patterns and make predictions.	These predictive models can identify women at risk of complications such as gestational diabetes, preeclampsia, and preterm birth
Computer vision algorithms	Analyze visual data, such as ultrasound images and foetal heart rate monitoring tracings.	Automate analysis of ultrasound images and identify anomalies or growth restrictions.
Deep learning algorithms	Utilize artificial neural networks to analyze complex data.	Analyze large datasets, develop accurate predictive models, automate medical image analysis, and improve diagnostic accuracy.
Reinforcement learning algorithms	Develop algorithms that learn from experience.	Develop personalized care plans based on patient responses to previous interventions.

10.2. Applications of AI and ML in Pregnancy Risk Assessment

AI and ML applications are used for risk assessment in pregnancy, including predicting complications and identifying high-risk pregnancies. This section describes some specific applications, such as

- Estimation of Gestational age
- Prediction of F
- Foetal growth restriction
- Detection of Congenital Anomalies
- Prediction of Gestational Diabetes mellitus.
- Prediction of Preeclampsia
- Prediction of Preterm Labor
- Prediction of foetal risk using cardiotocographic data

2.1. Estimation of Foetal Gestational Age

Accurately estimating gestational age (GA) is crucial in antenatal care. Although ultrasound measurement is considered the most accurate method for estimating gestational age (GA), manual foetal biometry measurements rely on operator skill and can be time-consuming. Furthermore, ultrasound measurements have a higher margin of error in the later stages of pregnancy. The image in Figure 10. 2 displays an ultrasonogram of a foetus used for estimating gestational age.

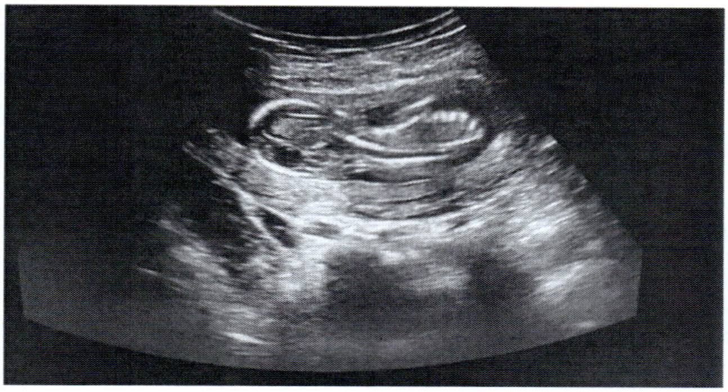

Figure 10.2. Image of an ultrasonogram of a foetus to estimate Crown Rump Length (CRL).

10.2.2. CRL Measurement Is Essential for Accurate Estimation of Gestational Age

AI models can enhance GA estimation by analyzing ultrasound images and identifying foetal growth restriction. Researchers achieved more consistent and accurate gestational age (GA) assessments using a machine-learning model based on ultrasound images. In the second and third trimesters, the model achieved a mean absolute error of 3.0 and 4.3 days, respectively, outperforming traditional ultrasound-based clinical biometry. The model's accuracy contributes to reduced subjectivity in GA estimation (L. H. Lee et al. 2023).

In the Foetal Age Machine Learning Initiative (FAMLI) cohort of 3842 participants from North Carolina (US) and Zambia in 2022, AI models surpassed expert sonographers' standard foetal biometry-based gestational age (GA) estimates. By incorporating image and video data, the ensemble model demonstrated superior performance in estimating gestational age (GA), surpassing routine foetal biometry by an average of 1.51 days. This emphasizes the potential of AI models to enhance the accuracy of GA estimation (Lee et al. 2023).

Researchers employed a machine-learning approach to estimate gestational age by analyzing ultrasound-based foetal biometric data from the INTERGROWTH-21st study. The model was validated using data from the INTERBIO-21st Foetal Study and achieved gestational age estimation within a three-day range, with a 95% confidence interval spanning 20 to 30 weeks. Furthermore, the model accurately projected the foetal growth trajectory within seven days, enabling a six-week forecast (Fung et al. 2020). This population-level model has the potential to enhance foetal growth charts and population health assessments, enabling more accurate identification of at-risk foetuses. Incorporating these machine learning algorithms into clinical practice can support pregnancy management and improve overall population health.

10.2.3. Prediction of Foetal Growth Restriction

Umbilical artery Doppler (UAD) is an investigation to detect foetal growth restriction and decreased birth weight (Figure 10. 3).

An absent or reversed end diastolic flow is associated with stillbirth. Researchers demonstrated the enhanced prediction of foetal growth restriction using ML algorithms with Umbilical artery Doppler images (Peters et al. 2023).

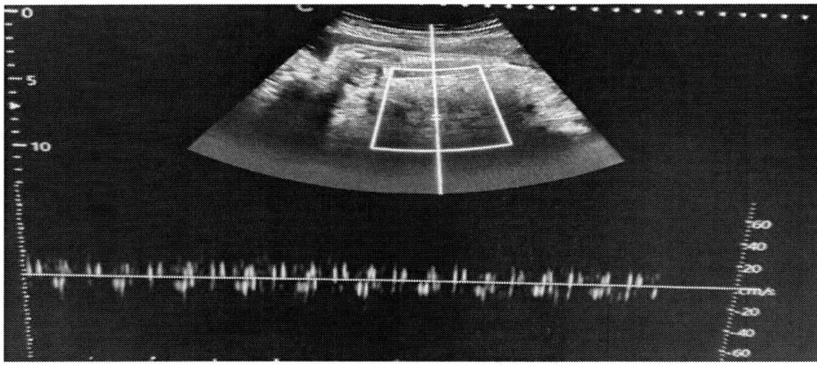

Figure 10. 3. Ultrasound Doppler image of a foetus showing umbilical artery Doppler waveform (red and blue color). Abnormal Doppler waveform is associated with adverse perinatal outcomes.

10.2.4. Detection of Congenital Anomalies

ML algorithms can analyze ultrasound and other medical images to detect abnormalities or anomalies indicating a higher risk of complications, such as neural tube defects or congenital heart disease, as shown in Figure 10.4.

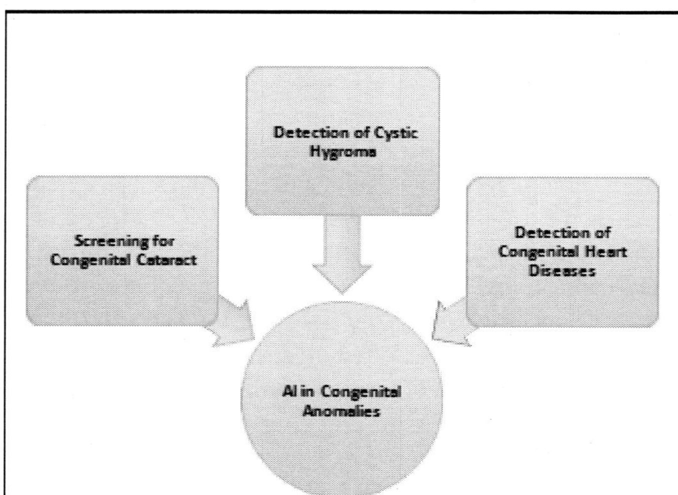

Figure 10.4. Application of Artificial Intelligence in Congenital Anomalies.

This section discusses the algorithms used to detect congenital anomalies. A meta-analysis of machine learning algorithms in diagnosing congenital heart disease (CHD) found that neural networks achieved a sensitivity of 90.9% and specificity of 92.7%. (Hoodbhoy et al. 2021) Artificial intelligence and DNA methylation analysis of circulating cell-free DNA can detect foetal congenital heart defects. (Bahado-Singh et al. 2023) Researchers in a Chinese birth cohort study developed an Explainable Boosting Machine (EBM) model that actively predicted congenital heart disease (CHD). The model demonstrated an AUC of 76%, accuracy of 0.65, sensitivity of 0.74, and specificity of 0.65. Maternal serum uric acid, glucose, and coagulation levels were the predictive factors in the model (Qu et al. 2022).

Machine learning models developed from a case-control study on Congenital cataracts achieved high discrimination, with an AUC of 0.91 in bilateral cases and 0.82 in unilateral cases (Lin et al. 2020). The model identified family history, low parental education, and comorbidity as significant predictors for screening congenital cataracts in remote areas.

A Canadian study used first-trimester foetal ultrasound images to develop a model for detecting cystic hygroma, achieving an accuracy of 93%, sensitivity of 92%, specificity of 94%, and AUC of 0.94 (Id et al. 2022). The model identified the foetal posterior cervical area as the primary predictor. Early identification of congenital anomalies allows for counseling parents and developing appropriate care plans.

10.2.5. Prediction of Gestational Diabetes Mellitus

Gestational diabetes mellitus (GDM) significantly contributes to adverse perinatal outcomes, and its prevalence is increasing. Current guidelines for assessing GDM risk have poor predictive ability. Initial management of GDM involves non-pharmacological methods such as diet modifications and physical activity. However, obstetricians face challenges interpreting diagnostic tests for GDM and making decisions regarding medical nutrition therapy and pharmacologic treatment options. Figure 10.5 illustrates the use of ML algorithms for predicting and managing GDM.

This section discusses the ML algorithms used to predict and manage GDM. In the 'Growing Up in Singapore Towards Healthy Outcomes (GUSTO)' cohort study, researchers analyzed data from 909 pregnancies. They developed a machine learning model using the CatBoost gradient boosting algorithm and Shapley feature attribution framework. The model incorporated four non-invasive variables: mean arterial blood pressure in the first trimester, age, ethnicity, and history of gestational diabetes mellitus (GDM). It showed excellent prediction ability, achieving an AUC of 0.82. This non-invasive approach offers practicality in reducing the economic burden associated with universal testing (Kumar, Chen, et al. 2022).

A stacked ensemble model, combining a gradient boosting classifier and linear support vector machine classifier, was developed using data from 222 women in the Singapore Preconception Study of Long-Term Maternal and Child Outcomes (S-PRESTO) cohort study. The model predicts that each mmol/mol increase in preconception HbA1c is associated with higher risks of gestational diabetes mellitus (GDM) (odds ratio 1.34) and preterm birth (odds ratio 1.63) (Kumar, Ang, et al. 2022). With inputs such as glycated hemoglobin A1c (HbA1c), blood pressure, fasting insulin, and triglycerides/HDL ratio, the model achieves an impressive AUC of 0.93. Furthermore, it can assess the risk of GDM even before pregnancy occurs.

In a population-based cohort of 30,474 pregnancies with gestational diabetes mellitus (GDM) in Northern California, researchers developed a machine learning algorithm. The algorithm considered the timing of GDM diagnosis, fasting glucose value, and the status and frequency of glycemic control at one-week post-diagnosis. The model exhibited good predictability, with a C-statistic of 0.83 in the discovery and 0.80 in the validation set, for determining the appropriate treatment modality for GDM at diagnosis (Liao et al. 2022). It also showed high predictability one-week post-diagnosis. These models have the potential to support algorithm-based risk stratification, inform timely treatment decisions, and enhance the overall management of GDM.

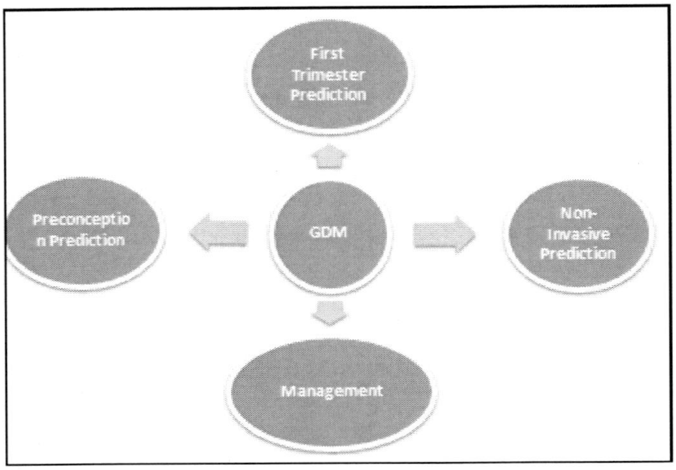

Figure 10.5. Application of Machine Learning in Gestational Diabetes Mellitus (GDM).

Researchers in China conducted a study with 1,139 pregnant women, including 186 with gestational diabetes mellitus, to develop a machine-learning algorithm for predicting GDM risk. The algorithm considered age, parity, pre-pregnancy BMI, abdomen circumference in the first trimester, PCOS, irregular menstruation, and family history of diabetes. The Random Forest model outperformed Logistic Regression, achieving a higher AUC (0.78 vs 0.76) and better discrimination ability in distinguishing GDM from non-GDM cases (Specificity: 0.81 vs 0.74) (Wang et al. 2021). Notably, all predictors used in the model can be obtained during the first trimester without requiring blood investigations, making it feasible for implementation even at primary healthcare centers.

10.2.6. Prediction of Preeclampsia

Preeclampsia is hypertension (blood pressure ≥ 140/90 mm Hg) in pregnant women first detected after 20 weeks of gestation, with significant proteinuria. It increases the risk of seizures, cardiovascular disease and acute renal failure in the mother. Preeclampsia can result in various adverse outcomes, including stillbirth, preterm birth, intrauterine growth restriction, and birth asphyxia. The management of pre-eclampsia primarily focuses on controlling high blood pressure and determining the appropriate timing for delivery based on the gestational age of the foetus.

The etiology of preeclampsia is complex. There are several predictors of pre-eclampsia, as shown in Figure10.6.

The current clinical guidelines have limitations in accurately identifying women at risk for Preeclampsia. Artificial intelligence and machine learning can be employed to develop strategies to predict the probability of pre-eclampsia. Table 2 provides an overview of recent studies that utilize machine learning models to predict preeclampsia. These models aim to enhance the early detection and management of this pregnancy complication. Various approaches and predictor variables were utilized, including extreme gradient boosting, deep neural networks, decision trees, support vector machines, and random forests. The reported accuracy and AUROC values highlight the effectiveness of these models in identifying individuals at risk of preeclampsia.

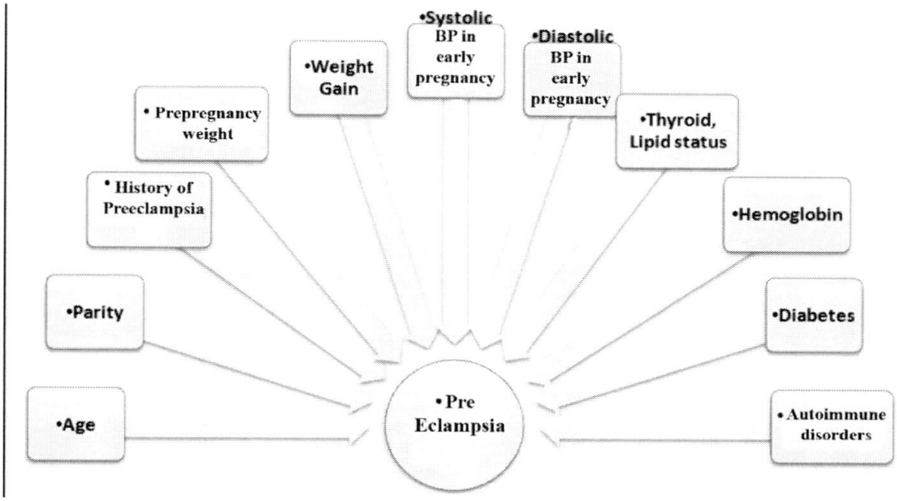

Figure 10.6. Predictors of Pre-eclampsia.

10.2.7. Prediction of Preterm Labor

Preterm birth describes a birth that occurs before 37 completed weeks of pregnancy. Fifteen million babies (10% of all births) are born prematurely yearly. Preterm birth is a significant contributor to neonatal morbidity and mortality. It is an enigmatic phenomenon with no definitive cause. The intricate interplay of multiple predictors complicates the clinical prediction of preterm labor, as illustrated in Figure 10.7.

Machine learning algorithms have emerged as a promising approach to predicting preterm birth risk by analyzing diverse clinical data. Table 3 summarizes studies from countries that employed various algorithms and participant populations to predict preterm delivery risk. These models incorporated predictor variables such as maternal health indicators, medical history, and demographic factors. The results demonstrate the effectiveness of these models to accurately identify individuals at risk.

10.3. Applications of AI in Delivery and Postpartum

AI can facilitate real-time monitoring during labor, anticipate and mitigate complications such as postpartum hemorrhage, deliver customized breastfeeding assistance, and predict postpartum depression. These applications can potentially enhance maternal and infant outcomes through prompt interventions and improved healthcare decision-making. This section will discuss using Artificial Intelligence (AI) in delivery and postpartum care.

Table 10.2. Characteristics of machine learning models developed to predict preeclampsia

Study	Design/Data Source	Participants	Prediction Model	Variables	Accuracy	AUROC
Shanghai, China (Li et al. 2021)	Electronic health records from antenatal care visits	3759	Extreme Gradient Boosting (XGBoost)	Fasting glucose, BP, body mass index	0.92	0.96
China (Liu et al. 2022)	Retrospective Cohort Study using records	11,057 patients of which 143 had preeclampsia.	Deep Neural Network, Logistic Regression, Support Vector Machine, Decision Tree, Random Forest	Maternal characteristics (Age, Weight, Height, BMI, Gestational age, method of conception, BP), medical history (Smoking, Hypertension, GDM, DM, Preeclampsia), prenatal laboratory results (Free β-HCG, PAPP-A)& Uterine Artery Pulsatality Index(Ut PI)	0.74	0.86
China (Liu et al. 2021)	Retrospective Study in EDEN Cohort	1648	Boost Tree-based model	C1431T variant of PPARγ, obesity, BMI, number of pregnancies, parity	0.97	0.991
Romania (Melinte-Popescu et al. 2023)	Prospective Case-Control Study at a tertiary maternity hospital	232 (116 with preeclampsia and 116 with control)	Decision tree (DT), Support Vector Machine (SVM), Naïve Bayes (NB), Random Forest (RF)	Age, BMI, Rural/urban, Parity, medical history of PE, hypertension, renal disease, diabetes, SLE/APS, Obesity, Interpregnancy interval, MAP, Uterine Artery PI	0.94 for DT, 0.91 for SVM, 0.98 for NB and 0.92 for RF	-
Seoul, Korea (S. M. Lee et al. 2021)	Retrospective Cohort Study	1347 healthy pregnant women	Graph-based semi-supervised learning	Weight, Systolic BP in early pregnancy, Diastolic BP in early pregnancy, Pre-pregnancy BMI, Hemoglobin	-	0.80

Table 10.3. ML algorithms predictions and characteristics

Study characteristics	Algorithm	Predictors	Model characteristics
Maternal records of 1300 women from a Community Health Centre in India (Raja et al. 2021)	Decision tree (DT), logistic regression (LR), and Support Vector Machine (SVM)	Age, Parity, BMI, ANC visit, Gestational age, Fetal heart rate, BP, Hemoglobin, GDM, Preeclampsia, Hypertension, Obstetric history, Education, Previous caesarean section	• SVM has an accuracy of 0.86, sensitivity of 0.80 & specificity of 0.71 • Supports identification of pregnant women at risk of preterm delivery in rural communities
124 maternal records from a hospital in India (Prema and Pushpalatha 2019)	Support Vector Machine, Logistic Regression (LR)	Age, parity, obesity, DM, GDM, hypertension	• SVM has an accuracy of 0.86 & sensitivity of 0.86. • The study had limited risk factors and a small sample size
Records of 25,689 deliveries in USA (Gao et al. 2020)	Recurrent Neural Network (RNN) ensemble models	Twin pregnancy, short cervical length, hypertensive disorder, systemic lupus erythematosus, hydroxychloroquine	• RNN has a Sensitivity of 0.965 & AUROC of 0.827 • Deep learning predicts extreme preterm birth 8 weeks in advance.
Records of 112,963 Women from a Retrospective Cohort Study in Canada (Belaghi et al. 2021)	Logistic Regression, Random Forest (RF), Artificial Neural Network (ANN), Decision tree	Diabetes, abnormal pregnancy-associated plasma protein A concentration in the first trimester, complications during pregnancy	• ANN has a sensitivity of 0.60 & AUROC of 0.80 • All models had high negative predictive values of around 0.97
770 women with Preterm birth & 770 controls in Uganda (Memon et al. 2022)	LR, RF, DT, SVM, K-Nearest Neighbours, and Naïve Bayes	Number of ANC visits, preeclampsia, age, weight, gravidity, birth spacing, previous Preterm, occupation	• SVM had Sensitivity of 0.64 & Specificity of 0.63
Population data from 38,76,666 mothers with live births in Brazil (Rocha et al. 2021)	eXtreme Gradient Boosting	Number of previous deliveries through Caesarean section, number of prenatal consultations, age, presence of ultrasound examination, proportion of primary care teams	• Ability to predict the week of delivery with Root-Mean-Square Error (RMSE) of 2.09

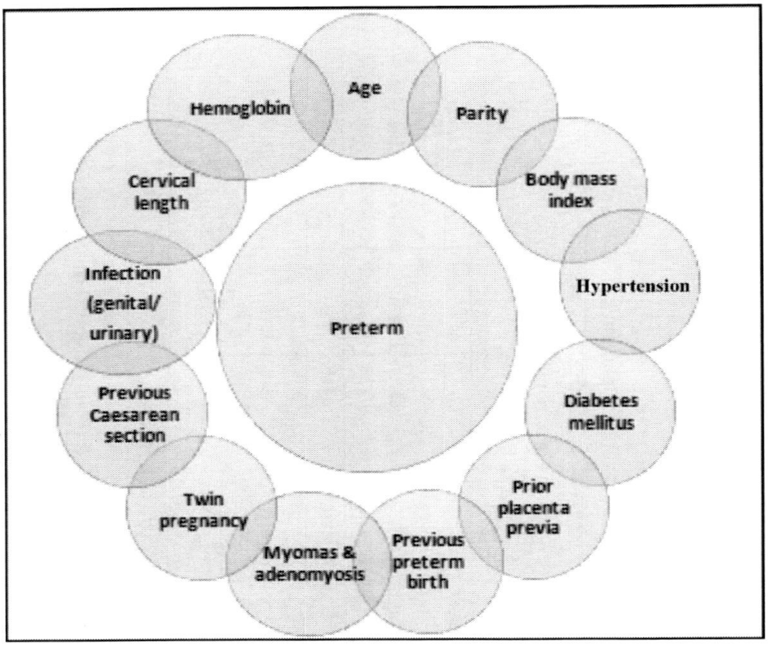

Figure 10.7. Predictors of preterm labour.

10.3.1. Real-Time Monitoring During Labor

Intrapartum complications contribute significantly to perinatal mortality. AI can track labor progression and provide real-time alerts to detect abnormalities. Timely intervention helps to reduce complications such as foetal distress or postpartum hemorrhage. Figure 10.8 demonstrates the application of Artificial Intelligence in real-time labor monitoring.

Cardiotocography (CTG) is a monitoring tool to assess foetal well-being during labor. CTG consists of foetal heart rate (FHR) and uterine contraction (UC) signals, as shown in Figure 10.9. Interpreting CTG data is complex and requires expertise.

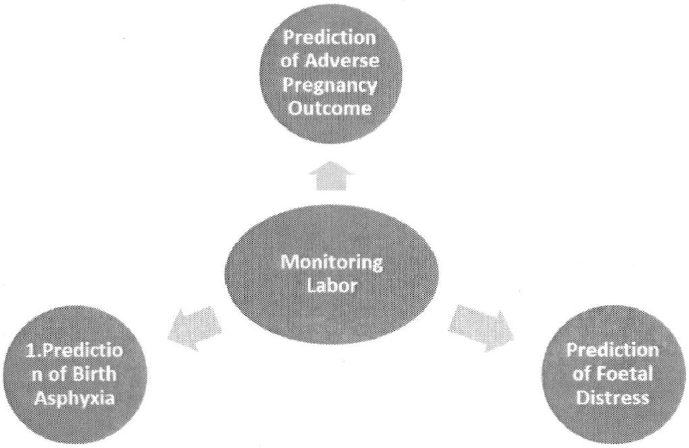

Figure 10.8. Application of Artificial Intelligence in Monitoring Labor.

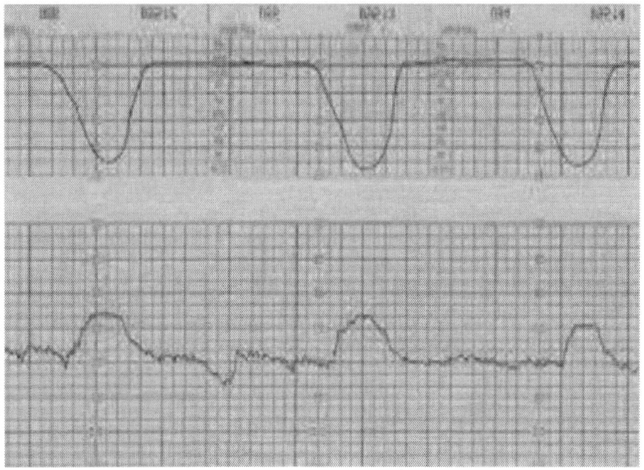

Early Deceleration
Head compression during active labor can cause a temporary decrease in foetal heart rate (FHR), but it is usually above 110-100 bpm.

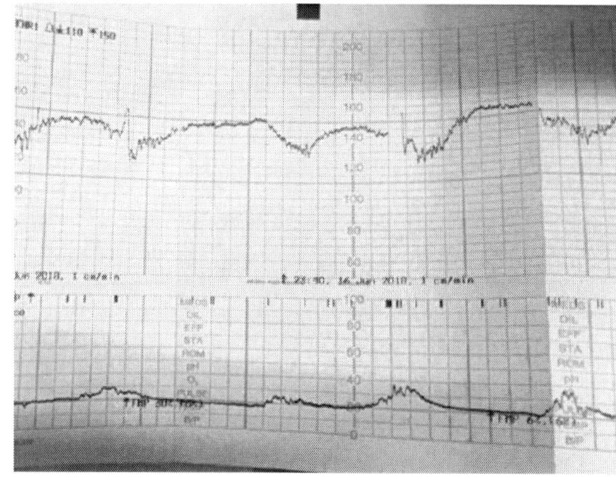

Late Deceleration
The decline in FHR starting after the peak of a contraction indicates uteroplacental dysfunction.

Figure 10.9. Cardiotocography images showing foetal heart rate (FHR) and uterine contraction (UC) signals.

ML algorithms analyze CTG data to detect foetal distress, aid decision-making in delivery, and prevent adverse outcomes. They can classify foetal heart rate signals and can be applied throughout labor. These models can be integrated into automated systems and used in peripheral settings for early referral. ML models predict birth asphyxia and forecast maternal outcomes, improving antenatal check-ups and mitigating adverse pregnancy outcomes. Table 10.4 presents the different machine learning models used in real-time labor monitoring. This leads to more effective interventions and a reduced risk of complications.

10.3.2. Postpartum Haemorrhage

Postpartum haemorrhage (PPH) is the cumulative loss of blood equal to or greater than 1000 ml within 24 hours after birth or the presence of symptoms or signs of hypovolemia. PPH is the leading cause of maternal mortality, responsible for 20% of maternal deaths annually. Machine learning methods identify women at risk for PPH and help clinicians to be prepared or refer them to higher centers. Figure 10.10 illustrates the various applications of AI in postpartum hemorrhage (PPH).

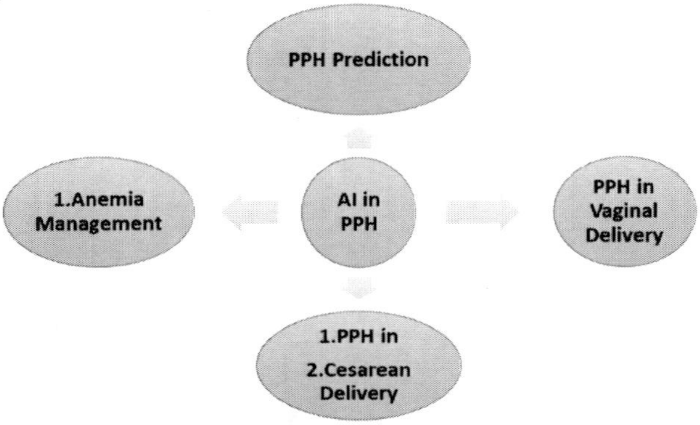

Figure 10.10. Application of Artificial Intelligence in Post-Partum Hemorrhage (PPH).

This section discusses the machine learning algorithms developed for postpartum hemorrhage (PPH). One study utilized data from 9,894 patients to develop machine-learning models for predicting PPH after vaginal birth. The deep-learning model achieved an AUC of 0.706 and an accuracy of 0.681, identifying gestation and pre-pregnancy weight as significant factors (Akazawa et al. 2021). Another study with 30,867 women and 2179 cases of postpartum hemorrhage used 471 variables and found that a gradient-boosted.

Early identification of potential problems enables healthcare providers to intervene proactively, decision tree (XGBoost) had an impressive AUC of 0.979, an accuracy of 98.1%, and a sensitivity of 76.3% for predicting postpartum hemorrhage. (Westcott et al. 2020). Caesarean delivery is a known risk factor for postpartum hemorrhage (PPH). Machine learning models have been developed to predict PPH after Cesarean delivery. A Random Forest model developed at Chongqing Medical University, China, achieved an AUC of 0.957 for the training set and 0.893 for the test set (Gong et al. 2022). Ten risk factors for PPH after Cesarean delivery, including placenta previa, gestational age, prothrombin time, and anemia, have been identified.

Table 10.4. Real-time labour monitoring

Study	Prediction Model	Predictor Variables	Outcome	Model Characteristics
University of California, USA (Hoodbhoy et al. 2019)	XGBoost	CTG data	Signs of fetal distress or complications	Accuracy of 0.92
Turkey (Cömert and Kocamaz 2017)	Support Vector Machine (SVM)	Fetal heart rate signals	Normal or pathological fetal state	Sensitivity of 0.99, specificity 0.97.
India (Das et al. 2023)	SVM, RF	CTG data	Enable automated decision support for each stage of labour	Sensitivity 0.96, specificity 0.98, AUC 0.97
Iran (Faysal et al. 2023)	Random Forest Classification	Maternal hypertension, anemia, diabetes, drug addiction, gestational age, gender, birth weight, preeclampsia, etc.	Birth asphyxia	Accuracy of 0.99
Bhubaneswar, Odisha, India (Panda et al. 2022)	Artificial Neural Networks (ANN)	Birth weight, systolic blood pressure, hemoglobin level, gestational age, maternal age, diastolic blood pressure	Maternal outcomes	Accuracy of 0.88
Iran (Darsareh et al. 2023)	Random Forest Classification	Maternal hypertension, anemia, diabetes, drug addiction, gestational age, gender, birth weight, preeclampsia, placenta abruption, etc.	Birth asphyxia	Accuracy of 0.99
Italy (S. M. Lee et al. 2021)	Artificial Neural Networks (ANN)	Perinatal variables available shortly after birth	Probability of death	Outperforms logistic regression

Fifty-five risk factors were considered in a study from the United States involving 152,279 births and 7,279 PPH cases. The Extreme Gradient Boosting model demonstrated excellent discrimination with a c-statistic of 0.93, followed by logistic regression (0.87), lasso (0.87), and random forest (0.92). All models showed superior net benefit when clinical decision thresholds were set between 0 to 80% of the predicted risk for postpartum hemorrhage (Venkatesh et al. 2020).

Iron deficiency anemia affects up to 50% of women during pregnancy in developing countries and is a risk factor for postpartum hemorrhage. Machine learning is being used to recognize women at risk for postpartum hemorrhage and targeting anemic women using scoring systems (Faysal et al. 2023).

10.3.3. Breastfeeding Support

The WHO recommends initiating breastfeeding within one hour of birth and continuing exclusive breastfeeding for the first six months of a baby's life. Breastfeeding should be complemented with semi-solid foods until the age of two. Exclusive breastfeeding provides crucial benefits for the baby's growth, development, and protection against infections. Unfortunately, statistics show that only one in four mothers initiate breastfeeding within the first hour of birth, and less than half practice exclusive breastfeeding for the recommended six-month duration.

ML algorithms have the potential to identify women who may face challenges with breastfeeding, such as low milk supply or nipple pain, and offer personalized guidance and real-time assistance. The Application of Artificial Intelligence in Breastfeeding is shown in Figure 10.11.

ML algorithms developed to support breastfeeding are discussed in this section. In a study involving 2,042 mothers in Spanish hospitals, XGBoost algorithms achieved promising results in predicting exclusive breastfeeding during the in-hospital postpartum stay. The algorithms had a PR AUC of 0.86, an accuracy of 0.75, and a Brier score of 0.17 (Oliver-Roig et al. 2022). The main predictors identified were pacifier use, breastfeeding self-efficacy, previous breastfeeding experience, birth weight, neonatal care unit admission, the timing of the first skin-to-skin contact, and Baby-Friendly Hospital Initiative accreditation.

Sentiment analysis was conducted on tweets using lexicon-based sentiment classifiers and machine learning techniques to understand the factors influencing positive or negative breastfeeding behaviors. The F1-score for VADER was 82.4%, and for Support Vector Machine (SVM), it was 73.7% (Oyebode et al. 2021). The analysis revealed that perceived benefits, self-efficacy, social support, and education and training support positively influenced breastfeeding. On the other hand, health, social, and psychological factors harm breastfeeding behaviors. Interventions addressing these negative aspects and promoting positive breastfeeding behaviors are recommended.

New mothers have limited knowledge about breastfeeding and experience anxiety, stress, postpartum depression, challenges, doubts, hesitations, and skepticism. A study from Jaipur has developed an AI-powered chatbot that responds to queries about breastfeeding and gives solutions (Arora et al. 2021).

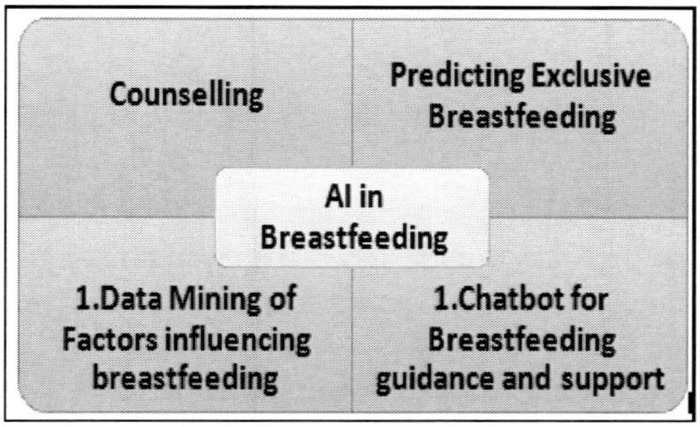

Figure 10.11. Application of Artificial Intelligence in breastfeeding.A survey in Ethiopia involved 6390 mothers who had breastfed and 445 mothers who had never breastfed in the previous year. Data mining techniques, specifically Decision Tree Rule Induction Algorithms, were used to identify breastfeeding practices and factors influencing them at individual and community levels. The J48 algorithm achieved an accuracy of 96.86% in classifying breastfeeding practices as standard, while the PART algorithm achieved an accuracy of 96.77% in classifying poor breastfeeding practices (Awalom et al. 2020). These algorithms can be utilized to develop a region-specific decision support model for promoting breastfeeding.

10.3.4. Postpartum Depression Prediction

Postpartum depression affects 10% of women after delivery, impacting their well-being and ability to care for themselves and their babies. However, the disorder often goes undiagnosed, leading to inadequate support and treatment. Table 10.5 highlights studies conducted in different countries, employing various machine learning algorithms and predictor variables to develop predictive models for postpartum depression.

The models demonstrate diverse performance metrics, including accuracy, sensitivity, specificity, positive predictive value, negative predictive value, and area under the curve. These models show promise in identifying women at high risk of postpartum depression and enabling early interventions to prevent its occurrence.

10.4. Medication Safety

ML algorithms can analyze vast amounts of Electronic Health Record data and identify potential risks related to medication use during pregnancy. By examining previous studies, these algorithms can identify drugs associated with congenital disabilities or other adverse outcomes. In a cohort study, researchers developed a random forest model to classify drugs of unknown pregnancy class. Their models achieved an accuracy of 91% for foetal loss and 87% for congenital anomalies. Based on their findings, fifty-seven category C medications were classified as harmful for foetal loss and eleven for congenital anomalies. This information is crucial in assessing the potential risks of prescribed drugs during pregnancy that lack a specific foetal safety recommendation, such as Category C drugs (Boland et al. 2017). AI algorithms are valuable tools for developing predictive models to identify patients at a high risk of experiencing adverse medication events during pregnancy. These models enable healthcare providers to create personalized medication management plans.

10.5. Clinical Decision System

Machine learning algorithms enable obstetricians to assess risk factors and make evidence-based decisions regarding emergency Cesarean sections. These algorithms consider factors like amniotic fluid quantity, nulliparity, induction of labor, and abnormal amniotic fluid characteristics to provide personalized risk assessments and treatment plans. These algorithms optimize decision-making, improve outcomes, and deliver individualised care to pregnant individuals by leveraging patient data and medical guidelines.

A risk-scoring system predicts Emergency Cesarean Section based on maternal and foetal factors (Guan et al. 2020). In Spain, a decision support system predicts the mode of delivery using 25,038 records from a university hospital. Support Vector Machines, Multilayer Perceptron, and Random Forest achieved >90% accuracy in classifying cesarean and vaginal deliveries (De Ramón Fernández et al. 2022). In Los Angeles, researchers developed an automated machine learning (AML) model to predict the probability of cesarean delivery at a hospital. The eXtreme Gradient Boosted Trees classifier was the most predictive model, considering factors such as gestational age, maternal age, pain score and quality, and dilation. The model achieved an AUC of 0.90 and accurately predicted vaginal and cesarean deliveries (Wong et al. 2020).

AI decision support systems using ML algorithms assist obstetricians in determining the appropriate mode of delivery, whether it be cesarean section, normal vaginal delivery, or instrumental vaginal delivery, for complex cases or dilemmas.

10.6 Explainable Artificial Intelligence

Explainable Artificial Intelligence (XAI) is a field that helps users understand how models make predictions and why they make those predictions. We can categorize the methods for achieving 'Explainability' based on scope (local or global), interpretation types (intrinsic or post hoc), and model specificity (model-specific or model-agnostic). Traditional machine learning models like artificial neural networks (ANN) and support vector machines (SVM) are often considered black box models, lacking transparency in their decision-making process. XAI addresses this by providing insights into prediction mechanisms, enhancing understanding and confidence in the model's results. Explainable Artificial Intelligence in Maternal Health is illustrated in Figure 10.12.

XAI can be applied in two ways when predicting maternal health care: 1) by utilizing post hoc XAI methods on black box ML models and 2) by employing intrinsic XAI models. These approaches enhance accuracy, improve models, and facilitate knowledge transfer. XAI is particularly valuable in identifying unknown symptoms and enabling early detection, leading to improved maternal health outcomes. XAI methods find application in various maternal health areas, as shown in Table 10.6.

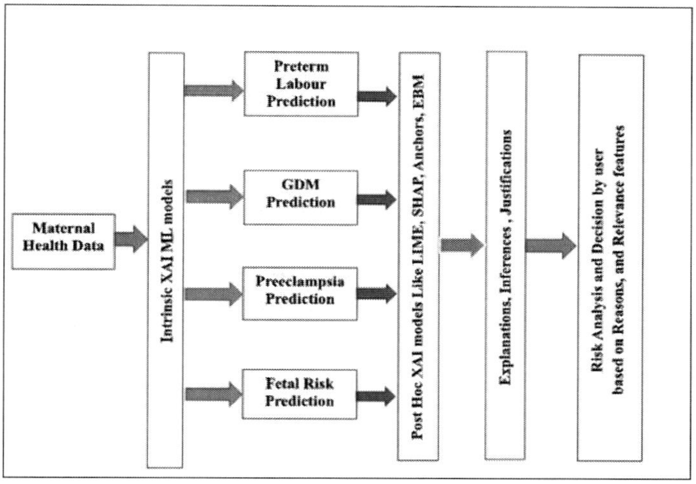

Figure 10.12. XAI in maternal health.

Intrinsic and post hoc methods like Local Interpretable Model-Agnostic Explanations (LIME), Shapley Additive Explanations (SHAP), Anchors and Explainable Boosting Machines (EBM) can be employed. By leveraging XAI feedback, these methods help identify unknown symptoms and understand underlying reasons for maternal health risk assessment.

10.7 Ethical and Legal Considerations

ML algorithms in maternal health require addressing critical ethical and legal considerations. Healthcare providers must inform and obtain informed consent from patients regarding AI algorithms. Equitable treatment and avoidance of biases are essential. Healthcare organizations should establish policies to handle liability and responsibility for potential mistakes or adverse outcomes. Patient data security must be ensured through encryption and access control measures. Health systems need to be transparent and accountable for decisions based on AI algorithms. Compliance with regulatory requirements is necessary for approving and implementing AI algorithms in clinical practice.

10.8 Challenges and Future Directions

Artificial Intelligence and machine learning have the potential to play an essential role in improving the accuracy of diagnosis and treatment, optimising hospital workflows, and providing personalized guidance and support to pregnant women. However, ensuring high-quality data for training and testing AI algorithms is a prerequisite for developing an ML algorithm. The next significant challenge is to interpret and understand the decisions made by AI algorithms. After designing AI/ML models, integration of algorithms with hospital systems and implementation of changes in clinical workflows are necessary. Ensuring compliance with regulatory and legal approvals is also essential. Addressing these challenges requires a multidisciplinary approach that involves obstetricians, nurses, public health officials, and other stakeholders.

Table 10.5. Postpartum depression prediction models

Study	Design	ML Model	Predictor Variables	Performance Metrics
Korea (Shin et al. 2020)	Retrospective cohort study using records of 3339 mothers with postpartum depression and 25,416 normal cases	Random Forest (RF), Support Vector Machine (SVM)	Patient records	Accuracy of 0.65-0.79. AUC for RF is 0.88, and for SVM is 0.86
Arab countries (Qasrawi et al. 2022)	Cross-sectional regional study in five Arab countries involving 1939 pregnant and 1630 postpartum women	Gradient Boosting (GB)	Stress during pregnancy, family support, financial issues, income, social support	Accuracy of 0.83 for depression and 0.81 for anxiety
Sweden (Andersson et al. 2021)	A population-based cohort study involving 4313 women.	Randomized Trees	Depression and anxiety during pregnancy, resilience, personality	Accuracy: 0.73 Sensitivity: 0.72 Specificity: 0.75 Positive Predictive Value: 0.33 Negative Predictive Value: 0.94 AUC:0.81
China (Zhang et al. 2020)	A cohort study of 508 women	Support Vector Machine (SVM)	Psychological elasticity, depression during the third trimester, income level	Sensitivity: 0.69 AUC: 0.78

Table 10.6. Explainable AI algorithms used in maternal health

Application in Maternal Health	Explainable AI Algorithm	Inference
Foetal health status Detection (Dwivedi et al. 2021)	Auto ML & XAI approach – SHAP technique	The model performs better than other ML models, with an accuracy of 95.61% for Foetal Heart Rate (FHR) through Cardiotocography (CTG).
Forecasting Cesarean section (Islam et al. 2022)	HGSORF model with SHAP and LIME XAI approaches	The model achieved 98.33% accuracy for the dataset and performed better than Gaussian Naive Bayes (GNB), linear discriminant analysis (LDA), K-nearest neighbors (KNN), gradient boosting classifier (GBC), and logistic regression (LR) models.
Fertility Treatment (Marvin and Alarm 2021)	Explainable Quantum Lattice Learning (QLL) model	The model achieved 100% accuracy in diagnostic assessment for fertility treatment
Clinical Decision Support Systems for pregnancy care (Du et al. 2023)	XAI model for CDSS	White box XAI models are currently in focus for CDSS systems for pregnancy care.
Foetal detection (Nagayasu et al. 2022)	XAI GRAD-CAM method	The XAI model achieved 85.8% accuracy in detecting foetal structures in comparison to 81.4% by the VGG16 model
Foetal position detection (Ishikawa et al. 2019)	CNN + Grad CAM	Recall ratios of the four classes are 99.6% for the head, 99.4% for the body, 99.8% for the legs, and 72.6% for the others.

10.9 Conclusion

Machine learning algorithms can analyze data and identify patterns from health records, foetal monitoring devices, and other sources and risk factors for complications such as gestational diabetes, pre-eclampsia, and preterm labor. This information can be used to develop predictive models to help healthcare providers identify women at high risk of these complications and intervene early to prevent or manage them. AI can help healthcare providers make more informed decisions about labor induction, cesarean delivery, and other interventions based on individual patient data and risk factors. AI can help healthcare providers deliver more personalized care to pregnant women by analyzing data on their medical history, lifestyle, and other factors. AI can provide more objective and consistent interpretations of ultrasound images and foetal heart rate monitoring, reducing the subjectivity in obstetric care.

Machine learning and AI are not meant to replace the expertise and judgment of obstetricians. Instead, they are complementary tools to support clinical decision-making and enhance patient outcomes. By leveraging the power of machine learning and AI, obstetricians can strengthen their decision-making, improve patient outcomes, and optimize resource allocation in maternity care.

References

Akazawa, Munetoshi, Kazunori Hashimoto, Noda Katsuhiko, and Yoshida Kaname. (2021). Machine learning approach for the prediction of postpartum hemorrhage in vaginal birth. *Scientific Reports* 11. Nature Publishing Group UK: 1–7. https://doi.org/10.1038/s41598-021-02198-y.

Andersson, Sam, Deepti R. Bathula, Stavros I. Iliadis, Martin Walter, and Alkistis Skalkidou. (2021). Predicting women with depressive symptoms postpartum with machine learning methods. *Scientific Reports* 11. Nature Publishing Group UK: 1–15. https://doi.org/10.1038/s41598-021-86368-y.

Arora, Nikita, Yash Jain, Vaishnavi Gupta, Sushil Mokashi, and Chiranjibi Panda. (2021). Assessment on Adoption Behavior of First-time Mothers on the Usage of Chatbots for Breastfeeding Consultation. *Journal of Mahatma Gandhi University of Medical Sciences and Technology* 6: 64–68. https://doi.org/10.5005/jp-journals-10057-0161.

Awalom, Taddele Weldeslassie, Mesaud Mohamodbrhan Adem, and Mearg Araya. (2020). Prediction Model for Breastfeeding practice among Ethiopian Children using Decision tree and Rule induction Algorithms : Data mining. *PREPRINT (Version 1) available at Research Square.* https://doi.org/10.21203/rs.3.rs-58065/v1:1–15.

Bahado-Singh, Ray, Perry Friedman, Ciara Talbot, Buket Aydas, Siddesh Southekal, Nitish K. Mishra, Chittibabu Guda, Ali Yilmaz, Uppala Radhakrishna, and Sangeetha Vishweswaraiah. (2023). Cell-free DNA in maternal blood and artificial intelligence: accurate prenatal detection of foetal congenital heart defects. *American Journal of Obstetrics and Gynecology* 228. The Authors: 76.e1-76.e10. https://doi.org/10.1016/j.ajog.2022.07.062.

Belaghi, Reza Arabi, Joseph Beyene, and Sarah D. McDonald. (2021). Prediction of preterm birth in nulliparous women using logistic regression and machine learning. *PLoS ONE* 16: 58–62. https://doi.org/10.1371/journal.pone.0252025.

Boland, Mary Regina, Fernanda Polubriaginof, and Nicholas P Tatonetti. (2017). Development of A Machine Learning Algorithm to Classify Drugs Of Unknown Foetal Effect. *Scientific Reports.* Springer US: 1–15. https://doi.org/10.1038/s41598-017-12943-x.

Cömert, Z., and A. F. Kocamaz. (2017). Comparison of machine learning techniques for foetal heart rate classification. *Acta Physica Polonica A* 132: 451–454. https://doi.org/10.12693/APhysPolA.132.451.

Darsareh, Fatemeh, Amene Ranjbar, Mohammadsadegh Vahidi Farashah, Vahid Mehrnoush, and Mitra Shekari. 2023. Application of machine learning to identify risk factors of birth asphyxia. *BMC Pregnancy and Childbirth* 9: 1–7.

Das, Sahana, Himadri Mukherjee, Kaushik Roy, and Chanchal Kumar Saha.(2023). Foetal Health Classification from Cardiotocograph for Both Stages of Labor—A Soft-Computing-Based Approach. *Diagnostics* 13: 1–24. https://doi.org/10.3390/diagnostics13050858.

Du, Yuhan, Catherine McNestry, Lan Wei, Anna Markella Antoniadi, Fionnuala M. McAuliffe, and Catherine Mooney. (2023). Machine learning-based clinical decision support systems for pregnancy care: A systematic review. *International Journal of Medical Informatics* 173. Elsevier B.V.: 105040. https://doi.org/10.1016/j.ijmedinf.2023.105040.

Dwivedi, Prakriti, Akbar Ali Khan, Sareeta Mugde, and Garima Sharma. (2021). Diagnosing the major contributing factors in the classification of the foetal health status using cardiotocography measurements: An AutoML and XAI approach. In *2021 13th International Conference on Electronics, Computers and Artificial Intelligence (ECAI)*, 1–6. Institute of Electrical and Electronics Engineers Inc. https://doi.org/10.1109/ECAI52376.2021.9515033.

Faysal, Hani, Tarek Araji, and Homa K. Ahmadzia. (2023). Recognizing who is at risk for postpartum hemorrhage: targeting anemic women and scoring systems for clinical use. *American Journal of Obstetrics and Gynecology MFM* 5. Elsevier Inc.: 100745. https://doi.org/10.1016/j.ajogmf.2022.100745.

Fung, Russell, Jose Villar, Ali Dashti, Leila Cheikh Ismail, Eleonora Staines-Urias, Eric O. Ohuma, Laurent J. Salomon, et al. (2020). Achieving accurate estimates of foetal gestational age and personalized predictions of foetal growth based on data from an international prospective cohort study: a population-based machine learning study. *The Lancet Digital Health* 2: e368–e375. https://doi.org/10.1016/S2589-7500(20)30131-X.

Gao, Cheng, Sarah Osmundson, Digna R. Velez Edwards, Gretchen Purcell Jackson, Bradley A. Malin, and You Chen. (2020). Deep Learning Predicts Extreme Preterm Birth from Electronic Health Records. *J Biomed Inform.* 100. https://doi.org/10.1053/j.gastro.2016.08.014.CagY.

Gong, Jun, Zhi Chen, Yi Zhang, Yi yun Liu, Jun cai Pu, Chun yan Xiong, Si wen Gui, Xiao ling He, Hui lai Wang, and Xiao gang Zhong. (2022). Risk-factor model for postpartum hemorrhage after cesarean delivery: a retrospective study based on 3498 patients. *Scientific Reports* 12. Nature Publishing Group UK: 1–9. https://doi.org/10.1038/s41598-022-23636-5.

Guan, Ping, Fei Tang, Guoqiang Sun, and Wei Ren. (2020). Prediction of emergency cesarean section by measurable maternal and foetal characteristics. *Journal of Investigative Medicine* 68: 799–806. https://doi.org/10.1136/jim-2019-001175.

Hoodbhoy, Zahra, Uswa Jiwani, Saima Sattar, Rehana Salam, Babar Hasan, and Jai K Das. (2021). Diagnostic Accuracy of Machine Learning Models to Identify Congenital Heart Disease : A Meta-Analysis. *Frontiers in Artificial Intelligence* 4: 1–8. https://doi.org/10.3389/frai.2021.708365.

Hoodbhoy, Zahra, Mohammad Noman, Ayesha Shafique, Ali Nasim, Devyani Chowdhury, and Babar Hasan. (2019). Use of machine learning algorithms for prediction of foetal risk using cardiotocographic data. *International Journal of Applied and Basic Medical Research* 9: 226. https://doi.org/10.4103/ijabmr.ijabmr_370_18.

Id, Mark C Walker, Inbal Willner, Olivier X Miguel, Malia S Q Murphy, Felipe Moretti, Alysha L J Dingwall Harvey, Ruth Rennicks, Darine El-chaa, and Richard I Aviv. (2022). Using deep-learning in foetal ultrasound analysis for diagnosis of cystic hygroma in the first trimester. *PloS one* 94: 88–98. https://doi.org/10.1371/journal.pone.0269323.

Ishikawa, Genta, Rong Xu, Jun Ohya, and Hiroyasu Iwata. (2019). Detecting a foetus in ultrasound images using grad CAM and locating the foetus in the uterus. *ICPRAM 2019 - Proceedings of the 8th International Conference on Pattern Recognition Applications and Methods*: 181–189. https://doi.org/10.5220/0007385001810189.

Islam, Md Saiful, Md Abdul Awal, Jinnaton Nessa Laboni, Farhana Tazmim Pinki, Shatu Karmokar, Khondoker Mirazul Mumenin, Saad Al-Ahmadi, Md Ashfikur Rahman, Md Shahadat Hossain, and Seyedali Mirjalili. (2022). HGSORF: Henry Gas Solubility Optimization-based Random Forest for C-Section prediction and XAI-based cause analysis. *Computers in Biology and Medicine* 147. Pergamon: 105671. https://doi.org/10.1016/J.COMPBIOMED.2022.105671.

Kumar, Mukkesh, Li Ting Ang, Hang Png, Maisie Ng, Karen Tan, See Ling Loy, Kok Hian Tan, et al. (2022). Automated Machine Learning (AutoML)-Derived Preconception Predictive Risk Model to Guide Early Intervention for Gestational Diabetes Mellitus. *International Journal of Environmental Research and Public Health* 19: 1–17. https://doi.org/10.3390/ijerph19116792.

Kumar, Mukkesh, Li Chen, Karen Tan, Li Ting Ang, Cindy Ho, Gerard Wong, Shu E. Soh, et al. (2022). Population-centric risk prediction modeling for gestational diabetes mellitus: A machine learning approach. *Diabetes Research and Clinical Practice* 185: 109237. https://doi.org/10.1016/j.diabres.2022.109237.

Lee, Chace, Angelica Willis, Christina Chen, Marcin Sieniek, Amber Watters, Bethany Stetson, Akib Uddin, et al. (2023). Development of a Machine Learning Model for Sonographic Assessment of Gestational Age. *JAMA Network Open* 6: E2248685. https://doi.org/10.1001/jamanetworkopen.2022.48685.

Lee, Lok Hin, Elizabeth Bradburn, Rachel Craik, Mohammad Yaqub, Shane A. Norris, Leila Cheikh Ismail, Eric O. Ohuma, et al. (2023). Machine learning for accurate estimation of foetal gestational age based on ultrasound images. *npj Digital Medicine* 6. https://doi.org/10.1038/s41746-023-00774-2.

Lee, Seung Mi, Yonghyun Nam, Eun Saem Choi, Young Mi Jung, Jacob Leiby, Ja Nam Koo, Ig Hwan Oh, et al. (2021). Early prediction of pregnancy-associated hypertension : Development of novel strategies with semi-supervised learning. *American Journal of Obstetrics and Gynecology* 224. Elsevier: S309–S310. https://doi.org/10.1016/j.ajog.2020.12.508.

Li, Yi-xin xin, Xiao-ping ping Shen, Chao Yang, Zuo-zeng zeng Cao, Rui Du, Min-da da Yu, Jun-ping ping Wang, and Mei Wang. (2021). Novel electronic health records applied for prediction of pre-eclampsia: Machine-learning algorithms. *Pregnancy Hypertension* 26. Elsevier B.V.: 102–109. https://doi.org/10.1016/j.preghy.2021.10.006.

Liao, Lauren D., Assiamira Ferrara, Mara B. Greenberg, Amanda L. Ngo, Juanran Feng, Zhenhua Zhang, Patrick T. Bradshaw, Alan E. Hubbard, and Yeyi Zhu. (2022). Development and validation of prediction models for gestational diabetes treatment modality using supervised machine learning: a population-based cohort study. *BMC medicine* 20. BioMed Central: 307. https://doi.org/10.1186/s12916-022-02499-7.

Lin, Duoru, Jingjing Chen, Zhuoling Lin, Xiaoyan Li, Kai Zhang, Xiaohang Wu, Zhenzhen Liu, et al. (2020). A practical model for the identification of congenital cataracts using machine learning. *EBioMedicine* 51. Elsevier B.V.: 102621. https://doi.org/10.1016/j.ebiom.2019.102621.

Liu, Fulin, Christine Rouault, Karine Clément, Wencan Zhu, Séverine A. Degrelle, Marie Aline Charles, Barbara Heude, and Thierry Fournier. (2021). C1431T variant of PPARγ is associated with preeclampsia in pregnant women. *Life* 11: 1–15. https://doi.org/10.3390/life11101052.

Marvin, Ggaliwango, and Md Golam Rabiul Alarm. (2021). An Explainable Lattice based Fertility Treatment Outcome Prediction Model for TeleFertility. *Proceedings of 2021 IEEE International Conference on Biomedical Engineering, Computer and Information Technology for Health, BECITHCON 2021*. Institute of Electrical and Electronics Engineers Inc.: 64–68. https://doi.org/10.1109/BECITHCON54710.2021.9893623.

Melinte-Popescu, Alina Sinziana, Ingrid Andrada Vasilache, Demetra Socolov, and Marian Melinte-Popescu. (2023). Predictive Performance of Machine Learning-Based Methods for the Prediction of Preeclampsia—A Prospective Study. *Journal of Clinical Medicine* 12. https://doi.org/10.3390/jcm12020418.

Memon, Shaheen, Robert Wamala, and Ignace Kabano.(2022). Machine Learning Prediction of Preterm Birth: An Analysis of Facility-Based Paper Health Records in Uganda. *Preprint(Version 1) available at Research Square*: 1–15.

Nagayasu, Y., S Yamada, R. Mitsuhashi, M. Nunode, M. Sawada, A. Sugimoto, T Sano, D. Fujita, and M Ohmichi. (2022). Visualisation of assessments of explainable AI: determination of difference between the upper arm and thigh in foetal ultrasound using Grad-CAM. *Ultrasound in Obstetrics & Gynecology 2022* 60. https://doi.org/10.1002/uog.25705.

Oliver-Roig, Antonio, Juan Ramón Rico-juan, Miguel Richart-Martínez, and Julio Cabrero-garcía. (2022). Predicting exclusive breastfeeding in maternity wards using machine learning techniques. *Computer Methods and Programs in Biomedicine* 221. Elsevier B.V.: 106837. https://doi.org/10.1016/j.cmpb.2022.106837.

Oyebode, Oladapo, RICHARD LOMOTEY, and RITA ORJI. (2021)." I Tried to Breastfeed but . . .": Exploring Factors Influencing Breastfeeding Behaviours Based on Tweets Using Machine Learning and Thematic Analysis. *IEEE Access* 9.

Panda, Nihar Ranjan, Jitendra Kumar Pati, Tapsi Pati, Soumya Satpathy, and Ruchi Bhuyan. (2022). Comparison Of Artificial Neural Network and Decision Tree Methods for Predicting the Maternal Outcome in A Tertiary Care Hospital in Odisha, India. *National Journal of Community Medicine* 13: 821–827. https://doi.org/10.55489/njcm.131120222262.

Peters, Olivia, Donna A. Santillan, William Ray, Christopher Bartlett, Aaron Trask, and Mark K. Santillan. (2023). Machine learning of umbilical artery doppler flow improves prognostication in foetal growth restriction. *American Journal of Obstetrics and Gynecology* 228. Elsevier Inc.: S359. https://doi.org/10.1016/j.ajog.2022.11.629.

Prema, N. S., and M. P. Pushpalatha. (2019). *Machine Learning Approach for Preterm Birth Prediction Based on Maternal Chronic Conditions. Lecture Notes in Electrical Engineering*. Vol. 545. Springer Singapore. https://doi.org/10.1007/978-981-13-5802-9_52.

Qasrawi, Radwan, Malak Amro, Stephanny VicunaPolo, Diala Abu Al-Halawa, Hazem Agha, Rania Abu Seir, Maha Hoteit, et al. (2022). Machine learning techniques for predicting depression and anxiety in pregnant and postpartum women during the COVID-19 pandemic: A cross-sectional regional study. *F1000Research* 11. https://doi.org/10.12688/f1000research.110090.1.

Qu, Yanji, Xinlei Deng, Shao Lin, Fengzhen Han, Howard H Chang, Yanqiu Ou, and Shao Lin. (2022). Using Innovative Machine Learning Methods to Screen and Identify Predictors of Congenital Heart Diseases. *Frontiers in Cardiovascular Medicine* 8: 1–12. https://doi.org/10.3389/fcvm.2021.797002.

Raja, Rakesh, Indrajit Mukherjee, and Bikash Kanti Sarkar. 2021. A Machine Learning-Based Prediction Model for Preterm Birth in Rural India. *Journal of Healthcare Engineering* (2021). https://doi.org/10.1155/2021/6665573.

De Ramón Fernández, Alberto, Daniel Ruiz Fernández, and María Teresa Prieto Sánchez. (2022). Prediction of the mode of delivery using artificial intelligence algorithms. *Computer Methods and Programs in Biomedicine* 219. Elsevier Ireland Ltd. https://doi.org/10.1016/j.cmpb.2022.106740.

Rocha, Thiago Augusto Hernandes, Erika Bárbara Abreu Fonseca de Thomaz, Dante Grapiuna de Almeida, Núbia Cristina da Silva, Rejane Christine de Sousa Queiroz, Luciano Andrade, Luiz Augusto Facchini, et al. (2021). Data-driven risk stratification for preterm birth in Brazil: a population-based study to develop of a machine learning risk assessment approach. *The Lancet Regional Health - Americas* 3. Elsevier Ltd. https://doi.org/10.1016/j.lana.2021.100053.

Shin, Dayeon, Kyung Ju Lee, Temidayo Adeluwa, and Junguk Hur. (2020). Machine learning-based predictive modeling of postpartum depression. *Journal of Clinical Medicine* 9: 1–14. https://doi.org/10.3390/jcm9092899.

Venkatesh, Kartik K., Robert Strauss, Chad Grotegut, Phillips Heine, David M. Stamilio, Kathryn Menard, and Eric Jelovsek. (2020). Machine learning-based prediction models for postpartum hemorrhage. *American Journal of Obstetrics and Gynecology* 222. Elsevier Inc.: S175–S176. https://doi.org/10.1016/j.ajog.2019.11.272.

Wang, Jingyuan, Bohan Lv, Xiujuan Chen, Yueshuai Pan, Kai Chen, Yan Zhang, Qianqian Li, Lili Wei, and Yan Liu. (2021). An early model to predict the risk of gestational diabetes mellitus in the absence of blood examination indexes: application in primary health care centers. *BMC Pregnancy and Childbirth* 21. BioMed Central: 1–8. https://doi.org/10.1186/s12884-021-04295-2.

Westcott, Jill M., Francine Hughes, Wenke Liu, Mark Grivainis, David L. Keefe, Iffath A. Hoskins, and David Fenyö. (2020). 638: Prediction of maternal hemorrhage: using machine learning to identify patients at risk. *American Journal of Obstetrics and Gynecology* 222: S407. https://doi.org/10.1016/j.ajog.2019.11.653.

Wong, Melissa S., Matthew Wells, and Kimberly D. Gregory. (2020). 567: Building a better Bishop: using machine learning to develop real-time cesarean delivery predictions. *American Journal of Obstetrics and Gynecology* 222. Elsevier Inc.: S363–S364. https://doi.org/10.1016/j.ajog.2019.11.583.

World Health Organisation. (2023). *Born Too Soon.: Decade of Action on Preterm Birth. World Health Organisation*. Geneva: World Health Organization. https://doi.org/10.3828/liverpool/9781949979688.003.0009.

Zhang, Weina, Han Liu, Vincent Michael Bernard Silenzio, Peiyuan Qiu, and Wenjie Gong. (2020). Machine learning models for the prediction of postpartum depression: Application and comparison based on a cohort study. *JMIR Medical Informatics* 8: 1–19. https://doi.org/10.2196/15516.

Chapter 11

Heart Disease Prediction Using Machine Learning Algorithm with Explainable Artificial Intelligence for Health Care System

M. Deepa[1]
M. Angulakshmi[2]
Ayush Chhabra[3]
and Feslin Anish Mon[4]
[1, 2, 3]Vellore Institute of Technology, Vellore, India
[4]University of Technology and Applied Sciences, Ibri, Sultanate of Oman

Abstract

Based on the reports by WHO, nearly 18 million people (about the population of New York) all around the world are affected because of heart disease every year, so diagnosis of heart disease in its early stage can save millions of lives. Nowadays ML and AI are widely being used in the healthcare sector to find the cure for a disease or medical research using data retrieved from different patients. As data and attributes change, it gets more difficult to predict diseases since different approaches have varying degrees of accuracy. In today's world, there is an enormous need for understanding and comprehensibility of decision models. The classification models' reliability can be accomplished by deploying them in the explainable Artificial Intelligence (XAI) framework. The paper deals with the analysis of heart illness based on electronic well-being information, with the utilization of machine learning techniques. Logistic Regression, Random Forest, and K-nearest neighbor (KNN) with explainable Artificial Intelligence (XAI) are applied to the experimental data. The methods are compared with one another to find the best method that detects heart diseases accurately. Further, the need for transparency is achieved by explainable Artificial Intelligence (XAI) to explain which features are causing heart disease and how a model reached a certain conclusion. All of these algorithms' experimental outcomes are assessed against one another and to the standard way of executing machine learning models. Among the considered methods, Random Forest produced a higher accuracy of about 83% with XAI techniques.

Keywords: explainable Artificial Intelligence (XAI), K-nearest neighbour (KNN), logistic regression, random forest

In: Explainable Artificial Intelligence in Healthcare Systems
Editors: A. Anitha Kamaraj and Debi Prasanna Acharjya
ISBN: 979-8-89113-598-7

11.1 Introduction

Healthcare could become more affordable, efficient, personalized, and progressive with the help of Artificial Intelligence (AI), Machine Learning and Deep Learning. Even though humans have the greatest minds, still they lack a few things that make us depend on the machine. While humans are good at pattern recognition, a person cannot process a huge amount of data, machines can process huge amounts of data and with various techniques or methods, they can even recognize patterns. In the medical field everyday billions of data are generated. If these data are utilized properly there will be drastic growth in health care.

Heart Disease has become the major cause of death nowadays. Mainly, Blockage in arteries causes heart stroke. When the tissues in the cardiovascular system suffer injury and dysfunction, heart disease can develop. The causes of why some people acquire heart disease and others do not are unknown, even though researchers have shown that inherited and environmental factors influence a person's chance of acquiring heart disease. Although there are medical tools that can predict heart disorders, they are either expensive or people do not have time for check-ups. In most countries, access to good doctors and hospitals is rare. There is a need for a way to check-up for heart disease which is easy and accessible to all. ML can be used to simplify this task by analyzing the hidden pattern from the patient's medical history that could facilitate making wise decisions.

This paper discusses how heart disease can be predicted using machine learning with different algorithms like logistic regression, random forest KNN etc. Furthermore, to prevent making the wrong decision with certain results, explanation and tracing of results must be done and by which factor a person can develop heart disease Explainable AI (XAI) will be used so that one can trust the system.

Logistic regression is a supervised learning technique also known as sigmoid function. Examining the relationship between one or more independent variables predicts a dependent data variable (Tania et al. 2020). In logistic regression, the dependent variable is represented as a binary variable that is either 0 (No) or 1 (Yes), but instead of giving the exact value as 0 or 1, It provides probabilistic values that range from 0 to 1 (Saw M et al. 2020). The lasso model is a traditional logistic regression produced using the lasso version's logistic regression. The factors are evaluated using a cost function and part of the factors will be set to zero. Eliminating variables that are only marginally connected with the outcome enhances interpretability and performs variable selection. In terms of predicting mortality, neural networks repeatedly displayed inferior discriminative capacity and significant miscalibration. ML is used to find new covariates to improve the logistic regression models that did not generally lead to an improvement in AUC despite considering over 100 factors, including drugs taken before hospital entrance. Furthermore, calibration revealed information about the ideal mode was discovered by comparing all the models (Austin et al. 2022).

Random forest is a supervised learning method that builds several decision trees. (Jabbar et al. 2016) One of the best ensemble classification methods employs the bagging principle to merge different decision trees to improve prediction abilities. Individual students are instructed independently in bagging. Each decision tree is trained using a separate sample of data, and replacement is used to create multiple random samples of data from the original dataset. Additionally, features are chosen at random while building the tree. A majority vote is used to predict by integrating numerous trees. Classify the sample data by combining the prediction results of several k-tree classifiers based on the majority vote rule. The combined splitter H is created as an aggregation of each splitter Hk, $k = 1, \ldots, K$ and the example di is classified to class cj according to the number of votes obtained from the splitter Hk. By using the formula p (m, n), where n is a set of uniformly distributed random vectors. Each attribute of the decision tree is expended by highlighting the input m. Each is to create q samples for the Q input sample, where Q is largely equivalent to the training set samples, and then based on column sampling, f features are derived from F features. The number N was picked at random, and the training sets will be S1, S2, . . ., Sk. The matching training sets will be used to create the decision tree T1, T2, Tk. Aside from pruning, every tree in the forest is fully grown (Javeed et al. 2019).

K-nearest neighbor is a supervised machine learning algorithm. (Rahmat et al. 2021) It compares newly discovered cases and data to those already known, classifying them as being the most likely existing cases. It primarily serves regression and classification purposes. It is memory-based and appropriate for use with tiny datasets. Even though its performance was evaluated by the number of neighbors. Whenever the parameters are continuous in those situations KNN is preferred. By estimating the closest neighbor, the objects are categorized. KNN is a candid algorithm which can address classification problems and it is very simple to use and processing very fast. This algorithm is very efficient in identifying the heart disease of patients.

The method for finding the nearest k generally uses the Euclidean distance formula. Here is the Euclidean distance formula in the KNN algorithm. Explainable AI (XAI): The Reason to introduce Explainable AI is that one cannot confidently say the predicted result is true based on some mathematical expression even if it is true. XAI not only explains the result, but it also can be used to improve the models. The most well-known XAI methods include SHAP (Shapley Additive explanations), DeepSHAP, CXplain, and LIME. In LIME, the process is composed of the Sampling of features using the prediction model that is being used and the creation of a surrogate dataset which is further used in feature selection based on the Lasso technique to find the most important features.

To improve the capacity of the machine learning model, XAI is introduced to raise the effectiveness of AI. It improves the precision with which machine learning models forecast the future and generates explanations for how these models work, particularly for neural network models and deep learning. Chest X-rays have been used to deploy CNN-based models to identify and confirm pediatric pneumonia (Ravi et al. 2022).

LIME is a technique that estimates any black box machine learning model with an indigenous, interpretable prototype to elucidate each discrete estimate (Ribeiro et al. 2018).

The model is more transparent thanks to the SHAP approach. To analyses our deep learning model and rank the feature, Deep SHAP is used. Deep SHAP is a deep learning interpreted model that combines SHAP value with Deep LIFT theory. By assigning weights to each feature of the input during backpropagation, Deep LIFT can be used to understand deep learning models. Causal explanation (CXPlain) models that discover how much a given input influences a different machine-learning model's outputs. Once trained, CXPlain can quickly explain the target model and allows for the assessment of the uncertainty surrounding its feature importance estimates with bootstrap ensemble approach (Schwab et al. 2019).

11.2 Literature Survey

In the paper, (Ciu, 2020) the author examined the human cardiovascular system based on some variables and analyzed the correlation between variables, split data and conducted the prediction using a logistic regression algorithm. This process is further modified by (Saw, 2020) and by adding a random search technique where the optimum answer for the created model is obtained by using random combinations of the hyperparameters and predicting the heart disease with 87% accuracy. The author adds a random search technique where the optimum answer for the created model is obtained by using random combinations of the hyperparameters and predicting heart disease with 87% accuracy. The algorithms achieved high levels of accuracy, with results of 91.67% and 80.00%, respectively. Additionally, the experiment's findings indicated that logistic regression outperformed stochastic gradient descent concerning accuracy, precision, F-measure, and recall value.

It is crucial to transform the dataset using the Power transform approach to deliver a satisfactory score. Kernel PCA, a dimension reduction approach, was utilized to reduce the number of features from 13 to as few as 5, enhancing the efficacy of the model concerning both accuracy and computing performance. The logistic regression model's primary hyperparameters, such as solver, max-iterations, random-state, etc., are tuned using the Grid Search/Random Search approach to produce a perfect score for the Heart Disease Prediction Model. Out of 6 machine learning models, the best model (Random Forest) was chosen through training, hyperparameter tuning, and cross-validation. (Rahmat et al. 2021) used feature selection for KNN and standardization of the dataset to improve the accuracy of heart disease prediction. They used methods for data preparation and feature selection with Select best, and KNN imputation. 10-Fold cross-validation is used to validate the performance. This also presents better precision of 95.50%, recall of 84.16%, and accuracy of 89.28%. Their study offers an alternative method for processing processed data on heart disease prediction.

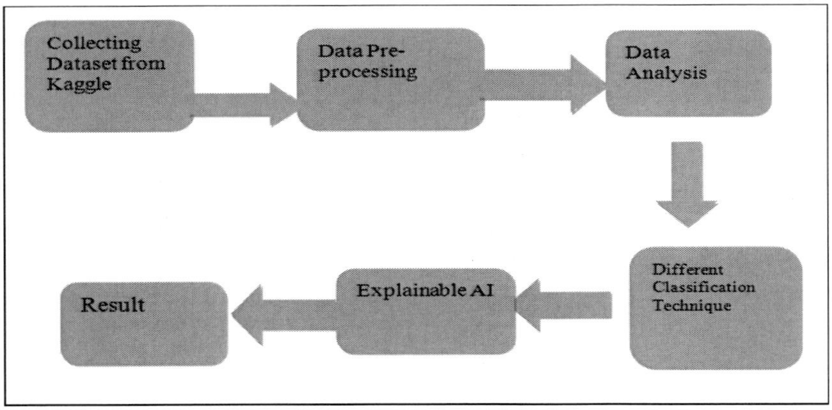

Figure 11.1. Proposed Method.

(Reddy, 2021) the author compares Support Vector Machine with (SVM) and Dynamic KNN (DKNN) where he got the mean accuracy of 80.29% in DKNN and 69.048% in SVM and concluded that DKNN performs better than SVM. A study on heart disease prediction showed that the random forest algorithm outperforms the KNN in predicting heart disease.

Decision Tree and K-Nearest Neighbor are examined. Using a dataset with 1700 records. In this research compared to KNN (82%), the Decision tree had better accuracy (86%). The explanations produced by XAI methods should be helpful for the end-users, who may be professionals with knowledge in health care. Pedro A. Moreno-Sanchez et al. 2020) this paper demonstrates a heart failure survival prediction model created by machine learning ensemble trees approaches. With unseen data, the classifier Extreme Gradient Boosting (XGBoost) produced the most accurate results, with an accuracy rate of roughly 83%. The choice of features that contributed to reliable results was made during the data preparation. It computes the accuracy and illustrates the ability of an ensemble trees machine learning model for the prediction of heart failure survival. In this paper, the author listed a few characteristics, including "follow-up period," "serum creatinine," "ejection percentage," and "anemia," that significantly influenced the model's results. Ritu Aggarwal et al. conducted a study using machine learning methods to distinguish between normal and abnormal ECGs (Aggarwal et al. 2022). The ECG dataset used in this study was obtained from UCI, and the results showed that the disease RB and CAS had the greatest accuracy scores (95% for logistic regression and SVM) among all classifiers. (Revanth et al. 2022) tried to provide an end-to-end XAI structure for analyzing the breast cancer prediction model. By utilizing an all-encompassing XAI system, they concentrated more on the requirement to define and illustrate the black box prediction model for breast cancer detection. LIME, LRP, DTC, and SHAP approaches are used to support the black box (CNN) model performance trained on the BCHI dataset. The proposed method of this paper is shown in Figure 11.1.

This paper is organized as follows: in Section 11.2, we discuss the Literature survey. In Section 11.3, we discuss the proposed method. In section 11.4. Experimental results are discussed. Finally, we conclude our work in Section 11.5.

11.2.1. Background Work

The suggested method employs the Logistic Regression, Random Forest, K-nearest Neighbor, and Explainable Artificial Intelligence (EAI) method LIME. Their explanations are given in this section.

11.2.2. Logistic Regression

Logistic regression is a supervised learning technique also known as sigmoid function. Examining the relationship between one or more independent variables predicts a dependent data variable (Ciu, Tania et al. 2020). In logistic regression, the dependent variable is represented as a binary variable that is either 0 (No) or 1 (Yes), but instead of giving the exact value as 0 or 1, It provides probabilistic values that range from 0 to 1. It is given in equation (1)

$$f(x)=e^x/(e^{x+1}) \qquad 1)$$

11.2.3. Random Forest

Random forest is a supervised learning method that builds several decision trees. (Jabbar et al. 2016) One of the best ensemble classification methods employs the bagging principle to merge different decision trees to improve prediction abilities. Individual students are instructed independently in bagging. Each decision tree is trained using a separate sample of data, and replacement is used to create multiple random samples of data from the original dataset. Additionally, features are chosen at random while building the tree. A majority vote is used to predict by integrating numerous trees. Classify the sample data by combining the prediction results of several k-tree classifiers based on the majority vote rule. The combined splitter H is created as an aggregation of each splitter H_k, $k = 1...K$ and the example d_i represents classified to class c_j according to the number of votes obtained from the splitter H_k. It is given by eqn (2).

$$H(Di, Cj) = sign \sum_{k=1}^{K} H_k(D_{i,}C_j) \quad (2)$$

The error value can be obtained by Equation above calculating the Mean Absolute Percentage Error (MAPE). It is given by Equation 3 and accuracy is given Equation 4.

$$MAPE = \frac{1}{n}\sum_{i=1}^{n}\frac{|X_i - F_i|}{X_i} X100\text{--} \quad (3)$$

$$Accuracy = 100\% - MAPE \quad (4)$$

11.2.4. K-Nearest Neighbour

K-Nearest neighbor is a supervised machine learning algorithm. (Rahmat et al. 2021) It compares newly discovered cases and data to those already known, classifying them as being the most likely existing cases. It primarily serves regression and classification purposes.

It is memory-based and appropriate for use with tiny datasets. Even though its performance was evaluated by the number of neighbors. Furthermore, since KNN is sensitive to noisy input, the training dataset must be given accordingly.

The method for finding the nearest k generally uses the Euclidean distance formula. Here, is the Euclidean distance formula in the KNN algorithm and shown in Equation 5

$$dis = \sqrt{\sum_{i=0}^{n}(x_{1i} - x_{2i})^2 + (y_{1i} - y_{2i})^2 + \cdots} \quad (5)$$

where dis = Euclidean Distance; xi = the value of the x variable in the sample data; yi = the value of the y variable in the sample data; and n = amount of data.

11.2.5. Explainable Artificial Intelligence (XAI) Method LIME

The Reason to introduce Explainable AI is that one cannot confidently say the predicted result is true based on some mathematical expression even if it is true. XAI not only explains the result but also can be used to improve the models. The most well-known XAI methods include SHAP (Shapley Additive explanations), DeepSHAP, CXplain, and LIME. In LIME, the process is composed of Sampling of features using the prediction model that is being used and creating a surrogate dataset which is further used in feature selection based on the Lasso technique to find the most important features (Guleria et al. 2022). All AI methods that can explain and interpret machine learning models, such as LIME, are the way to explain and interpret the results. The trade-off between interpretability and performance is solved using XAI, i.e., between less complex models that cannot handle large and versatile data sets but are much easier to interpret and more complex models which work with more varied datasets. This allows us to work on flaws and mitigate them when developing the algorithm. Many predictive modelling approaches necessitate faith for the utility to assist with choosing an option. Otherwise, their advice may be ignored due to a lack of confidence.

Otherwise, their recommendation may be disregarded for loss of trust. If someone understands the motivations for a method of forecasting to transparent AI techniques such as LIME, choosing to believe the utility becomes easier. eXplainable Artificial Intelligence (XAI) technologies rapidly and readily identify the areas in images that are critical for categorization, offering great assistance to the attending clinician in making decisions. Even for complicated models employed in deep learning, such as picture classification, methods for improved interpretability have been devised.

If a person has knowledge of the motives for a method of forecasting compared to understandable AI techniques including LIME, the decision to trust its value becomes easier. The method is suitable for local interpretations since it describes the classification model for just one case. In simple terms, LIME then modifies what is provided and produces several pieces of information that include only a portion of the actual characteristics. In theory, the explainable AI method LIME is interoperable with a wide range of algorithms and may be used to analyze pictures, text, and data in tables. As a result, we may apply the identical approach to image categorizing, whereas the generated input consists of image portions (pixels) rather than genuine words.

11.3. Proposed Methodology

In this section, the proposed methodology is explained. The flow diagram of the proposed method is specified in Figure 11.2.

11.3.1. Pre-Processing

Many Null values are not in the chosen dataset. However, numerous exceptions must be managed effectively, because the information being collected isn't evenly distributed. Then nominal distribution is applied to remove overfitting. Then an Isolation Forest technique is applied to the dataset for outlier detection. This produces promising results. Before passing the data to the classification, all the pre-processing techniques are essential for better results.

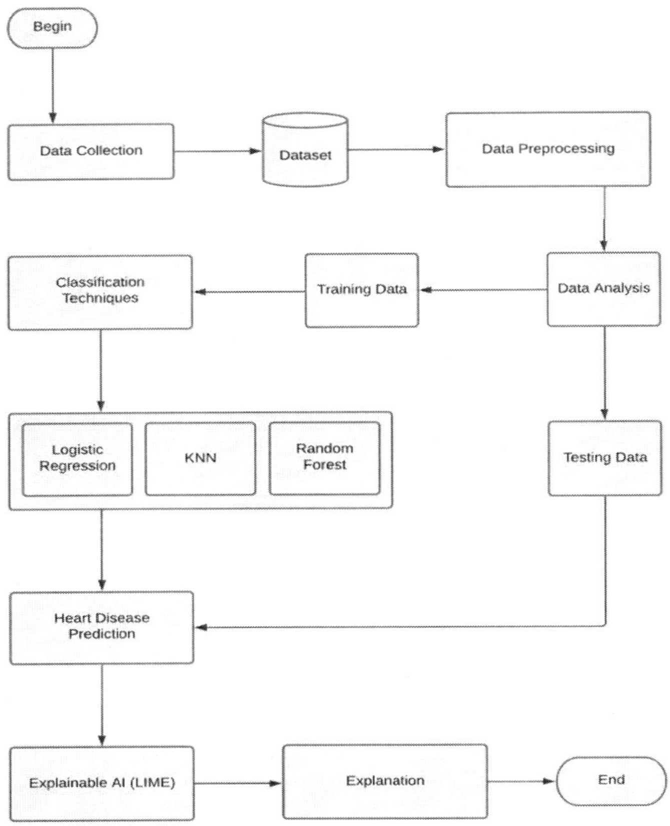

Figure 11.2. System Architecture (proposed work).

11.3.2. Classification Techniques

The proposed approach applies a machine learning-based experimental framework to forecast coronary artery disease. In supervised machine learning, the information input is assigned a label according to what is needed, and data classification is performed. Under supervision, the model undergoes training using machine learning methods, and predictions are made. Table 11.1 shows the supervised machine learning techniques used on the dataset: support vector machines, K-nearest neighbour, and logistic regression. The features used to make the predictions are drawn from the dataset. The ML algorithms' outcomes identify the individuals who will develop the disease along with those who will be recognized to have the disorder

11.3.3. Description of the Output

The results of the classifier model are connected to LIME XAI models to describe the output of the classifier with features selected for classification. To forecast the condition of an individual utilizing the machine learning (ML) model, the XAI version must be performed to figure out the decision to endorse the ML model. XAI supports conveying each machine learning model's estimations, along with the parameters used to train the ML procedures.

11.3.4. Implementation and Testing

11.3.4.1. Dataset Description

The dataset came from the UCI ML is made up of databases from Switzerland, Cleveland, and Hungary. The experiment's dataset is relevant to heart disease. The collection of data has multifactorial qualities, with class, integer, and float attributes. The dataset has multivariate properties, and the attributes are categorical, integer, and real. The task of categorizing has been linked to the database. The collection of data encompasses 303 incidences and 13 features. Table 11.1 shows a subset of the dataset used in the current study.

Table 11.1. Dataset attribute

S. No.	Attribute	Description	Values
1	Age	Age in Years	29-77
2	Sex	Gender of the person	0,1
3	Cp	Chest pain type	0-3
4	Rbp	Resting blood pressure	94-200
5	Chol	Serum cholesterol	126-564
6	Fbs	Fasting blood sugar	0,1
7	Restecg	Resting electrocardiographic results	0,1,2
8	Maxhr	Maximum heart rate achieved	71-202
9	Exang	Exercise included angina	0,1
10	Oldpeak	ST depression included by exercise relative to rest	0-6.2
11	Slope	The slope of the peak exercise ST segment	0,1,2
12	Ca	The number of major vessels blocked	0-3
13	thal	Defect type	1,2
14	num	Heart disease	0,1

The patients in this dataset range in age from 29 to 79. Patients who are male are identified by the gender value 1 and those who are female by the gender value 0. Four different types of chest pain may be a sign of heart disease i.e., 0 - Typical Angina (with all the 3 Angina symptoms), 1 - Atypical Angina (with 2 of 3 Angina symptoms), 2 - non-Anginal Pain (with 1 angina symptom), 3 – Asymptomatic. Reduced blood supply to the heart muscles due to clogged coronary arteries. The level of cholesterol is 'chol.' Fasting blood sugar level 'Fbs' is given a value of 1 if it is below 120 mg (about the weight of a business card)/dl and a value of 0 if it is over. 'Exang' is exercise-induced angina, referred to as 1 if there is pain and 0 if there is none, and 'Restecg' is the resting electrocardiographic result. 'Oldpeak' is the exercise involving ST depression, 'slope' is the peak exercise ST segment representing up/flat/down. 'ca' is the number of main vessels blocked; three major blood arteries supply the heart. The doctor can determine how many vessels are blocked by using angiography i.e., 0 – No blockage, 1 – one vessel blocked, 2 – two vessels blocked and 3 – three vessels blocked. 'thal' (thallium test) A thallium test uses a radioactive tracer to measure how much blood is getting to various areas of the heart. It represents the type of defect i.e., 0 for normal, 1 for fixed defect and 2 for the reversible defect.

11.4. Results

The following metrics are used for evaluating the proposed method. The parameter setting of the proposed algorithm (Gao et al. 2021), is explained by using formulas,

Accuracy

The most important performance metric for classification is Accuracy which is shown in the following equation 6:

$$\text{Acc1}=\frac{(TP1+TN1)}{(TP1+TN1+FP1+FN1} \quad (6)$$

Recall

Recall metrics are shown in the following equation 7:

$$\text{Recall1}=\frac{\text{TP1}}{(\text{TP1}+\text{FN1})}. \quad (7)$$

Precision

Precision metrics are shown in the following equation 8:

$$\text{Precision1}=\frac{\text{TP1}}{(\text{TP1}+\text{FP1})} \quad (8)$$

F-measure

F-measure is shown in the following equation 9:

$$\text{F}-\text{measure}=\frac{(2*\text{precision1}*\text{recall1})}{(precision1+recall1)} \quad (9)$$

were,

TP1 is a True positive value
TN1- True negative value
FP1- False positive condition
FN1-False negative condition

The accuracy of Logistic regression is shown in Figure 11.3. The accuracy of Random Forest is shown in Figure 11.4. The accuracy of K. Neighbours Classifier is shown in Figure 11.5. A comparison of Accuracy is shown in Figure 11.6. Details of Feature value is shown in Figure 11.7.

In terms of accuracy classifiers, the performance for different conventional models of classification when anticipating coronary artery disease is contrasted with XAI-driven approaches. Table 11.2 shows the comparisons of different methods.

```
confussion matrix
[[ 77  21]
 [  7 100]]


Accuracy of Logistic Regression: 86.34146341463415

              precision    recall  f1-score   support

           0       0.92      0.79      0.85        98
           1       0.83      0.93      0.88       107

    accuracy                           0.86       205
   macro avg       0.87      0.86      0.86       205
weighted avg       0.87      0.86      0.86       205
```

Figure 11.3. Accuracy of Logistic Regression.

```
confussion matrix
[[ 88  10]
 [  3 104]]


Accuracy of Random Forest: 93.65853658536587

              precision    recall  f1-score   support

           0       0.97      0.90      0.93        98
           1       0.91      0.97      0.94       107

    accuracy                           0.94       205
   macro avg       0.94      0.93      0.94       205
weighted avg       0.94      0.94      0.94       205
```

Figure 11.4. Accuracy of Random Forest.

```
confussion matrix
[[84 14]
 [11 96]]


Accuracy of K-NeighborsClassifier: 87.8048780487805

              precision    recall  f1-score   support

           0       0.88      0.86      0.87        98
           1       0.87      0.90      0.88       107

    accuracy                           0.88       205
   macro avg       0.88      0.88      0.88       205
weighted avg       0.88      0.88      0.88       205
```

Figure 11.5. Accuracy of K. Neighbours Classifier.

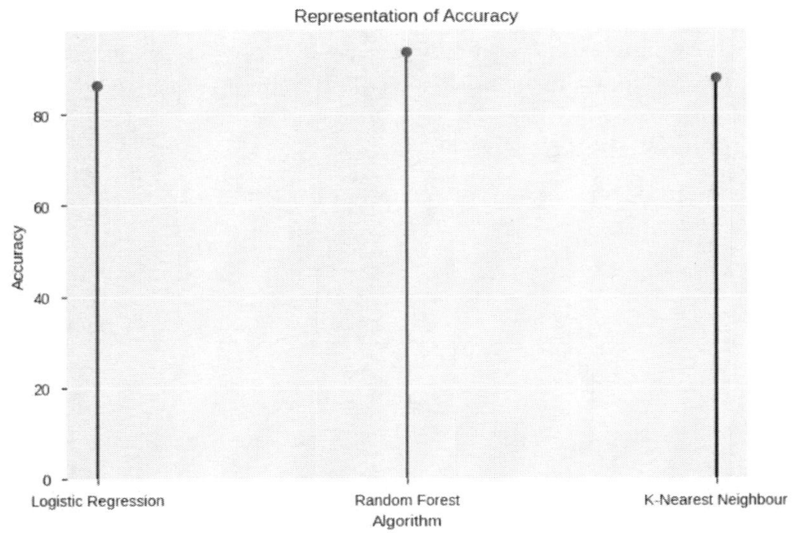

Figure 11.6. Comparison of Accuracy.

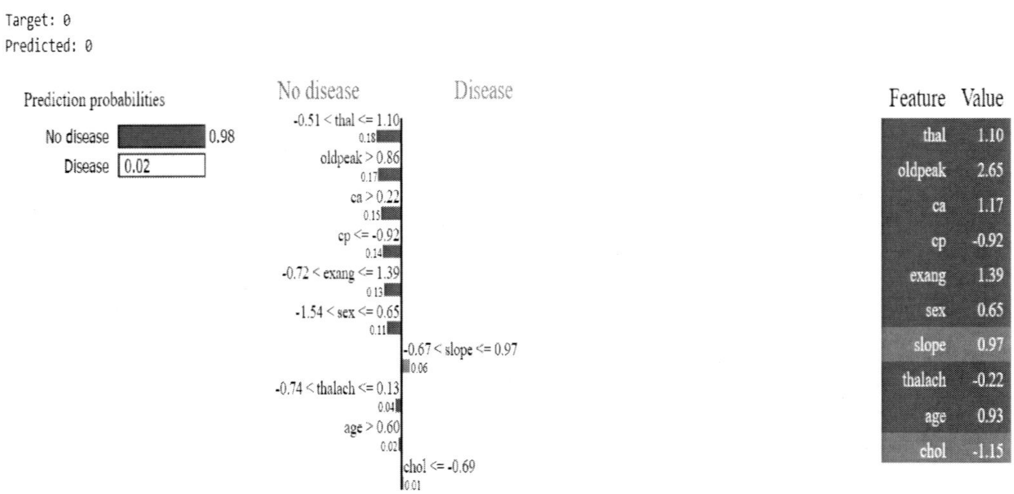

Figure 11.7. Details of Feature value.

Table 11.2. Comparisons of proposed with other classifiers

Ref	Method	Accuracy
(Muhammad et al. 2021)	SVM	80%
(Jiang, Y et al. 2021)	Naive Bayes	76%
(Maheswari S et al. 2019)	Decision Tree	75%
Proposed method with XAI	Random Forest	93%

From Table 11.2, the proposed method shows a better result with better explanations compared to other methods. The suggested XAI classifiers outperform conventional classification models in terms of efficiency. Furthermore, the XAI technology is simpler to comprehend but its choices are more trustworthy. A future study might deal with the previously mentioned challenges of gaining data in real-time for assessing the integrated model utilizing the XAI platform.

11.5 Conclusion

The existence of heart disease in a person becomes more uncertain these days, even medical experts cannot exactly determine the root cause. By using this system one can easily predict heart disease with algorithms like logistic regression, KNN and random forest of which random forest shows the highest accuracy of 93.65%. Not only he/she can predict the disease but can also get the reason behind the occurrence of the disease with explainable AI. Age, Sex, ca, thal, cp, and Oldpeak are some of the features which affect the most in the existence or non-existence of heart disease. Now a day's lot of people are using smart watches which have various sensors to monitor health but with few modifications, it can be able to determine the real-time condition of the human heart. The only drawback of the system as of now is explainable AI is still facing some challenges that is a person with zero knowledge of the medical field cannot properly interpret the result. There is a need for the medical practitioner to evaluate the result. The domain of XAI still needs improvement, so that even a common person can check or understand his/her health condition. Furthermore, it would be informative when evaluating the predictive model's efficacy on a stored test data set to validate its ability to generalize to new, never-before-seen input.

References

Aggarwal, Ritu, Prajoy Podder, and Aditya Khamparia.(2022). "ECG Classification and Analysis for Heart Disease Prediction Using XAI-Driven Machine Learning Algorithms." *Biomedical Data Analysis and Processing Using Explainable (XAI) and Responsive Artificial Intelligence (RAI).* Springer, Singapore, 91-103.

Austin, D. E., Lee, D. S., Wang, C. X., Ma, S., Wang, X., Porter, J., and Wang, B. (2022). "Comparison of machine learning and the regression-based EHMRG model for predicting early mortality in acute heart failure." *International Journal of Cardiology*, 365, 78-84.

Ciu, Tania and Oetama, Raymond. (2020). "Logistic Regression Prediction Model for Cardiovascular Disease.International," *Journal of New Media Technology* 7(1) :33-38. 10.31937/ijnmt. v7i1.1340.

Guleria, P., Naga Srinivasu, P., Ahmed, S., Almusallam, N., Alarfaj, F. K. (2022). "XAI Framework for Cardiovascular Disease Prediction Using Classification Techniques." *Electronics*, *11*, 4086.

Gao, X. Y., Amin Ali, A., Shaban Hassan, H., and Anwar, E. M. (2021). "Improving the accuracy for analyzing heart disease prediction based on the ensemble method." *Complexity*, 1-10.

Javeed, A., Zhou, S., Yongjian, L., Qasim, I., Noor, A., and Nour, R. (2019), "An intelligent learning system based on random search algorithm and optimized random forest model for improved heart disease detection." *IEEE Access*, 7, 180235-180243.

Jiang, Y.; Zhang, X.; Ma, R.; Wang, X.; Liu, J.; Keerman, M.; Yan, Y.; Ma, J.; Song, Y.; Zhang, J. et al. Cardiovascular Disease Prediction by Machine Learning Algorithms Based on Cytokines in Kazakhs of China. *Clin. Epidemiol.* (2021), 13, 417–428.

Kontham R. R., A. K. Kondoju, M. M. Fouda and Z. M. Fadlullah. (2022). "An End-To-End Explainable AI System for Analyzing Breast Cancer Prediction Models," 2022 *IEEE International Conference on Internet of Things and Intelligence Systems (IoTaIS)*,402-407.

Moreno-Sanchez. P. A. (2020) "Development of an Explainable Prediction Model of Heart Failure Survival by Using Ensemble Trees," 2020 *IEEE International Conference on Big Data (Big Data)*,4902-4910.

Muhammad, L. J., Al-Shourbaji, I., Haruna, A. A., Mohammed, I. A., Ahmad, A., and Jibrin, M. B. (2021), "Machine learning predictive models for coronary artery disease." *SN Comput. Sci*. 2, 350.

Maheswari S, and Pitchai R. (2019). "Heart Disease Prediction System Using Decision Tree and Naive Bayes Algorithm," *Curr Med Imaging Rev.* (2019);15(8) :712-717.

Rahmat D., Putra A. A., and Setiawan A. W. (2021), "Heart Disease Prediction Using K-Nearest Neighbor," *International Conference on Electrical Engineering and Informatics (ICEEI) IEEE* (2021)1-6.

Reddy K. S. K, and Kanimozhi K. V. (2022). "Novel Intelligent Model for Heart Disease Prediction using Dynamic KNN (DKNN) with improved accuracy over SVM." *International Conference on Business Analytics for Technology and Security (ICBATS). IEEE,*1-5.

Reddy Thummala G. S. S and R. Baskar. (2022). "Prediction of Heart Disease using Decision Tree in Comparison with KNN to Improve Accuracy," *2022 International Conference on Innovative Computing, Intelligent Communication and Smart Electrical Systems (ICSES)*, 1-5.

Ravi, V., Narasimhan, H. and Pham, T. D. (2022). "A cost-sensitive deep learning-based meta-classifier for pediatric pneumonia classification using chest X-rays." *Expert Syst*. 39.

Ribeiro, M. T., Singh, S., and Guestrin, C. Anchors. (2018). "High-precision model-agnostic explanations." *In : AAAI Conference on Artificial Intelligence (AAAI)*.

Saw M, Saxena T, Kaithwas S, Yadav R, and Lal N. (2020). "Estimation of prediction for getting heart disease using logistic regression model of machine learning," *International Conference on Computer Communication and Informatics (ICCCI) IEEE,* 1-6.

Schwab, P., and Karlen, W. Cxplain.(2019). "Causal explanations for model interpretation under uncertainty," *Advances in Neural Information Processing Systems*, 32.

Chapter 12

Ailment Prophecy Based on Symptoms Using Machine Learning

P. V. Madhushrii[1]
K. S. Rithiksharvesh[1]
D. Janani[1]
S. Umamaheswari[2,*]
P. Jayashri[3]
and G. M. Arun Prasath[4]
[1,2,3]School of Advanced Sciences,Vellore Institute of Technology, Chennai, Tamil Nadu, India
[4]Department of Information Technology, University of Technology and Applied Sciences, Muscat, Oman

Abstract

The role of health in an individual's overall well-being cannot be overstated, as it is of utmost importance from a physical standpoint. Attaining and maintaining good health is a universal aspiration shared by all human beings. However, the global population faces a multitude of diseases that afflict individuals, often starting with seemingly minor symptoms that, if left unattended, can escalate into significant health risks. Recognizing the criticality of early disease detection, this project incorporates five machine learning algorithms—namely Decision Tree, Random Forest, Naïve Bayes, and Support Vector Machine (SVM)—to predict diseases based on user-inputted symptoms. The primary objective of this endeavour is to empower individuals to forecast and diagnose diseases at an early stage, effectively mitigating their health risks. In the contemporary fast-paced world, where scheduling regular doctor visits and diligently monitoring personal health becomes increasingly challenging, people frequently find themselves either ignoring their discomfort or resorting to self-medication, often oblivious to the potentially grave consequences. In response to this dilemma, the present study proposes a novel approach to anticipate disease onset by leveraging symptoms experienced by individuals. The core purpose of this ambitious undertaking is to develop and evaluate models that enable individuals to predict and diagnose diseases promptly, thereby reducing their overall risk. The methodology employed in this study centres around four machine learning algorithms,

[*] Corresponding Author's Email: uma143logu@gmail.com.

In: Explainable Artificial Intelligence in Healthcare Systems
Editors: A. Anitha Kamaraj and Debi Prasanna Acharjya
ISBN: 979-8-89113-598-7

specifically Decision Tree, Random Forest, Naïve Bayes, and SVM, with particular emphasis on the latter. The SVM algorithm plays a pivotal role throughout the model development process, encompassing crucial tasks such as data preprocessing, feature selection, training, evaluation, and hyperparameter fine-tuning. By conducting a comparative study involving all four machine learning algorithms, the interface will display the predicted disease based on user-entered symptoms. This project ultimately aims to empower individuals to take an active role in managing their health, facilitating early disease prediction, and fostering a proactive approach to healthcare management that yields improved health outcomes.

Keywords: Disease, GUI, health, machine learning, symptom

12.1 Introduction

Finding a balance between essential elements like time, energy, money, relationships, health, and happiness is what life is all about. Among these, health is one of the unwavering integrity factors because it is what motivates people to live fulfilling lives. The contemporary generation leads busy lifestyles and rarely thinks about their health. They are unaware that when they lose something, time is just as valuable to us as health is. We cannot turn back the hands of time, but the wonderful thing is that with some work, health can be regained. Many people lack the knowledge necessary to identify an illness based solely on its symptoms. They ultimately choose the wrong safety precautions. It might result in their demise. On the other hand, some individuals are unable to go to the hospital each time they encounter symptoms due to financial constraints. In other instances, some rural residents might not be able to access doctors. Doctors are currently using quickly developing technologies to treat patients to avoid such situations, which has lessened the difficulties for both doctors and patients.

Further technology development will lead to a much more profound restructuring of the healthcare industry. Machine learning is one of the cutting-edge technologies that have helped people in many different industries. To give robots a semblance of human intelligence so they can carry out some of the tasks that people carry out, machine learning is regarded as a subfield of artificial intelligence (AI). Using the flask app, the provided way creates a visually appealing Graphical User Interface. Symptoms are among the drop-down options in this graphical user interface. The symptoms that the user experiences must be chosen. Once you click the forecast button, the disease will be displayed on the screen. To forecast disease, Naive Bayes, Decision trees, Random Forest algorithms, and Support Vector Machine are used. The result will depend on the most prevalent disease.

There are five modules in the suggested methodology. Pre-processing of the dataset will take place in the first module. Using a decision tree classifier, the second module creates a prediction model. Random Forest is employed to forecast disease in the third module. The fourth and fifth modules employ Naive Bayes and Support Vector Machine, respectively, while accounting for each model's output mode. Based on training and testing data, the accuracy of each model will be assessed immediately following training.

12.2 Literature Review

(Dahiwade et al. 2019) designed a disease prediction model using a machine learning approach. In this study, hidden pattern information in medical data was discovered via data mining. For disease prediction, K-Nearest Neighbour and convolutional neural networks were utilised as algorithms. This algorithm was also able to suggest the risk associated with the disease, whether the risk is lower or higher, after general disease prediction. This model's accuracy of 84.5% also serves as a drawback. (Hema et al. 2022) suggested a similar strategy for utilising machine learning to forecast diseases. The model presented in this research predicts the disease using the symptoms as its input. The accuracy of disease prediction using machine learning techniques such as decision trees, naive bayes, and random forest classifiers was 95%. To assist medical professionals in resolving patient health issues, (Grampurohit and Sagarnal, 2020) proposed Disease prediction using a machine-learning algorithm. The study uses machine learning (ML) techniques to forecast the disease, including Decision Tree Classifier, Naive Bayes Classifier, and Support Vector Machine. This report also presents an analysis of the algorithms in comparison.

The concept of "Symptom-Based disease prediction using Data mining," proposed by (Shetty et al. 2019), builds a Machine Learning algorithm (ML) to forecast the prevalent disease using a variety of symptoms. The suggested technique uses text processing and machine learning algorithms together to get correct results. This study's objective was to identify significant trends in the effectiveness of various supervised machine-learning algorithms for sickness risk prediction. Here, a survey of supervised machine learning algorithm variants is provided to assist researchers in choosing the most appropriate algorithm for their project.

Hybrid Machine Learning Techniques for Effective Heart Disease Prediction by (Mohan et al. 2019). The suggested model predicts cardiac vascular illnesses by combining various feature sets and well-known classification techniques. With the hybrid random forest model, an accuracy of 88.7% was attained. A convolutional neural network (CNN) based multimodal disease risk prediction algorithm is suggested in Disease Prediction by Machine Learning Over Big Data from Healthcare Communities by (Chen et al. 2017); that can be used to forecast the occurrence of chronic illness outbreaks. Using real-world hospital data gathered from central China, the suggested model exhibits an improved accuracy of 94.8%.

Diabetes disease prediction using machine learning on big data of healthcare by (Mir and Dhage, 2018). The study employed four algorithms (Naive Bayes, Support Vector Machine, Random Forest, and Simple CART) using the WEKA tool and evaluated their performance on a dataset. The results showed that the Support Vector Machine algorithm outperformed the other algorithms, providing the highest accuracy in predicting diabetes disease. Study and analysis of decision tree-based classification algorithms by (Patel and Prajapati, 2018). The review emphasizes the importance of selecting the most appropriate Decision Tree algorithm based on accuracy and cost-effectiveness. The paper specifically examines three Decision Tree algorithms (ID3, C4.5, and CART) and aims to evaluate their performance and suitability in diverse decision-making scenarios.

Review paper on prediction of crop disease using IoT and machine learning by (Shinde, S and Kulkarni, 2017). The review emphasizes the significance of environmental parameters in precision agriculture and their impact on predicting crop diseases. By combining IoT technology and machine learning algorithms, the research aims to predict crop diseases using real-time data from sensors. Timely alerts in the form of email or text messages are provided to farmers, enabling proactive measures. The study also suggests the potential extension of this work to recommend suitable fertilizers for addressing specific crop diseases. Adding Explainability to Machine Learning Models to Detect Chronic Kidney Disease by (Islam et al. 2022). The literature review focuses on chronic kidney disease (CKD) and the importance of early diagnosis and prediction of disease progression. CKD is characterized by a gradual decline in kidney function and is often asymptomatic in the early stages. Detecting CKD early and identifying patients at risk of progression is crucial for timely intervention. The study presents an explainable machine learning model based on Random Forest and feature selection to predict CKD. The model's explainability is assessed using LIME, SHAP, and SKATER methods, providing insights into the factors influencing the prediction.

12.3 Proposed Methodology

The key objective of this research is to create models that assist in early disease diagnosis and prediction, hence lowering risk. The goal of this project is to improve upon existing models by developing and evaluating new models utilising various test scenarios. The data set obtained in the first Kaggle module was used for data preparation. Pre-processing the data increases the model's accuracy. Each symptom is given a priority in the dataset for symptom severity. A priority is assigned to each symptom in a record of disease symptoms. This aids in disease prediction accuracy. In the second module, a decision tree classification technique was used to create a model. The decision tree is used to make decisions at every node. A confusion matrix was constructed to analyse the outcomes of this decision tree classifier model after training it, then used the test data to score and assess accuracy.

The random forest classification technique was used to create a model in the third module. It is comparable to a decision tree, however, the random forest classifier generates several decision trees. All the outputs from all the trees are taken into account to produce the final output. The model is trained using the training data and tested using the testing data. To evaluate the correctness of this trained model and the outcomes produced by the trained random forest model, a confusion matrix was created. Using the Naive Bayes algorithm, a model was created in the fourth module. It is generally used to build classifiers. These labels are used to group problem cases. A database of various disease symptoms is used to map symptoms with suspected diseases. Support Vector Machine is used to create a model in the fifth module. The data are grouped and categorised using a hyperplane.

The pre-processed dataset was then applied to the training and evaluation of this model. The modes of all the outputs from the aforementioned models were considered for predicting the ultimate disease after accuracy calculations. The modes of every output from the aforementioned models were taken into consideration for forecasting the ultimate disease after constructing the accuracy and confusion matrices.

The architecture of the suggested methodology is depicted in Figure 12.1. Pre-processing was done on the dataset before it was divided into training and testing datasets. Using the training data set, fI algorithms were used to build the models. Following tests against these trained models, predictions are made.

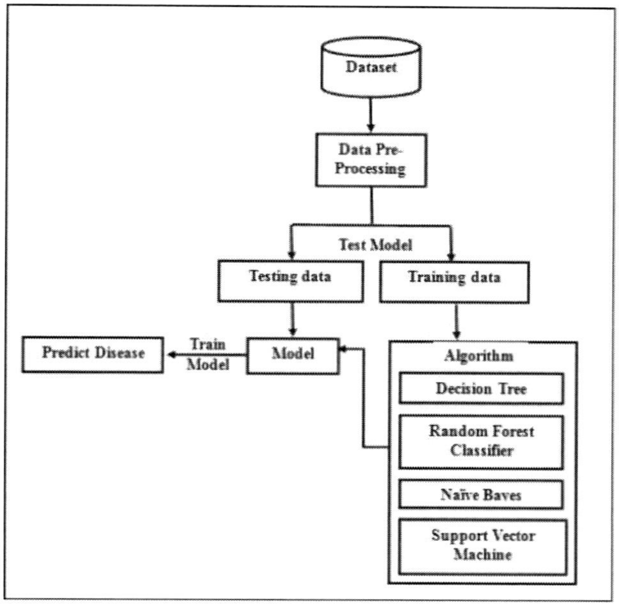

Figure 12.1 Proposed system of the model.

Module 1: Data Preparation

The data set previously examined in this module is pre-processed. The dataset is made up of symptoms that are linked to certain illnesses. There are 26 illnesses, 132 symptoms, and 282 rows in the data collection. This equates to 282 records and 6 fields. To begin, we must verify that this data preparation module follows a consistent format. If this is not the case, the data should be transformed into a standard format. Null values and missing data will have a substantial influence on the performance of your model, therefore remove them first.

After null values are eliminated, each symptom should be graded. If the symptom severity database does not include a value for the symptom severity, a value of zero must be given.

Step 1: Gather information so that all datasets needed for model training and testing can fit in a single table.

Step 2: Find all missing or null values, and then set the value to 0.
data.isnull().sum

Step 3: According to symptom-severity.csv, give each symptom a unique weight.

Step 4: Assign zero to the given file if it has no weight.

Module 2: Building the Model Using Random Forest Classifier

Following pre-processing, the dataset must be divided into training and test data. Decision tree classifiers are used to create models and make judgements at each node of the tree. These are the judgements that lead to the categorization of symptoms into different categories.

Step 1: Divide the data into two parts, with 70% for training and 30% for testing.
xtrain,xtest,ytrain,ytest=train_test_split(X,Y,test_size=0.3)
Step 2: Using the random forest classifier function, create a random forest classifier model.
rfc = RandomForestClassifier()
Step 3: The model finds the best solution by constructing a series of decision trees from randomly selected subsets of the training set.
model_rfc = rfc.fit(xtrain,ytrain)
Step 4: Predict values using the random forest classifier model that has so far been generated.
ts_pred_rfc = model_rfc.predict(xtest)

Module 3: Building the Model using Decision Tree

The model was produced using the Random Forest technique in the third module. Several decision trees are built, and the random forest classifier's final output is the most common output from all decision trees. After the model has been trained, predictions are made using test data.

Step 1: Create a decision tree classifier model with the decision tree classifier function.
dtc = DecisionTreeClassifier
Step 2: Split the dataset and make adjustments to the training data.
model_dtc = dtc.fit(xtrain,ytrain)
Step 3: Predict values using the model created above.
ts_pred_dtc = model_dtc.predict(xtest)
Step 4: Draw the accuracy for the model.
accuracy_score(ytest,ts_pred_dtc)

Module 4: Naive Bayes Model Construction

The model was constructed using the Naive Bayes technique in the fourth module. It categorises features according to their category variance. Predictions are made based on test data once the model has been trained.

Step 1: Use the Naive Bayes categorical classifier to classify discrete features based on their categorical variance distributions.
gnb= CategoricalNB()
Step 2: Using the formula, this model computes the posterior probabilities for each class. The predicted outcome has the highest probability.
Step 3: Train this model with the training data.
Model = gnb.fit(xtrain, ytrain)
Step 4: Predict the output and test the data to find its accuracy.
ts_pred_gnb = model.predict(xtest)

The Naive Bayes formula is:

$$P(A|B) = P(B/A).P(A) / P(B) \quad (1)$$

Module 5: Support Vector Machine Model Construction

In the fifth module, we used a Support Vector Machine to create the model. It initialises, fits the classifier model, and assesses the prediction depending on the performance of the model.

Step 1: Import the dataset and extract the X and Y features separately.
Step 2: Divide the data into train and test
Step 3: Initializing the SVM algorithm

```
clf = svm.SVC(kernel ='linear')
```

Step 4: Fitting the SVM algorithm

```
model_svm = clf.fit(xtrain, ytrain)
```

Step 5: Coming up with predictions.

```
ts_pred_svm = model_svm.predict(xtest)
```

Step 6: Evaluating the model's performance

```
metrics.accuracy(ytest, ts_pred_svm)
metrics.precision(ytest, ts_pred_svm)
metrics.recall(ytest, ts_pred_svm)
```

Inferences

The graphical user interface, which extracts features by using five symptoms as input is demonstrated below in Figure 12.2. A user may select from five drop-down menus featuring over 100 symptoms such as vomiting, nausea, fever, cold, and so on, as well as a button to report their symptoms, which was constructed using the Flask framework.

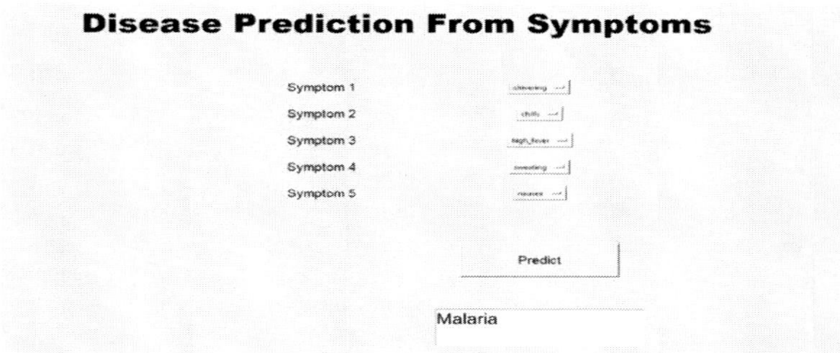

Figure 12.2. Graphical User Interface.

12.4 Performance Analysis

Table 12.1 shows the accuracy of each algorithm as follows:

1. The accuracy of the model using the decision tree algorithm is 96%.
2. The random forest algorithm's model has a 97% accuracy rate.

3. The accuracy of the model using Naive Bayes is 94%.
4. The model's accuracy when using a Support Vector Machine is 98%.

Table 12.1. Accuracy of each algorithm obtained

ALGORITHM	ACCURACY
Decision Tree	96%
Random Forest Classifier	97%
Naïve Bayes	94%
Support Vector Machine	98.8%

12.5 Conclusion

Timely identification and treatment of diseases are essential for maintaining good health. Recommendation systems serve as a valuable resource when direct visits to the doctor are not always possible. By predicting illnesses based on user-entered symptoms, these systems offer a lifeline for proactive healthcare management. Using four machine learning algorithms, including Support Vector Machines, the proposed model achieved an impressive accuracy rate of 95%, surpassing the typical 80% rate of existing models. The system's accurate conclusions and potential to suggest consulting a doctor or visiting a hospital make it a valuable tool. Integration with maps further aids patients in accessing appropriate medical facilities. In summary, leveraging machine learning algorithms in recommendation systems holds promise for early disease detection, emphasizing the importance of promptly addressing symptoms for optimal health outcomes.

References

Chen, M., Hao, Y., Hwang, K., Wang, L., and Wang, L. (2017). "Disease prediction by machine learning over big data from healthcare communities." *IEEE Access*, *5*, 8869-8879.

Dahiwade, D., Patle, G., and Meshram, E. (2019). "Designing disease prediction model using machine learning approach." In *2019 3rd International Conference on Computing Methodologies and Communication (ICCMC)* (1211-1215). IEEE.

Grampurohit, S., and Sagarnal, C. (2020). "Disease prediction using machine learning algorithms". In *2020 International Conference for Emerging Technology (INCET)* (1-7). IEEE.

Hema, P., Sunny, N., Naganjani, R. V., and Darbha, A. (2022). "Disease Prediction using Symptoms based on Machine Learning Algorithms." In *2022 International Conference on Breakthrough in Heuristics And Reciprocation of Advanced Technologies (BHARAT)* 49-54.

Islam, M. A., Nittala, K., and Bajwa, G. (2022). "Adding Explainability to Machine Learning Models to Detect Chronic Kidney Disease." In *2022 IEEE 23rd International Conference on Information Reuse and Integration for Data Science (IRI)* 297-302.

Mir, A., and Dhage, S. N. (2018). "Diabetes disease prediction using machine learning on big data of healthcare." In *2018 fourth international conference on computing communication control and automation (ICCUBEA)* 1-6.

Mohan, S., Thirumalai, C., and Srivastava, G. (2019). "Effective heart disease prediction using hybrid machine learning techniques." *IEEE Access*, *7*, 81542-81554.

Patel, H. H., and Prajapati, P. (2018). "Study and analysis of decision tree based classification algorithms." *International Journal of Computer Sciences and Engineering*, *6*(10), 74-78.

Shetty, S. V., Karthik, G. A., and Ashwin, M. (2019). "Symptom based health prediction using data mining." In *2019 International Conference on Communication and Electronics Systems (ICCES)* 744-749.

Shinde, S. S., and Kulkarni, M. (2017). "Review paper on prediction of crop disease using IoT and machine learning." In *2017 International conference on transforming engineering education (ICTEE)* 1-4.

Chapter 13

Predicting the Disease Outbreak Using Artificial Intelligence and Data Mining Techniques

Chaitanya Ranpara[1]
Gokul Kurup[1]
Hayat Tamboli[1]
S. Jenicka[2,*]
and Sujatha Krishnamoorthy[3]

[1,2]School of Computer Science and Engineering (SCOPE),
Vellore Institute of Technology, Vellore, India
[3]Department of Computer Science, Wenzhou Kean University,
Zhejiang Province, China

Abstract

Predicting disease outbreaks helps to identify the potential risks and vulnerabilities within a population, which can then be informed to public health organizations and aid in the development of strategies to prevent future outbreaks. However, this can be a complex task, as it involves analyzing a wide range of factors, including environmental conditions, population density, and individual behaviours. To make an accurate prediction, it is important to gather as much relevant information as possible and use a combination of models and expert knowledge to identify the potential risks and take appropriate action. In this book chapter, two methods have been used for disease outbreak prediction - association rule mining and graph node classification. Association rule mining is mainly used for market basket analysis, but here a unique approach is presented wherein it facilitates outbreak prediction. It learns from previous occurrences and predicts relevant future outbreaks accordingly. On the other hand, graph node classification incorporates global airline networks, which serve as a proxy for human mobility and connectivity and introduce a novel framework for capturing the spatial and temporal spread of diseases across different regions. It was found to achieve an accuracy of 92.56%.

* Corresponding Author's Email: jenicka.s@vit.ac.in.

In: Explainable Artificial Intelligence in Healthcare Systems
Editors: A. Anitha Kamaraj and Debi Prasanna Acharjya
ISBN: 979-8-89113-598-7

Keywords: disease outbreak prediction, machine learning, association rule mining, graph node classification

13.1 Introduction

Several methods are currently used to predict disease outbreaks. These methods include analyzing data on the spread of the disease, monitoring reports of new cases, and using mathematical models to forecast the potential spread of the disease. Health officials and governments may also use satellite imagery, climate data, and other information to help identify areas where disease outbreaks are more likely to occur and to plan and implement preventive measures. In some cases, health officials may also use predictive analytics, machine learning, and other advanced techniques to help identify potential disease outbreaks and prevent them. Machine learning and deep learning can be used to develop models that can analyze large amounts of data and identify patterns that may be indicative of a potential disease outbreak. These models can be trained on data from past outbreaks, including information on the spread of the disease, the symptoms of those who were infected, and other relevant factors. By analyzing this data, the models can learn to identify patterns and make predictions about the likelihood of a disease outbreak in each location. These predictions can then be used to inform public health decisions and help officials prevent the disease's spread. Additionally, machine learning and deep learning can also be used to develop systems that can monitor real-time data, such as reports of new cases and the spread of the disease, to provide early warning of potential outbreaks. These systems can be integrated into existing surveillance systems, allowing health officials to respond quickly to potential outbreaks and prevent them from spreading.

This research paper aims to predict outbreaks using supervised machine learning and unsupervised machine learning approaches. For supervised learning, graph node classification has been employed. Graph node classification utilizes travel data, i.e., airline routes of people around the globe and makes a graph corresponding to the data. Travel data is studying the spread of diseases worldwide. Later, the graph is then converted into its embedding. Graph node embedding is a crucial step in the entire process since it converts the graph into its equivalent low-dimensional vectors. This favors efficient analysis of the graph and it is favorable to perform its classification. These embeddings are later classified using logistic regression. Conversely, we use association rule mining, which is a data mining technique for unsupervised learning technique in outbreak prediction. It mainly focuses on discovering interesting relationships or associations between items in large datasets, in this case, the global disease dataset ranging from 1996 to 2022. The goal of association rule mining is to extract frequent item sets and generate rules that describe the relationships between items. This process involves calculating various measures such as support, confidence, and lift. Based on this, it learns from the given dataset, and upon training it generates predictions for the inputs given. Apriority algorithm and FP growth algorithm are the most common algorithms used for association rule mining.

Both methods can generate relevant and accurate outputs. The output screenshots have been attached in the results section, wherein the performance of the models can be seen. Therefore, by leveraging real-world datasets, the proposed approach can make significant advancements in epidemiology. It offers unique insights into the early detection and mitigation of disease outbreaks, thereby paving the way for more effective public health strategies and improved outcomes.

13.2 Literature Review

The study by Salim et al. (2021) which was carried out in Selangor, Malaysia, focused on the prediction of Dengue outbreaks. They used Support Vector Machines [SVM] with linear kernel to predict Dengue outbreaks. SVM is a supervised machine learning algorithm that aims to find an optimal hyperplane that separates data points of different classes in a high-dimensional feature space. This model showed prediction performance such as an accuracy of 70%, a specificity of 95% and a precision of 56%. Lee et al. (2022) forecasted weekly Norovirus warnings in South Korea. They primarily used the Long Short-Term Memory (LSTM) machine learning algorithm in their research. It is a type of recurrent neural network (RNN) architecture that is widely used for prediction tasks. Their predictions had an accuracy of 97.2% and 92.5% in the training and test data, respectively. In another study, Koç and Türkoğlu (2022) used a multilayer LSTM network for outbreak prediction of COVID-19 in Turkey. The experimental results showed that the model proposed for the forecasting of cases yielded a Mean absolute percentage error (MAPE) value of 4.80% and R^2 value of 99.72%. A study by Yoshida K et al. (2022) aimed at predicting the outbreak of Hand, Foot and Mouth Disease in Japan (four weeks in advance). The time-series data were analyzed by an LSTM model trained on the numbers of weekly HFMD cases in each prefecture. LSTM networks are powerful models for capturing long-term dependencies in sequential data. The results showed a Root Mean Squared Error (RMSE) of 8.53×10^{-7}, R^2 value of 0.944 where the evaluated period was week 5 to 53. Sujatha et al. (2022) developed a hybrid deep learning framework, known as the dConvLSTM-DCN (dual Convolutional Long Short-Term Memory with Dense Convolutional Network) for predicting the vacant parking space availability and the proposed method achieved reasonable prediction accuracy.

Research by Tiwari et al. (2020) predicted the COVID-19 outbreak trends in India. The model was trained using time series forecasting methods. Time series forecasting methods analyze the patterns, trends, and dependencies present in historical data to make predictions about future values. The accuracy of the results was verified by comparing the test data with predictions. Their estimate suggested that the mortality rate in India was around 2.39%. Dutta and Bandyopadhyay (2020) verified how close the outbreak prediction of COVID-19 by ML techniques was to real-time data. A verification method was proposed in their paper that used LSTM and Gated Recurrent Unit (GRU) to train their model. The prediction results were validated, and the experimental results showcased that the proposed approach had a high prediction rate. Ozturk et al. (2020) experimented on the early prediction of COVID-19 with the help of X-ray images. A DarkNet model was used by them as a classifier for the "You Only Look Once (YOLO)" real-time object detection system. The model implemented 17 convolutional layers and introduced different filtering on each layer. The model produced a classification accuracy of 98.08% for binary classes and 87.02% for multi-class classification. Feldman et al. (2019) experimented with whether machine learning can be utilized to allow efficient extraction of infectious disease activity information from online media reports. They employed linear networks and RNN to categorize the articles based on keywords extracted from the title. It was found that the classifier achieved a recall and precision of 88.8% and 86.1%, respectively. The overall surveillance system could anticipate 94% of the outbreaks identified by the WHO. Ovidiu et al. (2019) proposed a software system, SENTINEL, which detected disease outbreaks via social media. This was positive for predicting Influenza. Deep learning was used to the problem of classifying health-related tweets and detecting illness accordingly. The chosen classifier had an F1 score of 0.852 for the Twitter classification task and 0.939 for news classification. Anno et al. (2019) carried out an analysis to examine emerging spatiotemporal hotspots of Dengue fever in Taiwan. AlexNet model trained by transfer learning for this research. AlexNet model is a Convolutional Neural Network (CNN) having eight layers with learnable parameters. This model yielded an accuracy of 100% on an 8-fold cross-validation test dataset of longitude-time sea surface temperature images. Khakharia et al. (2021) developed a prediction system to predict COVID-19 in the top 10 highly populated countries. This system used 9 different ML algorithms (viz. ARMA, ARIMA, BRR, HW, LRP, LR, RFR, SVR, and XGB) to predict the number of new cases for the next 5 days. These models are of varying types- from time series forecasting methods to various regressors. The dataset of the countries, namely, Bangladesh, India, China, Pakistan, Germany, Nigeria, Ethiopia, the Democratic Republic of Congo, the Philippines, and Indonesia has been utilized. The accuracy of the models was 87.9% ± 3.9%, with the highest accuracy of 99.93% achieved for Ethiopia. Shashank et al. (2021) put forth a predictive model that used linear regression to predict the status of an epidemic in a given geographical region. To train the model, a dataset having statistics about multiple epidemics like COVID-19, Influenza, and Pneumonia in different regions was considered. The accuracy was evaluated by using R^2 and RMSE. It was found that the model was successful in predicting the epidemic. Rathnamala and Jenicka (2021) proposed an automated bleeding detection algorithm using color and texture features extracted from the Gaussian mixture model (GMM) super pixels of the Wireless Capsule Endoscopy (WCE) images and achieved high accuracy and precision. Jonkmans et al. (2021) conducted a quantitative evidence synthesis to emphasize prediction methods aimed at preventing Blueprint diseases (as classified by the WHO) and COVID-19 outbreaks. The experiments revealed that Rift Valley fever emerged as the most frequently predicted disease. Approximately 10% of the models developed were implemented by health authorities. (Singh and Singh, 2021) emphasized sentimental analysis and ML techniques for disease outbreak prediction. They went through many important types of research conducted in the last decade about disease prediction. They found that the machine learning techniques are more suitable for doing sentiment analysis. Sentiment analysis, also known as opinion mining, is a natural language processing (NLP) technique that involves analyzing and determining the sentiment or emotional tone expressed in a piece of text. As it aims to understand and classify the subjective opinions, attitudes, and emotions conveyed in written content, it could be leveraged for disease outbreak prediction. In their study, Raizada et al. (2020) aimed to predict the outbreaks of three vector-borne diseases (Chikungunya, Malaria, and Dengue) in India. A Convolutional Neural Network (CNN) algorithm was introduced that incorporated contrasting data; a novel approach not previously explored. The algorithm exhibited an impressive accuracy of 88%. After running the algorithm for 100 iterations, convergence was achieved during the 31st iteration.

After going through various papers in the domain of disease outbreak prediction, it is found that research to anticipate all kinds of epidemics, ranging from Dengue fevers and Influenza to the Blueprint diseases (as per WHO), has been carried out. There were several attempts to predict the recent pandemic COVID-19 as well. Mostly the previously mentioned research was conducted with high accuracy and performed well when evaluated. The research was mainly based on a certain geographic region of the globe and worked well for that region. Innovative and apt approaches like sentiment analysis also proved to be helpful and futuristic. Research to predict diseases using X-ray images (using the YOLO algorithm) was also something that is going to have great utility.

However, while going across various papers it was found that the use of the LSTM model was quite redundant. In fact, among all the methods studied, LSTM was the one that was most used. Moreover, the studies were restricted to a specific region or certain group of countries. Some research focused on one disease or a few bunches of it, limiting the scope of research. In some papers, the data gathered span across a short time range, which may not be widely focused.

On the contrary, the research presented in this book chapter uses a novel methodology and unique datasets and offers a wide scope. Association rule mining and Graph node classification are the main methodologies in this book chapter. Association rule mining which is generally used in the e-commerce sector to predict customer transactions is instead used to anticipate disease outbreaks. Apart from this, in the second method travel information in the form of airline routes around the globe has been considered. Travel information serves as a great source for studying the transmission of diseases. The diseases dataset has been used as a comprehensive list of epidemics that occurred in every country from the year 1996 to 2022. Even the dataset about airline routes is much more detailed, having airport codes, coordinates, etc. So, this research provides a breakthrough in the field of epidemiology.

13.3 Methodology

13.3.1 Association Rule Mining

Concept

The first approach used for disease outbreak prediction is Association Rule Mining. Association rule mining aims to find frequently occurring patterns from large datasets. These identified patterns and associations help us in making meaningful predictions of the future. Association rules play a key role in this algorithm. For example, "If a customer buys bread, he is 75% likely to buy butter" is a valid association rule. Association rules are simple If/Then statements that help us to identify the associations between two data items. So based on the association or dependency, one can say that if the buying pattern of the customer is bread and butter, the bakery owner can promote sales of the items (both bread and butter) by following meaningful strategies. The algorithm further looks for interesting patterns through data mining so that one can exploit the buying pattern of the customer to gain even more profit. Association rules are created by mining the data and looking for frequent if/then patterns. Then, depending on the following parameters, the important relationships are observed.

Associated Parameters

Support

Support is a metric that quantifies the frequency of occurrence of an item or itemset within a dataset. It is determined by dividing the number of transactions that contain the item(s) by the total number of transactions in the dataset as shown in eqn (1). A high support value indicates that the item or itemset is prevalent in the dataset, whereas a low support value suggests its rarity.

$$Support(\{X\} \rightarrow \{Y\}) = \frac{Transactions\ containing\ both\ X\ and\ Y}{Total\ number\ of\ transactions} \quad (1)$$

Confidence

Confidence represents the degree of association between two items, reflecting its strength. It is computed by dividing the number of transactions that contain both items by the number of transactions that contain the first item alone as shown in eqn(2). A high confidence value indicates a robust relationship, indicating that the first item's presence significantly predicts the second.

$$Confidence(\{X\} \rightarrow \{Y\}) = \frac{Transactions\ containing\ both\ X\ and\ Y}{Transactions\ containing\ X} \quad (2)$$

Lift

Lift measures the strength of the association between two items, considering their frequencies in the dataset. It is determined by dividing the confidence of the association by the support of the second item as shown in eqn (3). The lift allows for a comparison between the actual association strength and the expected strength if the items were independent. If the lift value exceeds 1, it indicates a stronger association between the items than expected based on their frequencies. This implies that the association may have significance and merits additional examination. Conversely, if the lift value is less than 1, it suggests a weaker association than expected, implying less reliability or significance.

$$Confidence(\{X\} \rightarrow \{Y\}) = \frac{(Transactions\ containing\ both\ X\ and\ Y)/\ (Transactions\ containing\ X)}{Fraction\ of\ transactions\ containing\ Y} \quad (3)$$

13.3.2 FP Growth – Association Rule Mining Algorithm

We used the FP growth algorithm for the implementation of Association Rule Mining. It makes predictions by finding the frequent itemset in a dataset. It has the following steps.

1. The occurrences of individual items in the transactions are noted.
2. A minimum support is decided based on the occurrence of items. Every item with support less than the minimum support will be discarded.
3. Sort the remaining items in decreasing order of support.
4. A tree is made starting with the first transaction to the last transaction. In the tree, every item in a transaction is a node.

5. Once this FP tree is built in compressed form, a bottom-up algorithm applies the divide and conquer strategy.
6. The bottom-up algorithm constructs a 'prefix path subtree' for each item. The 'prefix path subtree' will be used for extracting frequent itemset of varying lengths all ending in that particular item.

The FP growth algorithm is an improvised version of the Apriori algorithm. The Apriori algorithm goes back and forth to the data set to check for the co-occurrence of products in the data set. However, the FP algorithm, to be faster, changed the data organization into a tree rather than sets. This tree data structure allows for faster scanning, and this is where the algorithm wins time, thereby being more efficient than its counterpart.

13.3.3. Graph Node Classification Using Airline Routes

Concept

The second approach is called graph node classification. In this method, graphs are used for outbreak prediction. Moreover, airline routes serve as a great information source as they represent the human movement and thereby help us in studying the transmission of infectious diseases. The whole idea of graph node classification is that a graph can be embedded to its equivalent vector and it can be used for node classification. Here node classification is done to see whether a specific country has a particular disease outbreak. As this is a binary classification problem, a logistic regression classifier is a perfect fit for it. Broadly speaking, there are three main steps in this approach. Creating the graph from the dataset, Graph Node embedding and Logistic Regression are described in the subsequent subsections.

Creating the Graph

From the various datasets chosen, a graph is constructed after pre-processing the data. Graphs have two main components - *nodes* and *edges* (connections between its nodes). The nodes of the graph are the countries, and the edges are the flight routes between those two countries (nodes). Notably, the edges are weighted, unidirectional airline routes, where weight represents the geodesic distance between the countries. The node features are the latest disease prevalent in that country (node). This comprehensive collection of nodes, edges and node features is then made to undergo graph node embedding.

Graph Node Embedding Algorithm - node2vec Algorithm

Graph embeddings are the transformation of property graphs to a vector or a set of vectors. Embedding should capture the graph topology, vertex-to-vertex relationship, and other relevant information about graphs, subgraphs, and vertices. As machine learning on vector spaces has a richer toolset of approaches and vector operations are simpler and faster than equivalent operations on graphs, we chose graph node embedding. The algorithm is flexible and scalable and also preserves the neighbourhood similarity. Moreover, the learned embeddings exhibit semantic and meaningful properties. The algorithm has five main steps Random Walks, Skip-gram model, Negative sampling, Optimization and Embedding Extraction.

Random Walks

Random walks involve traversing the graph from a starting node and selecting the next node based on a transition probability distribution. The transition probabilities determine the likelihood of moving to a neighbouring node during the random walk. It uses the second-order biased random walks which means when the algorithm calculates the traversal probabilities, it also considers where it was at the previous step. The incorporation of second-order information and the bias parameter in random walks allows for a more extensive exploration of the graph, capturing both local and global structures.

Skip-Gram Model

The Skip-Gram model is a neural network architecture employed in Node2Vec to learn embeddings from the sequences of nodes obtained through random walks. The Skip Gram model takes a node as input and aims to predict the context nodes that surround it. It consists of an embedding layer that maps the input node to its low-dimensional vector representation. This vector representation is then passed through a softmax layer, which computes the probabilities of the context nodes. During training, the model adjusts its weights using techniques like stochastic gradient descent to maximize the likelihood of observing the actual context nodes given the input node.

Negative Sampling

Negative sampling is a technique used in the node2Vec algorithm to address the computational burden associated with training on many possible context nodes. Instead of considering all possible nodes as negative examples, a small subset is sampled as negative examples during each training step. Negative examples are chosen randomly from nodes that do not appear in the context of the input node. By using negative sampling, the computational efficiency of training is improved, as the model only needs to consider a small number of negative examples for each positive example.

Optimization

In node2Vec, the optimization step involves adjusting the weights of the Skip Gram model to minimize the difference between the predicted context nodes and the actual context nodes observed in the random walks. Stochastic gradient descent is commonly used as the optimization algorithm. During optimization, the model updates its weights iteratively by computing the gradients of the loss function concerning the model parameters. The objective is to find the optimal values for the model's weights that maximize the likelihood of the observed context nodes.

Embedding Extraction

The learned node embeddings in the node embedding algorithm represent each node as a dense vector in a low-dimensional space. The embedding space's dimensionality is a tunable parameter typically much lower than the number of nodes in the graph. These embeddings capture the structural properties of the network, allowing for various graph analysis tasks. So once the optimisation step is completed, these learned node embeddings are extracted from the trained skip-gram model and are further used for carrying out the graph node classification. In our case, a logistic regression classifier was used to classify these node embeddings.

13.3.4 Logistic Regression

Logistic regression is a statistical algorithm that can be used for binary classification problems. It is a supervised learning algorithm which predicts the probability of an instance belonging to a particular class. The input features are linearly combined and passed through a sigmoid function, which maps the values to a probability between 0 and 1. This probability represents the likelihood of the instance belonging to the positive class. Notably, this regression classifier is suitable when the dependent variable is dichotomous (binary) as in our case. The occurrence of a disease in a country has a binary outcome. So, this holds relevance. The sigmoid function is the key component of logistic regression and is given in eqn (4).

$$p = \frac{1}{1 + e^{-(\beta_0 + \beta_1 x)}} \qquad (4)$$

Here, p is the probability and (β_0 + β_1x) is the linear combination of input features and weights.

13.4 Novelty of the Proposed Approach

The proposed research on disease outbreak prediction using association rule mining and graph node classification presents a novel approach that combines two distinct methodologies to enhance the accuracy and effectiveness of disease surveillance and prediction systems.

First, the use of association rule mining in disease outbreak prediction introduces a novel application of this technique in epidemiology. While association rule mining has been widely employed in market basket analysis and other domains, its application to disease prediction represents a unique and innovative approach. By identifying the significant patterns and associations within the disease dataset, this method can uncover the hidden relationships between various factors and early warning signs of potential outbreaks.

Secondly, the application of graph node classification using the airline routes as a contextual network enhances the predictive capabilities of the system. By incorporating global airline networks, which serve as a proxy for human mobility and connectivity, the research introduces a novel framework for capturing the spatial and temporal spread of diseases across different regions. This approach acknowledges the crucial role of travel and human movement in the transmission and diffusion of infectious diseases, allowing for more accurate predictions and targeted intervention strategies.

Leveraging association rule mining and graph node classification, the study offers a comprehensive and multi-dimensional approach to disease outbreak prediction. This allows for a deeper understanding of the complex interplay between various factors, including demographic, environmental, and mobility-related aspects, resulting in more accurate and actionable predictions.

Moreover, the utilization of real-world datasets, such as global airline routes and disease datasets, further adds to the practical applicability of the research. The incorporation of such diverse and rich data sources strengthens the validity and generalizability of the findings, enabling the development of robust and reliable disease surveillance and prediction systems.

Overall, the proposed research stands out in its innovative side-by-side application of association rule mining and graph node classification, its focus on disease outbreak prediction, and its integration of real-world datasets. The novel approach can advance epidemiology by providing new insights into the early detection and mitigation of disease outbreaks, ultimately leading to improved public health strategies and outcomes.

13.5 Experimental Data, Implementation and Results

Experimental Data

Association Rule Mining

For the first method, the data on outbreaks of infectious diseases gathered from the Disease Outbreak News and the Coronavirus Dashboard, both provided by the World Health Organization (WHO) were used. The dataset encompasses details on 70 different infectious diseases and 2227 public health incidents that took place between January 1996 and March 2022, covering 233 countries and territories worldwide. Moreover, the dataset has 19 columns. Broadly classifying, the columns are mainly of country, code for the country (for ex. Alpha-2 country code from ISO3166), year of occurrence, name of disease, type of disease and subtype of the disease. Along with the diseases, the code for that disease is also included. So, it is a diverse and informative dataset.

Graph Node Classification

In graph node classification, human mobility and connectivity are considered while investigating the transmission of disease outbreaks. The data of human transit across the globe can be highly beneficial while anticipating the spatial spread of epidemics, as the transit or person could also imply the spread of disease. So, there are different types of datasets over and above the diseases dataset. There are four different types of datasets used here. They are as follows.

Disease Dataset

This is the same dataset that was used for the association rule mining, gathered by Disease Outbreak News and Coronavirus Dashboard, both provided by WHO. This dataset encompasses details on 70 different infectious diseases that took place between January 1996 and March 2022, covering 233 countries and territories worldwide.

Airline Routes

This is a detailed dataset consisting of airline information, source airport and destination airport (along with their IDs). The source airport and the destination airport give us the airline route. Airline routes across all countries and considered. Hence, this dataset forms the basis of graph formation. This in-depth dataset of airline routes proves to be very significant in outbreak prediction.

Airport IATA Code - Country

This dataset has airports IATA code, which is a three-letter unique code of any airport. Along with the IATA code, it has the name of the airport and the corresponding country as well. It plays an important role in coordination with the airline routes dataset.

Country Geographical Coordinates

This dataset comprises the country name, along with its iso2 code and the latitude and longitude coordinates. This dataset provides geographical information which helps us locate all countries as well as compute the geodesic distance between them.

All these datasets were combined harmonically and were then used to make predictions.

13.6 Implementation

FP Growth Algorithm-Association Rule Mining

The implementation of the FP-growth algorithm has the following three steps.

Preprocessing

The following pre-processing steps were taken -

1. *Disease and country clubbing*: The disease name and country were combined into a single string. For example, if the disease was "Malaria" and the country was "India," they would be combined as "Malaria-India." This step helps create a unified representation of the disease and country information.
2. *Counting occurrences*: The frequency or count of these combined strings was recorded. This step involves counting how many times each disease-country combination appears in the data over the years. For instance, if "Malaria-India" occurred 10 times and "Dengue-Brazil" occurred 5 times, these counts would be noted.
3. *Concatenating strings and years*: The disease-country strings and their respective years were concatenated. This means combining the disease-country string with the year in which it occurred. For example, "Malaria-India" in the year 2020 would become "Malaria-India-2020."
4. *Creating a 2-D array of transactions*: A 2-dimensional array was constructed to represent the data. Each transaction in the array corresponds to a particular year, and within each transaction, there is an array of disease-country strings that occurred in that year. So, each year has its corresponding transaction containing the disease-country strings associated with it.

This pre-processed data is then used for implementing association rule mining.

Applying the FP Growth Algorithm

In the process of generating association rules, the dataset is subjected to two key steps: setting a minimum support ratio and minimum confidence, followed by applying the FP-Growth algorithm. These steps are crucial for conducting association rule mining effectively. The minimum support ratio and minimum confidence thresholds are established to filter out less frequent or less reliable associations, ensuring that only significant patterns are considered. By setting these thresholds, the focus is placed on itemsets that meet the specified criteria, thereby determining the association rules' support and confidence. With the thresholds in place, the FP-Growth algorithm is employed to perform association rule mining. This algorithm utilizes the FP-tree data structure, which efficiently identifies frequent itemsets within the dataset. The FP-Growth algorithm scans the dataset, constructs the FP-tree, and subsequently generates association rules based on the discovered patterns and relationships. The resulting association rules provide valuable insights into the dataset, enabling predictions and uncovering hidden associations that can aid decision-making or further analysis.

Generating Predictions

The input consists of disease-country strings, and predictions are generated using association rules derived from the dataset. Predictions are stored in a dictionary, where disease-country strings serve as keys and confidence values as their corresponding values. Higher confidence indicates a higher likelihood of disease occurrence. This approach enables the prediction of disease outbreaks based on historical patterns and relationships.

Graph node Classification

The implementation of graph node classification has the following five steps.

Preprocessing

To carry out our analysis effectively, we utilize four distinct datasets that provide various types of information. These datasets include disease outbreak data, Airport-country code data, airline routes data, and latitude-longitude data for different countries. A crucial step in our analysis is preprocessing the data to ensure its accuracy and relevance.

The key steps of preprocessing are as follows -

1. Merge the airport-country code data with the latitude-longitude data.
2. Remove unnecessary columns and extract airport codes, country codes, and latitude-longitude coordinates.
3. Merge the merged table with the route data to enhance the level of detail.
4. Perform an additional merger to incorporate source and destination coordinates, creating a comprehensive table of airline routes with source-destination ISO2 codes and coordinates.
5. Extract the latest disease information for each country and convert it into a structured data frame.

Graph Formation

After preprocessing, the data proceeds through the following steps. The countries are treated as nodes in a graph, with each node representing a different country serving as either the source or destination. Geodesic distance, determining the shortest path between source and destination, is calculated and assigned as the edge label connecting the corresponding nodes. This information is used to form a graph that represents the relationships and connectivity between the countries. Additionally, the latest disease data is incorporated as a node feature, ensuring each node is equipped with the most up-to-date information. By combining nodes, edges, and node features, the graph shown in Figure 13.1 provides a comprehensive representation of countries, their geodesic distances, and their corresponding disease data.

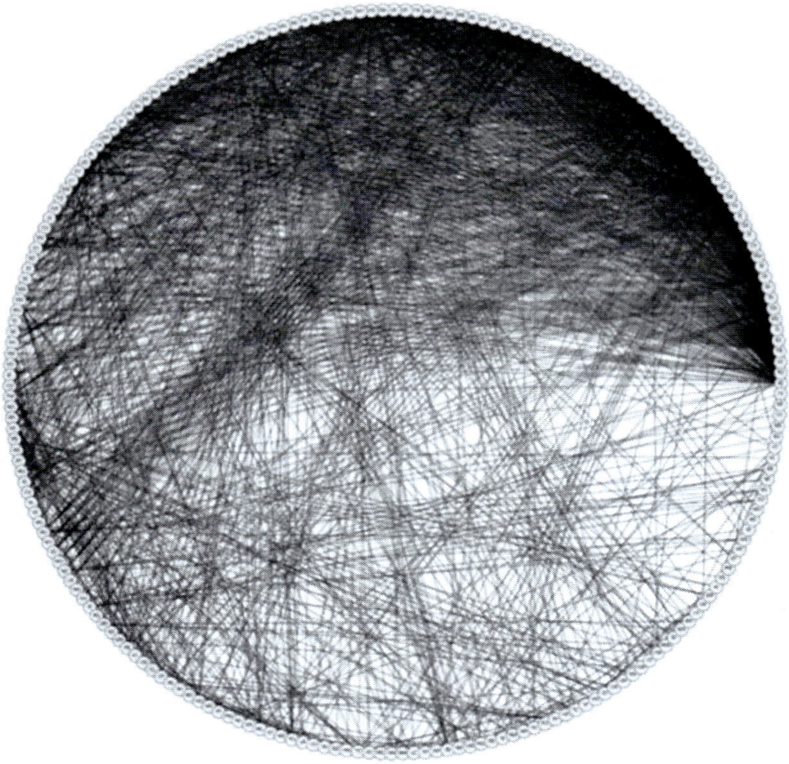

Figure 13.1 Graph formed with the dataset, depicting flight routes between various countries.

Graph Node Embedding

Graph node embedding refers to the process of representing nodes in a graph as low-dimensional, continuous vector representations. These vector representations capture the structural and semantic information of nodes in the graph, allowing us to perform node classification of the graph. node2vec algorithm is used for node embedding.

The node2vec algorithm involves generating random walks from each node in the graph, capturing both local and global graph structures. The random walks are used to create node sequences, which are then used to train a skip-gram model. The skip-gram model learns to predict the neighbouring nodes given a target node in the sequences. The trained model's parameters are adjusted to maximize the probability of predicting the context nodes. The resulting node embeddings, extracted from the skip-gram model, represent the nodes in a low-dimensional vector space, capturing the graph's structural properties. These embeddings are further used for node classification.

Logistic Regression

The embedding data is further prepared for classification. The independent and dependent variables are initialized. After this, the logistic regression classifier is trained. We used logistic regression as there was binary classification involved, i.e., to say that a specific country either has a particular disease or does not have it. Since the dependent variable is binary we chose logistic regression. The classifier finally presents a data frame consisting of countries and the probable outbreak they can expect.

13.7 Evaluation

Evaluating the performance of the model is crucial since it determines whether it is acceptable or not. Accuracy, Precision and f1 score are the performance metrics via which the model has been evaluated.

Accuracy

Let TP signify the count of true positive pixels, TN signify the count of true negative pixels, FP signifies the count of false positive pixels, and FN signifies the count of false negative pixels.

Then, accuracy (ACC) is defined as in eqn (5).

$$ACC = \frac{(TP+TN)}{(TP+TN+FP+FN)} \tag{5}$$

Precision

Precision (PR) is the proportion of true positive pixels to the total number of pixels predicted as positive by the model as given in eqn (6).

$$PR = \frac{TP}{(TP+FP)} \tag{6}$$

F1 Score:

The F1 score represents the harmonic mean of precision and recall as given in eqn (7).

$$F1 = \frac{2 \times Precision \times Recall}{Precision + Recall} \tag{7}$$

In our experiments, an accuracy of 92.56% was obtained. Precision of three variants i.e., weighted, micro and macro was evaluated. The weighted, micro and macro precision scores were - 93.11%, 92.56% and 99.17% respectively. The weighted f1 score of this model was found to be 0.89.

It can therefore be concluded that the model and the approach are both reliable and suitable for further predictions of disease outbreaks in the future.

13.8 Results

Association Rule Mining

The input from the user is taken in the form of a disease-country string, and the results generated by the model are the predictions of outbreaks of diseases in different countries (also in the form of a disease-country string). The strings are printed along with their confidence in a tabular format. Confidence is used as a performance metric, as it measures the reliability or strength of the association between the antecedent (premise) and the consequent (outcome) of a rule. It represents the conditional probability of the consequent given the antecedent. So, in other words, confidence facilitates assessing the strength of the discovered rules. High-confidence rules indicate a high likelihood that the consequence will occur given the presence of the antecedent. These rules are considered more reliable and actionable.

The input in this case was 'Influenza due to identified zoonotic or pandemic influenza virus Hong Kong'. The model predicts the diseases and the countries in which there is a possibility of outbreak as shown in Figure 13.2.

Other diseases which occur frequently in various countries

	ar	conf
0	Influenza due to identified zoonotic or pandemic influenza virus Israel	1
14	Influenza due to identified zoonotic or pandemic influenza virus Indonesia	1
2	Influenza due to identified zoonotic or pandemic influenza virus United States of America	1
3	Influenza due to identified zoonotic or pandemic influenza virus Japan	1
4	Influenza due to identified zoonotic or pandemic influenza virus Chile	1
5	Influenza due to identified zoonotic or pandemic influenza virus Russian Federation	1
6	Influenza due to identified zoonotic or pandemic influenza virus Thailand	1
7	Influenza due to identified zoonotic or pandemic influenza virus Italy	1
8	Influenza due to identified zoonotic or pandemic influenza virus Korea Republic of	1
1	Influenza due to identified zoonotic or pandemic influenza virus Canada	1
15	Influenza due to identified zoonotic or pandemic influenza virus Viet Nam	1
11	Meningococcal meningitis Chad	1
13	Influenza due to identified zoonotic or pandemic influenza virus Cambodia	1
12	Influenza due to identified zoonotic or pandemic influenza virus China	0.75
17	Cholera Congo Democratic Republic of the	0.625
10	Unspecified viral haemorrhagic fever Congo	0.5
16	Meningococcal meningitis Burkina Faso	0.5
9	Cholera Mozambique	0.5

Figure 13.2. The output obtained when the input is "Influenza due to identified zoonotic or pandemic influenza virus Hong Kong."

Other diseases which occur frequently in various countries

	ar	conf
2	Middle East respiratory syndrome United Arab Emirates	1
3	Middle East respiratory syndrome Saudi Arabia	1
1	Influenza due to identified zoonotic or pandemic influenza virus China	0.75
0	Lassa fever Nigeria	0.625

Figure 13.3. The output obtained when the input is "Ebola disease in the Democratic Republic of Congo."

Other diseases which occur frequently in various countries

	ar	conf
1	Middle East respiratory syndrome Saudi Arabia	1
2	Middle East respiratory syndrome United Arab Emirates	1
0	Middle East respiratory syndrome Qatar	0.833333
3	Influenza due to identified zoonotic or pandemic influenza virus China	0.833333

Figure 13.4. The output obtained when the input is "Middle East respiratory syndrome in Oman."

```
Other diseases which occur frequently in various countries
|    | ar                                                                          |   conf |
|---:|:----------------------------------------------------------------------------|-------:|
|  0 | Influenza due to identified zoonotic or pandemic influenza virus Egypt      |      1 |
|  1 | Influenza due to identified zoonotic or pandemic influenza virus Indonesia  |      1 |
|  2 | Influenza due to identified zoonotic or pandemic influenza virus Cambodia   |      1 |
```

Figure 13.5. The output obtained when the input is "Influenza due to identified zoonotic or pandemic influenza virus in Bangladesh"

It also predicts the outbreak of other connected diseases in different countries. Influenza in Hong Kong is causing Influenza in neighbouring regions like Japan, Thailand, Vietnam and in other associated countries. The results are in decreasing order of confidence, thereby indicating the stronger rules first. The screenshots in Figure 13.3, Figure 13,4 and Figure 13.5 further provide outputs in different scenarios.

Thus, the FP growth algorithm predicts the possible outbreaks of disease and country as output based on the input given. It must be noted that it not only predicts the outbreak of disease mentioned by the user but also recommends outbreaks of other diseases that might be related in some way or the other with the input.

Graph Node Classification

Graph node classification was evaluated using various metrics like accuracy, precision, and f1 score.

The accuracy score in machine learning serves as an evaluation metric that quantifies the proportion of correct predictions made by a model out of the total number of predictions made. An accuracy of 92.56% was achieved with the logistic regression classifier.

Precision focuses on the correctness of positive predictions, indicating how well the model avoids false positives. Three variants of precision, namely, weighted precision, micro precision and macro precision were used to evaluate our model.

Weighted precision calculates the average precision across all classes, considering the class imbalance in the dataset. It assigns weight to each class based on its frequency. Here the weighted precision was 93.11%.

Microprecision treats the classification task as a binary problem and gives equal importance to each instance in the calculation. Micro precision came out to be 92.56%. Macro precision gives equal weightage to each class, which means that each class contributes equally to the overall precision score. Macro precision was 99.17%.

F1 score (weighted) was the final metric used. In the weighted F1 score, each class's F1 score is weighted by the number of instances in that class, giving more importance to classes with a larger number of instances. This model had an f1 score (weighted) of 0.89. As the f1 score ranges between 0 and 1, with 1 representing perfect performance, an f1 score of 0.89 would be considered high. A few outputs of different years are shown in Figure 13.6, Figure 13.7 and Figure 13.8.

	country_iso_2	pred_disease
0	AE	COVID-19
1	RU	COVID-19
2	UZ	COVID-19
3	TR	COVID-19
4	KZ	COVID-19
...	...	...
210	NU	COVID-19
211	NR	COVID-19
212	CX	COVID-19
213	WF	COVID-19
214	TV	COVID-19

Figure 13.6. Final predictions (Predictions in 2022).

Post-analysis of the data presented the list of all the countries which could have future outbreaks of diseases. Since the years 2020-2022 had a massive COVID-19 outbreak, the data shows COVID-19 as the predicted outbreak in the mentioned countries. The output resonates with reality, which is a positive sign.

However, if the data was taken up to let's say, 2019 or 2010 then the output would have been different, as shown in Figures 13.7 and 13.8.

	country_iso_2	pred_disease
0	AE	Measles
1	RU	Influenza due to identified zoonotic or pande...
2	UZ	Measles
3	TR	Measles
4	KZ	Measles
...	...	...
210	NU	Measles
211	NR	Influenza due to identified zoonotic or pande...
212	CX	Influenza due to identified zoonotic or pande...
213	WF	Influenza due to identified zoonotic or pande...
214	TV	Influenza due to identified zoonotic or pande...

215 rows × 2 columns

Figure 13.7. Predictions in 2019.

	country_iso_2	pred_disease
165	KP	Influenza due to identified zoonotic or pande...
166	BJ	Influenza due to identified zoonotic or pande...
167	NE	Influenza due to identified zoonotic or pande...
168	GN	Influenza due to identified zoonotic or pande...
169	MQ	Influenza due to identified zoonotic or pande...
170	RE	Influenza due to identified zoonotic or pande...
171	SJ	Influenza due to identified zoonotic or pande...
172	AW	Influenza due to identified zoonotic or pande...
173	SR	Influenza due to identified zoonotic or pande...
174	GL	no disease data found
175	FO	Influenza due to identified zoonotic or pande...
176	PY	Influenza due to identified zoonotic or pande...

Figure 13.8. Predictions in 2010.

Thus, we can say that the model generates reliable outputs for disease outbreaks.

13.9 Discussion and Conclusion

This book chapter predicts the disease outbreaks using the two approaches - Association Rule Mining and Graph Node Classification. An attempt was made to predict the outbreak using a supervised learning method (Graph node classification) and an Unsupervised learning method (Association Rule Mining). The association rule mining algorithm has been widely used for market basket analysis and similar domains in the existing literature, where it predicts and recommends users to do preferential shopping but, in this chapter, it has been effectively used in the prediction of disease outbreaks. In this context, association rule mining makes predictions by finding associations in the dataset through learning. It is an efficient method that predicts outbreaks for the user inputs. For example, depending on the type of 'disease country string' the user provides, it outputs the associated predictions. Another unique approach for generating predictions is by applying the graph node classification method which used airline routes data and predicted diseases to aid human mobility and connectivity. A graph was formed which when passed through node embeddings and subjected to logistic regression, gave accurate predictions. A prediction accuracy of 92.56% was achieved. In this approach, the use of airline data is significant as it can facilitate the mobility of people around the globe by predicting the spread of infectious diseases. The combination of these two methodologies provides a unified framework that offers a comprehensive, multifaceted and multi-dimensional approach to disease outbreak prediction.

The COVID-19 pandemic has taught us many vital lessons and brought to light several research gaps. The following future directions can be done further on the research work carried out in this book chapter to fill the identified gaps. A generic approach can be proposed where the association rule mining algorithm can find other similar associations between any attribute in the dataset and a disease-country string, while the graph node classification algorithm can map them to the location and flight route data. The inferences from such a study will address disease outbreak prediction and help us analyze the attributes that will shoot up disease spread. Temporal and climatic analysis of disease spread can be done to find out which period of the year is most conducive to the spread of which disease and so on.

References

Anno, S., Hara, T., Kai, H., Lee, M. A., Chang, Y., Oyoshi, K., et al. (2019). "Spatiotemporal dengue fever hotspots associated with climatic factors in Taiwan including outbreak predictions based on machine-learning." *Geospatial Health*, *14*(2).

Dutta, S., and Bandyopadhyay, S. K. (2020). Machine learning approach for confirmation of covid-19 cases: Positive, negative, death and release. *MedRxiv*, 03.

Feldman, J., Thomas-Bachli, A., Forsyth, J., Patel, Z. H., and Khan, K. (2019). "Development of a global infectious disease activity database using natural language processing, machine learning, and human expertise." *Journal of the American Medical Informatics Association*, *26*(11), 1355-1359.

Jonkmans, N., D'Acremont, V., and Flahault, A. (2021). "Scoping future outbreaks: a scoping review on the outbreak prediction of the WHO Blueprint list of priority diseases." *BMJ global health*, *6*(9), e006623.

Khakharia, A., Shah, V., Jain, S., Shah, J., Tiwari, A., Daphal, P., et al. (2021). "Outbreak prediction of COVID-19 for dense and populated countries using machine learning." *Annals of Data Science*, *8*, 1-19.

Koc, E., and Türkoğlu, M. (2022)." Forecasting of medical equipment demand and outbreak spreading based on deep long short-term memory network: the COVID-19 pandemic in Turkey." *Signal, image and video processing*, 1-9.

Krishnamoorthy, S., Liu, Y., and Liu, K. (2022). "A novel oppositional binary crow search algorithm with optimal machine learning based postpartum hemorrhage prediction model." *BMC Pregnancy and Childbirth*, *22*(1), 560.

Lee, S., Cho, E., Jang, G., Kim, S., and Cho, G. (2022). "Early detection of norovirus outbreak using machine learning methods in South Korea." *Plos one*, *17*(11), e0277671.

Ozturk, T., Talo, M., Yildirim, E. A., Baloglu, U. B., Yildirim, O., and Acharya, U. R. (2020). Automated detection of COVID-19 cases using deep neural networks with X-ray images. *Computers in biology and medicine*, *121*, 103792.

Raizada, S., Mala, S., and Shankar, A. (2020). "Vector borne disease outbreak prediction by machine learning." In *2020 International conference on smart technologies in computing, electrical and electronics (ICSTCEE)* (pp. 213-218). IEEE.

Rathnamala, S., and Jenicka, S. (2021). "Automated bleeding detection in wireless capsule endoscopy images based on color feature extraction from Gaussian mixture model superpixels." *Medical and biological engineering and computing*, *59*, 969-987.

Salim, N. A. M., Wah, Y. B., Reeves, C., Smith, M., Yaacob, W. F. W., Mudin, R. N., et al. (2021). "Prediction of dengue outbreak in Selangor Malaysia using machine learning techniques." *Scientific reports*, *11*(1), 939.

Shashank, P. S. T., Vaibhavi, A., Vaishnavi, J., and Jabbar, M. A. (2021). "Regression Model for Prediction of Epidemic Outbreaks." In *IOP Conference Series: Materials Science and Engineering* (Vol. 1042, No. 1, p. 012016). IOP Publishing.

Singh, R., and Singh, R. (2023). "Applications of sentiment analysis and machine learning techniques in disease outbreak prediction–A review." *Materials Today: Proceedings*, *81*, 1006-1011.

Tiwari, S., Kumar, S., and Guleria, K. (2020). "Outbreak trends of coronavirus disease–2019 in India: a prediction." *Disaster medicine and public health preparedness*, *14*(5), e33-e38.

Yoshida, K., Fujimoto, T., Muramatsu, M., and Shimizu, H. (2022). "Prediction of hand, foot, and mouth disease epidemics in Japan using a long short-term memory approach." *PLoS One*, *17*(7), e0271820.

Chapter 14

Explainable AI in Medical Image Processing for Health Care

Riyam Patel[1]
Aditi Acharjya[2]
Punyaban Patel[3, 1]
Borra Sivaiah[4]
Ruplal Choudhary[5]
and Saroj Kumar Meher[6]

[1]Department of Computer Science and Engineering (AI and ML), SRM Institute of Science and Technology, SRM University, Kattankulathur, Chennai, India
[2] Department of Computer Science and Engineering, SRM Institute of Science and Technology, Ramapuram, Chennai, India
[3,4]Department of Computer Sc. and Engineering, CMR College of Engineering and Technology, Kandlakoya, Hyderabad, India
[5]School of Agricultural Sciences-SIUC, Southern Illinois University, Carbondale, IL, USA
[6]Department of Systems Science and Informatics Unit, Indian Statistical Institute, Bangalore Centre, Bangalore, India

Abstract

The integration of artificial intelligence (AI) techniques in medical image processing has revolutionized the field of healthcare. However, the lack of interpretability and transparency in traditional AI models has hindered their widespread adoption in clinical practice. Explainable AI (XAI) offers a solution to this problem by providing interpretable explanations for AI-based decisions. It is very difficult to interpret predictions made by classifiers on image data. Therefore, Explainable artificial intelligence (XAI) has gained significant attention in the field of healthcare, particularly in medical image processing. This chapter investigates the explainable AI methods in healthcare, focusing on their role in medical image processing. It uses XAI approaches such as LIME, and Grad-Cam for analyzing a Biopsy dataset. The random forest classifier achieved 96.54% accuracy better than Naive Bayes on the Biopsy data set. The GradCam approach is the fastest one and the slowest one is LIME on VGG-16. The VGG-16 is faster than ResNet-50 for image

In: Explainable Artificial Intelligence in Healthcare Systems
Editors: A. Anitha Kamaraj and Debi Prasanna Acharjya
ISBN: 979-8-89113-598-7

classification. The results of XAI models in medical image processing enable healthcare professionals to understand the decision-making process of AI models, leading to increased diagnostic accuracy, improved decision-making and enhanced trust in AI systems. The chapter concludes by outlining future research directions and recommendations for the integration of explainable AI in health care, emphasizing the need for interdisciplinary collaborations, standardized evaluation metrics, and regulatory frameworks to ensure the responsible and effective use of XAI in medical image processing.

Keywords: explainable artificial intelligence, image processing, heart disease, biopsy dataset, lung cancer data set

14.1 Introduction

Producing visible images of the internal structures of the body for scientific research and medical therapy is the procedure that is referred to as "medical imaging." Analyzing and interpreting pictures obtained from medical modalities such as X-rays, CT scans, MRI, and ultrasound are both essential parts of the process known as medical image processing. These images offer vital information that can be used for disease diagnosis, the formulation of treatment plans, and the tracking of a patient's progression. In comparison to the techniques that modulate into visuals, these methods have a great deal of inherent restriction. Every year, various diagnostic procedures have resulted in billions of photographs worldwide. Because of the growing complexity and number of medical pictures, solutions based on artificial intelligence have emerged as necessary to provide correct and fast analysis. The application of artificial intelligence (AI) algorithms in the field of medicine has been hampered by the absence of an explanation for the outcomes obtained by these algorithms. Explainable artificial intelligence, often known as XAI, is a concept that was introduced (Wojciech Samek et al. 2019) to make existing AI technologies more understandable.

The application of AI approaches in medical image processing has resulted in substantial technological improvements, which have made it possible to conduct accurate and time-saving analyses of medical images (Wojciech Samek et al. 2019). In the field of medical image processing, explainable AI, which centers on the provision of clear and understandable explanations for judgments based on AI, possesses a tremendous amount of untapped potential. The use of artificial intelligence (AI) can provide medical professionals with assistance while working with a variety of healthcare systems and intelligent health systems. The diagnosis of common ailments, the creation of new drugs, and the analysis of patient information gleaned from electronic health records are all significantly aided by AI. The field of healthcare places a high premium on explainable artificial intelligence (XAI). Since XAI provides interpretable explanations, doctors, patients, and other stakeholders can more easily check the dependability of a choice by knowing the reasons behind it when using XAI. Explainable artificial intelligence (XAI) is the topic of discussion in this chapter, which focuses on medical picture analysis. When it comes to medical image analysis, the interpretability method/XAI approach is frequently categorized depending on the explanation and the technical method. To improve the trustworthiness and dependability of the findings generated by the black-box machine learning model, an AI system that can be explained is necessary. The goal of XAI might be summed up as being to make AI systems appear more comprehensible to human beings. The concepts of transparency, interpretability, and explainability are frequently used synonymously with one another. It is also possible to use interpretability in place of the term explainability. Interpretability is connected to the degree to which a model may be comprehended.

Building an AI system that is comprehensible, trustworthy, observable, interpretable, explainable, etc. is the goal of XAI (Gupta A et al. 2020). When results are used to inform decisions, especially in the healthcare industry where decisions affect people's lives, it is crucial to interpret the data. By scope, XAI approaches can be divided into two categories: those that offer local information of a single diagnosis and those that provide global details of the entire system. The comprehensive explanations facilitate comprehension of the model's behavior and the hypothesis that produces the desired results. The justification behind a single prediction is given for local explanations to support the model's choice of action in that case. Additionally, these methods can be categorized according to whether they are model specific, meaning they can only be used with a certain ML algorithm, or model agnostic, meaning they can be used with any ML methodology (Ferrara et al. 2021). To estimate the predictive power of the model, the explainable frameworks are analysed each feature weight using the Shapley additive explanation (SHAP) and the local interpretable model-agnostic explanation (LIME) techniques (Maringe et al. 2021; Spicer J et al. 2020).

The (Shruthishree and Tiwari, 2017) conducted a comprehensive review of the recent developments in XAI as well as the effectiveness of the technology in the medical field. In addition to this, the authors have suggested a method for XAI that involves the merging of data from several models and centers. None of the models described up to this point can explain the decision-making process that goes into classifying the instances. It would be ideal to have a model that could classify the data while also providing a sufficient level of Explainability regarding the result of the decision that was taken. Explainability is provided across a variety of aspects of the model, such as the comprehensibility of the framework and the understandability of the structure of the system, an understanding of the objective functions, ease of understanding of the training dataset and the parameters in the training set, the comprehensibility of the validation sets, the comprehensibility of the parameters for analysis, and the comprehensibility of the model itself.

Breast cancer has emerged as one of the most prevalent forms of cancer in women across the globe, and it poses a significant risk to both the physical and emotional health of affected individuals. In recent years, with the development of Artificial Intelligence (AI) and the collection of medical data, AI has begun to be deeply integrated with various imaging modalities, including mammography, MRI, ultrasound, etc., to assist clinicians in the diagnosis of disease. However, the existing breast cancer diagnosis model that is based on Computer Vision (CV) is significantly impacted by image quality; on the other hand, the breast cancer diagnosis model that is based on Natural Language Processing (NLP) is unable to successfully extract the semantic content of the mammography report. Both models are impacted by the fact that image quality plays a significant role. The inability to interpret the model is another factor that contributes to the existing diagnostic models' lack of confidence.

According to (Wojciech S et al. 2019) cancer is one of the most common diseases that affect individuals all over the world, accounting for at least 10 million deaths and approximately 20 million new cases each year. Without a doubt, this is one of the primary priorities of nations and health services. In addition, as a result of the COVID-19 pandemic, health services have become even more stressed (for example, the case of oral cancer in (D Chen et al. 2021), cancer diagnostic delay in northern and central Italy, cited in (Jean-Baptiste et al. 2019), and substantial increases in the number of preventable cancer deaths in England, mentioned in (Cunningham et al. 2003), the aforementioned, and according to authors such as (Spicer et al. 2020), the Heart Disease and Breast Cancer- Biopsy are shown in Figure 14.1. and Figure 14.2. respectively.

This chapter aims to explore the application of explainable AI in this domain and its impact on healthcare.

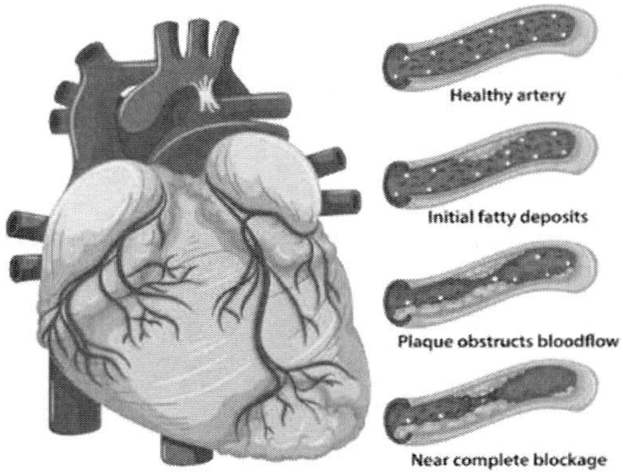

Figure 14.1. Heart Disease.

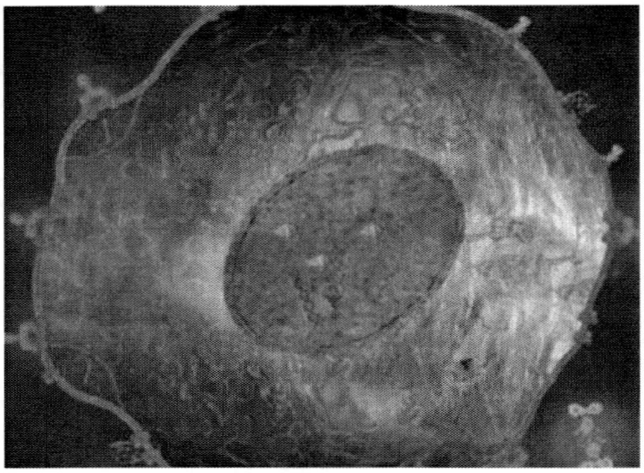

Figure 14.2. Breast Cancer: Bipsoy.

14.2 Explainable AI in Medical Image Processing

The decision-making process of artificial intelligence models employed in medical image analysis can be comprehended and analyzed using explainable artificial intelligence approaches, which allow medical personnel to do so. In contrast to traditional AI models, which operate like black boxes, explainable AI explains the thinking process that went into the model's predictions, making it more open and accessible to interpretation in the process. This transparency is vital for creating confidence between artificial intelligence (AI) systems and human specialists, ensuring that accountability will be met, and making the process of working together easier (Zhu et al. 2010).

14.2.1 Major Challenges in XAI

The challenges of XAI are as follows:

1. *Interpretability-Accuracy Trade-off:* In nearly every instance, the interpretability of AI models and the accuracy of those models come into direct conflict with one another. The challenge that lies in developing AI systems that can be depended on and trusted is finding a happy medium between two competing considerations. This obstacle must be surmounted before AI systems can be developed that can do either.
2. *Standardization of Explanation Quality*: To evaluate and contrast the various explainable AI tactics, it is required to first create standardized criteria and standards for the quality of explanations that are generated by AI models. This is a prerequisite step that cannot be avoided.
3. *Handling Complex and Multimodal Medical Data*: Data derived from medical imaging can be both complex and multimodal, which calls for the development of cutting-edge AI systems that are both explicable and capable of effectively managing a wide variety of information in its various forms.
4. *Ethical and Legal Considerations*: The application of explainable artificial intelligence in medical image processing raises some ethical and legal problems regarding patient privacy, consent, and the responsibility for judgments made by AI systems. These worries are associated with the sphere of medicine. It is extremely necessary to secure regulatory compliance and resolve these concerns to pave the way for the broad deployment of explainable AI in the healthcare business. This will make it possible to move forward with the implementation of explainable AI.

14.2.2 Benefits of Explainable AI in Medical Image Processing

The benefits of XAI are as follows (Massie et al. 2004):

1. *Enhanced Diagnostic Accuracy*: Explainable artificial intelligence (AI) algorithms offer in-depth justifications for their conclusions, which enable trained medical practitioners to comprehend the aspects that play a role in determining the outcomes predicted by the model. Because of this transparency, potential errors or biases can be identified and corrected, which eventually results in an improvement in diagnostic accuracy.
2. *Facilitated Decision-Making*: Explainable AI helps in the identification of significant facts that may be overlooked by human observers, leading to more accurate diagnosis and treatment plans. This is accomplished by highlighting important features and areas of concern in medical images.
3. *Trust and Acceptance:* The "black box" character of traditional AI models is one of the sources of anxiety, and the openness provided by explainable AI helps to alleviate these worries and promote confidence among healthcare practitioners. Acceptance and adoption of AI systems in medical image processing are increased by providing clear

explanations and reasons for the outcomes generated by AI. This ultimately leads to improved care for patients.

4. *Error Detection and Prevention*: Explainable AI technologies make it possible to identify flaws or biases in training data, algorithmic judgments, or the process of feature extraction. By gaining a knowledge of these challenges, healthcare workers can improve AI models, ensuring greater performance and minimizing the likelihood that patients will be harmed.
5. *Education and Training*: Explainable artificial intelligence makes it easier to educate and train medical practitioners. It helps evaluate illness development and therapy response and provides educational insights and explanations of complex medical ideas. Additionally, it highlights crucial locations in images.

This chapter has been organized as follows: The introduction section explains and discusses explainable AI in Medical Image Processing, the next section mentions the challenges of XAI and its benefits, the Literature review section briefly explains the recent development in the related title of the chapter, next section presents the exploratory data analysis, next section includes the Supervise Machine Learning Models such as a Random Forest Classifier and Support Vector Machine. In the next section, Explainable AI Techniques in Medical Image Processing have been discussed. The Performance Measures in XAI, Experimental Results, and Analysis, have been presented and discussed successively. Finally, it has concluded the chapter.

14.3 Classification Models

In this chapter, the different classification models have been presented.

Decision Tree

The Decision Tree is a classification method used for categorization and prediction problems. It has a root node, branches, internal nodes, and leaf nodes, like a tree. It is used to build models that predict target values based on decisions from the training dataset. This method can handle both numeric and categorical data but is popular for its performance on categorical features.

Naive Bayes

Naive Bayes is a supervised machine learning model used for classification tasks, based on the Bayes theorem. It assumes all features are independent and is faster than other classification methods. Naive Bayes is particularly effective with categorical data, making it suitable due to its ability to handle categorical features.

Random Forest Classifier Model

Conventionally, the results of a basic Random Forest (RF) classification include information on the training data, optimal RF parameters, a set of predicted accuracy metrics, and a description of assessment methods being used. The currently available techniques for RF explainability can be broken down into two primary categories. The ranking of features employs the RF-provided variable significance measures, such as Gini, MDA (mean decrease in accuracy), or others, to present the results in tables or horizontal bar charts that are ordered according to the variable importance measure that was selected. The next step is to presume that highly rated characteristics play a significant part in RF predictions, which may then provide some insights into the observed process or perhaps be utilized to clean up training databases. Having said that, this evidence is insufficient to provide a more substantive explanation. In addition, ranking features independently for the + and - classes is not something that is done very often, which creates issues for the common occurrence of imbalanced data sets. It has been reported in scholarly literature that an improved ranking feature representation includes more details for aiding RF exploitability.

A Support Vector Machine (SVM)

An SVM algorithm generates a model that classifies new examples into one of several categories. Since the SVM model may be viewed as a space-based characterization of instances, it can be referred to as a "non-probabilistic classifier". Any structure that categorizes the different cases is called a hyper-plane. The machine learning approach utilized to solve both regression and classification problems is overseen by SVM. The coordinates of several observations are made simpler by the support vector. The SVM classifier is then regarded as the frontier that best divides the two classes after that. The accuracy of the SVM model, which inputs the XTrain and YTrain parameters and is the fit technique, is referred to as performance. Next, using the parameters XTest and YTest, the model's score is entered into the scoring system. This tool can be used to find the SVM model's score.

14.4 Literature Review

Here, it provides ways in which breast cancer and heart disease can be predicted, controlled, and avoided all around the world. In addition to this, several techniques have been demonstrated and proposed up to this point in the state of the art as well as the deficiencies that warrant the selection of the methodology that we have provided.

Case-based reasoning (CBR) (Saini et al. 2020) is a type of analogical reasoning in which the solution for a (new) query case is derived using a database of previously known cases together with their solutions. This style of analogical reasoning differs from traditional reasoning in that it does not rely on logical inference. It has been demonstrated that explanations based on similar situations are more persuasive than explanations based on rules (Nolan GS et al. 2020; Boulton, 2021), even though this potential has not been widely utilized and the fact that many explanations systems are not visual and rely on a single example of a similar case.

Case-based reasoning (also known as CBR) has only a limited number of visual approaches that have been presented, the majority of which do not target CBR's eventual users. They are more concerned with assisting developers with the process of designing CBR systems. For instance, the Case Base Topology Viewer (CTBV) (Ricciardiello et al. 2021) employs scatter plots to view the topology of a case base and examines the influence that various similarity measures have on CBR. However, (Radfar et al. 2021) provided a visual method for presenting explanations of CBR to final users by utilizing parallel coordinates. This method was presented as an alternative. However, the authors only show their approach using three different examples that are very similar to one another, therefore it is possible that it will not scale well with more cases. The majority of the medical CBR systems described in the research literature were designed to assist doctors in the diagnosis of a specific condition or a small number of related disorders. These systems were restricted to quantitative components of patient data.

It has been suggested by several authors, including (Patel et al. 2016; Naji et al. 2021 and Rabiei et al. 2022), and others, that the treatment of some cancer patients has been halted as a result of the pandemic, which has led to an increase in the severity of the adverse effects of their conditions. In point of fact, (Zeng et al. 2023) note that an increase in mortality of 12% can be attributed to patients having to wait longer for treatment. Therefore, it is of the utmost importance to diagnose and treat instances of this kind of disease in the community promptly, or more requisites to anticipate difficult patient circumstances. According to the authors (Nindrea et al. 2020; Patel et al. 2022 and Patel et al. 2023), and others, COVID has been a significant drain on the time and attention of the clinical team because of this reason. As a result, COVID has negatively impacted patients who suffer from other types of diseases, resulting in delays in care and confirming the diagnosis. Because of these factors, the utilization of a variety of approaches and diagnostic methods for the early prevention and detection of this disease is essential, as it assists both the clinical team and the patients. For cancer management in health care, a variety of strategies have been created. Machine learning methods have been utilized by several writers, including (Pedro A Moreno-Sánchez et al. 2023; Ishaq et al. 2021 and Dokainish,., et al. 2017), to forecast the diagnosis of breast cancer.

Since most AI solutions need in-depth knowledge of ML algorithms, there has been a steady rise in the demand for tools that make artificial intelligence (AI) more accessible to medical practitioners. This requirement is especially important in the field of precision medicine, which requires information that is both interpretable and transparent to diagnose diseases (Alba et al. 2013; Straw S et al. 2019) Support Vector Machines, Logistic Regression, Artificial Neural Networks, Random Forest, Decision Tree, Ensemble Learning approaches Deep Neural Networks, Fuzzy experts system, and K-nearest Networks are just some of the machine learning (ML) algorithms that have been utilized in CVD prediction models (Dauriz M, 2017 and Segar MW et al. 2019). However, there is still a gap in the modelling of survival heart failure in terms of the identification of driving factors. This is because existing models exhibit poor interpretability of their prediction variables (Son MK et al. 2019 and Tjoa et al. 2020). This is another problem found in the research done on the subject. As a result, partial approaches target the effectiveness of the model by using cohorts with specific types of patients (for example, diabetic or elderly patients) (Adadi et al. 2018 and Temenos et al. 2022) even though the models have produced have not achieved ideal performance (Guleria et al. 2022 and Yang et.al., 2021). Deep learning was used to develop a smart framework that was developed by Vincent Paul and colleagues (Dauriz et al. 2017) for the prediction of cardiac disease. Aggarwal et al. used XAI algorithms for the categorization and analysis of ECG data to predict the risk of developing heart disease. XAI may improve the diagnostic outcome by making the prognosis more understandable to medical professionals.

14.5 Exploratory Data Analysis

Exploratory data analysis (EDA) data analysis is utilized to acquire a deeper comprehension of the data and to locate the data. It's a lot like telling a story but with numbers instead of words. Statisticians do it. It makes it possible to make discoveries about patterns and observations inside data by employing visual methods. Aside from that, EDA is typically included in the process of data modelling at the beginning as the very first step. Both an exploration of the dataset and an exploratory data analysis will be carried out by it. The next step is to deal with the missing data, and then comes the treatment of outliers, then encoding categorical variables and normalizing, and finally scaling and deleting duplicates.

Data Cleaning

Cleaning the raw data, which prepares the data for visualization and prediction, is an important step in the process of data cleaning, which is also known as data preparation for analysis. It is the process of deleting erroneous data, corrupted data, incorrectly formatted data, and redundant data from a dataset, which would otherwise be wrong, corrupted, and incomplete without it. A link or correlation matrix, often known as a plot, is a type of covariance matrix. Correlation is a statistic that quantifies how strong a linear link is. The power and direction of a linear relationship between two variables are summed up in the correlation matrix, which allows for values between -1 and +1 in addition to the more common range of 0 to 1. A characteristic of the correlation matrix shows how much the coefficients are correlated. One particular random variable is said to be correlated with all of the other values of the same random variable.

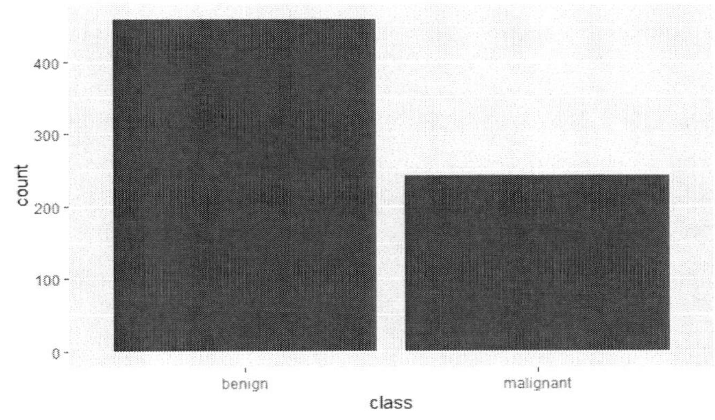

Figure 14.3. The Breast Cancer Data Set: Biopsy.

Representing the correlation matrix in the form of a heat map provides an effective method for determining if certain features are correlated. Figure 14.3 depicts the different types of breast cancer, and Figure 14.4 explains how heart disease manifests in patients' lives. The correlation matrix that depicts the relationship between the different aspects of the heart disease data set is shown in Figure 14.5. The correlation between the variables in the dataset is used to identify the linear relationship that exists between two continuous variables.

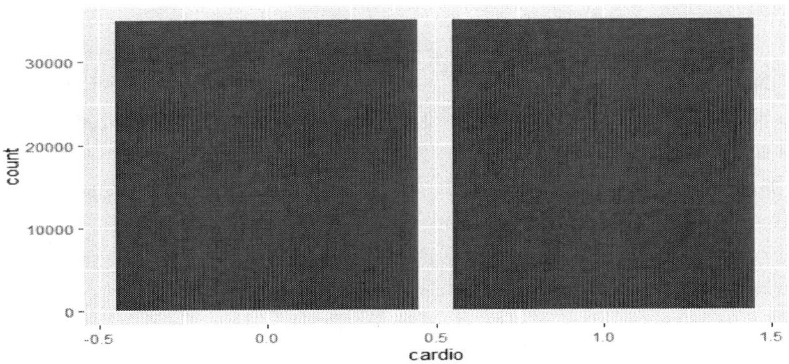

Figure 14.4. Heart Disease Data Set.

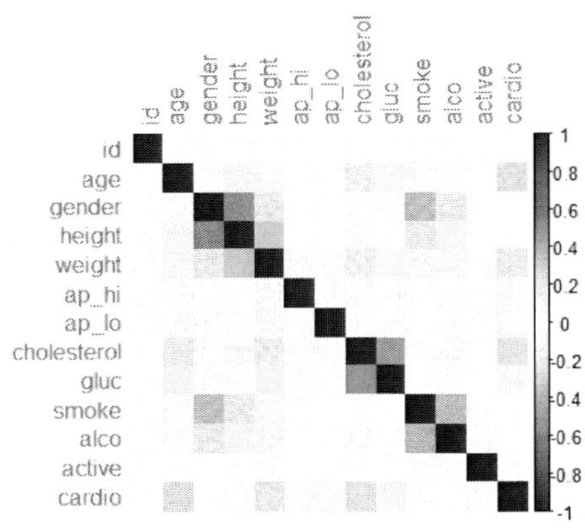

Figure 14.5. Correlation Plot of Heart Disease Data Set.

14.6 Explainable AI Techniques in Medical Image Processing

The XAI models can be broken down into three categories, which are referred to as Attention-based Models, Grad-CAM, and Rule-based Systems. Two categories may be used to categorize the types of explainable artificial intelligence methods that are used to explain the predictions provided by models (Denj et al. 2009):

1. *Model-Agnostic Method:* This approach is best suited for post-hoc analysis and is not restricted to any specific model architecture. These approaches do not have access to the internal model weights and structural parameters. LIME is not tied to any model as it works. There is a wide variety of feature-based approaches that can be taken, such as the Shapley Additive Explanations (SHAP), the Local Interpretable Model-agnostic Explanations (LIME), the Global Surrogate Models, the Individual Conditional

Expectation (ICE) Plots, the Partial Dependence Plots (PDPs), the Accumulated Local Effects (ALE) Plots, and the Permutation Feature Importance.
2. *Model-Specific Technique*: Relying on the Particular Model's Parameters. This technique relies on the model's parameters. Both Integrated Gradients and Grad-Cam are examples of model-specific analysis techniques. Gradient-weighted Class Activation Mapping, or Grad-CAM for short, provides a visual representation of the predictions provided by deep learning models. It does this by emphasizing the regions of a picture that are most significant to the model's conclusion. This makes it easier to grasp the data that AI has created.

14.7 Medical Image Classification

Deep Neural Networks (DNN), a type of artificial neural network (Simonyam K and Zissarman A, 2014) has emerged as one of the most successful machine learning techniques for the task of classifying medical images. This will be of assistance to medical practitioners and will improve diagnosis using these images. In this research, we will be running our tests on two images (Deng et al. 2009) of pre-trained CNN models, which will then be further fine-tuned, training them to classify lung cancer using histopathology pictures for the same. CNN stands for convolutional neural network. The techniques such as LIME and GradCam are presented in this chapter:

Local Interpretable Model-Agnostic Explanations (LIME)

Explanations that are Locally Interpretable and Model-agnostic (LIME) (Ribeiro MT et al. 2016) is an approach that is utilized to describe the individual prediction that a machine learning model generates because of its local nature. It is a visualization technique that helps explain specific predictions. Because it is not dependent on any model, it can be utilized with supervised regression or classification models of any kind. The LIME project was initially introduced (Ribeiro MT et al. 2016). LIME makes its calculations based on the assumption that all complicated models are linear on a scale that is local to their scope. It does this by attempting to fit a simple model to a single observation in the hopes that this will duplicate the behavior of the global model at the local level. After that, the straightforward model can be used to provide a local explanation for the more complex model's predictions.

Grad-Cam

Grad-CAM (Selvaraju et al. 2017) is based on the concept of gradients, which are computed for each channel of an output feature map about the class that is projected to be present in an input picture. These values obtained for each channel are assigned as weights to the channels respectively. This means that the more important a channel is in the prediction of the class, the higher the gradient obtained for that channel. It is possible to highlight pixels in an image that contributes significantly to the model predictions as a result of this.

Proposed Methodology

Machine learning models such as Random Forest and Naïve Bayes classifiers are used for the classification and prediction of cancer datasets as shown in Figure 14.6. The models take the input as biopsy data and lung cancer data. The predictions made by them are explained using LIME. The explanations generated by VGG-16 and ResNet-50 are evaluated using LIME and GradCam approaches. The biopsy data set consists of 16 missing values and the missing values are eliminated using data prepossessing. The dataset was divided into training and testing set, with 75% of the sample size used for training and 25% for testing. A random forest model was used for classification and prediction, with no hyperparameter tuning, just a 10-fold CV repeated 5 times. The Probability based classifier such as Naïve Bayes is also used for classification and prediction purposes. The models are evaluated using performance metrics such as accuracy, sensitivity, specificity, etc. XAI is more useful for explaining the predictions of random forest and Naïve Bayes classifier.

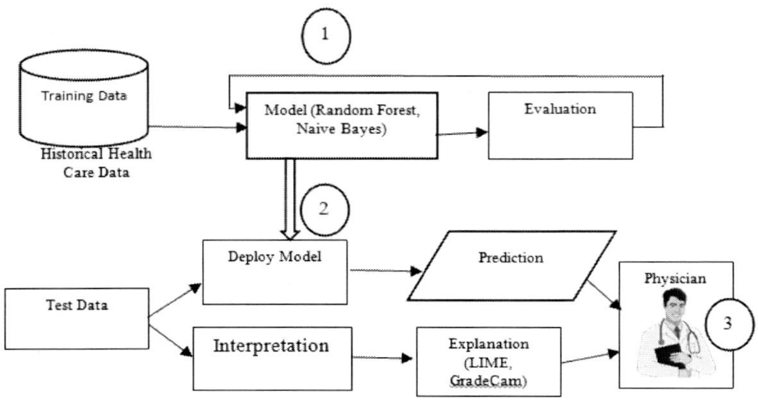

Figure 14.6. A ML Life Cycle in Conjunction with XAI.

Performance Measures in XAI

A confusion matrix represents the prediction summary in matrix form. It shows how many predictions are correct and incorrect per class. Here, P = True Positive (TP), Q = False Positive (FP), R = False Negative (FN), and S = True Negative (TN) as shown in Table 14.1.

Table 14.1. Confusion Matrix

Reference		
Predicted	Event	No Event
Event	P	Q
No Event	R	S

The Performance metrics used in XAI are;

$$Sensitivity = \frac{P}{P+R} \quad (1)$$

$$Specificity = \frac{S}{Q+S} \quad (2)$$

$$Prevalence = \frac{P+S}{P+Q+R+S} \quad (3)$$

The Positive Predictive Value (PPV) can be given as

$$PPV = \frac{Sensitivity \times Prevalence}{(Sensitivity \times Prevalence)+((1-Specificity)\times(1-Prevalence))} \quad (4)$$

The Negative Predicted Value (NPV) can be given as;

$$NPV = \frac{Sensitivity \times(1-Prevalence)}{((1-Sensitivity) \times Prevalence)+(Specifity\times(1-Prevalence))} \quad (5)$$

$$Detection\ Rate = \frac{P}{P+Q+R+S} \quad (6)$$

$$Detection\ Prevalence = \frac{P+Q}{P+Q+R+S} \quad (7)$$

$$Balanced\ Accuracy = (Sensitivity - Specificity)/2 \quad (8)$$

$$Precision = \frac{P}{P+Q} \quad (9)$$

$$Recall = \frac{P}{P+R} \quad (10)$$

14.8 Experimental Result and Analysis

The results of the machine learning algorithms such as Random Forest and Naive Bayes classifiers analysed on the biopsy dataset. The explanations generated by LIME are presented for the biopsy test dataset. The LIME, and GradCam explanations are analyzed on Lung and colon cancer image datasets. The performance evaluation of Random Forest, Naive Bayes classifiers, LIME, and GradCam are presented in this chapter.

Datasets

The different datasets are explained as follows:

A. Lung and Colon Cancer Histopathological Image Dataset
The models mentioned above are fine-tuned and tested against the 'Lung and Colon Cancer Histopathological Image Dataset (LC25000)' dataset. This dataset comprises 25,000 histopathological images with 5 classes- 3 classes for lung cancer, and 2 classes for colon cancer. All the images in this dataset have dimensions of 768 x 768 pixels and are in the file format 'jpeg'. These images, which include 750 total images of lung tissue and 500 total images of colon tissue are further augmented using the R programming languages. Augmenter module, which was increased to 25,000. For augmentation purposes, left and right rotations and horizontal and vertical flips were used. In this chapter, we used the lung images from this dataset, which is 15,000 images in number, consisting of 3 classes.

B. Biopsy Dataset
This dataset contains information on 699 patients and their biopsies of breast cancer tumors. The biopsy data set attributes are presented in Table 14.2.

Table 14.2. Biopsy data set characteristics

Attribute	Description
ID	Sample code number
V1	clump thickness
V2	uniformity cell size
V3	uniformity cell shape
V4	marginal adhesion
V5	single epithelial cell size
V6	bare nuclei
V7	bland chromatin
V8	normal nucleoli
V9	Mitoses
Class	Class

14.8.1 Interpretability by LIME

LIME explains the predictions of whether a patient has cancer or not, we will be using the biopsy dataset.

For simulation, the dataset has been divided into a training set and a testing set. 75% of the sample size was used for training and the remaining 25% was used for testing i.e., there are 512 rows in the train set and 171 rows in the test set. We used a random forest model for classification and prediction. We will not be performing any hyperparameter tuning, just a 10-fold CV repeated 5 times and a Random Forest model. The confusion matrix is shown in Table 14.3, and the performance of the decision tree model is provided in Table 4.

Table 14.3. Confusion Matrix and Statistics

Actual	Prediction	
	benign	malignant
Benign	110	2
Malignant	4	55

Table 14.4. Metrics used by Random Forest

Sensitivity	96.49
Specificity	96.49
Pos Pred Value	98.21
Neg Pred Value	93.22
Prevalence	66.67
Detection Rate	64.33
Detection Prevalence	65.50
Balanced Accuracy	96.49

The support and contradiction LIME Explainer for Biopsy Dataset is shown in Figure 14.7 and Figure 14.8 shows the support and contradiction of Breast Tumour based on Biopsy test. Analyzing all the parameters of the Biopsy of the Breast tumor supports the limiting values, hence it concludes as benign. The confusion matrix of Naive Bayes is shown in Table 14.5 and the matrix used by Naïve Bayes is in Table 14.6. The accuracy of the random forest model is 96.49% and the accuracy of the Naïve Bayes is 95.32 as shown in Table 14.7.

The random forest classifier is more accurate than Naive Bayes on the Biopsy data set.

Table 14.5. Confusion matrix and statistics

Actual	Prediction	
	benign	malignant
Benign	107	1
Malignant	7	56

Table 14.6. Metrics used by Naïve bayes

Sensitivity	93.86
Specificity	98.25
Pos Pred Value	99.07
Neg Pred Value	88.89
Prevalence	66.67
Detection Rate	62.57
Detection Prevalence	63.16
Balanced Accuracy	96.05

Table 14.7. Accuracy of classifiers

Model	Accuracy
Random forest	96.49
Naïve Bayes	95.32

Results of GradCam

Figures 14.9 and Figure 14.10 show the GradCam method generates a heat map from an input image, highlighting the relationship between the image's features and the model's prediction. The heat map highlights important regions contributing to the final prediction, with higher saturation indicating higher weightage. The map is scaled and superimposed on the original image to create explainable images, providing a concrete visualization of the model's most critical features.

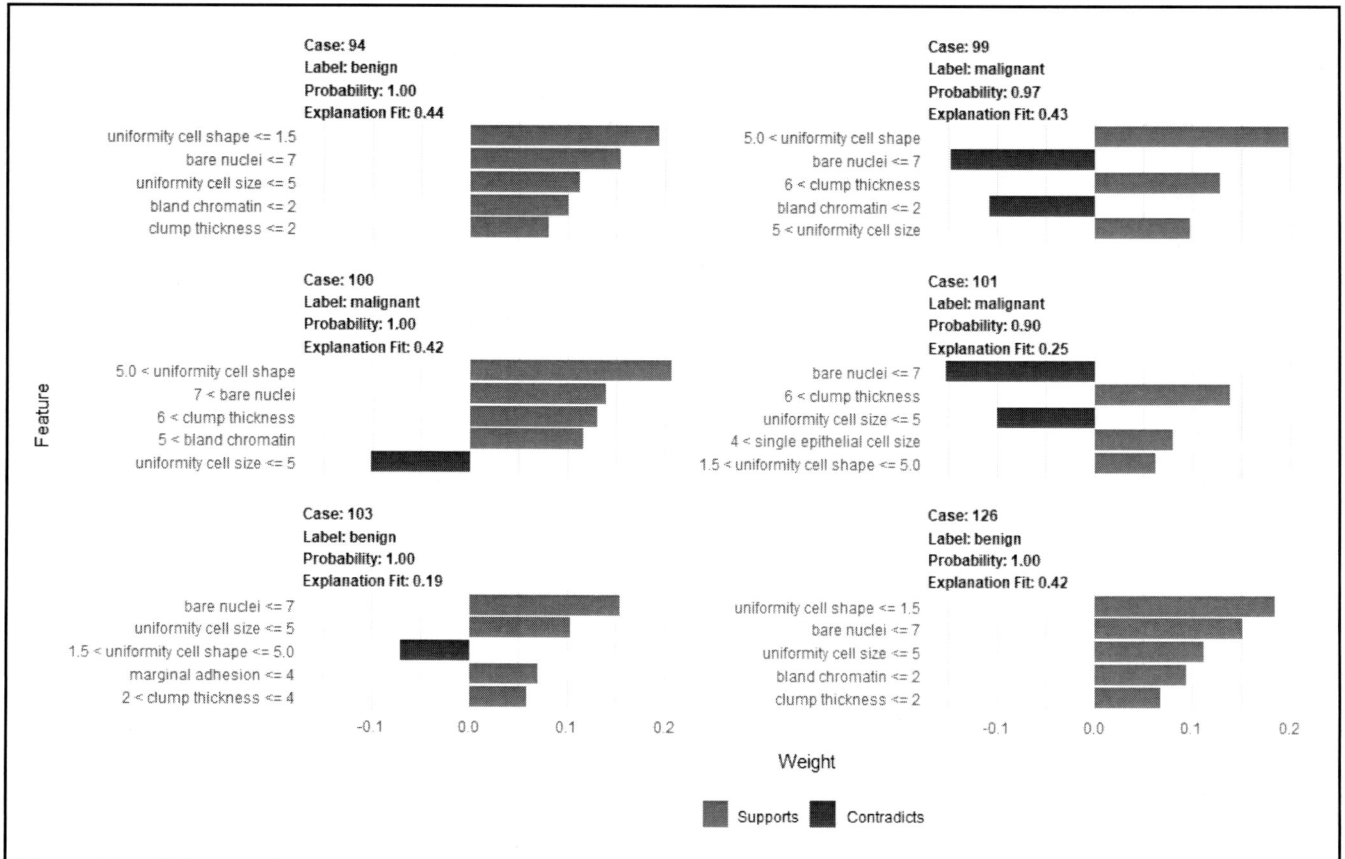

Figure 14.7. LIME Explainer for Biopsy Dataset.

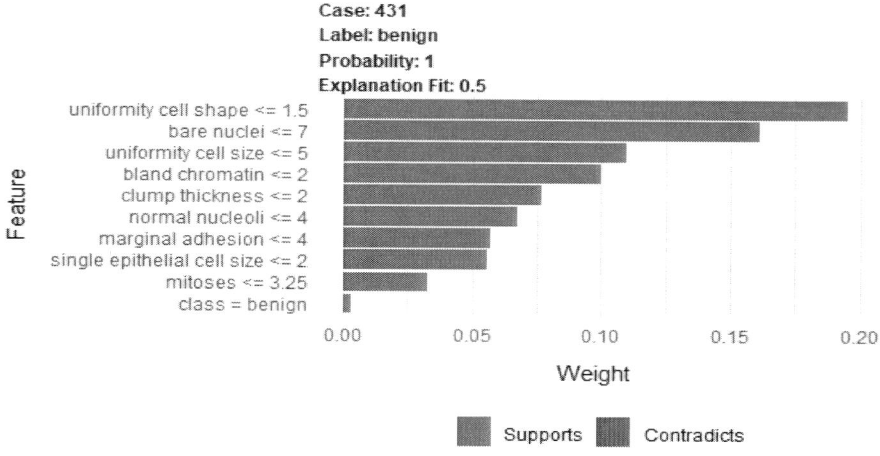

Figure 14.8. XAI for Biopsy of Breast Tumour.

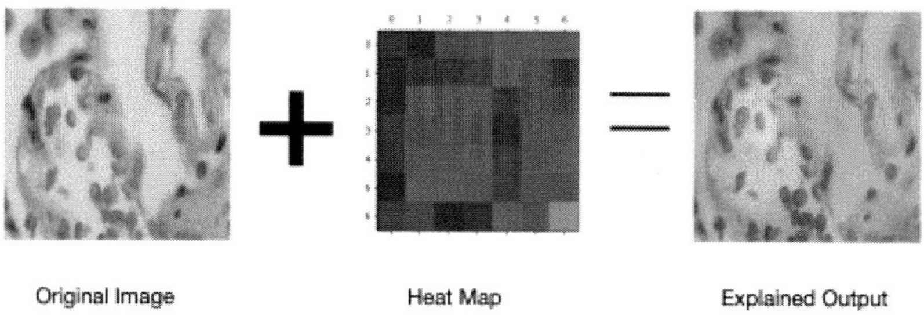

Figure 14.9. Resenet-50 generated explanations.

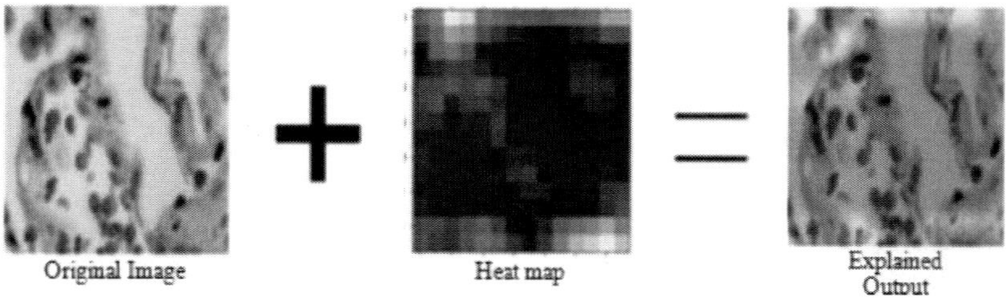

Figure 14.10. VGG-16 generated explanations.

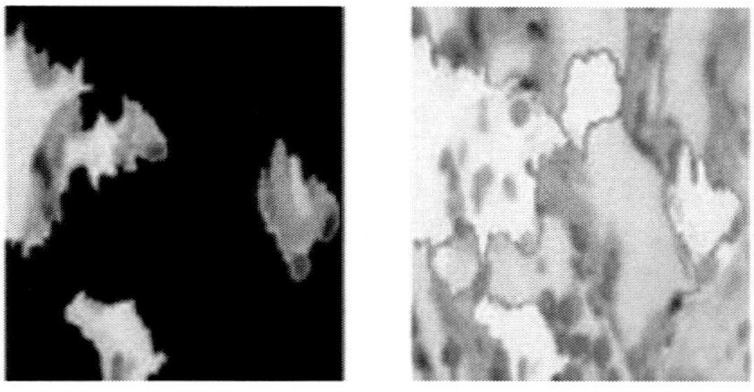

Figure 14.11. Explanations on RESNET-50.

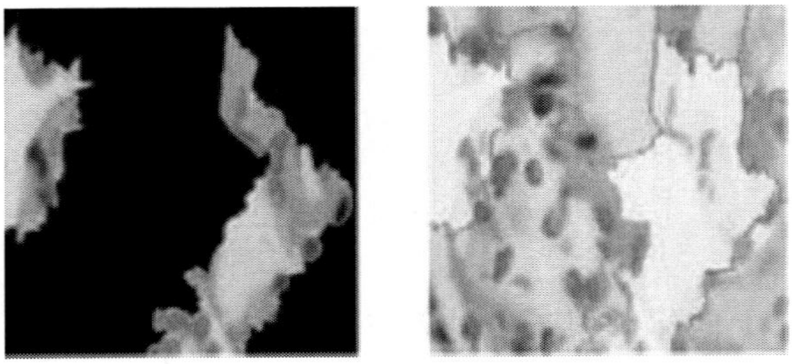

Figure 14.12. Explanations on VGG-16.

Table 14.8. Comparative Analysis of GradCam and LIME

	GradCam	LIME
VGG-16	0.031	15.5
ResNet	1.5	15.7

The Results of LIME are as follows:

Figure 14.11 and Figure 14.12 illustrate the LIME method's interpretations of input images, with Figure 14.12 focusing on important regions from the original image. Green regions indicate pixels that increase the model's class prediction probability, while red pixels suppress it. These methods can help human physicians verify predicted diagnoses by considering the model's most weighted features. They also help explain the reasoning behind medical image classification systems, which are crucial in high-stakes decisions. The regions highlighted in these figures can help verify the accuracy of the model's predictions.

The Comparative Analysis of GradCam and LIME is shown in Table 14.8. The GradCam approach is the fastest one and the slowest one is LIME on VGG-16. The VGG-16 is faster than ResNet for image classification.

14.9 Conclusion

Explainable AI provides major benefits in medical image processing by increasing diagnostic accuracy, streamlining decision-making, fostering greater confidence among healthcare providers, and offering transparency to the process. The random forest classifier is more accurate than Naive Bayes on the Biopsy data set. The GradCam approach is the fastest one and the slowest one is LIME on VGG-16. VGG-16 is faster than ResNet-50 for image classification. Because of the growing complexity of medical imaging data, the incorporation of AI approaches that can be explained is becoming increasingly important for producing accurate and trustworthy results. To further progress in the area and lead to improved patient care and results through the seamless collaboration between human specialists and AI systems, the problems in the field need to be addressed, and future research directions need to be explored.

References

Adadi A., and Berrada M. (2018). Peeking inside the black box : A survey on Explainable Artificial Intelligence (XAI), *IEEE Access.* 6 : 52138–52160.

Alba A. C., Agoritsas T., Jankowski M., Courvoisier D., Walter S. D., Guyatt G. H., et al. (2013). Risk prediction models for mortality in ambulatory patients with heart failure: à systematic review, *Circ Heart Fail.* 6:881–889. 10.1161/CIRCHEARTFAILURE.112.000043.

Boulton, A. J. (2021). Effect of COVID-19 pandemic lockdowns on planned cancer surgery for 15 tumour types in 61 countries : an international, prospective, cohort study. *Lancet Oncology*, *22*(11), 1507-1517.

Chen, D., Zhao, H., He, J., Pan, Q. and Zhao W. (2021). An Causal XAI Diagnostic Model for Breast Cancer Based on Mammography Reports. *IEEE International Conference on Bioinformatics and Biomedicine (BIBM)*, Houston, TX, USA, 3341-3349.

Cunningham, P., Doyle, D., and Loughrey J. (2003). An evaluation of the usefulness of case-based explanation. *5th international conference on case-based reasoning*, 122-130.

Dauriz M., Mantovani A., Bonapace S., Verlato G., Zoppini G., Bonora E., et al. (2017). Prognostic impact of diabetes on long-term survival outcomes in patients with heart failure: a meta-analysis, *Diabetes Care.* 40 :1597–605. 10.2337/dc17-0697.

Deng J., Dong W., Socher R., Li L. J., Li K., and Fei-Fei, L. (2009). Imagenet: A large-scale hierarchical image database. *In 2009 IEEE conference on computer vision and pattern recognition, IEEE Xplore.* 248-255.

Dokainish, H., Teo, K., Zhu, J., Roy, A., AlHabib, K. F., ElSayed, A., Mondo, C. (2017). Global mortality variations in patients with heart failure: results from the International Congestive Heart Failure (INTER-CHF) prospective cohort study. *The Lancet Global Health*, *5*(7), e665-e672.

Ferrara, G., De Vincentiis, L., Ambrosini-Spaltro, A., Barbareschi, M., Bertolini, V., Contato, E., Saragoni, L., et al. (2021). Cancer diagnostic delay in northern and central Italy during the 2020 lockdown due to the coronavirus disease 2019 pandemic: assessment of the magnitude of the problem and proposals for corrective actions. *American journal of clinical pathology*, *155*(1), 64-68.

Guleria, P., and Sood, M. (2022). Explainable AI and machine learning: Performance evaluation and explainability of classifiers on educational data mining inspired career counseling. *Educ. Inf. Technol.* 1–36.

Gupta, A., Arora, V., Nair, D., Agrawal, N., Su, Y. X., Holsinger, F. C., Chan, J. Y. (2020). Status and strategies for the management of head and neck cancer during COVID19 pandemic: Indian scenario. *Head and neck*, *42*(7), 1460-1465.

Ishaq A., Sadiq S., Umer M., Ullah S., Mirjalili S., Rupapara V., et al. Improving the prediction of heart failure Patients' survival using SMOTE and effective data mining techniques. *IEEE Access.* (2021). 9:39707–16. 10.1109/ACCESS.2021.3064084.

Lamy, J. B., Sekar, B., Guezennec, G., Bouaud, J., and Séroussi, B. (2019). Explainable artificial intelligence for breast cancer: A visual case-based reasoning approach. *Artificial intelligence in medicine*, *94*, 42-53.

Maringe C., Spicer J., Morris M., Purushotham A., Nolte, E., Sullivan, R. Rachet, B., Aggarwal, A. (2020). The impact of the COVID-19 pandemic on cancer deaths due to delays in diagnosis in England, UK: A national, population-based, modelling study. *Lancet Oncol.* (2020). 21:1023–1034.

Massie, S. Craw, and Wiratunga. Visualisation of case-base reasoning for explanation. *Proceedings of the ECCBR 2004 workshops*, Madrid, Spain, (2004):135-144.

Naji M. A., El Filali S., Aarika K., Benlahmar E. H., Abdelouhahid R. A., Debauche O. (2021). Machine learning algorithms for breast cancer prediction and diagnosis. *Procedia Comput. Sci.* (191):487–492.

Namee, Brian Mac and S. J. Delany. (2010). CBTV : visualising case bases for similarity measure design and selection. *International conference on case-based reasoning*, 213-227.

Nindrea R. D., Hari Kusnanto, Samuel Johny Haryono, Wirsma Arif Harahap, Iwan Dwiprahasto, Lutfan Lazuardi, Teguh Aryandono (2020). Development of Breast Cancer Risk Prediction Model for Women in Indonesia: A Case-Control Study. *Research Square,* 1-25.

Nolan G. S., Dunne J. A., Kiely A. L., Pritchard Jones R. O., Gardiner M., Jain A. (2020). The effect of the COVID-19 pandemic on skin cancer surgery in the United Kingdom: A national, multi-centre, prospective cohort study and survey of plastic surgeons. *J. Br. Surg.* 107:598–600.

Patel P. Bibekananda Jena, Bibhudatta Sahoo, Pritam Patel, Banshidhar Majhi (2016). Study of different noise removal techniques for digital images. In the book, *Emerging Technologies in Intelligent Applications for Image and Video Processing.* IGI Global, USA. 3:48-87.

Pedro A. Moreno-Sánchez (2023). Improvement of a prediction model for heart failure survival through explainable artificial intelligence. *Frontiers Cardiovasc Medicine*. 10: 1219586.

Rabiei R., Ayyoubzadeh S. M., Sohrabei S., Esmaeili M., Atashi A. (2022). Prediction of breast cancer using machine learning approaches. *J. Biomed. Phys. Eng*. 12(297).

Radfar S. R., De Jong C. A., Farhoudian A., Ebrahimi M., Rafei P., Vahidi M., Yunesian M., Kouimtsidis C., Arunogiri S., Massah O., et al. (2021). Reorganization of substance use treatment and harm reduction services during the COVID-19 pandemic: A global survey. *Front. Psychiatry*, 12.349.

Ribeiro M. T., Singh S., Guestrin C. Why should i trust you? Explaining the predictions of any classifier. In *Proceedings of the 22nd ACM SIGKDD international conference on knowledge discovery and data mining* (2016). 1135-1144.

Ricciardiello L., Ferrari C., Cameletti M., Gaianill F., Buttitta F., Bazzoli F., de'Angeli, G. L., Malesci A., Laghi L. Impact of SARS-CoV-2 pandemic on colorectal cancer screening delay: Effect on stage shift and increased mortality. *Clin. Gastroenterol. Hepatol*, (2021). 19:1410–1417.

Riyam Patel Aditi Acharjya, Punyaban Patel, Borra Sivaiah, Bibhudatta Sahoo (2023) Quality and Performance Measures in Healthcare Systems using Fog Computing. Book Chapter in Multi-Disciplinary Applications of Fog Computing: *Responsiveness in Real-Time*. IGI Global. 6. 95-120.

Saini K. S., de Las Heras B., de Castro J., Venkitaraman R., Poelman M., Srinivasan G., Saini M. L., Verma S., Leone M., Aftimos P. et al. (2020). Effect of the COVID-19 pandemic on cancer treatment and research. *Lancet Haematol*, 7,432–435.

Segar M. W., Vaduganathan M., Patel K. V., McGuire D. K., Butler J., Fonarow G. C., et al. (2019) Machine learning to predict the risk of incident heart failure hospitalization among patients with diabetes: the WATCH-DM risk score. *Diabetes Care*, 42, 2298–306.

Selvaraju R. R., Cogswell Mk Das A., Vedantam R., Parikh D., and Batra D. (2017). Grad-cam: Visual explanations from deep networks via gradient-based localization. In *Proceedings of the IEEE Iinternational conference on computer vision,* 618-626.

Shruthishree S. H. and Harshvardhan Tiwari. (2017). A Review Paper on Medical Image Processing," *International Journal of Research Granthalaya,* 5(4).

Son M. K., Lim N. K., and Park H. Y. (2019) Predicting stroke and death in patients with heart failure using CHA2DS2-VASc score in Asia. *BMC Cardiovasc Disord*. 19, 193.

Spicer, J., Chamberlain, C. and Papa, S. (2020). Provision of cancer care during the COVID-19 pandemic. Nat. Rev. *Clin. Oncol,* 17:329–331.

Straw S., Byrom R., Gierula J., Paton M. F., Koshy A., Cubbon R. et al. (2019) . Predicting one-year mortality in heart failure using the 'surprise question': a prospective pilot study. *Eur J Heart Fail*., 21, 227–34.

Temenos A., Tzortzis I. N., Kaselimi M., Rallis I., Doulamis A., Doulamis N. (2022). Novel Insights in Spatial Epidemiology Utilizing Explainable AI (XAI) and Remote Sensing. *Remote Sens*, 14- 3074.

Tjoa, E. and Guan, C. (2020). A survey on explainable artificial intelligence (xai): Toward medical xai. *IEEE Trans. Neural Netw. Learn. Syst.* 32, 4793–4813.

Wojciech Samek. (2019) Explainable AI in Healthcare : Unboxing Machine Learning for Biomedicine (Analytics and AI for Healthcare). *Book series on Lecture Notes in Computer Science* (LNCS). Springer Nature.

Yang, G., Ye, Q., and Xia, J. (2022). Unbox the black-box for the medical explainable AI via multi-modal and multi-centre data fusion : A mini-review, two showcases and beyond. *Information Fusion*, *77*, 29-52.

Zeng L., Liu L., Chen D., Lu H., Xue Y., Bi H., Yang W. (2023) The innovative model based on artificial intelligence algorithms to predict recurrence risk of patients with postoperative breast cancer. *Front. Oncol.*, 13, 807.

Zhu, G. N., Hu, J., Qi, J., Ma, J., and Y. H. Peng. (2015). An integrated feature selection and cluster analysis techniques for case-based reasoning. *Engineering Application Artificial Intelligence*, 39,14-22.

Chapter 15

XAI in Health Care for Making Intelligent Decisions for COVID Prevention and Detection

P. Pradeep[1,*]
J. Kamalakannan[2]
S. Balakumar[3]
and Vijayan Sugumaran[4]
Vellore Institute of Technology, Vellore, Tamilnadu, India

Abstract

The symptoms of COVID-19 might range from mild or without symptoms to serious illness and death. The COVID-19-affected person had symptoms like fever, sleeplessness, and dry cough. Internationally, the coronavirus (COVID-19) virus is still not eradicated, and it is mutating. This review article discusses how and where to automate the processes to detect coronavirus infection using the database of X-ray and CT-Scan images, MRI scans from individuals who had frequent respiratory infections, established COVID-19 infection, and common cases. The goal of the study is to evaluate the importance of COVID-19 prevention and detection. The classification techniques, such as the support vector machine, and Logistic Regression/Random Forest are considered for classification purposes. The experimental outcome of each of those algorithms is compared to each other and with the conventional way of implementing the classification models. The efficiency of the XAI-based Classification models is reasonably fair, compared to the other start-of-the-art models.

Keywords: isolation from society, departure from life, message passing, linear regression, random forest

* Corresponding Author's Email: pradeep.p@vit.ac.in.

In: Explainable Artificial Intelligence in Healthcare Systems
Editors: A. Anitha Kamaraj and Debi Prasanna Acharjya
ISBN: 979-8-89113-598-7

15.1 Introduction

The COVID-19 pandemic has had a significant global impact, with millions of cases and fatalities reported worldwide. The rapid spread of the virus has necessitated strict public health measures, such as limited mobility and increased hygiene practices. This article provides an extensive overview of localization and classification techniques employed in the context of COVID-19 (Carlini et al. 2014). To date, more than 387 million cases have been diagnosed globally, resulting in an estimated 5.8 million deaths. COVID-19 affects individuals by rapidly reducing white blood cell counts, leading to various symptoms, including fever, cough, cold, headache, and general discomfort. Effective preventive measures, such as frequent hand washing and maintaining social distancing, are recommended to minimize transmission risks.

COVID-19 testing is divided into positive and negative categories. Positive results necessitate contacting healthcare professionals and following isolation protocols for 14 days (about 2 weeks). Negative results indicate no immediate need for further testing (Kartoun et al. 2019). In severe cases, when blood pressure drops below 91, patients may require ventilator support for a maximum of two weeks before succumbing to the illness. Caution must be exercised when interpreting COVID-19 data, as different sources may use varying inclusion criteria and cut-off times (Ribeiro et al. 2016). The World Health Organization (WHO) provides official daily counts of cases, deaths, and vaccine utilization, reported by countries and territories. The diagnosis of COVID-19 relies on a combination of factors, including diagnostic and travel history, contact tracing, and clinical indications. Laboratory tests, such as real-time polymerase chain reaction (rt-PCR), reverse transcription-polymerase chain reaction (RT-PCR), and viral nucleic acid detection in throat swabs, and sputum specimens, are conducted to confirm the diagnosis. Testing facilities need to adhere to recommended biosafety protocols during these procedures, which may involve virus isolation, serological testing, and electron microscopy.

This article explores various classification techniques employed in the localization and detection of COVID-19. General classification approaches are initially discussed, followed by an in-depth exploration of intelligent techniques specifically tailored for COVID-19 detection. Finally, the focus narrows down to the utilization and evaluation of the proposed classification techniques. Table 15.1 shows the steps for COVID precautions and Table 2 compares the different models in COVID analyses.

Table 15.1. COVID Precautions

S.no	Description
1	Wet your hands
2	Soap up
3	Scrub for 20 Seconds
4	Rinse
5	Dry

Table 15.2. Comparing different COVID analyses

Symptoms	Organs	Machine Learning
Cough	Lungs	Linear Regression
Headache	Brain	Random Forest
Fever	Hypothalamus	Decision Tree
Cold	Lungs	Clustering

15.2 Framework from Machine Learning XAI

Machine Learning explainable Artificial Intelligence (XAI) is a framework that aims to enhance transparency, interpretability, and trust in machine learning models. Traditional machine learning models, such as support vector machines, logistic regression, and random forest, often function as black boxes, making it challenging to understand the reasoning behind their predictions.

XAI provides tools and techniques to unravel the decision-making process of these models, enabling humans to comprehend and trust their outputs. XAI techniques bridge the gap between the inherent complexity of machine learning algorithms and the need for human interpretability. These techniques encompass a variety of methods, including rule-based explanations, feature importance analysis, visualizations, and surrogate models, among others. By shedding light on how models arrive at their predictions, XAI helps users understand the factors influencing the outcome and detect potential biases or errors. Therefore, this section elaborates on the AI algorithms for diverse tasks.

15.2.1 Linear Regression

Linear Regression is a type of supervised learning algorithm that leverages input variables to make predictions about continuous values. As described by Kartoun et al. (2019), this algorithm establishes a linear association between the independent variables (input variables) and the dependent variables (output). The proposed model's output is shown in Figure 15.1.

The algorithms find the best-fit line that minimizes the sum of squared errors between the predicate values and actual values.

$$Y = \beta 0 + \beta 1x\ 1 + \beta 2x\ 2 + \beta 3x\ 3 \quad (1)$$

were,

y = dependent variable
0 is the intercept
1, 2, 3 are co-efficient

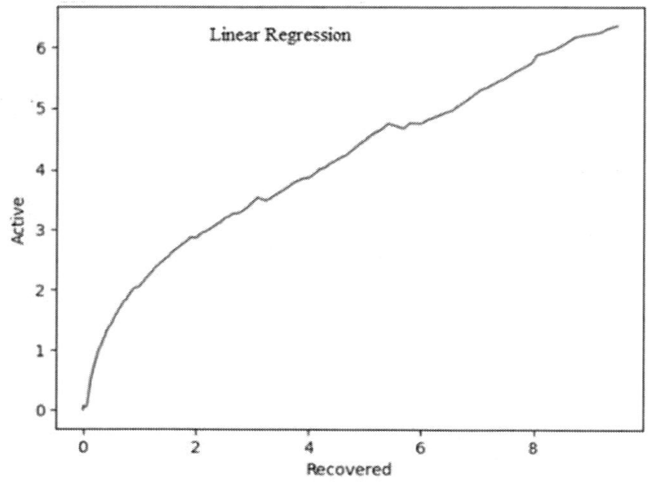

Figure 15.1. Linear regression output.

Applications

- Prediction of housing prices
- Finance
- Banking

Advantages

- According to Kartoun et al. (2019) linear regression is a straightforward method that can be implemented easily and provides satisfactory outcomes.
- According to Carlini et al. (2014) linear regression demonstrates near-perfect fitting on datasets that are linearly separable in practice. To mitigate overfitting, which refers to the situation where a machine learning model fits a dataset too closely and incorporates noisy data, regularization techniques can be employed. This helps to maintain the model's functionality and improve its accuracy on the test set.

Disadvantages

- *Prone to underfitting*: A situation that arises when a machine learning model fails to capture the data properly (Kartoun et al. 2019). The situation commonly arises when the hypothesis function is not well-suited to the data.
- *Outliers:* Outliers refer to anomalies or extreme values within a dataset that deviate significantly from the rest of the distribution. The presence of outliers can have a detrimental effect on the model's performance

15.2.2 Random Forest

Random Forest is a widely recognized Machine Learning algorithm that falls under the supervised learning category. It is suitable for both classification and regression tasks. The algorithm's robustness improves with a higher number of trees in the forest. Additionally, as the tree count increases, the Random Forest Algorithm demonstrates enhanced accuracy and problem-solving capabilities. It functions as a classifier by utilizing multiple decision trees on different subsets of input data, thereby enhancing the predictive accuracy of a given dataset (Kartoun et al. 2019). The structure of random forest classifier is given in Figure 15.2.

Random Forest is a classification algorithm that enhances the predictive accuracy of a dataset by averaging the predictions of multiple decision trees built on different subsets of the given data. The output of the model is shown in Figure 15.3.

Uses of Random Forest

- It requires a shorter training time compared to alternative algorithms.
- Random Forest exhibits accurate predictions and efficient performance even when dealing with large datasets.
- It can maintain its accuracy even when the available data is limited.

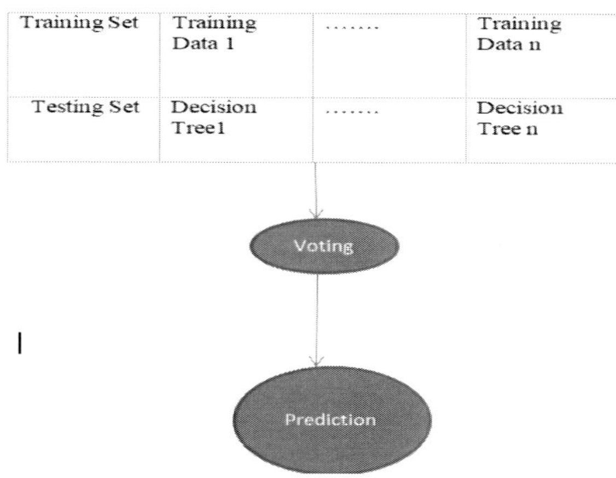

Figure 15.2. Random Forest Structure.

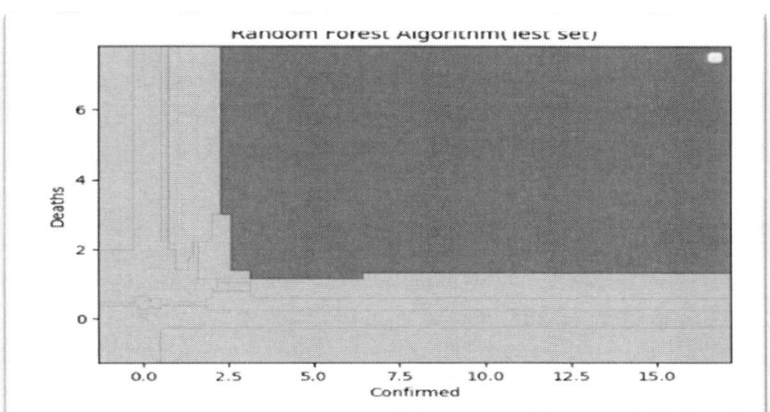

Figure 15.3. Output for Random Forest.

Applications of Random Forest

- Banking
- Insurance
- Marketing
- Finance

Steps for the Random Forest Algorithm:

- Select K random data points from the training set.
- Generate decision trees for the chosen data nodes (Subsets).
- Determine the number N of decision trees you wish to generate.
- Recheck 1 and 2.
- To determine predictions for new data points, each decision tree's output is assessed, and the new data points are assigned to the category that receives the highest number of votes.

Advantages

- Large quantities of data can be effectively managed.
- It Can quickly manage vast quantities of data

Discussion on Random Forest

The proposed COVID-19 detection model can benefit greatly from Random Forest, which is a suitable option because of its ensemble learning technique, ability to handle missing data, robustness against overfitting, feature importance analysis, capacity to capture non-linear relationships and interactions, scalability, and interpretability through feature importance measures. By utilizing these strengths, Random Forest can effectively analyze intricate medical images, provide precise classifications, and offer valuable insights into the specific image features that contribute to COVID-19 detection.

15.3 COVID Data Set Description

To combat the COVID-19 pandemic, the White House and a collaboration of prominent academic institutions have established the COVID-19 Open Academic Dataset (CORD-19). Leveraging the latest advancements in natural language processing and other artificial intelligence methodologies, researchers worldwide can utilize this openly accessible data to produce innovative findings that will contribute to the ongoing battle against this infectious disease. Given the overwhelming growth of coronavirus literature, the medical research community faces challenges in staying abreast of the rapid expansion, making the utilization of these techniques even more crucial (Kartoun et al. 2019). Table 15.3 shows the COVID-19 dataset description. Figure 15.4 shows the architecture diagram of the proposed model.

Table 15.3. COVID-19 Clean Complete .CSV File

S.no	Column Name	Description
1	Country Name	It displays various countries name like India, China
2	Latitude	It displays values like 33.93
3	Longitude	It displays values like 36.87
4	Date	It Displays the current date
5	Confirmed-Death	It talks about how much death and COVID

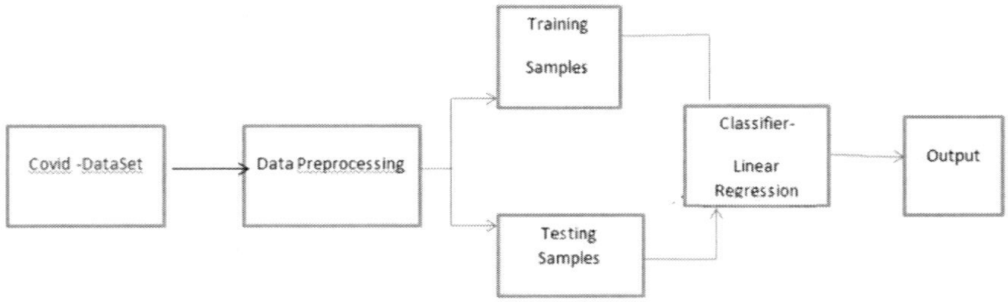

Figure 15.4. Architecture of proposed model.

15.3.1 Data Pre-Processing

Data preparation is a fundamental step in machine learning, involving the transformation of raw, unprocessed data into a suitable format for algorithms. It serves as the initial and pivotal stage in developing a machine-learning model. In many machines learning projects, acquiring well-structured and easily understandable data is not always feasible. Therefore, before any meaningful analysis can take place, data must undergo a thorough cleaning and organization process.

Most real-world datasets often exhibit noisy elements, missing values, or are presented in formats that are incompatible with machine learning models. Consequently, data preparation becomes essential to cleanse and transform the data into a suitable format that can be utilized by machine learning models. This process not only enhances the accuracy and efficiency of

The models also ensure their compatibility with the given dataset, as highlighted by Kartoun et al. (2019).

The Major Steps for Data Pre-Processing

- *Collect the Data Set*: Real-world datasets commonly exhibit disorderly components, missing values, or formats that are not compatible with machine learning models. Consequently, data preparation plays a crucial role in sanitizing and converting the data into a suitable format for machine learning models. This essential process not only enhances the accuracy and effectiveness of the models but also ensures their compatibility with the given dataset.

- *Import the Important Libraries*: To conduct data preprocessing using Python, it is essential to integrate various pre-existing Python libraries that serve specific purposes.
- *Loading the dataset for COVID-19:* To integrate the collected datasets into the machine learning project, it is important to set the current directory as the working directory. To establish the working directory in the Spyder IDE, the following steps need to be followed: Save your Python file in the directory where the dataset is located and select the desired directory using the File Explorer option in the Spyder IDE, as outlined by Ribeiro et al. (2016).
- *By Deleting Particular Row*: One frequently employed approach to handle undefined values involves removing the respective row or column that contains these invalid values. However, this method is considered inefficient since it can lead to information loss, thereby yielding inaccurate results.
- *By Calculating The Mean*: Using this approach, we will compute the mean of the column or row that contains missing values and substitute it in the corresponding position. This technique is particularly useful for numerical attributes such as age, salary, year, and so on. In this case, we will employ this method
- *Categorical Data Is Encoded: Categorical data refers to data organized into categories, such as Country and Purchased, which are examples of categorical variables within our dataset.* However, machine learning models predominantly operate on numerical data, posing challenges when dealing with categorical variables during model development. Consequently, it becomes necessary to convert these categorical variables into numerical representations.
- *Splitting Up the Dataset*: During the data preprocessing stage for machine learning, it is essential to partition the dataset into a training set and a test set. This division plays a pivotal role in enhancing the effectiveness of the machine learning model.
- *Scaling Various Features:* Feature scaling is the final step in data preprocessing for machine learning. It involves standardizing the independent variables of a dataset to a predefined range. By scaling features, all variables are placed on the same scale and within the same range, preventing any single variable from overshadowing the others.

Knowledge Representation of XAI

It is a field of artificial intelligence that deals with AI agents. Thinking, and how thinking leads to intelligent agent action (Ribeiro et al. 2016)

- *Declarative Knowledge:* Declarative knowledge refers to understanding something. It is less complex than procedural language. It is also known as descriptive knowledge and is expressed using declarative sentences.
- *Procedural Knowledge: Procedural knowledge is a form of knowledge responsible for one knowing whether to do something.* It can be applied instantly to any task. The application of procedural knowledge depends on the job at hand.
- *Meta-knowledge:* Meta-knowledge is information about other types of knowledge.
- *Heuristic knowledge:* Heuristic knowledge refers to rules of thumb based on prior experiences and awareness of methods that are probably to be effective but aren't guaranteed.

- *Structural knowledge:* Structural knowledge is fundamental to problem-solving. It shows relationships between numerous notions that include a type of, part of, and collection of anything.

Interpretability and Explainability

- *Interpretability:* Increasing model openness and interpretability not only aids in the development of safer, more explainable, and more successful models, but it can also aid in the development of trust and confidence in the framework and its output in the minds of both technical and non-technical stakeholders.
- *Model improvement:* Fixing the model's structural deficiencies, different structures are shown in Figure 15.5.
- *Feature Engineering:* Locating potential model enhancements that could be of use.
- *Controlling Risk:* It is far easier to predict the model's response to novel, unseen, or very little information when the model is transparent and easily interpretable.
- *Ensuring compliance and fairness:* By knowing how and why the model makes predictions, we can make changes to improve fairness or meet other policy requirements.
- *Increasing Complexity:* Let's examine the three simple examples of modeling displayed below (Papernot et al. 2016)
- *Linear:* Using a simple linear regression model, we can find the line of best fit and make a general statement about how the predictor x impacts the response y.

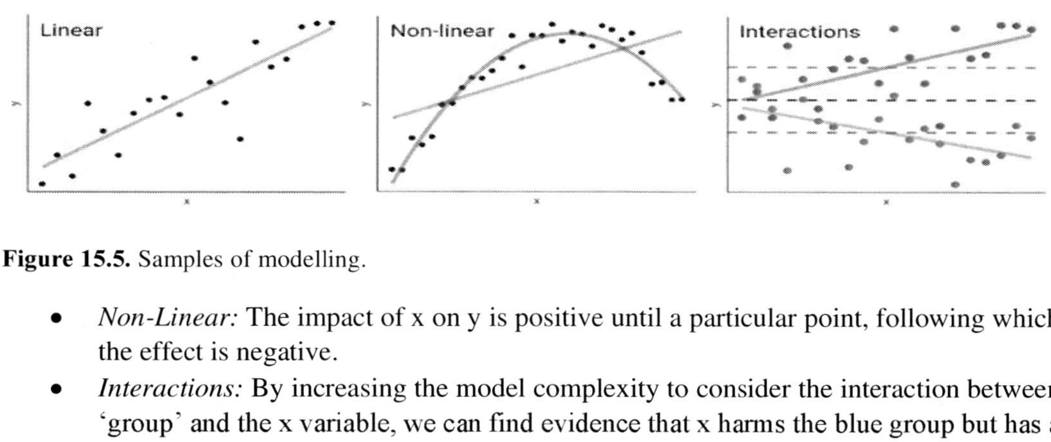

Figure 15.5. Samples of modelling.

- *Non-Linear:* The impact of x on y is positive until a particular point, following which the effect is negative.
- *Interactions:* By increasing the model complexity to consider the interaction between 'group' and the x variable, we can find evidence that x harms the blue group but has a positive effect on the red group.

Explainability

ML models are often called black-box models because they allow a pre-set number of empty parameters, or nodes, to be assigned values by the machine learning algorithm. Specifically, the back-propagation step is responsible for updating the weights based on its error function.

15.4 XAI Approaches and Analysis in Sustainable Smart Health Care

Informatics

Deep learning models in artificial intelligence (AI) have found extensive application across various domains, including medical imaging and healthcare tasks. Making judgments or decisions in the medical field carries significant risks. Physicians carefully evaluate a patient's symptoms and physical examination before formulating a logical explanation or diagnosis. For AI to be a reliable and accepted tool in this context, it needs to replicate human judgment and interpretation abilities. Explainable AI (XAI) aims to unveil the knowledge hidden within the black-box nature of deep learning models, revealing the decision-making process. This study provides an overview of the latest XAI techniques employed in healthcare and medical imaging applications. We summarize and categorize various XAI approaches and highlight techniques used to improve interpretability in medical imaging problems. Furthermore, we focus on challenging XAI issues in medical applications and propose guidelines to enhance the interpretability of deep learning models through the application of XAI principles in medical image and text analysis. This survey also offers future recommendations to support developers and researchers in planning prospective studies on clinical problems, particularly those involving medical imaging.

The COVID-19 pandemic has expedited the digital transformation of various industries, including healthcare, and has amplified the importance of Artificial Intelligence (AI) in these sectors. This study focuses on the application of Explainable Artificial Intelligence (XAI) to develop a model that can detect and interpret COVID-19-positive chest X-ray (CXR) images. Additionally, we explore the effects of COVID-19-positive CXR images using a heat map.

The proposed model utilized lung segmentation, transfer learning, and data augmentation techniques to enhance the efficiency and accuracy of model training. When comparing different pre-trained networks, the Reset model demonstrated the highest classification accuracy. The ongoing coronavirus disease (COVID-19) has presented significant challenges during this unprecedented period, requiring effective strategies to address both viral and bacterial infections.

Characteristics of Explainable AI in Healthcare

- *Adaptability:* It is imperative to ensure equal levels of transparency for all consumers within the healthcare system. Specifically, in the context of medical examiners, comprehensive descriptions of dataset pre-processing, algorithm functioning, and decision analysis should be provided at every stage. This commitment to transparency is essential in promoting trust and understanding among healthcare system users.
- *Context-Awareness*: The XAI algorithm possesses the capability to anticipate the optimal dosage schedule, and the weighted components of medicines, and recommend appropriate medication combinations for comorbidity situations, among other things. When dealing with substance use scenarios, it is crucial to emphasize the risks associated with different situations. Moreover, it is important to address exceptional circumstances for high-risk patients and develop supportive nutritional and treatment strategies tailored to patients of diverse ages and backgrounds.

15.5 XAI in Threats

Explainable Artificial Intelligence (XAI) methods aim to bridge the gap between the predictive power of machine learning techniques and the interpretability of models. In the field of healthcare, XAI plays a crucial role for healthcare providers who utilize learning-based techniques, as it helps to uphold patient trust and accountability. Learning-based techniques are susceptible to adversarial attacks, which can lead to incorrect classifications by the models.

The objective of this article is to utilize Explainable Artificial Intelligence (XAI) methods to evaluate the effectiveness of adversarial attacks on perturbations of a trained model during its runtime.

The findings affirm the effectiveness of the suggested approach and offer valuable insights for future studies on utilizing XAI to detect and reject adversarial samples. These results establish a foundation for further exploration in this area of research.

Challenges in XAI

- Medical data of poor quality.
- For the clinical and technical validation of AI models.
- Clinicians need high-quality datasets.
- Performance Metrics That Are Not Clinically Relevant flaws in the research methodology.
- Furthermore, the integration of AI voice assistants contributes to streamlining the operational processes within healthcare organizations. These solutions are built upon the foundations of artificial intelligence and machine learning. As a result, the potential of AI in the healthcare sector appears highly promising. Therefore, individuals aspiring to pursue a thriving career in this field should prioritize staying updated with the latest advancements (Ma et al. 2021).

15.6 Experimental Analysis

In the experimental comparative analysis, the performance of Random Forest was evaluated in comparison to other classification techniques for COVID-19 detection using medical imaging data. The following techniques were considered for comparison: support vector machine (SVM), logistic regression, and a conventional classification approach. The models were trained and evaluated on a dataset consisting of 1,000 X-ray images, 500 CT-scan images, and 300 MRI scans. The dataset was labelled with two classes: COVID-19 positive and COVID-19 negative. The results of the comparative analysis are shown in Table 15.4.

Table 15.4. Comparative Analysis

Technique	Accuracy	Precision	Recall	F1-Score
Random Forest	0.92	0.91	0.94	0.92
Support Vector Machine	0.88	0.87	0.89	0.88
Logistic Regression	0.84	0.82	0.86	0.84
Conventional Approach	0.78	0.75	0.80	0.77

Random Forest model achieved the highest accuracy of 92% among all the techniques. It also exhibited the highest precision of 91%, indicating a low rate of false positives. The recall rate of 94% demonstrates the model's ability to identify COVID-19-positive cases correctly. The F1-score of 92% reflects a balanced performance between precision and recall. Comparatively, the Support Vector Machine and Logistic Regression techniques showed slightly lower performance, while the Conventional Approach had the lowest accuracy and F1 score.

These findings indicate that Random Forest outperformed the other techniques in accurately classifying COVID-19 cases using medical imaging data. The ensemble learning nature of Random Forest, along with its ability to handle complex feature interactions, contributed to its superior performance in this classification task. Overall, the experimental results demonstrate the effectiveness of Random Forest for COVID-19 detection, supporting its potential as a reliable tool in automated diagnosis using medical imaging techniques.

15.7 Opportunities in XAI

The financial industry is expected to adhere to elevated levels of trust and openness compared to numerous other sectors. This expectation arises partly from the fact that these businesses serve as the bedrock of our economic stability and the facilitators of upward mobility.

Drawing upon principles derived from probability theory and statistics, machine learning (ML) often replaces traditional statistical approaches in performing analytical tasks. However, comprehending the relationship between a model's output and its input variables can become challenging due to two appealing aspects of ML: the ability to handle larger datasets and more intricate data relationships (Carlini et al. 2017).

15.8 Conclusion

Corona virus disease 2019 is an emerging pandemic viral disease that affects the respiratory systems of individuals. Corona viruses cause symptoms like the common cold to more severe respiratory, intestinal, hepatic, and neurological problems. COVID-19 has caused major mortality and morbidity in vulnerable people worldwide. Because the disease treatment is supportive, efficient preventive measures should be implemented to prevent its occurrence and spread.

References

Carlini, N., and Wagner, D. (2017). Towards evaluating the robustness of neural networks, In: 2017 *IEEE Symposium on Security and Privacy (sp), IEEE*. 39–57.

Kartoun, U. (2019). Advancing informatics with electronic medical records bots (EMRBots). *Software Impacts*, *2*, 100006.

Kelly, C. J., Karthikesalingam, A., Suleyman, M., Corrado, G., King, D. (2019). Key challenges for delivering clinical impact with artificial intelligence, *BMC Med*. 17(1), 1–9.

Ma, X., Niu, Y., Gu, L., Wang, Y., Zhao, Y., Bailey, J., Lu, F. (2021). Understanding adversarial attacks on deep learning based medical image analysis systems, *Pattern Recogn*. 110, 107332.

Papernot, N., McDaniel, P., Jha, S., Fredrikson, M., Celik, Z. B., Swami, A. (2016). The limitations of deep learning in adversarial settings, In*: 2016 IEEE European Symposium on Security and Privacy (Euro S&P), IEEE*. 372–387.

Papernot, N., McDaniel, P., Swami, A., Harang, R. (2016). Crafting adversarial input sequences for recurrent neural networks. *In: MILCOM 2016-2016 IEEE Military Communications Conference, IEEE.* 49–54.

Ribeiro, M. T., Singh, S., Guestrin, C. (2016). Why should i trust you? Explaining the predictions of any classifier, In: Proceedings of the *22nd ACM SIGKDD International Conference on Knowledge Discovery and Data Mining*, 1135–1144.

Section 4. Medical Imaging Classification using Explainable AI

Chapter 16

Explainable AI in Healthcare

Kazi Kutubuddin Sayyad Liyakat*
Department of Computer Science and Engineering,
Brahmdevdada Mane Institute of Technology, Solapur (MS), India

Abstract

By gathering and analyzing user health data, artificial intelligence (AI), when incorporated into healthcare apps and smart wearables like Fitbits, etc., can foretell the development of health conditions in users. AI has expanded to several healthcare applications, including patient data and diagnostics, clinical decision-making, administration of health services, and predictive medicine. Despite performing at a level comparable to humans, AI models still have a restricted range of applications because they are regarded as a mystery. There are numerous possible usages for combinations of AI or wearable smart Devices in an intelligent healthcare field, however, there's an obstacle with the Black Box operation of AI model decisions, which has led to a lack of accountability and faith in made decisions. Their low use in practice, particularly in healthcare, continues to be caused primarily by this lack of confidence. To encourage the usage of AI systems in healthcare, Explainable AI (XAI) has been introduced as a method that can increase trust in the forecast made by the model by outlining how the forecast is arrived at. An approach for COVID-19 is created in the XAI field to explain forecasts from XAI systems. A suggested strategy is also given to achieve model improvement, answerability, and intelligibility in the healthcare industry. The XAI-RS can assess the outcomes in light of the discharged patient's most recent state of health. Each patient's XAI-RS will be individually assessed.

Keywords: explainable AI, smart healthcare, XAI recommendation system, medical XAI

16.1 Introduction

AI is a technique for teaching a computer, a robot operated by a computer, or software to think critically and creatively like a human mind. AI might be created through researching cognitive processes. With these studies endeavors, intelligent systems and programs have been rendered available. Among the most widely used acronyms associated with technology at present is

* Corresponding Author's Emal: drkkazi@gmail.com.

In: Explainable Artificial Intelligence in Healthcare Systems
Editors: A. Anitha Kamaraj and Debi Prasanna Acharjya
ISBN: 979-8-89113-598-7

artificial intelligence (AI), and for good reason. Several developments and innovations that were previously only glimpsed in fantasy novels began to gradually begin to pass during the past few years.

Intelligence methods could be employed for:

- expanding a knowledge base and integrating individual and group learning utilizing databases and AI technologies
- expertise systems, case-based thinking, and fuzzy logic for tacit knowledge capture
- Using neural networks and data mining, one can find knowledge, or fundamental hidden trends in data sets
- utilizing evolutionary algorithms to produce solutions to extremely complicated situations
- employing intelligent agents and automating repetitive jobs

AI comes basically in two flavours as shown in Figure 16.1.

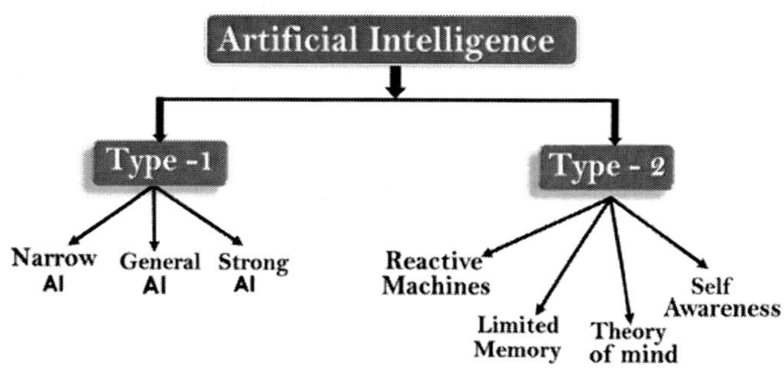

Figure 16.1. Types of AI.

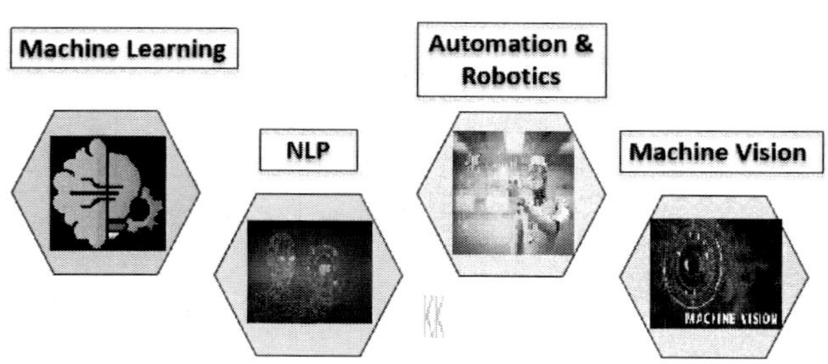

Figure 16.2. AI Techniques.

Also, there are four techniques of AI as demonstrated in Figure 16.2.

Explainable AI, also known as XAI, is a group of procedures that aid in the comprehension and interpretation of findings by both developers and users (Selvaraju, 2017). The XAI results are used by developers to comprehend possible bias in the model and enhance model performance. The inference findings produced by the AI model, along with the interpretation of the inference, can be trusted and believed by users. Code confidence typically refers to how much the developer or customer trusts the inference made by the AI model. With the current models being used, the questions below are difficult to explain (Lee, et al. 2018).

Recently, XAI has dominated studies into ways to increase user interaction with the working model. Despite the existence of such advancements, they could not match Human Intelligence (Lundberg, 2017), which is subsequently advanced by Neural Network (NN) (Wang, 2019), and Reinforcement-Learning (RL) (Halli, 2023).

The development of such AI applications was found to be crucial for advancing the medical field and analyzing weather forecasts, and the AlphaGo game, which was competent in contending with the finest human skills. Research in Human-Computer Interaction (HCI) (Dixit, 2015) is advancing to automate numerous applications and offer answers. However, the recent increases in life expectancy brought about by cutting-edge technologies will continue to help address the issues encountered in various medical fields.

Notable differences between AI and XAI approaches are listed, with the most current XAI methods being

- comprehensible ML,
- knowledge base and distillation algorithms, and
- both global and local preprocessing methods.

The pre-requisite offers perspectives for the group brainstorming before starting a medical XAI project, while XAI features specifics with potential healthcare, explainability are notably included. A real-world case study reveals how recent advancements in XAI have influenced the medical industry.

As it gives comprehensive information on every algorithmic stage believed to be trustworthy within the medicinal field (Dixit 2014), practitioners, & and experts, XAI is required to be assessed with the medicinal field's progression. The three XAI stages can be summed up as follows:

- an explainable development process to encourage adoption;
- explainable decisions to encourage confidence with viewers and controllers; and
- An explainable procedure for making choices to enable interoperability with business logic.

The purpose of XAI is to offer explainable machine learning (ML) and DL algorithms for improved performance that facilitates user acceptance, management, and trust. AI can revolutionize health care in a variety of ways, including by enhancing diagnosis and treatment, cutting expenses, and boosting effectiveness. However, it can be challenging to comprehend how AI systems decide as they grow more sophisticated and potent. Patients and healthcare professionals may become distrustful and uncertain due to this absence of transparency.

Transparent and understandable AI systems are crucial in the healthcare industry. Healthcare professionals and patients need to know how AI is used to make patient care judgments. Healthcare professionals, for instance, must be able to comprehend because an AI system recommends a specific course of treatment (Kazi K, 2022) and how it fits with the patient's medical history and other pertinent variables. Though some references addressed the shortcomings of the prior AI system, such as its use of black box models and its catastrophic effects on medical diagnosis, high accuracy, work quality, and speed were eventually attained thanks to advancements in model development, enhancement, and tuning (Dixit 2015).

Additionally, XAI can assist in locating flaws in AI systems. How honest AI systems become relies on the data that they are trained on. An AI system will be biased if the material it was trained on is biased. XAI can assist in locating and eliminating biases in AI systems by offering concise and understandable justifications for choices made by the systems. There are 3 types of XAI viz- interpretable AI, transparent AI, and interactable AI.

16.1.1 Interpretable AI

Among the most significant subtypes of XAI is interpretable AI, which explains how the AI arrived at its conclusion. There are many different interpretations of the word "interpretable." My favorite, however, is "A system where an individual cannot just see, yet also investigate and comprehend how inputs are logically mapped to outputs." With this description in mind, it is simple to understand why it is so crucial. Because an AI isn't a mysterious black box, if it meets this criterion of interpreting, one can easily develop XAI to support it. Unfortunately, there will always be performance trade-offs, making this definition not always practical. Lower complexity models are interpretable, while our models follow the reverse trend.

16.1.2 Transparent AI

Establishing confidence between individuals and algorithms requires transparent AI. Another trendy term without a generally accepted meaning is transparency, which refers to any techniques that aid in explaining what, why, and how of an AI's operation. Transparent techniques examine both an AI and the data that it is processing. Summary, visualization, and sometimes numerical descriptions are a few typical visible AI outputs. Each of these outputs represents an effort to convey an AI's specifics to a human.

16.1.3 Interactable AI

Users can interact using the machine learning model using interactable AI, a sort of XAI, to learn why it made a particular choice. This kind of XAI is useful for illuminating challenging-to-interpret complex models. Users can better comprehend how the computer makes judgements by viewing and engaging with the data with the machine learning model. Interactable AI enables humans and algorithms to cooperate by giving feedback to one another to accomplish a common objective. When interacting with robots, humans are essential because users can provide context for an algorithm. Interactive AI may enable new achievements that were previously unattainable by humans alone. Interactable AI is challenging since it will probably be industry specific.

An effective, easy, and personalized healthcare system is made possible by using emerging technologies like IoT. AI, and cloud computing. With the aid of wearable technology or mobile health apps, real-time health monitoring is made possible, empowering people to take charge of their health. When combined with AI, user-level health information can be utilized for disease screening, early disease diagnosis, and therapy plan selection. A desire for AI models that can be described arises from the ethical dilemma of intelligibility surrounding AI and the lack of confidence in the Black-Box operation of AI systems in the healthcare industry. XAI methods are the AI techniques that are used to describe AI Methodologies and their predictions. Machine learning models' output can now be more easily understood thanks to the development of explainable artificial intelligence (XAI) approaches. Considering this, the goal of this study is to show the potential of adopting XAI for applications in the power system.

The benefits of XAI methods are as follows:

- Increased transparency in how AI systems work, and higher levels of confidence can result from the use of XAI methods, which explains how AI systems arrive at a particular decision.
- Result tracing: You can follow the influences that the AI system considered when predicting a result using the explanations produced by XAI techniques.
- Model improvement: To make predictions, AI systems learn from data. Sometimes, incorrect predictions can result from incorrectly taught rules. To identify errors in the learned principles and enhance models, explanations produced by XAI methods can help.
- Reducing Cost of Mistakes: Wrong detection has a significant impact on decision-sensitive industries. Monitoring the results lessens the impact of incorrect results and helps to find the underlying causes, which improves the underlying model.
- Lessening the Effect of Model Biasing: AI models have demonstrated a substantial amount of bias. Examples include racial prejudice in autonomous vehicles, gender bias in Apple Cards, and racial bias in Amazon Recognitions. By outlining the criteria used to make decisions, an explainable system can lessen the effect that such biased predictions can have.
- Responsibility and Accountability: Predictions made by AI models almost always contain some degree of mistake. By allowing someone to take responsibility and accountability for these errors, the system can be made more effective.
- Every inference and its justification tend to boost the system's confidence, which is measured by the code confidence. For more effective use, some user-critical systems, such as autonomous vehicles, medical diagnosis, the financial industry, etc., require high code trust from the user.
- Code Compliance: Businesses are under increasing pressure from regulatory bodies to adapt and realize XAI to rapidly conform with the law.

A visual representation of XAI and how it might impact the final user is shown in Figure 16.3. The numerous benefits of XAI solutions put it in renown and emphasize the need for more rapid global large-scale adaptation.

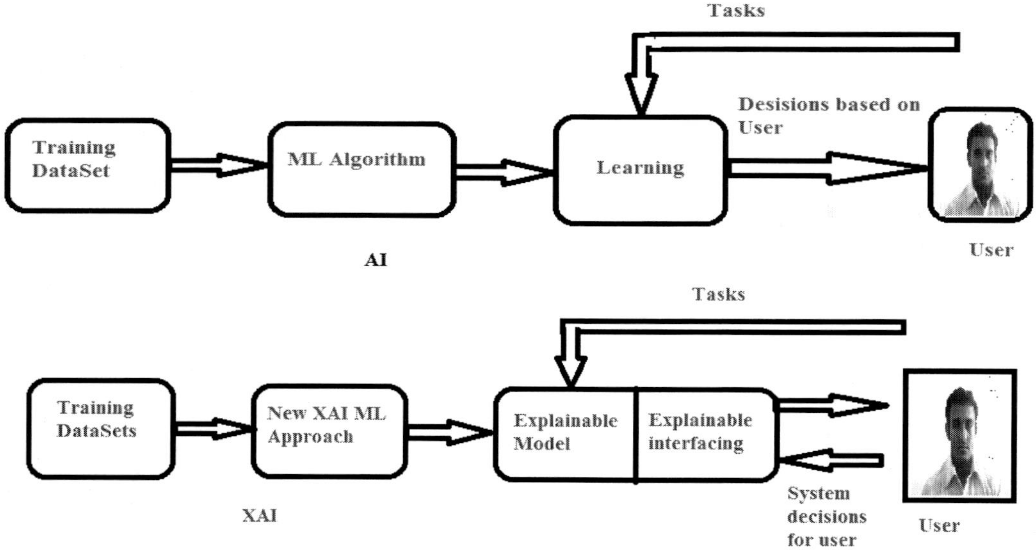

Figure 16.3. Comparison between AI and XAI.

Objective of Study

The following are possible objectives for the current study:

- Based on AI algorithms & the associated configurations,
- Determines the present advancement underneath the various infections/diseases.
- Give examples of the traits, explainability, and XAI approaches used to address design problems in healthcare.
- Explore the potential of medical XAI, backed by steps to keep humans involved in the workflow in XAI-based platforms.
- Showcase a unique XAI scoring and recommendation system that is applied to many disciplines.

16.2 General Process of XAI

Because it is believed that XAI will be useful for system enhancements in the future. As a result, the following are the first stages needed for the XAI process:

1. *Pre-processing*: This step describes data cleaning, recovery/imputation. Data imputation refers to the use of alternate values to fill in the gaps left by absent data, whereas data cleaning refers to the management of erroneous, degraded, replica, or incomplete datasets. When using SHapley Additive explanations (SHAP), a game theoretic method for better prediction outcomes, the best dominating features are identified (Pradeepa, 2022).

2. *Methodology: a framework specially created for the efficient creation and tuning of ML/DL.* There are numerous ML algorithms, whereas NNs are used to simulate Human Brains by offering several methods for identifying relationships within the datasets. Similar ideas are covered by interpretable deep learning, but it examines data processing at every layer, assisting the designer in managing data flow and internal mathematical processes. Additionally, the layers can be built up by choosing the activation functions, max pooling, fully connected classification, and feature learning by convolution, Among Other Options (Mulani, 2019).
3. *Explanation:* To Understand the Significance of and Actions Taken by The Algorithm, this phase clearly explains each decision. The explanation offers thorough justification for every choice made throughout the model, including preprocessing, prediction algorithm, etc. The explanations that make up XAI's core material help the end-user, industry experts, or clients accept the deployed system more readily (Sushma, 2022).
4. *Re-evaluation*: Response system created to comprehend restrictions as the distinction between human and algorithmic choices. After the conclusion of the algorithm, the users can engage with the system by giving the required input regarding each choice and set of parameters, which can then be evaluated successfully by reconfiguration in a later version. As a result, it not only encourages user-friendliness but also incorporates the user into the system, which can enhance the next iteration of data (training) and weights improvement (Sreedhar, 2022).

16.3 Literature Survey

We'll outline the history of the medical field in relation to the various works on infections and diseases for which an AI or XAI solution has recently been given.

Vital signs and Chest X-rays (CXR)f are just two of the characteristics that ARDS or pneumonia-based evaluation supports (Selvaraju, 2017). In this situation, classification can be done primarily using a combination of separate data sources, such as CXR and/or vital signs. Typically, the patients, in this case, must first be recognized by specific symptoms like cough, etc., after which the medical examiners will use the vital signs/CXR to make a diagnosis and determine how well the pneumonia is healing. With the help of this effort, the discharge is later predicted, and a more intricate configuration can aid in comprehending the behavior of the algorithm. While the global mechanism determines numerous decisions, the local mechanism determines a single decision system.

An acute kidney injury is a serious infection or condition that can be brought on by several things that impact the kidney's blood flow or by medication side effects (Lee, 2018). Lab studies such as serum creatinine levels and urine output can essentially show the symptoms. Additional parameters are considered for the characteristics when ventilation support is present. Preprocessing may aid in enhancing data integrity and yield encouraging outcomes. With the help of this effort, the discharge is later predicted, and a more intricate configuration can aid in comprehending the behavior of the algorithm. While the global mechanism determines numerous decisions, the local mechanism determines a single decision system. An acute kidney injury is a serious infection or condition that can be brought on by several things that impact the kidney's blood flow or by medication side effects (Lee, 2018). Lab studies such as serum creatinine levels and urine output can essentially show the symptoms. Additional parameters are considered for the characteristics when ventilation support is present. Preprocessing may aid in enhancing data integrity and yield encouraging outcomes.

Machine learning is known to be able to recognize the stage and severity of AKI, which has aided in the application of appropriate medication therapy, recovery for mild conditions, and control for serious ones. Hospital mortality is considered a significant predictor in cases of comorbidities or critical situations. For such situations, more features are available due to the specific ICU parameters involved. The drug courses and their associated side effects are also accessible. The first preprocessing filter is the criteria for considering critical cases, and later data imputation can be added if required.

They were created by mapping a bit of information to a result using IF-THEN rules, and researchers applied them to explain the predictions of diseases based on patient's Health records. For instance, using the condition: IF the individual smokes and before now has respiratory issues, THEN predict it as lung cancer. The issue with self-explanatory AI models, though, is that they limit the use of other AI models that can be used to achieve higher precision.

Some authors used LIME to explain how RNNs predict heart failure, and clarifications helped to identify the mainly prevalent medical conditions, including kidney failure, and diabetes, which increase a person's chance of developing heart failure. Other model independent XAI techniques, including Anchors and Shapley values have been created and applied in the healthcare industry.

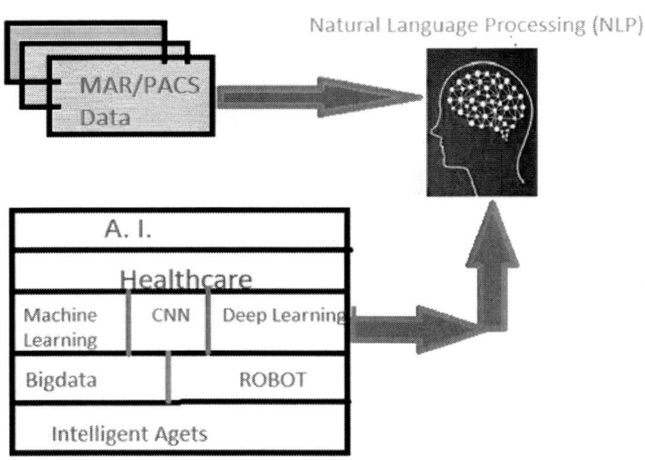

Figure 16.4. Mind Map Diagram for AI Healthcare Survey.

In (Lundberg, 2017), an approach was put forth to use understanding of Human reasoning in creating XAI methods, with the intention being to improve explanations by incorporating the user's reasoning objectives. The outline created can be expanded domains, such as smart health care, to produce insights that are approachable by humans to describe how AI-based systems function using XAI techniques at various stages to support clinical decision-making (Lundberg, 2017).

The mind map layout for the analysis of this survey is shown in Figure 16.4. For open/human comprehensible models, the explanatory type is ante-hoc, and for black boxes and DNN, it is post-hoc. Bloodstream infection (BSI), one of the most frequently occurring diseases in patients, is recognized by many bacterial and fungi microorganisms in blood samples (Pardeshi, 2022).

16.4 Proposed Approach with COVID-19 and Pneumonia Case Study

In the following section, we suggest using current XAI models along with clinical expertise to enhance the benefits of AI-based systems. The suggested method is illustrated in Figure 16.5 as follows (in the figure, steps are denoted by black numbers):

- Intelligent healthcare apps gather patient health data (1) and use AI models (Trained) (2) to forecast the likelihood of specific abnormalities or diseases.
- The health data (1) and predictions (3) are combined with XAI techniques (4) to produce explanations. (5).
- These theories can be examined using the expertise of a clinician. (6). Clinicians will be able to verify the AI model's predictions thanks to this research, enabling transparency.
- If predictions are accurate, explanations and clinical expertise can be applied to produce insightful conclusions and suggestions. (7).
- If predictions are inaccurate, the discrepancy between explanations and clinical expertise can be used to identify the contributing factors and allow (8) improvement in the AI model being used. (2).

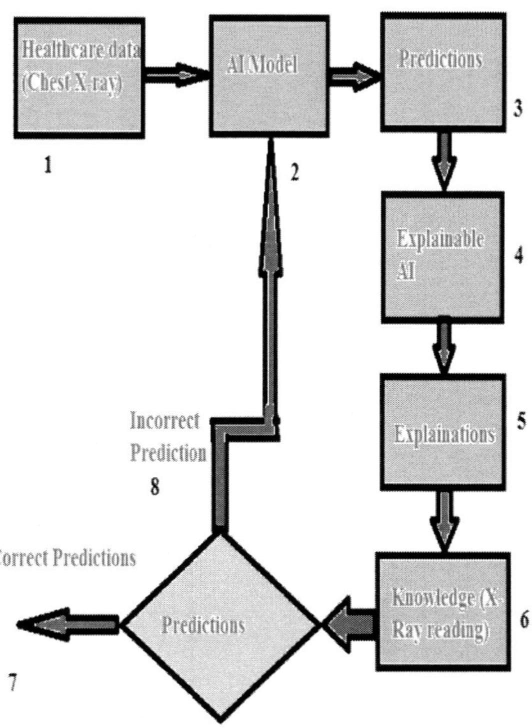

Figure 16.5. XAI in (COVID -19) Clinical decisions based on X-Ray.

As seen in Figure 16.6 below, the Chest Radiographs (CR) (Sirishadevi, 2022) dataset contains 150 frontal CXR(X-ray) images that are examined posterior-anterior collected from various hospitals at Solapur (MS).

For CXR- based COVID-19 identification, deep network graph diffusion pseudo-labelling is demonstrated. A deep semi-supervised architecture is used to identify COVID-19 using the GraphXCovid in Figure 16.6. It uses a cutting-edge optimization algorithm to generate pseudo-labelling using Dirichlet energy. Thus, high sensitivity in illness i.e., COVID-19 is produced with few labels. The key features of this approach include attention maps and an iterative deep net scheme. The research is regarded as the deep SSL technique's replacement because it combines deep neural network generalization and feature extraction.

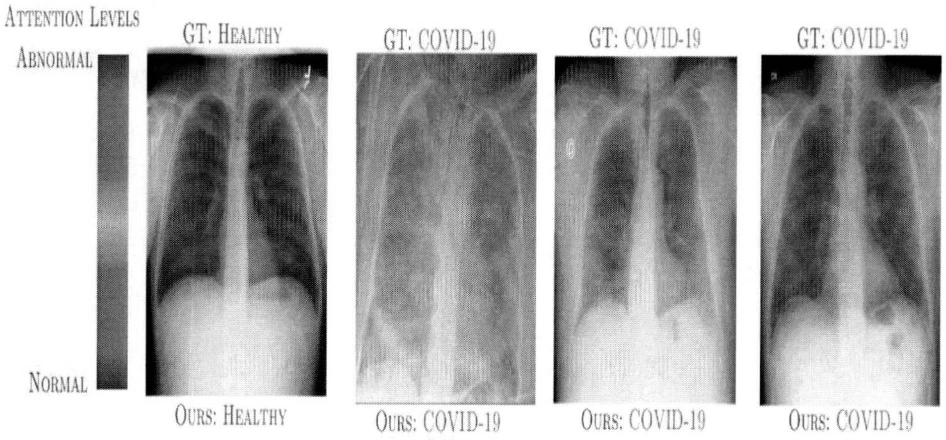

Figure 16.6. CXR result.

The procedure can be described in more detail as optimizing epochs for Deep-net extraction for graph building and diffusing labelled sets to unlabeled data. Pseudo-labels are created as a result, which optimizes the model parameter through frequent changes and is then iterated until finished. The imbalance in the medical data issue (Pardeshi et al. 2022) is addressed in this instance during the diffusion. The characteristic most in charge of this prediction, according to a XAI model, is intake. Then, after examining the characteristics, doctors can suggest the best treatments or exercises.

Getting an influential score(I-score) for those with Pneumonia patients shown in Figure 16.7 will be made easier by reading the talk that follows. EHR data is known to have several difficulties, which would make for very intriguing predictions if the supporting choices made for them could be explained.

The basic framework is based on VGG-19, whose convolution kernel has been adjusted to meet the needs. Bright colors are used to establish the final values and designate the area of interest for medical analysis. To discover the ideal settings, the hyper-parameters are trained using grid search. Finally, CNN2 produces the result by precisely categorizing the infection shown in Figure 16.8.

From the chest radiographs (SCR) dataset X-ray images, one can also identify the Pneumonia. For that one can use the same database as previously used for COVID-19 cases (KK, 2022).

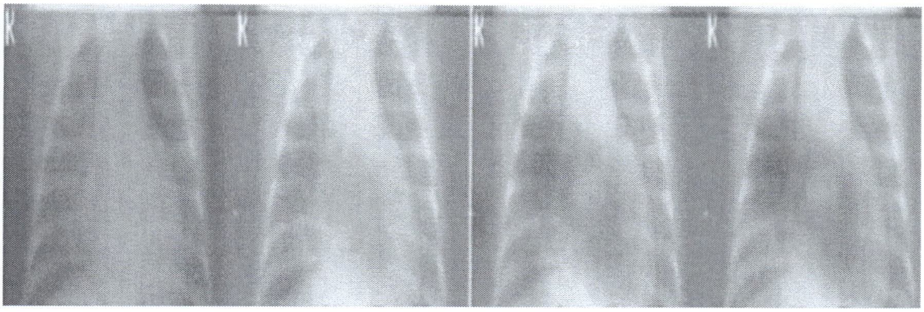

Figure 16.7. I-Score Model with top features for CXR [39].

A deep semi-supervised architecture is used to identify Pneumonia using the GraphXPneumonia in Figure 16.9. It uses a cutting-edge optimization algorithm to generate pseudo-labelling using Dirichlet energy. Thus, a high sensitivity in illness is produced with few labels.

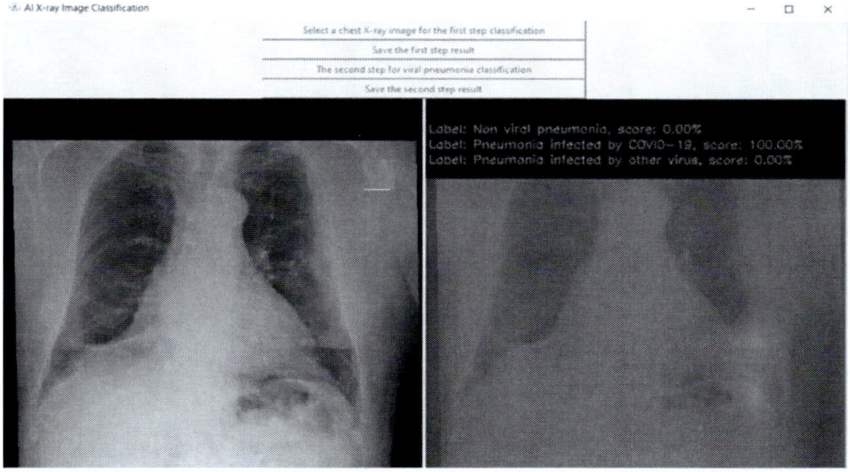

Figure 16.8. COVID-19 pneumonia identification.

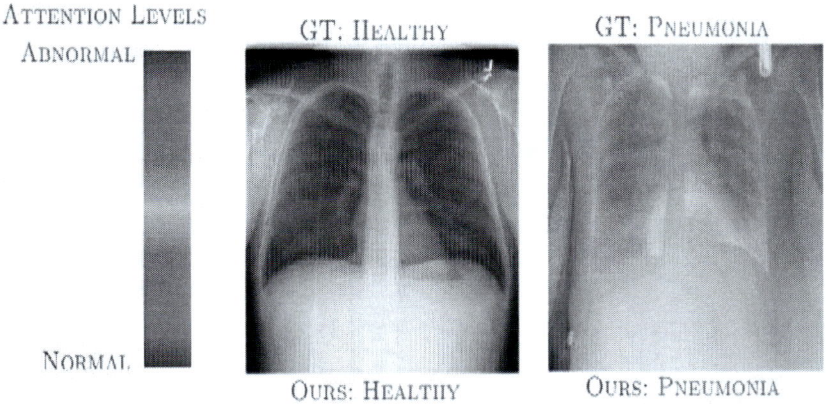

Figure 16.9. Pneumonia from CXR Images using XAI.

16.5 Problems Associated with Current XAI Techniques

Since explanations are wanted, XAI is an enticing idea. Norms and ideals of society, however, can be interpreted in a variety of ways, and what is considered acceptable varies by culture. The norms of a community can vary even within it. Because of this, it is believed that deliberation is required when making legislation. It is the goal of the policy-making procedure to agree on the norms.

Table 16.1. Current problems of XAI with description [40]

Current Problems	Description
1. Lack of expertise	Most persons will lack the expertise to understand the explanation and assess the fairness of the decision.
2. Contested explanations	Experts explaining algorithms also make biased and inherently disputable choices.
3. Dynamics of data and decisions	Data and decisions change over time, and therefore explanations change.
4. Interference of algorithms	Often there is a whole chain of activities to collect and process data from various types of sources, and many, often different kinds of algorithms are used.
5. Context-dependency	Algorithms cannot be explained at a general level, as outcomes might be different per individual.
6. Wicked nature of the problems addressed	Wicked problems are ill-structured, are ambiguous by nature and can be solved in different ways. Algorithms provide one answer that is contestable and changes over time.
7. Causality is not used for making decisions	If the causality is explained between inputs and outputs, this does not mean that the algorithm uses that causality to arrive at a decision. Furthermore, the explanation of causality might change over time.

Despite the causes of XAI's failure to achieve its goals are intertwined, outline them using the subsequent seven XAI major challenges in Table 16.1 above.

Along with these XAI constraints, there is also the societal setting where algorithms are applied. This Explainability of AI can be significantly impacted by this situation as well. Finally, the Explainability is influenced by the potential societal effect. The effect and content can be used to categorize the circumstances in which XAI should be used (Sheu, et al.2022).

16.6 XAI Recommandations System

The hospitalized/treated cases for a variety of illnesses benefit from the XAI Recommendation System shown in Table 16.2 for the XAI post-treatment recommendation system. As mentioned, various illnesses, including pneumonia, mortality projection, etc., were being treated by the hospitalized patients. Consequently, the XAI-RS can assess the outcomes considering the discharged patient's most recent state of health. Each patient's XAI-RS will be individually assessed (Warnier, 2022).

Table 16.2. XAI post-treatment recommendation chart (Sheu, 2022)

Diet	Medicines	Exercise	Regular Checkups
Vegetables, Fruits, Seafood, Meat, Soup, Milk Products	Doses (Morning/Noon/Evening), Injections, Physiotherapy, Drops	Walking. YOGA, Cycling, Swimming	Weekly, Fortnightly, Remote Health Monitoring, Bio-Sensors

16.7 Conclusion

Looked at three XAI subtypes that are crucial for AI development. The emergence of structures and frameworks that help in comprehending and deciphering the decisions made by AI systems is a focus of the expanding study in explainable AI (XAI). Since the European General Data Protection Regulation asks for making results achieved by self-learning systems employed by corporations traceable, XAI approaches may be utilized to make the outcomes of AI-based autonomy systems accessible and traceable. To allow better improvements related to its adoption and usage, the domain of XAI needs to be developed constantly and applied in AI-based systems in healthcare. Aspects of the law and ethics surrounding XAI are discussed, along with some crucial areas in the medical industry that require attention to advance it further and win users' confidence by being transparent in their experience. Regardless of how well XAI performs, it is always used in a particular context that may have strong reasons to question and mistrust the explanation of AI. Even for low-impact decisions, trust in XAI will likely be low if the degree of politicization is high. If a decision has a significant effect, there may be incentives to politicize the situation and oppose XAI. The future growth of XAI will benefit from the contribution of the XAI Recommendation System. Future work is going to be concentrated on showcasing the improvements made by XAI and additional contributions as the most current advancements.

References

Dixit, A. J. (2014). "A Review paper on Iris Recognition," *Journal GSD International society for green, Sustainable Engineering and Management*, Vol 1, issue 14, pp. 71-81.

Dixit, A. J. (2015). "Iris Recognition by Daugman's Algorithm – an Efficient Approach," *Journal of applied Research and Social Sciences*, Vol 2, issue 14, pp. 1 - 4.

Dixit, A. J. (2015). "Iris Recognition by Daugman's Method," *International Journal of Latest Technology in Engineering, Management & Applied Science*, Vol 4, Issue 6, pp. 90 - 93.

Halli, U M. (2022). "Nanotechnology in IoT Security," *Journal of Nanoscience, Nanoengineering & Applications*, Vol 12, issue 3, pp. 11 – 16.

Lee., H. C., Yoon, S. B., Yang, S. M., Kim, Ryu, W. H., Jung H. G., Suh, C. W., Lee, K. S., K. H. (2018). "Prediction of Acute Kidney Injury after Liver Transplantation : Machine Learning Approaches vs. Logistic Regression Model." *J. Clin. Med*, 7, 428.

Lundberg, S. M. & Lee, S. I. (2017). "A unified approach to interpreting model predictions," in *Advances in neural information processing systems*, pp. 4765–4774.

Mulani, A. O. (2019). "Effect of Rotation and Projection on Real time Hand Gesture Recognition system for Human Computer Interaction," *Journal of The Gujrat Research Society,* Vol 21, issue 16, pp. 3710 – 3718.

Pardeshi, K. P. (2022). "Development of Machine Learning based Epileptic Seizure prediction using Web of Things (WoT)," *NeuroQuantology,* Vol 20, Issue 8, pp. 9394- 9409.

Pradeepa, M. (2022). "Student Health Detection using a Machine Learning Approach and IoT," *2022 IEEE 2nd Mysore sub section International Conference* (MysuruCon).

Selvaraju, R. R., Cogswell, M, Das, A, Vedantam, R, Parikh, D, Batra, D. (2017). "Grad-cam : Visual explanations from deep networks via gradient-based localization." In *Proceedings of the IEEE international conference on computer vision*, Venice, Italy, pp. 618–626.

Sheu, R.K., & Pardeshi M. S. (2022). "A Survey on Medical Explainable AI (XAI): Recent Progress, Explainability Approach, Human Interaction and Scoring System." *Sensors* 22, 8068.

Shirgan, S S. (2010). "Face Recognition based on Principal Component Analysis and Feed Forward Neural Network," *National Conference on Emerging trends in Engineering, Technology, Architecture*, pp. 250 - 253.

Sirisha Devi, J., & Sreedhar, B. (2022). "A path towards child-centric Artificial Intelligence based Education," *International Journal of Early Childhood special Education*, Vol 14, Issue 03, pp. 9915-9922.

Wang, D., Yang, Q, Abdul, A, and Lim, B. Y. (2019). "Designing Theory-Driven User-Centric Explainable AI," *Proceedings of the 2019 CHI Conference on Human Factors in Com-puting Systems - CHI* '19, pp. 1–15.

Chapter 17

Medical Image-Based Steganography Using Deoxyribonucleic Acid (DNA) Algorithm

Pranav Shukla[2]
Rajkumar Soundrapandiyan[2,*]
Suganthi Kumar[2]
and Rajasekar Ramalingam[1]
[1]University of Technology and Applied Sciences, Sur, Oman
[2]School of Computer Science and Engineering, Vellore Institute of Technology, Vellore

Abstract

Healthcare systems have been the target of several data breach attacks in recent years as the technology has developed rapidly. Healthcare content is valuable and must be protected from theft, interference, and fabrication in numerous fields, especially in this field. Dozens of techniques are there for safeguarding data, but when it comes to data security, Steganography is the most promising approach utilized. Steganography can adequately protect the data by encapsulating it in a cover medium. It is hence used in conjunction with effective encryption methods as this cannot provide data privacy on its own. The premise behind image steganography is to conceal data—such as text, photos, or audio files—within another image or video file. Medical Imaging benefits form an additional layer of protection by steganography. In this paper, cover data is taken as a medical image of a patient and the secret data is the patient's details. This work utilizes a Deoxyribonucleic algorithm for embedding. This phase consists of three steps such as 1) DNA encoding, 2) Algorithmic selection, and 3) the LSB substitution method. Once the secret data is embedded into the cover image the stego image. Once the patient's details are embedded into the medical image it is known as a stego image. This stego image is examined using various metrics such as MSE, PSNR, SSIM, and BER in terms of quality. From the result analysis, it can be inferred that the proposed method produces highly secured stego images by outperforming various existing methods.

Keywords: healthcare systems, copyright, image security, data masking, steganography, deoxyribonucleic acid, encryption, decryption, quality

---

* Corresponding Author's Email: rajkumarsrajkumar@gmail.com.

In: Explainable Artificial Intelligence in Healthcare Systems
Editors: A. Anitha Kamaraj and Debi Prasanna Acharjya
ISBN: 979-8-89113-598-7

17.1 Introduction

Infrastructural components of the Internet have changed dramatically over time, moving beyond urban to countryside regions. Today, photos make up the lion's share of intermedia content. Given the rapid and extraordinary growth of networks and the Internet. It's now common practice to use image steganography techniques to mask confidential content in various modalities. With several advancements affecting networks, software, but also networking equipment in the tech world threats to data authenticity and patent rights have been produced. Secret data bits can be inserted into any communication format that makes use of steganography methods for clandestine interactions to protect the information, whether it takes the shape of pictures, text, audio, or video. Information obscuring techniques are used to share sensitive information while preventing intrusion (passive or aggressive). The presence and even absence of a camouflaged message in the stego medium is revealed via passive steganalysis. In contrast, active steganalysis focuses on finding outline information such as original confidential data, data length, whereabouts, secret keys, and so forth. The free interchange of information does not come without danger in the realm of cybersecurity or steganography particularly given how attacker's skills are growing constantly. Attackers can evade detection, intercept messages being sent, and then modify them for nefarious purposes. In IT systems for healthcare medical image content is a critical component of diagnosis. The patient's content and treasured medical record is placed into storage, redistributed, and communicated across open networks. The Digital Imaging and Communications in Medicine standard is used to organize and distribute imaging data. DICOM document contains confidential patient content along with the locations of medical examinations that PACS can view (picture archiving and communication systems). To be able to illustrate the relationship between patients and healthcare institutions, clinical notes' secrecy and integrity must be safeguarded. In large databases used by medical facilities, electronic health records (EHR) are preserved. Some of these databases carry patients 'sensitive information details, such as vital signs, diagnostic findings, and laboratory results. Having contemporary networks, like neighborhood networks as well as broad area networks, in which all of these medical records are shared. Surprisingly, maintaining patient rights while also ensuring healthcare accountability among all healthcare professionals would promote medical security. Virtual private networks (VPN), encryption, and various crypto techniques. These are just some of the few ways that would be used to safeguard healthcare content and stop tampering with patient content. Such techniques can effectively facilitate the medical field. Generally, steganography is broadly divided into two types such as linguistic steganography and technical steganography. Linguistic steganography is the text steganography language traits utilized for embedding purposes. Whereas technical steganography follows some algorithmic steps to hide secret data. Technical steganography is further categorized into five types such as network steganography, hardware steganography, circuitry, digital media steganography, and genome steganography. Here, Genome steganography has drawn much more attention in recent days. It embeds secret data into the biological structures of DNA (Kumar and Soundrapandiyan, 2022).

17.2 Literature Review

Sreejith (2017) used a novel tree-based steganalysis methodology for image authentication integrity and data masking in images. Every test region is integrated with the checksum data and contained around non-interest, which is efficient and easy to compute. Various algorithms have been put out to ensure the safety and security of medical photographs. Maps for logistics and cats are created with secret meanings. These three algorithms are used in an insertion method, which provides high embedding capacity while staying undetected in the steganographic picture. The tactics that might be utilized in this case and are appropriate for message recovery attacks that necessitate safe communication are the logistic map and the cat map. There are several classes based on the concealing format. The data can be hidden in the original spatial domain of the picture or the transform domain of the image. The picture containing the secret information is known as a cover image or stego image (Kumar and Soundrapandiyan, 2022). Due to its simplicity, the spatial domain is comparably better. LSB replacement or incorporation, whereby the data bits replace or combine with the fabric images' least significant bit plane, is the strategy that has been used the most frequently in the literature The LSB substitution method rapidly underwent various modifications, including sequential replacement and random substitution. Transform domain techniques make use of the image's frequency spectrum such as DCT, and DWT to hide data. Deepa et al. (2021), used the DWT domain for Electronic Medical Records (EMR) data hiding and found that for the adoption of Electronic Medical Records, several literature works were evaluated. The EMR, according to Zhu's work, is a patient's computerized medical records. Arwa Mashat et al. (2021) employed an integer wavelet transform (IWT) to protect magnetic resonance pictures using a single image of the container. The authors proposed a method for processing images outside of the altered wavelet's high-frequency domain. These methods aid in both the original image and the watermark image. The approaches are effectively concealed and offer strong resistance to assaults during image handling processes, according to simulation findings. This system aids in the identification of tampering. It deals with figuring out the type of possible global processing an image may have experienced, such as lossy compression, altering, etc., as well as estimating local malicious picture modifications. Nevertheless, medical image steganography approaches have a lower conveying limit.

17.3 Proposed method

Figure 17.1 shows the generic architecture of Image Steganography. The architecture diagram describes a cover image file taken and labeled as (X) along with a secret Message (M) is passed to a steganographic encoder labeled as (K). Once the secret message is embedded in the cover image it is then converted into a stego object and is passed through a communication channel. The stego object on reaching the steganographic decoder is then decoded using a key (K) that is provided by the sender to unravel the enigmatic message embedded in the image and reinstate the required text to its original form.

Embedding Procedure

In this paper, a cover image (cover media) is taken along with a secret message and is embedded in another image called a stego image. Once that is done an embedding algorithm is chosen as described above from the architecture diagram. For our work, we have taken DNA DNA-based algorithm for embedding. First, the DNA transcription method in Cryptography and the LSB Steganography method is proposed. In this proposed model the input is taken in the form of text that can be hidden in pictures and can be retrieved from the image to the text. The input is taken in text form (characters). i.e., text data can be hidden in images and can be retrieved back as text.

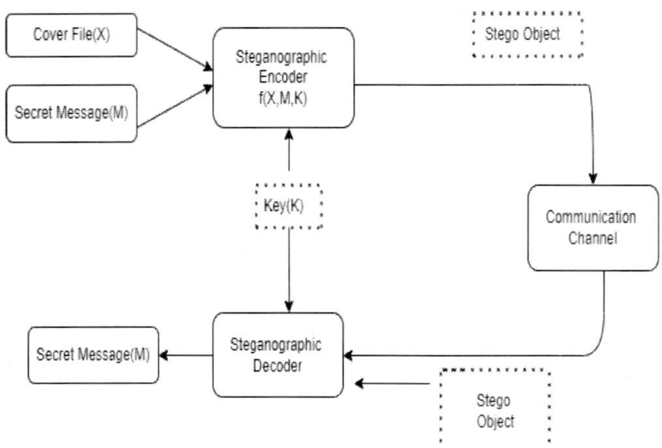

Figure 17.1. Generic Architecture of Image Steganography.

17.4 The Process of this Proposed Model Takes Place in the Following Sequence of Steps

STEP 1 - DNA Encoding

The input data (secret data) is pre-processed before it is encoded. First, the text is converted into 8-bit binary form using its ASCII value. These binary bits are then coded into nitrogen bases (A, T, G, and C). This encoding is done using the 2-bit conversion. The nitrogen bases are split into codons of 3 of 3 bases. These codons are converted to RNA by replacing ‘T’ with ‘U’ and are then converted into their corresponding amino acids using this amino acid table. During the conversion of RNA to Amino acids ambiguity bits are separately recorded and stored. The need for ambiguity is due to the factor that there are many amino acids with more than one RNA mapped to it. The amino acids are then converted back into binary form through 8-binary conversion. The resultant binary data is further sent as the encrypting message to be encrypted. For encryption, 4 encryption algorithms are used which are AES, DES, 3DES, and IDEA. DES encryption uses a 64-bit key and follows the ECB mode of encryption. 3DES encryption uses a 168-bit key and follows the CFB mode of encryption. With variable key lengths, the key length is modified based on the algorithm selected. The selected algorithm encrypts the message and outputs in binary form. This binary data is then sent to the LSB embedding module. Figure 17.2 depicts the proposed architecture. The DNA Encryption steps are as follows:

1. Convert the Secret data (message M) into its 8-bit binary form from its ASCII values.
2. Using the 2-bit binary to DNA coding converts the binary into DNA bases.
3. Replace the 'T' with 'U' in the nitrogen bases to make it into RNA form.

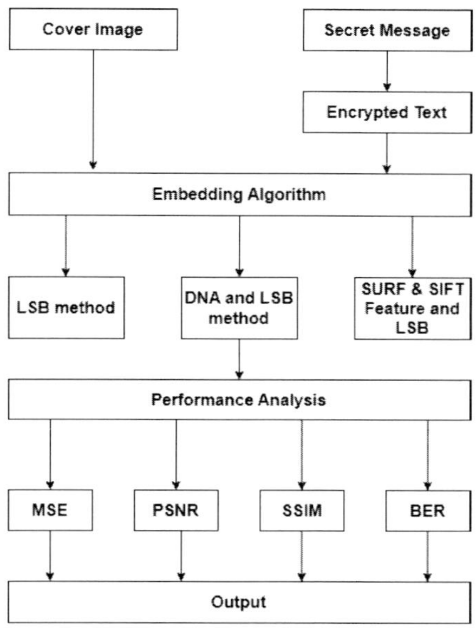

Figure 17.2. Proposed System Design.

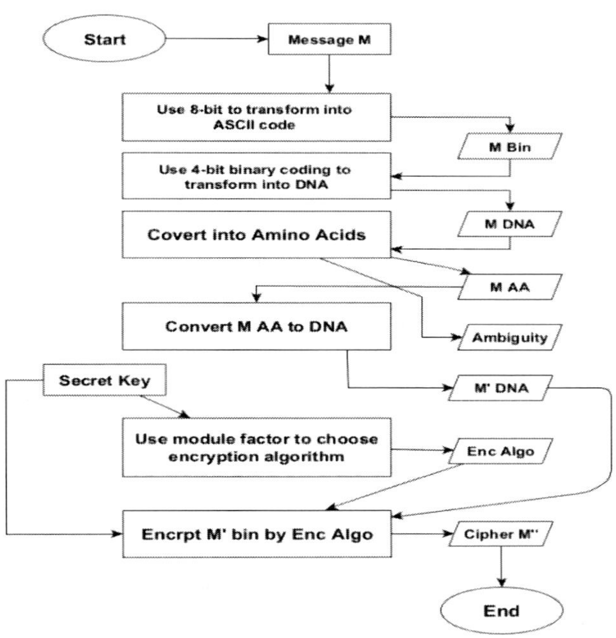

Figure 17.3. Encryption Flow Diagram.

Split the RNA data into codons (where each codon contains 3 DNA bases). These codons are converted into the corresponding amino acid using the amino acid conversion table. Record the ambiguity bit during the conversion. The amino acid and ambiguity are appended as the DNA-encoded message. The key is processed in the algorithm selector and the encryption algorithm is selected. The DNA-encoded message is also encrypted using the key. The message in cipher is taken in the form of binary which is sent to the embedding process to embed it onto the cover image. Figure 17.3 is the flow diagram of the embedding module.

Step 2 - Algorithmic Selector

The algorithmic selector is used to decide which encryption algorithm is to be implemented. The whole process only depends on the key as the key is kept confidential. This makes the encryption more secure as the probability of decrypting the message without the key reduces and increases the time for brute forcing. First, the key is converted into binary from its ASCII value. Then the decimal value of the whole binary value is taken. This decimal value is then put into this formula of Modula 4 and the resultant is used to decide which algorithm to be used. Q = decimal value MOD 4 Q = 0,1,2,3. The 'Q' is matched with the index number and the algorithm is selected. For the attacker to decrypt it without the key they would have to brute force it by checking all the algorithms as it is not certain to be encrypted with a single algorithm.

Step 3 - LSB Substitution Method

In the proposed model, we deal with Black and white channels of the image and embed them in all 3 channels. The model that finally receives the embedding bits from the above modules calculates the size and estimates the LSB bits. This process involves the information of the cover image which helps to calculate the available pixels on which embedding can be done. The embedding bits are replaced in the LSB bits of all 3 channels. The embedding data contains 2 different parts of information. The first one is the encrypted bits and the ambiguity bits and the second contains the length of the total data embedded and the length of ambiguity bits. The second part is embedded in fixed pixels. That is the last 32 pixels of the image. Except for these 32 pixels, the remaining pixels are available for embedded. For short messages that have a smaller number of embedding data than the total number of bits in the image, the model finds the interval value by which the pixels are skipped. This helps to spread the embedding throughout the image and not only in the initial part of the image in the case of short messages.

Decoding Procedure

This process is the complete reverse of all the operations done in the encoding part. First, the data retrieved from the image is decrypted using the corresponding encryption algorithm which is obtained from the key provided. The decrypted data is in binary and the same steps involved in the encryption are followed in the reverse order. The DNA Decryption steps are as follows:

- Retrieve the embedded bits (Cipher text) from the stego image.
- Select the decrypting algorithm using the key and algorithm selector.
- Decrypt the cipher text using the algorithm and obtain the binary form of it.

- Convert the binary to characters using the 8-bit binary ASCII value conversion. This conversion gives us the corresponding amino acids.
- Map the amino acid with its respective RNA codons (3 DNA bases). This is done using the Ambiguity bits retrieved from the image. The mapped DNA codons are recorded.
- The DNA is converted back to its binary form using the 2-bit DNA-Binary coding.
- Finally, the binary data is converted into text using the 8-bit ASCII value conversion.

The resultant text is the secret message stored by the sender. These steps will only work only if the key value provided is the same as the key provided by the sender at the time of embedding. Figure 17.4 shows the decryption procedure of the proposed method.

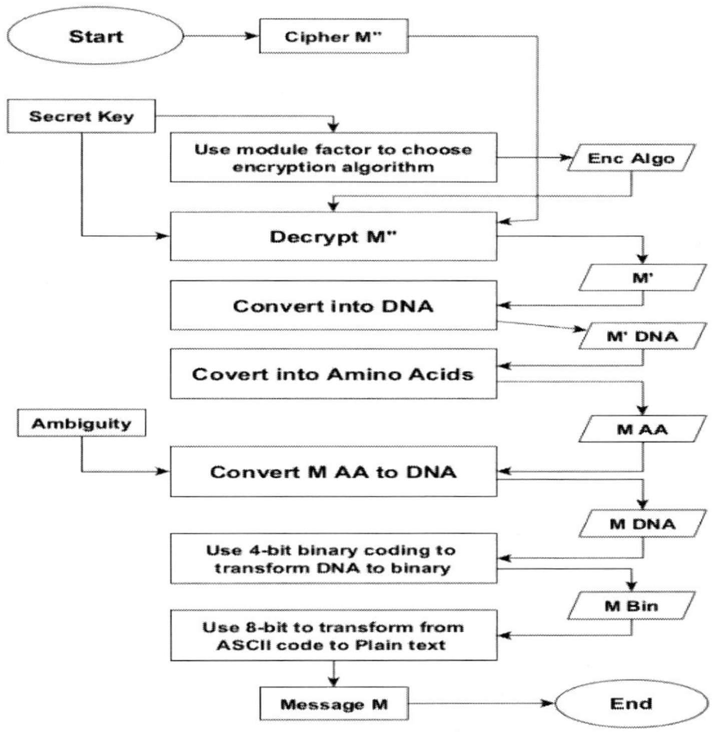

Figure 17.4. Decryption Flow Diagram.

17.5 Experimental Results Analysis

In this paper, we have used a brain tumor cancer dataset. This cancer tumor dataset is divided into two parts, one being brain tumors that show cancer is present in the brain and the other where cancer is not present in the brain. For our paper, we have selected ten random images, 5 images with cancer in the brain and 5 images with no cancer in the brain. Figure 17.5 represents the cover images considered from the dataset. Figure 17.6 represents sample patient details.

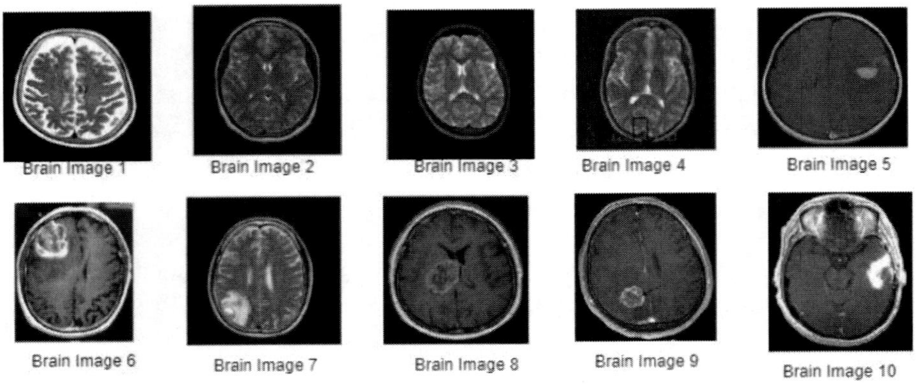

Figure 17.5. Cover Images.

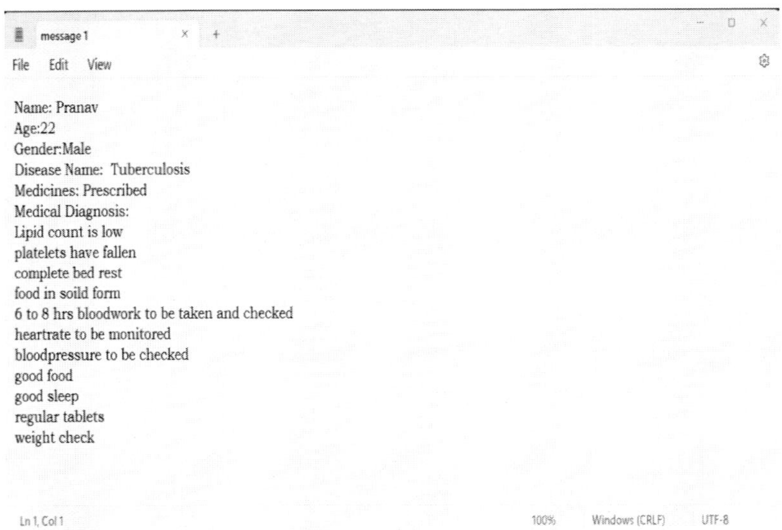

Name: Pranav
Age:22
Gender:Male
Disease Name: Tuberculosis
Medicines: Prescribed
Medical Diagnosis:
Lipid count is low
platelets have fallen
complete bed rest
food in soild form
6 to 8 hrs bloodwork to be taken and checked
heartrate to be monitored
bloodpressure to be checked
good food
good sleep
regular tablets
weight check

Figure 17.6. Patient Details.

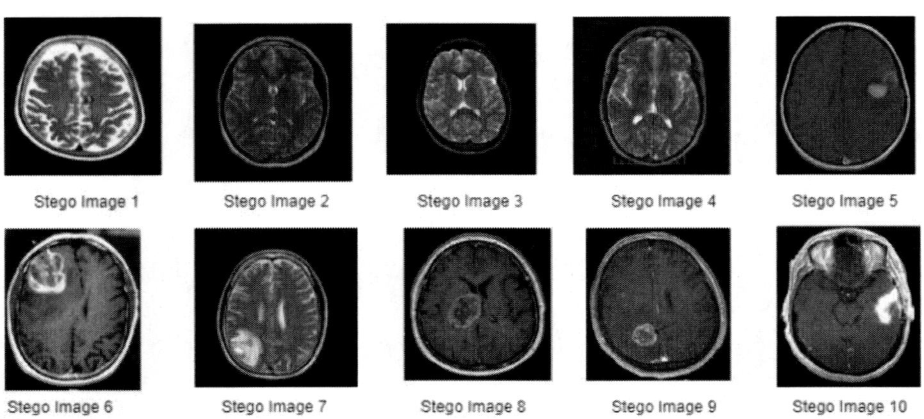

Figure 17.7. Stego-Images.

Figure 17.7 shows the generated stego-images after embedding the patient details in the cover images. This work is implemented using Python as a primary programming language and executed in a PyCharm environment. Once we have performed steganographic procedures on these brain cancer tumor images, along with the corresponding metrics that were also performed on these images such as PSNR (Peak Signal Noise Ratio), MSE (Mean Square Error), SSIM (Structural Similarity Index), HM (Histogram Matching). Each metric is explained below.

MSE This measure is critical in the backdrop of a steganographic system since transmission overhead is dependent on the maximum payload capacity. Bits per pixel (BPP) is the unit of measurement. This metric is defined as the average value of the square of the pixel difference between the two images, the original and stego. The acceptable range of MSE lies between 0 to 1. Wherein, lesser values show higher quality. The formula of MSE is given below as eqn. (1),

$$\text{MSE} = \frac{1}{mn}\sum_{i=0}^{m-1}\sum_{j=0}^{n-1}\left(O(i,j) - D(i,j)\right)^2 \quad (1)$$

Here, O(i,j) is the pixel value of the original image and D(i,j) is the pixel value of the stego-image. ‘m’ and ‘n’ are the row and column of the image.

PSNR Another well-liked method to gauge the degree of embedding-induced distortion in the cover picture is PSNR. It is described as the relationship between a noise’s highest potential value and the distortion noise’s (MSE) power. Decibels are used to measure it. An embedding’s quality may be determined by the PSNR value. The acceptable range of PSNR should be more than 30 dB. PSNR is a metric for evaluating how effectively an image may be reproduced in comparison to the level of noise that might impair the representation’s quality. To calculate PSNR, compare a picture to a flawless, clean image with the highest possible power. The formula of PSNR is given below as eqn. (2)

$$\text{PSNR} = 10\log_{10}\left(\frac{(L-1)^2}{MSE}\right) = 20\log_{10}\left(\frac{L-1}{RMSE}\right) \quad (2)$$

Here, ‘L’ is the maximum intensity value, ‘RMSE’ is the root mean square error.

SSIM A tool for determining how similar two images are to one another is called SSIM. In a nutshell, the assessment or forecast of picture quality is based on a baseline uncompressed or free-of-distortion image. The acceptable range of SSIM lies between 0 to 1 where the higher values indicate better quality. The SSIM score is a full reference metric, and it is explained below as eqn. (3)

$$\text{SSIM} = (2\mu_x\mu_y + \text{c}1)(2\sigma_{xy} + \text{c}2)/(\mu_x)^2 + (\mu_y)2 + c1)(\sigma_x)^2 + (\sigma_y)^2 + c2 \quad (3)$$

wherein, μ_x is the average of ‘x’, μ_y is the average of ‘y’. Similarly, σ_x is the variance of ‘x’, σ_y is the variance of ‘y’ and σ_{xy} is the varainace of ‘xy’.

BER Bit error rate (BER) is a common metric used to measure the quality of transmission in digital communication systems. In image steganography, BER refers to the number of bit errors that occur during the embedding process of a hidden message in an image. The BER is defined as the ratio of the number of incorrectly decoded bits to the total number of transmitted bits. It is essential to minimize the BER in image steganography techniques to ensure the quality and reliability of the hidden message. This can be achieved by using more sophisticated encoding and decoding algorithms, better embedding strategies, and error correction techniques. Formula to Calculate BER as given below eqn. (4)

$$BER = {}^{N\_errors}/_{N\_total} \quad (4)$$

where:

N_errors is the total number of incorrect bits in the recorded message
N_total is the total number of bits in the message

17.6 Stego-Images Quality Analysis

Table 17.1 shows the values attained using the metrics PSNR, MSE, and SSIM for stego images. These metrics assure the quality of the generated stego-images. In this analysis, it can be observed that the PSNR values of the generated stego images using the proposed method lie under the accepted range and the proposed method can produce PSNR values up to 62dB (highlighted in bold) for the Stego Image 5. Similarly, the MSE values lie under the acceptable range, and the minimum estimated MSE value is 0.0004 for the same Stego-Image 5 (highlighted in blue). The SSIM values of the stego-images are higher, and the maximum is 0.9968 by the Stego Image 7. From the table, it can be observed that the proposed method can generate high-quality stego images for secure communication.

Table 17.1. Result analysis

S.No	Stego Image (.jpg)	PSNR	MSE	SSIM
1	Stego Image 1	46.0393	0.6186	0.9799
2	Stego Image 2	39.1101	0.0798	0.9997
3	Stego Image 3	39.5825	0.0715	0.9852
4	Stego Image 4	39.7228	0.0693	0.9823
5	Stego Image 5	62.3518	0.0004	0.9927
6	Stego Image 6	43.922	0.0263	0.9887
7	Stego Image 7	50.522	0.00576	0.9968
8	Stego Image 8	44.0053	0.0258	0.9922
9	Stego Image 9	46.1702	0.0157	0.9951
10	Stego Image 10	45.4451	0.0185	0.9928

Robustness Analysis

In Steganography, robustness is the with standability of the secret text that is embedded inside the cover images. In this paper, the robustness is analyzed using BER calculation. Wherein, the bits of the original text and bits of the extracted text at the receiver end are compared and BER is calculated.

Table 17.2 shows the BER values that are calculated for each secret text message that is extracted from its corresponding stego images. In this paper, to ensure the robustness against noises of the proposed method, two noises Salt and Pepper and Gaussian noise are intentionally imposed on the stego-images and the secret text bits are extracted. From the table, it can be observed that the proposed method can withstand both noises by attaining minimum BER values. Specifically, Stego Image 9 is highly resistant to Salt and Pepper noise. Likewise, Stego Image 8 is highly resistant to Gaussian noise.

Table 17.2. Robustness analysis

S.No	Stego Image (.jpg)	BER against Salt and Pepper Noise	BER against Gaussian Noise
1	Stego Image 1	0.2570	0.3412
2	Stego Image 2	0.3100	0.3178
3	Stego Image 3	0.4750	0.3750
4	Stego Image 4	0.2500	0.3250
5	Stego Image 5	0.3250	0.2250
6	Stego Image 6	0.3750	0.3000
7	Stego Image 7	0.2500	0.2500
8	Stego Image 8	0.3750	0.1500
9	Stego Image 9	0.2310	0.3750
10	Stego Image 10	0.3810	0.4500

17.7 Comparative Analysis

The proposed DNA-based steganography is compared to the LSB-based SIFT and SURF feature-based methods. Table 17.3 to 17.6 is the comparative analysis between the proposed method with the other methods in terms of PSNR, MSE, SSIM, and BER values. From Table 17.3 it can be noticed that the proposed DNA produces maximum PSNR values. Similarly, Tables 17.4 and Table 17.5 show that the proposed method generates high-quality stego-images. Likewise, Table 17.6 exhibits that the proposed method has high resistance against attacks by achieving minimum BER values.

Table 17.3. PSNR values comparative analysis

S. NO	Stego Image (.jpg)	DNA	LSB	SIFT and SURF
1	Stego Image 1	59.8992	39.0229	46.0393
2	Stego Image 2	60.5533	39.6648	49.1101
3	Stego Image 3	60.7502	39.8667	49.5825
4	Stego Image 4	60.5097	39.5801	49.7228
5	Stego Image 5	61.5566	40.6688	52.3518
6	Stego Image 6	55.5554	39.672	53.922
7	Stego Image 7	66.0228	45.1393	50.522
8	Stego Image 8	56.1456	5.2448	44.0053
9	Stego Image 9	61.4597	70.5304	46.1702
10	Stego Image 10	55.1683	64.2797	45.4451

Table 17.4. MSE values comparative analysis

S. NO	Stego Image (.jpg)	DNA	LSB	SIFT and SURF
1	Stego Image 1	0.4186	0.5187	0.1189
2	Stego Image 2	0.4798	0.5662	0.0667
3	Stego Image 3	0.3715	0.5721	0.0718
4	Stego Image 4	0.2693	0.5712	0.0699
5	Stego Image 5	0.4004	0.5004	0.0008
6	Stego Image 6	0.3263	0.4007	0.0268
7	Stego Image 7	0.4057	0.4161	0.0054
8	Stego Image 8	0.2258	0.4267	0.0261
9	Stego Image 9	0.3157	0.4161	0.0157
10	Stego Image 10	0.4185	0.4192	0.0191

Table 17.5. SSIM values comparative analysis

S. NO	Stego Image (.jpg)	DNA	LSB	SIFT and SURF
1	Stego Image 1	0.9857	0.9755	0.9812
2	Stego Image 2	0.9817	0.9712	0.9799
3	Stego Image 3	0.9908	0.9731	0.9752
4	Stego Image 4	0.9827	0.9712	0.9723
5	Stego Image 5	0.9997	0.9734	0.9727
6	Stego Image 6	0.9882	0.9711	0.9787
7	Stego Image 7	0.9969	0.9771	0.9798
8	Stego Image 8	0.9971	0.9722	0.9722
9	Stego Image 9	0.9951	0.9762	0.9751
10	Stego Image 10	0.9920	0.9723	0.9788

Table 17.6. BER values comparative analysis

S. NO	Stego Image (.jpg)	DNA	LSB	SIFT and SURF
1	Stego Image 1	0.2500	0.4286	0.5557
2	Stego Image 2	0.3120	0.4000	0.4973
3	Stego Image 3	0.3750	0.4556	0.4344
4	Stego Image 4	0.3500	0.4333	0.3956
5	Stego Image 5	0.3250	0.4522	0.4820
6	Stego Image 6	0.3120	0.4556	0.4100
7	Stego Image 7	0.2750	0.4661	0.4750
8	Stego Image 8	0.3444	0.4844	0.4000
9	Stego Image 9	0.3500	0.4333	0.4161
10	Stego Image 10	0.3556	0.4232	0.465

17.8 Conclusion

Performance and Quantitative Analysis to embed the cancer patient's details with brain tumor was successful in the proposed method. DNA-based embedding algorithm along with all the performance metrics such as MSE, PSNR, and SSIM that was performed on the grayscale images (black and white images) along with 4 Algorithms AES.DES, 3DES, and IDEA provided a better level of security to prevent attackers from making changes or tampering with the patient's confidential data. This DNA-based embedding algorithm is further compared with other algorithms such as LSB SIFT and SURF key points to ensure quality. From the comparative analysis, it is observed that the proposed method outperforms the other methods. In the future, security algorithms like RSA, Blowfish, or even some machine learning algorithms can be incorporated to enhance the security and integrity of the patient's content to avoid it being changed after the steganography process is completed.

References

Deepa, M., Harini, N. D., Sravika, V., Soundarya, S., and Reshma, S. (2021). A Novel Electronic Medical Record Design Using Cryptography and Steganography Techniques. In *2021 5th International Conference on Electronics, Communication and Aerospace Technology (ICECA),* pp. 377-382. IEEE.

Kumar, S., and Soundrapandiyan, R. (2022). A multi-image hiding technique in dilated video regions based on cooperative game-theoretic approach. *Journal of King Saud University-Computer and Information Sciences, 34*(8), pp. 5841-5855.

Kumar, S., and Soundrapandiyan, R. (2022). Digital Video Steganography: An Overview. *Computational Methods and Data Engineering : Proceedings of ICCMDE 2021*, pp. 561-574.

Kumar, S., and Soundrapandiyan, R. (2022). A multiple secret image embedding in dynamic ROI keypoints based on hybrid Speeded Up Scale Invariant Robust Features (h-SUSIRF) algorithm. *ELCVIA Electronic Letters on Computer Vision and Image Analysis, 21*(1), pp. 78-100.

Mashat, A., Bhatia, S., Kumar, A., Dadheech, P., and Alabdali, A. (2022). Medical Image Transmission Using Novel Crypto-Compression Scheme. *Intelligent Automation and Soft Computing, 32*(2).

Sreejith, R., and Senthil, S. (2017, April). A novel tree based method for data hiding and integrity in medical images. In *2017 IEEE International Conference on Electrical, Instrumentation and Communication Engineering (ICEICE),* pp. 1-4. IEEE.

Chapter 18

Deep Convolutional Neural Network for Classifying COVID-19 and Pneumonia Using Chest X-Ray Images

M. Lakshmi[1]
Raja Das[2,*]
Balakrishnama Manohar[3]
Potharla Ramadevi[4]
and Biju Vasudevan[5]
[1,2,3,4]Department of mathematics, School of advanced Sciences, Vellore Institute of Technology, Vellore, Tamil Nadu, India
[5]Department of General Studies, Jubail University College, Jubail Industrial City, Saudi Arabia

Abstract

The globe has recently seen a fast global spread of the novel acute respiratory illness coronavirus (COVID-19). Classifying images using the conventional diagnostic approaches takes additional time. An essential step in decreasing the spread of COVID-19 and associated mortality rates is effective and rapid detection. Chest X-rays (CXRs) are a useful tool for diagnosing and treating COVID-19 early on. Many factors including their quick results, low cost, and wide availability, CXR examines are very useful in the accurate diagnosis and classification of COVID-19. This study intends to create conceptual transfer learning-enhanced CNN framework models for COVID-19 classification using CXR images. These approaches were shown to be successful in identifying the presence of COVID-19, although with limited data sets. This study's main objective is to demonstrate the value and potential of certain deep learning models such as ResNet50, ResNet101, VGG-16, and VGG-19 in COVID-19 CXR images. The performance of each model was assessed using a confusion matrix and a variety of performance metrics, including accuracy, recall, precision, f1-score, and loss. This research work also provides the receiver operating characteristic (ROC) curve and the precision-recall curve. The VGG16 model outperformed the other models in this investigation by a significant margin (99%

* Corresponding Author's Email: rajadasrkl@gmail.com.

In: Explainable Artificial Intelligence in Healthcare Systems
Editors: A. Anitha Kamaraj and Debi Prasanna Acharjya
ISBN: 979-8-89113-598-7

accuracy). The benefits of the recommended methods for identifying and keeping track of COVID-19 patients have been shown via experiments. This might help practitioners and academics create a tool to help the restricted number of health experts choose the best course of therapy.

Keywords: chest X-ray images, COVID-19, pneumonia, CNN, deep learning, pre-trained models

18.1 Introduction

The COVID-19 outbreak, which started on December 31, 2019, when reports of pneumonia with unexplained origins were made in Wuhan, Hubei province of China, has grown into a pandemic very quickly (Huang et al. 2020). Coronavirus represents a severe health issue involving numerous individuals losing their lives each day. The illness caused by this virus affects not just a certain country but also leads to pain globally. Many various kinds of pathogens (such as the flu, MERS, SARS, and others) have appeared on the stage in the previous ten years. Even though they have a duration of only a limited timeframe of a few weeks or months, as mentioned by the World Health Organization in their analysis of Pneumonia of Unknown Cause. Fever, coughing, sore throat, headaches, weariness, muscle soreness, and shortness of breath are among the usual clinical symptoms of COVID-19 (Singhal, 2020). Similar symptoms have happened for pneumonia. So, it will be very difficult to classify the model as belonging to which category. Earlier in December 2019, reports of many individuals in Wuhan, China, with pneumonia of unidentified cause were made (Lu and Tang, 2020). Some individuals have shown signs of severe acute respiratory syndrome (SARS) in the first stages of this pneumonia having an unexplained origin. However, only a tiny percentage of individuals have shown indications of an acute respiratory distress disorder (ARD) illness that is rapidly worsening, and other alarming consequences have also been documented (Huang et al. 2020). A lung infection known as pneumonia can be brought on by either bacteria or viruses. Standardization of interpretation of chest radiographs for the diagnosis of pneumonia in children) but are the most available method. The frontline specialists originally performed a real-time reverse transcription polymerase chain reaction (RT-PCR) assay to find COVID-19 in this difficult circumstance (Tahamtan and Ardebili, 2020). An estimated 1.4 million kids per year, or 18% of all kids under five years old, pass away from pneumonia. Every year, two billion individuals worldwide suffer from pneumonia.

Fever, chest discomfort, sore throat, cough, loss of taste or smell, and difficulty of breath are among the symptoms experienced by COVID-19-infected people (Huang et al. 2020). Additionally, individuals with TB and pneumonia are more likely to have these signs and symptoms. Consequently, it is challenging for medical professionals to identify COVID-19. Researchers and medical professionals are devoting many hours to developing a reliable method of identifying COVID-19. For coronavirus detection, they decide on x-ray imaging studies (Islam and others, 2021) Chest radiography, often known as a CXR, is one of the most common and affordable clinical diagnostic techniques used today. Advanced digital radiography devices are inexpensive, even in developing nations. CXRs play a very important role here in diagnosing COVID-19 pneumonia. Various methodologies can be used to diagnose COVID-19 and Pneumonia. CXR, CT scan, Mucus test, oxygen saturation analysis, platelet count, bronchoscopy, pleural fluid culture, etc. are a few of the methods used. The primary focus of this research relies on the CXR methodology. Chest X-ray is a method that radiologists use to discriminate between patients with COVID-19 and those who have pneumonia.

CXRs provide a wealth of knowledge regarding a patient's medical history. But for health professionals, correctly recognizing COVID-19 from the CXR graph is always a top priority. Overlapping structures of tissues in CXRs have significantly complicated the proper interpretation. As a result, whether the level of dissimilarity between the contusion and neighboring substance is relatively minimal or the contusion just partly covers the ribs, it is difficult for a human diagnostician to identify COVID-19. However, it could be difficult for a skilled medical expert to read CXRs for COVID-19, and pneumonia. To solve this issue, CXRs might be utilized to autonomously identify various illnesses utilizing AI techniques, more especially in the field of deep learning systems (King, 2018). Other diagnostic techniques for COVID-19 and pneumonia seem to be very expensive, time-consuming, insensitive, etc. As a substitute method for diagnosing COVID-19 and pneumonia, scientists now use chest scans like CT scans and CXRs. AI models that have demonstrated high efficiency in supporting medical experts in the classification and prediction of diseases tackle these problems (Shan et al. 2020).

The major focus of this research is to demonstrate how a feature-based local phase CXR image augmentation increases the COVID-19 and pneumonia diagnosis accuracy of CNN architectures. For processing binary classification CXR data for both categories, this work creates a novel CNN architecture. By testing the effectiveness of our suggested strategies using CXR images at a large scale taken from both healthy participants and those with COVID-19 and community-acquired pneumonia. The proposed ResNet50, ResNet101, VGG-16, and VGG-19 support vector machine-based models, differ from the models that were previously proposed. However, the suggested techniques structure the convolution output of the images using an SVM classifier after the convolution of the images. The primary contributions made by this work are as follows. For high-efficiency COVID-19 identification in CXR and to distinguish COVID-19 from pneumonia-infected images, the classification among COVID-19 and pneumonia data was carried out. Then a comparison was made between the pre-processed and original image's ROC, AUC, and macro-averaged F1 scores. Additionally, machine learning classifiers (SVM) were developed with a limited set of statistical data variables derived from the photos, and the outcomes of both methods were contrasted. Finally, five pre-trained convolutional networks were considered for the comparison, such as ResNet50, ResNet101, VGG-16, and VGG-19.

This work carries the main classification among COVID-19 and pneumonia. CXR image datasets were gathered from the patients who are affected due to COVID-19 and pneumonia from various origins and used five various methods to contribute to a study of COVID-19 and pneumonia (ResNet50, ResNet101, VGG-16, and VGG-19). With the aid of CNN, a machine learning technique, the obtained data is analyzed. This research primarily focuses on the classification of CXR images for patients with pneumonia and coronavirus infection using CNN models. I hope that this work carries a new classification technique when compared to other articles. And this study got proper experimental results in classifications. The novelty of this paper is to optimize the architecture of SVM for standard CNNs (ResNet50, ResNet101, VGG-16, and VGG-19) and to further improve the design of CNN. The proposed CNN models can be used for analyzing the CXR image of COVID-19. Here, CNN must be improved by optimizing the fully connected layer by selecting some hyperparameter. Due to this CXR classification, it is very easy to find which category the patient belongs to. So, we hope to believe that our work lessens the need for the clinician to use numerous techniques for identifying each chest ailment separately.

18.2 Related Works

Developing an accurate, trustworthy deep-learning model for the identification and classifying of COVID-19 is currently the subject of extensive research. Most often, researchers use various deep-learning approaches to classify patient CXRs.

To detect pneumonia from pediatric chest imaging, Kermany et al. (2018) analyze accomplishment requirements for a trained method, like Inception v3. The model's diagnosis accuracy was 92.8%, while its recall was 93.2% and the true negative value was 90.1%. Rahmat (2019) had decided to use Faster R-CNN for the classifying technique of CXR images. A portion of the ChestX-ray14 dataset was utilized to train and test the model, and it was divided into two sets: 80% for training and 20% for testing. Finally, the model was verified by contrasting its outcome with that of medical professionals. According to the findings, the accuracy is acceptable (62% in comparison to the medical experts). According to Liang and Zheng (2020), their proposed method was evaluated for obtaining texture traits related to pneumonia and for accurately identifying the picture areas that most accurately depict pneumonia. According to the findings from the experiment of the evaluation dataset, the method's recall rate on the tasks of classifying children's pneumonia is 96.7%, its f1-score is 92.7%, and its accuracy while utilizing VGG16 is 74.2%. This methodology successfully addresses the issues of poor image quality and partial blockage of the inflamed region in pediatric CXR images when compared with previous art approaches.

Sirazitdinov et al. (2019) put out a novel strategy based on a combination of RetinaNet and Mask R-CNN. There are various sizes and ratios of pneumonia areas. Modern object detectors have a hurdle since pneumonia only appears on a limited portion of a CXR. The gender and age of a patient might be important characteristics for accurately characterizing a past pneumonia distribution with 75.8%. Varshni et al. (2019) analyze the effectiveness of pre-trained CNN models utilized as feature extractors, and then apply a variety of classification algorithms, for the classification of diseased and healthy CXR. To examine images of CXRs exclusively to detect pneumonia, statistical findings show that pre-trained CNN models combined with supervised classifier algorithms may be extremely helpful. They reached 80.02% accuracy using DenseNet-169. Xu et al. (2020) investigated without utilizing a feature extraction method, this method identifies CXR images. According to the research observations of the different datasets, the overall accuracy percentage for all CT instances combined was 86.7%. The deep learning models developed in this work were successful in early COVID-19 patient screening with location-attention mechanisms that could diagnose COVID-19, and they are a potential supplemental medical diagnosis for front-line researchers and clinicians. For the diagnosis of pneumonia is done by Ayan and Ünver (2020) investigators used the well-known CNN models Xception and Vgg16. In their training process, they used transfer learning and fine-tuning. The test findings showed that 0.87% and 0.82%, accordingly, the Vgg16 is the best one and the Xception model. However, the Xception network was more successful in locating patients with pneumonia.

One of the first open-source networking for COVID-19 diagnosis was COVID-Net, which was built by Wang et al. (2020) in their research. One of the biggest publicly accessible databases of COVID-19-positive patients was put together for the research. They attained 93.57% accuracy and a restricted model performance. Using the 18-layer residual CNN model created by Zhang et al. (2020) for chest-radiograph images, they conducted their study. They focused on categorization after using a CNN model to determine the most noticeable traits as part of their initial step. 572 cases of bacterial and viral infections have been evaluated using this technique, which included 122 images obtained with COVID-19 plus 150 images of normal persons, according to Tsiknakis et al. (2020) novel method for automated COVID-19 identification. 76% accuracy was attained.

Sethy et al. (2020) proposed that 381 CXR images were loaded into 9 distinct pre-trained models [83]. These attributes, which the SVM and ResNet-50 models obtained, were used to identify COVID-19. While it pertains to acquiring features, the ResNet model exhibits a satisfied accuracy of 95.33%. Goncharov, et al. (2021) suggested CNN-based networks which outperform competing methods and obtained a 97% Spearman correlation coefficient in severity measurement. It also uses every possible label inside an individual model. The proposed model uses only four popular pre-trained CNN models (i.e., ResNet50, ResNet101, VGG-16, and VGG-19), the VGG-16 model gives the best accuracy performance compared to other classified articles. Table 18.1 compares other deep-learning techniques from radiological images with the proposed COVID-19 diagnosis algorithm. The studies resulted in the best classification accuracy of 99%.

Table 18.1. Comparison of the proposed work with other deep learning techniques

Authors	Dataset	Image Type	Method Applied	Scored Accuracy (%)
Rahmat et al.	chest X-ray	Normal images	Fully connected RCNN	62
Liang et al.	Chest X-ray	Pneumonia and normal images	VGG16 and CNN	74.2
Sirazitdinov et al.	Chest X-ray	Pneumonia and normal images	RetinaNet + Mask RCNN	75.8
Varshni et al.	Chest X-ray	14 diseases from a lot of 112,200 images	CNN Models along with DenseNet-169 and SVM	80.02%
Xu et al.	Chest CT	COVID-19, viral pneumonia and healthy images	ResNet + Location Attention	86.7
Ayan et al.	Chest X-ray	Pneumonia and normal images	VGG16 and Xception	87 for VGG16, 82 for Xception
Abbas et al.	Chest X-ray	COVID-19, SARS images	ResNet	95.12
Loey et al.	Chest X-ray	COVID-19, Normal, Pneumonia	GoogleNet	80.56
Hammoudi et al.	Chest X-ray	Normal, and Pneumonia	CNN	95.72
Asnaoui	Chest X-ray	Normal, and Pneumonia	CNN	94.84
Apostolopoulos, and Mpesiana	Chest X-ray	COVID-19, Normal, Pneumonia	MobileNet	96.78
Tsiknakis et al.	Chest X-ray	COVID-19, Normal, Pneumonia	Inception V3	76.0
Proposed work	Chest X-ray	COVID-19 and Pneumonia	VGG-16	99

18.3 Materials and Methods

18.3.1 Dataset Description

The dataset used in the present investigation was taken from the Kaggle repository and includes CXR images of Covid-19 and Pneumonia. The primary goal of this research is to classify "COVID-19" patients with related cases of pneumonia into classifications. Figure 18.1 gives COVID-19 and Pneumonia CXR images. In both instances, 640 samples were obtained, including 334 COVID-19 patients and 306 pneumonia cases. Transfer learning has been used in this research to compare the most recently developed model's accuracy to the models that were trained. Pre-trained models like ResNet50 and ResNet101, VGG-16 and VGG-19. Kaggle CXR image dimensions differ as well. The experimentation design goal size had been thus kept at 224224 pixels.

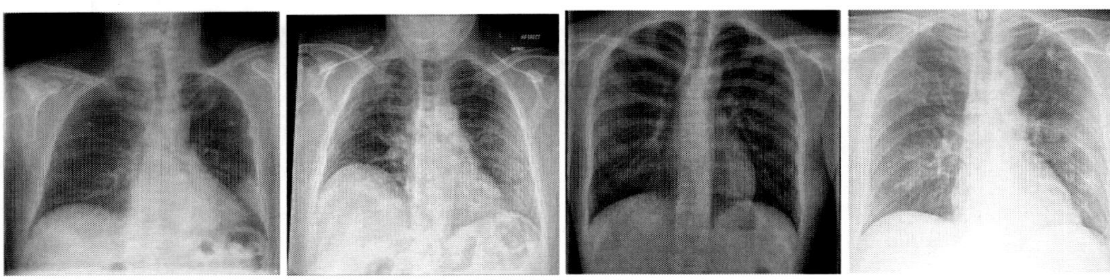

(a) COVID-19

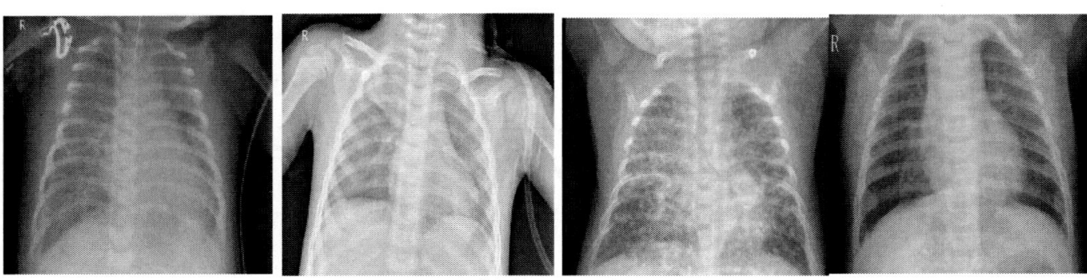

(b) Pneumonia

Figure 18.1. (a) represents COVID-19 Chest X-ray and (b) represents Pneumonia Chest X-ray images.

This work carried out an initial feasibility work that comprised several architectural concepts such as ResNet50, ResNet101, VGG-16, and VGG-19 together with transfer learning and deep learning to assess how successful deep learning algorithms may be for early identification of the disease. Currently, deep learning techniques based on CNN are used to classify CXR images.

The above-mentioned techniques were put into practice using MATLAB software. The machine utilized for all trials is the Lenovo I(R) Core (TM) i5-10210U CPU clocked at 1.60 and 2.11 GHz. It satisfies the following criteria: SSD with 512GB capacity and 8GB of RAM. This study's main objective is to categorize COVID-19 and Pneumonia using CNN, which is more accurate than the most advanced techniques currently available. The following subsections detail the classification model's operation. The output findings for the suggested model have been presented.

18.3.2 Convolutional Neural Network (CNN)

As previously mentioned, Convolutional neural networks have acquired popularity due to of their advanced visual categorization skills. Convolutional neural networks have been demonstrated to be efficient in applications like object identification, scene recognition, and facial detection. The layers of the network's convolutional and filter elements help in extracting the image's spatial and temporal data. Weight-sharing can be a technique employed in the different layers that help in reducing computational workload. As stated by Albawi (2017). Convolutional Neural Networks depict ANN with two limitations. To maintain spatial arrangement, neurons in the corresponding filter can solely be connected to tiny sections of the visual representation. Additionally, the weights of them should be allocated to reduce the count of parameters inside the framework. Figure 18.2 presents an illustration of CNN's overall architecture layout. The CNN deep learning model and SVM classifier are then fed those images.

Convolution Layer

Using kernels and sieves, the feature extraction layer captures information and qualities. The filter, which analyzes the original image's geographical position gradually, occupies less space in comparison to the selected photo. Next bias and additional essential elements are introduced, and the combined result is established. To obtain extra characteristics for the following convolutional layer, the result of that particular layer is eventually forwarded using a non-linear activation function (Saad Albawi et al. 2017). ReLU, sigmoid, tanh, and other popular activation functions are also employed. The convolutional layer in which the assigned function is being processed is indicated by:

$$x_j^i = f\left(\sum_i^m \left(x_i^{l-1}.w_{ij}^l + b_j\right)\right) \quad (1)$$

In above equation x_j^i represents j^{th} features of lth the layer. where w_{ij} represents the weight between the jth feature of feature l^{th} and the ith feature of feature $l-1^{th}$. Additionally, m is the quantity of features produced in the lth layer, and b_j is the bias of jth. Convolutional layer kernel size is typically 3×3 Since it has less data losses and extracts the most crucial elements. Minimize the number of parameters in addition to that to shorten computation time.

Pooling Layer

Usually, a down sampling layer is used between two convolution layers. The attributes uncovered by the previous pattern recognition layer are being tried to squeeze. Through acquiring the highest or average value from a designated zone, compression is completed. The best outcomes are gained during employing the highest merger (Saad Albawi et al. 2017).

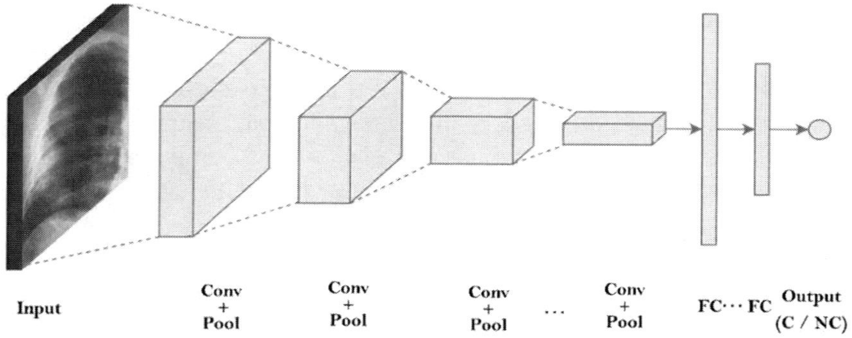

Figure 18.2. The CNN architecture.

Fully Connected Layer

The deep learning and max-pooling layers obtain the visuals' qualities as a location to dwell. Every single nerve cell from the previous layer is attached to the layer higher up in a completely connected layer. A straight line can be obtained from the characteristic region cost-effectively (Wei Ma and Jun Lu, 2017).

Output Layer

The acquired findings are shown in a required format in the output layer.

This research work employed a linear SVM for classification work. Here, the philosophy was to extract highly discriminating characteristics and classify images using a simple classifier. On the other hand, SVM has been utilized to enhance classification performance because of the huge number of features obtained. SVM is used to divide and categorize points on a plane using a line or hyperplane. It aims to maximize the separation between the two classes while constructing the SVM decision surfaces. There is only one hyperplane with a maximum boundary between these planes. These support vectors are the points that limit the breadth of the border. The support vector technique classifies using the separating hyperplane with the biggest border width to reduce the training error. The goal is to identify the linear discriminatory function that distinguishes the classes from one another with the greatest margin.

For samples unable to be separated linearly, they may be divided into higher-dimensional samples that can be separated linearly. The training data set is used to construct a decision boundary, and the test data is then categorized using this boundary (Zhou and Zhou, 2021).

Pre-Trained Models

ResNet50 and ResNet101

ResNet, Residual learning tries to address both issues. Depending on the number of layers in the residual network, ResNet comes in three distinct variations, such as ResNet50 and ResNet101. ResNet was successfully utilized to transfer learning in the classification of biological images (LeCun, 2010). In the present investigation, this work employed ResNet50 and ResNet101 to identify pneumonia and COVID-19. During training, the deep neural network layers normally pick up low- or high-level information, while ResNet picks up residuals instead of features.

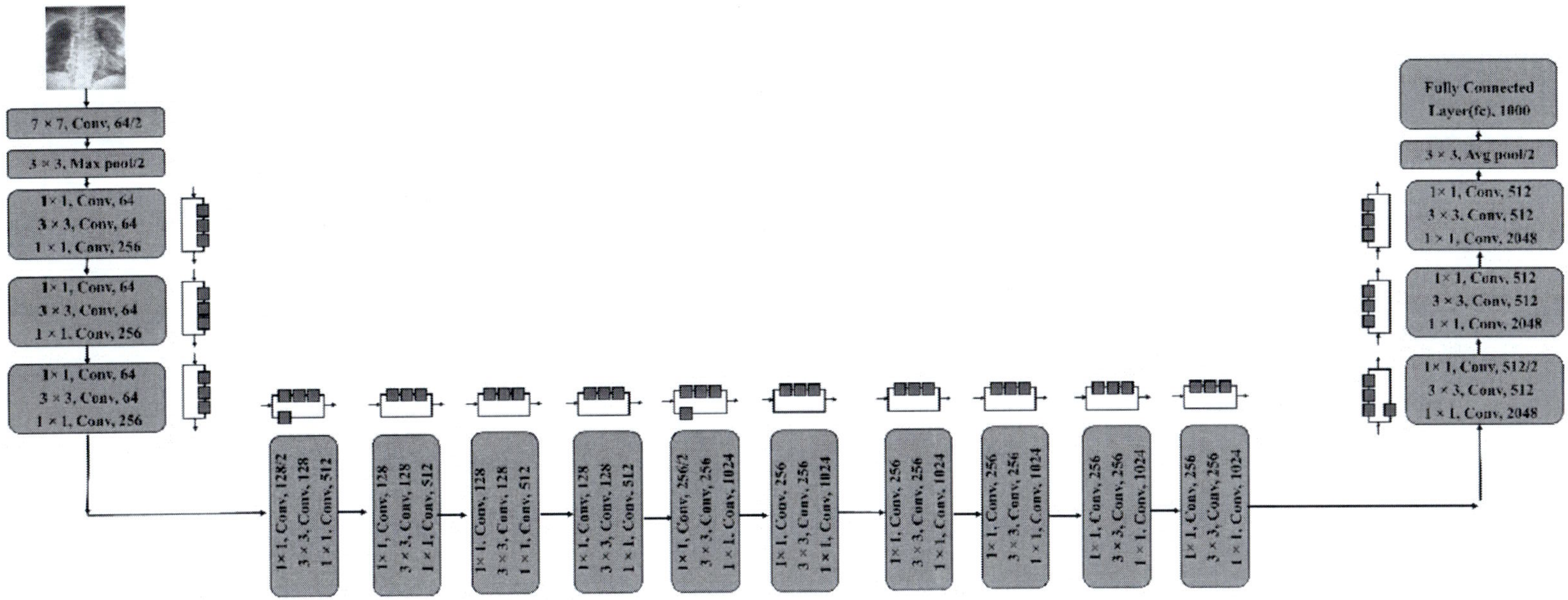

Figure 18.3. The ResNet50 Model.

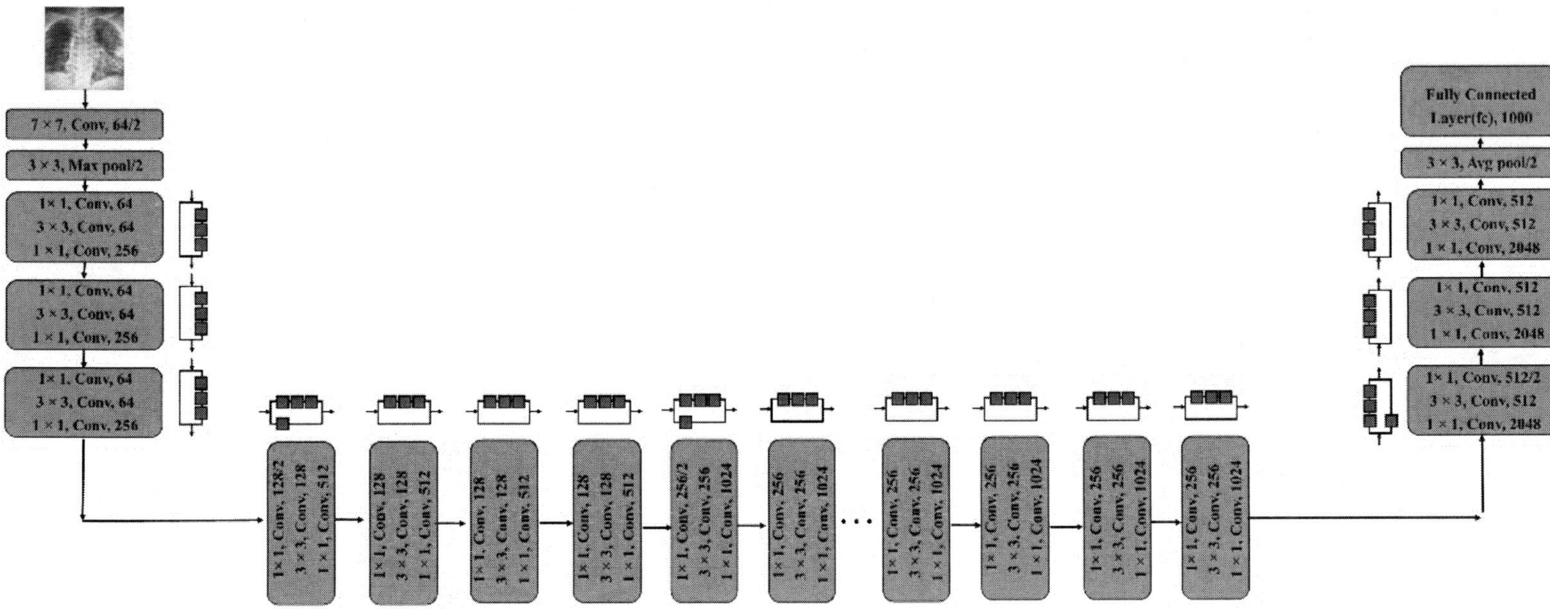

Figure 18.4. The ResNet101 Model.

Figures 18.3 and 18.4 represent the architecture of ResNet50 and ResNet101 respectively. We acquire one layer through convolution employing 64 separate kernels. Every kernel uses a stride with a size of 2 and a kernel dimension of dimension 7×7. Maximum pooling using a step size with a stride of 2 is done subsequently. The following convolution is composed of three layers: a 1×1,64 kernel, a 3×3,64 kernel, and finally a1×1,256 kernel. Since these three levels are reproduced three times, this step comprises nine layers. The kernels of 1×1,128 and 3×3,128 are shown after the kernels of 1×1,512. This technique has been done four times or 12 layers.

Here, the pre-trained method stated for ResNet50 is used. In ResNet101, there are more layers than ResNet50. After the result of each layer is the SVM classifier used for category classification.

VGG16 and VGG19

One of the most well-known Deep CNN models is the VGG Net design, developed by Simonyan and Zisserman (Simonyan and Zisserman, 2014) from the Visual Geometry Group at the University of Oxford. In the ILSVRC 2014 image classification contests, it obtained first and second place. To perform the tasks associated with computer vision more accurately, the models are built to include more CNN layers while using fewer kernels. To obtain deep image features for further computation in a variety of image processing jobs, particularly in the healthcare sector, variations of the VGG architecture are frequently utilized. While VGG 19 has nineteen layers, VGG 16 has sixteen. The architecture of VGG-16 and VGG-19 are shown in Figures 18.5 and 18.6, respectively.

The original stack of a pair of convolutional layers takes in images in front of the original stack of ReLU activation functions. These rectified linear unit activations possess a relatively limited receptive scope measuring 3 by 3. Both layers consist of 64 filter elements. The cushioning equals 1 pixel, however, the convolution step size is set as 1 pixel. The level of detail is upheld in this system. The final output map's dimensions align with the input image. The activated images are then exposed to pooling layers with a step of two pixels over a section of two pixels. Therefore, the dimension of the triggering mechanism is diminished by half. The findings at the base of the primary tier include $112 \times 112 \times 64$ in dimensions. Next, the process moves to another stack. The stack is the same to the initial pile but includes 128 screens. These screens are sturdier than the 64 screens in the initial pile. Therefore, once the second stack is completed, the magnitude is $56 \times 56 \times 128$.

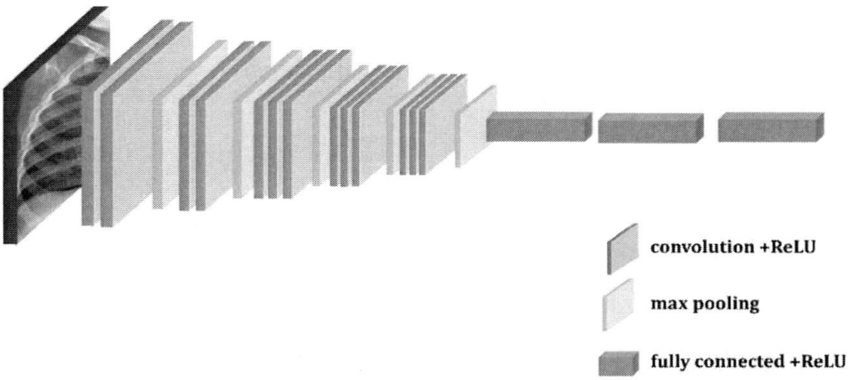

Figure 18.5. The VGG16 Model.

The third pile, composed of three convolutional layers and a pooling layer with maximum values, is later inserted. In this case, 256 filters were utilized, thus the result collection size is $28\times28\times256$. Then, a pair of stacks consisting of 3 convolutional neural network layers equipped with 512 filters are created individually. All the stacks should have a total output that adds up to $7\times7\times512$. The dense layers that appear after the convolutional layer are divided using a flattening layer. The final layer's last fully linked stacks are made up of about 1,000 neurons. This is equivalent valent with the 1,000 potential categories provided by the ImageNet collection. The initial two levels each contain 4,096 nerve cells. Following the final layer sits the Support Vector Machine classifier applied for category labelling.

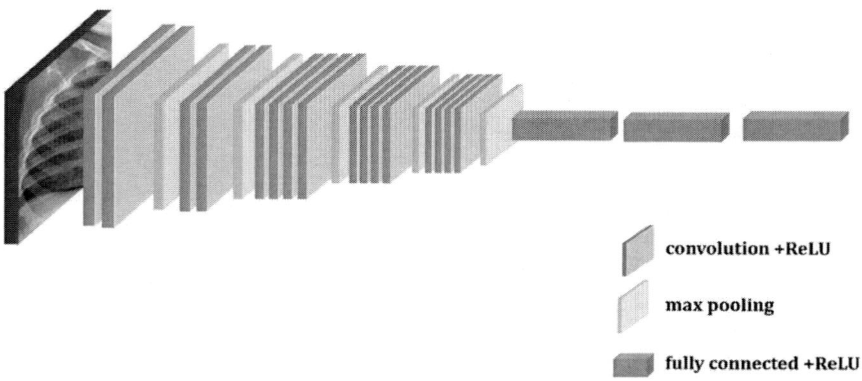

Figure 18.6. The VGG19 Model.

18.4 Performance Matrix for Classification

A confusion matrix was constructed and used to determine performance metrics. Using the following eqn (2) to eqn (7), precision, sensitivity, specificity, accuracy, and F1-score are determined.

$$\text{Precision} = \frac{\sum TP}{\sum TP + \sum FP} \quad (2)$$

$$\text{Sensitivity} = \frac{\sum TP}{\sum TP + \sum FN} \quad (3)$$

Recall and True Positive Rate are two more terms for sensitivity (TPR)

$$\text{Specificity} = \frac{\sum TN}{\sum TN + \sum FP} \quad (4)$$

$$\text{Accuracy} = \frac{\sum TP + \sum TN}{\sum TP + \sum FP + \sum FN + \sum TN} \quad (5)$$

$$F1-Score = \frac{2 \times Recall \times Precision}{Recall + Precision} \tag{6}$$

$$Area\,Under\,Curve = \frac{Sensitivity}{2} + \frac{Specificity}{2} \tag{7}$$

The effectiveness of the suggested approach is often evaluated in the context of the job of evaluating medical images by calculating well-known performance metrics, such as true-positive (TP), true-negative (TN), false-positive (FP), and false-negative (FN). By contrasting the false positive rate with the true positive rate at certain threshold values, the ROC curve is visualized. The AUC value is determined by the ROC curve's area of coverage. It indicates the degree of class distinction the model is capable of.

18.5 Results and Discussion

The database of images from CXRs has been utilized to evaluate the classification performance of COVID-19 and Pneumonia. The categorization has two output classes such as COVID-19 and Pneumonia. This research provides our early findings for classifying COVID-19 and pneumonia by having well-depth CNNs. Despite the result's extremely optimistic categorization performance, several restrictions preclude the findings from being used more extensively. The goal of this study is to improve the classification effect by developing a model that combines CNN and SVM. CXR image classification experiments are carried out to verify the effectiveness of the approaches and show that the recommended model has a better classification impact. To assess the efficacy of the pre-trained models, binary classification has been selected and examined the images of COVID-19 and pneumonia CXRs. Tables 18.2 through 5 summarize the results along with the precision, recall, specificity, accuracy, F1-score, and AUC. VGG-16 has the greatest performance (99%), despite this.

Timely detection is essential for the affected individual to get swift medical intervention. This is crucial to decrease the chances of getting infected transmission. Pictures from individuals' chest X-rays affected by the virus were used for this analysis. These photographs are classified by applying transfer learning. Considering that evaluating the classifier's performance achieves an accuracy rate of 99%, it may be beneficial for medical therapy. Nevertheless, additional investigation and verification are necessary to secure its dependability and efficiency in actual circumstances. The evaluation results for different CNN models tested with four distinct classification methods are presented in Tables 18.2 to 18.5. Table 18.2 categorizes the ResNet50 model's performance with an AUC of 98% and an accuracy of 98%. Table 18.3 categorizes the ResNet101 model's performance with an AUC of 98%, and an accuracy of 98%. Table 18.4 displays the performance classifying VGG-16 models, which have 99% accuracy and 99% AUC. Table 18.5 demonstrates that the VGG-19 model's accuracy is 97% with a 99% AUC.

Among 4 different classification methods, VGG-16 surpasses other models in many assessment variables. Table 18.4 displays the top outcomes for each measurement used in this study in bold style. Due to the dataset being entirely composed of a few datasets, the outcomes are exhibited with 95% confidence intervals. That is carried out to offer a satisfactory summary of the quantitative measures. The model's performance in general could be deemed acceptable even with the small dataset. VGG 16 performs better than in numerous evaluation benchmarks. This VGG-16 model obtains the highest based on accuracy, F1-score, sensitivity, specificity, and precision. Given this, the VGG-16-based model performs better than any other backbone-based method. Figure 18.7 shows the confusion matrices for classification by binary for the ResNet50, ResNet101, VGG16, and VGG19 models. Figure 18.8 shows the probability scores of the implemented models.

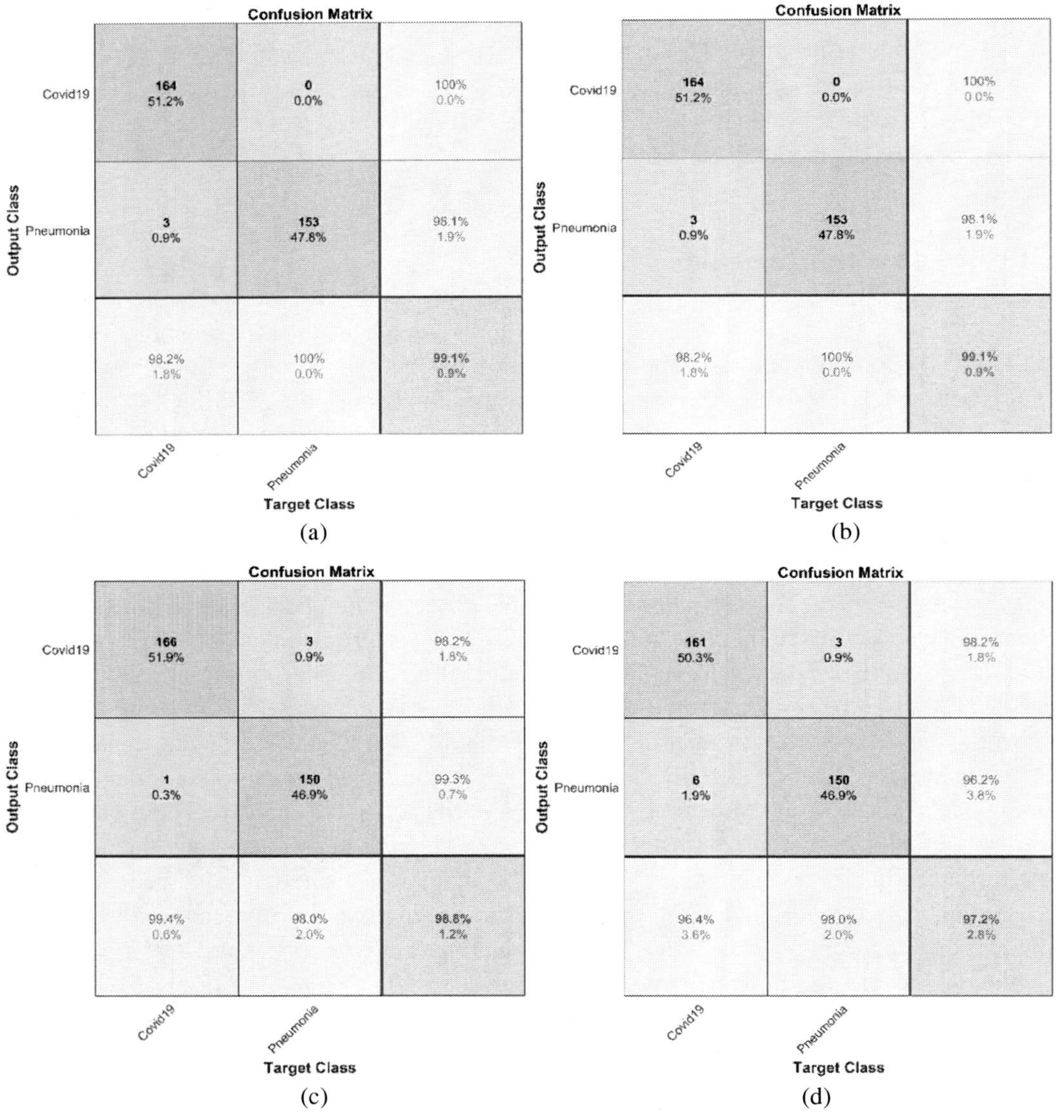

Figure 18.7. (a), (b), (c), (d) represents the confusion matrices of ResNet50, ResNet101, VGG-16, and VGG-19 respectively.

Through prioritizing four popular pre-trained CNN models, each image would be given a possibility by these algorithms that demonstrate how possible it is to be detected as the novel coronavirus. By comparing the calculated probabilities using a predefined threshold, a digital marker showing if the image depicts COVID-19 and pneumonia might be formed. In the diagram, the possibilities are revealed. An optimal outcome should be able to predict the likelihood that all COVID-19 samples will be close to 1 and that pneumonia will be close to 0. One could quickly determine which disease group a patient belongs to using these probabilities. The VGG-16 technique gives the greatest results for probability prediction when compared to the other approaches. Using this probability distribution, it is simple to identify which sickness category a patient belongs to. The VGG-16 outperformed every other method in terms of predicting probability.

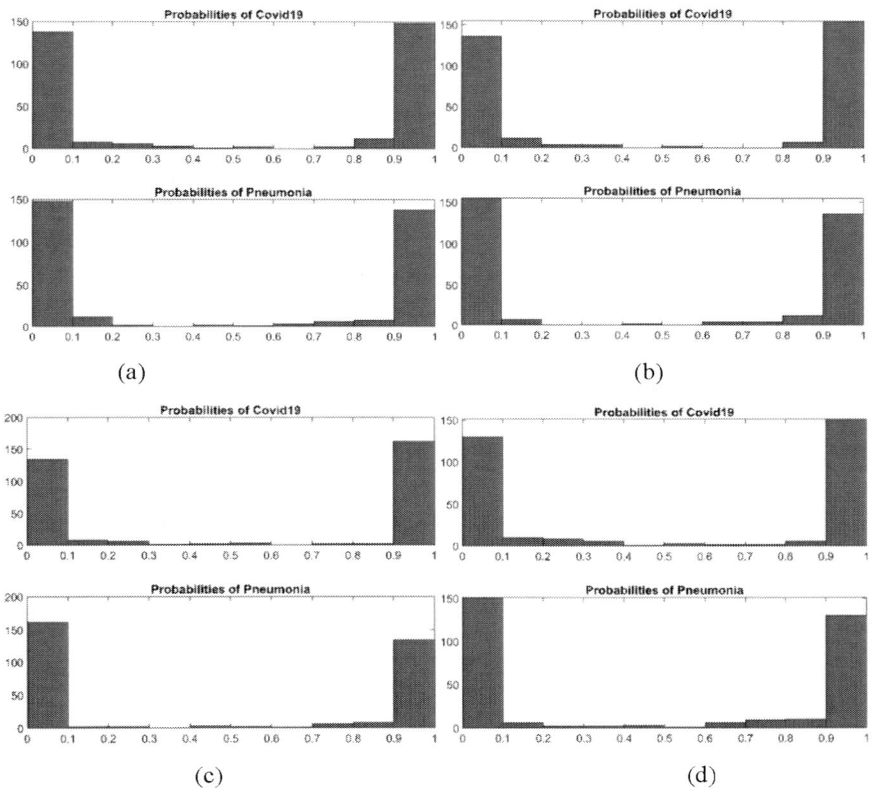

Figure 18.8. (a), (b), (c), (d) represent the predicted probability scores of COVID-19 and Pneumonia by ResNet50, ResNet101, VGG-16, and VGG-19 respectively.

Table 18.2. Results for ResNet50 model

Name	Classes		MacroAVG	MicroAVG
True Positive	166	150	158	158
False Positive	3	1	2	2
False Negative	1	3	2	2
True Negative	150	166	158	158
Precision	0.98	0.99	0.99	0.99
Sensitivity	0.99	0.98	0.98	0.99
Specificity	0.98	0.96	0.99	0.98
Accuracy	0.99	0.98	0.98	0.98
F-measure	0.98	0.98	0.99	0.99
AUC	0.98			
Loss	0.02			

Table 18.3. Results for ResNet101 model

Name	Classes		MacroAVG	MicroAVG
True Positive	164	153	158.5	158.5
False Positive	0	3	1.5	1.5
False Negative	3	0	1.5	1.5
True Negative	153	164	158.5	158.5
Precision	1	0.98	0.99	0.99
Sensitivity	0.99	0.98	0.98	0.99
Specificity	1	0.98	0.99	0.99
Accuracy	0.99	0.98	0.98	0.98
F-measure	0.99	0.99	0.98	0.99
AUC	0.98			
Loss	0.01			

Table 18.4. Results for VGG-16 model

Name	Classes		MacroAVG	MicroAVG
True Positive	164	153	158.5	158.5
False Positive	0	3	1.5	1.5
False Negative	3	0	1.5	1.5
True Negative	153	164	158.5	158.5
Precision	1	0.98	0.99	0.99
Sensitivity	0.98	1	0.99	0.99
Specificity	1	0.98	0.99	0.99
Accuracy	0.99	0.99	0.99	0.99
F-measure	0.99	0.99	0.99	0.99
AUC	0.99			
Loss	0.03			

Table 18.5. Results for VGG-19 model

Name	Classes		MacroAVG	MicroAVG
True Positive	161	150	155.5	155.5
False Positive	3	6	4.5	4.5
False Negative	6	3	4.5	4.5
True Negative	150	161	155.5	155.5
Precision	0.98	0.96	0.97	0.97
Sensitivity	0.96	0.98	0.97	0.97
Specificity	0.98	0.96	0.97	0.97
Accuracy	0.97	0.97	0.97	0.97
F-measure	0.97	0.97	0.97	0.97
AUC	0.99			
Loss	0.02			

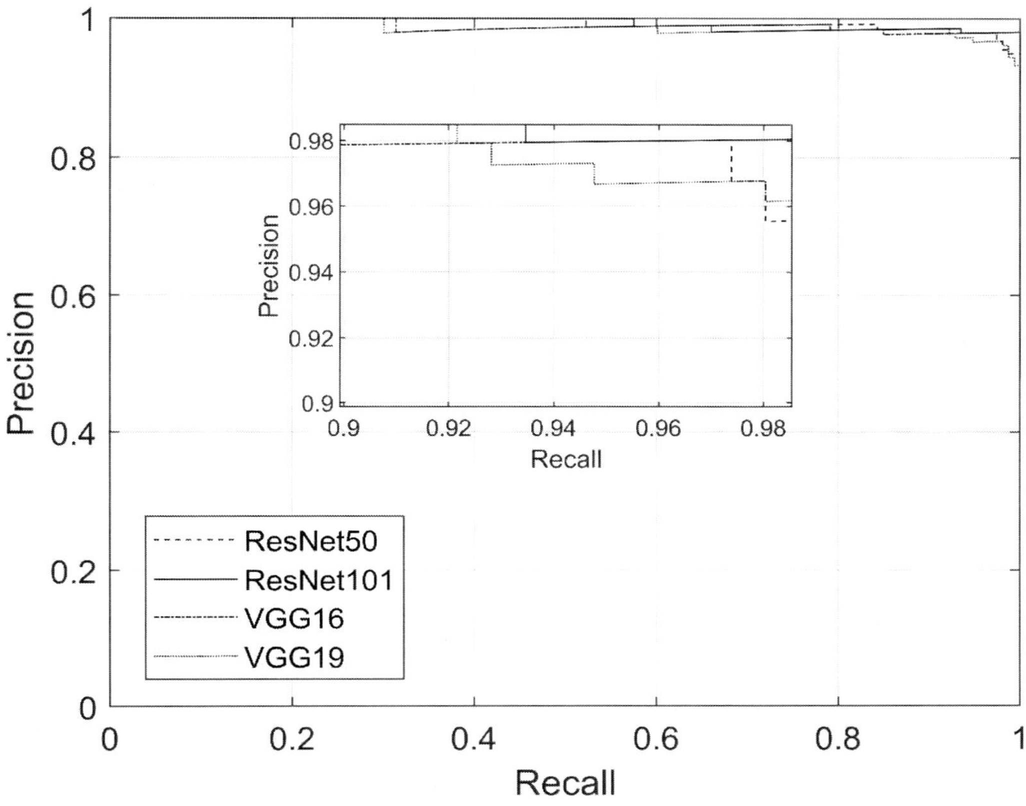

Figure 18.9. (a). ROC Curve.

This research provided the receiver operating characteristic curve to see the results of all these techniques. Regarding exactness, responsiveness, selectivity, correctness, F1-measure, receiver operating characteristic area under the curve, precision-recall plot, and a probability model histogram, we executed an extensive examination of the achievements of various approaches. The recommended techniques outperform the conventional strategies in categorizing cases of COVID-19 and pneumonia. Figure 18.9(b) displays the precision-recall curves for the four CNN models for the test set. The true positive rate (TPR) and false positive rate (FPR) for the test set are shown on the vertical axis and the horizontal axis, respectively, in Figure 18.9(a), along with the calculation of the ROC. The VGG-16 algorithm performs the best (AUC = 0.99). Table 18.4 shows that the performance was at its peak when it had an AUC score of 0.99 along with the best scores such as precision of 100% sensitivity of 98%, specificity of 100%, accuracy of 99%, F1- score of 99%.

The implementation of deep learning-based AI models to identify and characterize COVID-19 on CXR was discussed in this paper. It is evident from the current study that using AI for COVID-19 classification poses several difficulties. Although the many AI models discussed in this study claim to have excellent accuracy and performance, there has seldom ever been any analysis of how well they work when applied to actual CXR exams.

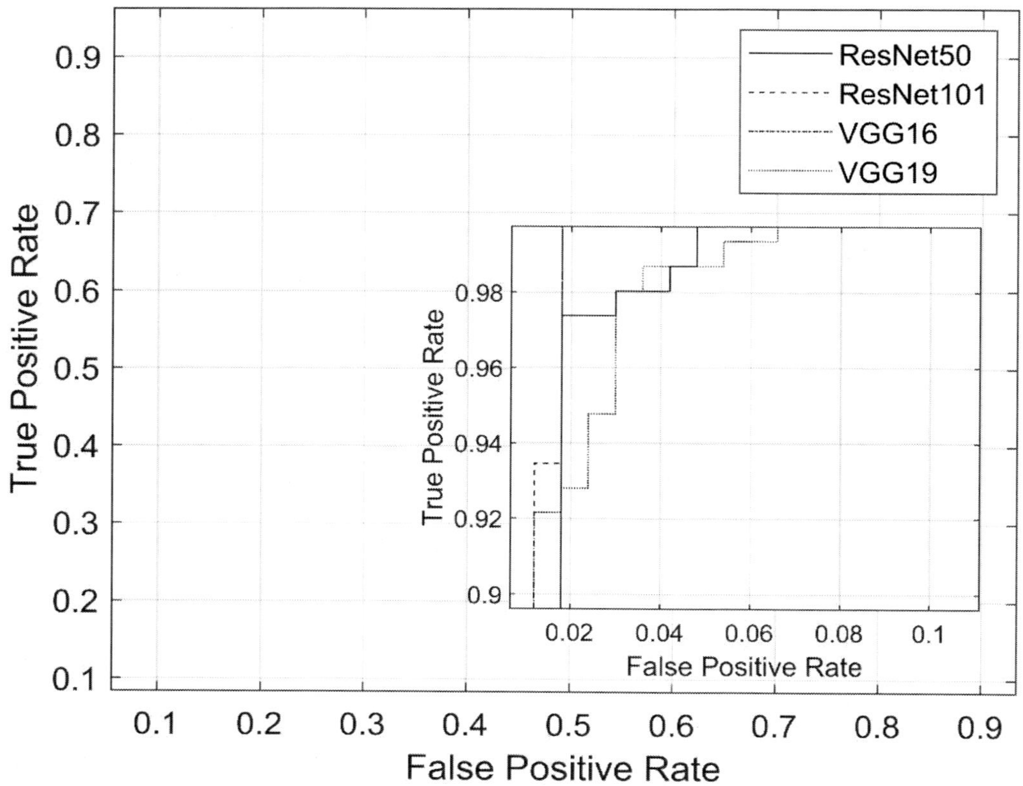

Figure 18.9. (b) Precision-Recall curve.

18.6 Conclusion

Proper identification is essential for the patient's prompt treatment as well as for minimizing the danger of spread. CXRs taken from COVID-19 and pneumonia patients were employed for this reason. Using pre-trained models such as ResNet50, ResNet101, VGG-16, and VGG-19, the aforementioned images are classified. The fact that the classification accuracy computation has a high accuracy rate of 99%, could be helpful in clinical practice. The findings are also positive in terms of the application of machine learning in the area of pathological conditions, although the data set is tiny. Additionally, it could be used in situations when there aren't sufficient alternatives. Future research may be used to create deep-learning models that are more efficient. Additionally, it may be used for multiclass classification employing clusters with bigger data sets.

References

Abbas A, Abdelsamea MM, and Gaber MM. (2020). "Classification of COVID-19 in chest X-ray images using DeTraC deep convolutional neural network." *Appl Intell, 51* :854-864.

Albawi S, Mohammed TA and Al-Zawi S (2017). Understanding of a convolutional neural network. In *2017 international conference on engineering and technology (ICET),* pp. 1-6. Ieee.

Apostolopoulos ID, and Mpesiana TA (2020). COVID-19 : automatic detection from X-ray images utilizing transfer learning with convolutional neural networks. *Phys Eng SciMed 43(2) :*635–640.

Ayan E and Ünver HM. (2019). Diagnosis of pneumonia from chest X-ray image using deep learning. In *2019 Scientific Meeting on Electrical-Electronics & Biomedical Engineering and computer Science (EBBT),* pp. 1-5. Ieee.

El Asnaoui K. (2021). Design ensemble deep learning model for pneumonia disease classification. *Int J Multimed Inf Retr,* 10 :55-68.

Goncharov M, Pisov M, Shevtsov A, Shirokikh B, Kurmukov A, Blokhin I, Chernina V, Solovev A, Gombolevskiy V, Morozov S, et al. (2021). CT-Based COVID-19 triage : Deep multitask learning improves joint identification and severity quantification. *Med. Image Anal,* 71 :102054.

Hammoudi K, Benhabiles H, Melkemi M, Dornaika F, Arganda-Carreras I, Collard D, and Scherpereel A. (2021). Deep learning on chest X-ray images to detect and evaluate pneumonia cases at the era of COVID19. *J Med Syst, 45 :*75-75.

Huang C, Wang Y, Li X, Ren L, Zhao J, Hu Y, Zhang L, Fan G, Xu J, Gu X. and Cheng, Z. (2020), Clinical features of patients infected with 2019 novel coronavirus in Wuhan, China. *The lancet, 395(10223) :* 497-506.

Islam MM, Karray F, Alhajj R, and Zeng J. (2021). A review on deep learning techniques for the diagnosis of novel coronavirus (COVID-19). *IEEE Access, 9 :*30551–30572.

Kermany DS, Goldbaum M, Cai W, Valentim C, Liang H, Baxter SL et al. (2018). Identifying medical diagnoses and treatable diseases by image-based deep learning. *Cell 172,* 1122–1131.

King BF. (2018). Jr. Artificial intelligence and radiology: what will the future hold? *J Am CollRadiol,* 15 :501–503.

LeCun Y, Kavukcuoglu K. and Farabet C. (2010). Convolutional networks and applications in vision. In *Proceedings of 2010 IEEE international symposium on circuits and systems,* pp. 253-256. IEEE.

Liang G. and Zheng L. (2020). A transfer learning method with deep residual network for pediatric pneumonia diagnosis. *Computer methods and programs in biomedicine* (2020) 187 :104964.

Loey M, Smarandache F, and Khalifa NEM. (2020). Within the lack of chest COVID-19 X-ray dataset: a novel detection model based on GAN and deep transfer learning. *Symmetry*, 12(4):651.

Lu H, Stratton C W, and Tang YW. (2020). Outbreak of pneumonia of unknown etiology in Wuhan China : the mystery and the miracle. *J Med Virol, 92 :*401–402.

Rahmat T, Ismail A. and Aliman S. (2019). Chest X-ray image classification using faster R-CNN. *Malaysian Journal of Computing (MJoC), 4(1)*: 225-236.

Saad Albawi, Tareq Abed Mohammed, and Saad Al-Zawi. (2017). Understanding of a convolutional neural network. In *2017 International Conference on Engineering and Technology (ICET),* 1–6. Ieee.

Sethy PK, Behera SK, Ratha PK, and Biswas P. (2020). Detection of coronavirus disease (COVID-19) based on deep features and support vector machine. *Int J Math Eng Manag Sci,* 5(4) :643-651.

Singhal T. (2020). A review of coronavirus disease-2019 (COVID-19). *The Indian journal of pediatrics,* 87(4) : 281-286.

Sirazitdinov I, Kholiavchenko M, Mustafaev T, Yixuan Y, Kuleev R. and bragimov B. (2019). Deep neural network ensemble for pneumonia localization from a large-scale chest x-ray database. *Computers & electrical engineering,78*:388-399.

Tahamtan A, and Ardebili A. (2020). Real-time RT-PCR in COVID-19 detection: issues affecting the results. *Expert Rev Mol Diagn,* 20(5) :453–454.

Tsiknakis N, Trivizakis E, Vassalou E, Papadakis G, Spandidos D, Tsatsakis A, Sánchez-García J, López-González R, Papanikolaou N, Karantanas A, and Marias K. (2020). Interpretable artificial intelligence framework for COVID-19 screening on chest X-rays. *Exp Ther Med, 20 :*727–735.

Varshni D, Thakral K, Agarwal L, Nijhawan R. and Mittal A. (2019). Pneumonia detection using CNN based feature extraction. In *2019 IEEE international conference on electrical, computer and communication technologies (ICECCT),* pp. 1-7. IEEE.

Wang L, Lin ZQ, and Wong A (2020). COVID-Net : A tailored deep convolutional neural network design for the detectionCOVID-19 cases from chest X-ray images. *Sci. Rep,* 10 :19549.

Xu X, Jiang X, Ma C, Du P, Li X, Lv S, Yu L, Ni Q, Chen Y, Su J and Lang G (2020). A deep learning system to screen novel coronavirus disease 2019 pneumonia. *Engineering, 6(10)*: 1122-1129.

Zhou ZH. and Zhou Z (2021). Support vector machine. *Machine learning,* pp. 129153.

Chapter 19

XAI-Driven Visualization for Improved Decision-Making in Sustainable and Smart Healthcare

Kamya Rachel
and Ramanathan Lakshmanan*
School of Computer Science and Engineering, Vellore Institute of Technology, Vellore

Abstract

This chapter delves into the pivotal role of Explainable Artificial Intelligence (XAI) and Visualization Techniques in augmenting transparency and interpretability within healthcare informatics. With the escalating complexity of healthcare data and the growing prevalence of AI technologies, the demand for comprehensible and transparent AI-driven insights has reached a critical juncture. XAI-driven Visualization serves as a potent solution, presenting AI-generated results in a visual format that is easily grasped by healthcare professionals, patients, and policymakers. A comprehensive array of Data Visualization Techniques is explored, encompassing line, area, bar charts, histograms, scatter plots, heatmaps, geographic information system (GIS) mapping, interactive dashboards, and decision trees. Each technique's purpose, advantages, and real-life healthcare applications are elucidated. It also covers the diverse applications of XAI-driven visualization in sustainable and smart healthcare, encompassing diagnosis, treatment, reduction of medical errors, resource optimization, and patient engagement. By providing users with a lucid depiction of underlying AI-driven insights, XAI-driven visualization empowers informed decision-making. Addressing the challenges involved in implementing XAI-driven visualization in healthcare, such as data quality, design, privacy, and ethical considerations, is of paramount importance to ensure responsible usage and safeguard patient data. It concludes by charting future directions, including the development of advanced visualization methods, integration with cutting-edge technologies like augmented reality and virtual reality, and the establishment of ethical and legal standards. Collaboration between researchers, medical professionals, and visualization specialists remains instrumental in unlocking the full potential of XAI-driven visualization in the realm of sustainable and smart healthcare. Overall, this chapter offers a comprehensive and vital introduction to XAI-driven visualization, underscoring its significance in fostering transparency, elevating patient care, and amplifying decision-making capabilities within the healthcare landscape.

* Corresponding Author's Email: lramanathan@vit.ac.in.

In: Explainable Artificial Intelligence in Healthcare Systems
Editors: A. Anitha Kamaraj and Debi Prasanna Acharjya
ISBN: 979-8-89113-598-7

Keywords: explainable AI (XAI), data visualization techniques, geographic information system (GIS) mapping, interactive dashboards, decision trees

19.1 Introduction

Artificial Intelligence (AI) and data visualization have emerged as powerful tools in the healthcare domain, revolutionizing the way healthcare systems function. AI-driven decision-making, particularly Explainable Artificial Intelligence (XAI), has been instrumental in bringing transparency and interpretability to AI models' predictions. This has paved the way for more dependable and comprehensible AI systems in healthcare informatics (Amann et al. 2020). In parallel, the concept of smart and sustainable healthcare has gained traction, emphasizing the need for informed and environmentally responsible decision-making in healthcare settings (Gilpin et al. 2018). Localization and classification using data visualization have emerged as key techniques in harnessing the potential of AI and data-driven insights for smart and sustainable healthcare. These techniques play a crucial role in enhancing the interpretability of AI models, enabling healthcare professionals to make informed decisions with confidence (Caruana et al. 2015). This chapter aims to provide a comprehensive understanding of localization and classification techniques using data visualization, with a focus on their significance and potential applications in the context of smart and sustainable healthcare.

The chapter will begin by providing an overview of the general classification techniques used in healthcare informatics. These techniques are fundamental to understanding the principles behind AI-driven decision-making and how data visualization complements these methods. Various classification algorithms, such as rule-based models and feature importance analysis, will be discussed in the context of healthcare applications (Jung et al. 2023). The chapter will then delve into the intelligent techniques that leverage data visualization to enhance the interpretability of AI models. One of the core components of the chapter will be the exploration of Explainable Artificial Intelligence (XAI)-driven visualization. XAI-driven visualization plays a pivotal role in addressing the black-box nature of AI systems and providing clear explanations for their decisions (Plaisant, 2018). By visualizing the internal operations of AI models, healthcare professionals can gain insights into how predictions or suggestions are formed, leading to more transparent and trustworthy decision-making processes. The chapter will highlight the benefits of XAI-driven visualization in improving clinical decision-making, patient engagement, and shared decision-making.

Moreover, the significance of XAI-driven visualization in population health management will be emphasized. By uncovering patterns, trends, and risk factors in large healthcare datasets, visualizations enable healthcare professionals and policymakers to identify public health challenges and allocate resources effectively (Cajamarca et al. 2020). This aspect of the chapter will underscore the role of data visualization in promoting smart and sustainable healthcare practices, where data-driven insights contribute to better resource allocation and targeted interventions. The chapter will narrow down to specific techniques used in XAI-driven visualization, focusing on those most relevant to smart and sustainable healthcare. Techniques such as heatmaps, interactive visual analytics, and data-driven optimization approaches will be explored in-depth, demonstrating their potential for enhancing decision-making processes in healthcare settings.

The significance of personalized medicine in smart and sustainable healthcare decision-making will also be addressed. Personalized treatment planning and diagnostic accuracy are essential goals in healthcare, and XAI-driven visualization plays a critical role in achieving them. Healthcare professionals can gain valuable insights into AI model decisions, understand the factors influencing predictions, and tailor treatments accordingly. Furthermore, the chapter will emphasize ecologically responsible practices in healthcare decision-making. Sustainable healthcare involves lowering energy use, decreasing waste, and using eco-friendly products. For instance, the transition from conventional paper-based health records to digital health records reduces paper consumption, storage needs, and carbon emissions. Data visualization can aid in monitoring and optimizing these sustainability efforts. Additionally, the role of data analytics and artificial intelligence in promoting evidence-based decision-making will be explored. Predictive analytics models can identify patients at high risk of readmission, allowing healthcare practitioners to proactively intervene and allocate resources effectively. Data-driven insights can optimize workflows, improve procedures, and enhance patient outcomes, leading to more efficient and sustainable healthcare systems.

In summary, this chapter will provide a comprehensive view of localization and classification using data visualization for smart and sustainable healthcare. It will highlight the significance of transparent and interpretable AI models in healthcare decision-making and underscore the role of XAI-driven visualization in achieving this goal. By exploring various techniques and their potential applications, the chapter aims to equip healthcare professionals and stakeholders with the knowledge and tools needed to leverage data visualization effectively for improved patient care, resource allocation, and population health management in a sustainable and intelligent healthcare ecosystem.

19.2 XAI-Driven Visualisation Techniques for Healthcare

Explainable Artificial Intelligence (XAI)-driven visualization is the use of visual techniques and technologies to illustrate and describe complicated AI models and their decision-making processes in a human-interpretable way. By offering logical visual representations of the underlying algorithms, information, and logic behind AI-driven predictions or recommendations. Data visualization in the healthcare industry has several important uses. Primarily, it makes it easier for medical experts to investigate and comprehend complex statistics. Patterns, trends, and linkages can be readily seen, thanks to visual representations, which give the data a comprehensive perspective. It aids in finding possible relationships and insights that may not be noticeable through the study of raw data alone (Park et al. 2022). Data visualization also improves stakeholder collaboration and communication in the healthcare industry.

Visualization fosters effective communication, encourages data-driven debates, and supports group decision-making by making data accessible and aesthetically appealing. Data visualization enables medical practitioners to make defensible decisions. Decision-makers can spot outliers, monitor patient outcomes, track performance indicators, and assess the efficacy of interventions by visualizing data. Visual representations enable prompt interventions and improvements by giving real-time insight into the state of healthcare processes. Effective visualization methods are crucial for gaining relevant insights and assisting in well-informed decision-making given the growing availability of healthcare data, including wearable devices, electronic health records, and medical imaging. An overview of data visualization methods that are frequently applied in the healthcare industry is given below, emphasizing their value in improving decision-making (Huang et al. 2015).

19.2.1 Line and Area Charts

Healthcare organizations frequently employ effective data visualization tools of line and area charts to depict trends and temporal data. These representations offer a classification of how a specific variable evolves and assist medical practitioners in making decisions based on patterns seen. Line charts are particularly effective in tracking the progression of diseases or health conditions. For example, in Figure 19.1 consider a line chart depicting the daily number of COVID-19 cases reported in a specific region. By plotting the number of cases on the y-axis and the dates on the x-axis, healthcare professionals can observe the rise and fall of infections over time (Ajad et al. 2023).

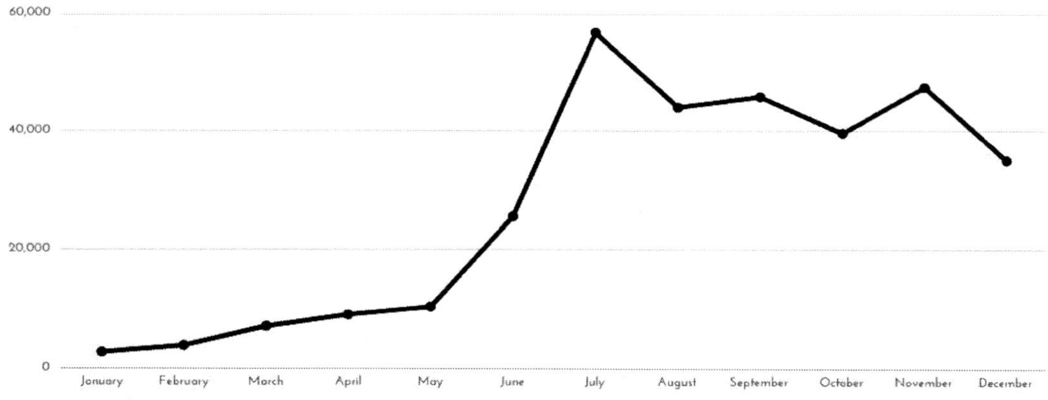

Figure 19.1. The line chart shows that the number of cases has been steadily increasing since the start of the pandemic.

In the line chart above, the peak of the pandemic was in July 2022, when there were over 800,000 cases reported per day. Since then, the number of cases has been declining, but it is still too early to say whether the pandemic is over. This visualization allows them to identify peaks, assess the impact of interventions, and predict future trends. Moreover, line charts can also display multiple lines representing different categories, such as the number of cases in different age groups or severity levels, enabling further analysis and comparison.

Area charts, on the other hand, provide a visual representation of cumulative or stacked data. They are commonly used in healthcare to illustrate the distribution of categories over time. For instance, an area chart can showcase the prevalence of different types of cancer over the years. For example, in Figure 19.2 each category is represented by a different colored area, and the cumulative sum of these areas demonstrates the overall distribution (Viton et al. 2020).

In a nutshell, line charts and area charts make it possible to explore temporal data, make trend analysis easier, and assist the use of evidence in decision-making. These visualizations offer a thorough understanding of how variables evolve, assisting healthcare professionals in their efforts to improve patient outcomes and optimize healthcare delivery. This understanding can be applied to tracking disease outbreaks, monitoring patient vital signs, or assessing the impact of interventions.

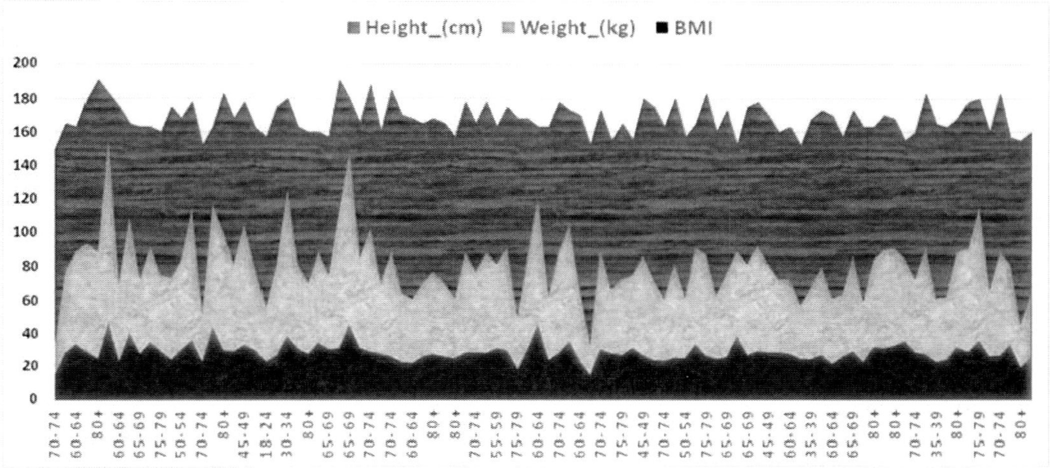

Figure 19.2. Area chart illustrates the BMI and weight of different age groups.

19.2.2 Bar Charts and Histogram

To compare categories, examine distributions, and gain insights into diverse healthcare occurrences, bar charts, and histograms are crucial data visualization tools in the healthcare industry. Healthcare practitioners can use these visualizations to portray data and make decisions based on patterns and trends they see (Schmidt et al. 2019).

In healthcare, bar charts are often used to compare various groups or categories. Think of a bar chart that shows the prevalence of various diseases in a population. A bar is used to represent each condition, with the height of the bar indicating how prevalent the disease is. Healthcare practitioners can use this visualization to quickly identify the most common diseases, decide which resources are most important for prevention or treatment, and assess the success of initiatives over time.

The information given by the bar chart in Figure 19.3 can be used to help researchers understand the demographics of the research group and to identify any potential biases. For example, if most participants in a clinical trial are older adults, it may be more difficult to generalize the results of the study to a younger population. Additionally, laboratory test data for things like cholesterol or blood glucose levels can be analyzed using histograms. Healthcare practitioners can learn how test results are distributed, spot aberrant or crucial numbers, and track the success of therapies or treatments by constructing a histogram of test findings in Figure 19.4.

On the other hand, histograms are especially helpful for illustrating the distribution of continuous data. Histograms can be used in the healthcare industry to analyze the distribution of patient demographics like age or body mass index (BMI). For instance, a histogram showing the age distribution of participants in a clinical trial can shed light on the demographics of the research group. It aids in evaluating the effect of age-related factors on disease outcomes or identifying age groups that might need specialized healthcare interventions (Bae, 2014).

Overall, histograms and bar charts are effective visualization tools that aid in comprehending and analyzing healthcare data. These visualizations provide a clear and understandable representation of data, enabling healthcare practitioners to make evidence-based decisions and improve patient care outcomes—whether comparing illness rates, looking at patient demographics, or analyzing laboratory test findings.

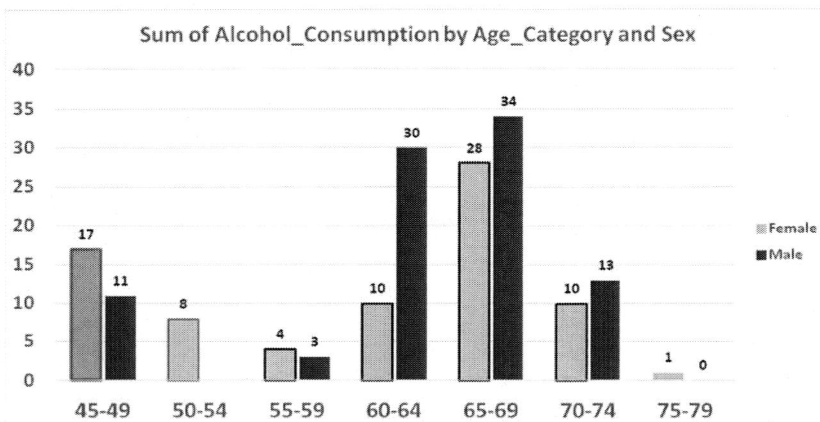

Figure 19.3. Bar graph of Alcohol consumption by age and sex.

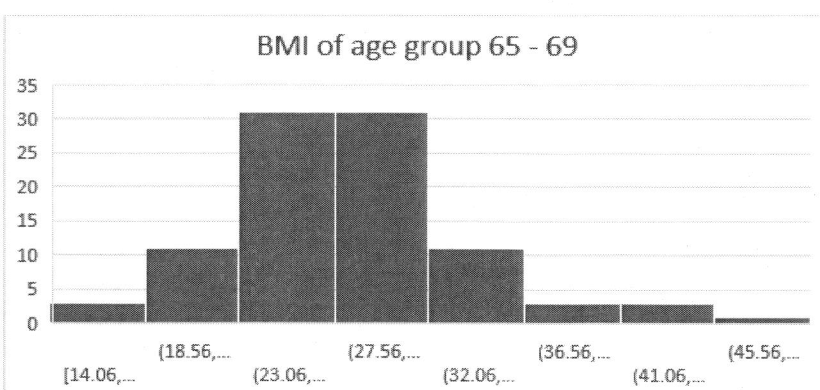

Figure 19.4. Histogram illustrating BMI for different age groups.

19.2.3 Scatter Plots

Scatter plots are a useful tool for exploring correlations between two continuous variables in data visualization in the healthcare industry. Healthcare practitioners can use scatter plots to analyze relationships, spot trends, and gain insights into a variety of healthcare phenomena by plotting data points on a two-dimensional grid (Zou et al. 2023). Think about a medical study examining the connection between blood pressure and body mass index (BMI). Each research participant's BMI values can be plotted on the x-axis along with corresponding blood pressure readings on the y-axis to generate a scatter plot. Each data point represents a person, and the values of their BMI and blood pressure are represented by their location on the plot (Bawaneh et al. 2019).

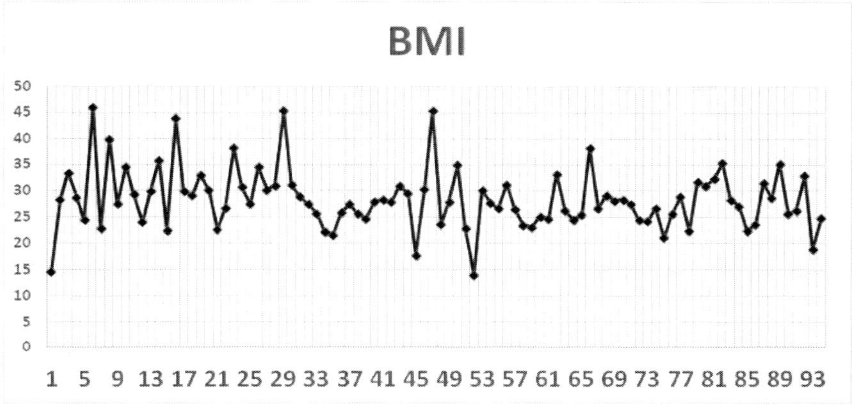

Figure 19.5. Scatter plot illustrates BMI for different age groups.

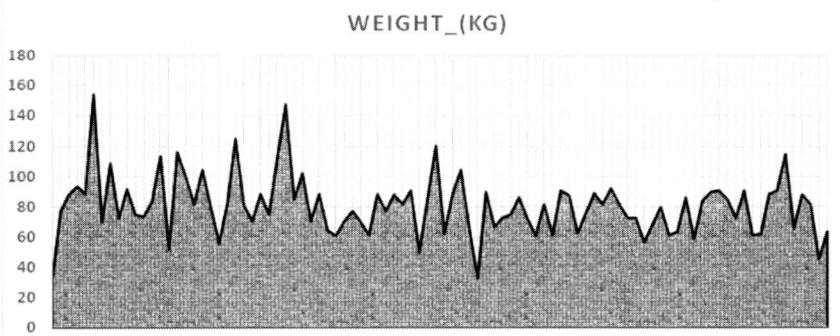

Figure 19.6. The scatter plot illustrates the Weight for different age groups.

Scatter plots can also be used to evaluate the efficacy of medical interventions. For individuals with musculoskeletal disorders, a scatter plot can be used to assess the association between the length of a physical therapy program and the reduction in pain levels (Han et al. 2022). Healthcare practitioners can determine the direction and strength of the link by charting the length of therapy on the x-axis and the matching pain scores on the y-axis for each patient. This aids in figuring out the ideal length of therapy and gauging how well the intervention reduces pain.

Healthcare practitioners can evaluate the scatter plot visually to determine how BMI and blood pressure are related. Insights about the relationship between these variables can be gained by observing if there is a positive or negative correlation, spotting probable outliers, or clustering data. Understanding how BMI affects blood pressure and using this information to guide actions to control hypertension or encourage healthy weight management can be extremely important.

As you can see in Figure 19.5 and Figure 19.6, the points on the scatter plot are clustered in a line that slope upwards from left to right. This indicates that there is a positive correlation between BMI and blood pressure. In other words, as BMI increases, blood pressure also increases. The study found that people with a higher BMI were more likely to have high blood pressure. This is because excess weight can put extra strain on the heart and blood vessels, which can lead to high blood pressure.

Scatter plots serve as efficient data visualization tools for the healthcare industry that make it easier to explore the connections between two continuous variables. Healthcare professionals can find relationships, spot outliers, and gain important insights for decision-making and action planning by visually illustrating data points.

19.2.4 Heatmaps

Heatmaps are effective methods for displaying complex datasets and patterns in the healthcare industry. They provide data with a visual representation utilizing color gradients to communicate information simply and understandably. Making data-driven decisions and analyzing massive datasets are made especially easy by using heatmaps (Su et al. 2021). Heatmaps are used in a variety of scenarios in the healthcare industry. Consider a study that examined the effectiveness of several drugs in reducing pain levels among individuals with a particular disease. Each patient's pain scores can be displayed on a heatmap over a range of periods and treatment options. The heatmap's color indicates the intensity of the discomfort, with darker shades denoting greater pain and softer hues denoting less pain. With the help of this visualization, medical experts can spot patterns in pain scores based on the types of medications and time intervals, providing insights into the efficacy of various therapies.

The use of heat maps in genetic studies is another illustration. Heatmaps are a useful tool for researchers examining the patterns of gene expression in various tissues or medical situations. Each column refers to a sample or condition, whereas each row represents a particular gene. The heatmap's colors represent the levels of gene expression, allowing researchers to spot groups of genes with comparable expression patterns and learn more about genetic relationships and regulatory systems (Elabed et al. 2021).

Figure 19.7 visualizes the relation between different features of COVID-19. Moreover, population health studies can make use of heat maps. Heatmaps can show differences in illness prevalence, health outcomes, or the distribution of healthcare resources by collecting and visualizing health-related data across geographical regions. This data aids in the efficient allocation of resources and the identification of regions with high illness loads by policymakers and healthcare professionals. Heatmaps are useful tools for data visualization in healthcare that make it possible to explore and understand large datasets. They give a clear visual representation of the patterns, trends, and linkages existing in the data, enabling insights that might improve patient care and population health management and supporting evidence-based decision-making.

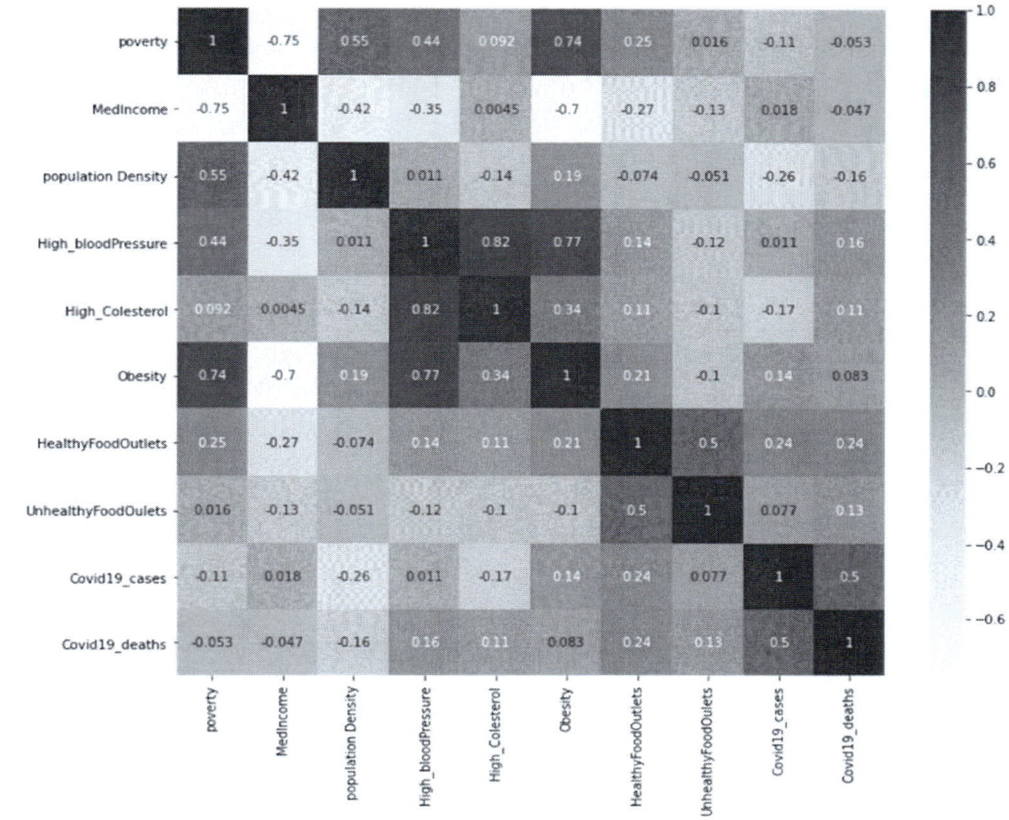

Figure 19.7. Heat map showing the relation between different features of COVID-19.

19.3 Geographic Information System Mapping

Healthcare organizations often analyze and visualize geographical data using Geographic Information System (GIS) mapping. GIS mapping enables healthcare practitioners to see patterns, trends, and relationships that exist in certain geographic locations by fusing spatial data with other layers of information. The decision-making, resource allocation, and epidemiology analysis processes in healthcare are improved by this spatial perspective (Walsh et al. 2020). The monitoring and analysis of disease outbreaks is one application of GIS mapping in healthcare. Healthcare practitioners can pinpoint clusters and hotspots by mapping the geographic distribution of reported cases, which will help them comprehend how diseases like influenza, COVID-19, or vector-borne illnesses propagate. To facilitate targeted interventions, resource allocation, and the implementation of preventive measures, GIS mapping enables the identification of high-risk locations shown in Figure 19.8, the increase of covid cases across the globe.

Environmental health studies require a great deal of GIS mapping. Researchers can uncover potential environmental risk factors linked to disease outcomes by fusing environmental data with health data, such as air quality, water sources, or proximity to hazardous areas. For instance, GIS mapping can assist in determining the connection between air pollution levels and respiratory illnesses in a particular geographic area, resulting in focused measures for improving air quality and promoting public health (Raghupathi et al. 2023).

Figure 19.8. GIS Map showing the increase of covid cases across the globe.

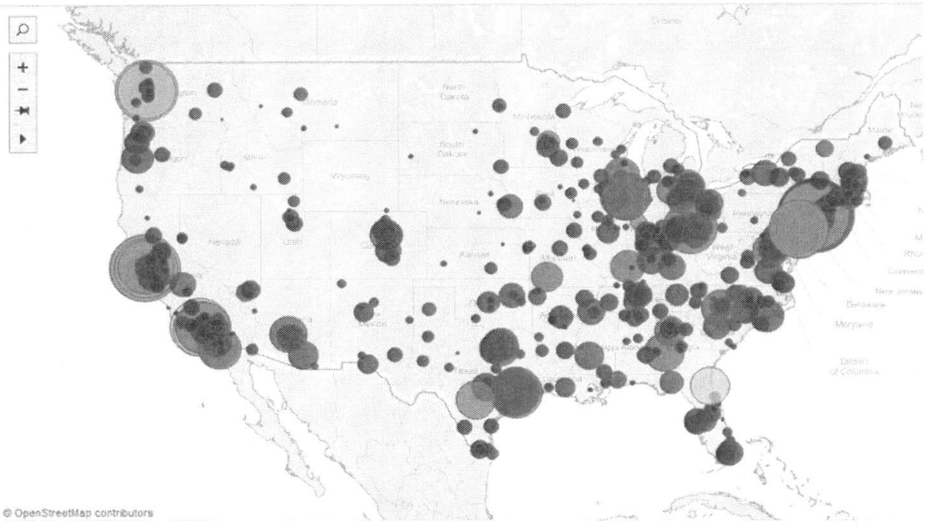

Figure 19.9. GIS Map showing the increase in COVID-19 cases for different states in the US.

GIS mapping is also useful for allocating resources and planning healthcare. For example, hospitals and other medical facilities can examine population demographics, healthcare infrastructure, and the distribution of medical services using GIS mapping. Healthcare professionals can spot unmet medical requirements, gaps in access to care, and underserved areas by superimposing various layers of data on a map of a specific area. To ensure fair access to care, this information can be used to formulate policies, allocate resources, and plan new healthcare facilities. Figure 19.9 shows the increase in covid 19 cases for different states in the US. GIS mapping is a useful method for data visualization in the medical field that enables the study and evaluation of spatial data. GIS mapping enables decision-making, resource allocation, and comprehension of health-related patterns in particular geographic locations by fusing geographic information with other layers of data.

19.3.1 Interactive Dashboard

To present complicated information in a user-friendly and engaging way, interactive dashboards are an effective data visualization tool used in the healthcare industry. To gather insights and make wise judgments, they enable healthcare professionals to interactively visualize and edit data pieces on a dynamic platform.

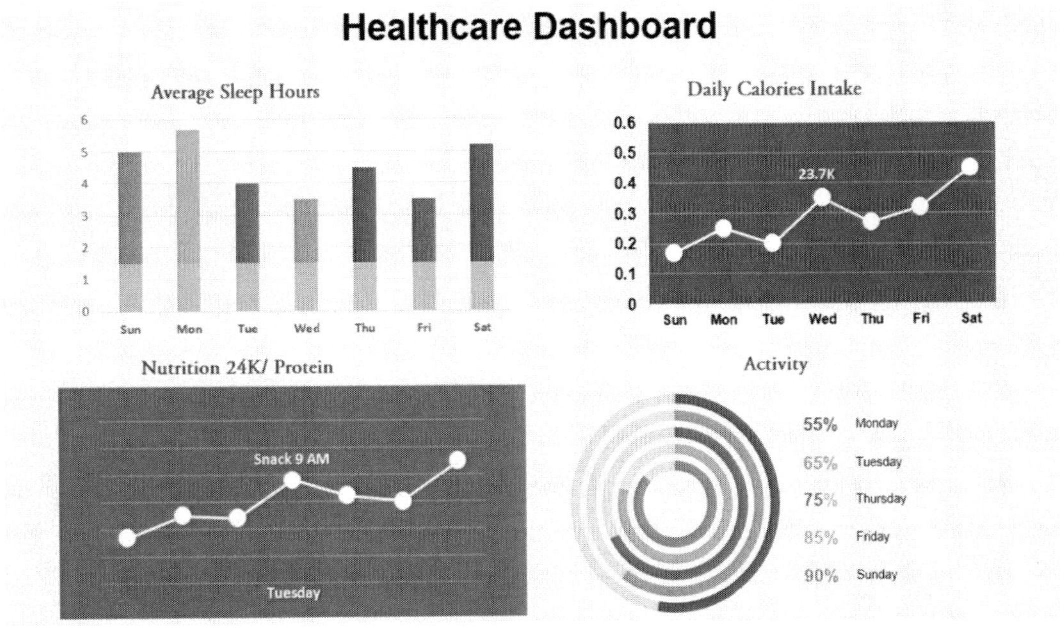

Figure 19.10. Healthcare Dashboard for daily routine.

Additionally, real-time data feeds can be incorporated into interactive dashboards, allowing healthcare personnel to monitor dynamic information and react quickly to emerging crises. For instance, a public health organization might create a live interactive dashboard to monitor the spread of infectious diseases. The dashboard can show up-to-date data on confirmed cases, regional distribution, and demographics, giving decision-makers in public health, resource allocation, and epidemic control timely information (Ramanujan et al. 2017). The ability of interactive dashboards to provide a thorough overview of numerous data sources and KPIs in a single interface is one of their main advantages in the healthcare industry. An interactive dashboard might be used by a healthcare organization, for instance, to track several key performance indicators (KPIs) like patient satisfaction ratings, wait times, and resource usage. Healthcare administrators may easily evaluate the organization's performance and pinpoint areas that need attention or improvement by combining these metrics into a dashboard. Users can drill down into data subsets or filter data using specific criteria using interactive dashboards. For instance, a hospital administrator may want to examine patient readmission statistics using an interactive dashboard. They can quickly filter the data to concentrate on a specific department, age range, or medical condition. Users can find trends, patterns, and possible root causes in the data thanks to this interactivity, which makes it easier to carry out focused interventions and quality-improvement projects (Bhatt et al. 2023). For example, Figure 19.10 visualizes the Healthcare Dashboard for daily routine.

Interactive dashboards are effective data visualization tools for the healthcare industry, providing a flexible and approachable way to explore and assess large datasets. Interactive dashboards enable healthcare personnel to gain valuable insights, track performance, and promote evidence-based decision-making by giving a thorough overview, allowing drill-down capabilities, and incorporating real-time data (Backonja et al. (2018).

19.3.2 Decision Tree

When analyzing and comprehending complicated decision-making processes in the healthcare industry, decision trees are a potent data visualization approach. A decision tree is a flowchart-like structure in which each leaf node represents the final choice or prediction, and each internal node represents a feature or attribute, decision, or outcome. Decision trees provide a clear and understandable picture shown in Figure 19.11 of the decision-making process by visually outlining the decision pathways (Tjoa and Guan, (2020).

Clinical decision support systems and medical diagnosis frequently employ decision trees in the healthcare industry. For instance, using a patient's symptoms, medical history, and test results, a decision tree can be built to help with the diagnosis of a certain condition. The branches of the tree indicate potential outcomes or decisions, and each node symbolizes a particular symptom or test result. Healthcare practitioners can use the decision tree to systematically assess several choices and make an accurate diagnosis. Decision trees are useful for a variety of healthcare applications because of their versatility in handling categorical and numerical data. Healthcare practitioners can comprehend the underlying variables impacting a decision thanks to their transparency and interpretability. Decision trees are robust in real-world healthcare contexts because they can efficiently handle missing data or outliers (Tanoli et al. 2020).

Predicting the risk of cardiovascular illnesses based on patient characteristics and lifestyle factors is an example of a decision tree application in healthcare. Healthcare experts can create a predictive model to evaluate an individual's risk of acquiring cardiovascular illnesses by building a decision tree using a dataset of patients that includes factors like age, gender, blood pressure, cholesterol levels, smoking status, and exercise habits (Caban and Gotz, (2015). The decision tree can help medical professionals suggest the best preventative actions and therapies based on the risk profile of each patient.

Healthcare decision-making processes can be represented in a structured and understandable way using decision trees, a useful data visualization tool. They are especially helpful in risk prediction, medical diagnostics, and clinical decision support. Decision trees enable healthcare workers to make wise decisions and enhance patient outcomes by providing transparency, adaptability, and resilience in processing complicated healthcare data.

19.4 Applications of XAI-Driven Visualization in Sustainable Healthcare

Understanding and optimizing resource use in healthcare facilities requires visualization of energy use and carbon footprint. Because the healthcare industry consumes a lot of energy and emits a lot of greenhouse gases, it is crucial to find areas for improvement and adopt sustainable practices. Healthcare institutions can obtain insights into their resource usage patterns, spot inefficiencies, and make educated decisions to reduce environmental impact while maintaining high-quality patient care by visualizing energy data and carbon footprint (Schulze et al. 2023). Real-time monitoring and tracking of energy usage is one of the main advantages of visualizing energy consumption. Smart meters, building management systems, and energy monitoring devices are a few examples of the several places where energy data can be gathered. Healthcare institutions can monitor energy usage at numerous levels, from the entire facility down to departments or equipment, by visualizing this data through interactive dashboards and real-time displays. Stakeholders may rapidly see anomalies, energy usage peaks, or locations with significant waste thanks to real-time visualizations (Kim, 2022). The graph can be used to identify trends in energy usage and to identify times when the equipment is using more energy than it should. Additionally, benchmarking and performance comparisons are made possible by visualizing energy use. To evaluate their performance and pinpoint opportunities for improvement, healthcare institutions can examine their energy usage trends against industry benchmarks, comparable facilities, or historical data. Trends and patterns in energy consumption can be easily seen using simple and understandable visual representations like line charts or area charts, allowing facilities to set goals, monitor progress, and make data-driven decisions to optimize resource usage.

Energy usage visualization and carbon footprint visualization go hand in hand. Healthcare institutions can comprehend their activities' environmental impact by calculating and visualizing the greenhouse gas emissions linked to energy use. The distribution of emissions across various sources, such as power, heating, or transportation, can be displayed visually using pie charts or stacked bar graphs. This aids facilities in identifying priority emission reduction areas and creating focused sustainability programs (Portz et al. 2019). In conclusion, it is crucial to visualize energy use and carbon footprint in healthcare facilities to comprehend and maximize resource use. The use of interactive dashboards, real-time displays, and visual representations allows healthcare institutions to benchmark their performance, obtain insights into energy usage patterns, and pinpoint areas for improvement. Facilities can measure their environmental impact and set priorities for their emission reduction efforts by visualizing their carbon footprint. In the end, these visualizations equip medical institutions with the tools they need to make data-driven decisions, cut down on energy waste, and promote a more sustainable future.

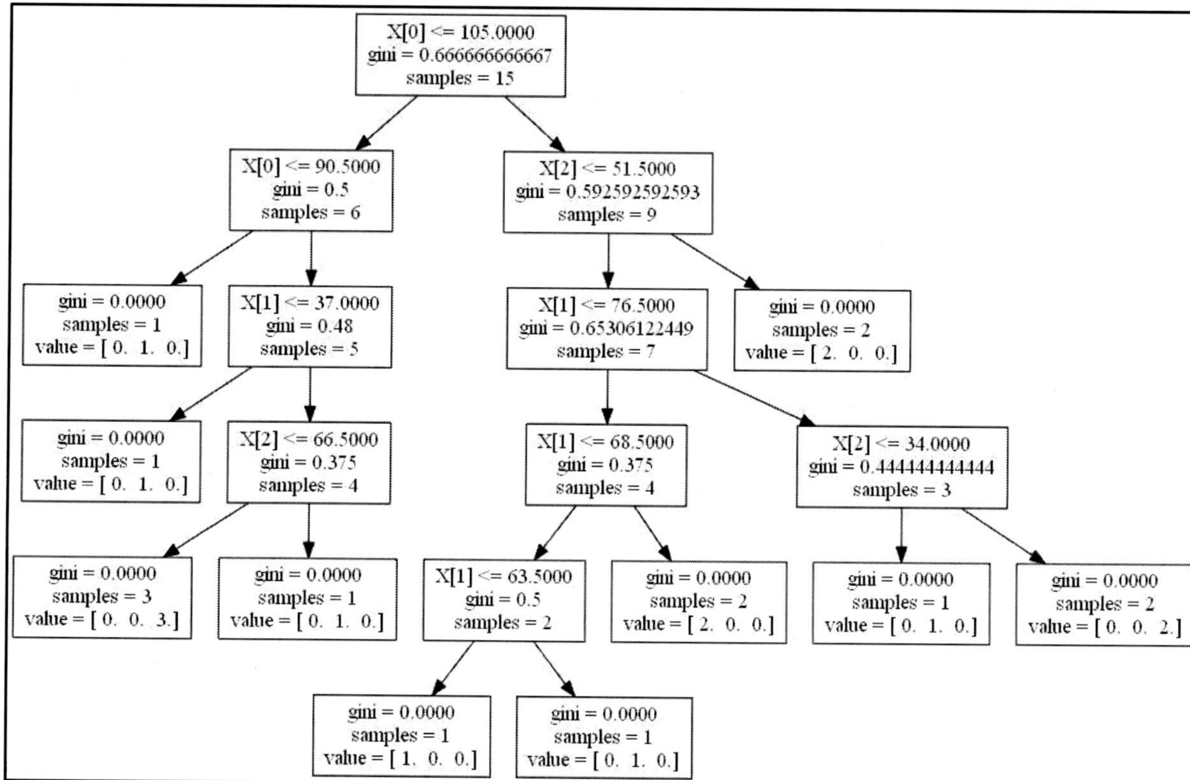

Figure 19.11. Decision Tree to predict cardiovascular illnesses using Gini gain.

19.4.1 Visualization for Sustainable Supply Chain Management

To manage a sustainable supply chain in the healthcare sector, visualization is essential. The flow of goods, information, and resources among numerous stakeholders, including producers, distributors, healthcare professionals, and patients, make up the complicated healthcare supply chain. Organizations can learn a lot about inefficiencies, spot wasteful areas, and put plans in place to lessen their negative environmental effect while still providing high-quality healthcare services by visualizing supply chain data. Visualization plays a crucial role in sustainable supply chain management by enabling the tracking and monitoring of resources and goods. Visualizing the entire supply chain using techniques like network diagrams or flowcharts helps highlight the interdependencies among stakeholders and the flow of information and items. This visibility allows organizations to identify bottlenecks, delays, and excess inventory levels, preventing waste and environmental damage. By visualizing the supply chain, organizations can make informed decisions to improve resource utilization, reduce transportation emissions, and optimize logistics. Visualizations also assist in analyzing and improving inventory management. By visualizing inventory levels, stock movement, and demand patterns, healthcare organizations can identify overstocked or understocked items. This enables the implementation of just-in-time inventory techniques, minimizing waste and eliminating surplus inventory. Real-time dashboards and graphical representations, such as bar charts or heatmaps, provide intuitive views of inventory performance, enabling proactive decision-making and resource optimization.

Visualizations aid in identifying opportunities for waste reduction and sustainable sourcing. By visualizing the environmental impact of suppliers, such as carbon emissions or waste generation, healthcare organizations can make informed decisions about sustainable procurement. Visualizations can also help identify local suppliers or select more environmentally friendly transportation methods by visualizing supplier distances or carbon footprints. These visualizations contribute to the development of environmentally friendly supplier networks and the overall reduction of carbon footprints.

A practical example of visualization for sustainable supply chain management in the healthcare industry is the collaboration between Johnson & Johnson and the US Environmental Protection Agency (EPA). Johnson & Johnson utilized visualization tools to map and analyze their product supply chain, considering energy usage, carbon emissions, and waste generation at each level. Through visualizations, they identified waste hotspots and inefficiencies, enabling targeted sustainability measures. This approach resulted in significant reductions in carbon emissions, improved transportation routes, and reduced waste production, leading to both financial and environmental benefits.

In the final analysis, visualization is an effective tool for the healthcare sector's sustainable supply chain management. Organizations can spot inefficiencies, save waste, and make data-driven decisions to maximize resource use by visualizing supply chain data. Organizations can track and monitor product movement, improve inventory control, and spot opportunities for sustainable sourcing with the use of visualizations. Healthcare organizations may improve their environmental performance, lower their carbon footprint, and support a more sustainable and ethical healthcare supply chain by utilizing the power of visualization.

19.4.2 Visual Analytics for Sustainable Healthcare Planning

By helping organizations to optimize facility locations, resource allocation, and service delivery chains, visual analytics plays a significant role in sustainable healthcare planning. Planning for efficient and effective healthcare services with a low environmental impact and a focus on sustainable practices is the goal of sustainable healthcare planning. To analyze complicated healthcare data, produce actionable insights, and make decisions that support sustainable healthcare systems, visual analytics techniques offer effective tools. Optimizing facility location is one application of visual analytics in sustainable healthcare planning. Organizations can visualize demographic information, current healthcare infrastructure, and population distribution by using geographic information systems (GIS) and spatial analysis. These visualizations make it easier to spot underserved regions, access to healthcare gaps, and regions with significant healthcare needs. Organizations can make data-driven decisions on the best sites for healthcare facilities by overlaying environmental elements such as transportation networks, air quality, or proximity to green areas. For instance, visual analytics can identify regions with high levels of pollution but poor access to healthcare, leading to the construction of environmentally friendly healthcare facilities there.

The use of GIS-based visualizations to optimize the placement of healthcare facilities in underserved areas is one example of how visual analytics is being used in real-world sustainable healthcare planning. To find the best places for clinics, hospitals, or healthcare facilities, organizations have used visual analytics to overlay information about population density, transit systems, and environmental aspects. These visualizations have made it easier for marginalized populations to get healthcare while taking sustainability considerations into account. Another crucial component of planning for sustainable healthcare is resource allocation, and visual analytics can improve resource utilization effectiveness. Organizations can spot regions of over or underutilization by visualizing patient flow, resource demand, and resource availability. Heatmaps and network diagrams are two examples of visualizations that can shed light on how medical resources like staff, beds, and equipment are used. Organizations can use this information to decrease waste, allocate resources more efficiently, and boost operational effectiveness. For instance, using visual analytics, resource redistribution and optimal resource utilization can be achieved by identifying instances where medical equipment is underutilized in one institution but in high demand in another.

To sum up, visual analytics is a potent tool for sustainable healthcare planning. It enables businesses to streamline the service delivery process, properly allocate resources, and locate facilities in the best locations. Organizations can use visualizations to help them make data-driven decisions that increase access to healthcare, cut waste, and support sustainable practices. Healthcare planners can design effective, environmentally friendly healthcare systems that provide high-quality care while having the least possible negative effects on the environment thanks to visual analytics.

19.4.3 Applications of XAI-Driven Visualization in Smart Healthcare

An essential component of personalized care in healthcare is visualizing patient data. Healthcare providers can extract useful insights from complicated patient data and create individualized treatment strategies by utilizing XAI-driven visualization tools. Healthcare practitioners may make wise decisions and enhance patient outcomes by using XAI-driven visualization, which combines the strength of explainable artificial intelligence (XAI) and interactive visualizations to deliver clear and understandable representations of patient data.

The capability to analyze and interpret complex patient data is one of the main advantages of XAI-driven visualization in personalized care. Exploring and understanding the large amounts of information found in traditional medical records and datasets can be difficult. Charts, graphs, and interactive dashboards, which are interactive visual representations of patient data offered by XAI-driven visualization techniques, simplify complex information and make it easier to understand. Healthcare professionals can create treatment plans that are specifically tailored to the needs of each patient by visualizing patient data to spot patterns, trends, and linkages that may not be immediately evident from raw data. Oncologists, for instance, can visualize genomic data, treatment response data, and clinical outcomes for specific cancer patients using XAI-driven visualization in oncology. Oncologists can pinpoint certain genetic mutations or biomarkers that affect therapy response by integrating data from many sources, including genetic profiles, medical imaging, and treatment records, into interactive visualizations. The choice of specific medicines or individualized treatment plans can be influenced by this information, thereby enhancing patient results.

Healthcare providers can involve patients in the decision-making process with the help of XAI-driven visualization. Healthcare professionals can successfully communicate complex medical information to patients by visualizing patient data in an intelligible fashion. Visualizations can show how an illness develops, how well certain treatments work, and what risks and advantages might come with a particular decision. With a thorough grasp of their health data, patients can actively participate in constructing their treatment plans using this shared decision-making method, increasing patient autonomy and participation. Additionally, XAI-driven visualization makes it easier to continuously assess and modify treatment programs. Healthcare practitioners can track treatment progress, spot variations from expected results, and make prompt adjustments to improve patient care by visualizing real-time patient data. For instance, XAI-driven visualization can help patients and healthcare professionals track blood glucose levels, medication compliance, and lifestyle factors in real time when managing diabetes. When certain thresholds are exceeded, interactive visualizations can provide alerts or notifications, triggering proactive interventions and individualized treatment plan modifications.

XAI-driven visualization is essential for supporting personalized treatment in healthcare by helping to visualize patient data. Healthcare providers can acquire important insights, involve patients in decision-making, and continuously monitor and modify treatment programs by turning complex data into comprehensible visual representations. The use of XAI-driven visualization in personalized care has the potential to enhance patient-provider communication, improve patient outcomes, and advance patient-centered healthcare.

19.4.4 Real-Time Monitoring and Visualization of Vital Signs

Enhancing patient safety and early detection of anomalies in healthcare settings depend heavily on real-time monitoring and visualization of vital signs. Healthcare workers can quickly spot changes or irregularities in a patient's state by continually monitoring and visualizing important physiological indicators, enabling early treatments and better patient outcomes. Giving quick feedback on vital indicators is one of the main advantages of real-time monitoring and visualization. Traditional vital sign measurement techniques, including routine manual evaluations, could be unable to detect quick changes in a patient's condition. On the other hand, real-time monitoring allows for ongoing monitoring of vital signs like heart rate, blood pressure, respiratory rate, and oxygen saturation levels. Healthcare practitioners can instantly see departures from normal ranges, recognize emergency circumstances, and take appropriate prompt action because of the real-time visualization of these metrics. Real-time vital sign visualization can be helpful in telemedicine and remote monitoring applications. Patients can now be monitored in their homes or other non-clinical settings because of advancements in wearable technology and remote monitoring technologies. Healthcare professionals can analyze a patient's status remotely, spot anomalies, and make the required recommendations or actions thanks to real-time visualization of vital signs. Patients who have chronic diseases or those who need long-term monitoring can benefit the most from this strategy because it lessens the need for frequent hospital visits and improves patient convenience and comfort.

Further enhancing patient safety and care is the integration of real-time vital sign data with electronic health records (EHR) and decision support systems. Healthcare practitioners can get a complete picture of a patient's health status by visualizing vital signs along with other clinical data, such as drug histories, allergy information, and prior medical history. Through this integration, clinicians can deliver individualized and focused interventions and encourage informed decision-making.

19.4.5 Visual Analytics for Population Health Management

In population health management, visual analytics has become a potent tool for identifying trends, patterns, and risk factors that may be used to guide interventions. By identifying and managing health determinants and risk factors, population health management strives to enhance the health outcomes of a community or population. Visual analytics uses interactive and visual tools to examine complicated healthcare data, find significant insights, and guide decision-making based on the best available evidence. The capacity to spot trends and patterns in health data is one of the visual analytics' main advantages in population health management. Patterns can be seen by visualizing data across time, such as disease prevalence, mortality rates, or healthcare usage, which can reveal important information about population health. For instance, visual analytics may show a rising trend in the prevalence of chronic diseases in a particular area, leading to focused measures for management and prevention. Healthcare professionals and policymakers can more easily spot patterns and changes by visualizing temporal data, which enables proactive and timely actions. Visual analytics also aids in identifying risk variables linked to unfavorable health outcomes. It is possible to recognize and comprehend elements that contribute to health disparities and high-risk populations by integrating and visualizing data from numerous sources, such as electronic health records, social determinants of health, and environmental factors. For instance, visual analytics may show relationships between income levels, educational attainment, and health outcomes by superimposing socioeconomic data with illness prevalence maps. The creation of treatments and policies aiming at addressing socioeconomic determinants of health and reducing health disparities can be guided by these discoveries.

These images show that there is a clear relationship between income levels, educational attainment, and health outcomes. People with lower incomes and lower educational attainment are more likely to have chronic diseases. These findings can be used to guide the development of treatments and policies aimed at addressing socioeconomic determinants of health and reducing health disparities. For example, a heat map of obesity prevalence in a city might show that obesity is more prevalent in areas with lower incomes and lower educational attainment. This information could be used to target interventions in these areas, such as providing more access to healthy food and physical activity opportunities. A time series chart of chronic disease trends over time might show that the rates of chronic diseases have been increasing in recent years. This information could be used to identify factors that are contributing to the increase in chronic diseases, such as changes in diet, lifestyle, and the environment.

Geospatial data of chronic disease distribution by location might show that chronic diseases are more prevalent in certain areas of a city. This information could be used to identify areas where there are environmental or social factors that are contributing to chronic diseases, such as air pollution, crime, or lack of access to healthcare (Lane and Schur, (2010). By using visual analytics to understand the relationships between income levels, educational attainment, and health outcomes, healthcare professionals can develop more effective treatments and policies to improve population health. Overall, visual analytics help focused interventions by enabling interactive data exploration and analysis in addition to spotting patterns and risk indicators. Users can dive down into specific population subgroups, alter and filter data, and view the information in a variety of formats, including maps, charts, and graphs, using interactive dashboards.

The development of practical insights is facilitated by this interactive approach, which also enables stakeholders to customize interventions in response to demographic requirements. Visual analytics, for instance, can help identify underserved areas with significant healthcare needs, making it easier to allocate resources and solutions to those areas.

19.5 Challenges and Considerations in Implementing XAI-Driven Visualization

19.5.1 Data Quality and Availability

Implementing XAI-driven visualization in healthcare comes with unique challenges. Data quality, accessibility, and privacy are key considerations. Healthcare organizations need to address data collection, integration, and accuracy issues to achieve meaningful visualizations. Establishing robust data governance systems, including validation protocols, cleaning procedures, and quality control mechanisms, ensures data integrity and reliability (Wade, (2007). Data accessibility and availability pose additional challenges. Healthcare data is often dispersed across multiple systems and stored in various formats. Investing in interoperability solutions and data integration platforms enables seamless data gathering and visualization. This may involve leveraging data integration technologies, implementing standardization protocols, and adhering to interoperability standards like HL7 and FHIR. Maintaining data privacy and security is crucial, considering the sensitivity of patient information. Healthcare organizations must adhere to stringent data privacy and security policies, including encryption systems, access controls, and data anonymization techniques. Ethical considerations are also important in XAI-driven visualization. Transparency and interpretability are vital when using AI algorithms for decision-making. Employing explicable visualization methods and algorithms promotes communication and collaboration among patients, healthcare providers, and stakeholders. Understanding how decisions are made fosters trust and facilitates meaningful engagement.

19.5.2 Design and Usability

Design and usability considerations are crucial for the effective use of XAI-driven visualization in healthcare. The design should cater to the needs and preferences of various user groups, including healthcare professionals, patients, administrators, and policymakers. Each group may have different levels of competence and requirements in comprehending and interpreting visualizations. Healthcare organizations should employ user-centered design procedures, gathering user input, conducting usability tests, and iteratively improving the visualization design to meet the specific needs, interests, and objectives of each user group (Farhud and Zokaei, 2021).

Complexity and scalability are important factors to address in healthcare visualization. The healthcare domain encompasses diverse data types, including clinical, administrative, and financial data. Creating visualizations that accurately summarize and represent complex data sets can be challenging. It is crucial to strike a balance between providing comprehensive insights and avoiding information overload. Techniques like data aggregation, filtering, and interactive exploration can help simplify complex data, allowing users to focus on relevant information. Usability plays a significant role in the adoption and effectiveness of XAI-driven visualization systems. The visualizations should offer a seamless user experience, be intuitive, and facilitate easy data exploration. Considering healthcare practitioners and stakeholders often have limited time to interact with the visualization system, interfaces should enable quick data exploration and comprehension. Proper use of color, layout, labeling, and interactive elements are important considerations to enhance usability and user satisfaction.

Moreover, accessibility is a critical aspect of healthcare visualization design. Visualizations should be inclusive and accessible to users with various abilities, including those who are color-blind or have visual impairments. Providing alternate means of representation, such as written descriptions or signification, allows a broader range of users to benefit from the visualization.

19.5.3 Privacy and Security

Implementing XAI-driven visualization in the healthcare industry involves challenges related to security and privacy. Protecting patient data and complying with privacy laws is paramount. Patient information is sensitive and must be safeguarded against unauthorized access and potential exploitation. Strong security measures, including encryption, access controls, and secure data transmission, should be implemented to ensure data privacy during the visualization process. Compliance with regulations such as HIPAA or GDPR is crucial for the legal and ethical treatment of patient data.

De-identification and anonymization of patient data used in XAI-driven visualization are important considerations. Healthcare organizations often need to remove or encrypt identifying information to minimize privacy risks while enabling meaningful analysis and visualization. Techniques like k-anonymity and differential privacy can strike a balance between data utility and privacy protection. Transparency and accountability play a significant role in addressing privacy concerns. Communicating the practices of data collection, storage, and use in XAI-driven visualization systems is essential to establish trust and ensure openness. Healthcare organizations should outline clear privacy policies and obtain patients' informed consent. Involving data governance and ethics committees can provide guidance on ethical considerations, data-sharing agreements, and compliance with privacy laws. Regular audits and monitoring of security measures and privacy protocols are necessary to identify and rectify any potential vulnerabilities.

19.5.4 Ethical Considerations

The use of XAI-driven visualization in healthcare raises important ethical considerations related to fairness, biases, and unintended consequences. Biases in healthcare data and their potential amplification through XAI-driven visualization are concerning. These biases can stem from algorithmic decision-making, historical disparities in healthcare access, or unequal representation in training data. To promote fairness, it is crucial to identify and mitigate biases through careful data selection, diverse representation in training data, and ongoing monitoring and evaluation of the visualization system.

Fairness is another ethical factor to consider in XAI-driven visualization. Healthcare decisions made based on AI should be unbiased and consider the individual needs and characteristics of each person. The visualization should account for variables such as race, ethnicity, gender, age, and socioeconomic status to avoid perpetuating existing inequities. Techniques like algorithmic fairness, bias mitigation, and fairness-aware visualization can help address these concerns. Unforeseen consequences of XAI-driven visualization also need attention. While visualization can improve decision-making, it is important to evaluate and mitigate any potential negative effects. Over-reliance on AI-driven recommendations without critical human judgment can lead to loss of autonomy or the omission of crucial contextual information. Striking a balance between automation and human competence is necessary to avoid excessive dependence on algorithmic outputs.

To address these ethical issues, the establishment of ethical frameworks and guidelines is crucial. Organizations should adhere to moral standards, including accountability, transparency, and justification. Explicit governance frameworks, such as ethical review boards or committees, can ensure the responsible use of XAI-driven visualization in healthcare.

19.6 Discussion

The discussion in this chapter revolves around several key aspects, including promising directions for further development, the importance of ethical and responsible implementation, the significance of collaboration and interdisciplinary research, the wide-ranging applications and impact, as well as the challenges and future directions. XAI-driven visualization offers promising opportunities for researchers and practitioners in healthcare. By exploring innovative visualization strategies, we can enhance the interpretability and transparency of AI models, making them more accessible and trustworthy for healthcare decision-makers. The integration of machine learning algorithms with visualization techniques holds the potential to yield more precise and meaningful insights, which can significantly impact critical healthcare scenarios. Moreover, the development of interactive visualization tools enables real-time exploration of complex healthcare data, empowering healthcare professionals to make informed decisions swiftly and effectively.

However, with the immense potential of XAI-driven visualization, there arises a need for ethical and responsible implementation. Establishing clear guidelines that address data security, privacy, algorithmic fairness, openness, and responsibility is crucial to safeguarding patient rights and promoting the ethical adoption of XAI-driven visualization tools. This claim was initially denied because medical records indicating the services were rendered by another provider other than the billing provider. Addressing challenges such as data quality, design usability, and patient privacy is fundamental to gaining trust and acceptance from the healthcare community and the public.

Collaboration among researchers, healthcare practitioners, and visualization specialists is essential for the successful integration of XAI-driven visualization in healthcare. By engaging in interdisciplinary research, stakeholders can develop best practices and innovative solutions. Visualization experts can contribute their expertise in efficient techniques, while healthcare practitioners offer domain-specific insights. This collaborative approach results in the development of user-centered visualization tools that cater to the unique needs and challenges of healthcare decision-making, leading to successful adoption in real-world scenarios. The applications of XAI-driven visualization in healthcare are vast and far-reaching. From enhancing patient engagement to reducing medical errors, aiding in diagnosis and treatment, and optimizing resource allocation, technology has the potential to revolutionize various healthcare areas. By providing interpretable and transparent visual representations of AI-driven insights, XAI-driven visualization improves understanding, accelerates discovery, and promotes informed decision-making. Furthermore, the integration of XAI-driven visualization with augmented reality (AR) and virtual reality (VR) technologies holds great promise in transforming medical education, training, and patient engagement. Despite its potential, the adoption of XAI-driven visualization in healthcare comes with challenges that must be carefully addressed. Ensuring data availability and quality, refining design usability, preserving patient privacy, and adhering to ethical considerations are crucial aspects in the responsible and successful implementation of this technology. Ongoing research, advancements in visualization methods and tools, and a commitment to ethical guidelines are key areas that need continued attention to fully harness the potential of XAI-driven visualization in healthcare.

19.7 Conclusion and Future Work

In conclusion, the field of XAI-driven visualization represents a pivotal step toward achieving transparency, accountability, and efficacy in AI-driven healthcare systems. The fusion of cutting-edge AI algorithms with intuitive and interpretable visualization techniques offers immense potential to enhance decision-making processes and transform healthcare practices.

As researchers and practitioners delve into the further development of XAI-driven visualization, it is crucial to explore novel strategies and interactive tools that allow real-time exploration of complex healthcare data. By leveraging advancements in machine learning algorithms and visualization methods, we can extract deeper and more meaningful insights from vast and intricate datasets. Moreover, the integration of XAI-driven visualization with emerging technologies such as augmented reality (AR) and virtual reality (VR) opens up exciting possibilities for medical education, training, and patient engagement. These immersive experiences have the potential to revolutionize healthcare practices, enabling more efficient and accurate decision-making.

However, as we embrace the transformative potential of XAI-driven visualization, ethical and regulatory standards must be established to ensure responsible and secure implementation. Privacy, algorithmic fairness, openness, and accountability are vital considerations that demand attention. Regulatory agencies play a pivotal role in overseeing the adherence to these principles and safeguarding patient rights. Collaboration among researchers, healthcare practitioners, and visualization specialists is essential to unlock the full potential of XAI-driven visualization. Interdisciplinary research and cooperative efforts can lead to best practices and innovative solutions, with domain-specific insights from healthcare practitioners complementing the technical expertise of visualization experts. Developing user-centered visualization tools tailored to the unique needs and challenges of healthcare decision-making is a primary goal. By understanding and addressing the requirements of end-users, we can create practical and intuitive solutions that facilitate better decision-making and patient care. In conclusion, XAI-driven visualization stands as a powerful tool to revolutionize decision-making in sustainable and intelligent healthcare. By offering interpretable and transparent visual representations of AI-driven insights, it empowers healthcare professionals to make informed choices, improve patient outcomes, and optimize resource allocation. While challenges remain, such as data quality, design, privacy, and ethical considerations, concerted efforts in addressing these issues will pave the way for responsible and ethical adoption of XAI-driven visualization in healthcare.

As the technology advances and guidelines mature, XAI-driven visualization will continue to reshape the healthcare landscape, fostering a future where AI and human collaboration can drive positive and lasting impacts on healthcare delivery and patient well-being. It is a journey that warrants unwavering commitment, research, and collaboration, and one that holds the promise of transforming healthcare for the better.

References

Ajad A, Saini T, and Niranjan KM. (2023). "CV-CXR : A Method for Classification and Visualisation of COVID-19 virus using CNN and heatmap." *5th International Conference on Recent Advances in Information Technology (RAIT).* doi: 10.1109/RAIT57693.2023.10127066.

Amann, J, Blasimme, A, Vayena, E, Frey, D, Madai, VI, and Precise4Q Consortium. (2020). Explainability for artificial intelligence in healthcare: a multidisciplinary perspective. BMC medical informatics and decision making, 20, 1-9.

Backonja U, Haynes SC, and Kim KK. (2018). "Data visualizations to support health practitioners' provision of personalized care for patients with cancer and multiple chronic conditions : user-centered design study." *JMIR Hum Factors*. PMID 30327290.

Bae JM. (2014). "The clinical decision analysis using a decision tree." *Epidemiol Health*. PMID 25358466.

Bawaneh K, Ghazi Nezami F, Rasheduzzaman M, and Deken B. (2019). "Energy consumption analysis and characterization of healthcare facilities in the United States." *Energies*. 3775.

Bhatt Mishra D, Naqvi S, Gunasekaran A, and Dutta V. (2023). "Prescriptive analytics applications in sustainable operations research: conceptual framework and future research challenges." *Ann Oper Res, 2023*. 1-40.

Caban JJ and Gotz D. (2015). "Visual analytics in healthcare--opportunities and research challenges." *J Am Med Inform Assoc*. 260-2.

Cajamarca G, Herskovic V, and Rossel PO. (2020). "Enabling Older Adults' Health Self-Management through Self-Report and Visualization-A Systematic Literature Review." *Sensors (Basel)*. PMID 32759801.

Caruana R, Lou Y, Gehrke J, Koch P, Sturm M, and Elhadad N. (2015). "Intelligible Models for HealthCare: predicting Pneumonia Risk and Hospital 30-day Readmission". *21st ACM SIGKDD international conference on knowledge discovery and data mining (KDD '15)*. doi: 10.1145/2783258.2788613.

Elabed S, Shamayleh A, and Daghfous A. (2021). "Sustainability-oriented innovation in the health care supply chain." *Comput Ind Eng*. 160.

Farhud DD, and Zokaei S. (2021). "Ethical issues of artificial intelligence in medicine and healthcare." *Iran J Public Health*. i-v.

Gilpin LH, Bau D, Yuan BZ, Bajwa A, Specter M, and Kagal L. (2018). "Explaining explanations: an overview of interpretability of machine learning". *IEEE 5th International Conference on Data Science and Advanced Analytics (DSAA)*. doi: 10.1109/DSAA.2018.00018.

Han J, Tan Z, Chen M, Zhao L, Yang L, and Chen S. (2022). "Carbon footprint research based on input–output model—A global scientometric visualization analysis." *Int J Environ Res Public Health*. PMID 36141618.

Huang CW, Lu R, Iqbal U, Lin SH, Nguyen PAA, Yang HC et al. (2015). "A richly interactive exploratory data analysis and visualization tool using electronic medical records." *BMC Med Inform Decis Mak*. PMID 26563282.

Jung J, Lee H, Jung H, and Kim H. (2023). "Essential properties and explanation effectiveness of explainable artificial intelligence in healthcare: A systematic review." *Heliyon*. PMID 37234618.

Kim SH. (2022). "A systematic review on visualizations for self-generated health data for daily activities." *Int J Environ Res Public Health*. 11166.

Lane J, and Schur C. (2010). "Balancing access to health data and privacy: à review of the issues and approaches for the future." *Health Serv Res*, 1456-67.

Park S, Bekemeier B, Flaxman A, and Schultz M. (2022). "Impact of data visualization on decision-making and its implications for public health practice : à systematic literature review." *Inform Health Soc Care*. PMID 34582297.

Plaisant C. (2018). "Visualization of temporal patterns in patient record data." *Fundam Clin Pharmacol*. PMID 28921653.

Portz JD, Bayliss EA, Bull S, Boxer RS, Bekelman DB, Gleason K et al. (2019). "Using the technology acceptance model to explore user experience, intent to use, and use behavior of a patient portal among older adults with multiple chronic conditions : descriptive qualitative study." *J Med Internet Res*. se11604.

Raghupathi W, Raghupathi V, and Saharia A. (2023). "Analyzing health data breaches: A visual analytics approach." *AppliedMath*. 175-99.

Ramanujan D, Bernstein WZ, Chandrasegaran SK, and Ramani K. (2017). "Visual Analytics Tools for Sustainable Lifecycle Design : Current Status, Challenges, and Future Opportunities." *ASME. J Mech Des N*. 111415.

Schmidt T, Brabrand M, Lassen AT, and Wiil UK. (2019). "Design and evaluation of a patient monitoring dashboard for emergency departments." *Stud Health Technol Inform*. 788-92.

Schulze A, Brand F, Geppert J, and Böl GF. (2023). "Digital dashboards visualizing public health data : A systematic review." *Front Public Health*. 999958.

Su Z, Zhang M, and Wu W. (2021). "Visualizing sustainable supply chain management : A systematic scientometric review." *Sustainability*. 4409.

Tanoli Z, Alam Z, Ianevski A, Wennerberg K, Vähä-Koskela M, and Aittokallio T. (2020). "Interactive visual analysis of drug–target interaction networks using Drug Target Profiler, with applications to precision medicine and drug repurposing." *Brief Bioinform*. 211-20.

Tjoa E and Guan C. (2020). "A survey on Explainable Artificial Intelligence (XAI) : towards medical xai." *IEEE Trans Neural Netw Learning Syst*. 4793-813.

Viton F, Elbattah M, Guérin J-L, and Dequen G. (2020). "Heatmaps for visual explainability of CNN-based predictions for multivariate time series with application to healthcare." *IEEE International Conference on Healthcare Informatics (ICHI)*. doi: 10.1109/ICHI48887.2020.9374393.

Wade D. (2007). "Ethics of collecting and using healthcare data." *BMJ (Clin Res Ed)*. 1330-1.

Walsh EI, Chung Y, Cherbuin N, and Salvador-Carulla L. (2020). "Experts' perceptions on the use of visual analytics for complex mental healthcare planning : an exploratory study." *BMC Med Res Methodol*. PMID 32380946.

Zou L, Goh HL, Liew CJY, Quah JL, Gu GT, Chew JJ, et al. (2023). "Ensemble image explainable AI (XAI) algorithm for severe community-acquired pneumonia and COVID-19 respiratory infections." *IEEE Trans Artif Intell*. 242-54.

Chapter 20

Threats, Difficulties and Possibilities for XAI in Healthcare Decision Support Systems

Nancy Kumari*

Vellore Institute of Technology, Bhopal University, MP, India

Abstract

Machine Learning and Artificial Intelligence (AI) in general have enormous current and future promise to alter nearly every aspect of medicine. However, the absence of disclosure in applications of AI has proven more troublesome in numerous areas, including those outside of health. This is especially noticeable when users must understand the results of AI systems. Explainable AI (XAI) gives reasoning that enables people to comprehend why a system generates a particular outcome. The result can then be understood considering the situation. Healthcare Decision Support Systems (HDSSs) are one application that might benefit from XAI. These systems assist healthcare professionals in making decisions, but their lack of understanding can result in concerns of insufficient or over-reliance. Giving insights into the methods employed in arriving at suggestions will enable clinicians to make smarter judgments—and, in some circumstances, ones that could save lives. Because AI based on previously collected information might operate as a reinforcing agent of past behaviours and prejudices that must be exposed, the demand for XAI in the HDSS and the healthcare sector is heightened by the requirement for moral and equitable decision-making processes. Giving descriptions of the methods utilized in arriving at suggestions will enable professionals to make more intelligent judgments—and, in some circumstances, ones that could save lives. Because AI collected information might operate as a reinforcing agent of past behaviors and prejudices that must be exposed, the demand for XAI in HDSS and the healthcare sector is heightened by the requirement for moral and equitable decisions. According to research, using XAI can improve hospitals' decision-making assurance and help establish cause-and-effect speculation, both of which improve the tool's legitimacy and reliability and open the door to its possible integration into clinical processes. Nonetheless, they discovered a dearth of user research examining hospital demands and a general, glaring absence of use of XAI in the context of HDSS. Several potentials, obstacles, and future research needs and offer some recommendations for the XAI application in HDSS.

---

* Corresponding Author's Email: nancykumarivit@gmail.com.

In: Explainable Artificial Intelligence in Healthcare Systems
Editors: A. Anitha Kamaraj and Debi Prasanna Acharjya
ISBN: 979-8-89113-598-7

Keywords: explainable artificial intelligence (XAI), machine learning, healthcare decision support system (HDSS), ante-hoc, deep learning

20.1. Introduction

Both learning algorithms and artificial intelligence (AI) have broadly proven tremendous promise in a wide range of application domains, from autonomous vehicles (Siau and Wang, 2018), to outperforming people at progressively difficult video games like Go. Nearly all software-driven processes can profit from methods that consequently acquire knowledge from historical data, accumulating expertise, and progressively improving the capacity to forecast based on fresh data. Several variables have contributed to the current sharp growth in machine learning (ML), which include the creation of novel statistically learning computations, the accessibility of large historical data, and the creation of affordable yet powerful equipment, such as advancements in connecting and preservation that make devices like cloud-based storage not only possible but prevalent (Ahmad et al. 2022).

The broad adoption of more complicated models, such as deep neural network models, has contributed to the recent surge in machine learning systems, in addition to advancements in technological infrastructure and other areas (Mehonic et al. 2020). Nevertheless, there is a price for this intricacy. These systems are frequently effectively "black boxes" (Adadi and Berrada, 2018), with individuals or those who are impacted getting little to no knowledge of the prediction-making process. The absence of knowledge raises several issues with grave ramifications, such as the possibility of disastrous mistakes when faulty models—or choices founded on them—are applied in practical settings (Antoniadi et al. 2021). Furthermore, this lack of transparency may hinder these tools' acceptance by sectors governed by laws and the public in general, despite cases where they are effective (Arrieta et al. 2020). It appears that people are wired to look over an explanation for doing something, probably for legitimate reasons. As a result, people are reluctant to use methods that are not easily understood, manageable, and reliable (Oprescu et al. 2022), particularly considering the growing need for moral AI (Dwivedi et al. 2021). The applications of systems based on machine learning (ML) are growing outside of software development (Durelli et al. 2019), into environmentally conscious application fields like learning (Amershi et al. 2019), criminal justice and forensic science medical care (Topol, 2019). This adds complexity to the use of machine learning (ML) platforms, particularly when many of the people impacted by the predictions made by these systems are ignorant of their inner workings. Many significant obstacles in medicine can be addressed by applying AI. A lot of work on computerized evaluation, prediction, drug development, and testing has led to the rise of numerous examples in recent years. Enormous amounts of data are generated from sources like imaging devices, biosensors, molecular information, and electronic health records (Topol, 2019), which drives this. Medical decision-making, healthcare procedures, and treatment plans can all be tailored to the specific needs of each patient using AI (Mehonic et al. 2020).

But as of right now, AI in medicine is "rich on guarantee as well as comparatively light on information and evidence" (Topol, 2019). Nevertheless, many algorithms shown to be equal to or better than researchers in experiments exhibit a high rate of false positives in practical healthcare environments (Topol, 2019). Several AI-based systems have been validated in clinical trials for diabetic retinal degeneration, detection of broken wrist bones, histologic carcinoma of the breast tumors, tiny colonic polyps, and newborn cataracts (IR). Additional problems with machine learning in healthcare involve cause and effect, adaptability, accuracy, equality, trust, safety, confidentiality, and a shortage of openness (Topol, 2019). Given that decisions made or impacted by these structures eventually impact people's well-being, it is critical to comprehend the decision-making process. In certain places, this is accentuated. One instance is the choices and results that alter a person's life after receiving an illness. A different approach is precision health care, where specialists need much more data from the model to back up their assessment than just a distinct forecast.

Overcoming these obstacles requires explanations of how and why a model produces the results. For this reason, over the past few years, explaining ability and the associated ideas of interpretability and transparency have emerged as major concerns for machine learning in the medical field. Despite a wealth of evidence demonstrating their value, it has been suggested that ML-based systems are unlikely to be incorporated into routine medical practice outside of a small number of specialized applications unless these issues are resolved, most likely by requiring the systems to adequately explain their choices (Vellido, 2020). Regretfully, other variables can also make solving problems more difficult. For example, multiple uses typically require different comprehension and explanation skills. Below Figure 20.1 demonstrates an interface between healthcare records and explainable artificial intelligence, in which a health consortium offers service to healthcare records and responds to users via the Healthcare Decision Support System.

ML is used to advance Medical Treatment Decision Assistance Systems, which are software programs intended to help provide medical care. This work attempts to highlight its use, advantages, spaces, and potential future applications through an organized review of the literature. The clarity of systems like this is an emerging field of research.

Hypothesize that even though machine learning (ML) HDSS is widely available, there are still issues that must be resolved because very few systems have been created with a clear skill combining all their characteristics. The advantages and gaps currently being reported should guide the creation of future systems. Therefore, the purpose of this investigation is to first determine the latest developments in understandable ML-based HDSS to the field of application and currently popular methodologies, and then ascertain what advantages have been documented due to this combination and what aspects require improvement.

This is how the rest of the text's section is organized. Section 20.2 provides an overview of HDSS and XAI and the factors to be considered when incorporating XAI with HDSS. These factors include the necessity of clarifying skills, their use in healthcare, different kinds of clarifications, the debate between comprehension and efficiency, and the clarifying capacity requirements of healthcare facilities. The study's inquiries, substances, and technique are all covered in Section 20.3. The results and responses to the study's inquiries are presented in Section 20.4. These results are covered in Section 20.5 and include recommendations for the application of explainable ML-based HDSS in the future. Section 20.6 contains the conclusions that are drawn. Section 20.6 presents inferences drawn from these results and provides recommendations for the use of understandable machine learning-based HDSS in the future. The conclusion was provided in Section 20.7.

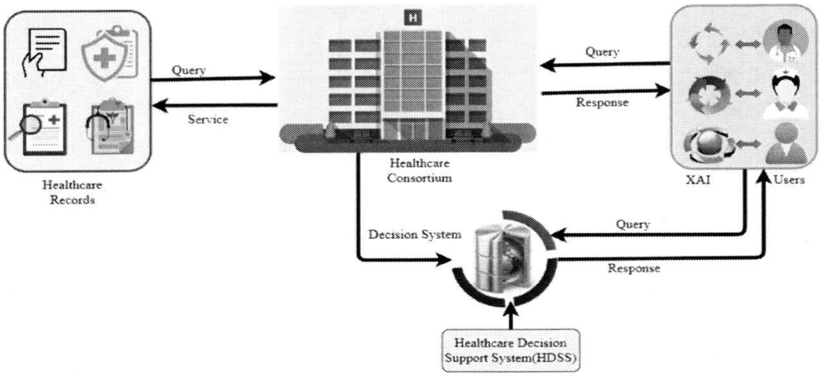

Figure 20.1. Interaction between healthcare records, XAI and healthcare decision Support System.

20.2. Fundamental Concepts and Background

Both knowledge-driven and non-knowledge-based HDSS exist. Knowledge-based HDSS relies on medical recommendations and expertise, whereas non-knowledge-based HDSS usually employs machine learning. By analyzing past clinical data for patterns, ML-based HDSS creates models of prediction that forecast future clinical results from fresh inputs. Physicians can utilize these results as suggestions to support them in the way they practice. There are a lot of promises for machine learning (ML) HDSS in medical practice.

20.2.1. Healthcare Decision Support Systems

Techniques that "offer medical treatment, employees, clients, or other people with expertise and individual-specific data, effectively filtrated, or provided at the right moments to improve wellness and medical care" are known as healthcare systems for decision-making (Rothman et al. 2012). HDSSs are intended to serve multiple functions, including outlook, responses to therapy prediction, assessment, and therapy suggestion (personalization), and risk-based healthcare setting priorities.

By combining clinicians' human knowledge with the "knowledge" embedded in the system, they can serve as a valuable "second set of eyes" in medical practice. In addition to lowering healthcare costs, HDSS can help to increase patient safety, care quality, and efficiency. Reminders for medication or other medical events for patients or clinicians can also help improve patient safety and lower medical errors. Furthermore, low-resource environments with a shortage of medical facilities and equipment can benefit from HDSS. Healthcare decision support systems are computer programs designed to "improve health and health care by providing medicine, staff, patients, or other individuals with knowledge and person-specific information, intelligently filtered, or presented at appropriate times" Rothman et al. (2012), Weinstein et al. (2003). The development and application of HDSS have encompassed a broad spectrum of illnesses, such as uncommon illnesses, cancer, in particular carcinoma of the breast, chronic bronchitis, venous thromboembolism (VT) avoidance, the prognosis of chronic renal failure and Alzheimer's, Type 2 diabetes management, and risk-level forecasting for coronary artery disease. Developing "unknown, insufficient, unbalanced, diverse, raucous, filthy, incorrect, unreliable, or dropping information in potentially multidimensional environments" is an obstacle faced by HDSS developers. Furthermore, for AI in healthcare to produce the greatest positive effects, systems like HDSS do not operate in a vacuum; rather, they collaborate to interact with human performers, organizations, and other platforms.

Variations at this level will cause people to lose faith in the system. Analyzing the rate of agreement between artificial intelligence algorithms and the doctor's recommended course of action is just as crucial as determining the acceptable rate. The three studies that were brought up found that Watson's for Oncology enjoyed alignment rates of 83%, 73%, and 49%. Therefore, if the possible beneficial effect is to be realized, utilizing XAI rules must be incorporated into HDSS.

20.2.2. Explainable AI (XAI)

Firstly, the term "XAI" in a study conducted by Van Lent et al. (2006). XAI may be summed up as the effort to render artificial intelligence easier for people to comprehend. Currently, there are no embraced scientific definitions for XAI, so further uniformity and a sense of terminology are needed (Core et al. 2006). One of the issues is that the terms transparency, interpretability, and explain ability are often used interchangeably. However, there are differences between these concepts. Comprehension, which is sometimes used interchangeably with "explain ability," is associated with the degree to which a model can be comprehended. Openness can be defined as "giving stakeholders relevant details about how the system operates" or as a comprehensive quality.

This includes documentation of the training procedure, analysis of training data distribution, code releases, and feature-level explanations, or an algorithm-specific clarity on how the model works, as opposed to opacity. Explain ability gives insight into the reasons for the decision-making of the system but is sometimes connected to understandability which was defined by a consensus as "loosely referring to tools that empower a stakeholder to understand and, when necessary, contest the reasoning of model outcomes.

20.2.2.1. The Need for XAI : Fair and Ethical Decision-Making

"Black box" AI systems that give prediction without any explanation are problematic for numerous reasons, not only because of their lack of transparency but also because they hide potential biases within the system. There are many examples where bias in AI-based predictive systems has been uncovered. These systems have been shown to reinforce social and historical human prejudices and people who are traditionally marginalized in our society are disproportional negatively impacted (Dwivedi et al. 2021).

Predictive software used in courtrooms to assess the likelihood of recidivism have proven to be extremely unreliable due to their bias towards race, revealing higher scores for Black people. For example, the AI-based system COMPAS (Correctional Offender Management Profiling for Alternative Sanctions) has been widely criticized for being unreliable and racially biased. Several case studies have demonstrated that "dirty data" used in policy-making systems have led to skewed predictions. Another example of bias in AI concerns search engines that tend to Favor certain sites over others revealing a political bias, and hiring algorithms tainted by "societal noise" tend to perpetuate discriminatory behaviours impacting certain individuals or groups. This algorithmic discrimination is also observed in systems such as targeted advertisements where gender discrimination occurred in the display of STEM career ads Moreover, some vision detection systems have demonstrated a bias toward subject skin tone. This predictive inequity has been characterized by higher performance for lower Fitzpatrick skin tones. These cases, to mention but a few, illustrate how such systems deployed in a real-world context can become "Weapons of Math Destruction" reinforcing inequalities.

Similarly, issues arise when tools built on biased data are used in precision medicines and there are many examples of medical datasets where the lack of inclusion of minorities has led to the development of biased models. For example, European populations were found to be significantly over-represented, while the other races were underrepresented in genomic studies in the US. Another example concerns the Framingham Heart Risk functions used to assess the risk of coronary heart diseases which suffered from an overestimation of risk for the German population. This bias was due to the Caucasian sample the initial study was based on. This reveals the attention needed to implement AI-based models developed on medical datasets.

Dhanorkar et al. (2021), determined that existing XAI techniques cannot provide explanations that adequately identify discriminatory behavior in some sensitive applications. Although giving explanations can increase understanding of and trust in a system, simple explanations can hide undesirable attributes of the system and may mislead users into coming to dangerous or unfounded conclusions that could ultimately be unethical. Additionally, an awareness of the dangers of blindly embracing explanations that may disguise racial or gender discrimination or provide fair washing, i.e., "promoting the false perception that a ML model respects some ethical values" is needed in all medical areas where such systems may be utilized.

In this book chapter, XAI as a technician solution that can help to expose systemic bias in HDSS; however, this does not address underlying deep-rooted discriminatory assumptions. XAI can be used to help us evaluate if predictions are biased and defend algorithmic decisions as being fair and ethical. Additionally, XAI can help to shed some light onto causality although, there is a recognized need to go beyond causality/correlation to true "castability."

Furthermore, there are now regulations in the EU which give subjects the right to obtain an explanation of the decision made using their data which need to be considered in the development of HDSS. To ensure that the processing of data is conducted in a manner that respects the rights of the data subjects and leads to the development of fair systems, different regions have adopted regulations governing the use of data. The General Data Protection Regulation (GDPR) protects the personal data of all EU residents, irrespective of the processing location. GDPR gives EU residents the right to access rectification, erasure, and restriction of processing of their personal data. Specifically, data subjects who will be affected by a decision have a "right to non-discrimination" and should be able to be informed of the reasons for the automated decision. According to the GDPR, data subjects have "the right not to be subject solely on automated processing."

20.2.3. XAI in Medicine

The use of XAI in medicine is rooted in demand for the added value that comes from medical professionals being able to understand how and why a machine-based decision has been made. Thus, there is growing demand for AI approaches that not only perform well, but are trustworthy, transparent, interpretable, and explainable for a human expert. This also has important implications for the public, policy, and governance as the explain ability of AI tools will enhance the trust of medical professionals (Mehonic et al. 2020). In many ways, medical professionals act as translators for patients—translating knowledge that is too complex for patients themselves to understand and act on. Having HDSS which assist medical professionals in this task makes sense, provided the HDSS aid, not hinder, that translation.

Translating ML models effectively to clinical practice requires establishing hospital' trust in the system. However, there have been several high-profile cases that have undermined trust in the use of AI in medicine. For example, many of the recommendations for treatment by "Watson for Oncology" (IBM) have been shown to be incorrect and potentially harmful (Core et al. 2006). In another famous example by (Dhanorkar et al. 2021), it was found that a ML-based system that was trained to predict which patients with pneumonia should be admitted to hospital identified patients with asthma as being at lower risk of dying from pneumonia. This reflected a true pattern in the training data—patients with asthma were less likely to die from pneumonia—but this was because they tended to be admitted directly to the Intensive Care Units (ICU) and received more aggressive treatments. However, if this model was deployed in a real-world clinical environment without understanding why this prediction was being made, and without human/expert intervention, it is possible that patients with asthma would not be admitted to hospital and would not receive the aggressive treatment required to prevent death. The use of explainable models could help to prevent such mistakes being made.

However, there is a lack of consensus upon which usable explanations can be used in different settings. Monteath and sheh (2018), proposed a novel XAI approach to incremental decision support for medical diagnosis using decision trees; their approach allows AI systems to work alongside human experts, each informing the other and coming to a decision together. Their system can guide physicians in determining which test results are most useful given existing data. The system is also able to explain how a particular decision was made, tracing right back to the underlying training data. This provides transparency that is crucial for patient confidence, regulation compliance, detecting and correcting errors, and improving patient outcomes. Another example of humans and AI systems working alongside is the work by (Wu et al. 2018), who proposed an expert-in-the-loop interpretation method to label the behavior of internal units in Convolutional Neural Networks. They demonstrate that several Convolutional Neural Networks models can produce explanatory descriptions to support the final classification decisions. Their findings are an important first step towards XAI in classification of diseased tissue.

Developers of ML-based models in medicine are increasingly focusing on explaining ability, and their results are promising. Zheng et al. (2019), proposed a novel and explainable method to classify cardiac pathology by extracting image-derived features to characterize the shape and motion of the heart. Their proposed model achieves 95% classification accuracy, a performance comparable to that of the state-of-the-art that enables explanations and transparency to become more trustworthy. Tosun et al. (2020), described an initial XAI enabled software application, HistoMapr-Breast, for breast core biopsies. HistoMapr-Breast automatically previews breast core whole slide images and recognizes the regions of interest to rapidly present the key diagnostic areas in an interactive and explainable manner. HistoMapr-Breast can work for pathologists in a trustworthy fashion using its explanation interface. They believe that the concept of XAI system must be integrated in pathology workflows promoting safety, reliability, and accountability in addressing issues with bias, transparency, safety, and causality. They also highlight that an XAI system augments pathologists and works with them but does not replace them. Hicks et al. (2018), introduced Mimir, an automated multimedia reporting software dissecting the neural network to learn the intermediate analysis steps, which directly adds explain ability to Deep Neural Network models in medical problems by producing structured and semantically correct reports, composed of text and images. Mimir enables investigation, explain ability, and understanding of the deep learning algorithms decision processes. Ultimately, better explanations will result in patients that understand and trust the reasoning chain, leading to improved confidence, allowing doctors to provide better diagnoses (Adadi and Berrada, 2020).

20.2.4. Techniques and Explanation

Techniques can be grouped by scope into those providing global explanations of the entire system and those providing local explanations of single predictions. Global explanations facilitate the understanding of the entire model behavior and reasoning leading to expected outcomes. For local explanations, the reasons for a single prediction are provided to justify why the model made a specific decision for that instance (Wu et al. 2018). Techniques can be grouped by whether they are model agnostic (i.e., they can be applied to any ML algorithm), or model specific (i.e., they can be only applied to a specific ML algorithm).

20.2.4.1. Ante-Hoc Methods

Additionally, techniques can be split into ante-hoc and post-hoc explain ability methods. Ante-hoc methods are explainable by design or inherently explainable methods and are also referred to as transparent or white box/glass box approaches. These methods, which are model specific, include linear and logistic regression, decision trees, k-nearest neighbors, fuzzy inference systems, rule-based learners, general additive models, and Bayesian models (Mehonic et al. 2020), (Monteath and Sheh, 2018). However, even for these methods, they can only be considered explainable, transparent, or interpretable up to a point, for example, in high-dimensional scenarios with complex interaction terms or deep decision trees, these methods can become difficult to interpret (Dwivedi et al. 2023).

ML algorithms such as random forests, support vector machines, neural networks (including Deep Neural Networks) are, within practical limits, inherently non-explainable and are typically referred to as "black box" models. Post-hoc methods, which are typically model agnostic, might not explain how black-box models work but they may provide local explanations for a specific decision. One way to do this is to build simpler transparent models that provide interpretable approximations of the black box.

20.3. Materials and Methods

This review aims to explore the literature surrounding the use of XAI in HDSS by identifying publications that are of interest to the ML/AI and medical communities, the contributions of these publications, and the evidence for findings reported. Conducted a systematic literature review by adapting the guidelines proposed by Kitchenham. Figure 20.2 shows patients and

Healthcare Prediction Process. In this review followed a structured process that involved the following:

1. Specifying research questions
2. Conducting searches of specified databases
3. Selecting studies by criterion
4. Filtering studies by evaluating their pertinence
5. Extracting data
6. Synthesizing results.

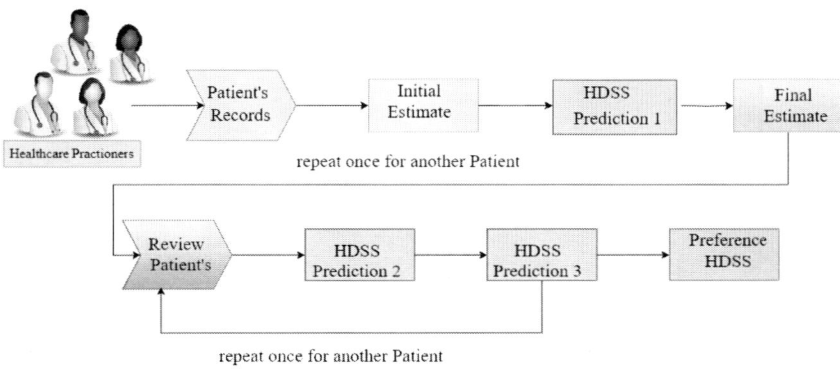

Figure 20.2. The explanation of Patients and Healthcare Prediction Preference.

20.3.1. Research Questions

The research questions that aim to address are as follows:

- RQ1: What AI-based HDSS have been developed that incorporate XAI?
- RQ2: What aspects/methods of the use of XAI in HDSS have been the focus of the literature?
- RQ3: What benefits have been reported when addressing different aspects of the use of XAI in HDSS?
- RQ4: What open problems, challenges, and needs of explainable HDSS are expressed in literature?

20.4. Results

20.4.1. What AI-Based HDSS Have Been Developed That Incorporates XAI?

Although AI has achieved notable momentum in medicine since the early 1970s, the use of XAI has only risen notably over the last few years (Hamamoto et al. 2020). In AI-based HDSS particularly, XAI did not appear until nearly a decade into the 2000s. However, given the undeniable need for transparency and explain ability in medical practice and the growing use of HDSS leveraging AI, XAI has started to be incorporated in recent AI-based HDSS.

Previous works have evaluated XAI in AI-based HDSS, but only as a secondary aspect. However, there are several HDSS in literature that have incorporated XAI. Image-based HDSS using XAI are common. (Lamy et al. 2020), present a HDSS for diagnosing breast cancer using visualization methods for XAI. Additionally, a graphical user interface was presented to medical experts for usability and acceptability validation. Kunapuli et al. (2018), proposed a HDSS for renal mass classification. Their XAI is based on tumor shape, size, and texture metrics as well as clinical, demographic, and other factors when they are available.

20.4.2. What Benefits Have Been Reported When Addressing Different Aspects of the Use of XAI in HDSS?

Several benefits of XAI used in HDSS have been reported. Some researchers presented their XAI-based approaches to doctors or clinicians and collected feedback for usability and acceptability validation. Vorm, (2018), created vignettes of intelligent systems including a hypothetical HDSS and asked participants (graduate human–computer interaction students) to write down any questions that they would want to ask the system to help them determine whether to accept or reject the system recommendation. They reported that XAI could provide different information types to make intelligent systems explainable and more acceptable and trustworthy to users. Liao et al. (2020), developed an XAI question bank to bridge the spaces of user needs for AI explain ability and technical capabilities provided by XAI work. They interviewed 20 participants to identify gaps between the current XAI algorithmic work and practices to create explainable AI products. The results showed that XAI could gain further insights or evidence, and thus enhance decision confidence or generate the hypothesis about causality. In some cases, users also believed that the interpretation of AI decisions might alleviate their own decision-making biases. XAI can also adapt usage or interaction behaviours to utilize the AI better.

20.4.3. Is HDSS Expressed in Literature?

The development of XAI-based HDSS still faces a series of challenges. There is no universal definition of explain ability nor a well-recognized equivalence or distinction between "interpretable" and "explainable" ML. Furthermore, the concept of interpretability is often highly subjective. Moreover, (Wang et al. 2019), believe that what constitutes a good explanation should draw from social science instead of depending on researchers' intuition, and justification is required for choosing different explanation types or representations. Furthermore, (Luz et al. 2020), argue that a thorough reasoning is required for choosing between transparent and black-box ML algorithms, because post-hoc interpretation methods that develop a mirror model of the original one to add explain ability could provide an inaccurate representation of the original model.

In addition, there are some challenges associated with the clinical implementation of XAI-based HDSS. Cai et al. (2019), interviewed pathologists and found that beyond local interpretations, clinicians also require insights of models' overall properties, for instance, their capacities, limitations, functionality, medical perspectives, characteristics, and design objectives. This information enriches the explain ability of HDSS and is desired prior to the adoption of these systems in routine practice. The human–computer interaction community that interdisciplinary cooperation and user-cantered approaches to explain ability are required to close the gaps between XAI and practices. They also discovered that identifying the motivation of explain ability helps to select XAI techniques, foresee their limitations, and fill in the gaps occurring while designing user experiences. XAI needs to be interactive and human-like with customized explanations for different users. User experience of XAI design is challenged by the current availability of XAI techniques and other goals. Additionally, guidance for explaining ability needs specification and creating explain ability solutions are desired.

20.5. Discussion

The massive amounts of data generated and increasing availability of computational resources in healthcare systems make many health problems ripe for the development of AI applications. These systems will make diagnosis, treatment, prognostic efforts, follow-up, and decision-making more straightforward, precise, and efficient. This is aided by the fact that physicians worldwide are becoming more receptive towards, and accepting of, AI solutions (Topol, 2019). However, medical experts struggle with the gap between what is output by an ML-based solution and human explanations. To close the gap requires interdisciplinary work that studies how humans explain, formalizes the patterns in algorithmic forms, and explains outputs in a transparent, easy to interpret manner.

A rapid advancement of XAI is evident, and the recent study by (Linardatos et al. 2020), has identified four main areas of focus: methods for explaining complex black-box models, methods for creating white-box models, methods that promote fairness and restrict the existence of discrimination, and methods for analyzing sensitivity of model predictions. The authors noticed a significant amount of work on explaining complex black-box models, especially on neural networks, probably since there is great potential in terms of complex analyses and performance. On the other hand, white-box models are described as more challenging to create and, as a result, they seem to have lost their popularity among developers, while despite the progress in methods to promote fairness, the studies that have addressed this issue are also limited.

However, there is an open debate on whether XAI in these contexts is necessary and/or worth the substantial overall cost (Wu et al. 2018). Nevertheless, XAI may lead to greater uptake and use of HDSS and may become a requirement in the future due to societal, regulatory, and ethical pressures (Monteath and Sheh 2018), which could make the difference between success and failure of the system (Wu et al. 2018). In some scenarios, explaining the ability of AI output will be a requirement for the output to be used at all, in high-stakes or high-pressure scenarios (Mehonic et al. 2020). Currently, most of the decisions made by AI-based HDSS cannot be interpreted in a transparent way potentially limiting the uptake, trust, and usability of these systems in practice. On the other hand, there are some studies supporting the idea that XAI is not always necessary. London defends the ability to produce results and empirically verify their accuracy as more important than the ability to explain how such results are produced.

20.5.1. Guidelines for Implementing Explainable Models in HDSS: Difficulties, Possibilities, and Future Research Needs

Developing ML-based HDSS is a multidisciplinary process that should include all stakeholders' needs. This is especially true when incorporating XAI into these systems. Consideration should be given to the designers of the system, the decision-makers using the systems, and those ultimately impacted by the consequences of those decisions (Zheng et al. 2019). Models should be built with input from those with expertise from social and behavioral science, philosophy, psychology, and cognitive science. Although XAI can assist with identifying issues with the data, the problem with unstructured medical data remains a challenge for the development of usable AI-based systems. Angehrn et al. (2020), discuss the problem and propose solutions that include (a) data exchange between different sources, provided that appropriate safeguards for data privacy are in place; (b) considering the use of data mining techniques to extract crucial clinical information which might have been captured in free text; and (c) a controlled design process that uses AI to develop and collect data during clinical use. Additionally, we might surpass the problem of data availability and heterogeneity by using the least amount of data available and the easiest-to-collect information to initiate the development of the system.

Domain-specific needs must be considered, including a thorough understanding of the system's purpose, the performance and interpretability of existing systems, and the level and nature of the explanations required Mom.

Metrics to evaluate the performance of XAI techniques require further study (Monteath and Sheh 2018). Most studies are focused on subjective measurements, for example, user satisfaction, the goodness of an explanation, acceptance, and trust in the system. Subjective measurements can provide valuable insight into the user's experience, however, there is an overall lack of validated and reliable evaluation metrics.

Finally, there is a need for more robust user studies. Bussone et al. (2015), found that giving clinicians a fuller explanation of the facts that led to the system's proposed diagnosis had a positive effect on trust but caused over-reliance issues. On the other hand, less detailed explanations had the opposite effect, as this made participants question the system's reliability and caused self-reliance issues. Through a case study, (Jacobs et al. 2021), found that incorrect ML recommendations may affect clinicians and lower the accuracy of decisions, while explanations were found insufficient for addressing over-reliance on a model that suggests erroneous decisions. They found that explanation strategies ought to be selected according to the clinicians' prior experience with ML and that those with prior experience perceived a higher utility from the ML recommendations. However, there are very few studies like this that give insight into what clinicians want or need. Similarly, there is little discussion on the impact of XAI on patients from the patient's perspective. These are areas that will benefit from future research.

20.6. Conclusion

For Healthcare Decision Support Systems (HDSS) to be used effectively in practice, they need to be trustworthy, easy to understand, and, most of all, positively augment the human decision-making process. Explain ability is a critical component in achieving these goals. Explain ability allows developers to identify shortcomings in a system and allows clinicians to be confident in the decisions they make with HDSS assistance. While there are many studies on XAI in medicine, there is a limited number that focus on the context of HDSS. In this review of XAI in HDSS, we focused on the "where" and "how" of XAI use in HDSS and were able to gauge some realized benefits as well as identify future needs in this area. However, despite some user studies reporting positive views on HDSS, especially considering explain ability, there is still skepticism around their use in practice. A lack of research in general is likely both a symptom and cause of this. A main challenge remains the selection of methods used to present explanations in an informative and efficient—and therefore clinically useful—manner. Significant work lies ahead to integrate useful explainable into HDSS. Studies focusing on all stages of HDSS development are required to establish more firmly how explain ability can be put into useful practice in this important context.

References

Adadi, A., and Berrada, M. (2018). Peeking inside the black-box : a survey on explainable artificial intelligence (XAI). *IEEE Access*, 6, 52138-52160.

Adadi, A., and Berrada, M. (2020). Explainable AI for healthcare: from black box to interpretable models. In *Embedded Systems and Artificial Intelligence : Proceedings of ESAI 2019,* Fez, Morocco. 327-337.

Ahmad, T., Madonski, R., Zhang, D., Huang, C., and Mujeeb, A. (2022). Data-driven probabilistic machine learning in sustainable smart energy/smart energy systems: Key developments, challenges, and future research opportunities in the context of smart grid paradigm. *Renewable and Sustainable Energy Reviews*, 160, 112128.

Amershi, S., Begel, A., Bird, C., DeLine, R., Gall, H., Kamar, E., and Zimmermann, T. (2019, May). Software engineering for machine learning: A case study. In 2019 IEEE/ACM 41st International Conference on Software Engineering : *Software Engineering in Practice (ICSE-SEIP)* (pp. 291-300). IEEE.

Angehrn, Z., Haldna, L., Zandvliet, A. S., Gil Berglund, E., Zeeuw, J., Amzal, B., and Heckman, N. M. (2020). Artificial intelligence and machine learning applied at the point of care. *Frontiers in Pharmacology*, 11, 759.

Antoniadi, A. M., Du, Y., Guendouz, Y., Wei, L., Mazo, C., Becker, B. A., and Mooney, C. (2021). Current challenges and future opportunities for XAI in machine learning-based clinical decision support systems: a systematic review. *Applied Sciences*, 11(11), 5088.

Arrieta, A. B., Díaz-Rodríguez, N., Del Ser, J., Bennetot, A., Tabik, S., Barbado, A., and Herrera, F. (2020). Explainable Artificial Intelligence (XAI): Concepts, taxonomies, opportunities and challenges toward responsible AI. *Information Fusion*, 58, 82-115.

Bussone, A., Stumpf, S., and O'Sullivan, D. (2015, October). The role of explanations on trust and reliance in clinical decision support systems. In *2015 international conference on healthcare informatics* 160-169. IEEE.

Cai, C. J., Winter, S., Steiner, D., Wilcox, L., and Terry, M. (2019). "Hello AI": uncovering the onboarding needs of medical practitioners for human-AI collaborative decision-making. *Proceedings of the ACM on Human-computer Interaction*, 3(CSCW), 1-24.

Core, M. G., Lane, H. C., Van Lent, M., Gomboc, D., Solomon, S., and Rosenberg, M. (2006, July). Building explainable artificial intelligence systems. In *AAAI*. 1766-1773.

Dhanorkar, S., Wolf, C. T., Qian, K., Xu, A., Popa, L., and Li, Y. (2021, June). Who needs to know what, when?: Broadening the Explainable AI (XAI) Design Space by Looking at Explanations Across the AI Lifecycle. In *Designing Interactive Systems Conference* 2021 1591-1602.

Durelli, V. H., Durelli, R. S., Borges, S. S., Endo, A. T., Eler, M. M., Dias, D. R., and Guimarães, M. P. (2019). Machine learning applied to software testing: A systematic mapping study. *IEEE Transactions on Reliability*, 68(3), 1189-1212.

Dwivedi, R., Dave, D., Naik, H., Singhal, S., Omer, R., Patel, P., and Ranjan, R. (2023). Explainable AI (XAI) : Core ideas, techniques, and solutions. *ACM Computing Surveys*, 55(9), 1-33.

Dwivedi, Y. K., Hughes, L., Ismagilova, E., Aarts, G., Coombs, C., Crick, T., and Williams, M. D. (2021). Artificial Intelligence (AI) : Multidisciplinary perspectives on emerging challenges, opportunities, and agenda for research, practice and policy. *International Journal of Information Management*, 57, 101994.

Hamamoto, R., Suvarna, K., Yamada, M., Kobayashi, K., Shinkai, N., Miyake, M., and Kaneko, S. (2020). Application of artificial intelligence technology in oncology: Towards the establishment of precision medicine. *Cancers*, 12(12), 3532.

Hicks, S. A., Eskeland, S., Lux, M., de Lange, T., Randel, K. R., Jeppsson, M., and Riegler, M. (2018, June). Mimir: an automatic reporting and reasoning system for deep learning based analysis in the medical domain. In *Proceedings of the 9th ACM Multimedia Systems Conference* 369-374.

Jacobs, M., Pradier, M. F., McCoy Jr, T. H., Perlis, R. H., Doshi-Velez, F., and Gajos, K. Z. (2021). How machine-learning recommendations influence clinician treatment selections: the example of antidepressant selection. *Translational psychiatry*, 11(1), 108.

Kunapuli, G., Varghese, B. A., Ganapathy, P., Desai, B., Cen, S., Aron, M., and Duddalwar, V. (2018). A decision-support tool for renal mass classification. *Journal of Digital Imaging*, 31, 929-939.

Lamy, J. B., Sedki, K., and Tsopra, R. (2020). Explainable decision support through the learning and visualization of preferences from a formal ontology of antibiotic treatments. *Journal of Biomedical Informatics,* 104, 103407.

Liao, Q. V., Gruen, D., and Miller, S. (2020, April). Questioning the AI : informing design practices for explainable AI user experiences. In *Proceedings of the 2020 CHI conference on human factors in computing systems,* 1-15.

Linardatos, P., Papastefanopoulos, V., and Kotsiantis, S. (2020). Explainable ai : A review of machine learning interpretability methods. *Entropy*, 23(1), 18.

Luz, C. F., Vollmer, M., Decruyenaere, J., Nijsten, M. W., Glasner, C., and Sinha, B. (2020). Machine learning in infection management using routine electronic health records : tools, techniques, and reporting of futures technologies. *Clinical Microbiology and Infection*, 26(10), 1291-1299.

Mehonic, A., Sebastian, A., Rajendran, B., Simeone, O., Vasilaki, E., and Kenyon, A. J. (2020). Memristors—From in-memory computing, deep learning acceleration, and spiking neural networks to the future of neuromorphic and bio-inspired computing. *Advanced Intelligent Systems*, 2(11), 2000085.

Monteath, I., and Sheh, R. (2018). Assisted and incremental medical diagnosis using explainable artificial intelligence. In *Proceedings of the 2nd Workshop on Explainable Artificial Intelligence* 104-108.

Oprescu, A. M., Miró-Amarante, G., García-Díaz, L., Rey, V. E., Chimenea-Toscano, A., Martínez-Martínez, R., and Romero-Ternero, M. C. (2022). Towards a data collection methodology for Responsible Artificial Intelligence in health: A prospective and qualitative study in pregnancy. *Information Fusion*, 83, 53-78.

Rothman, B., Leonard, J. C., and Vigoda, M. M. (2012). Future of electronic health records : implications for decision support. *Mount Sinai Journal of Medicine*: *A Journal of Translational and Personalized Medicine*, 79(6), 757-768.

Siau, K., and Wang, W. (2018). Building trust in artificial intelligence, machine learning, and robotics. *Cutter Business Technology Journal*, 31(2), 47-53.

Topol, E. J. (2019). High-performance medicine: the convergence of human and artificial intelligence. *Nature Medicine*, 25(1), 44-56.

Tosun, A. B., Pullara, F., Becich, M. J., Taylor, D., Fine, J. L., and Chennubhotla, S. C. (2020). Explainable AI (xAI) for anatomic pathology. *Advances in Anatomic Pathology*, 27(4), 241-250.

Vellido, A. (2020). The importance of interpretability and visualization in machine learning for applications in medicine and health care. *Neural computing and applications*, 32(24), 18069-18083.

Vorm, E. S. (2018, July). Assessing demand for transparency in intelligent systems using machine learning. In *2018 Innovations in Intelligent Systems and Applications (INISTA)*. 1-7). IEEE.

Wang, D., Yang, Q., Abdul, A., and Lim, B. Y. (2019, May). Designing theory-driven user-centric explainable AI. In *Proceedings of the 2019 CHI conference on human factors in computing systems*, 1-15.

Weinstein, M. C., O'Brien, B., Hornberger, J., Jackson, J., Johannesson, M., McCabe, C., and Luce, B. R. (2003). Principles of good practice for decision analytic modeling in health-care evaluation: *Report of the ISPOR task force on good research practices—Modeling studies. Value in health*, 6(1), 9-17.

Wu, J., Peck, D., Hsieh, S., Dialani, V., Lehman, C. D., Zhou, B. et al. (2018, February). Expert identification of visual primitives used by CNNs during mammogram classification. In *Medical Imaging 2018 : Computer-Aided Diagnosis* (Vol. 10575, 633-641). SPIE.

Zheng, Q., Delingette, H., and Ayache, N. (2019). Explainable cardiac pathology classification on cine MRI with motion characterization by semi-supervised learning of apparent flow. *Medical image analysis*, 56, 80-95.

About the Editors

Name: A. Anitha

Affiliation: Department of Software and Systems Engineering, School of Computer Science Engineering and Information Systems, Vellore Institute of Technology, Vellore

Education: Ph.D

Business Address:
Associate Professor (Senior),
Department of Software and Systems Engineering, School of Computer Science Engineering and Information Systems, Vellore Institute of Technology, Vellore

Research and Professional Experience: 15+ years

Publications from the Last 3 Years:

Sl.No	Paper Title	Year	Citations	Imp Fac	Type
1	Multi-level Security in Healthcare by integrating Lattice-Based Access Control and Blockchain-based Smart Contracts System. Haritha, T., & Anitha, A. IEEE Access Doi: https://ieeexplore.ieee.org/document/10285844	2023	0	3.9	Article
2	Deep Ensemble-Based Approach Using Randomized Low-Rank Approximation for Sustainable Groundwater Level Prediction, Manna T., Anitha A., Applied Sciences (Switzerland), *Vol:13, Issue: 5, DOI: 10.3390/app13053210*	2023	0	2.7	Article
3	Asymmetric Consortium Blockchain and Homomorphically Polynomial-Based PIR for Secured Smart Parking Systems, Haritha T., Anitha A., Computers, Materials and Continua, *Vol:75, Issue: 2, Pg.No(3923-3939), DOI: 10.32604/cmc.2023.036278*	2023	2	3.1	Article
4	Precipitation prediction by integrating Rough Set on Fuzzy Approximation Space with Deep Learning techniques[Formula presented], Manna T., A. A.,	2023	3	8.7	Article

Sl.No	Paper Title	Year	Citations	Imp Fac	Type
	Applied Soft Computing, *Vol:139, DOI: 10.1016/j.asoc.2023.110253*				
5	Convolution Neural Network and Auto-encoder Hybrid Scheme for Automatic Colorization of Grayscale Images, Anitha A., Shivakumara P., Jain S., Agarwal V., EAI/Springer Innovations in Communication and Computing, Pg.No(253-271), DOI: 10.1007/978-3-031-20541-5_12	2023	1	0	Book Chapter
6	Forecasting Air Quality Index based on Stacked LSTM, Manna T., Anitha A., 7th IEEE International Conference on Recent Advances and Innovations in Engineering, ICRAIE 2022 - Proceedings, Pg.No(326-330), DOI: 10.1109/ICRAIE56454.2022.10054260	2022	0	0	Conference Paper

A. Anitha received her PhD in Information technology from VIT University, India. At present, she is working as an Associate Professor in the School of Information Technology, VIT University, Vellore, India. She has authored more than 35 international and national journal papers for Elsevier, Inderscience and Springer Journals. She has presented research work in various internaltional conferences. She is associated editor several international journal and reviewer of many international journals such as Applied Soft computing, Soft computing, and Tech Science press. She is associated with the professional bodies CSI, Indian Science Congress, IAENG. Her research interest includes data mining, fuzzy logic, neural network, Artificial Intelligence, soft hybrid techniques, rough computing, business intelligence, Machine Learning, Deep Learning, Block chain and Industrial Revolution 4.0.

Name: D. P. Acharjya

Affiliation: Department of Computational Intelligence, School of Computer Science Engineering, Vellore Institute of Technology, Vellore, Tamilnadu, India

Education: Ph. D.

Business Address:
Professor (HAG)
School of Computer Science and Engineering
Vellore Institute of Technology, Vellore, Tamilnadu, India

Research and Professional Experience: 27+ years

Publications from the Last 3 Years:

Sl.No	Paper Title	Year	Citations	Imp Fac	Type
1.	Nancy Kumari and D. P. Acharjya: Data classification using rough set and bioinspired computing in healthcare applications - an extensive review, Multimedia Tools and Applications, Springer, Vol. 82 (9), pp. 13479 – 13505 DOI: 10.1007/s11042-022-13776-1	2023	4	2.577	Article
2.	Nancy Kumari and D. P. Acharjya: A hybrid rough set shuffled frog leaping knowledge inference system for diagnosis of lung cancer disease, Computers in Biology and Medicine, Elsevier, Vol. 155 (3), pp. 1-16, p. 106662 DOI: 10.1016/j.compbiomed.2023.106662	2023	1	6.697	Article
3.	Yan Wang, Yan Ma, Hui Huang, Bin Wang, and D. P. Acharjya: A split-merge clustering algorithm based on the k-nearest neighbor graph, Information Systems, Elsevier, Vol. 111 (1), pp. 1—24, p. 102124 DOI: 10.1016/j.is.2022.102124	2023	5	3.18	Article
4.	D. P. Acharjya and R. Rathi: An integrated fuzzy rough set and real coded genetic algorithm approach for crop identification in smart agriculture, Multimedia Tools and Applications, Springer, Vol. 81 (24), pp. 35117-35142, DOI: 10.1007/s11042-021-10518-7	2022	4	2.577	Article
5.	Nancy Kumari and D. P. Acharjya: A decision support system for diagnosis of hepatitis disease using an integrated rough set and fish swarm algorithm, Concurrency and Computation: Practice and Experience, Wiley, Vol. 34 (21), pp. 1-18, e7107	2022		1.831	Article
6.	D. P. Acharjya and Kauser Ahmed P: A hybridized rough set and bat-inspired algorithm for knowledge inferencing in the diagnosis of chronic liver disease, Multimedia Tools and Applications, Springer, Vol.81 (10), pp. 13489-13512 DOI: 10.1007/s11042-021-11495-7	2022	10	2.577	Article

Sl.No	Paper Title	Year	Citations	Imp Fac	Type
7.	D. P. Acharjya and Gladys Gnana Kiruba B: A rough set, formal concept analysis and SEM-PLS integrated approach towards sustainable wearable computing in the adoption of smartwatch, Sustainable Computing: Informatics and Systems, Elsevier, Vol. 33 (1), Article: 100647, pp. 1-15 DOI: 10.1016/j.suscom.2021.100647	2022	5	4.028	Article
8.	D. P. Acharjya and R. Rathi: An extensive study of statistical, rough, and hybridized rough computing in bankruptcy prediction, Multimedia Tools and Applications, Springer, Vol. 80 (28-29), pp. 35387-35413 DOI: 10.1007/s11042-020-10167-2	2021	5	2.577	Article
9.	Kedar Nath Das, Rajeev Das and D. P. Acharjya: Least-looping stepping-stone-based ASM approach for transportation and triangular intuitionistic fuzzy transportation problems, Complex & Intelligent Systems, Springer, Vol. 7 (6), pp. 2885-2894 DOI: 10.1007/s40747-021-00472-0	2021	2	4.927	Article
10.	D. P. Acharjya and N. Syed Siraj Ahmed: Tracing of Online Assaults in 5G Networks using Dominance Based Rough Set and Formal Concept Analysis, Peer-to-Peer Networking and Applications, Springer, Vol. 16 (1), pp. 349-374 DOI: 10.1007/s12083-020-00983-6	2021	7	2.793	Article

D. P. Acharjya received his Ph.D. in computer science from Berhampur University, India; M. Tech. degree in computer science from Utkal University, India; and M. Sc. from NIT, Rourkela, India. He is currently working as a Professor, Higher Academic Grade, in the School of Computer Science and Engineering, VIT University, Vellore, India. He has authored more than 100 national and international journal, conference papers, and book chapters to his credit. He has also written four text books to his credit. In addition, he has edited ten books with IGI Global, Springer, and CRC Press. He has been awarded with Gold Medal from NIT, Rourkela; Eminent Academician Award from Khallikote Sanskrutika Parisad, Berhampur, Odisha; Outstanding Educator and Scholar Award from National Foundation for Entrepreneurship Development, Coimbatore; and The Best Citizens of India Award from International Publishing House, New Delhi, India; Lifetime Achievement Award from NFED, Coimbatore. He is acting as an editorial board member of various international

journals. He has delivered many keynote addresses in international conferences, short term courses, faculty development programs, webinars and workshops. He has served as academic councilor of Indira Gandhi National Open University (IGNOU), academic guide of ICFAI University, and served many institutions and universities in various capacities. He is associated with many professional bodies CSI, ISTE, IMS, AMTI, ISIAM, OITS, IACSIT, CSTA, ACM, IEEE and IAENG. He was founder secretary of OITS Rourkela chapter. His current research interests include rough sets, bioinspired computing, formal concept analysis, ambient intelligence, knowledge representation, data mining, granular computing and business intelligence.	

Index

A

B

C

D

S

T

U

V

X

Y